MACR ECONO

LAURENCE S. SE
University of Delaw

HARCOURT BRACE JOVAN
and its subsidiary, A

San Diego   New York
London   Sydney

To The Instructor

As macroeconomists who enjoy our subject, we would like to be able to cover virtually every topic presented in a standard text. But few of us can do so in a one-semester course. That reality leads to one of two responses.

Some instructors follow the chapters of a standard text in sequence, but inevitably they have to omit the last few chapters. Such important topics as capital accumulation and economic growth or open-economy macroeconomics are simply not covered. Even inflation and unemployment are sometimes treated hurriedly at the end of the course.

Other instructors elect to skip whole chapters or large sections of chapters in order to cover all the essential topics. Because the standard text is written to be read in sequence, however, students and instructors may be plagued by references to earlier material they have not covered.

Core and Supplement

One purpose of this book is to address such problems. The strategy has been to divide the material into two categories: Core (Chapters 1–11) and Supplement (Chapters 12–16). The eleven Core chapters can be completed in one semester. The Core consists of the following:

Part 1   Aggregate Demand and Aggregate Supply
   Chapter 1   National Income Accounting and Equilibrium Output
   Chapter 2   *IS–LM* Analysis
   Chapter 3   Aggregate Demand and Aggregate Supply
Part 2   Inflation and Unemployment
   Chapter 4   The Inflationary Process
   Chapter 5   Inflation: History, Prevention, and Consequences
   Chapter 6   Disinflation and Transitional Recession
   Chapter 7   Unemployment

Part 3   Stabilization
   Chapter 8   Stabilization Policy
   Chapter 9   Fiscal and Monetary Policy
Part 4   Accumulation and Growth, and the Open Economy
   Chapter 10   Capital Accumulation and Economic Growth
   Chapter 11   Macroeconomics in an Open Economy

An instructor can assign the eleven Core chapters knowing that all the essential topics of macroeconomics will be examined in sequence.

The five Supplement chapters are designed to serve the diverse priorities of individual instructors while avoiding the problem of addressing subjects out of sequence. At the beginning of each Supplement chapter, the prerequisite (Pr) Core chapter or chapters are indicated. Most instructors should find time to cover one or two Supplement chapters during a one-semester course. The Supplement consists of the following:

   Chapter 12   Consumption and Investment (Pr: Ch. 2)
   Chapter 13   Money, Banking, and the Federal Reserve System (Pr: Ch. 2)
   Chapter 14   Unemployment and Vacancies (Pr: Chs. 4–7)
   Chapter 15   Topics in Accumulation and Growth I (Pr: Ch. 10)
   Chapter 16   Topics in Accumulation and Growth II (Pr: Ch. 10)

For example, the prerequisite for Chapter 13, on money, banking, and the Federal Reserve system, is Core Chapter 2, on $IS-LM$ analysis. The instructor who wants a detailed treatment of money creation can assign Chapter 13 at any time after the completion of Chapter 2. Or, the instructor whose students have already taken a money and banking course, or who places a higher priority on other topics, can omit Chapter 13, knowing that the essential facts about monetary institutions and policy are covered in Core Chapters 2, 8, and 9.

The Supplement strategy is carried one step further in Chapters 15 and 16 ("Topics in Accumulation and Growth" I and II). In these chapters, each of the eight topics is completely self-contained. Once the prerequisite (Chapter 10, "Capital Accumulation and Economic Growth") has been met, the instructor can assign one or more topics from Chapters 15 and 16. The instructor who gives very high priority to accumulation and growth can assign Chapters 10, 15, and 16.

Although this Core–Supplement division offers new options for the instructor, the standard options remain available as well. It is possible to substitute Supplement chapters for late Core chapters. The instructor who prefers to concentrate on inflation and unemployment and on stabilization can substitute Supplement Chapters 12, 13, and 14 for Core Chapters 10 and 11.

The *DG–SG* Diagram

This book moves the analysis of inflation and unemployment to a central position in the course (Chapters 4–7), and makes the demand growth–supply growth *(DG–SG)* diagram a key tool. The *DG–SG* diagram is a modification of the demand–supply diagram; the vertical axis of the *DG–SG* diagram plots the inflation rate instead of the price level.

A simple rule for shifting the demand growth and supply growth curves is derived so that the student will feel as comfortable with this tool as with the *IS–LM* diagram. The student learns how to use this simple rule to trace out the inflationary spiral path (Chapter 4, Figure 4.4), and the disinflationary spiral path (Chapter 6, Figure 6.1). Thus the *DG–SG* diagram, like the *IS–LM* and *D–S* diagrams, becomes a practical tool that the student can master and use.

The Option of a Deeper Treatment of Accumulation and Growth

Much of the current economic debate centers on policies to promote saving and investment—tax policy, budget policy, and "supply-side economics." Several of these topics are first introduced in Core Chapter 2 as an application of *IS–LM* analysis. All of them are treated in Core Chapter 10, on capital accumulation and economic growth, which emphasizes the analysis of policies.

In addition, Supplement Chapters 15 and 16 include eight self-contained topics on accumulation and growth: government deficits and debt; supply-side economics; Social Security and capital accumulation; policies to reduce consumption; policies to raise investment; the sources of economic growth; the neoclassical growth model; and accumulation, pollution, and depletion. The instructor can therefore assign only Chapter 10, Chapter 10 plus several of the self-contained topics in Chapters 15 and 16, or Chapter 10 and Chapters 15 and 16 in their entirety.

Numerical Examples That Correspond to Diagrams

Equilibrium output, *IS–LM* analysis, and aggregate demand and supply are taught through the presentation of simple equations and numerical examples that correspond to diagrams. The text focuses on numerical examples; the use of general form equations and formal derivations is reserved for the appendix.

A single numerical example unifies Part 1. To illustrate, in Chapter 2 the student is shown how to calculate the new values of consumption and investment when there is a shift to an easy fiscal–tight monetary policy mix. In the example, the student learns how to compute that investment falls from $380 billion to $204 billion, and that consumption increases from $1,520 billion to $1,696 billion. At the end of Chapter 3, the student learns how to solve the demand equation and supply equation for the price level and output, to use the *IS* or *LM* equation to find the interest rate, and to use the consumption and investment functions to find consumption and investment.

Early Introduction of Important Policy Issues

Student motivation can be stimulated by early exposure to important policy problems. A deep treatment must wait until model development is complete, but a meaningful introduction can come earlier than is sometimes realized.

With student motivation in mind, only essential national income accounting is presented in Chapter 1 (a more comprehensive treatment is found in Appendix 1A). Thus, in Chapter 1 the model of equilibrium output is presented, and the role of the tax system as an automatic stabilizer and the consequences of alternative balanced budget rules for economic stability are introduced.

In Chapter 2, a variety of policy topics is discussed: monetary policy to combat recession, why effective stabilization policy is difficult, the significance of the fiscal–monetary policy mix (and the budget deficit) at full-employment output for accumulation and growth, and supply-side economics. In Chapter 3, the key role of the hypothesis of price expectations (inertial vs. rational) for the behavior of the demand–supply model is reviewed.

Emphasis on Problems and Policy Analysis

With the demand–supply model completed in Part 1, the remainder of the Core gives high priority to the analysis of problems and policy options: inflation and unemployment (Chapters 4–7), stabilization (Chapters 8–9), capital accumulation and economic growth (Chapter 10), and open economy macroeconomics (Chapter 11).

The objective is to devote a large amount of course time to the analysis of problems and policy options. For example, Chapter 4 uses the *DG–SG* diagram to show how inflation arises, Chapter 5 focuses on how to prevent inflation, Chapter 6 considers policy options for disinflating and the role of inertial vs. rational expectations in determining the disinflation path, Chapter 7 reviews supply-oriented policies to reduce the normal unemployment rate, Chapter 8 discusses why effective stabilization policy is difficult, Chapter 9 examines the design of fiscal and monetary policy, Chapter 10 analyzes policies to raise the saving and investment rate of the economy, and Chapter 11 explains why policies that raise the saving rate should reduce the trade deficit.

Other Features

Several other features should be noted:

1. In Chapter 6, the student is shown how econometric technique can be used to estimate the responsiveness of inflation to unemployment. This section gives the student a better grasp of the empirical aspect of macroeconomics.

2. In Chapter 8, on stabilization, numerical examples from the model of equilibrium output are used to compare counter-cyclical and constant policy under uncertainty.

3. The design and impact of alternative balanced budget rules are discussed in Chapter 9.

4. In Chapter 3, diagrams show the interaction of $D-S$ and $IS-LM$ under inertial and rational expectations in response to a fiscal policy expansion and a monetary policy expansion.

5. While Core Chapter 7 on unemployment presents the essential facts, concepts, and policy options, Supplement Chapter 14 presents a labor market model that generates equilibrium employment, unemployment, and vacancies and that can be used to analyze the impact of supply-oriented policies on the normal unemployment rate.

6. The appendix to Chapter 6 gives an exposition of the $DG-SG$ model using simple algebra and numerical examples, for the instructor who prefers a more quantitative approach to inflation–output dynamics. Still greater depth can be achieved by adding Chapter 14, which presents a labor market model using simple algebra.

Instructor's Manual and Study Guide

The author of this text is the sole author of the accompanying Instructor's Manual and a joint author, with Professor Jeffrey Miller of the University of Delaware, of the Study Guide. Both items are therefore fully integrated with the text.

A useful feature of the Instructor's Manual is the provision of complete exams: a first exam on Part 1, a second exam on Parts 2 and 3, and a final exam covering all Core chapters. Each exam is presented twice using two different formats: multiple choice questions and problems.

The answers are worked out in full for the instructor's convenience. Different exams for three semesters are provided. The author of the text has used these exams to test the text material.

Acknowledgments

I am grateful to the following professors of economics for feedback on drafts of chapters: Jeffrey Miller, University of Delaware; Mark Kuperberg, Swarthmore College; Alan Auerbach, University of Pennsylvania; James Butkiewicz, University of Delaware; John McDermott, University of South Carolina; Richard T. Freeman, International Finance Division, Federal Reserve Board; Pierre Fortin, Université Laval; Eric Brucker, University of Delaware; Harry Hutchinson, University of Delaware; Saul Hoffman, University of Delaware; Lawrence Donnelly, University of Delaware; Anita Schwarz, University of Delaware; Kenneth Koford, University of Delaware; Burton Abrams, University of Delaware; Charles Link, University of Delaware; Kenneth Lewis, University of Delaware; James Thornton, University of Delaware.

I want to thank the following reviewers: Stuart Allen, University of North Carolina at Greensboro; Robert Archibald, College of William and Mary; John Boschen, Tulane University; Richard Cebula, Emory University; John W. Graham, Rutgers University; Manford Keil, University of Houston, Central Campus; Anne Mayhew, University of Tennessee at Knoxville; Steven McCafferty, Ohio State University; Andrew J. Policano, University of Iowa; James A. Richardson, Louisiana State University; Robert Yarbrough, Amherst College.

I wish to thank the many University of Delaware students who proofread and checked early drafts.

I owe a debt of gratitude to Tracy White, Diane Pella, Robin Risque, and Lynn Edwards, all of Harcourt Brace Jovanovich, for their care in the production process.

Finally, I am grateful to my wife, Ann, my son, Jesse, my daughter, Suzanna, my parents, Eleanor and Irv, and my brothers, Robbie and Leon.

To The Student

The Introduction describes what macroeconomics is about. Here, one suggestion is offered on how to approach this text and subject.

As you read, always have paper, pencil, and calculator available. Draw each diagram, write each equation, and work each calculation. In short, be an active reader who "scribbles." Experience shows that passive readers—those who read but never scribble—often think that they are following the material. But when they then try to draw a diagram, write an equation, or perform a calculation on that first exam, they often receive a sobering surprise.

The text itself should be regarded as a kind of workbook that stimulates writing, calculating, drawing, and scribbling. Terms, concepts, and questions at the end of each chapter provide a useful test of comprehension. As enjoyable as macroeconomics is, it is not a subject for the couch or easy chair. It is a subject for the desk and a hard chair. Be an active reader of this macroeconomics text. You'll master it better and enjoy it more.

Brief Contents

Detailed Contents

INTRODUCTION

Macroeconomics is concerned with inflation and unemployment, recession and recovery, economic stability and instability, economic growth and capital accumulation, productivity and the standard of living, the national economy and the world economy. Macroeconomics is also concerned with the policies that influence these phenomena: monetary and fiscal policy to maintain stability and to prevent inflation, or to achieve disinflation; supply-oriented policy to reduce the normal unemployment rate, to raise normal output, or to assist disinflation; tax policy to promote capital accumulation and productivity; exchange-rate policy to promote adjustment to the world economy.

Perhaps the best way to explain what macroeconomics is all about is to take a brief excursion through this text. We will pause only long enough to raise questions. The aim of this excursion is to whet — not to satisfy — your appetite.

An Excursion Through Macroeconomics

The three chapters in Part 1 lay the foundation and provide the necessary tools for our study of macroeconomics. Is this a time for patience, when only the promise of a future "return" must motivate you? Not at all. Even in Part 1, you will acquire useful economic tools and principles, confront important policy issues, and encounter valuable economic lessons. Let's consider a few.

Although paying taxes is a personally unpleasant task, you will learn that the tax system is an *automatic stabilizer* in that it reduces the magnitude of fluctuations in output and employment. You will also see how, in principle, it is possible for monetary and/or fiscal policy to combat a recession — although, in practice, a successful stabilization policy is difficult to achieve.

How fast will the standard of living advance over time? The answer depends partly on how much output is devoted to investment instead of consumption. You will see why the mix of monetary and fiscal policy at the full-employment level is a crucial determinant of the allocation of output between consumption and investment. Specifically, a "tight" fiscal/"easy" monetary mix favors investment relative to consumption and results in faster growth in the standard of living.

Next we will turn to Part 2, which covers inflation and unemployment—two of the most important economic problems in recent years. Most of us know that *inflation* means rising prices. We know that we do not like it. We are afraid that it will get out of control and seriously harm us. Yet not very many of us can answer the most important questions about inflation.

Why does inflation occur? The United States had almost no inflation in the early 1960s, but the U.S. inflation rate was close to 10% by the end of the 1970s. From 1955 to 1964, there was virtually no inflation; however, after this fine performance, the inflation story became more discouraging. From 1965 to 1980, inflation rose from 1% to almost 10%. This rise was briefly halted twice—in 1971 and 1975. The early1980s at last saw a significant decline in the inflation rate.

What accounts for the history of U.S. inflation over the last three decades? Could its rise have been prevented and, if so, how? How important is it to prevent inflation? How harmful is inflation?

If there is already significant inflation in the economy, then the key question becomes: How can inflation be brought down? In other words, how can *disinflation* be engineered?

In the early 1980s, the United States and several other economically advanced countries achieved significant disinflation. The United States began the decade with a 10% inflation rate; by 1983, this rate had decreased to less than 5%. But the early 1980s also witnessed a severe recession accompanied by high unemployment. In fact, when inflation was reduced in two earlier periods—1971 and 1975—recessions also occurred and the unemployment rate rose above normal.

This observation suggests several crucial questions: are a severe recession and a significant rise in the unemployment rate necessary to achieve disinflation? How much unemployment—and lost output—must be accepted to reduce, say, a 10% inflation rate to almost 0%? How do economists estimate these key magnitudes? Do the answers depend on how disinflation policy is conducted or on the "package" of disinflation policies?

Now let's assume that inflation has decreased. What unemployment rate can be sustained without causing inflation to increase again? Is a relatively high unemployment rate necessary to keep inflation from accelerating? Can policies be implemented to reduce the normal unemployment rate without rekindling inflation?

Once disinflation is achieved and the normal unemployment rate is reduced, the next challenge becomes: How can the economy be kept as close to the position of no inflation and a relatively low unemployment rate as possible? We will examine the conduct of such a *stabilization policy* in Part 3.

The federal government can attempt to stabilize the economy through fiscal policy by varying *tax rates* and *government expenditures* or through monetary policy by varying the *quantity of money* and/or the *interest rate*. A key question at this point is would an activist fiscal or monetary policy be likely to do more good than harm? Is it better to try to adjust fiscal or monetary policy continuously to perceived changes in the economy? Or is it better to set fiscal and monetary policy according to the "normal" state of the economy and to avoid continuous adjustment?

How does fiscal and monetary policy operate? Do important lags and uncertainties confront fiscal and monetary policymakers? How does an *econometric model*—a model based on the statistical analysis of actual data—capture the interaction of all the basic elements of the macroeconomy? Can such a model be used to guide stabilization policy? What criticisms does the use of an econometric model invoke?

In Part 4, we will consider two important aspects of macroeconomics: capital accumulation and economic growth, and "open-economy" macroeconomics. Let's examine both briefly here.

When you study what determines the growth rate of the standard of living over time, you will see that the key to improving the standard of living is to raise *productivity*, or to raise the output per hour worked. How does productivity rise, and how can we make it grow faster?

Basically, a society must decide how much current output to devote to current consumption and how much current output to allocate to capital accumulation (investment) to raise future output and consumption. Economic growth, capital accumulation, saving and investment, and productivity growth will all be examined in depth.

Part 4 begins with an analysis of growth and accumulation but soon turns to policy. What policies can raise capital accumulation? What are the pros and cons of alternative policies? How much capital accumulation is desirable? (You will discover that tax policy influences capital accumulation.) We will also discuss *supply-side economics*, which has received much attention in recent years. You will learn that the size of the budget deficit when the economy is at normal output is very important to capital accumulation and economic growth. This observation will raise the question: How desirable is a balanced budget?

Our excursion through macroeconomics concludes with the recognition that our national economy is an "open economy"; it is part of the world economy. We must review and reevaluate our earlier conclusions in light of our link with this world economy. Can the world economy cause a permanent depression in the United States? Are trade deficits harmful? What causes a trade deficit? What are the pros and cons of *flexible* versus *fixed* exchange rates?

Macroeconomics is concerned with all of these substantive issues —with how the economy works and with what economic policies are desirable or undesirable. The central motivation for studying macroeconomics is to tackle these critical issues and to devise policies to improve the well-being of people.

But you should also appreciate macroeconomics from another perspective. The subject of macroeconomics illustrates the skill of model construction and the use of analytical techniques. How do economists try to understand a very complex economy? How are such basic tools as diagrams, mathematics, and statistics used? How are economic models constructed, tested, and applied?

As you study macroeconomics, keep these questions in mind. Are these the proper techniques for analyzing the problem at hand? Why do economists use these techniques and not others? Does the use of a particular tool make sense? Is a particular model plausible? Is there a better way to understand a phenomenon or to answer a question?

Macroeconomics, then, is not only substantively important; it also illustrates how human beings, confronted with a complex subject, develop analytical tools and techniques to try to bring order and understanding to an intricate mechanism called "the economy."

Science and Values

Economics is an objective science. At the same time, every economist holds particular philosophical and ethical views. It is important to keep the distinction between *objective analysis* and *personal values* clearly in mind as you study macroeconomics. The following example illustrates this point.

Suppose that two economists wish to determine how much unemployment will accompany a 5% reduction in the inflation rate under policy 1. This is an *objective* determination with an *objective* answer. The correct answer has nothing to do with the personal values of either economist; it depends on the objective properties of the economy.

Suppose that these two economists arrive at the same answer. They agree about how much unemployment policy 1 will generate while it reduces inflation by 5%. Does this also mean that they agree on whether or not to advocate policy 1? Not necessarily.

Each economist's attitude toward policy 1 also depends on his or her personal values. As a citizen (not as an economist per se), suppose that economist A is strongly opposed to generating unemployment. She opposes policy 1, and prefers either to tolerate the inflation or to try to bring it down by implementing policy 2, which—although she admits it is costly and inefficient—at least does not generate unemployment.

As a citizen, suppose that economist B is strongly opposed both to tolerating inflation and to the use of costly and inefficient policy 2. He concludes that policy 1 should be adopted.

Note that although economists A and B disagree over whether or not to use policy 1, they both agree on the objective consequences of policy 1 and policy 2. The general public, however, may observe that economists A and B disagree about whether or not to pursue policy 1. The public may mistakenly conclude that A and B disagree about the objective properties of the economy (how the economy will respond to the particular policy) and may reason that economics cannot be an objective, scientific subject because economists often disagree. But in our example, the policy disagreement is due solely to the different personal values of the economists; there is no economic disagreement.

Of course, A and B could arrive at different objective estimates. Economist A could estimate that a large rise in unemployment is necessary to reduce inflation by 5% under policy 1, but economist B could estimate that only a small rise is necessary. Even if they both have the same personal values, A may oppose policy 1 because she estimates it will generate severe unemployment and B may support policy 1 because he estimates it will cause only mild unemployment.

In this case, the disagreement over policy is not due to values but to different assessments of the objective properties of the economy. Such differences arise because it is difficult to obtain a precise estimate of economic properties. Economists cannot place the economy in a laboratory and conduct repeated experiments under controlled conditions.

Despite this obstacle, we will see that professional economists have achieved a significant degree of agreement concerning the objective properties of the economy and the appropriate techniques and tools with which to analyze these properties. Important differences do remain, but common ground is shared by most economists.

As you study macroeconomics and as you observe the debates over the macroeconomic issues in our society, you should keep this distinction in mind. Always ask: What is the *source* of the disagreement over a particular policy? Is it due to a different assessment of the objective properties of the economy? Or is it due to a difference in personal values?

▶ Differences in personal values probably will always remain among economists — and among citizens in general. Economics is an objective science; its goal is to minimize disagreements concerning the objective properties of the economy. Economists should be judged on how well they succeed in this scientific task and not on whether they continue to disagree over specific policies — for such disagreements will always remain as long as personal values differ.

1 Aggregate Demand and Aggregate Supply

CHAPTER

1

National Income Accounting and Equilibrium Output

Imagine you are the first macroeconomist. In front of you stands the real economy—with its many products and transactions. Its complexity is awesome. No one before you has ever tried to make any sense of it. How do you begin?

The first thing most economists would advise you to do is to establish some basic *accounting relationships*. How do you react to their advice? You may respond with enthusiasm (some people have a natural zest for accounting) or trepidation (which would be understandable but unjustified). *National income accounting* is absolutely essential to constructing macroeconomic theory and devising macroeconomic policy; it is also interesting in its own right. The best way to demonstrate this is simply to say: be patient and follow the economists' advice.

In Chapters 1–10, we will consider a *closed economy*—an economy with no foreign trade (exports or imports) or capital flows. We will postpone the inclusion of exports and imports in our accounting system until Chapter 11, where we will analyze macroeconomics in an *open economy* with foreign trade and capital flows.

1.1 Total Output, Value-Added, and Income

Macroeconomists focus on *totals* or *aggregates* of economic activity. They must determine how to count the total output of the economy during a given year. This may seem difficult because the economy is in a never-ceasing *circular flow*. At all times, goods are being produced and income is being generated and used to buy goods; the cycle repeats itself, without end. Let's consider a simple, common-sense example. We will simplify the economy and assume that there are only three producers: a farmer, a miller, and a baker. How do you count the total output of this simple economy?

You might initially make the mistake of *double-counting*. The farmer sells the miller $100 worth of wheat on August 1; the miller transforms this wheat into flour and sells $250 worth of flour to the baker on September 1; the baker transforms the flour into bread and sells $350 worth of bread to consumers during October. Is it sensible to add $100 + $250 + $350 to obtain a total economic output of $700?

No, it is not. In pricing the flour, the miller takes into account the cost of the wheat; the price of the flour must cover this cost. Thus, the $250 worth of flour includes the value of the wheat that the miller used to make it. If you add the $100 worth of wheat to the $250 worth of flour, when the value of the wheat is already included in the $250, then you are double-counting.

Furthermore, only $350 worth of bread is available for *final* use. The wheat has been transformed into flour and the flour into bread. The values of the transformed wheat and flour are built into the value of the bread. A consumer cannot use the $100 worth of wheat, the $250 worth of flour, and the $350 worth of bread simultaneously. Only *final goods and services* can be counted to obtain *total (final) output*.

One of the most familiar terms in economics — *Gross National Product* (GNP) — now makes its entrance:

GROSS NATIONAL PRODUCT (GNP) is the *total (final) output* — the total value of all (final) goods and services.

In our simple economy, the Gross National Product is $350.

Now let's consider another way of looking at the problem. Each producer — the farmer, the miller, and the baker — *adds value* to the final product (the bread). If the farmer uses only wheat seeds (at no cost) and transforms them into $100 worth of wheat, then the farmer's *value-added* is $100. The miller uses the $100 worth of wheat and transforms it into $250 worth of flour; thus, the miller's value-added is $150. Finally, the baker uses the $250 worth of flour and transforms it into $350 worth of bread; thus, the baker's value-added is $100.

The total value-added for the farmer, the miller, and the baker is therefore $100 + $150 + $100 = $350. It is not a coincidence that $350 is also the value of the final product — the bread. The *total output* is the *total (final)* product or the *total value-added*.

Now suppose that the farmer, the miller, and the baker join together to form a single firm. Each producer continues to add the same value-added as before ($100 for the farmer, $150 for the miller, and $100 for the baker, or a total of $350), but now no buying or selling occurs among them. The only sale is the $350 worth of bread to consumers. Because production is the same as before, the total output is also the same and is not influenced by whether the three producers are independent or whether each producer is part of a single firm. This is the case if we define "total output" as "final product." It is not the case if we define "total output" as "total sales," which will be $100 + $250 + $350 = $700 if the producers are independent but $350 if they work in a single firm.

Thus far, the farmer, the miller, and the baker have been viewed as three individuals who work entirely alone. But this is not so. Actually, each manages a small business firm, pays wages to workers, interest to creditors, and rent to the owners of land and facilities, and retains a profit.

Consider the miller who buys $100 worth of wheat from the farmer, adds value of $150, and sells $250 worth of flour to the baker. The $150 in income to the miller's "firm" is then paid out to the *factors of production:* wages to laborers, $80; interest to creditors, $30; rent to the owner of the mill, $20. The $20 that remains — the "residual" — is the miller's "profit." If, for example, rent were $60, then the miller's profit would be − $20, or a loss of $20.

Profit is the *residual* income that is not paid to the factors of production (the producers of the final product). Subtracting the sum of wages, interest, and rent from total value-added yields the *profit.* If the result is negative, then profit is negative and we call it a *loss.* Profit takes on whatever value is necessary to assure that the sum of all income categories equals the value-added.

For each firm, therefore, the sum of all incomes — wages, interest, rent, and profit — must equal the total value-added of that firm. In our simple economy, the total income of the farmer's firm is $100; of the miller's firm, $150; and of the baker's firm, $100. The sum of all incomes — wages, interest, rent, and profit — in our simple economy is $350, which is equal to the total (final) product and to the total value-added.

Therefore

(1.1)   Total (Final) Output ≡ Total Value-Added ≡ Total Income

This triple equality is a fundamental accounting relationship that always holds. It is called an *accounting identity.* (The symbol consisting of three horizontal bars (≡) indicates an *identity.*)

To summarize, the economy is in a circular flow that never stops to help us track, account for, or analyze it. At all times, production is occurring, value is being added, goods are being sold, income is being generated and paid to the factors of production, and people are buying goods. However, the fundamental accounting identity of triple equality can help us to analyze these various economic activities.

You can better appreciate the accounting identity of triple equality by considering some refinements of our simple example. We will now assume that (believe it or not) $50 of the bread sold by the baker in October was in fact produced in the previous year. (Investigators discover that the bread, after being frozen for months, was secretly thawed in September for October sale.)

Imagine the outcry from economists. The eating of old bread would not disturb them (although it could well incense consumers). But the distortion of the true total output of the economy would certainly evoke their concern. Clearly, the value of the final product produced this year (the total output) was only $300, not $350; yet, $350 worth of bread was sold in October.

To obtain the total output, the sale of the final product must be adjusted by the change in the *stock of inventory* that occurs during the year. At the beginning of the year, the baker had an inventory of frozen bread valued at $50. By the end of the year, the stock of inventory was zero, so that the change in inventory was (−$50). To obtain the final product produced this year, the change in inventory (−$50) must be added to the value of the final product ($350).

Now what about the triple equality of equation (1.1)? The baker's value-added for this year was clearly only $50, not $100. It is true that the baker sold $350 and purchased $250. But to properly compute this year's value-added, the change in inventory must be added to this difference. If the baker's value-added this year is $50, then total value-added is $300 and is equal to total output.

Now let's consider the total income. At first glance, the total income generated by the baker's firm might still appear to be $100 ($350 − $250). But although wages, interest, and rent remain the same, inventory is reduced by $50; therefore, profit (the residual income) should also be reduced by $50 to reflect this loss to the firm. For example, if wages, interest, and rent sum to $60, then the firm retains $40 but loses $50 worth of inventory. Its profit is then the difference between $40 and $50, or (−$10), the total income of the firm equals the value-added, and the triple equality holds.

In the following year, the baker does not freeze any bread and, once again, the sale of the final product (bread) is $350. Everything else remains the same, with one exception: The miller is holding an additional $50 worth of flour at year's end. Total output for the year is actually $400 (not $350), because the stock of inventory had been raised by $50.

What about the triple equality? The miller's value-added is clearly $200 (not $150), so the $50 increase in inventory must be added to obtain the value-added. The total value-added in our simple economy is then $400, which is equal to total output. The miller's profit is also $50 greater due to the $50 increase in inventory, and the total income in our economy is again $400.

Let's consider another refinement. We will now assume that our three producers each use machinery, or *capital equipment*, that wears down, or *depreciates*, each year. (*Depreciation* is the allowance made for a decrease in the value of capital equipment that wears down during the year.) Where did this machinery come from? Imagine that a fourth producer—a machine manufacturer who mines his own metal—generates $100 of value-added and sells $100 worth of machinery. In our previous simple economy with *no* inventory, with a total final product valued at $350, total output is now $450.

But while $100 worth of new machinery is being set up for use by the farmer, the miller, and the baker, some old machinery is depreciating. If the value of the old machinery declines (by, say, $60), then the income category of depreciation must be added to wages, interest, and rent. The residual continues to be profit, but the profit is now further reduced by the amount of depreciation. The triple equality still holds.

Depreciation raises a further issue. The *gross* final product—the machinery—is $100, but the *net* increase in the value of the machinery is only $40 ($100 less the $60 depreciation). Thus, although the *gross output* of the economy is $450, the *net output* is only $390 ($350 worth of bread and a net output of $40 for machinery). Therefore, for the economy

(1.2)   Net Output ≡ Gross Output − Depreciation

But what happens to the triple equality? We can make Net Output = Net Value-added = Net Income by subtracting depreciation from gross value-added to obtain net value-added and by subtracting depreciation from gross income to obtain net income.

By now, you should be appreciating the art of accounting. It consists of seeing the same thing from different angles or perspectives and of making adjustments that preserve important identities.

Finally, we will distinguish between "flow" and "stock." We have already been measuring *flow*—the output, value-added, or income generated during a given time period. By contrast, *stock* is measured at any particular moment in time. For example, at any moment, there is a certain stock, or *quantity*, of machinery in the economy, or the public holds a certain stock or quantity of money at a given time. Machinery is a component of *real wealth*, as are land and natural resources. Money is a component of *financial wealth*; other components include shares of stocks and bonds. Imagine, at any moment in time, totaling up the value of all machines or the sum of all money. Wealth is a stock, but output and income are flows. We measure flows over a time period, not at a particular moment in time.

1.2 The Components of Output and Income

In our simple economy with only four producers, there are two final products: bread and machines. Bread is clearly a consumer good; it is produced to directly satisfy consumer wants. But machinery is an *investment* or a *capital good* that is produced to raise *future* productive power; it does not directly satisfy consumer wants. Of course, machinery produced this year is expected to raise the output of consumer goods and help satisfy consumer wants in the future.

It is useful to divide total (final) output Q into two categories: (1) output actually consumed this year; (2) output to be utilized in future years. We will call the first category *consumption* and the second category *investment:*

(1.3) $$Q \equiv C + I$$

where Q = output

C = consumption

I = investment

Note that investment I is a component of output; I is *not* financial investment. Therefore, the purchase of a machine is an investment; the purchase of bonds or securities (stock) is not investment. It is important to keep this distinction in mind.

In our example with no inventory, $C = \$350$, $I = \$100$, and $Q = \$450$. Here, we are defining Q as *gross* output and I as *gross* investment; we are not subtracting depreciation. (If we did subtract the $60 depreciation from I, we would have a net investment of $40; we would then subtract $60 from Q to obtain a net output of $390.)

Now let's consider the examples with inventory. In one example, the miller adds $50 of flour to his inventory, so that Q becomes $500. We must place this increase in inventory on the right-hand side of equation (1.3) to maintain the equality. Because the flour is not yet consumed but can be utilized in the future, it is regarded as investment; thus, investment increases by $50 to $150. Note that the increase in inventory is a component of investment.

Next, consider the example of the frozen bread (and assume that there is no change in the miller's inventory). With a $50 reduction in the baker's inventory, Q becomes $400. This reduction in inventory reduces investment by $50 ($50 less is available for future use). Thus, C

becomes $350, and I becomes $50 ($100 of new machinery minus a $50 inventory change).

Equation (1.3) is an identity. It must always hold. Every final product must be assigned to either C or I, and any adjustment in inventory must be accounted for in I.

▶ Note that an increase in the inventory of a consumer good is a component of investment because it is not yet consumed and is available for future use.

To show that equation (1.3) is an accounting identity that must be true, we use an equal sign composed of three bars instead of two. Pay attention to this distinction throughout the text. Later, we will learn why it is crucial to distinguish between an *equilibrium condition* (which holds only for a particular value of each variable) and an *identity* (which holds at all values).

From our triple equality, Q is not only total (final) output; it is also *total income*. Total income has two uses in our simple economy with no government: it is either consumed or saved. In fact, we define *saving* as income minus consumption:

(1.4) $$S \equiv Q - C$$

where Q = total income

In our simple economy, wages, interest, and rent are paid out to individuals, who save the income that they do not consume. Depreciation is retained by the firm to replace worn-out capital. Part of the firm's profit is paid out to stockholders who own the firm and who have previously invested financial capital in it. These payments, called *dividends*, are either consumed or saved. Profit that is not paid out in dividends is called *retained earnings*. Depreciation plus retained earnings equals *business saving* (retained earnings alone equals *net* business saving).

Thus, income is divided between consumption and saving (the sum of personal and business saving):

(1.5) $$Q \equiv C + S$$

Equation (1.5) is an identity; it is always true. Any income that is not consumed is considered to be saved.

From equations (1.3) and (1.5), it follows that

(1.6) $$I \equiv S$$

Equation (1.6) is an identity; it is always true.

1.3 Real Output, the Price Level, and Nominal Output

We will now simplify our economy even more by assuming that it produces only one product. Last year, 100 units were produced at a price of $1.00 per unit, so that the value of the total output was $100. This year, the value of total output — the *nominal output* — is $110; hence, nominal output has increased 10%. What has happened?

One possibility is that the price per unit is still $1.00 but that 110 units of output were produced. Another possibility is that 100 units were again produced but that the price per unit is now $1.10. Still another explanation is that the price per unit is now $1.05 and that approximately 105 units were produced. The possibilities are infinite. If Q is the number of units of *real output* and P is the price per unit, all we know is that $PQ = \$110$. Thus

(1.7) $$Y \equiv PQ$$

where Y = nominal output

P = price level

Q = real output

If we know the value of nominal output in a given year and the price per unit, then we can find real output by deflating nominal output by price. Dividing both sides of equation (1.7) by P, we obtain

(1.7') $$Q \equiv \frac{Y}{P}$$

For example, if we are told that nominal output is $110 and that the price per unit is $1.10, then real output is $110/$1.10 = 100.

In an economy with many goods and services, there is no single price; instead, we must use a *price index* to represent the average price (see Appendix 1A). But the principle is the same. Real output (real GNP) — also called *constant-dollar* GNP — can be obtained by deflating nominal output (nominal GNP) — also called *current-dollar* GNP — by the price level (the price index).

Note that when P is a price index, real output Q is measured in dollars. For example, if $Y = \$110$ billion and $P = 1.10$, then $Q = Y/P = \$110/1.10 = \$100$ billion.

The official base year for the United States is 1982. This means that the 1982 price index is 1.00. In 1982, nominal GNP was $3,166 billion; with $P = 1.00$, real GNP was also $3,166 billion. In 1985, nominal GNP was $3,993 billion; hence, nominal GNP in 1985 was 26% higher than in 1982. But in 1985, $P = 1.117$; the price index was 11.7% higher in 1985 than in 1982. Thus, in 1985, real GNP was $3,574 billion (3,993/1.117).

Hence, real GNP was only 13% higher in 1985 than in 1982, even though nominal GNP was 26% higher.

INFLATION is a rise in the *price level* (in the *average price* of goods and services).

▶ During an inflationary period, the rise in real GNP or Q is less than the rise in nominal GNP or Y.

Why is it important to distinguish between real GNP and nominal GNP? Let's suppose that we want to determine if the standard of living is improving. Looking at nominal GNP, we cannot tell; an increase in nominal GNP may be solely due to a rise in the price level. To find out if more goods and services are actually being produced, we must look at real GNP.

This is not to suggest that real GNP is a perfect measure of social well-being. For example, real GNP ignores environmental pollution. The point is that the change in real (not nominal) GNP is relevant to social and economic well-being.

Now suppose that we want to know whether employment will change. We cannot tell by looking at nominal GNP. An increase in nominal GNP may not increase employment, because it may be solely due to a rise in the price level — not to an increase in the production of goods and services. To find out if employment will increase, we must look at real GNP.

Thus, the change in real GNP influences the standard of living and employment, but nominal GNP is what we directly measure. It is important to measure the price increase (see Appendix A) so that nominal GNP can be deflated by the price index to obtain real GNP.

The symbol Q will always designate real output (real GNP). Once again, consider equation (1.3):

(1.3) $$Q \equiv C + I$$

This equation shows that real output is the sum of two components: *real consumption* and *real investment*. Real consumption is obtained by deflating nominal consumption by a *consumption price index;* real investment is obtained by deflating nominal investment by an *investment price index* (see Appendix 1A).

▶ Throughout our analysis, we will usually not repeat the word "real." It should be understood, in an equation like (1.3), that all variables are real, not nominal.

1.4 Equilibrium Output

A basic assumption of the analysis of equilibrium output should be emphasized at the outset.

▶ Throughout Chapter 1, we will assume that the *price level P* is constant and that the *interest rate r* is constant.

Does this mean that we believe P and r are constant in the real economy? Not at all. Our strategy is as follows. In this chapter, we will investigate what happens to output Q when P is constant. In Chapter 2, we will continue to hold P constant but let r vary. Finally, in Chapter 3, we will let both P and r vary to see how the output Q and the price level P of the economy are simultaneously determined.

Consider the hypothesis that the *demand for output D* (the amount of real goods and services that buyers seek to purchase) depends on actual output Q. Why might this hypothesis be true?

Recall a basic national income accounting relationship: total output equals total income. Thus, if Q is total output, then Q is also total income. If we assert that D depends on Q, then we are saying that D depends on actual total income. This seems plausible because consumer demand for output C—the largest component of the total demand for output D—almost certainly varies directly with total income Q. When households earn more income, they demand more output.

Is there a level of Q at which the demand for output D equals actual output Q? Will there normally be only one value of Q at which $Q = D$? Let's consider a simple economy in which the answer to both questions is "yes." As we will see shortly, we call the value of Q, where $D = Q$, the *equilibrium output*. If the economy is at this equilibrium output, then

$$(1.8) \qquad Q = D$$

If we assume that there is no government and no foreign trade, then total demand for output is defined as the sum of consumption demand C and investment demand I in the identity

$$(1.9) \qquad D \equiv C + I$$

▶ Note that in this section, C and I indicate consumption and investment *demand,* respectively—the levels that buyers *plan* or *intend.* By contrast, in the accounting identities (1.3) and (1.5), C and I indicate *actual* consumption and investment. Shortly, we will see that our model assumes that the economy moves rapidly to an output level at which actual consumption equals consumption demand and actual investment equals investment demand. Based on this assumption, we will use the same symbol C to denote actual and planned consumption and the same symbol I to denote actual and planned investment.

Our simple economy consists of two production sectors: (1) the C-sector, which produces consumer goods and services (such as food, clothing, and shelter), and (2) the I-sector, which produces investment goods (such as machinery and equipment). The C-sector responds to consumption (consumer) demand C from households, which buy such goods and services as food, clothing, and shelter. The I-sector responds to investment demand I primarily from business firms, which buy such goods as machinery and equipment. We will soon see that, in equilibrium, the output of consumer goods equals consumer demand and the output of investment goods equals investment demand.

THE CONSUMPTION FUNCTION

From national income accounting, we know that the income earned by each sector of the economy exactly equals the output produced by that sector. The income is received by the suppliers of labor (workers) and the suppliers of financial capital (savers) to that sector. The households that receive this income will use part of their income to finance consumption (consumer) demand C. It seems plausible that the greater their income Q, the greater consumption C will be. A *consumption function* expresses the hypothesis:

(1.10) $C = C_a + cQ$ *Example:* $C = 100 + 0.8Q$

Here, $C_a = \$100$ billion and $c = 0.8$. Figure 1.1 illustrates this consumption function. Note that its slope is 0.8, and that its intercept is 100. If $Q = \$1,000$ billion, then $C = \$900$ billion; if $Q = \$1,500$ billion, then $C = \$1,300$ billion.

In equation (1.10), C has two components: C_a, the component of consumption demand that is independent *(autonomous)* of total income Q, and cQ, the component of consumption demand that depends on Q. (We will see in a moment that c is the *marginal propensity to consume* MPC.)

If consumers become more optimistic, then C_a may increase; then C would increase at a given Q. Thus, the term C_a in equation (1.10) incorporates the fact that C may change even if Q remains constant.

In equation (1.10), the MPC $= c$:

The MARGINAL PROPENSITY TO CONSUME MPC is the ratio of the change in *consumption* C to the change in *total income* Q that precipitates it; hence, the MPC $\equiv \Delta C / \Delta Q$, where Δ indicates *change*.

FIGURE 1.1 A CONSUMPTION FUNCTION

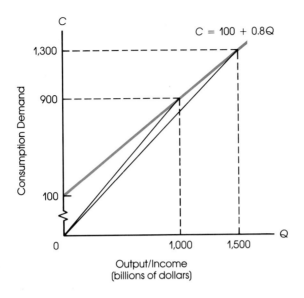

At any point on the C line, the MPC equals the slope of the line; the slope is the same (0.8) at all points on the line. By contrast, at any point on the C line, the APC equals the slope of a line drawn from the point to the origin; hence, the APC at (1,500, 1,300) is less than the APC at (1,000, 900).

In our example, if Q increases by $100 billion and $c = 0.8$, then C will increase by $80 billion; thus, $\Delta C/\Delta Q = 80/100 = 0.8 = c$. Note that for any value of C_a, the MPC $= c$.

It is important to distinguish between the *marginal* propensity to consume MPC and the *average propensity to consume* APC:

The AVERAGE PROPENSITY TO CONSUME APC is the ratio of *consumption C* to *total income Q;* hence, the APC $\equiv C/Q$.

To illustrate the difference between the APC and the MPC in our example, suppose that $Q = $1,000 billion. Then

$$C = 100 + 0.8Q = 100 + 0.8(1,000) = 100 + 800 = 900$$

Hence, the APC $\equiv C/Q = 900/1,000 = 0.9$.

Now suppose that Q increases by $500 billion to $1,500 billion. Since the MPC is 0.8, we know that C will increase by $400 billion to $1,300 billion. We can easily confirm this:

$$C = 100 + 0.8(1,500) = 100 + 1,200 = 1,300$$

Hence, the APC = 1,300/1,500 = 0.87 (approximately).

Thus, in our example, the APC differs from the MPC and varies with Q, while the MPC remains constant. The MPC and the APC can be seen in Figure 1.1. There, at any point on the C line, the MPC equals the slope of the line; the slope is the same (0.8) at all points on the line. By contrast, at any point on the line, the APC equals the slope of a line drawn from the point to the origin because the vertical distance is C and the horizontal distance is Q; hence, the APC varies at each point on the line.

EQUILIBRIUM OUTPUT

To keep our example as simple as possible, we will assume that investment demand I is independent of Q. Investment demand is intended or planned investment — the expenditure on machinery and other investment goods and the increase in inventory that the firm desires. We will also assume that firms determine investment demand based on expectations of future demand for output, so that I is independent of current output Q.

If I and C_a are $100 billion and if c is still 0.8, then solve for the value of Q at which $Q = D$. Substituting equations (1.9) and (1.10) into equation (1.8) and solving for Q, we obtain

$$Q = D = C + I = (100 + 0.8Q) + 100$$
$$0.2Q = 200$$
$$Q = 1,000$$
$$C = 100 + 0.8(1,000) = 900$$

If output $Q = \$1,000$ billion, then income $Q = \$1,000$ billion and consumption demand $C = \$900$ billion. Because investment demand $I = \$100$ billion, total demand $D = \$1,000$ billion; thus, $D = Q$. The C-sector will produce $900 billion, and the I-sector will produce $100 billion.

Now suppose that Q is any value other than $1,000 billion. If, for example, $Q = \$500$ billion, then $C = \$500$ billion. With I at $100 billion, $D = \$600$ billion, so that D exceeds Q. Symmetrically, if $Q = \$1,500$ billion, then $C = \$1,300$ billion. With I at $100 billion, $D = \$1,400$ billion, so that D is less than Q.

Figure 1.2 graphically illustrates the *equilibrium output* — the only value of Q for which $Q = D$, or $Q = \$1,000$ billion. Actual Q is plotted on the horizontal axis, and D and its two components, C and I, are plotted on the vertical axis. The *aggregate-demand line* is given by

$$D = C + I = (100 + 0.8Q) + 100 = 200 + 0.8Q$$

FIGURE 1.2 EQUILIBRIUM OUTPUT

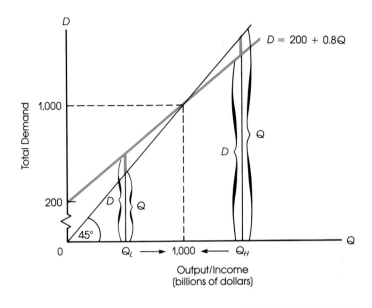

At $Q = \$1{,}000$ billion, $D = Q$. At Q_L, D exceeds Q and so producers will increase Q toward \$1,000 billion. At Q_H, D is less than Q and producers will decrease Q toward \$1,000 billion.

Thus, its slope is 0.8 and its vertical intercept (where $Q = 0$) is 200.

In Figure 1.2, we want to find the point at which $D = Q$. If we draw a 45° line from the origin, we can see that the vertical distance is equal to the horizontal distance at any point on the line. Because the horizontal distance is Q, the vertical distance is also Q. Hence, $D = Q$ where this aggregate-demand line intersects the 45° line. This occurs at only one value of Q. We have just calculated that this special value of Q is \$1,000 billion. It is clear from Figure 1.2 that if Q is less than \$1,000 billion (for example, at Q_L), then D exceeds Q, and if Q is greater than \$1,000 billion (for example, at Q_H), then D is less than Q.

Let's ask two questions concerning this special value of Q (in this example, \$1,000 billion), where $D = Q$. First, if this Q is produced, will producers judge that they have produced the proper Q, or will they want to change Q?

If output is \$1,000 billion, producers will observe that buyers demand exactly \$1,000 billion. It seems plausible that these producers will not want to change Q. Raising Q would probably result in an unwanted increase in unsold inventory, and reducing Q would forego profitable sales. Producers wish to maintain Q at the equilibrium output of $1,000 billion.

▶ If producers have no tendency to change a particular level of Q, then it is an *equilibrium level* of Q. If at a particular level of Q, demand for output is equal to actual output ($D = Q$), then Q is an equilibrium level.

The second question is if Q initially differs from $1,000 billion, so that D does not equal Q, will producers choose to adjust Q to $1,000 billion, so that $Q = D$?

If Q is less than $1,000 billion, then producers will observe that D exceeds Q and will be given a signal to raise Q accordingly. Symmetrically, if Q is greater than $1,000 billion, then producers will observe that D is less than Q and will be given a signal to reduce Q accordingly.

What form will the signal take? If Q is less than D, then, to satisfy demand, inventory will be cut below the level that firms desire. If inventory reaches 0, the demand cannot be satisfied. In either case, firms will have an incentive to raise Q. Symmetrically, if Q exceeds D, then inventory will be increased above the level that firms desire; firms will therefore have an incentive to cut Q.

Thus, the unintended and undesired decumulation or accumulation of inventory signals firms to raise or cut production, respectively, to move Q toward D. In our example, $1,000 billion is a *stable* equilibrium output that eliminates the discrepancy between Q and D.

▶ An equilibrium output Q is *stable* if producers always have a tendency to adjust actual output toward that particular level of Q.

But won't firms want to adjust the price level P as well as the output level Q? Probably. However, the premise of the analysis in this chapter is to take the price level P as given. We are asking what will happen to output Q if price P remains constant? We ignore any price adjustment at this stage; in Chapter 3, the price level will be permitted to vary.

The fact that the equilibrium output is stable provides some justification for our assumption that the actual Q is $1,000 billion. But isn't it possible that producers will make a mistake and produce output at some other level than $Q = $1,000 billion? Yes, but once they observe their mistake, producers will attempt to adjust Q toward $1,000 billion —although this will not happen instantaneously.

Our strategy is to ignore such potential mistakes and to assume that output will tend to gravitate toward its equilibrium value. In the short run, however, it is possible for some discrepancy to exist between actual output Q and the demand for output D generated at that level of Q. Some time may elapse before the gap is closed. By that time, economic conditions may have changed, and a gap may open once again between

Q and D. However, most macroeconomists believe that it is a sensible strategy to develop a macroeconomic model that ignores such discrepancies and to assume that Q will be equal to its equilibrium value.

▶Note that from now on, we will assume that actual consumption equals consumption demand (planned or intended consumption) and that actual investment equals investment demand (planned or intended investment). Based on this assumption, we will use the same symbol to indicate both the actual and the planned levels of a variable. Hence, C will indicate both *actual* and *planned consumption,* and I will indicate both *actual* and *planned investment.*

THE MULTIPLIER

Initially, in the preceding example, investment demand $I = \$100$ billion and, as a result, equilibrium output $Q = \$1,000$ billion. If I increases to $\$200$ billion, what happens to equilibrium output Q? Your response might be that Q will also increase by $\$100$ billion. But this is incorrect because consumption demand C will not remain constant at $\$900$ billion. As soon as Q begins to increase, C will also increase, according to equation (1.10). The rise in Q will equal the initial rise in I ($\$100$ billion) plus the induced rise in C. The consumption function "multiplies" the increase in I, so that Q rises more than the increase in I that provoked the change.

The new equilibrium output Q can be found simply by repeating our earlier calculation, with $I = \$200$ billion instead of $\$100$ billion:

$$Q = D = C + I = C_a + cQ + I = (100 + 0.8Q) + 200$$
$$0.2Q = 300$$
$$Q = 1,500$$
$$C = 100 + 0.8(1,500) = 1,300$$

Thus, when I increases by $\$100$ billion, Q increases by $\$500$ billion. Note that C increases by $\$400$ billion (from $\$900$ billion to $\$1,300$ billion). This result is shown in Figure 1.3.

The MULTIPLIER m is the ratio of the change in *equilibrium output* Q to the change in *investment* I that precipitated the change in Q:

(1.11) $$m \equiv \frac{\Delta Q}{\Delta I}$$

In our example, $m = 500/100 = 5$.

FIGURE 1.3 AN INCREASE IN *I* RAISES EQUILIBRIUM OUTPUT Q

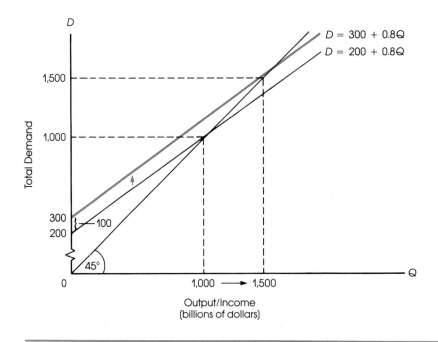

When *I* increases by $100 billion (from $100 billion to $200 billion), the *D* line shifts upward $100 billion (from Q = 200 + 0.8Q to Q = 300 + 0.8Q). Equilibrium output increases by $500 billion (from $1,000 billion to $1,500 billion).

What is happening to the economy in this example? Initially, the C-sector produces $900 billion of output (such as food and clothing) and the I-sector produces $100 billion of output (such as machinery and equipment). Total output Q is therefore $1,000 billion. Now what happens when investment demand increases to $200 billion — that is, when business firms decide they want to buy $200 billion (not $100 billion) worth of investment goods?

The I-sector responds by raising production from $100 billion to $200 billion. Those who receive the income generated by the I-sector — the suppliers of labor and capital to the I-sector — enjoy an increase in income of $100 billion. Since the *propensity to consume c* = 0.8, these income earners raise their consumption demand by $80 billion. In response, the C-sector raises its production by $80 billion (from $900 billion to $980 billion).

Those who receive the income generated by the C-sector — the suppliers of labor and capital to the C-sector — enjoy an increase in income of $80 billion. Because the propensity to consume *c* = 0.8, these income earners raise their consumption demand by $64 billion (0.8 × 80). When the C-sector responds by raising production $64 billion (from $980 billion to $1,044 billion), income earners raise their consumption demand by $51.2 billion (0.8 × 64). And the process continues to repeat itself. Thus, the increase in output is

(1.12)
$$\Delta Q = 100 + \quad 80 \quad + \quad 64 \quad + \cdots$$
$$\Delta Q = 100 + 0.8(100) + 0.8[0.8(100)] + \cdots$$

Earlier, we calculated the new equilibrium output Q to be $1,500 billion, so that $\Delta Q = $500 billion. The sum in series (1.12) should therefore be $500 billion. Is it?

At first glance, it might seem that the sum will grow without limit as additional terms are added, because the series never ends; there is always another round. But no matter how many terms you add to, say, the sum $1 + \frac{1}{2} + \frac{1}{4} + \frac{1}{8} + \frac{1}{16} + \cdots$, the sum gets closer and closer to 2 but never exceeds 2. Thus, an *infinite series* can have a *finite* sum. In this example, the sum is 2.

Our series (1.12) has a finite sum, which can be obtained by multiplying every term on both sides by 0.8:

$$\Delta Q = \quad 100 + \quad 0.8(100) + 0.8[0.8(100)] + \cdots$$
$$0.8(\Delta Q) = 0.8(100) + 0.8[0.8(100)] + \cdots$$

Subtracting the second series from the first cancels every term except 100 on the right side:

$$\Delta Q - 0.8\Delta Q = 100$$
$$0.2\Delta Q = 100$$
$$\Delta Q = 500$$

The sum in series (1.12) is, indeed, $500 billion. Whether we trace the impact on output "round by round" or calculate the new equilibrium output Q directly, we obtain the same answer: $\Delta Q = $500 billion; therefore, Q increases from $1,000 billion to $1,500 billion.

We can use series (1.12) to obtain the formula for the multiplier m in terms of the marginal propensity to consume MPC. Instead of selecting particular numerical values for ΔI and c let's consider series (1.12') for *any* ΔI and c (MPC):

(1.12')
$$\Delta Q = \Delta I + c(\Delta I) + c[c(\Delta I)] + \cdots$$

Again, we multiply each term on both sides by c to obtain

$$c(\Delta Q) = c(\Delta I) + c[c(\Delta I)] + \cdots$$

Subtract this result from series (1.12′), all terms on the right side cancel except ΔI and we obtain

$$\Delta Q - c(\Delta Q) = \Delta I$$

Factoring out ΔQ on the left gives us

$$(1 - c)\Delta Q = \Delta I$$

and dividing by ΔI and $(1 - c)$ yields

$$\frac{\Delta Q}{\Delta I} = \frac{1}{1 - c}$$

From equation (1.11), the left side of this equation is the multiplier m. Since MPC $= c$, we have shown that in our simple model

(1.13) $$m = \frac{1}{1 - \text{MPC}}$$

If, in our example, $c = \text{MPC} = 0.8$, then $m = 1/(0.2) = 5$. The MPC is always a fraction between 0 and 1.

▶ As the marginal propensity to consume MPC becomes greater, the denominator on the right side of equation (1.13) becomes smaller and the multiplier m becomes greater.

1.5   An Economy with Government

We will now introduce government into our simple economy. Government receives *tax revenue T* from households and firms, it gives *government transfers R* to some households and firms, and it directly purchases some *final product G*. How do we integrate government into our national income accounting relationships?

Let's begin by emphasizing that government expenditure has two components:

GOVERNMENT EXPENDITURES equals *government purchases G* plus *government transfers R.*

An example of a government purchase G is the government purchase of labor and materials to build a highway. Examples of government transfers R are the payment of Social Security benefits, unemployment compensation, or welfare benefits to households. It therefore is important to distinguish between these two components of government spending.

We can now divide output into three categories. It is *consumed* or *invested* in the private sector or it is *purchased* by government. Thus, equation (1.3) becomes

(1.14) $Q \equiv C + I + G$

where G = government purchases of goods and services

If, for example, a machine manufacturer in the private sector also makes \$100 worth of military equipment for government purchase, then $G = \$100$. Here, a private firm produces the equipment and the government purchases it. The government itself may also be a producer; that is, it may add value. For example, if the government employs workers to provide a service — say, the maintenance of the national park system — then this government purchase of a service is included in G; moreover, the government is regarded as a "firm" that contributes value-added when it provides this service.

Now let's reconsider equation (1.4)

(1.4) $S \equiv Q - C$

which defines saving as income minus consumption. In an economy that includes government, *private saving* (personal saving plus business saving) equals *private net income* less consumption C, where private net income equals total income Q less tax revenue T plus government transfers R:

(1.15) $S \equiv (Q - T + R) - C$

where S = private saving

T = tax revenue

R = government transfers

$(Q - T + R)$ = private net income

Moving C to the left side, we have

(1.16) $C + S \equiv Q - T + R$

which states that private net income is used for consumption and saving.

It is useful to isolate Q in equation (1.16). Moving T and R to the left side, we obtain

(1.17) $C + S + (T - R) \equiv Q$

Here, $T - R$ is the *net tax* (tax revenue less government transfers). Thus, equation (1.17) tells us that total income is divided between consumption, private saving, and net tax.

Combining equations (1.14) and (1.17) gives us

$$C + I + G \equiv C + S + T - R$$

Canceling C and subtracting G from both sides yields

(1.18) $\qquad I \equiv S + (T - R - G)$

Here, $T - R - G$ is government (tax) revenue less government expenditures or the *government budget surplus Su:*

(1.19) $\qquad Su \equiv T - R - G$

If Su is negative, then the government budget is said to be "in deficit." For example, if the government budget surplus Su is $-\$100$ billion, we say that the *government budget deficit Df* is $\$100$ billion. Hence, $Df \equiv -Su$.

Substituting equation (1.19) into equation (1.18) yields

(1.20) $\qquad I \equiv S + Su$

$\qquad$ where I = private investment

$\qquad\qquad S$ = private saving

$\qquad\qquad Su$ = government surplus

Equation (1.20) is an important identity. It states that private investment must equal the sum of private saving and the government budget surplus. If the budget is in deficit (Su is negative), then private investment will be less than private saving by the amount of the deficit. For a given level of private saving S, as the budget deficit increases, private investment will decrease.

Dividing each term in equation (1.20) by Q, we obtain

(1.21) $\qquad \dfrac{I}{Q} \equiv \dfrac{S}{Q} + \dfrac{Su}{Q}$

I/Q is the ratio of private investment to total output, S/Q is the ratio of private saving to total output, and Su/Q is the ratio of the government surplus to total output. Equation (1.21) holds whether I and S are both gross or both net (gross less depreciation) values. We will consider the case in which both I and S are net values.

Some forecasters have projected that in the second half of the 1980s in the United States, S/Q will average roughly 7% and Su/Q will average roughly -3%. Ignoring the impact of foreign trade, this implies an I/Q ratio of approximately 4%. In other words, the projected government deficit implies that private investment would be half of private saving.

Equations (1.20) and (1.21) are accounting identities that must be true. They do not depend on behavioral relationships (such as whether deficits cause high interest rates), nor do they imply causality. We can only conclude, at this point, that I will be less than S if the government budget is in deficit (ignoring the impact of foreign trade).

TOTAL INVESTMENT AND TOTAL SAVING

Equation (1.20) may seem to imply that, with government in the economy, investment and saving are no longer equal. But this inference is incorrect. Equation (1.20) states that *private* investment is not equal to *private* saving (unless the surplus is 0). We will now show that when government is included in the economy, it remains true that total investment must equal total saving.

When the government purchases goods and services, part of these expenditures provide current satisfaction for the public (for example, expenditure on recreational services or on operation of the national parks). This component of government expenditures, denoted by G_C, should be regarded as consumption. People derive current satisfaction from services purchased on their behalf by government, just as they do from the goods and services they consume privately. (Note that *consumers* — not the government — derive satisfaction from government consumption.) Thus, *total consumption* C_T is the sum of private consumption C and *government consumption* G_C:

(1.22) $$C_T \equiv C + G_C$$

where C_T = total consumption

C = private consumption

G_C = government consumption

Government purchases that do not provide current satisfaction are intended to raise future productivity. This component of government expenditures is *government investment*, denoted by G_I. For example, government construction of roads, bridges, and schools are included in G_I. Thus, *total investment* I_T is the sum of private investment and government investment:

(1.23) $$I_T \equiv I + G_I$$

where I_T = total investment

I = private investment

G_I = government investment

Thus, equation (1.14) can be rewritten

$$Q \equiv C + I + G$$
$$\equiv C + I + G_c + G_I$$
$$\equiv (C + G_c) + (I + G_I)$$
(1.24) $$Q \equiv C_T + I_T$$

to show that total output equals total consumption plus total investment.

Incidentally, it is not obvious whether certain military expenditures should be categorized as government consumption or government investment. Military expenditure on capital goods can be regarded as an investment, because these durable goods provide a flow of "security" over a number of years (just as private capital goods provide a flow of output). However, when the improvement in the material standard of living based on a rise in consumption of "ordinary" goods and services is to be measured, military expenditure cannot be included in G_I. This choice does not affect the equality of total investment and total saving.

Now let's turn to *total saving* S_T—the sum of private and government saving. We have already focused on private saving (the sum of personal saving and business saving). We must now recognize that there is also *government saving* S_G. Just as private saving is defined as net income less consumption, government saving is defined as *government net income* $(T - R)$ less government consumption:

(1.25) $$S_G \equiv T - R - G_c$$

where S_G = government saving

G_c = government consumption

Note that government saving S_G differs from the government surplus Su. To show the relationship between Su and S_G, we recall equation (1.19):

(1.19) $$Su \equiv T - R - G$$

Splitting government expenditures G into its two components

$$Su \equiv T - R - G_c - G_I$$

and substituting equation (1.25) into equation (1.19), we obtain

(1.26) $$Su \equiv S_G - G_I$$

which states that the government surplus equals government saving less government investment.

For example, if tax revenue $T = \$200$ billion, government transfers $R = \$100$ billion, and government consumption $G_C = \$40$ billion; then from equation (1.25), government saving $S_G = \$60$ billion. If government investment $G_I = \$50$ billion, then from equation (1.26) the government surplus $Su = \$10$ billion.

Just as we defined total investment I_T in equation (1.23), we can now define total saving S_T as

(1.27) $\qquad S_T \equiv S + S_G$

where $S_T =$ total saving

$\qquad\qquad S =$ private saving

$\qquad\qquad S_G =$ government saving

Let's restate equations (1.15) and (1.25):

(1.15) $\qquad S \equiv (Q - T + R) - C$

(1.25) $\qquad S_G \equiv T - R - G_C$

If we add these two equations, T and R are eliminated, giving us

$$S + S_G \equiv Q - (C + G_C)$$

By identity (1.22), the term in parentheses on the right side of this equation is total consumption C_T; by identity (1.27), the term on the left side is total saving S_T. Thus, we can see that total saving equals total income minus total consumption:

(1.28) $\qquad S_T \equiv Q - C_T$

Combining identities (1.24) and (1.28), we find that total investment equals total saving:

(1.29) $\qquad I_T \equiv S_T$

Several conclusions deserve emphasis at this point. In an economy with government (but no foreign trade), the following conclusions hold true:

▶ *Total saving* equals *total income* minus *total consumption.*

▶ *Total investment* equals *total saving.*

▶ Total investment does not consist solely of private investment; government investment is an important component of total investment.

▶ Total saving does not consist solely of private saving; government saving is an important component of total saving.

1.6 Equilibrium Output in an Economy with Government

We will now extend our simple model of equilibrium output to include government expenditures and taxes. Our model consists of three equations:

(1.30) $$Q = C + I + G$$

(1.31) $$C = C_a + c(Q - T + R) \qquad \textit{Example: } C = 0 + 0.8(Q - T + R)$$

(1.32) $$T = tQ \qquad \textit{Example: } T = 0.25Q$$

where $t =$ the *tax rate*

Equation (1.30) states that when the economy is in equilibrium, actual output Q will equal D, which consists of three components: consumption demand, investment demand, and government demand.

Equation (1.31) is a consumption function. It takes the same form as equation (1.10). First, it includes C_a—a component of C that is independent (autonomous) of total income. (Of course, C_a may be 0.) The second component of equation (1.10) is cQ, where Q denotes total income; the second component in equation (1.31) is $c(Q - T + R)$, where $(Q - T + R)$ denotes *net income*, which was introduced in equation (1.15). Recall that government transfers R consist of government payments, such as Social Security benefits, unemployment compensation, and welfare payments.

Because net income $Q - T + R$ replaces total income Q, we must modify our earlier definitions of the average propensity to consume APC and the marginal propensity to consume MPC:

The AVERAGE PROPENSITY TO CONSUME APC is the ratio of *consumption* to *net income*, or $C/(Q - T + R)$. The MARGINAL PROPENSITY TO CONSUME MPC is the ratio of the *change in consumption* to the *change in net income*, or $\Delta C / \Delta (Q - T + R)$.

Note the distinction between government purchases G and government transfers R. Both are government expenditures. But if the government buys military or road-construction equipment, then the purchase is included in G. If the government raises Social Security payments to households, then this expenditure is included in R, not in G. G is a direct demand for goods and services from producers; R is not a direct demand. When R increases, net income increases and households will decide how much their consumption demand will change through the consumption function given in equation (1.31).

To simplify this discussion, let's assume that R, like G, is independent of Q. (In reality, most government transfers, such as unemployment compensation and welfare payments, increase when Q decreases. We will consider a more realistic *transfer function* in Chapter 9.)

In equation (1.31), MPC $= c$. If net income increases by $100, then consumption increases by $80 and MPC $= 0.8$. Equation (1.32) is a simple *tax function*, where T is tax revenue and t is the tax rate. In this economy, it is assumed that taxes T are simply the fraction t of income Q. This is the case if the only tax is an income tax with a single rate t that applies to all income.

An example will illustrate how our extended model determines the equilibrium output Q. If $I = \$380$ billion, $G = \$300$ billion, $C_a = 0$, $c = 0.8$, $R = \$250$ billion, and $t = 25\%$, then we can obtain equilibrium output Q by substituting equation (1.32) into (1.31) and equation (1.31) into (1.30) as follows:

$$Q = 0.8(Q - 0.25Q + 250) + 380 + 300$$
$$Q = 0.8(0.75Q + 250) + 680$$
$$Q = 0.6Q + 200 + 680$$
$$0.4Q = 880$$
$$Q = 2{,}200$$
$$T = 0.25(2{,}200) = 550$$
$$C = 0.8(2{,}200 - 550 + 250) = 1{,}520$$

Thus, equilibrium output $Q = \$2{,}200$ billion. It is convenient to assume that $2,200 billion happens to be the *full-employment level of output*. This means that to produce output of $2,200 billion, firms must employ everyone who wants to work (except for an inevitable *frictional level* of unemployment). (*Unemployment* will be examined in depth in Chapter 7.) We will regard $Q = \$2{,}200$ billion as the desired or *target level* of output Q. This equilibrium at $Q = \$2{,}200$ billion is shown in Figure 1.4.

THE MULTIPLIER

Now suppose that investment demand declines (by $80 billion) from $380 billion to $300 billion, perhaps because business managers have become more pessimistic. What happens to equilibrium output Q? We simply repeat the steps just taken, but with $I = \$300$:

FIGURE 1.4 A DECREASE IN *I* REDUCES EQUILIBRIUM OUTPUT Q

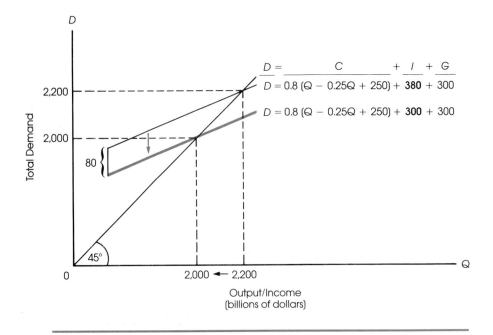

Initially, *I* is $380 billion and equilibrium output *Q* is $2,200 billion. Then *I* decreases by $80 billion to $300 billion, shifting the *D* line down by $80 billion. The equilibrium output *Q* decreases by $200 billion (from $2,200 billion to $2,000 billion).

$$Q = 0.8(Q - 0.25Q + 250) + 300 + 300$$
$$Q = 2,000$$
$$T = 0.25(2,000) = 500$$

The decline in equilibrium output *Q* to $2,000 billion is shown in Figure 1.4. It is not surprising that *Q* declines below $2,200 billion. But why does *Q* decrease by $200 billion (from $2,200 billion to $2,000 billion) when *I* declines by only $80 billion?

Earlier, in our model of a simple economy without government, we divided the economy into two sectors: the I (investment goods)-sector, and the C (consumer goods)-sector. Now, we consider the economy to be divided into three production sectors: the I-sector, the C-sector, and the G-sector, which produces government goods and services.

Initially, when investment demand declines by $80 billion, the I-sector responds by reducing its output by $80 billion. Consequently, income earned in the investment sector decreases by $80 billion.

Through the consumption function, this decrease in income reduces the demand for consumer goods, and the C-sector then responds by reducing its output.

Thus, the initial decline in I *multiplies* through the consumption function, so that the total decrease in equilibrium output Q exceeds the decrease in I that precipitated it. Let's check to be sure that if $Q = \$2,000$ billion, then $Q = D$. If $Q = \$2,000$ billion, then

$$C = C_a + c(Q - T + R) = 0 + 0.8(2,000 - 500 + 250) = 1,400$$
$$I = \qquad\qquad\qquad\qquad\qquad\qquad\qquad\quad = \quad 300$$
$$G = \qquad\qquad\qquad\qquad\qquad\qquad\qquad\quad = \quad 300$$
$$D = \qquad\qquad\qquad\qquad\qquad\qquad\qquad\quad = 2,000$$

When Q decreases by $\$200$ billion (from $\$2,200$ billion to $\$2,000$ billion), the I-sector reduces its output by $\$80$ billion (from $\$380$ billion to $\$300$ billion) and the C-sector reduces its output by $\$120$ billion (from $\$1,520$ billion to $\$1,400$ billion). The $45°$ diagram in Figure 1.4 illustrates how the decline in I reduces equilibrium output Q.

Recall from equation (1.11) that the multiplier is the ratio of the change in equilibrium output Q to the change in investment I that precipitated it:

(1.11) $$m \equiv \frac{\Delta Q}{\Delta I}$$

In this example, $m = 200/80 = 2.5$. This means that a decrease in I results in a decrease in Q that is 2.5 times as great.

THE DEFICIT

Now let's examine how the decrease in I and in equilibrium output Q affect the government budget. The *government budget deficit Df* is defined as government expenditure $G + R$ less tax revenue T:

(1.33) $$Df \equiv G + R - T$$

Recall that the government budget surplus Su is defined in equation (1.19), and note that $Df \equiv -Su$.

We calculated that when $I = \$380$ billion, $T = \$550$ billion; with $R = \$250$ billion and $G = \$300$ billion, the deficit is 0 and the budget is balanced. When I decreases to $\$300$ billion, we saw that, through the tax function (1.32), the decline in Q causes an automatic decrease in T. We calculate that if T decreases to $\$500$ billion, then the deficit becomes

$$Df \equiv G + R - T = 300 + 250 - 500 = 50$$

Note that the deficit does not occur because G or R is raised or because the tax rate t is cut. G, R, and t are all held constant: G at \$300 billion, R at \$250 billion, and t at 25%. The deficit occurs because when income falls, tax revenue declines automatically given the tax function (1.32).

This brings us to an important distinction. Although there is an actual deficit of \$50 billion in our example, it is solely due to the fact that Q is only \$2,000 billion instead of the full-employment level of \$2,200 billion. At the current level of government expenditure ($G = \$300$ billion, $R = \$250$ billion) and tax rate ($t = 25\%$), the government budget would be balanced if Q were at the full-employment level of \$2,200 billion. It is therefore useful to define the *full-employment surplus (deficit)* which can be contrasted with the *actual surplus (deficit)*:

The FULL-EMPLOYMENT SURPLUS (DEFICIT) is the *budget surplus (deficit)* that would occur at the *full-employment level* of output Q, given current government expenditures $G + R$ and the tax rate t.

In our model, G, R, and t are independent of Q, and would therefore be the same if Q were at the full-employment level. It is tax revenue T that varies directly with Q. As we will see in Chapter 9, in our actual economy, government transfers R do in fact vary with Q; for example, as Q increases, payments for unemployment compensation and welfare decrease. Thus, the R that would occur at the full-employment level of Q should be used to calculate the full-employment surplus (deficit).

Initially, if $I = \$380$ billion, actual output Q is at the full-employment level of \$2,200 billion, so that the actual deficit equals the full-employment deficit; in fact, both are initially 0. When I declines to \$300 billion, the actual deficit becomes \$50 billion. But the full-employment deficit remains at 0 because if Q were still at \$2,200 billion, with $G = \$300$ billion, $R = \$250$ billion, and $t = 25\%$ (yielding tax revenue T of \$550 billion), then the deficit would be 0.

If we look only at the actual deficit, which moves from 0 to \$50 billion, we cannot tell if government spending or tax policy has changed or if output has changed because, for example, investment demand has changed. But the fact that the full-employment deficit does not change (it remains at 0) tells us that the change in the actual deficit is not due to a change in government policy but, rather, to a change in actual output Q resulting from some other cause (such as a change in investment demand).

We will now address the following question: Is it desirable that tax revenue vary directly with income, as given by the tax function $T = tQ$ in equation (1.32)? You might be inclined to view this tax system as harmful. If tax revenue T were not influenced by Q, then the budget would remain balanced, despite a decline in Q.

What kind of a tax would keep total tax revenue independent of Q? If a *per-capita tax* were implemented, then each person would owe the government $X in tax, regardless of his or her income, and the total tax revenue owed to the government in a given year would be independent of Q. If an IQ (intelligence quotient) tax were implemented, then each person would owe the government a tax proportional to his or her IQ (measured by the score on an aptitude test), regardless of his or her income; once again, total tax revenue owed the government would be independent of Q. Try to think of other examples.

If tax revenue T is independent of Q, then when I decreases from $380 billion to $300 billion, an even greater decline in Q occurs. Why? If T is constant when Q decreases, then net income $Q - T + R$ will decline as much as Q. But if T decreases automatically with Q, as is the case when $T = tQ$, then net income $Q - T + R$ will decline less than Q. For example, when Q declines by $100 billion, if T decreases by $25 billion, then $Q - T + R$ will decline by only $75 billion. Thus, according to the consumption function, C will not decrease as much.

To show this, we replace equation (1.32) with equation (1.34), which states that tax revenue T is *constant* (independent of Q) and is always equal to $550 billion:

(1.34) $$T = 550 \quad \text{for any } Q$$

First, let's make sure that at the initial $I = $380 billion, Q is still $2,200 billion. Substituting equation (1.34) into equations (1.31) and (1.30) yields

$$Q = 0.8(Q - 550 + 250) + 680$$
$$Q = 2,200$$

Thus, with tax revenue held constant at $550 billion, $Q = $2,200 billion when $I = $380 billion.

If I decreases by, say, $80 billion (from $380 billion to $300 billion), we simply repeat the same steps with $I = $300 billion:

$$Q = 0.8(Q - 550 + 250) + 600$$
$$Q = 1,800$$

This time the multiplier is

$$m \equiv \frac{\Delta Q}{\Delta I} = \frac{400}{80} = 5.0$$

Thus, our original tax function (1.32) results in a smaller multiplier ($m = 2.5$) than a constant tax ($m = 5.0$). When I decreases, the equilibrium output Q of the economy decreases less with our original tax function than with a constant tax revenue, because the automatic decline in tax revenue cushions net income and consumption demand.

This brings us to an important conclusion:

▶ A tax system that makes tax revenue automatically vary in the same direction as income is called an *automatic stabilizer;* it makes the multiplier smaller than it would be under a constant tax revenue.

Many economists believe that the automatic stabilizer in our tax system is an important defense against economic depression.

THE CONSEQUENCES OF BALANCED BUDGET RULES

We will now extend our example to address an important policy issue. Is it desirable to require that the government budget should be *balanced*? A balanced budget rule, implemented by either a statute or a constitutional amendment, has been seriously considered in recent years. We will begin with the *always-balanced budget rule*.

Suppose that such a rule were in effect when investment demand I decreases from $380 billion to $300 billion. We have seen that the resulting decline in equilibrium output Q from $2,200 billion to $2,000 billion changes a balanced budget to a deficit of $50 billion. Under this balanced budget rule, Congress would be required to cut government spending $(R + G)$ or raise the tax rate t immediately to achieve a balanced budget. What would be the consequence of such fiscal action for Q?

A reduction in government transfers R or an increase in the tax rate t would reduce net income $(Q - T + R)$ and consequently reduce consumer demand C. This impact is evident in consumption function (1.31). Hence, C, one component of total demand D, would decrease in equation (1.30). A cut in government purchases G would reduce another component of total demand D in equation (1.30). Thus, fiscal action to balance the budget would reduce total demand D and cause equilibrium output Q to fall below $2,000 billion.

▶ Implementation of an *always-balanced budget rule* would require fiscal action that would worsen a recession. Such a rule would therefore be *destabilizing*.

To confirm this intuitive conjecture, let's calculate the Q that would result from an effort to balance the budget during a recessionary period. We will consider a reduction in R and an increase in t. (Try to calculate the effect of a cut in G yourself.)

If R is cut to balance the budget

$$R + G = T$$
$$R + G = tQ$$
$$R + 300 = 0.25Q$$
$$R = 0.25Q - 300$$

Substituting this expression for R into our equation for Q yields

$$Q = 0.8(Q - 0.25Q + R) + 300 + 300$$
$$Q = 0.8[Q - 0.25Q + (0.25Q - 300)] + 300 + 300$$
$$Q = 1,800$$
$$R = 0.25(1,800) - 300 = 150$$
$$T = 0.25(1,800) = 450$$

Thus, the budget would be balanced (spending and tax revenue would equal $450 billion), and Q would fall to $1,800 billion.

If t is raised to balance the budget

$$R + G = T$$
$$250 + 300 = T$$

Setting $T = 550$ in our equation for Q yields

$$Q = 0.8(Q - 550 + 250) + 300 + 300$$
$$Q = 1,800$$
$$t = \frac{T}{Q} = \frac{550}{1,800} = 30.6\%$$

Thus, the budget would be balanced (spending and tax revenue would equal $550 billion), and Q would fall to $1,800 billion.

▶ Our analysis shows that it would be undesirable to require that the government budget *always* be balanced, because such an always-balanced budget rule would be destabilizing.

This conclusion, however, applies only to the always-balanced budget rule. Other versions of a balanced budget rule are not destabilizing. For example, under an alternative rule, which we will call the *full-employment balanced budget rule*, government expenditures and the tax rate would be set so that the budget would be balanced if the economy is producing at the full-employment level of output.

Suppose that $R = \$250$ billion, $G = \$300$ billion, and $t = 25\%$. If $Q = \$2,200$ billion at the full-employment level of output, then the budget would be balanced (spending and tax revenue would equal $550 billion). These values of R, G, and t therefore satisfy the full-employment balanced budget rule.

But the key point to emphasize here is that these values of R, G, and t would satisfy this balanced budget rule regardless of the actual state of the economy or the actual government budget deficit. If I decreases from, say, $380 billion to $300 billion, then Q decreases (from $2,200 billion to $2,000 billion) and the deficit increases (from 0 to $50 billion). But the balanced budget rule does not require any change in R, G, or t, because these values *would* yield a balanced budget *if* the economy were operating at the full-employment level of output ($Q = $2,200 billion).

▶ A *full-employment balanced budget rule* would not be destabilizing; it would not require fiscal action that would worsen a recession.

Although a full-employment balanced budget rule would not be destabilizing, it would prevent the adjustment of government expenditures and/or the tax rate to try to hit the targeted output level of $Q = $2,200 billion. Thus, the rule would not permit implementation of an *activist* fiscal policy designed to maintain full-employment output.

The rule could be modified, however, to implement an activist fiscal policy. We will call this rule the *full-employment normally balanced budget rule*. According to this rule, if Q is on target this year, then government expenditures and the tax rate must be set so that the budget would be balanced next year if the economy is operating at the full-employment level of output. But if Q is below target this year, then government expenditures must be raised and/or the tax rate must be lowered to stimulate demand. If Q is above target this year, then government expenditures must be cut and/or the tax rate must be raised to restrain demand. The amounts by which government expenditures and the tax rate must be adjusted could be specified in a formula.

▶ A *full-employment normally balanced budget rule* would not be destabilizing and would prescribe fiscal action that tries to keep the economy operating at the full-employment level of output.

Is some version of a balanced budget rule desirable? Our analysis will address this question when we further analyze budget deficits and fiscal policy in Chapters 2, 8, 9, 10, and 15. Here, we simply emphasize the following point:

▶ An *always-balanced budget rule* is destabilizing. It is possible, however, to devise a balanced budget rule that is not destabilizing and that prescribes stabilizing fiscal action.

1. An important *national income accounting identity* is the triple equality

   Total (Final) Output ≡ Total Value-Added ≡ Total Income

2. *Gross National Product* (GNP) is the *total (final) output*—the total value of all (final) goods and services.

3. Net Output ≡ Gross Output − Depreciation.

4. In an economy with no government or foreign trade, *output Q* is divided between *consumption C* and *investment I*. Since *saving S* is defined as income Q not spent on consumption C, output Q is also divided between consumption C and saving S. It therefore follows that investment I must be equal to saving S.

5. *Nominal output Y* changes due to a change in the *price level P* and/or a change in *real output Q*. Thus, $Y = PQ$. Q, not Y, is a critical determinant of both the standard of living and employment. *Inflation* is defined as a rise in the average price P.

6. The simple model of *equilibrium output* assumes that the price level P and the *interest rate r* are constant.

7. The condition for equilibrium is that output Q equals the *demand for output D*. If D exceeds Q, then producers will increase Q; if Q exceeds D, then producers will reduce Q.

8. In an economy with no government, the two components of D are *consumption demand C* and *investment demand I*. I is assumed to be independent of Q. But C is assumed to vary directly with Q; this relationship is called the *consumption function*.

9. The *multiplier m* is defined as $\Delta Q/\Delta I$. For example, if $m = 5$ and I increases by 100, then equilibrium output Q increases by 500. The *marginal propensity to consume* MPC is defined as $\Delta C/\Delta Q$. For example, if the MPC $= 0.8$ and Q increases by 100, then C will increase by 80. It can be shown that $m = 1/(1 - \text{MPC})$. As the MPC increases, the multiplier increases.

10. In an economy with government, Q is divided among C, I, and G *(government purchases)*; Q is also divided among C, S, and $T - R$, where T is *tax revenue* and R is *government transfers*.

11. Government Expenditures ≡ Government Purchases G + Government Transfers R.

12. Two important accounting identities are:

    Private Investment I ≡ Private Saving S + the *government surplus Su*

    where $Su \equiv T - R - G$; and

Total Investment $I_T \equiv$ Total Saving S_T

where $I_T \equiv I + G_I$ (*government investment*)

$S_T \equiv S + S_G$ (*government saving*, or $T - R - G_C$)

13. The *full-employment surplus (deficit)* is the *budget surplus (deficit)* that would occur at the *full-employment level of output Q*, given current *government expenditures G + R* and the *tax rate t*.

14. A tax system that makes tax revenue T automatically vary directly with income Q is an *automatic stabilizer*. In response to a given decrease in I, equilibrium output Q decreases less than it would if tax revenue were independent of income; therefore, an automatic stabilizer reduces the multiplier. Many economists believe that this automatic stabilizer is an important defense against economic depression.

15. An *always-balanced budget rule* is destabilizing in that it would require fiscal action that would worsen a recession. It is possible to devise a balanced budget rule that is not destabilizing.

TERMS AND CONCEPTS

accounting identity
actual investment (I)
aggregate demand line
always-balanced budget rule
automatic stabilizer
average propensity to consume
 (APC)
balanced budget
capital
circular flow
closed economy
constant-dollar GNP
consumption demand (C)
consumption function
current-dollar GNP
demand for output (D)
depreciation
dividends
double counting
equilibrium
equilibrium output (Q)
factors of production
final goods and services
flow

full-employment balanced
 budget rule
full-employment level of output
 (Q)
full-employment normally
 balanced budget rule
full-employment surplus
 (deficit)
government budget deficit (Df)
government budget surplus (Su)
government consumption (C_C)
government expenditures
 ($G + R$)
government investment (G_I)
government purchases of goods
 and services (G)
government saving (S_G)
government transfers (R)
Gross National Product (GNP)
gross output
infinite series
inflation
inventory
investment demand (I)

marginal propensity to consume (MPC)
multiplier (m)
national income accounting
net income ($Q - T + R$)
net output
net taxes ($T - R$)
nominal GNP
nominal output
open economy
planned (intended) investment
price index
price level (P)
private investment (I)
private saving (S)

profit
real GNP
real output
real wealth
retained earnings
stock
tax function
the tax rate (t)
tax revenue (T)
total (final) output (Q)
total income (Q)
total saving (S_T)
transfer function
value-added

QUESTIONS

1.1 If a farmer sells a miller $200 worth of wheat on August 1, the miller sells $500 worth of flour to a baker on September 1, and the baker sells $700 worth of bread to consumers during October:
   a. What is *total output*?
   b. What is the *value-added* of each producer; what is *total value-added*?

1.2 Suppose that each producer in Question 1.1 manages a firm; each pays wages to workers, interest to creditors, and rent to owners of land and facilities, and retains a profit. What is the *income* generated by each firm? What is the *total income*?

1.3 If $100 worth of the bread sold in October in Question 1.1 was produced in the previous year and frozen for a year:
   a. What is the *value-added* of the baker this year?
   b. What is *total value-added*?
   c. What is the *change in inventory*?
   d. What is the *total (final) output*?
   e. What is the income generated in the baker's firm?
   f. What is *total income*?

1.4 If the miller in Question 1.1 held an additional $100 worth of flour at the end of the year than was held at the beginning of the year:
   a. What is the *total output*?
   b. What is the miller's *value-added*?
   c. What is *total value-added*?
   d. What is the *income* generated by the miller's firm?
   e. What is the *total income* of the farmer, the miller, and the baker?

1.5 Assuming an economy with no government, with $C = 0.75Q$:

a. If investment demand $I = \$200$ billion, then what is the *equilibrium output* Q?
b. If *I increases* to $300 billion, then what is the *equilibrium output* Q?
c. What is the value of the *multiplier m*? Does $m = 1/(1 - \text{MPC})$?
d. Draw a diagram to illustrate (a), (b), and (c).
e. What is the increase in *consumption*?
f. Explain how the increase in *I* first stimulates the production of *investment* goods, but then stimulates the production of *consumption* goods.
g. Show that successive increases in consumption add up to the total increase in consumption in part (e).
h. Suppose that $C = 120 + 0.6Q$, and rework parts (a), (b), and (c).

1.6 In an economy with government, show that:
a. *Private investment* equals *private saving* plus *the government surplus* $(I \equiv S + Su)$.
b. *Total investment* equals *total saving* $(I_T = S_T)$.

1.7 Assuming that $C = 0.75(Q - T + R)$, $T = 0.20Q$, $G = \$300$ billion, $R = \$200$ billion, and $I = \$550$ billion:
a. What is the *equilibrium output* Q?
b. What is the *budget surplus* (or *deficit*)?
c. If *I decreases* to $450 billion, what is the *equilibrium output* Q?
d. What is the value of the *multiplier*?
e. What is the budget surplus (or deficit)?

1.8 If *T* is constant at $500 billion (instead of $0.20Q$), rework Question 1.7. What did you learn from doing this?

APPENDIX 1A

NATIONAL INCOME ACCOUNTING

Appendix 1A extends our treatment of national income accounting.

1.A.1 Real versus Nominal Output and Income

In Chapter 1, we distinguished between nominal and real output in a simple economy producing only one good. For convenience, let's rewrite equation (1.7) here:

(1.7) $Y \equiv PQ$

Y = nominal output

P = price level

Q = real output

We then found that if we know the value of nominal output in a given year and the price per unit, we can determine real output by *deflating* nominal output by price. Dividing both sides of equation (1.7) by P, we obtained

(1.7′) $$Q \equiv \frac{Y}{P}$$

For example, if we are told that nominal output is $110 and that the price per unit is $1.10, then real output is $110/$1.10 = 100.

Now let us turn to an economy with many goods and services. We are now confronted with many prices, and we need to work with a price index.

Let's begin by recalling our definition of *gross national product* (GNP) as the total value of all *(final)* goods and services.

At this point, we want to focus on the distinction between nominal GNP and real GNP. To do this, we arbitrarily choose a year and call it the *base year*. Currently, the official base year in the United States is 1982. We then assign a price index of 1.00 to that base year. Next, we use equation (1.7′) to define real GNP, where P assumes the value of the price index. Thus, in the base year 1982, equation (1.7′) becomes

(1.A.1) $$Q_b \equiv \frac{Y_b}{P_b} = \frac{Y_b}{1.00} = Y_b$$

In the base year, real GNP (measured in dollars) is the same as nominal GNP. For example, real and nominal GNP both equal $3,166 billion in the official national income accounts in 1982.

Consider 1983 when the *average price* is 3.8% higher than it is in the base year of 1982. The price index for 1983 is therefore 1.038. Nominal GNP in 1983 is $3,402 billion. Thus, real GNP in 1983 can be obtained by deflating nominal GNP by the price index according to equation (1.7′):

$$Q \equiv \frac{Y}{P} = \frac{\$3,402}{1.038} = \$3,278$$

In 1983, real GNP is therefore $3,278 billion. We say that 1983 *current-dollar GNP* (nominal GNP) is $3,402 billion but that 1983 *constant-dollar GNP* (real GNP) is $3,278 billion.

▶ Real GNP is called *constant-dollar* GNP because it equals the value that nominal GNP would have been if the price level had remained constant at its level in the base year (if the dollar had maintained a constant value in terms of *purchasing power*).

Now consider any year t. Real GNP in year t can be obtained in the same way. In year t, equation (1.7') becomes

(1.A.2) $$Q_t \equiv \frac{Y_t}{P_t}$$

For example, in 1985, nominal GNP is \$3,993 billion and the price index is 1.117. Note that this means that the *average price* is 11.7% higher in 1985 than it is in 1982. Hence, from equation (1.A.2), we obtain

$$Q_t \equiv \frac{Y_t}{P_t} = \frac{\$3,993}{1.117} = \$3,574$$

Real GNP in 1985 is therefore \$3,574 billion. From 1982 to 1985, the rise in real GNP is much smaller than the rise in nominal GNP. The reason, of course, is the *inflation*—the rise in the price level—that occurred over this time. If we look only at nominal GNP, we will *overestimate* the actual increase in the real production of goods and services during this period.

Yet it is the nominal GNP that we directly measure. Let us look more carefully at how this deflation is performed. We can illustrate the method in a simple economy with no government. Let's begin by writing the accounting identity (1.3) in nominal (instead of real) terms. In other words, instead of real GNP Q, we will write nominal GNP Y; instead of real consumption C, we will write nominal consumption C'; and instead of real investment I, we will write nominal investment I':

(1.3) $$Q \equiv C + I$$
(1.A.3) $$Y \equiv C' + I'$$

The prime (') indicates the nominal or current-dollar value. To obtain the corresponding equation for real output, each component must be deflated by its own price index. For example, if the *price index for consumption goods* (the *personal consumption deflator*) $P_C = 1.25$ in a given year, then the price of consumption goods is, on average, 25% higher than it is in the base year (1982). Then

(1.A.4) $$C \equiv \frac{C'}{P_C}$$

(1.A.5) $$I \equiv \frac{I'}{P_I}$$

where P_I = the price index for investment goods

Equation (1.A.4) shows how real consumption C is obtained from nominal consumption C' and equation (1.A.5) shows how real investment I is obtained from nominal investment I'. According to accounting identity (1.3), real output Q is defined as the sum of real consumption C and real investment I:

(1.3) $\qquad Q \equiv C + I$

Then the *implicit price deflator* for the economy is given by

(1.A.6) $\qquad P \equiv \dfrac{Y}{Q}$

1.A.2 Gross National Product

Our definition of gross national product (GNP) now needs to be refined:

GROSS NATIONAL PRODUCT (GNP) is the total value of all final goods and services produced during a given year to be sold through the market.

In Chapter 1, we learned how to avoid double counting by counting only the value of the *final* product. We also were interested only in production during the current period and excluded the sale of goods produced in previous periods.

The phrase "to be sold through the market," however, requires comment. In the real economy, not all production results in goods and services intended for sale through the market. For example, work in the home—food preparation, care of children, and housecleaning—are all valuable services not usually sold through the market. When goods and services are not sold through the market, they are excluded from GNP. When they are, they are included.

Thus, if both the husband and wife work outside the home and hire a housekeeper to perform services in the home, then these services are included in GNP; their value is measured by the fee charged by the housekeeper. If either the husband or the wife performs the services, then no market transaction occurs and the service is not counted in GNP. For example, if a man marries his housekeeper—or a woman marries her housekeeper—the GNP will decline even if there is no change in behavior or in services actually produced.

Because we wish to measure total production, it might seem desirable to include all final goods and services in our measure of GNP—whether or not they are sold through the market. But doing this would present us with a severe practical obstacle—the difficulty of estimating the value of goods and services that are not actually sold—and so we exclude them from the GNP measurement.

This exclusion should be kept in mind when comparing the GNPs of different countries in different stages of economic development. In less economically advanced countries, a greater share of total production is not sold through the market. Many people live on farms and grow their own food. The production and preparation of food and clothing; the production, maintenance, and repair of dwellings; and recreation often require no market transaction.

To see how GNP is determined for the U.S. economy, let's begin with the *National Income and Product Accounts* (NIPA)—the official government accounts for the U.S. economy. NIPA statistics are published monthly in the *Survey of Current Business* by the U.S. Department of Commerce. A convenient cumulative source of NIPA data is the annual volume of the *Economic Report of the President*, which contains numerous tables of such data. Rare is the economist who does not have the latest Report and its valuable tables close at hand.

In these official national income accounts, the base year is 1982. Only in that year are nominal and real values identical.

Before we can examine actual data, however, we must recognize that the United States is an *open* economy with foreign trade. Because we will ignore trade until Chapter 11, exports and imports were omitted from our discussion in Chapter 1. But we must recognize here that output can be allocated to *net exports* (exports *minus* imports) as well as to consumption C, investment I, and government purchases G. With this modification (to be explained further at the beginning of Chapter 11), our basic identity for nominal output becomes

(1.A.7) $$Y \equiv C' + I' + G' + NX'$$

where NX' = net exports

The actual values of each component of nominal GNP for 1985 follow:

Nominal GNP	(billions of dollars)
C' = Consumption	2,582
I' = Investment	670
G' = Government Purchases	815
NX' = Net Exports	(−74)
Y = Nominal GNP	3,993

An important problem regarding national income accounts is when to categorize a particular good or service as consumption or investment. In principle, a consumer durable should be counted as an investment good in the year it is purchased; but in each year it is used (including the first), the service it provides should be counted as consumption.

In practice, we cannot easily measure the service that is generated without a market transaction. In U.S. national income accounts, consumer durables — with one important exception — are counted as consumption in the year of purchase. The exception, housing, is counted as investment in the year of purchase; in subsequent years, the estimated *service* (shelter) is counted as consumption (estimated on the basis of the rental payment for a comparable house that is not owner-occupied).

Now let's consider real output. The official base year is 1982. The price index for each component of GNP is assigned the value 1.00 for 1982. When each component is deflated by its price index, the result is real GNP:

(1.A.8) $$Q \equiv C + I + G + NX$$

where NX = net exports

For example, between 1982 and 1985, the average price of consumer goods and services rose 11.6%. Therefore, in 1985, the value of the personal consumption deflator $P_C = 1.116$. If 1985 nominal consumption $C' = \$2,582$ billion is divided by $P_C = 1.116$, the result, $2,313 billion, is real consumption C in 1985.

The actual values of each component of real GNP for 1985 follow:

Real GNP	(billions of dollars)
C = Consumption	2,313
I = Investment	651
G = Government Purchases	715
NX = Net Exports	(−105)
Q = Real GNP	3,574

From now on, our example will focus on nominal values. If we subtract depreciation — *capital consumption allowances* — from nominal GNP, we obtain *net national product* NNP:

	(billions of dollars)
Nominal GNP	3,993
Less: Capital Consumption Allowances (Depreciation)	438
Net National Product (NNP)	3,554

Business firms must pay taxes (called *indirect taxes*, because they are not levied on persons, although people ultimately bear the burden) before national income can be made available to the factors of production that produce the output. Thus

	(billions of dollars)
Net National Product (NNP)	3,554
Less: Indirect Business Tax	329
Other	9
National Income	3,216

Earlier, through the analysis of our simple economy, we derived the triple equality: total output equals total value-added equals total income. Note that "income" in the triple equality includes depreciation and indirect taxes. In U.S. accounts, national income is total income less depreciation and indirect taxes.

How is national income divided among the factors of production?

	(billions of dollars)
Compensation of Employees	2,373
Proprietor's Income	242
Rental Income of Persons	14
Corporate Profits	299
Net Interest	288
National Income	3,216

Roughly three-quarters of national income is labor income and approximately one-quarter is capital (property) income.

The steps that lead from GNP to personal outlays and personal saving are

GNP − Capital Consumption Allowances ≡ NNP

NNP − Indirect Taxes ≡ National Income

National Income ≡ Compensation of Employees + Proprietor's Income + Rental Income of Persons + Corporate Profits + Net Interest

National Income − Corporate Profits − Social Insurance Contributions − Net Interest + Personal Interest + Dividends + Transfer Receipts ≡ Personal Income

Personal Income − Personal Tax and Nontax Payments ≡ Disposable Personal Income

Disposable Personal Income ≡ Personal Outlays
+ Personal Saving

The *GNP deflator* is the price index that is used to deflate nominal GNP to obtain real GNP. Each component of GNP has its own price deflator, which is used to convert the nominal value of the component to its real value. The sum of all of these real values is the real GNP. When nominal GNP is divided by real GNP, the result is the GNP deflator.

Thus far, we have based our analysis on the simplifying assumption that there is a single price index for each major component of GNP, such as consumption. In practice, the conversion from nominal to real GNP occurs at the subcomponent level. Each subcomponent has its own price index. When the real values of all subcomponents of, say, consumption are summed, the result is real consumption. The sum of the major real components yields real GNP. Thus, the GNP deflator ultimately depends on the price indexes for each subcomponent of GNP.

The U.S. Bureau of Labor Statistics (BLS) computes the price indexes for each subcomponent for the U.S. Commerce Department. The BLS records the actual prices of individual items.

The GNP deflator is the broadest price index. Most economists regard its growth rate as the best single measure of inflation in the economy. Moreover, in the process of generating the GNP deflator, a deflator for each major component (for example, the consumption deflator) is generated. The *consumption deflator* is simply the ratio of nominal consumption to real consumption. Thus, the national income accounts generate a whole set of price deflators.

Two other price indexes deserve mention: the *consumer price index* (CPI) and the *producer price index* (PPI). Both are produced by the U.S. Bureau of Labor Statistics.

The CPI focuses on the prices paid for consumption; the GNP deflator includes all goods and services. A more useful comparison is between the CPI and the consumption deflator that is generated in the process of computing real GNP and the GNP deflator.

One disadvantage of the CPI is that it is a *fixed-weight index.* In contrast, the consumption deflator is a *current-weight index;* it changes each year to reflect current expenditure patterns. The CPI weights the price of different items according to the expenditure proportions in a base year (1972–1973). In contrast, the consumption deflator employs current expenditure weights; if the share of a subcomponent of consumption declines, then due to the way the consumption deflator is computed, the weight of the price index for this subcomponent will automatically be reduced.

Consider what happened when energy prices rose relative to other prices in the 1970s. Consumers gradually responded by shifting away from energy consumption. But the CPI continued to assign the 1972–1973 weight to energy prices; in contrast, the consumption deflator automatically reduced the weight as energy use declined.

Most specialists also believe that, in the past, the CPI has assigned too much weight to current changes in mortgage rates, without fully recognizing that most homeowners are subject to fixed mortgage rates. Although the consumption deflator may not measure the price of housing services perfectly, it probably does a better job than the CPI. Recently, the CPI has altered its treatment of mortgage rates in an attempt to correct this defect.

Despite these shortcomings, the CPI (not the consumption deflator) is currently used in cost-of-living contracts for wages and in such government transfer programs as Social Security.

The producer price index (PPI) focuses on the producer prices of goods that are not directly purchased by consumers.

APPENDIX 1B

THE ALGEBRA OF THE MODEL OF EQUILIBRIUM OUTPUT

In Appendix 1B, we will develop the model of equilibrium output algebraically. We have already examined the basic equations of this model using numerical illustrations. Here, more formal derivations will be presented.

1.B.1 Equilibrium Output in an Economy with No Government

We begin with the simple equilibrium output model, excluding government:

(1.8) $Q = D$

(1.9) $D \equiv C + I$

(1.10) $C = C_a + cQ$

In equation (1.10), C_a is the *autonomous* component of consumption demand—the component that is independent of total income Q. Consider the consumption function given by equation (1.10). The marginal propensity to consume MPC is defined as $\Delta C/\Delta Q$. The MPC is therefore equal to c. The average propensity to consume APC is defined as C/Q. Dividing both sides of equation (1.10) by Q yields

$$\text{APC} \equiv \frac{C}{Q} = \frac{C_a}{Q} + c$$

Only if $C_a = 0$ will the APC $= c$. If C_a is positive, then the APC will exceed the MPC; if C_a is negative, then the APC will be less than the MPC.

Also, the APC depends on the value of Q; if Q rises, the APC declines. The MPC is always equal to c, regardless of Q.

When we substitute equation (1.8) into equation (1.9), we obtain

(1.9′) $Q = C + I$

(1.10) $C = C_a + cQ$

Our system now has two equations. It can therefore be solved for only two unknowns. Thus, we must be given the values of all but two variables. Our two unknowns are Q and C, so we must be given I, C_a, and c.

We will assume that the parameter c has a constant value, based on consumer behavior; it must be given. C_a and I can vary; but because they must be given (determined outside the model), they are called *exogenous* variables. Q and C are determined within the model and are therefore called *endogenous* variables.

Equations (1.9′) and (1.10) are the *structural equations* of our model. They describe behavioral relationships or identities (equations that are true by definition or accounting principles) that generally involve more than one endogenous variable. Because a structural equation usually contains more than one unknown, it alone cannot tell us the value of any particular endogenous variable.

To solve for equilibrium output Q, we substitute equation (1.10) into equation (1.9′):

$$Q = C_a + cQ + I$$
$$Q - cQ = C_a + I$$

Factoring out Q gives us

$$(1 - c)Q = C_a + I$$

Dividing by $(1 - c)$ yields

(1.B.1) $$Q = \left(\frac{1}{1 - c}\right)(C_a + I)$$

It will be convenient to name the second term in equation (1.B.1). In our model, C_a and I are the two components of demand that are independent of Q—that are autonomous. Thus, we will call this term *autonomous demand* (demand independent of total income Q):

(1.B.2) $$D_a \equiv C_a + I$$

Using equation (1.B.2), we can rewrite equation (1.B.1) as

(1.B.3) $$Q = \frac{1}{1-c} D_a$$

When we substitute equation (1.B.3) into equation (1.10), we obtain

(1.B.4) $$C = C_a + \frac{c}{1-c} D_a$$

Equations (1.B.3) and (1.B.4) are the *reduced-form equations* of our system. Each endogenous variable Q and C is given by a reduced-form equation, in which an endogenous variable appears alone on the left side and every term on the right side is either an exogenous variable or a parameter. No other endogenous variable appears on the right side of the reduced-form equation. Recall that D_a, which equals $C_a + I$, is assumed to be exogenous.

The reduced-form equations (1.B.3) and (1.B.4) contrast with the two structural equations (1.9') and (1.10). Each reduced-form equation has only one unknown (endogenous) variable; the equation can therefore be used to obtain the value of this endogenous variable from the given exogenous variables and parameter. Let's check the results we obtained in Chapter 1 (page 20). With $C_a = \$100$ billion, $c = 0.8$, and $I = \$100$ billion:

$$Q = \frac{1}{1-c} D_a$$

$$Q = \left(\frac{1}{1-0.8}\right)(100 + 100)$$

$$Q = 1,000$$

Thus, the reduced-form equation (1.B.3) for Q can be used to find equilibrium output Q directly.

Equation (1.B.3) identifies the multiplier for us at a glance. Recall that in equation (1.11), the multiplier $m = \Delta Q/\Delta I$. If Q increases by $\$500$ billion when I increases by $\$100$ billion, then $m = 5$. From equation (1.B.3), we can see that if C_a (rather than I) increases by $\$100$ billion, then the increase in D_a will still be $\$100$ billion; because Q depends on D_a, the increase in Q will be the same. We can now define the multiplier m more generally as

(1.B.5) $$m \equiv \frac{\Delta Q}{\Delta D_a}$$

where D_a is autonomous demand $C_a + I$, as defined in equation (1.B.2).

In other words, if $m = 5$, then Q will increase by \$500 billion when D_a increases by \$100 billion — whether the increase in D_a is due to C_a, or to I, or to both. The impact on Q is the same. But it should be noted that if C_a increases by \$100 billion, then the C-sector of the economy will initially increase production by \$100 billion; if I increases by \$100 billion, then the I-sector of the economy will increase production by \$100 billion. The composition of output Q (consumption goods versus investment goods) will be affected by whether C_a or I increases by \$100 billion.

In equation (1.B.3), if D_a increases by 1 unit, then Q will increase by $1/(1 - c)$. It is clear that the multiplier, defined as $m = \Delta Q / \Delta D_a$, must equal $1/(1 - c)$, so that

(1.B.6)
$$m = \frac{1}{1 - c} = \frac{1}{1 - \text{MPC}}$$

Note that the multiplier depends only on the marginal propensity to consume MPC.

Substituting equation (1.B.6) into equation (1.B.3) gives us the reduced-form equation for equilibrium output Q

(1.B.7)
$$Q = mD_a$$

1.B.2 Equilibrium Output in an Economy with Government

Now let's introduce government into our equilibrium output model. Our model consists of three equations:

(1.30) $Q = C + I + G$
(1.31) $C = C_a + c(Q - T + R)$

and in place of equation (1.32)

(1.B.8) $T = T_a + tQ$

where T_a = autonomous tax revenue

Note that equation (1.B.8) differs from equation (1.32) in that it includes the term T_a. If autonomous tax revenue $T_a = 0$, then the two equations will be the same. In Chapter 1, in effect, we set $T_a = 0$. Thus, any result we obtain by using equation (1.B.8) can easily be applied to the equilibrium output model that includes equation (1.32) simply by setting $T_a = 0$. T_a may be positive or negative. The inclusion of T_a may make equation (1.B.8) yield a more accurate relationship between tax revenue T and total income Q.

In the *tax function* given by equation (1.B.8), we define the *marginal tax rate* MTR as $\Delta T/\Delta Q$; the MTR will always equal t. For example, if $t = 25\%$ and Q increases by $100 billion, then T will increase by $25 billion and $\Delta T/\Delta Q$ will be 25% (equal to t).

We define the *average tax rate* ATR as T/Q. The ATR results from dividing equation (1.B.8) by Q, so that

(1.B.9) $$\text{ATR} \equiv \frac{T}{Q} = \frac{T_a}{Q} + t$$

If $T_a = 0$, then the ATR equals t and is therefore equal to the MTR, which always equals t. But if T_a is positive, the ATR will exceed the MTR (t); if T_a is negative, the ATR will be less than the MTR (t).

Equations (1.30), (1.31), and (1.B.8) are structural equations. The three unknowns or endogenous variables are Q, C, and T. Everything else must be given: C_a and I are exogenous variables, c is a parameter, and G, R, T_a, and t are fiscal policy variables. (Recall that we make the simplifying assumption that government transfers R is independent of equilibrium output Q.)

We want to find the reduced-form equation for Q—to express equilibrium output Q in terms of known parameters and variables. To solve for Q, we follow the steps in the numerical example in the text, where we found $Q = $2,200 billion. The only differences are that for $I = $380 billion, we leave I and for $G = $300 billion, we leave G, so that letters are retained in the equation. Therefore, instead of obtaining a numerical value for Q, we will derive an expression for Q in terms of I, G, and the other variables and parameters. You may find it useful to glance back at the steps we took to obtain equilibrium output $Q = $2,200 billion (see page 33) as you follow the algebra given here.

Substituting equations (1.31) and (1.B.8) into equation (1.30) gives us

$$Q = C_a + c(Q - T_a - tQ + R) + I + G$$
$$Q = C_a + c(Q - tQ) - cT_a + cR + I + G$$
$$Q - c(Q - tQ) = C_a + \qquad - cT_a + cR + I + G$$
$$Q - cQ + ctQ = C_a + \qquad - cT_a + cR + I + G$$

Factoring out Q, we obtain

$$(1 - c + ct)Q = C_a + \qquad - cT_a + cR + I + G$$

Note that $1 - c + ct = 1 - c(1 - t)$. Dividing by $1 - c(1 - t)$ gives us

$$(1.B.10) \qquad Q = \frac{1}{1 - c(1 - t)} (C_a - cT_a + cR + I + G)$$

Each term in the second parenthetical expression is a component of demand that is independent of total income Q. We therefore define the second term as autonomous demand D_a (demand independent of total income Q):

$$(1.B.11) \qquad D_a \equiv C_a - cT_a + cR + I + G$$

Comparing equation (1.B.11) with equation (1.B.2) reveals that autonomous demand D_a now has three new components ($-cT_a$, cR, and G) due to the presence of government.

We can now rewrite equation (1.B.10) as

$$(1.B.12) \qquad Q = \frac{1}{1 - c(1 - t)} D_a$$

Equation (1.B.12) is the reduced-form equation for equilibrium output Q. In our model without government, the multiplier $m = \Delta Q / \Delta D_a$ is the coefficient of D_a in equation (1.B.3). In our three-equation model with government, the multiplier m is the coefficient of D_a in equation (1.B.12):

$$(1.B.13) \qquad m \equiv \frac{\Delta Q}{\Delta D_a} = \frac{1}{1 - c(1 - t)}$$

Note that the multiplier depends on the marginal propensity to consume MPC, which equals c, and on the marginal tax rate MTR, which equals t. It does not depend on either the average propensity to consume APC or the average tax rate ATR.

Given the new definition of D_a, equation (1.B.7) still holds. We can rewrite equation (1.B.12) as

$$(1.B.7) \qquad Q = mD_a$$

For example, if $c = 0.8$ and $t = 0.25$, then $m = 1/[1 - (0.8)(0.75)] = 1/0.4 = 2.5$.

In our model without government, the multiplier $m = 1/1 - c$; if $c = 0.8$, then $m = 5$. In general, the value of m in equation (1.B.13) is less than $1/(1 - c)$. Because $1 - t$ is a fraction, $c(1 - t)$ is less than c; hence, $1 - c(1 - t)$ is greater than $1 - c$. Since the denominator is larger, the multiplier is smaller. Thus, in our three-equation model with government, the multiplier is smaller. Intuitively, why?

When D_a declines in our three-equation model with its tax function, tax revenue decreases automatically. Net income therefore declines less than total income; thus, C decreases less than it would otherwise.

We have called the tax system in this equilibrium output model an "automatic stabilizer." We can now give a more precise definition:

An AUTOMATIC STABILIZER is a policy that reduces the size of the multiplier m.

2 IS–LM Analysis

In Chapter 2, we will develop the *IS curve* and the *LM curve*. The intersection of these two curves will yield both *equilibrium output Q* and the *equilibrium interest rate r*. The *IS–LM model* therefore advances beyond the model given in Chapter 1 because it determines the interest rate as well as the output.

In our examples, it will be convenient to work with *IS* and *LM* "curves" that are, in fact, straight lines, because our examples use "linear" equations. We will generally use the word "curve" to remind us that *IS* and *LM* relationships do not need to be "linear."

In Chapter 1, we assumed that both the price level *P* and the interest rate *r* are constant. In this chapter, we will permit *r* to vary, but we will retain our assumption concerning *P*:

▶ Throughout Chapter 2, we will assume that the price level *P* stays constant.

▶ Throughout this text, we will occasionally need to "round off" answers that do not "come out even." Each answer will be slightly affected by previous round-off decisions. As you check each calculation, you may obtain a slightly different answer due to your previous round-off decisions.

2.1 Goods-Market Equilibrium: The *IS* Curve

Our model of equilibrium output in Chapter 1 consisted of equations (1.30), (1.31), and (1.32). In this chapter, we will add a fourth equation, known as "the investment function." From these four equations, we will then derive the *IS* curve.

THE INVESTMENT FUNCTION

Our simple *investment function* rests on two hypotheses. First, we will assume that a rise in the interest rate r reduces investment demand I. The basic idea is that if r rises, firms will find it less attractive to borrow to finance their investment projects. Fewer investment projects will be profitable at a higher interest rate.

Second, we will assume that investment demand I can change, even if the interest rate r stays constant. For example, if business managers become more pessimistic about future sales, I will fall at any given r. Similarly, if new capital is expected to be less productive — and therefore less profitable — I will fall at any given r. Hence, I has an autonomous component that is independent of the interest rate r.

In Part 1, we will adopt the simplest hypotheses that appear plausible. In the case of consumption demand, we will assume that C depends partly on net income and partly on an autonomous component. In the case of investment demand, we will assume that I depends partly on the interest rate and partly on an autonomous component. (Obviously, further explanation is required to understand consumption and investment. We will analyze their determinants in Chapter 12.) For now, we will accept these simple hypotheses and concentrate on working out their implications for the macroeconomy.

Our simple investment function is given by

(2.1) $I = I_a - jr$ *Example: $I = 700 - 4{,}000r$*

where r = the interest rate

I_a = the autonomous component of investment demand

j = the *investment responsiveness parameter*, which measures the responsiveness of I to a change in r; j is positive ($j > 0$)

For example, if $r = 8\%$, then investment $I = 700 - [4{,}000\,(0.08)] = 380$. If r rises to 10%, then I decreases to $700 - [4{,}000\,(0.1)] = 300$. Figure 2.1 shows the *investment-demand curve* (the I curve) for this example. It has a *negative slope;* thus, when r decreases, I increases.

In Figure 2.1, r is plotted on the vertical axis and I is plotted on the horizontal axis. Yet r is the independent variable and I is the dependent variable; the investment-demand I curve shows how I responds to r. In most mathematical graphs, the independent variable is plotted on the horizontal axis. But economists began putting r on the vertical axis, and that convention has become the norm.

In Chapter 1, we analyzed what happens to Q if I decreases from $380 billion to $300 billion, but we did not specify why I declines. Given the investment function (2.1), we can now see that one possible explanation for the decline in I is a rise in the interest rate; if the parameter j

FIGURE 2.1 AN INVESTMENT CURVE

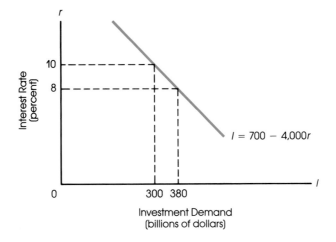

When the interest rate r decreases, investment demand I increases. The equation for this investment curve is $I = 700 - 4{,}000r$. For example, if $r = 8\%$, then $I = \$380$ billion; if $r = 10\%$, then $I = \$300$ billion.

in equation (2.1) is 4,000, then a 2% rise in r will reduce I by \$80 billion.

Another possible explanation is that when r is constant, I_a may decrease by \$80 billion because business managers have become more pessimistic about the future yield on current investment. Then the investment function will be

$$I = 620 - 4{,}000r$$

If $r = 8\%$, then investment I will be

$$I = 620 - [4{,}000(0.08)] = 300$$

Still another possibility is that both r and I_a may change in such a way that I decreases by \$80 billion. For example, if I_a declines by \$133 billion to \$567 billion and r declines by 1.33% to 6.67%, then

$$I = 567 - 4{,}000(0.0667) = 300$$

In this case, the drop in r partly offsets the drop in I_a, so that I decreases by only \$80 billion, even though I_a declines by \$133 billion.

Thus, we can interpret the decrease in investment demand I from \$380 billion to \$300 billion as the result of a rise in the interest rate r of

2%, a decline in the autonomous component of investment I_a of $80 billion, or a change in both I_a and r that, taken together, reduces I by $80 billion.

THE *IS* CURVE

Now let's consider the economic model comprised of the equations (1.30), (1.31), (1.32), and (2.1). Assume that I_a is given. Once the interest rate r is specified, then I is determined through the investment function given by equation (2.1). Once investment demand I is determined, then we can find the equilibrium output Q from equations (1.30), (1.31), and (1.32), just as we did in Chapter 1. Thus, our four-equation model implies a relationship between the interest rate r and the equilibrium output Q.

It is easy to see that when the interest rate r declines, equilibrium output Q increases. Why? When r decreases, through the investment function given by equation (2.1), I increases. When I increases, through equations (1.30), (1.31), and (1.32), equilibrium output Q increases. This relationship between the interest rate r and equilibrium output Q is called the *IS curve*. The *IS* curve for this example is shown in Figure 2.2.

FIGURE 2.2 AN *IS* CURVE

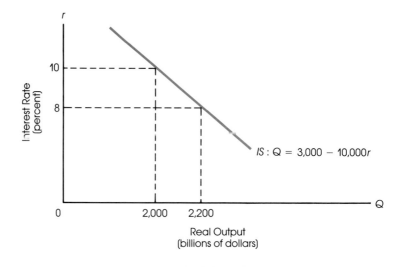

When the interest rate r decreases, equilibrium output Q increases. The equation for the *IS* curve is $Q = 3,000 - 10,000r$. For example, if $r = 8\%$, then equilibrium output $Q = $2,200 billion; if $r = 10\%$, then equilibrium output $Q = $2,000 billion.

When we solve equations (1.30), (1.31), and (1.32) for Q, we find the Q for which $Q = D$.

The *IS* CURVE consists of all points (r, Q) that result in equilibrium in the goods market. For any point (r, Q) on the *IS* curve, demand for goods D equals actual output Q.

▶ Note that although r is plotted on the vertical axis, we write point (r, Q) because r is the independent variable.

It is not a coincidence that the *IS* curve in Figure 2.2 and the *I* curve in Figure 2.1 both have a negative slope. The *IS* curve is based on the *I* curve. The *I* curve shows that when r decreases, *I* increases. But when *I* increases, equilibrium output Q increases; the *IS* curve shows this increase in Q when r decreases.

It is helpful to show how a point on the *IS* curve can be plotted in a particular example. Given the following numerical values:

(1.30)	$Q = C + I + 300$
(1.31)	$C = 0.8(Q - T + 250)$
(1.32)	$T = 0.25Q$
(2.1)	$I = 700 - 4{,}000r$

If $r = 8\%$, then $I = \$380$ billion. In Chapter 1, we calculated that if investment demand $I = \$380$ billion, then equilibrium output $Q = \$2{,}200$ billion. (If $r = 10\%$, then $I = \$300$ billion.) We also calculated that if $I = \$300$ billion, then equilibrium output $Q = \$2{,}000$ billion. Thus, in Figure 2.2, these two points (r, Q) lie on the *IS* curve: (8%, 2,200) and (10%, 2,000).

If you try other numerical values for r and calculate the corresponding Q, you will find that every point (r, Q) that you obtain lies on the straight line joining these two points. This line is the *IS* curve for this example.

We obtain the equation for the *IS* curve by substituting equations (1.31), (1.32), and (2.1) into equation (1.30), so that

$$Q = [0.8(Q - 0.25Q + 250)] + (700 - 4{,}000r) + 300$$
$$Q = [0.8(0.75Q)] + 200 + 700 - 4{,}000r + 300$$
$$Q = 0.6Q + 1{,}200 - 4{,}000r$$
$$0.4Q = 1{,}200 - 4{,}000r$$

(2.2)
$$Q = 3{,}000 - 10{,}000r$$

Equation (2.2) is the equation of the *IS* curve in this example. As a check, let's confirm our two points (8%, 2,200) and (10%, 2,000):

$$Q = 3{,}000 - 10{,}000(0.08) = 3{,}000 - 800 = 2{,}200$$
$$Q = 3{,}000 - 10{,}000(0.10) = 3{,}000 - 1{,}000 = 2{,}000$$

WHAT SHIFTS THE *IS* CURVE?

The *IS* curve given by equation (2.2) depends on the values that we have assigned to the variables and parameters in our system of equations: $G = \$300$ billion, $C_a = 0$, $c = 0.8$, $R = \$250$ billion, $t = 25\%$, $I_a = \$700$ billion, $j = 4{,}000$. If any one of these numerical values changes, then the *IS* curve will shift; for any interest rate r, a different equilibrium output Q will result.

For example, if business pessimism causes I_a to decrease by $133 billion (from $700 billion to $567 billion), while all other values remain constant, then the investment function will shift:

(2.1) $I = 700 - 4{,}000r$
(2.1') $I = 567 - 4{,}000r$

Let's consider what happens if $r = 8\%$:

Initially: $380 = 700 - [4{,}000(0.08)]$
Now: $247 = 567 - [4{,}000(0.08)]$

If $r = 10\%$:

Initially: $300 = 700 - [4{,}000(0.10)]$
Now: $167 = 567 - [4{,}000(0.10)]$

Figure 2.3 shows that the investment-demand I curve shifts to the left by $133 billion when I_a decreases by $133 billion (from $700 billion to $567 billion). At each interest rate r, I is now smaller by $133 billion. Note that the *coefficient of r* (the number that multiplies r) stays constant ($-4{,}000$); hence, there is no change in the slope of the I curve.

▶ Note that there is a fundamental difference between a *movement along* a curve and a *shift of* a curve. The I curve shifts left because investment demand I is smaller at each interest rate r.

If I_a remained at $700 billion, a rise in r would still reduce I. However, this would be a movement along (up) the I curve, not a shift of the curve to the left.

Now that the I curve is given by $I = 567 - 4{,}000r$, let's find the new *IS* equation. We repeat our earlier steps, substituting into equation (1.30) to obtain the equation for the *IS* curve, with $I_a = \$567$ billion:

FIGURE 2.3 A SHIFT OF THE INVESTMENT CURVE TO THE LEFT

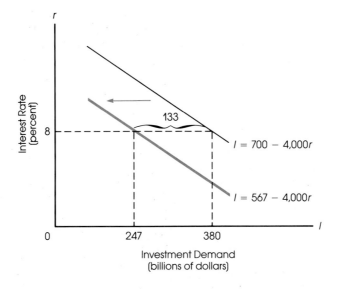

When business pessimism causes the autonomous component of investment I_a to decrease by $133 billion (from $700 billion to $567 billion), the I curve shifts to the left by $133 billion. At each interest rate r, investment demand I is now $133 billion less.

$$Q = [0.8(Q - 0.25Q + 250)] + (567 - 4,000r) + 300$$
$$Q = 0.8(0.75Q) + 200 + 567 - 4,000r + 300$$
$$Q = 0.6Q + 1,067 - 4,000r$$
$$0.4Q = 1,067 - 4,000r$$

(2.2′) $$Q = 2,667 - 10,000r$$

Compare equation (2.2′) with the equation for the *IS* curve, with $I_a = $700 billion:

(2.2) $$Q = 3,000 - 10,000r$$

Figure 2.4 shows the leftward shift of the *IS* curve for this example. The decrease in I_a from $700 billion to $567 billion reduces the constant term of the *IS* equation from 3,000 to 2,667 — a decrease of 333. Thus, at any r, Q is now $333 billion less and the *IS* curve shifts left by $333 billion. Note that the coefficient of r remains constant at $-10,000$; hence, there is no change in the slope of the *IS* curve.

FIGURE 2.4 A SHIFT OF THE *IS* CURVE TO THE LEFT

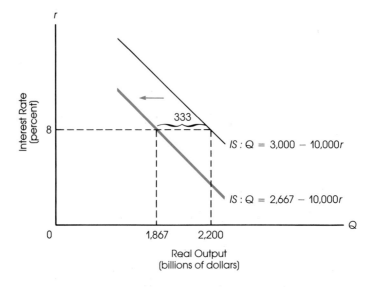

When business pessimism causes the autonomous component of investment I_a to decrease by \$133 billion (from \$700 billion to \$567 billion), the *IS* curve shifts to the left by \$333 billion. At each interest rate r, equilibrium output Q is now \$333 billion less.

Now let's examine the shift of the *IS* curve in more general terms. Consider a point (r_0, Q_0) on the initial *IS* curve in Figure 2.5. At this r_0, demand for output $D = Q_0$. Now suppose that a variable or parameter changes and that, at this same r_0, D exceeds Q_0. Then if r is held constant at r_0, producers will increase Q until D and Q are again equal at Q_1. Thus, the point (r_0, Q_1) will be on the new *IS* curve *IS'*. Since $Q_1 > Q_0$, the *IS* curve shifts to the right.

▶ Any change in a variable or parameter that raises demand for output D for a given interest rate r and level of output Q will shift the *IS* curve to the right.

If we rewrite the equations in our system, we can see what shifts the *IS* curve to the right. Substituting equation (1.32) into equation (1.31) yields equation (1.31′):

(1.30) $Q = C + I + G$

(1.31′) $C = C_a + c(Q - tQ + R)$

(2.1) $I = I_a - jr$

FIGURE 2.5 A SHIFT OF THE *IS* CURVE TO THE RIGHT

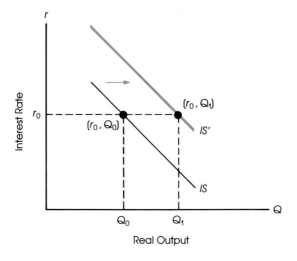

Initially, the *IS* curve passes through the point (r_0, Q_0), so that $Q = D$ at (r_0, Q_0). Then a variable or parameter in the model changes, so that D exceeds Q at (r_0, Q_0). Now equilibrium output Q must rise to Q_1 to make $Q = D$. Thus, the new *IS'* curve passes through point (r_0, Q_1), and the *IS* curve has shifted to the right.

The right side of equation (1.30) is the demand for output D. At a given Q and r, anything that raises D will shift the *IS* curve to the right. This means that anything (other than a change in Q or r) that raises any of the three components of demand for output D (C, I, or G) will shift the *IS* curve to the right.

First, consider the impact of fiscal policy. An increase in government transfers R or a cut in the tax rate t raises C at a given Q in equation (1.31'). Thus

▶ An increase in government purchases G or government transfers R or a cut in the tax rate t will shift the *IS* curve to the right.

Next, consider behavioral changes in the private sector. Any change in the autonomous component of consumption C_a and in the propensity to consume c that raises C at a given Q will shift the *IS* curve to the right. Any change in the autonomous component of investment I_a and in the investment responsiveness parameter j that raises I at a given r will also shift the *IS* curve to the right.

What happens at a point *off* the *IS* curve? For example, consider

FIGURE 2.6 THE STABILITY OF GOODS-MARKET EQUILIBRIUM

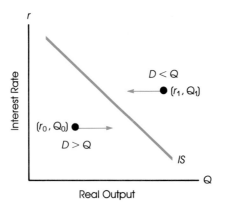

At any point to the *left* of the *IS* curve, such as (r_0, Q_0), D exceeds Q ($D > Q$). Hence, Q *increases*, moving the economy toward the *IS* curve. Symmetrically, at any point to the *right* of the *IS* curve, such as (r_1, Q_1), D is less than Q ($D < Q$). Hence, Q *decreases*, moving the economy toward the *IS* curve.

point (r_0, Q_0) to the left of the *IS* curve in Figure 2.6. With $r = r_0$, equilibrium output Q is greater than Q_0; it is the Q on the *IS* curve at $r = r_0$. Thus, with $r = r_0$ and $Q = Q_0$, demand for output D will exceed actual output Q_0. Why? Returning to Figure 1.2 tells us that D exceeds Q at any Q less than the equilibrium Q.

As before, we make the assumption that producers will respond to this excess demand for goods by increasing their output Q until the point on the *IS* curve directly to the right of (r_0, Q_0) is reached. Symmetrically, at a point to the right of the *IS* curve (r_1, Q_1), D will be less than Q; producers will respond to this excess supply of goods by reducing Q until the point on the *IS* curve directly to the left of (r_1, Q_1) is reached.

▶ Goods-market equilibrium is *stable*. If actual output Q differs from equilibrium output Q, then Q will move toward its equilibrium value.

2.2 Money-Market Equilibrium: The *LM* Curve

We can use our four-equation model, which yields the *IS* curve, to determine equilibrium output Q if we know the interest rate r. But what determines r? Anyone who has taken an introductory economics course knows that the monetary policy of a country's central bank (in the United States, the Federal Reserve System) has some influence on the interest rate r. Therefore, we now turn our attention to the *money market*.

Money is only one of many assets. *Wealth* can be held in several forms, including money, bonds, and corporate stock. In any period, *wealth-holders* (households, firms, and governmental units) must determine how much of their total wealth to hold in these various forms of wealth.

To simplify our analysis, we will consider only two assets: money (on which we will initially assume that no interest is paid) and an interest-bearing asset we will call a "bond." A *bond* is a promise to pay its holder a specific amount of money on a future date. To illustrate, a bond issued by a borrower on January 1 may state that the issuer will pay the holder $100 of principal and an additional $10 of interest on December 31 of the same year. Such a bond "matures" in one year and is called a "one-year bond."

If a one-year bond sells for $100 on January 1 and matures to $110 on December 31, then its interest rate is 10%. The buyer (lender) will receive $110 at the end of a year. The lender's gain on the loan is $10; as a percentage of the purchase price of $100, the gain is 10%.

If, however, despite its face value of $100, the bond sells for $95 on January 1, then the lender's gain will be $15. As a percentage of the purchase price of $95, the gain is 16%. The interest rate is therefore 16%.

If, instead, the bond sells for $105 on January 1, then the lender's gain will be only $5. As a percentage of the purchase price of $105, the gain is 5%. The interest rate is therefore 5%.

▶ The interest rate varies *inversely* with the price of a bond. As the price of the bond decreases, the interest rate increases.

In our two-asset economy, each wealth-holder must decide how much wealth to hold in the form of money and how much wealth to hold in the form of bonds. All wealth-holders are faced with a *wealth budget constraint;* they must *allocate wealth* between the two available assets (money and bonds). We say that each wealth-holder faces a *portfolio decision.*

Suppose that one wealth-holder, who has a total wealth of $1,000, decides to hold $400 in the form of money and $600 in the form of bonds. We say that the *demand for money* $M^D = \$400$ and the *demand for bonds* $B^D = \$600$ for this individual.

It is important to distinguish between *nominal* and *real* demand. If the public demands 5% more money this year than it did last year but the price level is also 5% higher, then the *nominal demand* for money has risen 5%. However, the *real demand* for money is unchanged. The *purchasing power* of the money demanded—or the quantity of real output that it can buy—remains the same.

Let W be *nominal wealth*, M be *nominal money*, B be *nominal bonds*, and P be the price level. *Real wealth* is then given by W/P; *real money*, by M/P; and *real bonds,* by B/P.

Thus, we can state the wealth budget constraint on each individual in our two-asset economy in *real* terms. The *real demand for money* M^D/P plus the *real demand for bonds* B^D/P equals the individual's *real wealth W/P:*

$$(2.3) \qquad \frac{M^D}{P} + \frac{B^D}{P} = \frac{W}{P}$$

where M^D = demand for money

$\qquad\ B^D$ = demand for bonds

If we aggregate overall wealth-holders (households, firms, and governmental units), then equation (2.3) holds for the whole economy. The total real demand for money plus the total real demand for bonds must equal the total real wealth.

Now let's turn to the *supply* of money and bonds. In any period, there is a given supply of money and a given supply of bonds. According to the *wealth identity,* the real supply of money plus the real supply of bonds equals the real wealth of the economy:

$$(2.4) \qquad \frac{M}{P} + \frac{B}{P} \equiv \frac{W}{P}$$

ASSET-MARKET EQUILIBRIUM occurs when the real demand for money equals the real supply of money $(M^D/P = M/P)$ and the real demand for bonds equals the real supply of bonds $(B^D/P = B/P)$.

Suppose that, initially, the real demand for money is less than the real supply of money. For example, the real wealth in the economy $W/P = \$1,000$ billion, the real money supply $M/P = \$500$ billion, and the real bond supply $B/P = \$500$ billion. But, initially, real money demand $M^D/P = \$400$ billion and real bond demand $B^D/P = \$600$ billion. What happens?

In the bond market, demand exceeds supply, so the price of bonds will rise (equivalently, the interest rate on bonds will decline). Assume that the supply of bonds and the demand for bonds eventually become equal. At that exact moment, it must be true that the supply of money and the demand for money will also be equal. When equilibrium occurs in one of two asset markets, it automatically occurs in the other asset market. Why?

Real wealth W/P is the same in equations (2.3) and (2.4). The total value of assets demanded must therefore equal the total value of assets supplied, or

$$(2.5) \qquad \frac{M^D}{P} + \frac{B^D}{P} = \frac{M}{P} + \frac{B}{P}$$

It is clear from equation (2.5) that if $B^D/P = B/P$, then, automatically, $M^D/P = M/P$. For example, suppose that the total value of assets demanded and supplied is \$1,000 billion, the money supply is \$500 billion, and the bond supply is \$500 billion. If bond demand is \$500 billion, then the bond market is in equilibrium and it must also be true that money demand is \$500 billion. Thus, the money market is in equilibrium.

To determine whether both asset markets are in equilibrium, we can focus on one of these two markets: the money market or the bond market. If the money market is in equilibrium, with money demand equal to money supply, then the bond market will automatically be in equilibrium as well, with bond demand equal to bond supply. We will focus on the money market.

THE DEMAND FOR MONEY

What determines the real demand for money M^D/P? We offer the hypothesis that real money demand depends on three variables: real income Q, the interest rate r, and an autonomous component that is independent of Q or r.

When individuals make their portfolio decisions, they weigh the pros and cons of each asset (money and bonds, in our example). Money is required for transactions. As incomes rise, the number of transactions increases, so that the demand for money increases. But bonds yield interest, whereas money (we assume initially) does not. Hence, as the interest rate on bonds rises, the demand for bonds becomes greater and the demand for money is reduced. Thus, our hypothesis says

▶ Real money demand M^D/P varies *directly* with real income Q and *inversely* with the interest rate r.

The autonomous component allows for a change in real money demand that is not due to a change in either *real income Q* or the interest rate r. What might influence the autonomous component of money demand? First, when individual wealth increases, even though real income and the interest rate remain the same, a person's demand for most assets — including money — will probably increase. Hence, an increase in wealth is likely to increase money demand. Second, a person's attitude toward risk, safety, and *liquidity* (the ability to convert wealth forms into cash) may change. For example, even with the same income and interest rate, a person who suddenly believes other assets are riskier or who needs to convert other assets to cash quickly may reduce the demand for other assets and increase the demand for money.

This *money-demand function* expresses our hypothesis:

(2.6) $$\frac{M^D}{P} = \frac{M_a}{P} + kQ - hr \quad \textit{Example:} \quad \frac{M^D}{P} = 0 + 0.5Q - 7,500r$$

where $\dfrac{M_a}{P}$ = an autonomous component (independent of Q or r)

Q = real income

r = the interest rate

k = a parameter that measures the responsiveness of M^D/P to a change in real income Q; k is positive ($k > 0$)

h = a parameter that measures the responsiveness of M^D/P to a change in the interest rate r; h is positive ($h > 0$)

This money-demand equation states that if real income Q increases, then real money demand M^D/P increases and that if the interest rate r on bonds increases, then real money demand M^D/P decreases. It also allows for a change in money demand due to an autonomous component M_a/P that is independent of real income or the interest rate.

If Q = $2,200 billion, then the money-demand equation simply relates M^D/P to r, given this particular Q:

$$\frac{M^D}{P} = [0.5(2,200)] - 7,500r$$

$$\frac{M^D}{P} = 1,100 - 7,500r$$

This equation is plotted in Figure 2.7. If r = 8%, M^D/P = $500 billion; if r = 10%, M^D/P = $350 billion. Hence, with Q held constant, if r increases, M^D/P decreases.

If Q increases to $2,500 billion, then the money-demand equation becomes

$$\frac{M^D}{P} = [0.5(2,500)] - 7,500r$$

$$\frac{M^D}{P} = 1,250 - 7,500r$$

This equation is also plotted in Figure 2.7. If r = 8%, then M^D/P = $650 billion. Clearly, the increase in Q shifts the money-demand curve to the right.

FIGURE 2.7 REAL MONEY DEMAND AND THE REAL MONEY SUPPLY

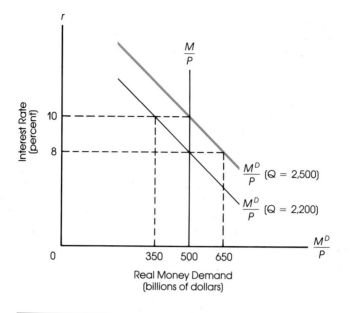

Real money demand M^D/P varies inversely with the interest rate r. For a given Q, we can plot the M^D/P that would result at each interest rate r. For example, if $Q = \$2,200$ billion, then at $r = 8\%$, $M^D/P = \$500$ billion. If Q increases to $\$2,500$ billion, then the M^D/P curve shifts to the right. But note that if r rises to 10%, M^D/P remains at $\$500$ billion. If the real money supply $M/P = \$500$ billion, then $M^D/P = M/P = \$500$ billion at point $Q = \$2,200$ billion, $r = 8\%$ and at point $Q = \$2,500$ billion, $r = 10\%$. These points are plotted in Figure 2.8.

Note that if r rises from 8% to 10% (with $Q = \$2,500$ billion), then M^D/P drops back to $\$500$ billion. Thus, when Q increases from $\$2,200$ billion to $\$2,500$ billion and r also rises from 8% to 10%, M^D/P stays constant at $\$500$ billion.

THE *LM* CURVE

Let us now turn to the money supply. Here, we will assume that the supply of money is controlled by a central bank — in the United States, the central bank is the Federal Reserve System, or the Fed. (We will examine the money-supply process more carefully in Chapter 13.) The Fed is assumed to control the nominal money supply. For a given price level, this implies a given real money supply.

The condition for MONEY-MARKET EQUILIBRIUM — and, therefore, for asset-market equilibrium — requires that real money demand equal real money supply, or

(2.7) $$\frac{M^D}{P} = \frac{M}{P}$$

Suppose that the real money supply $M/P = \$500$ billion and return to Figure 2.7. Earlier, we saw that if $Q = \$2,200$ billion and $r = 8\%$, then $M^D/P = \$500$ billion. We also saw that if Q increases to $\$2,500$ billion, then the M^D/P curve shifts to the right; but if r also increases to 10%, then M^D/P stays constant at $\$500$ billion.

The combinations of Q and r that will make real money demand M^D/P equal the available real money supply M/P ($\$500$ billion) are plotted in Figure 2.8. We have just seen that $M^D/P = \$500$ billion at these two points (r, Q): $(8\%, 2,200)$ and $(10\%, 2,500)$. The line joining these two points is called the *LM curve*.

FIGURE 2.8 AN *LM* CURVE

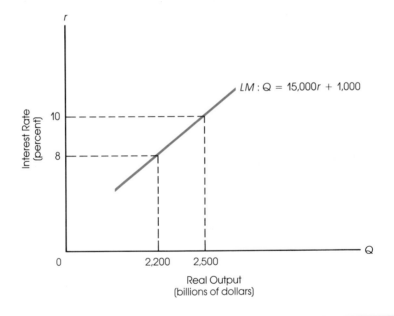

When real output Q increases, real money demand M^D/P tends to increase. Real money demand can be held constant (equal to the available real money supply M/P) if the interest rate r rises enough to discourage any shift in demand from bonds to money, notwithstanding the rise in Q. Hence, a rise in r of proper magnitude offsets the impact on real money demand of a rise in Q. The *LM* curve therefore has a positive slope.

▶ The *LM curve* has a positive slope because when Q increases, a rise in r is necessary to hold real money demand constant.

We can derive the equation for the *LM* curve by combining equations (2.6) and (2.7) to obtain

(2.8) $$\frac{M}{P} = 0.5Q - 7,500r$$

Although equation (2.8) is an *LM* equation, it is useful to isolate either r or Q. To solve for r, move $7,500r$ to the left and M/P to the right, so that

$$7,500r = 0.5Q - \frac{M}{P}$$

to obtain the *LM* equation in our example, with r isolated:

(2.9) $$r = \frac{1}{7,500}\left(0.5Q - \frac{M}{P}\right)$$

Given real income Q and the real money supply M/P, real money demand M^D/P will equal the given real money supply M/P if and only if r adjusts to the value given in equation (2.9). We assume that such an adjustment actually occurs in asset markets.

It is useful to think of r as the *dependent variable* in the *LM* relationship; given Q and M/P, it is r that adjusts to achieve equilibrium in asset markets. For this reason, we isolate r in equation (2.9).

It will also prove convenient to isolate Q. Returning to equation (2.8):

(2.8) $$\frac{M}{P} = 0.5Q - 7,500r$$

Moving the r term to the left side of the equation gives us

$$7,500r + \frac{M}{P} = 0.5Q$$

Thus, the *LM* equation, with Q isolated, is

(2.10) $$Q = 15,000r + 2\frac{M}{P}$$

Now suppose that the real money supply $M/P = \$500$ billion. Then the *LM* curve becomes

(2.11) $Q = 15{,}000r + 1{,}000$

Equation (2.11) is an example of an *LM* curve with specific values for the parameters k and h and the real money supply M/P. In equation (2.11), a higher r implies a higher Q. Hence, the *LM* curve has a positive slope, as shown in Figure 2.8. The "curve" is a straight line due to the simple linear form of the money-demand equation (2.6).

We can easily plot the *LM* curve. In equation (2.11), if $r = 8\%$, $Q = \$2{,}200$ billion; if $r = 10\%$, $Q = \$2{,}500$ billion. Joining these two points gives us the *LM* curve.

What does the *LM* curve mean? Equation (2.11) is obtained from equation (2.7), which states that real money demand equals real money supply. Thus, for each r, equation (2.11) gives the equilibrium output Q that would make money demand equal the given real money supply.

▶ The *LM curve* consists of all points (r, Q) that result in equilibrium in the money market. For any point (r, Q) on the *LM* curve, *real money demand* M^D/P equals *real money supply* M/P.

Since the money supply is given, it implies that every point (r, Q) on the *LM* curve will result in the same money demand — namely, the one equal to the given money supply. But why does money demand stay constant as Q and r rise together?

When Q rises, wealth-holders are encouraged to shift demand toward money to finance transactions and away from bonds. However, a rise in r of proper magnitude will encourage wealth-holders to shift demand toward bonds that pay interest and away from money. For a given rise in Q, a particular rise in r will keep money demand constant (equal to the available money supply).

Consider our example in equation (2.11), where real money supply $M/P = \$500$ billion. Does each point (r, Q) that satisfies equation (2.11) result in a real money demand of $\$500$ billion? Let's check one point. If r is 10%, then in equation (2.11)

$$Q = 15{,}000r + 1{,}000 = 15{,}000(0.1) + 1{,}000$$
$$= 1{,}500 + 1{,}000 = 2{,}500$$

What is real money demand M^D/P when $r = 10\%$ and $Q = \$2{,}500$ billion? Substituting into our money-demand equation (2.6), we obtain

$$\frac{M^D}{P} = 0.5Q - 7{,}500r = [0.5(2{,}500)] - [7{,}500(0.1)]$$
$$= 1{,}250 - 750 = 500$$

Therefore, this point on our *LM* curve will indeed cause real money demand to equal real money supply. The same is true for any point that satisfies *LM* equation (2.11).

Now let's return to the more general *LM* equation (2.10). We have just plotted the *LM* curve when $k = 0.5$, $h = 7,500$, and $M/P = \$500$ billion. A change in any one of these numerical values will shift the *LM* curve and, for any r, a different Q will result.

Suppose that the real money supply increases from $500 billion to $750 billion. At every point on the initial *LM* curve shown in Figure 2.8, $M^D/P = \$500$ billion, but the new *LM* curve must pass through points at which $M^D/P = \$750$ billion. Clearly, these points lie to the right of the initial *LM* curve because, at any r, a larger Q is now required to raise real money demand M^D/P to $750 billion.

From equation (2.10), the *LM* equation is

$$Q = 15,000r + 2\frac{M}{P} = 15,000r + 2(750)$$

(2.11′) $Q = 15,000r + 1,500$

Compare this equation with equation (2.11):

(2.11) $Q = 15,000r + 1,000$

Now, for any given r, Q is $500 billion greater than Q in equation (2.11). Thus, an increase in the real money supply M/P of $250 billion will shift the *LM* curve to the right by $500 billion.

▶ An *increase* in the real money supply shifts the *LM* curve to the right.

This rightward shift in the *LM* curve is shown in Figure 2.9.
Returning to the money-demand equation:

(2.6) $$\frac{M^D}{P} = \frac{M_a}{P} + kQ - hr$$

$$\frac{M^D}{P} = 0 + 0.5Q - 7,500r$$

Assume that the real money supply M/P is once again $500 billion. Then any point (r, Q) that makes real money demand $M^D/P = \$500$ billion in equation (2.6) lies on the initial *LM* curve. Consider point (r_0, Q_0) on the

FIGURE 2.9 A SHIFT OF THE *LM* CURVE TO THE RIGHT

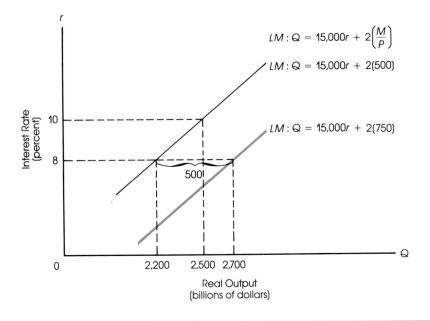

$$LM : Q = 15{,}000r + 2\left(\frac{M}{P}\right)$$

$$LM : Q = 15{,}000r + 2(500)$$

$$LM : Q = 15{,}000r + 2(750)$$

When the real money supply M/P increases by $250 billion (from $500 billion to $750 billion), the *LM* curve shifts to the right by $500 billion. At each interest rate r, the real output Q that is required to make real money demand equal real money supply ($M^D/P = M/P$) is $500 billion greater.

LM curve in Figure 2.10. Now suppose that at this (r_0, Q_0), real money demand M^D/P rises above $500 billion because M_a/P increases above 0.

Why would M_a/P increase? Real wealth may increase. Alternatively, wealth-holders may change their attitudes concerning risk, safety, and liquidity and decide that—at the same wealth, income, and interest rate—they want to reduce their demand for other assets and increase their demand for money.

But in our example, an increase in M_a/P above 0 will raise real money demand above $500 billion at point ($r_0$, Q_0), so that, at this point, real money demand will exceed real money supply. Point (r_0, Q_0) will not be on the new *LM* curve. As shown in Figure 2.10, at Q_0, a higher interest rate r_1 will be required to offset the increase in M_a/P and return real money demand to $500 billion (the value of the real money supply). The new *LM* curve goes through point (r_1, Q_0) instead of point (r_0, Q_0). Thus, the *LM* curve has shifted up (left) to *LM'*.

▶ An increase in real money demand at a given point (r, Q) shifts the *LM* curve up (left).

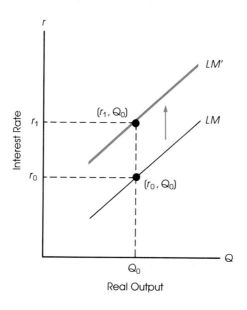

Initially, the *LM* curve passes through point (r_0, Q_0), so that $M^D/P = M/P$ at (r_0, Q_0). If the autonomous component of real money demand M_a/P increases, then M^D/P exceeds M/P at (r_0, Q_0). With Q at Q_0, r must rise to r_1 to reduce M^D/P back to equality with M/P. Hence, the new *LM'* curve passes through point (r_1, Q_0), and the *LM* curve has shifted up.

▶ An increase in real money demand at a given point (r, Q) has the same effect on the *LM* curve as a decrease in the real money supply. Each shifts the *LM* curve up (left).

What happens at a point *off* the *LM* curve? Consider the point (r_0, Q_0) to the left of the *LM* curve in Figure 2.11. At such a point, real money demand is less than real money supply ($M^D/P < M/P$) because, at a point directly to the right on the *LM* curve at which Q is higher (and therefore M^D/P is higher), money demand equals money supply. With $M^D/P < M/P$, the public attempts to shift out of money and into bonds. The excess *demand* for bonds raises the price of bonds (equivalently, lowers the interest rate). Hence, r declines until a point on the *LM* curve is reached.

Symmetrically, consider the point (r_1, Q_1) to the right of the *LM* curve in Figure 2.11. At such a point, real money demand is greater than real money supply ($M^D/P > M/P$) because, at a point directly to the left on the *LM* curve at which Q is lower (and therefore M^D/P is lower),

FIGURE 2.11 THE STABILITY OF MONEY-MARKET EQUILIBRIUM

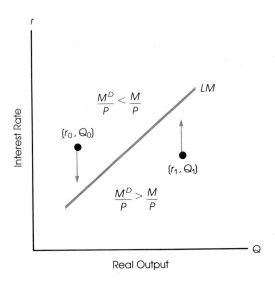

At any point to the *left* of the *LM* curve, such as (r_0, Q_0), M^D/P is less than M/P ($M^D/P < M/P$). Hence, the interest rate r *decreases*, moving the economy toward the *LM* curve. Symmetrically, at any point to the *right* of the *LM* curve, such as (r_1, Q_1), M^D/P exceeds M/P ($M^D/P > M/P$). Hence, r *increases*, moving the economy toward the *LM* curve.

money demand equals money supply. With $M^D/P > M/P$, the public attempts to shift out of bonds and into money. The excess supply of bonds reduces the price of bonds (equivalently, raises the interest rate). Hence, r rises until a point on the *LM* curve is reached.

▶ *Money-market equilibrium* is *stable*. If money demand exceeds money supply, then the interest rate rises, reducing money demand toward money supply. If money supply exceeds money demand, then the interest rate declines, raising money demand toward money supply. Hence, the interest rate always moves toward its equilibrium value, at which money demand equals money supply.

2.3 Equilibrium in the Goods and Money Markets

The intersection of the *IS* and *LM* curves gives the point (r, Q) at which both the *goods market* and the *money market* are in equilibrium simultaneously. At this r and Q, the goods market is in equilibrium (the demand for output D equals actual output Q) and the money market is in equilibrium (real money demand M^D/P equals the available real money supply

M/P). Moreover, at any other point (r, Q), at least one of these two markets will not be in equilibrium.

Let's use our earlier example to find the intersection of the IS and LM curves. Given

(2.2) $IS: Q = 3,000 - 10,000r$

(2.11) $LM: Q = 15,000r + 1,000$

We can solve for r:

$$15,000r + 1,000 = 3,000 - 10,000r$$
$$25,000r = 2,000$$
$$r = 0.08 = 8\%$$

Substituting back into equation (2.2), we obtain

$$Q = 3,000 - [10,000(0.08)] = 3,000 - 800 = 2,200$$

At $r = 8\%$ and $Q = \$2,200$ billion, demand for output will equal actual output and real money demand will equal real money supply. This intersection of the IS and LM curves is shown in Figure 2.12.

FIGURE 2.12 EQUILIBRIUM IN THE GOODS AND MONEY MARKETS

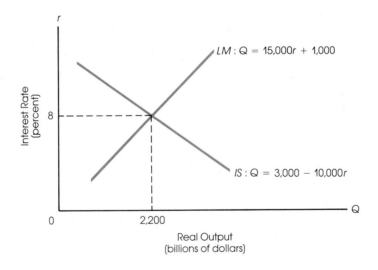

Given the particular monetary policy ($M/P = \$500$ billion), the equation for the LM curve is $Q = 15,000r + 1,000$. Given the particular fiscal policy ($G = \$300$ billion, $R = \$250$ billion, $t = 25\%$), the equation for the IS curve is $Q = 3,000 - 10,000r$. The IS and LM curves intersect at $r = 8\%$ and $Q = \$2,200$ billion. At this point, both the goods market and the money market are in equilibrium.

Let's recall what lies behind this solution. The *IS* equation (2.2) depends on the assumption that $G = \$300$ billion, $R = \$250$ billion, and $t = 25\%$; therefore, the *IS* equation depends on a particular *fiscal policy*. The *LM* equation (2.11) depends on the assumption that $M/P = \$500$ billion; therefore, the *LM* equation depends on a particular *monetary policy*. A different fiscal or monetary policy would result in a different intersection point for the *IS* and *LM* curves.

Suppose that the *IS* curve shifts to the right, perhaps due to an expansion of fiscal policy (an increase in G or R or a cut in t), but that the *LM* curve stays fixed. At the instant the shift occurs, there is a new intersection (shown in Figure 2.13), but the economy is still at the old intersection. How does the economy move to its new equilibrium point?

We saw earlier that if the economy is at a point off the *IS* curve, it will move *horizontally* toward that curve; if the economy is off the *LM* curve, it will move *vertically* toward that curve. If the economy is off both curves, it will move toward both curves. Although the speed of

FIGURE 2.13 THE PATH TO THE NEW EQUILIBRIUM FOLLOWING AN *IS* SHIFT

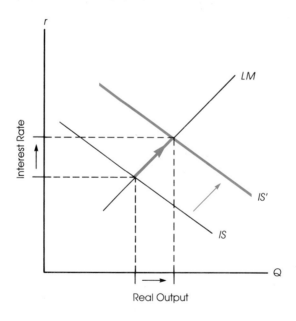

When the *IS* curve shifts right to *IS'*, it is plausible to assume that the money market remains in equilibrium. Hence, the economy moves along the *LM* curve to its new equilibrium; that is, the interest rate r and the level of output Q rise together such that, at each moment, point (r, Q) for the economy lies on the *LM* curve.

adjustment is not our main concern here, it seems plausible to assume that money-market equilibrium will be restored quickly through a movement of the interest rate r, but that goods-market equilibrium will be restored more slowly through a movement of equilibrium output Q.

To restore money-market equilibrium, the price of bonds (equivalently, the interest rate on bonds) must move until the demand for each asset equals its supply. To restore goods-market equilibrium, production must adjust until it equals demand. The asset-market price adjustment should occur more quickly than the goods-market quantity adjustment.

Thus, in Figure 2.13, when the IS curve shifts to the right, we assume that the economy stays on the current LM curve and moves along it to the intersection point with the new IS curve.

Now suppose that a monetary expansion shifts the LM curve to the right, as shown in Figure 2.14. We then assume that the economy moves vertically down to the new LM curve and along this curve to the new intersection point with the IS curve.

Let's consider each shift in more detail. When the IS curve shifts to the right, demand for goods exceeds production at the initial interest

FIGURE 2.14 THE PATH TO THE NEW EQUILIBRIUM FOLLOWING AN *LM* SHIFT

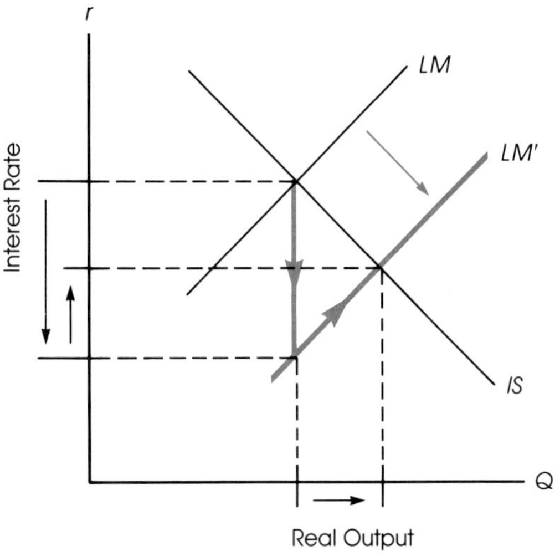

When the LM curve shifts right to LM', it is plausible to assume that the money market will move quickly toward equilibrium. Hence, the economy moves vertically down to the new LM' curve and then moves along (up) the LM' curve to a new equilibrium point. The interest rate should drop sharply and then rise to a final value below its initial value.

rate r; producers observe a reduction in inventories and respond by raising their output Q. But as income rises, the *transactions demand for money* also rises, and money demand exceeds money supply. As the public tries to shift out of bonds and into money, the price of bonds falls (equivalently, the interest rate r rises). The rise in r induces the public to reduce its money demand to correspond to the available money supply. Thus, the economy is on the *LM* curve at a higher point (r, Q). This process continues, and the economy moves along the *LM* curve to the intersection point with the new *IS* curve.

Now let's consider a shift of the *LM* curve to the right due to a *monetary expansion*. The most important method of monetary expansion is an *open-market purchase* of bonds by the central bank (the Federal Reserve System). The Fed pays for the bonds with money that it creates. The aim of the open-market operation is to change the relative supplies of money and bonds. The open-market operation raises the supply of money and reduces the supply of bonds held by the public.

If asset markets are initially in equilibrium, this shift in asset supplies causes a temporary portfolio *disequilibrium*. When the Fed substitutes money for bonds in the public's portfolio, the public will want to hold the new asset supplies only if the interest rate on bonds changes. Specifically, the reduction in the supply of bonds causes an excess demand for bonds at the initial bond price (equivalently, at the interest rate on bonds). This bids up the price of bonds and drives down the interest rate until the reduction in r is sufficient to reduce the demand for bonds to equal the new supply of bonds and to raise the demand for money to equal the new supply of money. The reduction in r then induces an increase in investment demand I and (through the multiplier) a rise in demand for output D, which is followed by an equal rise in equilibrium output Q.

Thus, a change in monetary policy causes temporary portfolio disequilibrium, which is quickly corrected by an adjustment in the price of bonds (equivalently, the interest rate on bonds). Then, more slowly, the change in the interest rate r induces a change in equilibrium output Q.

▶ The *IS–LM* model is a powerful analytical tool. At a glance, it enables you to see the impact of a change in fiscal or monetary policy or a change in autonomous private demand on the interest rate r and on equilibrium output Q. But the *IS–LM* model also has a dangerous limitation. By giving the "answer" so quickly and easily, it tempts the user to forget about the economic meaning and justification of each curve and about what is happening when a curve shifts and the economy moves from one point of *IS–LM* intersection to another. Resist the temptation to accept this easy "answer." Always test yourself to see if you can explain what is happening in words, and why.

2.4 Stabilization Policy

Now that we have presented the *IS–LM* system, let's return to our Chapter 1 example. Recall that, initially, *I* = $380 billion, *Q* = $2,200 billion, and the government budget is balanced (with the tax rate *t* = 25%). But then *I* declines to $300 billion, *Q* drops to $2,000 billion, and the reduction in tax revenue *T* creates a budget deficit.

We begin with the *IS–LM* diagram shown in Figure 2.15. Initially, with *I* = $380 billion and *t* = 25%, the *IS* and *LM* curves intersect at *Q* = $2,200 billion and *r* = 8%. In Chapter 1, we simply stated that *I* declined from $380 billion to $300 billion. But in this chapter, we can now introduce the investment function:

(2.1) $I = I_a - jr$
$I = 700 - 4,000r$

FIGURE 2.15 STABILIZATION BY MONETARY POLICY

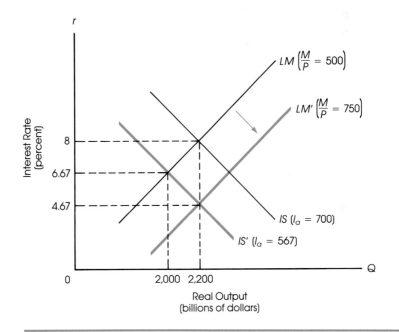

Real Output
(billions of dollars)

Initially, the economy is at *r* = 8% and *Q* = $2,200 billion. The equation for the investment curve is *I* = 700 − 4,000*r*, with *I_a* = $700 billion. The real money supply *M/P* = $500 billion. Then business pessimism reduces *I_a* to $567 billion and *I* = 567 − 4,000*r*. If *M/P* stays at $500 billion, so that the *LM* curve remains fixed, then *Q* decreases to $2,000 billion, *r* declines to 6.67%, and investment demand *I* drops from $380 billion to $300 billion. But if monetary policy raises *M/P* to $750 billion, shifting the *LM* curve to the right, then *Q* remains at $2,200 billion, *r* declines to 4.67%, and *I* stays at $380 billion.

At the initial IS–LM equilibrium, with $r = 8\%$

$$I = 700 - [4{,}000(0.08)] = 380$$

▶ We will now assume that a reduction in I_a, due to business pessimism about the future, provokes the decline in I (from $380 billion to $300 billion) and the decline in Q (from $2,200 billion to $2,000 billion).

It would be natural to think that I_a must decline by $80 billion (from $700 billion to $620 billion) to generate this outcome. But this is incorrect. If I_a declines, we know that the IS curve will shift to the left from IS to IS' in Figure 2.15. But if LM remains fixed, the interest rate r will drop below 8%. Thus, in equation (2.1), when I_a declines, it will cause r to decline also. It is the combined effect of these decreases in I_a and r that must make I decline by $80 billion.

How can we determine the decline in I_a that will cause Q to decrease from $2,200 billion to $2,000 billion? Because the real money supply is fixed at $500 billion, the LM equation remains unchanged:

(2.11) LM: $Q = 15{,}000r + 1{,}000$

At the intersection of the new IS curve IS' and this LM curve, $Q = \$2{,}000$ billion. We can then find the r at this intersection by substituting $Q = \$2{,}000$ billion into LM equation (2.11):

$$2{,}000 = 15{,}000r + 1{,}000$$
$$r = 6.67\%$$

Now we can use the investment function given by equation (2.1) to determine the required change in I_a. We seek the value of I_a that, with $r = 6.67\%$, will reduce I to $300 billion:

(2.1) $I = I_a - jr$
$$300 = I_a - 4{,}000(0.0667)$$
$$I_a = 567$$

▶ Thus, if business pessimism causes I_a to decline by $133 billion (from $700 billion to $567 billion), then r will decline by 1.33% (from 8% to 6.67%), I will decline by $80 billion (from $380 billion to $300 billion), and Q will decline by $200 billion (from $2,200 billion to $2,000 billion).

Note that the decline in I ($80 billion) is less than the decline in I_a ($133 billion). This is because the resulting reduction in r tends to raise I, so that I declines by only $80 billion instead of by $133 billion.

We can check our conclusion by making sure that the new *IS* curve *IS'* (with $I_a = \$567$ billion) and the *LM* curve in fact intersect at $r = 6.67\%$ and $Q = \$2,000$ billion. Earlier, we derived the equation of the *IS* curve when $I_a = \$567$ billion:

(2.2')   *IS':* $Q = 2,667 - 10,000r$ (with $I_a = 567$)

(2.11)   *LM:* $Q = 15,000r + 1,000$

Solving for r, we obtain

$$15,000r + 1,000 = 2,667 - 10,000r$$
$$25,000r = 1,667$$
$$r = 6.67\%$$

Substituting back into equation (2.2') yields

$$Q = 2,667 - 10,000(0.0667) = 2,667 - 667 = 2,000$$

Hence, a decline in I_a from \$700 billion to \$567 billion reduces r from 8% to 6.67% and reduces Q from \$2,200 billion to \$2,000 billion. The result is a *recession* — a decline in output below the full-employment level accompanied by a rise in unemployment.

MONETARY POLICY TO COMBAT RECESSION

Now let's consider a monetary policy designed to combat recession and restore Q to \$2,200 billion, given that I_a remains at \$567 billion. The Federal Reserve System must try to increase the real money supply so that the *LM* curve will shift right from *LM* to *LM'* in Figure 2.15, and the new *LM'* curve will intersect *IS'* at $Q = \$2,200$ billion.

Initially, the real money supply $M/P = \$500$ billion. To what value must the Fed raise M/P to achieve $Q = \$2,200$ billion? Under the monetary expansion, the *IS* equation will remain

(2.2')   *IS':* $Q = 2,667 - 10,000r$ (with $I_a = 567$)

If Q is to be \$2,200 billion, then r must be

$$2,200 = 2,667 - 10,000r$$
$$r = 4.67\%$$

The general *LM* equation is

(2.10)   *LM:* $Q = 15,000r + 2\dfrac{M}{P}$

Substituting in $Q = 2{,}200$ and $r = 4.67\%$ gives us

$$2{,}200 = [15{,}000(0.0467)] + 2\,\frac{M}{P}$$

$$\frac{M}{P} = 750$$

Thus, if the Fed raises the real money supply from \$500 billion to \$750 billion, the new *LM* equation becomes

(2.11′) LM': $Q = 15{,}000r + 1{,}500$ $\left(\text{with } \dfrac{M}{P} = 750\right)$

The intersection of the *IS'* and *LM'* curves given by equations (2.2′) and (2.11′), respectively, occurs at $r = 4.67\%$ and $Q = \$2{,}200$ billion, as shown in Figure 2.15. You can check this by solving equations (2.2′) and (2.11′) for r and then for Q. Note that investment demand I is

(2.1′) $I = 567 - 4{,}000r$
$I = 567 - [4{,}000(0.0467)]$
$I = 380$

The monetary expansion restores I to \$380 billion. Even though I_a remains at \$567 billion, the reduction in r from 6.67% to 4.67% raises I from \$300 billion back to \$380 billion.

Finally, note that the budget is now balanced. Recall that this example depends on $G = \$300$ billion, $R = \$250$ billion, and $t = 25\%$. If $Q = \$2{,}200$ billion, then $T = \$550$ billion, so that $G + R = T$.

We have just seen one example of *stabilization policy*—the attempt of the Federal Reserve System to combat recession by adjusting the money supply. As the economy slides into recession, the government may attempt to "stabilize" the economy by restoring output to the full-employment level of \$2,200 billion. In principle, our government may utilize one of two kinds of stabilization policy: monetary policy or fiscal policy.

Under *monetary policy*, the Federal Reserve adjusts the money supply. Under *fiscal policy*, the U.S. Congress and the President adjust the tax rate and/or government spending.

In our simple model, it may seem easy for the government to restore Q to \$2,200 billion by implementing the proper monetary or fiscal policy. In our example, raising M/P from \$500 billion to \$750 billion restores Q to \$2,200 billion. A similar calculation could be made for the tax rate or for government expenditures (either government transfers R

or government purchases *G*). But, in practice, there are serious obstacles to achieving the target *Q*.

Discretionary fiscal policy (changes in the tax rate or in government expenditures that require action by Congress and the President) is plagued by delays and political conflict. When the economy goes into recession, it is usually at least six months before Congress can enact a change in tax rates or spending and still another six months before this change actually goes into effect. By that time, the economy may already be recovering. If a *stimulus* enters the economy at this point, the result may be to "overheat" the economy, causing *inflation* (as we shall see in Chapter 4).

Moreover, discretionary fiscal policy appears to be subject to a basic *political asymmetry*. When the private sector generates too little demand, Congress and the President are usually willing to propose a stimulus — either in the form of a tax cut or an increase in government spending — because such a measure is popular. But when the private sector generates too much demand, which creates inflation, Congress and the President are often unwilling to propose a *restraint* — either a tax increase or a cut in government spending — because such a measure is unpopular.

Due to this political asymmetry, an active fiscal policy may raise the budget deficit over time because a stimulus, which increases the deficit, is enacted more often than a restraint, which reduces the deficit.

By contrast, the Fed appears able to act more quickly and more symmetrically. The Federal Open Market Committee (FOMC) meets each month to adjust monetary policy. It has twelve voting members — the seven Members of the Board of Governors of the Federal Reserve System, including the Chairman, and five of the regional Federal Reserve Bank presidents. The seven Board members are appointed by the President to serve fourteen-year terms. Clearly, the FOMC is not subject to re-election pressure.

Some economists believe that discretionary fiscal policy is still worthwhile. Others are persuaded that it is not worth attempting, except in an emergency — a *depression* (a severe, prolonged decline in output below the full-employment level accompanied by a sharp rise in unemployment). It should be emphasized, however, that most economists regard *automatic fiscal stabilizers* — the automatic variation of tax revenue with income — as very important.

Economists also disagree concerning the desirability of an active monetary policy. Although the institutional framework of monetary policy is promising (it permits relatively quick and symmetrical adjustments), even monetary policies must confront uncertainties and lags. The Fed can only estimate the direction in which the economy is moving and the precise monetary adjustment that is desirable. Moreover, there is a lag between the time the FOMC decides on an adjustment and the impact of that adjustment on the output of the economy.

▶ In Chapters 8 and 9, we will discuss stabilization policy in greater depth. Here, we simply issue the warning that stabilizing the economy is more difficult than our simple example may indicate.

2.5 The Significance of the Fiscal–Monetary Policy Mix at Full-Employment Output

We begin this section by emphasizing several important points:

▶ Throughout this section, we will assume that a change in the fiscal–monetary mix does not alter full-employment output; in particular, we will assume that a change in the tax rate t or in government transfers R does not alter the labor supply and, therefore, does not alter the output that is produced at full employment.

▶ We will also assume that the fiscal–monetary mix does not affect the propensity to consume or to save.

In Section 2.6, we will consider the possible impact of this policy mix on full-employment output and on the propensity to consume or to save.

▶ Throughout this section, we will assume that "an offsetting monetary policy" holds Q at the full-employment level ($Q = $2,200$ billion) for any fiscal policy. An *offsetting monetary policy* adjusts the money supply so that the *LM* curve will always intersect the *IS* curve at the full-employment level of Q.

If output is already at the full-employment level ($Q = $2,200$ billion) and is to be held at that level, then if government purchases G are held constant, an increase in investment can occur if and only if there is an equal decrease in consumption.

▶ At the full-employment level of output, there is a fundamental trade-off between *investment* and *consumption;* more investment requires less consumption.

In Chapter 10, we will see that more investment means that the economy will have a greater *real capital stock* next year. At the full-employment level of output next year, the economy will generate more output. It will therefore be possible to enjoy more consumption next year.

▶ The trade-off is really between present consumption and future consumption. A sacrifice in consumption this year will permit more consumption next year. The greater the share of output that we devote to investment becomes, the faster our standard of living will advance.

Suppose that policymakers estimate that business will normally keep I_a at $700 billion. Earlier, we calculated that $Q = \$2,200$ billion and $r = 8.0\%$ result from the following fiscal – monetary policy mix:

$$\text{Fiscal Policy:} \quad t = 25\%, R = \$250 \text{ billion}, G = \$300 \text{ billion}$$

$$\text{Monetary Policy:} \frac{M}{P} = \$500 \text{ billion}$$

Now, we focus on the composition of output. First, note that tax revenue T is

(1.32) $T = tQ = 0.25(2,200) = 550$

The budget is balanced because government expenditures $R + G = 250 + 300 = 550$.

It will prove useful to rewrite equation (1.33) for the government budget deficit

(1.33) $Df \equiv G + R - T$

as

(1.33') $Df \equiv G - (T - R)$

where $T - R = net revenue$ (tax revenue minus government transfers)

In this example, net revenue = \$300 billion and the deficit is 0:

$$T - R = 550 - 250 = 300$$
$$Df = G - (T - R) = 300 - 300 = 0$$

Hence, the deficit is 0 because both government purchases and net revenue equal \$300 billion.

Consumption is

(1.31) $C = c(Q - T + R) = 0.8(2,200 - 550 + 250) = 1,520$

With $G = \$300$ billion, $C + I = \$1,900$ billion, so that $C + I + G = \$2,200$ billion. Thus

$$I = 1,900 - C = 380$$

As a check, investment is given by

(2.1) $I = I_a - jr = 700 - [4,000(0.08)] = 380$

We will call this original fiscal policy "tight" relative to the fiscal policy we are about to consider. The impact of this tight fiscal policy (with an offsetting monetary policy) is shown in Figure 2.16(a), which includes a "pie" diagram indicating the composition of full-employment output, an $IS-LM$ diagram, and an investment diagram.

Suppose that some "high" R legislators give top priority to achieving a high level of government transfers and that other "low" t legislators give top priority to achieving a low tax rate. Also assume that "high" R legislators succeed in raising government transfers R above $250 billion and that "low" t legislators succeed in cutting the tax rate below 25%. Specifically, assume that R increases by $110 billion to $360 billion and that t declines by 5% to 20%. The fiscal policy that results is

$t = 20\%, R = \$360 \text{ billion}, G = \$300 \text{ billion}$

The impact of this "easy" fiscal policy (with an offsetting monetary policy) is shown in Figure 2.16(b), which you should compare to Figure 2.16(a).

Note that with an offsetting monetary policy keeping equilibrium output Q at $2,200 billion, the 5% cut in the tax rate t reduces tax revenue T by $110 billion. Consider the impact on the consumption function:

(1.31) $C = c(Q - T + R)$

Previously $C = 0.8(2,200 - 550 + 250) = 1,520$

Now $C = 0.8(2,200 - 440 + 360) = 1,696$

Note that C increases by $176 billion, 50% of which is due to the $110 billion tax cut and 50% of which is due to the $110 billion increase in government transfers. Thus, taxpayer consumption rises by $88 billion and transfer-recipient consumption rises by $88 billion.

This "easing" of fiscal policy raises consumption demand C and, consequently, total equilibrium output Q at any interest rate r. Therefore, in the $IS-LM$ diagram, the IS curve shifts to the right.

To offset this fiscal expansion and to hold Q at $2,200 billion, monetary policy must be tightened and the LM curve must shift to the left, as shown in Figure 2.16(b).

Because C rises by $176 billion, I must fall by $176 billion (from $380 billion to $204 billion) to keep Q at $2,200 billion. This new composition of output is shown in the pie diagram in Figure 2.16(b). We

FIGURE 2.16 (a) TIGHT FISCAL POLICY **(b)** EASY FISCAL POLICY

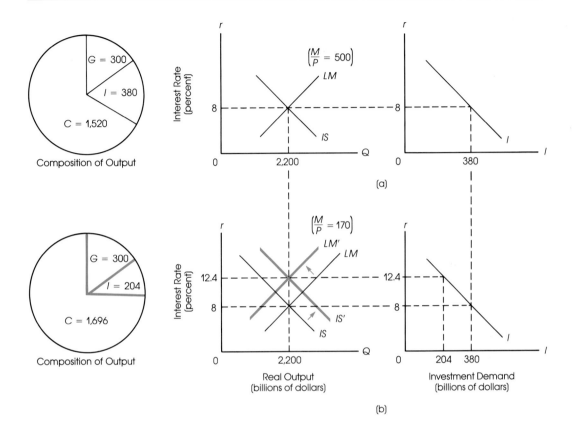

(a) These three diagrams show the impact of the original tight fiscal policy. The pie chart indicates the values of consumption C, investment I, and government purchases G. The $IS-LM$ diagram plots the $IS-LM$ intersection point ($r = 8\%$, $Q = \$2,200$ billion). The diagram of the investment function plots the interest rate r and investment demand I.

(b) These three diagrams show the impact of a switch from the original tight fiscal policy to an easy fiscal policy (with monetary policy tightened to keep real output Q at the full-employment level of \$2,200 billion). Comparing the pie chart here with the one in Figure 2.16(a), consumption C is larger and investment I is smaller. In the $IS-LM$ diagram, the rightward shift of the IS curve and the leftward shift of the LM curve hold Q constant and raise r. In the diagram of the investment function, the rise in the interest rate r causes a decline in investment demand I.

can easily calculate the required interest rate r from the investment function

(2.1) $I = I_a - jr$
              $204 = 700 - 4{,}000r$
              $r = 12.4\%$

This result is shown in the investment diagram in Figure 2.16(b). From the *LM* equation, the required real money supply is

(2.8) $\dfrac{M}{P} = 0.5Q - 7{,}500r = [0.5(2{,}200)] - [7{,}500(0.124)] = 170$

Thus, with the easing of fiscal policy, the real money supply must be cut from $500 billion to $170 billion to keep Q at $2,200 billion.
  Instead of a balanced budget, there is now a deficit of $220 billion:

(1.33) $Df \equiv G + R - T = 300 + 360 - 440 = 220$

It will prove useful to consider

(1.33′) $Df \equiv G - (T - R)$

Under the *tight* fiscal policy

              $T - R = 550 - 250 = 300$ (with $G = 300$, $Df = 0$)

Under the *easy* fiscal policy

              $T - R = 440 - 360 = 80$ (with $G = 300$, $Df = 220$)

Thus, the deficit rises from 0 to $220 billion because net revenue declines by $220 billion (from $300 billion to $80 billion) when "tight" fiscal policy becomes "easy."
  Comparing these two fiscal policies

    Tight fiscal policy:
              $t = 25\%$, $R = \$250$ billion, $Df = 0$;
              $C = \$1{,}520$ billion, $I = \$380$ billion
    Easy fiscal policy:
              $t = 20\%$, $R = \$360$ billion, $Df = \$220$ billion;
              $C = \$1{,}696$ billion, $I = \$204$ billion

Starting with the easy fiscal policy, with its high R and low t, how can we raise I from \$204 billion back to \$380 billion? One way is to return to the initial tight fiscal policy, cutting R from \$360 billion back to \$250 billion and raising t from 20% back to 25%. If this is done, then taxpayer consumption and transfer-recipient consumption would each decline by \$88 billion, enabling I to rise by \$176 billion. This would clearly require concessions from both "high" R and "low" t legislators.

If "high" R legislators have the votes to get what they want, can they maintain R at \$360 billion and still achieve a C of \$1,520 billion? Yes, if they are willing to raise the tax rate t sufficiently. We can find the required t by first obtaining the tax revenue T that would reduce C to \$1,520 billion:

$$C = c(Q - T + R)$$
$$1{,}520 = 0.8(2{,}200 - T + 360)$$
$$T = 660$$
$$t = \frac{T}{Q} = \frac{660}{2{,}200} = 30\%$$
$$Df \equiv G + R - T = 300 + 360 - 660 = 0$$

If "low" t legislators have the votes to get what they want, can they maintain t at 20% and still achieve a C of \$1,520 billion? Yes, if they are willing to cut government transfers R sufficiently. With $t = 20\%$, so that $T = 0.2(2{,}200) = 440$, we can find the R required to reduce C to \$1,520 billion:

$$C = c(Q - T + R)$$
$$1{,}520 = 0.8(2{,}200 - 440 + R)$$
$$R = 140$$
$$Df = G + R - T = 300 + 140 - 440 = 0$$

Note these options:

A "High" R ("High" t) Tight Fiscal Policy:
$t = 30\%$, $R = \$360$ billion, $Df = 0$; $C = \$1,520$ billion,
$I = \$380$ billion.
A "Low" t ("Low" R) Tight Fiscal Policy:
$t = 20\%$, $R = \$140$ billion, $Df = 0$; $C = \$1,520$ billion,
$I = \$380$ billion.

Under all three tight fiscal policies — high R (high t), low t (low R), and the original one — the IS curve intersects the LM curve (with $M/P = \$500$ billion) at $Q = \$2,200$ billion and $r = 8\%$. Net revenue $T - R = \$300$ billion and the budget is balanced. Total $C = \$1,520$ billion, total $I = \$380$ billion, and the tight fiscal policy pie diagram shown in Figure 2.16(a) is achieved. Then what consequence differs?

▶ Under a high R (high t) policy, the consumption of transfer recipients is higher and the consumption of taxpayers is lower than under a low t (low R) policy.

With an offsetting monetary policy holding output Q at the full-employment level, *deficit reduction* (achieved by raising net revenue $T - R$) will raise investment.

▶ Reducing the deficit either by raising taxes or by cutting government transfers (a tightening of fiscal policy), while maintaining full-employment output through an offsetting monetary policy, will reduce consumption and raise investment.

▶ Any citizen who favors increased investment relative to consumption should favor reducing the deficit that occurs at the full-employment level of output. A high R advocate should favor deficit reduction through an increase in taxes; a low t advocate should favor deficit reduction through a decrease in government transfers.

Suppose that an individual favors a consumption–investment mix that requires a deficit of 0 (a balanced budget) when the economy is held at the full-employment level of output by an offsetting monetary policy. Should this individual advocate a balanced budget rule?

Recall our discussion of balanced budget rules at the end of Chapter 1. Such a rule might be implemented by a statute or by a constitutional amendment. It is worth reemphasizing our conclusions:

▶ An *always-balanced budget rule* would be undesirable because it would be *destabilizing;* it would require fiscal action that would make a recession worse.

▶ A *full-employment normally balanced budget rule* would avoid destabilization and would prescribe fiscal action that tries to keep the economy at the full-employment level of output.

Thus, an individual who favors this consumption–investment mix might support a full-employment normally balanced budget rule. Recall that, under this rule, if Q is *on* target this year, then government expenditures and the tax rate must be set so the budget would be balanced next year if the economy is operating at the full-employment level of output. But if Q is *below* target this year, then government expenditures must be raised and/or the tax rate must be lowered to stimulate aggregate demand. And if Q is *above* target this year, then government expenditures must be cut and/or the tax rate must be raised to restrain aggregate demand.

THE IMPACT OF THE FISCAL–MONETARY POLICY MIX ON SAVING

Finally, let's consider our analysis of the fiscal–monetary policy mix from still another perspective. Recall that in our development of national income accounting relationships in Chapter 1, we showed that in an economy that includes government but has no foreign trade, total investment I_T must always equal total saving S_T:

(1.29) $I_T \equiv S_T$

In the discussion that follows, it will be crucial to bear in mind that total saving S_T consists of two components:

(1.27) $S_T \equiv S + S_G$
where S = private saving
       S_G = government saving
(1.25) $S_G \equiv T - R - G_C$

In our analysis of the fiscal–monetary policy mix thus far, we have ignored the concept of *saving*. We have seen, however, that switching to a tight fiscal policy (either high R or low t, or the original in our example) raises private investment I by \$176 billion (from \$204 billion to \$380 billion). With G constant, so that government investment G_I is constant, total investment I_T will increase by \$176 billion as well. From national income accounting relationships, it follows that total saving S_T should also rise by \$176 billion. Let's check to confirm that this is so.

To calculate the change in total saving S_T, we must consider the change in both of its components: private saving S and government saving S_G.

From equation (1.15), we know that private saving S equals private net income $(Q - T + R)$ minus consumption C, or

(1.15) $S \equiv (Q - T + R) - C$

Under the easy fiscal policy

$$S = (2{,}200 - 440 + 360) - 1{,}696$$
$$S = 424$$

Under the original tight fiscal policy

$$S = (2,200 - 550 + 250) - 1,520$$
$$S = 380$$

Under the high R tight fiscal policy

$$S = (2,200 - 660 + 360) - 1,520$$
$$S = 380$$

Under the low t tight fiscal policy

$$S = (2,200 - 440 + 140) - 1,520$$
$$S = 380$$

▶ Thus, the switch to any of the three tight fiscal policies will reduce private saving S by $44 billion (from $424 billion to $380 billion).

This makes sense. Starting from the easy fiscal policy—with its high R and low t—a switch to the high R (high t) tight fiscal policy raises taxes on households, forcing a reduction in both taxpayer consumption and saving. A switch to the low t (low R) tight fiscal policy reduces government transfers to households, forcing a reduction in both transfer–recipient consumption and private saving. A switch to the original tight fiscal policy both raises the tax rate t and cuts government transfers R. In each case, household net income decreases by $220 billion; with the propensity to consume $c = 0.8$, consumption is reduced by $176 billion and private saving is reduced by $44 billion.

But private saving S is only one of the two components of total saving S_T. Now let's consider government saving S_G, which is defined as government net income $(T - R)$ minus government consumption G_C, or

(1.25) $$S_G \equiv T - R - G_C$$

Assume that government consumption G_C stays constant. Starting from the easy fiscal policy, a switch to the original tight fiscal policy raises T by $110 and cuts R by $110. Thus, government net income $(T - R)$ and government saving S_G each increase by $220 billion. Starting from the easy fiscal policy—with its high R and low t—a switch to the high R (high t) tight fiscal policy keeps R constant at $360 billion but raises T by $220 billion (from $440 billion to $660 billion). Thus, government net income $(T - R)$ and government saving S_G again each increase by $220 billion. Starting from the easy fiscal policy—with its high R and low t — a switch to the low t (low R) tight fiscal policy keeps T constant at \$440 billion but reduces R by \$220 billion (from \$360 billion to \$140 billion). Thus, once again, government net income $(T - R)$ and government saving S_G each increase by \$220 billion.

▶ A switch to any of the three tight fiscal policies (with an offsetting monetary policy) will raise both government net income $(T - R)$ and government saving S_G by \$220 billion.

Since government saving S_G increases by \$220 billion and private saving S decreases by \$44 billion:

▶ A switch to any of the three tight fiscal policies (with an offsetting monetary policy) will raise total saving by \$176 billion (\$220 billion − \$44 billion). Thus, the increase in total saving S_T will in fact equal the increase in total investment I_T.

We can state this more generally:

▶ A switch to a tighter fiscal policy, with an offsetting monetary policy that holds total output constant, will reduce private saving S but will raise total saving S_T and total investment I_T.

▶ Our analysis of saving reveals an important point. If we want to know the impact of a policy change on total investment (or on private investment, if government investment is held constant), we must evaluate the impact of the policy change on *total* saving (private saving *plus* government saving) and not merely on private saving alone. Looking only at the change in private saving can give us the wrong answer.

Of course, it is possible to determine what would happen to total investment or to private investment (holding government investment constant) without ever using the concept of saving. Indeed, we never referred to the concept of saving when we performed our calculations. The point here is that if the concept of saving *is* used, it must be used properly. The change in total saving — not the change in private saving alone — must equal the change in total investment.

2.6 "Supply-Side Economics" and the Fiscal–Monetary Policy Mix

At the beginning of Section 2.5, we assumed that a change in the fiscal–monetary policy mix does not alter full-employment output or the propensity to consume (or to save). In our examples, we assumed that full-employment output $Q = \$2,200$ billion and that the propensity to consume $c = 0.8$ for each fiscal–monetary policy mix that we examined.

Here, we will consider the hypothesis that an increase in the tax rate will *significantly* lower the supplies of labor and capital and, hence, the full-employment level of output (the output that is produced when all those who seek work are working as much as they desire and when all those who seek to supply capital are supplying as much as they desire). A reduction in the supply of capital means a decrease in the propensity to save and, therefore, an increase in the propensity to consume.

Until now, our analysis has been entirely demand-oriented. We have implicitly assumed that the supplies of labor and capital and the *propensity to save s* are independent of the fiscal – monetary policy mix. If these supplies are fully employed, then a particular level of output — full-employment output — is produced ($2,200 billion in our examples). The task of fiscal – monetary policy has been to achieve an equilibrium output of $Q = \$2,200$ billion. We have assumed that the propensity to consume remains at $c = 0.8$ and that the propensity to save remains at $s = 0.2$, regardless of the policy chosen.

Economists have long recognized that an increase in the tax rate may reduce the supplies of labor and capital due to the *disincentive effect* of a higher tax rate. (A higher tax rate may discourage people from supplying labor and capital because they will keep a smaller share of their earnings.)

But most economists assume that, for a tax rate increase "in the relevant range" (that is, a moderate rate increase starting from the current tax rate), any reduction in the supply of labor or capital will be relatively small, so that an analysis of a shift to a tight fiscal – easy monetary policy mix could make use of the approximation (as we have) that full-employment output remains constant.

In recent years, however, some economists have challenged the validity of this approximation and proposed the *supply-side economics hypothesis:*

▶ According to the *supply-side economics hypothesis,* a tax-rate *increase in the relevant range* (a moderate rate increase starting from the current tax rate) will *significantly reduce* the supplies of labor and capital (and the propensity to save) and full-employment output. Symmetrically, a tax-rate *decrease* in the relevant range will *significantly increase* the supplies of labor and capital (and the propensity to save) and full-employment output.

But what is "significant?" Most advocates of the supply-side economics hypothesis contend that when the tax rate is raised, full-employment output will decline enough to keep full-employment tax revenue from increasing. Symmetrically, when the tax rate is cut, full-employment output will increase enough to keep full-employment tax revenue from decreasing.

▶ We will, however, use the term "supply-side hypothesis" to mean the assertion that a tax-rate increase will cause a *relatively large* decrease in full-employment output, even if this decline is not quite large enough to keep tax revenue from increasing.

In Chapters 10 and 15, we will consider supply-side economics at greater length. Here, rather than investigate the validity of the hypothesis, we ask: would its validity reverse our conclusion in Section 2.5 that a tighter fiscal policy raises investment?

Suppose that the economy is initially under the easy fiscal policy with its high R and low t. Then we shift to the high R (high t) tight fiscal policy, thereby raising the tax rate (with an offsetting monetary policy that keeps Q at full-employment output). It is possible that full-employment output will decrease and that the propensity to consume will increase. Previously, when we ignored these possible supply-side effects, we saw that with output held constant and consumption reduced, investment increased. Will supply-side effects reverse this conclusion? The answer is evident in the accounting identity

(1.24) $$Q \equiv C_T + I_T$$

Even if full-employment output Q decreases, I_T will increase as long as C_T declines more than Q declines.

▶ As long as the decrease in total consumption C_T is greater than any decline in full-employment output Q, a shift to a high R (high t) tight fiscal policy (entailing a higher tax rate) will raise total investment I_T.

To reverse the conclusion, the supply-side effects must be great enough to cause full-employment output to decline more than consumption. We will discuss the likelihood of this outcome in Chapters 10 and 15. Here, we note our conclusion from that discussion; most economists believe it is highly unlikely that the supply-side effects would be great enough to achieve this result. Thus, our conclusion from the last section will almost certainly remain valid. A shift to a high R (high t) tight fiscal policy (entailing an increase in the tax rate), complemented by an offsetting monetary policy, will increase investment.

SUMMARY

1. Investment demand I *increases* when the interest rate r *decreases*. Hence, equilibrium output Q *increases* when the interest rate *decreases*. This inverse relationship between the interest rate and equilibrium output is the *IS curve*. The *IS* curve consists of all points (r, Q) that result in equilibrium in the *goods market*.

2. Any change in a variable or parameter that raises demand for output D at a given point (r, Q) will shift the IS curve to the *right*. In particular, a fiscal policy expansion (an increase in government purchases G or government transfers R or a cut in the tax rate t) will shift the IS curve to the right. An increase in autonomous consumption or investment will shift the IS curve to the right.

3. In our two-asset economy, each wealth-holder must make *portfolio decisions* regarding the *allocation* of *wealth* between money and bonds. Money is demanded to finance transactions; bonds are demanded to earn interest. *Real money demand* increases when *real income* increases and when the interest rate on *bonds* decreases.

4. *Money-market equilibrium* occurs when real money demand equals the *real money supply*. The *LM curve* consists of all points (r, Q) at which real money demand is constant and equal to the available real money supply. The *LM* curve has a *positive slope;* it consists of all points (r, Q) that result in equilibrium in the *money market*.

5. An increase in the real money supply shifts the *LM* curve to the *right;* an increase in the autonomous component of money demand shifts the *LM* curve to the *left*.

6. The intersection of the IS and LM curves gives the point (r, Q) at which both the goods market and the money market are simultaneously in equilibrium.

7. *Stabilization policy* is an attempt by government to adjust *fiscal* or *monetary policy* to combat a recession caused by a decline in demand generated by the private sector. For example, if autonomous investment I_a declines, shifting the IS curve to the left, then an *expansionary* monetary policy can shift the LM curve to the right to restore full-employment output. In practice, effective stabilization may be difficult to achieve.

8. An *easing* of fiscal policy through a tax cut or an increase in government transfers, together with an *offsetting monetary policy* that maintains output at the full-employment level, shifts the IS curve to the right and the LM curve to the left. The result is an increase in consumption and a decrease in investment. Thus, an easing of fiscal policy, which entails an increase in the full-employment deficit, raises current consumption at the expense of investment and of future output and consumption.

9. Symmetrically, a tightening of fiscal policy through a tax increase or a government-transfer cut, together with an offsetting monetary policy that maintains full-employment output, shifts the IS curve to the left and the LM curve to the right. The result is a decrease in consumption and an increase in investment. Even if the *supply-side economics hypothesis* is correct and full-employment output de-

creases in response to a tax increase, investment will still rise as long as consumption decreases more than the decline in full-employment output.

QUESTIONS

Given $C = 0.75(Q - T + R)$, $R =$ \$200 billion, $T = 0.2Q$, $G =$ \$300 billion, $I = 950 - 4{,}000r$, $M^D/P = 0.5Q - 6{,}250r$, and $M/P =$ \$625 billion:

2.1 What is the IS equation?

2.2 What is the LM equation?

2.3 What is the equilibrium r and Q?

2.4 Suppose that I_a decreases from \$950 billion to \$770 billion. Why might this happen? What effect does this decrease in I_a have on the IS–LM diagram?

2.5 With $I_a =$ \$770 billion, what is the new IS equation?

2.6 With $I_a =$ \$770 billion, what is the new equilibrium r and Q?

2.7 Assume that the equilibrium output Q in Question 2.3 is the full-employment level of output. If $I_a = \$770$ billion, what value of r is required to restore full-employment output?

2.8 What value of M/P is required to restore full-employment output?

2.9 When the Federal Reserve System adjusts M/P to restore full-employment output, what happens to the $IS-LM$ diagram?

Once again, assume that $I_a = \$950$ billion and that the economy is at the full-employment equilibrium you found in Question 2.3.

2.10 What is the deficit Df?

2.11 What are consumption C and investment I?

If R is raised to $300 billion, t is cut to 16%, and the Fed adjusts M/P to maintain full-employment output:

2.12 What happens to the $IS-LM$ diagram?

2.13 What is the deficit Df?

2.14 What are consumption C and investment I?

Now consider some implications of Questions 2.1 – 2.14.

2.15 When I_a declines from $950 billion to $770 billion in Question 2.4, what happens to the deficit Df and to the interest rate r?

2.16 When R is raised, t is cut, and M/P is adjusted in Question 2.12, what happens to the deficit Df and to the interest rate r?

2.17 Compare the correct answers to Questions 2.15 and 2.16. Do Df and r always vary in the same direction? In the opposite direction?

2.18 How does a shift to an *easy* fiscal policy (with an offsetting monetary policy) affect current consumption? Future consumption?

APPENDIX 2A

THE ALGEBRA OF THE *IS-LM* DIAGRAM

In Appendix 2A, we will develop the $IS-LM$ model algebraically. We have already examined the basic equations of this model within the context of several numerical illustrations. Here, more formal derivations will be presented.

2.A.1 The *IS* Curve

We begin with our three-equation model of equilibrium output in an economy with government:

(1.30) $Q = C + I + G$

(1.31) $C = C_a + c(Q - T + R)$

(1.B.8) $T = T_a + tQ$

and add the investment demand equation given by

(2.1) $I = I_a - jr$

For any interest rate r, investment demand I is given by equation (2.1). For any given investment demand I, equations (1.30), (1.31,) and (1.B.8) determine equilibrium output Q. We want to derive an equation that gives Q as a function of r. This is the *IS* equation. To derive this equation, we substitute equation (1.B.8) into equation (1.31) to obtain

$$C = C_a + c(Q - T_a - tQ + R)$$

We then substitute both this expression for C and the expression for I given by equation (2.1) into equation (1.30), so that

$$Q = C_a + c(Q - T_a - tQ + R) + I_a - jr + G$$
$$Q = C_a + c(Q - tQ) - cT_a + cR + I_a - jr + G$$

Moving all terms that contain Q to the left side of the equation, we obtain

$$Q - c(Q - tQ) = C_a - cT_a + cR + I_a - jr + G$$

The left side can be rewritten

$$Q - c(Q - tQ) = Q - cQ + ctQ = (1 - c + ct)Q$$
$$= [1 - c(1 - t)]Q$$

giving us

$$[1 - c(1 - t)]Q = C_a - cT_a + cR + I_a - jr + G$$

Dividing by $1 - c(1 - t)$ yields the *IS* equation:

(2.A.1) $$Q = \frac{1}{1 - c(1 - t)}(C_a - cT_a + cR + I_a - jr + G)$$

We can rewrite equation (2.A.1) more concisely if we define the concept of autonomous demand D_a, first introduced in equation

(1.B.2) as demand that does not vary with r or Q, so that

(2.A.2) $D_a \equiv C_a - cT_a + cR + I_a + G$

The parenthetical term in equation (2.A.1) is identical to D_a as given by equation (2.A.2), except that it contains one more element $(-jr)$. Hence, the parenthetical term in equation (2.A.1) equals $D_a - jr$.

Also recall from equation (1.B.13) that the multiplier m in our three-equation system equals the first term in equation (2.A.1); we will designate this term $1/[1 - c(1 - t)]$ as *the IS multiplier* m_i.

Thus, we can rewrite equation (2.A.1) as

(2.A.3) $Q = m_i(D_a - jr)$

where $m_i \equiv \dfrac{1}{1 - c(1 - t)}$ is the *IS* multiplier given by equation (1.B.13).

For example, let's insert the numerical values we used in Chapter 2 into equation (2.A.1), so that $c = 0.8$, $t = 0.25$, $C_a = 0$, $T_a = 0$, $R = \$250$ billion, $I_a = \$700$ billion, $j = 4{,}000$, $G = \$300$ billion:

$$Q = \frac{1}{1 - [(0.8)(0.75)]} [0.8(250) + 700 + 300 - 4{,}000r]$$
$$Q = (2.5)(1{,}200 - 4{,}000r)$$
$$Q = 3{,}000 - 10{,}000r$$

This is *IS* equation (2.2).

Equation (2.A.3) sheds light on the *shifting* of the *IS* curve. Clearly, an increase in D_a that leaves m_i constant will shift the *IS* curve to the right; at any interest rate r, equilibrium output Q will increase. Thus, an increase in C_a, R, I_a, or G, or a decrease in T_a, will shift the *IS* curve to the right. Also, a decrease in t raises m_i and Q and therefore will shift the *IS* curve to the right.

Equation (2.A.3) also sheds light on the *slope* of the *IS* curve. $\Delta Q/\Delta r$ equals the coefficient of r

$$Q = m_i D_a - m_i jr$$

(2.A.4) $\dfrac{\Delta Q}{\Delta r} = -m_i j$

Hence, as both j (the responsiveness of investment demand I to the interest rate r) and the *IS* multiplier increase, $\Delta Q/\Delta r$ becomes greater (in absolute value) and the *IS* curve becomes flatter.

2.A.2 The *LM* Curve

We now add the money-demand equation (2.6) and the money-market equilibrium equation (2.7) to our model:

(2.6) $$\frac{M^D}{P} = \frac{M_a}{P} + kQ - hr$$

(2.7) $$\frac{M^D}{P} = \frac{M}{P}$$

Equation (2.6) tells us that real money demand depends on an autonomous component that is independent of Q or r, on real income Q, and on the interest rate r. Equation (2.7) tells us that real money demand must equal the available real money supply to achieve money-market equilibrium.

To solve for r, we substitute equation (2.7) into equation (2.6) to obtain

$$\frac{M}{P} = \frac{M_a}{P} + kQ - hr$$

Moving the hr term to the left and the M/P term to the right of the equation yields

$$hr = \frac{M_a}{P} + kQ - \frac{M}{P}$$

Dividing by h then gives us the *LM* equation with r isolated:

(2.A.5) $$r = \left(\frac{1}{h}\right)\left(\frac{M_a}{P} + kQ - \frac{M}{P}\right)$$

For any real income Q, the money market will be in equilibrium if the interest rate r adjusts to the value given by equation (2.A.5). We will assume that such an adjustment actually occurs in asset markets. It is useful to think of r as the dependent variable in the *LM* relationship; given Q, M/P, and autonomous money demand M_a/P, it is r that adjusts to achieve equilibrium in asset markets.

It will also prove convenient to isolate Q. Given

$$\frac{M}{P} = \frac{M_a}{P} + kQ - hr$$

If we isolate kQ, so that

$$kQ = hr - \frac{M_a}{P} + \frac{M}{P}$$

and divide by k, we obtain the *LM* equation with Q isolated:

(2.A.6) $$Q = \left(\frac{1}{k}\right)\left(hr - \frac{M_a}{P} + \frac{M}{P}\right)$$

Inserting the numerical values we used in Chapter 2 ($k = 0.5$, $h = 7{,}500$, and $M_a/P = 0$), we obtain

$$Q = (2)\left(7{,}500r + \frac{M}{P}\right)$$

$$Q = 15{,}000r + 2\left(\frac{M}{P}\right)$$

This is *LM* equation (2.10). For example, if the real money supply $M/P = \$500$ billion, then the *LM* equation becomes

(2.11) $$Q = 15{,}000r + 1{,}000$$

Equation (2.A.6) sheds light on the *shifting* of the *LM* curve. Clearly, if the real money supply M/P increases, then a higher Q will correspond to a given r and the *LM* curve will shift to the right. If autonomous money demand M_a/P increases, then a lower Q will correspond to a given r and the *LM* curve will shift to the left.

Equation (2.A.6) also sheds light on the *slope* of the *LM* curve. $\Delta Q/\Delta r$ equals the coefficient of r in equation (2.A.6):

$$Q = \left(\frac{h}{k}\right)r - \left(\frac{1}{k}\right)\left(\frac{M_a}{P} - \frac{M}{P}\right)$$

(2.A.7) $$\frac{\Delta Q}{\Delta r} = \frac{h}{k}$$

If h (the responsiveness of real money demand M^D/P to the interest rate r) is smaller, then the *LM* curve is more vertical.

2.A.3 *IS–LM* Equilibrium

The *IS* and *LM* equations are

(2.A.3) $$IS: \quad Q = m_i(D_a - jr)$$

$$(2.A.5) \qquad LM: \quad r = \left(\frac{1}{h}\right)\left(\frac{M_a}{P} + kQ - \frac{M}{P}\right)$$

These two equations contain two unknown, *endogenous* variables, r and Q. If we substitute equation (2.A.5) where r appears in equation (2.A.3), we eliminate r and obtain one equation with one endogenous variable, Q:

$$(2.A.8) \qquad Q = m_i\left\{D_a - j\left(\frac{1}{h}\right)\left[\frac{M_a}{P} + kQ - \frac{M}{P}\right]\right\}$$

Although this equation has only one unknown, Q, we have not yet isolated Q. To do this, we must move the Q term from the right side to the left side of the equation. First, we separate out the Q term on the right side and multiply both $-(j/h)$ and $M_a/P - M/P$ by -1 to obtain

$$Q = m_i\left[D_a + \frac{j}{h}\left(\frac{M}{P} - \frac{M_a}{P}\right)\right] - m_i\left(\frac{j}{h}\right)kQ$$

Next, we move the Q term from the right side to the left side:

$$Q + m_i\left(\frac{jk}{h}\right)Q = m_i\left[D_a + \frac{j}{h}\left(\frac{M}{P} - \frac{M_a}{P}\right)\right]$$

Factoring out Q on the left side gives us

$$\left[1 + m_i\left(\frac{jk}{h}\right)\right]Q = m_i\left[D_a + \frac{j}{h}\left(\frac{M}{P} - \frac{M_a}{P}\right)\right]$$

Dividing by the term multiplying Q, we then obtain

$$(2.A.9) \qquad Q = \left[\frac{m_i}{1 + m_i(jk/h)}\right]\left[D_a + \frac{j}{h}\left(\frac{M}{P} - \frac{M_a}{P}\right)\right]$$

If D_a increases by 1 unit, then Q will increase by the first bracketed term in equation (2.A.9). This term is the multiplier m in the *IS–LM* system. Our equation for Q can now be written

$$(2.A.10) \qquad Q = m\left[D_a + \frac{j}{h}\left(\frac{M}{P} - \frac{M_a}{P}\right)\right]$$

where $m \equiv \dfrac{m_i}{1 + m_i(jk/h)}$

$$m_i \equiv \frac{1}{1 - c(1 - t)}$$

$$D_a \equiv C_a - cT_a + cR + I_a + G$$

Equation (2.A.10) is the reduced-form equation for Q in the $IS-LM$ system of six equations: (1.30), (1.31), (1.B.8), (2.1), (2.6), and (2.7). The parameters and variables on the right side of this equation are assumed to be exogenous (given). Equation (2.A.10) will yield the value of equilibrium output Q at the $IS-LM$ intersection when numerical values are given for parameters c, j, k, and h; for the autonomous components of private demand C_a and I_a (consumption and investment); for the nominal money supply M and the autonomous component of money demand M_a; for fiscal policy variables G, R, T_a, and t; and for the price level P (which we assume is given throughout this chapter).

If D_a increases by ΔD_a, then Q will increase by $m\Delta D_a$. Hence, m is the multiplier for the $IS-LM$ system. Now it is easy to see that:

▶ The multiplier in the $IS-LM$ system m is less than the multiplier in the IS system m_i.

To see that this is true, we can look at the definition of m given in equation (2.A.10):

$$m \equiv \frac{m_i}{1 + m_i(jk/h)}$$

The denominator on the right of this equation is greater than 1 because the second term on the right is positive. Therefore, m is less than m_i.

Let's express the $IS-LM$ multiplier m in terms of c, t, j, k, and h. First, we divide the numerator and the denominator of the expression for m by m_i to obtain

$$m = \frac{1}{(1/m_i) + (jk/h)}$$

We then take the *reciprocal** of m_i, which is

$$\frac{1}{m_i} = 1 - c(1 - t)$$

---

* The reciprocal of X is $\frac{1}{X}$.

so that

$$(2.A.11) \qquad m = \frac{1}{[1 - c(1-t)] + (jk/h)}$$

Thus, m differs from m_i by jk/h in the denominator; again, it is evident that m is less than m_i.

Why is the IS–LM multiplier m smaller than the IS multiplier m_i? The IS multiplier denotes the increase in equilibrium output Q that follows from an increase in autonomous demand D_a in the absence of any feedback from the money market when real output Q expands. The four equations of the IS system treat the interest rate r as a constant, ignoring feedback from the money market. Hence, the IS multiplier tells us how much Q would increase on the assumption that r stays constant as Q expands, as shown in Figure 2.A.1.

FIGURE 2.A.1 WHY THE IS–LM MULTIPLIER IS LESS THAN THE IS MULTIPLIER

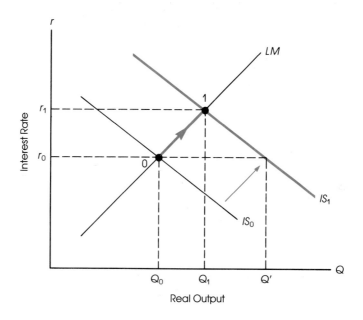

Initially, the economy is at point 0, the intersection of the IS_0 and LM_0 curves. Then the IS curve shifts to the right to IS_1. The IS multiplier indicates the increase in real output Q that would occur if the interest rate r stayed constant at r_0; this increase would be $Q' - Q_0$. But the interest rate r rises from r_0 to r_1, so that the increase in Q is only $Q_1 - Q_0$. The IS–LM multiplier yields this correct, smaller increase in Q.

But the $IS-LM$ multiplier does account for the feedback from the money market when Q expands. An increase in Q will raise real money demand M^p/P. Real money demand will then temporarily exceed real money supply M/P, and the interest rate r will rise to restore money-market equilibrium. The rise in r will reduce I, which will reduce the increase in Q. Therefore, when money-market feedback is recognized, the increase in Q in response to an increase in D_a is smaller. Hence, the $IS-LM$ multiplier is smaller than the IS multiplier.

This difference can be seen in the $IS-LM$ diagram in Figure 2.A.1. When D_a increases, the IS curve shifts to the right from IS_0 to IS_1. If r stayed constant at r_0, Q would increase from Q_0 to Q' (the amount of the rightward shift of the IS curve); this is the increase given by the IS multiplier m_i. Since Q increases by less than this amount, from Q_0 to Q_1, the change from the initial to the final $IS-LM$ intersection point is smaller than the rightward shift of the IS curve. The reason for this is that as Q increases, thereby raising the transactions demand for money, the interest rate r must rise to r_1 to keep the money market in equilibrium. The economy therefore moves "northeast" along the LM curve from point 0 to point 1 in Figure 2.A.1. The rise in r reduces investment demand I, so that the final increase in Q to Q_1 is less than it would be if r stayed constant.

3

Aggregate Demand and Aggregate Supply

In this chapter, we will accomplish three tasks. First, we will use the *IS–LM* analysis in Chapter 2 to develop the *aggregate demand curve*. Second, we will develop the *aggregate supply curve*. Third, we will show how aggregate demand and aggregate supply, taken together, determine the real output Q and the price level P of the economy.

3.1 The Aggregate Demand Curve

In Chapter 2, we developed the *IS* curve and the *LM* curve. The intersection of the *IS* and *LM* curves is a point (r, Q) at which both the goods market and the money market are in equilibrium. But the position of the *LM* curve—and, hence, the *IS–LM* intersection—depends on the price level P. Thus, the *IS–LM* intersection tells us the equilibrium output Q that will result at a specific price level P. Throughout Chapter 2, we assumed that P is constant.

A change in P will shift the *LM* curve, the *IS–LM* intersection, and equilibrium output Q. We will now trace the relationship between P and equilibrium output Q—the relationship that constitutes the *aggregate demand curve*.

Returning to our example in Chapter 2, the *IS* curve is given by equation (2.2) and the *LM* curve is given by equation (2.10):

(2.2) IS: $Q = 3,000 - 10,000r$

(2.10) LM: $Q = 15,000r + 2\dfrac{M}{P}$

If the *nominal money supply* $M = \$500$ billion, then the *LM* curve becomes

(3.1) $LM: \quad Q = 15{,}000r + 2\left(\dfrac{500}{P}\right)$

This is LM equation (2.10) with Q isolated, except that the nominal money supply is specified, so that the price level P is now the focus of our attention. P is a *price index*. In our examples, we will set the initial value of P at 1.00.

If, initially, the price level $P = 1.00$, then the real money supply $M/P = \$500$ billion and the LM equation is

(2.11) $LM: \quad Q = 15{,}000r + 1{,}000$

In Chapter 2, when we solved for equilibrium output Q, we found that $Q = \$2{,}200$ billion and that the interest rate $r = 8\%$.

Now suppose that the price level P is cut in half to 0.50. Then the real money supply will double, so that $M/P = \$1{,}000$ billion. Thus, our two equations become

(2.2) $IS: \quad Q = 3{,}000 - 10{,}000r$
(2.11″) $LM: \quad Q = 15{,}000r + 2{,}000$

Then, solving for r

$$15{,}000r + 2{,}000 = 3{,}000 - 10{,}000r$$
$$25{,}000r = 1{,}000$$
$$r = 0.04 = 4\%$$

Substituting back into equation (2.2), we obtain

$$Q = 3{,}000 - 10{,}000(0.04) = 3{,}000 - 400 = 2{,}600$$

With $P = 1.00$, we found earlier that, in equilibrium, $r = 8\%$ and $Q = \$2{,}200$ billion. With $P = 0.50$, we have just found that, in equilibrium, $r = 4\%$ and $Q = \$2{,}600$ billion. Thus, as P declines, Q increases.

This result is shown in Figure 3.1. In both graphs, Q is plotted on the horizontal axis. In our familiar $IS–LM$ diagram, shown in Figure 3.1(a), r is plotted on the vertical axis. In the new aggregate demand– aggregate supply diagram shown in Figure 3.1(b), P is plotted on the vertical axis.

The $IS–LM$ diagram in Figure 3.1(a) shows the equilibrium (r, Q) for $P = 1.00$ and for $P = 0.50$. When P declines from 1.00 to 0.50, the real money supply M/P doubles from \$500 billion to \$1,000 billion (with the nominal money supply constant at $M = \$500$ billion). The same change in the real money supply occurs if P remains fixed at 1.00 and

FIGURE 3.1 THE *IS-LM* DIAGRAM AND THE AGGREGATE DEMAND–
AGGREGATE SUPPLY DIAGRAM

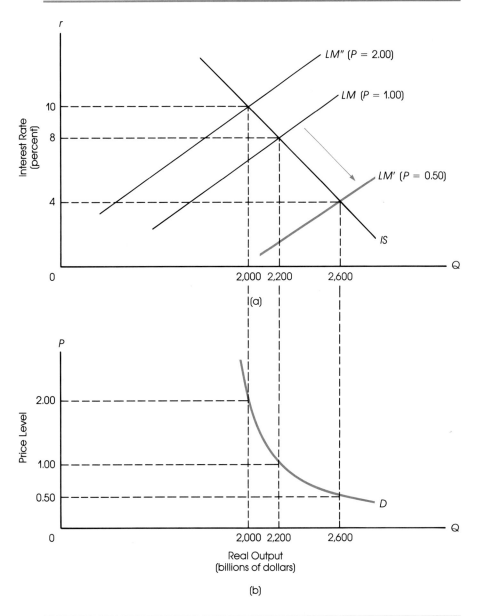

(a)

Real Output
(billions of dollars)

(b)

If the price level *P* declines from 1.00 to 0.50 in part (b), then the *LM* curve shifts to the right to *LM′* and real output *Q* increases from $2,200 billion to $2,600 billion in the *IS-LM* diagram shown in part (a). At *P* = 1.00 in part (b), *Q* = $2,200 billion in part (b); at *P* = 0.50, *Q* = $2,600 billion. If *P* rises from 1.00 to 2.00 in (b), then the *LM* curve shifts to the left to *LM″* and *Q* decreases from $2,200 billion to $2,000 billion in (a). At *P* = 2.00 in (b), *Q* = $2,000 billion in (b). Connecting the three points in diagram (b) yields the aggregate demand *D* curve.

the nominal money supply doubles (from $500 billion to $1,000 billion). Thus, we say that a reduction in P is equivalent to an increase in the nominal money supply M; specifically, halving P is equivalent to doubling M. In both cases, the real money supply M/P doubles. As we saw in Chapter 2, an increase in the real money supply shifts the LM curve to the right.

Shifting the LM curve to the right reduces the equilibrium r and raises the equilibrium Q, as shown in Figure 3.1(a). In our example, r declines from 8% to 4% and Q rises from $2,200 billion to $2,600 billion.

The same result is shown in the aggregate demand diagram in Figure 3.1(b), where we obtain two points: when $P = 1.00$, $Q = $2,200 billion; when $P = 0.50$, $Q = $2,600 billion. If we repeat the steps above for $P = 2.00$, we obtain $Q = $2,000 billion ($r = 10\%$). Thus, in our example, the aggregate demand curve is a *curve*, not a straight line, even though both IS and LM are straight lines. Its curvature is shown in Figure 3.1(b).

Let's derive the equation for the *aggregate demand D curve* in this example. The nominal money supply $M = $500 billion; hence, monetary policy is given. Government purchases $G = $300 billion, government transfers $R = $250 billion, and the tax rate $t = 25\%$; hence, fiscal policy is given. Moreover, the particular parameter values and exogenous variables (such as C_a and I_a) are given for each equation that yields the IS and LM curves.

Based on these monetary and fiscal policies and on these parameter and exogenous variable values, we have, once again

(2.2) IS: $Q = 3,000 - 10,000r$

(3.1) LM: $Q = 15,000r + 2\left(\dfrac{500}{P}\right)$

We want to eliminate r and obtain a single equation that shows how Q varies with P. This will be the *aggregate demand curve equation*. Perhaps the simplest way to do this is to multiply the IS equation by 3 and the LM equation by 2, which yields

(2.2) IS: $3Q = 9,000 - 30,000r$

(3.1) LM: $2Q = 30,000r + 4\left(\dfrac{500}{P}\right)$

Summing the two equations, r cancels out and leaves

$$5Q = 9,000 + \frac{2,000}{P}$$

Dividing by 5, we obtain the aggregate demand curve equation for our example:

(3.2) $$Q = 1,800 + \frac{400}{P}$$

This gives us the equilibrium output Q that occurs at the $IS-LM$ intersection for each level of P. For example, if $P = 1.00$, then $Q = \$2,200$ billion; if $P = 0.50$, then $Q = \$2,600$ billion; if $P = 2.00$, then $Q = \$2,000$ billion. These are the same values shown in Figure 3.1(b).

Equation (3.2) is not a linear equation, because P appears in the denominator; when plotted, it yields a curve. In plotting this equation, it is helpful to recognize that as P gets larger and larger, the last term in equation (3.2) approaches 0, so that Q approaches $\$1,800$ billion. Thus, in Figure 3.1(b), we can draw a vertical pole at $Q = \$1,800$ billion. The curve will approach this pole as P becomes larger and larger; we say that this pole is an *asymptote*. On the other hand, as P approaches 0, Q approaches infinity; thus, the horizontal axis is also an asymptote.

SHIFTING THE D CURVE

What will shift the aggregate demand D curve to the right? For a given price level P, anything that shifts either the IS curve or the LM curve to the right also shifts the $IS-LM$ intersection to the right, provided each curve has its "normal" slope (a negative slope for the IS curve; a positive slope for the LM curve) and ignoring the extreme cases when a curve is either vertical or horizontal. Hence, a rightward shift in the IS curve or the LM curve increases the equilibrium output Q that results at a given P. This means that a larger Q must be plotted at that P in the aggregate demand diagram. The same is true for any other level of P; at each P, Q becomes larger. Hence, the D curve shifts to the right.

▶ Any change that shifts either the IS curve or the LM curve to the right *for a given P* also shifts the aggregate demand D curve to the right.

Note the phrase "for a given P." A rightward shift of the D curve means that equilibrium output Q is greater at a given P. For example, an increase in the nominal money supply M, with P given, will raise the real money supply M/P, thereby shifting the LM curve to the right at the given P. Thus, equilibrium output Q (as determined by the $IS-LM$ intersection) will increase at that P, and the D curve will shift to the right.

Now suppose that the LM curve shifts to the right because P declines while the nominal money supply M remains constant. Equilibrium output Q (as determined by the $IS-LM$ intersection) will increase, but this does not mean that the D curve will shift. Instead, the increase in Q as P declines represents a move "southeast" down a fixed D curve. Indeed, this is exactly how the D curve is traced out: by reducing P and observing the increase in Q when the LM curve shifts to the right.

Let's review what will shift the IS curve to the right and what will shift the LM curve to the right for a given P. We begin with policy. A *fiscal* policy expansion—an increase in government spending (purchases G or transfers R) or a cut in the tax rate t—shifts the IS curve to the right; hence, a fiscal policy expansion shifts the D curve to the right. A *monetary* policy expansion—an increase in the nominal money supply M—shifts the LM curve to the right for a given P; thus, a monetary policy expansion shifts the D curve to the right.

▶ A fiscal policy expansion (which shifts the IS curve to the right) or a monetary policy expansion (which shifts the LM curve to the right) also shifts the aggregate demand D curve to the right.

Fiscal and monetary policies are not the only sources of shifts in the IS and LM curves. Anything that raises consumption demand C or investment demand I at a given r and Q will shift the IS curve to the right. For example, increases in the autonomous components of consumption or investment demand C_a or I_a will cause a rightward shift in the IS curve. Anything that decreases M^D/P at a given r, Q, and P will shift the LM curve to the right. For example, a decrease in the autonomous component of real money demand M_a/P for a given P will do this.

▶ Any change that raises consumption demand C or investment demand I at a given r and Q shifts the IS curve to the right and therefore shifts the aggregate demand D curve to the right. Any change that decreases real money demand M^D/P at a given r, Q, and P shifts the LM curve to the right and therefore shifts the aggregate demand D curve to the right.

Let's illustrate a shift in the aggregate demand D curve using our example (2.10). If the nominal money supply M increases from \$500 billion to \$600 billion, then (as we saw in Chapter 2) the LM curve shifts to the right. LM equation (2.10) then becomes

$$(3.3) \qquad Q = 15,000r + 2\left(\frac{600}{P}\right)$$

Repeating the derivation of the D curve equation, using equation (3.3) instead of equation (3.1), we obtain

$$(2.2) \qquad IS: \quad 3Q = 9,000 - 30,000r$$

$$(3.3) \qquad LM: \quad 2Q = 30{,}000r + 4\left(\frac{600}{P}\right)$$

Adding these two equations gives us

$$5Q = 9{,}000 + \frac{2{,}400}{P}$$

Dividing by 5, we obtain the *aggregate demand curve equation* with $M = \$600$ billion:

$$(3.4) \qquad Q = 1{,}800 + \frac{480}{P}$$

If we compare equation (3.4) with equation (3.2), we see that 480 replaces 400. Thus, when the nominal money supply M increases from \$500 billion to \$600 billion, converting equation (3.2) to equation (3.4), any level of P will result in a larger Q and the D curve will shift to the right. For example, at $P = 1.00$, Q increases from \$2,200 billion to \$2,280 billion.

NOMINAL DEMAND

Thus far, we have focused on the real output Q that is demanded at a given price level P. We will now define *nominal demand Y* as the expenditure PQ that buyers want to make, so that

$$(3.5) \qquad Y \equiv PQ$$

where Y = nominal demand

Q = real output demanded at a given P

Let's find the equation for nominal demand Y based on the aggregate demand curve equation (3.2), when $M = \$500$ billion:

$$(3.2) \qquad Q = 1{,}800 + \frac{400}{P}$$

Multiplying both sides of this equation by P, we obtain the *nominal demand equation*

$$(3.6) \qquad Y \equiv PQ = 1{,}800P + 400$$

Recall that the specific aggregate demand curve given by equation (3.2) is obtained from a specific monetary–fiscal policy mix and specific values of the parameters and exogenous variables. Once all of these parameters and variables have been set, a specific aggregate demand curve can be plotted, as we did in Figure 3.1(b). But from equation (3.6), we can see that nominal demand Y is *not* constant along the aggregate demand D curve; clearly, PQ varies as P changes along the D curve. Thus, it is not true that a particular monetary–fiscal policy mix fixes the nominal demand Y in the economy. Such a policy mix does, however, fix the aggregate demand D curve.

As we will see later in this chapter, the economy will actually move to the point (Q, P) at the intersection of the aggregate demand curve and the *aggregate supply curve*. Thus, the position of the aggregate supply curve determines the particular point on the aggregate demand D curve that results. The nominal demand Y therefore depends on the supply curve as well as on the demand curve.

To illustrate this important point, we will return to our example. With a nominal money supply of $M = \$500$ billion and the specific values for other variables and parameters previously given, the aggregate demand D curve is given by

$$(3.2) \qquad Q = 1,800 + \frac{400}{P}$$

An increase in the nominal money supply to $M = \$600$ billion (a growth rate of 20%) resulted in a new aggregate demand curve, given by

$$(3.4) \qquad Q = 1,800 + \frac{480}{P}$$

We will now show the change in nominal demand Y due to this 20% increase in the nominal money supply M. Initially, corresponding to equation (3.2), we derived the nominal demand equation when $M = \$500$ billion

$$(3.6) \qquad Y \equiv PQ = 1,800P + 400$$

After the 20% increase in M, corresponding to equation (3.4), we obtain the nominal demand equation when $M = \$600$ billion:

$$(3.7) \qquad Y \equiv PQ = 1,800P + 480$$

The actual values of P and Q will depend on the aggregate supply curve. Suppose initially that $P = 1.00$. If P happens to increase by 20% to 1.20, then Y will increase from $2,200 billion in equation (3.6) to $2,640 billion in equation (3.7). Hence, the *percentage growth rate of Y*, denoted by y, is 20%. In this case, a 20% growth rate in the nominal money supply M will result in a 20% growth rate in nominal demand y in the economy.

But suppose that P does not increase by 20% but instead increases by 10% to $P = 1.10$. Then Y will increase from \$2,200 billion to \$2,460 billion, as given by equation (3.7); hence, $y = 11.8\%$. In this case, the same 20% growth rate in the nominal money supply M results in a nominal demand growth rate y of only 11.8%.

Now suppose that P happens to increase by 30% to $P = 1.30$. Then Y will increase from \$2,200 billion to \$2,820 billion, as given by equation (3.7); hence, $y = 28.2\%$. In this case, the same 20% growth rate in the nominal money supply M results in a 28.2% growth rate in nominal demand y.

▶ Thus, a specific growth rate of the nominal money supply M does not fix the growth rate of nominal demand y. The value of y depends on the particular point (Q, P) on the new aggregate demand curve to which the economy moves, and this point (as we will soon see) depends on the aggregate supply curve.

It will prove convenient in the inflation–unemployment analysis in Part 2 to assume that nominal demand growth y is set at a specific rate. For example, we will examine what happens to the economy if y is raised permanently from 0% to 6% or reduced permanently from 6% to 0%.

In effect, we will assume that monetary and/or fiscal policy will be adjusted during each period to achieve the required nominal demand growth y. The necessary adjustment will depend on the aggregate supply curve.

To justify our simplifying assumption that y is fixed in advance, we imagine the following hypothetical procedure. Suppose that policymakers select a target y for the period and that they adjust monetary and/or fiscal policy as the period unfolds. If actual y appears to be less than the target y, they expand monetary and/or fiscal policy; if actual y appears to be greater than the target y, they contract monetary and/or fiscal policy. By alert, flexible adjustment, they manage to hit the required (targeted) y.

▶ To summarize, a specific monetary and/or fiscal policy, together with specific values for the other exogenous variables and parameters, determines a specific aggregate demand D curve. Nominal demand Y depends on the particular point (Q, P) on the aggregate demand D curve. Hence, a specific monetary and/or fiscal policy does not determine a particular nominal demand Y. Nevertheless, it may be useful to imagine monetary and fiscal policies adjusting during the period to hit a target for nominal demand Y and to assure a target rate of nominal demand growth y.

This completes our development and examination of aggregate demand. We will now turn to aggregate supply.

3.2 Long-Run Aggregate Supply

It is crucial to distinguish between *long-run* aggregate supply and *short-run* aggregate supply. In this section, we will explain why the *long-run aggregate supply curve* — the S_{LR} curve — is vertical, as shown in Figure 3.2. In Section 3.3, we will explain why the *short-run aggregate supply curve* — the S curve — has a positive slope, as shown in Figure 3.2.

A vertical S_{LR} curve implies that there is one and only one level of

FIGURE 3.2 THE LONG-RUN AGGREGATE SUPPLY S_{LR} CURVE AND THE SHORT-RUN AGGREGATE SUPPLY S CURVE

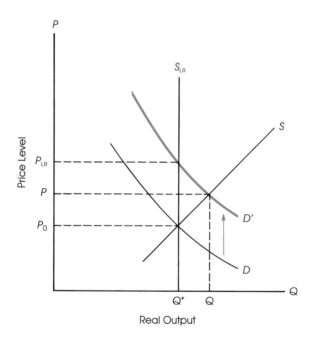

When the aggregate demand curve shifts permanently to the right from D to D', in the short run the economy moves along the short-run aggregate supply S curve to point (Q, P). But in the long run, the economy moves to the intersection of the vertical long-run aggregate supply S_{LR} curve and the new aggregate demand D' curve. Hence, in the long run, Q is once again Q^*, and the price level P is raised permanently to P_{LR}.

real output Q that producers will supply in the long run. Such a special level of Q deserves recognition; we will use the symbol Q^* to denote this level of real output. In Section 3.3, we will see that the supply of output Q can diverge from Q^* in the short run. Here, we will explain why long-run equilibrium cannot be reached until the supply of output returns to Q^*.

If the aggregate demand D curve is fixed, then real output Q and the price level P of the economy in the long run will be given by the intersection of the D curve and the S_{LR} curve, as shown in Figure 3.2. This means that real output will equal Q^* in the long run, regardless of the position of the D curve. The D curve, however, will determine the price level P.

Let's appreciate the significance of this conclusion. Suppose that a permanent increase in the nominal money supply raises the aggregate demand D curve permanently, shifting it from D to D' in Figure 3.2. In the long run, this increase in the nominal money supply will have no effect on the level of real output, which will remain at Q^*. The increase in the money supply will, however, cause a permanent increase in the price level P. More generally, the determinants of aggregate demand have no long-run impact on the real output of the economy. This is a striking conclusion.

But why should the S_{LR} curve be vertical? Why should Q^* be the only level of Q that is supplied in the long run?

To answer these questions, we must analyze the supply of and the demand for the two basic factors of production — *labor* and *capital*. In *long-run equilibrium* (regardless of the level of aggregate demand and the position of the aggregate demand D curve), one and only one level of *labor*, which we will designate L^*, can actually be employed and one and only one level of *capital*, which we will designate K^*, can actually be utilized. When L^* and K^* are utilized, a specific amount of real output, which we will designate Q^*, is produced or supplied.

Let's now turn to our analysis of factor markets. In a complete, general analysis, labor and capital would be treated symmetrically; such an analysis would show how K^* and L^* are simultaneously determined. A convenient simplification, however, is to assume that the quantity of capital utilized in long-run equilibrium is given by K^* and to analyze the supply of and the demand for labor. We will show that one and only one level of labor L^* can be utilized in long-run equilibrium, regardless of the position of the aggregate demand D curve.

THE DEMAND FOR LABOR

To simplify our analysis, we will assume that the *labor market* is *perfectly competitive*, so that each supplier (worker) and each demander (firm) is a *wage taker* and the wage is determined by the market. The supplier must decide what quantity to supply at the market wage, and the demander must decide what quantity to demand at the market wage. We will also assume that the product market is *perfectly competitive,* so that each firm faces a constant price for its output (the *market price*), regardless of the quantity it chooses to supply; the firm does not need to lower its price to sell additional output.

We will assume that each unit of labor is *homogeneous,* or that all units of labor are identical in quality. A *unit of labor* is the labor service provided in an hour of work by a worker with a specified skill who applies a specified intensity of effort. Note that two different persons may provide different units of labor, even though they work the same number of hours; also note that an individual may alter the units of labor supplied by changing either the number of hours worked or the skill or intensity with which the work is done.

Our basic tool will be the *labor demand–labor supply diagram* shown in Figure 3.3. Note that W/P, the ratio of the nominal wage W to the price of output P, appears on the vertical axis. We will explain the

FIGURE 3.3 LONG-RUN EQUILIBRIUM IN THE LABOR MARKET

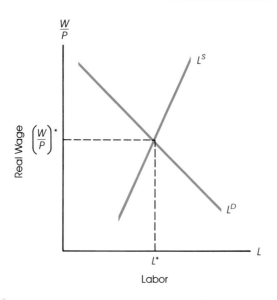

Long-run equilibrium in the labor market occurs at the intersection of the aggregate labor demand L^D curve and the aggregate labor supply L^S curve. In the long run, the real wage is W/P^* and labor utilized (ignoring frictional unemployment and vacancies) is L^*. The long-run equilibrium level of ouput Q^* in Figure 3.2 results when the long-run equilibrium level of labor L^* is utilized.

fundamental distinction between the *real wage W/P* and the *nominal (money) wage W* shortly.

Turning to the explanation of the labor demand – labor supply diagram, we begin with the *labor demand L^D curve*. To understand it, we will first consider a single, profit-maximizing firm that is trying to determine its optimal quantity of labor. We then will proceed to the whole economy.

Standard microeconomics teaches that the firm should use *marginal analysis* to determine what quantity of labor to demand at the nominal wage W. The manager should reason: "If I hire another unit of labor, how much will my cost increase? How much will my revenue increase? If the gain in revenue exceeds the increase in cost, I should do it and ask these questions again concerning the next additional unit of labor. If not, I should stop." Marginal analysis is therefore the evaluation of one unit of labor at a time.

The cost of hiring another unit of labor is the nominal wage W. What is the additional revenue? We obtain the answer in two steps. First, if another unit of labor is hired, while holding the capital stock constant, how much greater will physical output be? This increase in physical output is called the *marginal product of labor* MPL. At an initial level of 80 units of labor, with the given capital stock held constant, suppose that the MPL is 3 units of Q.

Now, how much greater will revenue be? The gain in revenue is obtained by multiplying the increase in Q by the selling price of the output. To illustrate, assume that a competitive firm faces a constant selling price of $8 per unit of Q. Then at the initial level of 80 units of labor, the increase in revenue from hiring an additional unit of labor — the *marginal revenue product of labor* MRPL — is $24 (3 × $8).

Thus, in a competitive industry where a firm can sell additional output at a constant price, the marginal revenue product of labor MRPL equals the marginal product of labor MPL multiplied by the price of the output P, or

(3.8) $$MRPL = MPL \times P$$

If the nominal wage per unit of labor W = $16, then at an initial level of 80 units of labor, it will be profitable for the firm to hire an additional unit of labor because the MRPL = $24. After hiring this unit, the firm should analyze whether or not to hire the next unit of labor. As more units are hired, given a constant real capital stock, *diminishing returns* will set in (the marginal product of labor MPL will decline as additional units of labor are hired). Even if the selling price remains constant, the marginal revenue product of labor MRPL, which equals MPL × P, will decline, as shown in Figure 3.4(a). Thus, the firm should hire additional units of labor until MPL × P decreases to equality with

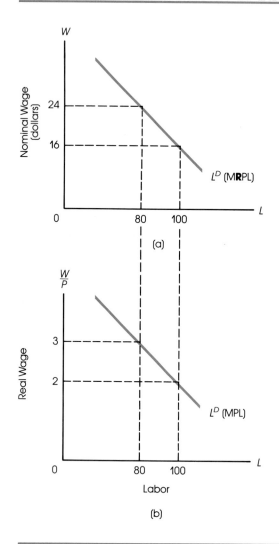

(a) Profit maximization occurs if the firm hires labor *L* until the marginal
revenue product of labor MRPL equals the nominal (money) wage *W*. If *W*
decreases from $24 to $16, then the firm maximizes its profits by raising *L* from
80 to 100 units.

(b) Profit maximization occurs if the firm hires labor *L* until the marginal
product of labor MPL equals the real wage *W/P*. If *W/P* decreases from 3 to 2,
then the firm maximizes its profits by raising *L* from 80 to 100 units.

W, achieving the condition for *profit maximization*:

(3.9) $W = \text{MRPL}$

Substituting equation (3.8) into equation (3.9) gives us

(3.10) $W = \text{MPL} \times P$

In this example, the firm should keep hiring additional units of labor until $\text{MPL} \times P$ decreases to $16, the *wage per unit of labor*, as shown in Figure 3.4(a). In this diagram, the nominal wage W (not the real wage W/P) is plotted on the vertical axis; Figure 3.4(a) differs from Figure 3.3 in this important respect.

To illustrate, if the MPL decreases to 2 units of Q (from its earlier value of 3) when 100 units of labor are employed, then $\text{MPL} \times P$ will decrease to $16 ($2 \times$8) from its earlier value of $24. Thus, at $W = $16, the demand for labor $L^D = 100$ units.

For any nominal wage W, the MRPL curve indicates the most profitable amount of labor for the firm to hire. Thus, the MRPL curve is the labor demand L^D curve in Figure 3.4(a), where the nominal wage W (not the real wage W/P) is plotted on the vertical axis.

It is useful to divide both sides of equation (3.10) by P to obtain

(3.10′) $\dfrac{W}{P} = \text{MPL}$

where $\dfrac{W}{P} = $ the real wage

Equation (3.10) tells us that the firm should hire additional units of labor until the MRPL equals the nominal wage W. Equivalently, equation (3.10′) states that the firm should hire additional units of labor until the MPL equals the real wage W/P.

The real wage W/P is the number of units of real output Q that the worker's compensation can buy. With the nominal wage $W = $16 and the price of the output $P = $8, the worker's compensation per unit of labor can buy 2 units of Q ($16/$8 = 2), so that the *real wage per unit of labor* is 2. Equation (3.10′) implies that the firm should hire additional units of labor until the marginal product of labor MPL declines to 2 units of Q, which is the real wage the firm must pay.

Just as equation (3.11) is equivalent to equation (3.10), Figure 3.4(b) conveys the same information as Figure 3.4(a). In Figure 3.4(a), with the nominal wage W on the vertical axis, we plot the marginal revenue product of labor curve MRPL. The MRPL curve is the L^D curve in this diagram; if $W = $16, then $L^D = 100$ units of labor. In Figure 3.4(b), with the real wage W/P on the vertical axis, we plot the marginal product of labor curve MPL. The MPL curve is the L^D curve in this diagram; if $W/P = \$16/\$8 = 2$, then $L^D = 100$ units of labor.

What determines the position and shape of the MPL curve (the L^D curve) in Figure 3.4(b)? The *production function* and the quantity of the other factor of production (capital K) being utilized are determinants of the MPL curve.

The production function is simply the technological relationship between the quantity of the factors of production being utilized *(input)* and the quantity of output that results. The production function can be written

(3.11) $Q = F(K, L)$

The symbol F simply means "a function of" (that is, "varies with"). Clearly, real output Q will increase when either capital K or labor L increases. If we hold K constant and increase L by 1 unit, then the resulting increase in Q is defined as the marginal product of labor MPL. With K held constant, each additional unit of L will raise Q, but probably by a smaller and smaller amount. In other words, as L increases, the MPL will decline. This is the phenomenon of diminishing returns.

The relationship between the production function and the MPL curve is illustrated in Figure 3.5. Figure 3.5(a) shows how Q varies with L for a given K. Note that each 1 unit increase in L raises Q; the increase in Q is the MPL. Figure 3.5(b) plots the MPL curve. Note that the curvature of the production function in Figure 3.5(a) causes the MPL to decline, as shown in Figure 3.5(b).

Consider the MPL at $L = 100$ units. We have just seen that as L increases above 100 units, the MPL should decline and the MPL curve should slope downward. But what determines the height of the MPL curve at $L = 100$? The quantity of K being held constant normally influences the MPL at any L, such as $L = 100$. As K increases (as the amount of machinery and equipment at the workplace increases), the MPL will probably increase. At $L = 100$ in our example, the MPL is 2 units of Q; but if K increased, the MPL would probably increase as well.

Thus, we cannot construct the MPL curve without specifying the quantity of K that is being held constant. We will make the plausible assumption that if K increases, then the MPL curve (the L^D curve) will shift up.

▶ In Figure 3.4(b), with the real wage W/P on the vertical axis, the L^D curve is the MPL curve. The position and slope of the MPL curve depend on the technological relationship between the quantities of the factors of production that are being utilized and the quantity of output that results, which is the *production*

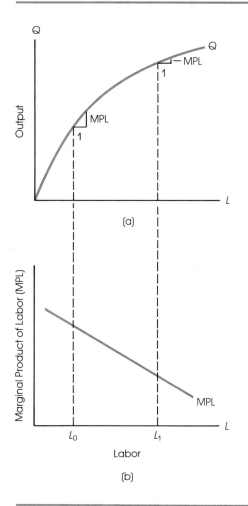

(a) The production function: as labor L increases (holding capital K constant), real output Q increases, but each additional unit of L raises Q by a smaller amount. (b) The MPL declines as L increases.

function $Q = F(K, L)$, and on the quantity of K that is fixed. If the quantity of K increases, then the MPL curve (the L^D curve) will probably shift up.

In Figure 3.4(b), we have focused on a single firm. To obtain the L^D curve for the whole economy, we horizontally sum the L^D curves for each firm at each real wage W/P. The curve that results is the *aggregate* *labor demand L^D curve* for the economy. The position and slope of the aggregate labor demand L^D curve will depend on the production functions governing the firms and on the quantity of capital held by each firm. Thus, the aggregate labor demand L^D curve shown in Figure 3.3 results from horizontally summing the individual L^D curves of all firms.

THE SUPPLY OF LABOR

We will now turn to the labor supply curve. Individuals must decide how they prefer to allocate their time. They can choose between hours of work or hours of leisure. What should matter to the individual is not the nominal wage W per se but the real wage W/P—the real output that the individual can obtain from working.

Why should the labor supply depend on the real wage? Suppose that after a person decides how many hours to work, the nominal wage W increases by 10% but the price of the output P also increases by 10%. This individual should not alter the number of hours worked per day. Despite the higher nominal wage W, the real output Q that can be obtained from working another hour has not changed. Some workers may not grasp this basic point, but most do appear to recognize that what counts is how their nominal wage W compares to the price of output P. Thus, we will assume that the real wage W/P (not the nominal wage W) determines labor supply.

What determines the slope of the *aggregate labor supply L^S curve*? As the real wage W/P increases, aggregate labor supply in the economy will increase if more individuals prefer to work or if the representative worker prefers to work more hours or with greater intensity.

It might seem that a higher real wage W/P will always increase the number of units of labor that workers prefer to supply and will therefore always result in a positively sloped labor supply curve (as shown in Figure 3.3). It is important to recognize that this is not necessarily true. Some workers who earn a higher real wage feel they can "afford" more leisure and prefer to work less. This, in itself, tends to give the labor supply curve a negative slope.

Standard microeconomics calls these two opposite effects the *substitution effect* and the *income effect,* respectively. In response to a higher real wage, the substitution effect tends to increase the labor supply and the income effect tends to reduce it. Economic theory cannot predict which effect will dominate. The slope of the aggregate labor supply L^S curve must be decided by the empirical evidence.

For much of the labor force, a vertical labor supply L^S curve (which implies that the substitution and income effects cancel each other out) appears to be empirically accurate. For some groups in the labor force, however, a positive labor supply L^S curve apparently results. We have therefore drawn the L^S curve in Figure 3.3 with a positive slope.

Now lets join the L^D and L^S curves in Figure 3.3. We will denote the level of labor at the L^D–L^S intersection by the symbol L^* and the level of the real wage at the L^D–L^S intersection by the symbol $(W/P)^*$. We must now make an important simplification.

▶ We will ignore *frictional unemployment* and *vacancies* (until Chapters 7 and 14). Here, we will make the standard assumption that equilibrium occurs when labor supply and labor demand are equal.

In Figure 3.3, given our simplifying assumption, L^* is the *long-run equilibrium level of labor* and $(W/P)^*$ is the *long-run equilibrium real wage*. If L^* is inserted into the production function given by equation (3.11), along with the *long-run equilibrium level of capital K^**, then the *long-run equilibrium level of output Q^** results.

In this frictionless model, if the real wage is less than $(W/P)^*$, then firms will find it profitable to demand more labor than workers are willing to supply and the real wage will rise as a result of a bidding competition until it reaches $(W/P)^*$. Symmetrically, if the real wage is greater than $(W/P)^*$, then firms will find it profitable to demand less labor than workers are willing to supply and the real wage will decline as a result of competition among unemployed workers until it reaches $(W/P)^*$.

A crucial point should be noted here. Equilibrium L^* and Q^* do not depend on the price of output P. L^* depends on the L^D and L^S curves. The L^D curve (the MPL curve) depends on the technological relationship between input and output. The L^S curve depends on the preferences of workers to allocate their time between leisure and real income. Neither curve depends on P.

But this means that long-run equilibrium output will be Q^* at any price level P. Hence, the long-run supply S_{LR} curve is vertical at Q^*, as shown in Figure 3.2.

Thus, if aggregate demand for output shifts outward permanently (from D to D' in Figure 3.2), then equilibrium output will return to Q^* in the long run and the sole impact of the demand shift will be to raise P.

3.3 Short-Run Aggregate Supply

It is important to specify the long-run equilibrium of the economy, but it is crucial to recognize that such an equilibrium may take several years to emerge. A central task of the macroeconomist is to describe what happens during the transition to long-run equilibrium. Thus, we employ a model with a supply curve that reflects short-run economic behavior. The *transition path* generated by our short-run model must eventually cause the economy to converge to the long-run equilibrium described by the labor demand–labor supply diagram shown in Figure 3.3.

In our development of the long-run aggregate supply S_{LR} curve, we asked: for any P, what Q will be supplied in long-run equilibrium? The answer was always the same: Q^*. We begin with P and determine the Q that will follow. In our short-run model, however, it will prove useful to reverse this order. We will ask: if Q is supplied, what P will firms set? We will begin with Q, and determine the P that will follow.

The SHORT-RUN AGGREGATE SUPPLY S CURVE indicates the price level P that producers will set at each output level Q.

THE PRICE–WAGE LINK

What determines the price level P that producers set? According to standard microeconomics, the more competitive are industries in the economy, the smaller the ratio of price to unit (average) cost will be. At any moment, the economy is characterized by a given degree of *competition* and a particular *price–unit cost ratio*. The largest component of unit cost is *unit labor cost* ULC. The *price–unit labor cost ratio P/ULC* will be denoted by K:[†]

$$(3.12) \qquad K \equiv \frac{P}{\text{ULC}}$$

Multiplying both sides of equation (3.12) by ULC, we obtain

$$(3.13) \qquad P \equiv K(\text{ULC})$$

where ULC = unit labor cost
$\quad K$ = the price–unit labor cost ratio

For example, if unit labor cost ULC = \$1 and the price–unit labor cost ratio K = 1.5, then P = \$1.50.

Unit labor cost, or *labor cost per unit of output*, is equal to *total labor cost* divided by *total output Q*. For example, if total labor cost is \$1,000 and 1,000 units of output Q are produced, then unit labor cost ULC is \$1,000/1,000 = \$1. Hence

$$(3.14) \qquad \text{ULC} \equiv \frac{WH}{Q}$$

[†] Note that the same symbol (K) is used to denote both *capital* and the *price–unit labor cost (P–ULC) ratio*. The meaning of the term K will be clear from its usage in specific discussions throughout the text.

where W = the wage per hour

H = total hours worked

WH = total labor cost

If we divide the numerator and the denominator of the right side of equation (3.14) by H, we have

(3.15) $$\text{ULC} \equiv \frac{WH}{Q} \equiv \frac{W}{Q/H} \equiv \frac{W}{A}$$

$$A \equiv \frac{Q}{H} = \text{output per hour (labor productivity)}$$

Equation (3.15) tells us that unit labor cost ULC is the ratio of the *wage per hour W* to *output per hour A* (equivalently, the ratio of the wage to labor productivity). In our example, total output $Q = 1,000$ units and total labor cost $WH = \$1,000$. If the wage per hour $W = \$1$ and the total hours worked $H = 1,000$, then output per hour (labor productivity) $A = 1,000/1,000 = 1$. Dividing the wage per hour $\$1$ by the output per hour 1, we obtain a unit labor cost ULC of $\$1$.

Substituting equation (3.15) into equation (3.13), we obtain

(3.16) $$P \equiv K \left(\frac{W}{A} \right)$$

Equation (3.16) states that the price level P which producers set at output level Q depends on three elements: the price–unit labor cost ratio K, the wage per hour W, and the output per hour (labor productivity) A. Because the degree of competition in the economy changes very slowly over time, we might expect the price–unit labor cost ratio K to change very slowly. (In Chapter 4, we will provide U.S. data to support the hypothesis that K changes slowly.)

▶ To simplify our analysis in Chapter 3, we will assume that the price–unit labor cost (P/ULC) ratio K is roughly constant in equation (3.16).

In a growing economy, where output per hour (labor productivity) A rises over time, if the wage per hour W changes by the same percentage as A, then the wage–labor productivity ratio W/A will stay constant; unit labor cost ULC will also remain constant and so, therefore, will P in equation (3.16).

For example, if both W and A increase by 2%, then ULC will stay constant. This makes sense because if output per hour A rises by 2% and the wage per hour W rises by 2%, then labor cost per unit of output will remain the same. In our example, if output per hour A rises from 1.00 to 1.02 (a 2% increase) and the wage per hour W rises from $1.00 to $1.02 (a 2% increase), then W/A will remain at $1.02/1.02 = $1. Thus, if W rises by the same percentage as A and K is held constant, then the price level P that producers set at output level Q will remain the same.

If W rises more than A, however, then W/A will increase (equivalently, ULC will increase); with the ratio K held constant, P will increase. Similarly, if W rises less than A, then W/A will decrease (equivalently, ULC will decrease); with the ratio K held constant, P will decrease.

▶ We have isolated an important determinant of the price level P that producers set at output level Q: the "race" between W and A — the wage per hour and output per hour (equivalently, the wage per hour and labor productivity). If the race is even, with W and A changing by the same percentage, then with the price–unit labor cost ratio K held constant, P will stay constant. But if W wins the race and rises by a greater percentage than A, then P will rise; if W loses the race and rises by a smaller percentage than A, then P will decline.

In Chapter 4, we will consider a growing economy in which output per hour (labor productivity) A normally increases each year. For the remainder of Chapter 3, however, we will consider a "no-growth" economy in which labor productivity A is normally constant from one year to the next.

When both K and A are assumed to be constant, the spotlight shines on W in equation (3.16), which links the price level P to the wage W. We ask two distinct questions about W:

1. What influences the W that firms set at a given Q?
2. As Q increases, what happens to W?

Note that if output per hour A is held constant and Q remains constant, then employment stays constant (so the unemployment rate U — the ratio of unemployed workers to the total labor force — stays constant). If Q increases, employment increases and the unemployment rate U decreases. Thus, we can restate our two questions as follows:

1. What influences the W that firms set at a given Q (and at a given U)?
2. As Q increases (and U decreases), what happens to W?

What is the significance of each question? The answer to the first — when Q is held fixed — will help us determine the *height* of the short-run aggregate supply S curve (the price level P) at that output level Q. The answer to the second — when Q varies — will tell us how P varies with Q and, therefore, the *slope* of the S curve.

Let's begin with the first question. We can construct the following hypothesis:

▶ A key determinant of the wage per hour W at a given real output Q (and the associated unemployment rate U) is the *expected price level P^e.*

Why is this hypothesis plausible? Both workers and managers probably recognize that the nominal (money) wage W must be compared to the price level that is expected P^e. Most workers realize that what counts is not the percentage increase in W per se but how this increase in W compares to the expected increase in P. If W and P both increase by 6%, workers will not gain any real income; the price increase will simply offset the wage increase. Similarly, most managers realize that the percentage increase in W that their firms can afford depends on the P they expect to charge for their output Q.

Thus, both workers and firms focus on the *expected real wage W/P^e,* rather than on the money wage W. At the time the wage is determined, workers and managers form an expectation of the price level that will occur over the life of the wage. If P^e is higher, then the wage per hour W at a given output level Q (and the associated unemployment rate U) are higher.

For example, if $P^e = \$1.50$, then W will be set at $1. If, instead, $P^e = \$3.00$ (an amount twice as great), it seems plausible that W will be set at $2.00 (also an amount twice as great). The same expected real wage W/P^e will result at that Q (and U).

If P^e increases, W may be constrained from rising immediately by a long-term labor contract. In some sectors of the economy, two- or three-year labor contracts are common. In most sectors, W cannot be changed more than once a year.

▶ At a given real output Q (and the associated unemployment rate U), if P^e increases by X%, we assume that the wage per hour W increases by X%, provided W is not constrained by a labor contract.

If W increases by X%, what happens to unit labor cost ULC? If, initially, $W = \$1$ and $A = 1$, then ULC $= \$1$. If W increases by 10% to $1.10, with A held constant, then ULC will increase to $1.10 (also a 10% increase).

▶ With output per hour (labor productivity) A held constant, if the wage per hour W increases by X%, then unit labor cost ULC increases by X%.

If ULC increases by X%, what happens to P? If $K = 1.5$ and, initially, ULC = \$1, then P = \$1.50. If ULC increases by 10% to \$1.10, then P also increases by 10% to \$1.65 (10% $\times$ \$1.50 = \$0.15).

▶ With the price–unit labor cost ratio K held constant, if unit labor cost ULC increases by X%, then the price level P also increases by X%.

To summarize:

▶ At a given real output Q, if the expected price level P^e increases by X%, then the P that firms will actually set (as measured by the height of the S curve at that Q) will also increase by X%, provided W is not constrained by a labor contract.

THE IMPACT OF UNEMPLOYMENT ON THE WAGE

We have thus far focused on the height of the S curve at a given level of output Q. But what determines the *slope* of the S curve; that is, how does P vary as Q changes? This brings us to our second question about W: as Q increases (and U decreases), what happens to W?

When Q increases, an increase in employment is required and the unemployment rate U decreases. But a decline in U tends to raise W. Why? As U declines, firms find it more difficult to locate workers to fill vacancies. Workers, on the other hand, find it easier to locate jobs. A decline in the unemployment rate, as we will explain in Chapter 14, implies that labor demand has risen relative to labor supply. Relative bargaining strength shifts away from the firms toward the workers; the result is that workers are able to obtain higher wages than they would have obtained if U had not declined. Thus, we can construct the following hypothesis:

▶ As real output Q increases (and the associated unemployment rate U decreases), the wage per hour W increases.

Since an increase in W will raise unit labor cost ULC, we can conclude from equation (3.16) that

▶ As real output Q increases (and the associated unemployment rate U decreases), the price level P increases. Hence, the short-run aggregate supply S curve has a positive slope.

Let's consider what would make the short-run aggregate supply S curve relatively flat. Suppose that, in most firms, W is fixed over the short run by long-term wage contracts. Then even if Q and U begin to change, W will remain fixed in most firms in the short run; only firms with wage contracts that are about to expire will be free to change W in the short run. Hence, the S curve will be relatively flat.

Long-term wage contracts in most firms are sufficient to yield a relatively flat S curve, but a relatively flat S curve can result even if such contracts are not pervasive. Suppose that relative bargaining strength proves fairly insensitive to changes in the unemployment rate U. Then, even if the wage W can be reset quickly when the unemployment rate U changes, W may not actually change very much.

What will result in a relatively steep short-run aggregate supply S curve? First, long-term wage contracts that fix W over the life of a contract must not be pervasive; many firms must be free to vary W during this period. Furthermore, suppose that W is very responsive to even a slight change in Q and U. In other words, if the relative bargaining strength of workers versus managers changes sharply in response to even a small change in U, then a small change in Q and U will cause a large change in W.

To summarize the most important conclusions we have drawn in this section:

▶ At a given real output Q, the height of the short-run aggregate supply S curve is the price level P that firms will set at that Q. If the price–unit labor cost ratio K is assumed to be roughly constant, then the height of the S curve varies directly with the wage W. In turn, the wage W that is set varies directly with the price level that is expected. Thus, the expected price level P^e is a key determinant of the height of the S curve at any Q; if the expected price level P^e is higher, then the height of the S curve—the P that firms will actually set—is greater at each Q.

▶ Any S curve is therefore drawn on the basis of a specific expected price level P^e. If P^e increases by $X\%$, then the S curve will shift up by $X\%$, provided W is not constrained by a labor contract.

▶ The S curve has a positive slope because as Q increases (and the unemployment rate U declines), labor demand L^D increases relative to labor supply L^S, thereby raising the wage W that is set. A higher wage results in a higher unit labor cost ULC and, hence, in a higher price level P. Thus, as Q rises, P rises.

3.4 Aggregate Demand, Short-Run Aggregate Supply, and IS–LM

We will now join the aggregate demand D curve and the short-run aggregate supply S curve to determine the real output Q and the price level P of the economy during a given period.

Suppose that in period 0, D_0 intersects S_0 at point (Q_0, P_0), in Figure 3.6. Recall that the height of the S curve depends on the expected price level P^e. It is convenient to assume that as long as the D curve remains constant, P^e also stays constant. It therefore follows that as long as the D curve remains constant, S (which depends on P^e) also stays constant.

Now if D shifts to the right to D_1 in period 1 (see Figure 3.6), what happens to Q and P in period 1? The answer, of course, depends on whether S_1 still coincides with S_0 (as it does in Figure 3.6) or whether the S curve shifts vertically (as it does in Figure 3.7). This in turn depends on whether P^e changes or stays constant. Recall that if P^e changes by $X\%$, then the S curve will shift vertically by the same $X\%$. We will consider two alternative assumptions concerning the expected price level P^e:

FIGURE 3.6 THE IMPACT OF A DEMAND SHIFT WITH INERTIAL EXPECTATIONS (*I*)

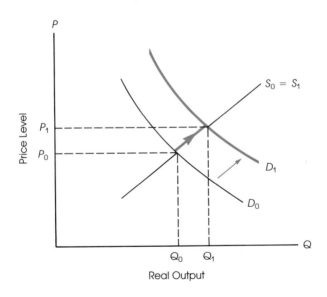

The S curve remains fixed, so that S_1 coincides with S_0. Hence, when the D curve shifts up from D_0 to D_1, both the price level P and real output Q increase.

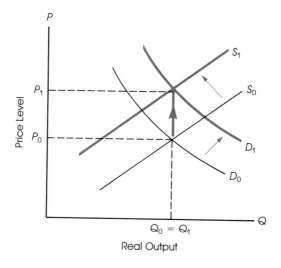

The S curve shifts up by the same amount as the D curve. Hence, when the D curve shifts up from D_0 to D_1, the price level P increases but real output Q remains constant.

I: P^e is not influenced in the short run by the shift in the D curve, so that the short-run aggregate supply S curve does not shift.

R: P^e is influenced in the short run by the shift in the D curve, such that the short-run aggregate supply S curve shifts vertically by the same amount as the shift in the aggregate demand D curve. Note that this implies that W is not constrained by a labor contract.

We use the letter I to designate the first hypothesis because it is illustrated by the case of *inertial expectations,* for which P^e equals the last period's actual price P_{-1}; if $P^e = P_{-1}$, then P^e is not influenced by this period's shift in the D curve. Hence, the S curve will be fixed in the short run when the D curve shifts.

We use the letter R to designate the second hypothesis because it is illustrated by the case of *rational expectations.* This case requires more explanation.

We have seen that P^e is a key determinant of the height of the S curve. A change in P^e of $X\%$ will vertically shift the S curve by the same $X\%$, provided that W is not constrained by a labor contract. The R hypothesis asserts that the S curve will shift vertically by the same amount as the D curve.

Why is it "rational" for people to change P^e immediately by the same amount as the vertical shift of the D curve? We will see shortly that this P^e equals the actual P for the period; hence, the expectations are accurate (rational).

RATIONAL EXPECTATIONS are the most accurate forecasts that can be made given the available information.

If information is perfect, then *rational expectations* will prove accurate ($P^e = P$). We will assume perfect information in our use of the term "rational expectations" in Chapter 3 (but see the discussion of *new classical macroeconomics* in Section 6.5, pages 273–74).

By contrast, in the case of inertial expectations, when $P^e = P_{-1}$, P^e in general will not equal the actual P for the period; hence, inertial expectations are generally inaccurate.

Under the I assumption, the height of the S_1 curve at any given real output Q is unaffected by the shift in the D curve, as shown in Figure 3.6. Thus, S_1 continues to coincide with S_0 as the D curve shifts to the right. The economy therefore moves along the constant S curve to its new equilibrium point (Q_1, P_1). The slope of the S curve determines the degree of change in Q and P. The flatter the S curve, the greater the change in Q and the smaller the change in P in the short run.

Under the R assumption, the height of the S_1 curve at any given real output Q is affected by a rightward shift in the D curve. Since the S curve shifts vertically by the same amount as the D curve, equilibrium output Q does not change, as shown in Figure 3.7. The entire impact of a shift in the D curve in the short run is to change P; Q remains unaffected.

Note that under the R assumption, the actual P in this period equals P^e. Why? Since the aggregate supply S and aggregate demand D curves shift by the same vertical amount, P changes by this amount. But this is exactly what people were expecting when they changed P^e by the same amount as the vertical shift in the D curve, thereby causing the S curve to shift vertically by that amount.

We have focused on the two polar cases, I and R, but an intermediate result is possible. The S curve may shift in the same vertical direction as the D curve but by a smaller vertical distance. In this intermediate case, the equilibrium point (Q, P) lies between the outcomes shown in Figure 3.6 and Figure 3.7.

In our analysis of inflation and disinflation in Chapters 4, 5, and 6, we will examine the inertial and rational expectations assumptions in more detail.

THE INTERACTION OF THE D–S AND THE IS–LM DIAGRAMS

We will now connect the D–S equilibrium point (Q, P) with the IS–LM diagram. We have just seen what happens when the D curve shifts to the right, but we also need to examine the shift in either the IS curve or the LM curve that generates this shift in the D curve.

With monetary and fiscal policy given, a particular D curve results. Recall how this D curve is obtained. With the nominal money supply M given, as P declines, the real money supply M/P rises and the LM curve shifts to the right; hence, equilibrium output Q at the $IS-LM$ intersection increases. Thus, as P decreases, Q increases; we plot this relationship as the D curve.

With monetary and fiscal policy given and the D curve specified, the D curve intersects the S curve at equilibrium point (Q, P). With the nominal money supply M given, this equilibrium P implies a particular real money supply M/P.

We saw in Chapter 2 that, once the real money supply M/P is given, a particular LM curve is specified. This LM curve intersects the IS curve at equilibrium point (r, Q).

Figure 3.8 shows the equilibrium points (Q, P) and (r, Q) in period 0. Here, D_0 and S_0 intersect at equilibrium point (Q_0, P_0). Given M_0 and this equilibrium P_0 in Figure 3.8(a), the real money supply is M_0/P_0, the LM curve is LM_0, and the intersection of LM_0 and IS_0 occurs at equilibrium point (r_0, Q_0) in Figure 3.8(b).

Given r_0, we can obtain investment from the investment function. Given Q_0, we can obtain consumption from the consumption and tax functions. Thus, by using the equations of the $IS-LM$ system, we can obtain the I_0 and C_0 that correspond to equilibrium point (Q_0, P_0) in the $D-S$ diagram.

Beginning with the equilibrium in period 0 (Figure 3.8), suppose that the D curve shifts to the right in period 1, so that D_1 lies to the right of D_0. What happens in the $IS-LM$ diagram? We must distinguish between two cases: *inertial expectations* (I), which implies a fixed S curve, and *rational expectations* (R), which implies that the S curve shifts up by the same amount as the D curve.

For each case, it is important to consider two sources of the rightward shift of the D curve:

IS: A rightward shift of the IS curve due to a fiscal expansion or an increase in autonomous consumption C_a or investment I_a.

LM: A rightward shift of the LM curve *at a given price level P* due to a monetary expansion (an increase in the *nominal* money supply M) or a decrease in *autonomous money demand M_a*.

We therefore have four situations to consider, as illustrated in Figures 3.9, 3.10, 3.11, and 3.12. As we analyze each case, keep in mind that the position of the LM curve depends on the *real* money supply M/P; whenever M/P increases, the LM curve shifts to the right. We will identify an LM curve by indicating the relevant real money supply M/P in brackets. For example, in period 0, with $M = M_0$ and $P = P_0$, the LM curve is $LM_0[M_0/P_0]$.

FIGURE 3.8 EQUILIBRIUM IN THE *D–S* AND *IS–LM* DIAGRAMS

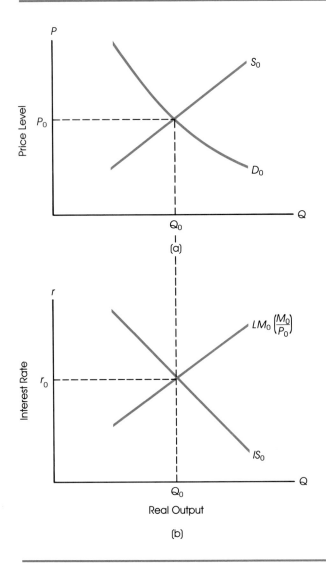

The *LM* curve LM_0 is graphed in (b) for a real money supply M_0/P_0, where P_0 is given by the intersection of D_0 and S_0 in (a).

(I) IS: This case is graphed in Figure 3.9. The source of the rightward shift in the *D* curve from D_0 to D_1 in Figure 3.9(a) is a shift in the *IS* curve from IS_0 to IS_1 in Figure 3.9(b). Note that if *P* remained constant at P_0 in the *D–S* diagram, then the new output would be Q', given by the intersection of IS_1 and

FIGURE 3.9 THE IMPACT OF AN *IS* SHIFT WITH INERTIAL EXPECTATIONS (*I*)

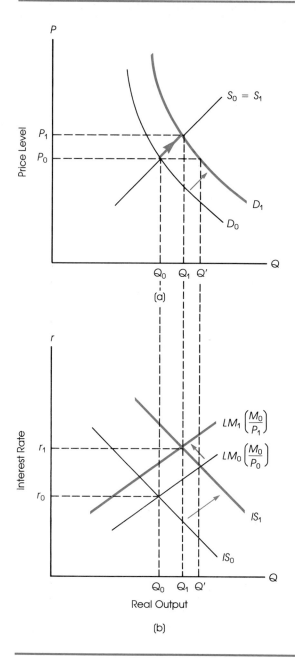

When the *IS* curve shifts to the right from IS_0 to IS_1 in (b), the *D* curve shifts to the right from D_0 to D_1 in (a). As *P* rises from P_0 to P_1, the real money supply decreases from M_0/P_0 to M_0/P_1, shifting the *LM* curve to the left from LM_0 to LM_1. The LM_1 curve at the new equilibrium is based on the real money supply M_0/P_1, where P_1 is given by the intersection of D_1 and S_1 in (a).

$LM_0[M_0/P_0]$. But since P rises to P_1, with M held constant at M_0, the real money supply M/P decreases from M_0/P_0 to M_0/P_1 and the LM curve shifts to the left from $LM_0[M_0/P_0]$ to $LM_1[M_0/P_1]$. Thus, r rises from r_0 to r_1, and Q increases from Q_0 to Q_1.

(I) LM: This case is graphed in Figure 3.10. The source of the right-ward shift in the D curve from D_0 to D_1 in Figure 3.10(a) is a shift in the LM curve from $LM_0[M_0/P_0]$ to $LM'[M_1/P_0]$ in Figure 3.10(b). Note that if P remained constant at P_0 in the $D-S$ diagram, then the new output would be Q', given by the inter-section of IS_1, which coincides with IS_0, and $LM'[M_1/P_0]$. But since P rises to P_1, the real money supply becomes M_1/P_1 and the LM curve becomes $LM_1[M_1/P_1]$, which lies between LM_0 and LM'. (Hence, the real money supply M_1/P_1 must be greater than M_0/P_0 but less than M_1/P_0.) Thus, r declines from r_0 to r_1; and Q increases from Q_0 to Q_1.

(R) IS: This case is graphed in Figure 3.11. The main differences be-tween this case and the (I) IS case graphed in Figure 3.9 are that the rise in P is greater and the leftward shift of the LM curve is greater, so that $Q_0 = Q_1$. Note that the rise in r is therefore greater.

(R) LM: This case is graphed in Figure 3.12. The main differences be-tween this case and the $(I)LM$ case graphed in Figure 3.10 are that the rise in P is greater, the real money supply M_1/P_1 equals the initial real money supply M_0/P_0, and LM_1 coincides with LM_0, so that $Q_0 = Q_1$. Note that r remains constant.

We will see in Chapters 4–6 that the R assumption does not appear to be strictly valid in the actual economy. Either the I assumption or an intermediate assumption between I and R is much more likely to be valid.

▶ If the R assumption is not strictly valid in the actual economy, then when either the IS curve or the LM curve shifts to the right (at a given price level P), so that the D curve shifts to the right, both Q and P will increase in the short run.

THE LONG-RUN IMPACT ON Q AND P

Thus far, we have focused on the short-run reaction in period 1. Now let's consider what happens in the long run. Returning to the I case, when P^e is not influenced in the short run by a shift in the D curve, assume that the S curve is relatively flat. If the D curve shifts to the right, most of the short-run demand shift "goes into Q" and relatively little "goes into P." It is important to recognize, however, that this is *only* the short-run effect. What happens next?

FIGURE 3.10 THE IMPACT OF AN *LM* SHIFT WITH INERTIAL EXPECTATIONS (*I*)

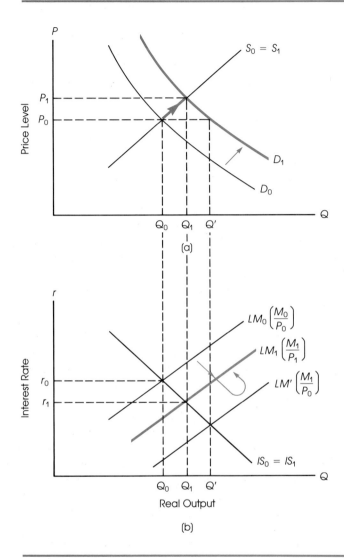

When the *LM* curve shifts to the right from LM_0 to LM' in (b) due to an increase in the nominal money supply to M_1 (with $P = P_0$), the *D* curve shifts to the right from D_0 to D_1 in (a). As *P* rises from P_0 to P_1, the real money supply decreases from M_1/P_0 to M_1/P_1, shifting the *LM* curve back to the left from LM' to LM_1. The LM_1 curve at the new equilibrium is based on the real money supply M_1/P_1, where P_1 is given by the intersection of D_1 and S_1 in (a).

FIGURE 3.11 THE IMPACT OF AN *IS* SHIFT WITH RATIONAL EXPECTATIONS (*R*)

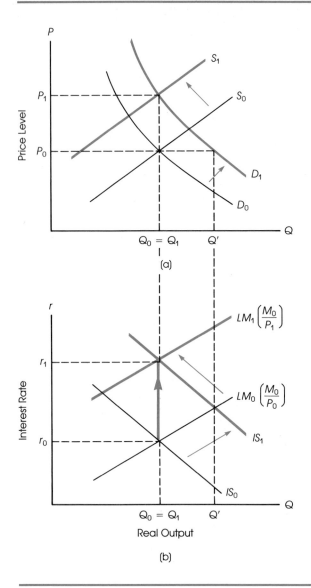

This situation differs from the *IS* shift with inertial expectations shown in Figure 3.9 in that the *S* curve here shifts up from S_0 to S_1, so that $Q_0 = Q_1$. The rise in *P* is greater here than it is in the inertial expectations case; hence, the reduction in the real money supply from M_0/P_0 to M_0/P_1 is greater here, as is the shift of the *LM* curve to the left from LM_0 to LM_1.

FIGURE 3.12 THE IMPACT OF AN *LM* SHIFT WITH RATIONAL
EXPECTATIONS (*R*)

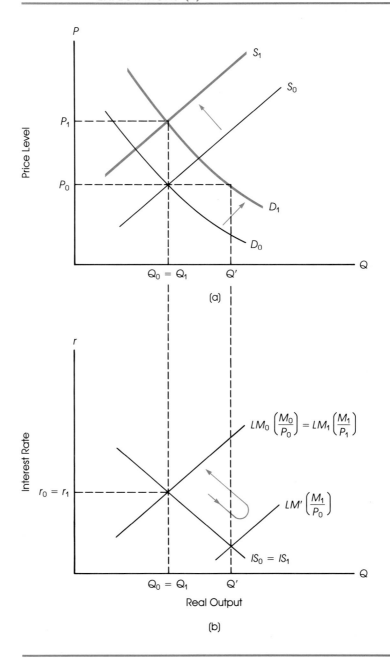

(a)

(b)

This situation differs from the *LM* shift with inertial expectations shown in Figure 3.10 in that the *S* curve here shifts up from S_0 to S_1, so that $Q_0 = Q_1$. The rise in *P* is greater here than it is in the inertial expectations case; hence, the reduction in the real money supply from M_1/P_0 to M_1/P_1 is greater, as is the shift of the *LM* curve to the left from LM' to LM_1.

Recall once again why the short-run aggregate supply S curve is relatively flat. First, long-term labor contracts may fix the wages in many firms in the short run. But in subsequent periods, these contracts will expire and firms will be free to raise W in response to the decline in the unemployment rate U. With the expiration of labor contracts, the S curve should become steeper. Second, the reduction in the unemployment rate U may initially be regarded as temporary and therefore have only a small impact on relative bargaining strength; but if the reduction in U persists, the impact on bargaining strength may grow, so that the S curve becomes steeper.

The most important change, however, will be in the expected price level P^e. As W and P increase, P^e will be adjusted upward. This adjustment will shift the S curve up, which will in turn raise P and further raise P^e. Hence, the S curve will continue to shift up. These shifts, given a fixed D_1 curve, will cause Q to move back toward its original position.

Now suppose that the economy is initially at long-run equilibrium output Q^*. In the long run (as we will see in Chapter 4), if the D curve remains fixed at its new permanent position, the economy will return to its initial equilibrium output level Q^* (and the corresponding unemployment rate U^*). In the long run, the demand shift will go completely into P and have no permanent effect on Q, even though the short-run S curve is relatively flat and P^e is independent of any shift in the D curve in the short run.

Thus, the position and the slope of the short-run S curve are very important for the short-run impact on P and Q of a shift in the D curve. But in the long run, they are not important. Whatever the position and the slope of the short-run aggregate supply S curve, we will see that in the long run, if the economy is initially at Q^*, the demand shift will go completely into P and have no effect on Q.

3.5 An Example of $D-S$ Equilibrium

At the beginning of this chapter, we derived an aggregate demand curve equation from our $IS-LM$ system, with the IS curve given by equation (2.2) and the LM curve given by equation (3.1):

$$(3.2) \qquad Q = 1{,}800 + \frac{400}{P}$$

If we can obtain a *short-run aggregate supply S curve equation,* then we can solve these two equations to obtain the $D-S$ equilibrium point (Q, P).

We know that the short-run aggregate supply S curve equation should have two properties:

1. When Q increases and P^e remains constant, P should increase.

2. When P^e increases by $X\%$ and Q remains constant, P should increase by $X\%$.

In the Appendix to this chapter, we derive the following example of a short-run aggregate supply S curve equation:

(3.17) $$P = \frac{4{,}000}{(6{,}200 - Q)} P^e$$

If we are given a numerical value for P^e, we can plot this curve in a Q–P diagram. For each value of Q, the equation will yield a corresponding value of P. For example, $P^e = 1.00$ yields these points:

Q	1,800	2,000	2,200	2,400	2,600
P	0.91	0.95	1.00	1.05	1.11

This table shows that as Q increases, P also increases. Equation (3.17) therefore yields a *positively sloped* supply curve. At any Q, an $X\%$ increase in P^e will result in an equal $X\%$ increase in P. For example, if P^e doubles, so that $X\% = 100\%$, then P also doubles, increasing by 100%. Thus, equation (3.17) possesses the two properties of a short-run aggregate supply S curve equation.

We now have an aggregate demand D curve equation (3.2) and a short-run aggregate supply S curve equation (3.17). Let's use these two equations to solve for the point (Q, P) at the D–S intersection. Just as we cannot draw a short-run aggregate supply S curve without specifying the value of P^e, we cannot solve these two equations unless we specify the value of P^e. Here, we will assume that $P^e = 1.00$. Then the aggregate demand D curve equation is

(3.2) $$Q = 1{,}800 + \frac{400}{P}$$

and the short-run aggregate supply S curve equation is

(3.18) $$P = \left(\frac{4{,}000}{6{,}200 - Q}\right)(1.00)$$

Equations (3.2) and (3.18) both contain two unknowns, P and Q. To solve for these unknowns, we multiply both sides of equation (3.2) by P, so that

$$PQ = 1{,}800P + 400$$

and both sides of equation (3.18) by $(6{,}200 - Q)$, so that

$$P(6{,}200 - Q) = 4{,}000$$
$$6{,}200P - PQ = 4{,}000$$
$$PQ = 6{,}200P - 4{,}000$$

Both the aggregate demand and short-run aggregate supply equations result in an expression for PQ. Setting these expressions equal to one another, we obtain

$$6{,}200P - 4{,}000 = 1{,}800P + 400$$
$$4{,}400P = 4{,}400$$
$$P = 1.00$$

In equation (3.2), if $P = 1.00$, then $Q = \$2{,}200$ billion. Thus, equilibrium $P = 1.00$ (note that $P = P^e$) and equilibrium $Q = \$2{,}200$ billion (assume that $Q^* = \$2{,}200$ billion, so that $Q = Q^*$).

The aggregate demand and short-run aggregate supply equations yield the equilibrium price level P and output Q of the economy. We can find the interest rate r by using the associated IS or LM equation:

(2.2) IS: $Q = 3{,}000 - 10{,}000r$

(3.1) LM: $Q = 15{,}000r + 2\left(\dfrac{500}{P}\right)$

where the nominal money supply $M = \$500$ billion and $P = 1.00$.
Using the IS equation (2.2), we obtain

$$2{,}200 = 3{,}000 - 10{,}000r$$
$$10{,}000r = 800$$
$$r = 8\%$$

Using the LM equation (3.1), we obtain

$$2{,}200 = 15{,}000r + 2\left(\dfrac{500}{1.00}\right)$$
$$1{,}200 = 15{,}000r$$
$$8\% = r$$

The $D-S$ equilibrium and the corresponding $IS-LM$ equilibrium are graphed in Figure 3.13.

We can also determine other variables, such as consumption C and investment I, by returning to the equations on which the IS curve is

FIGURE 3.13 A *D–S* EQUILIBRIUM AND THE CORRESPONDING *IS–LM* EQUILIBRIUM

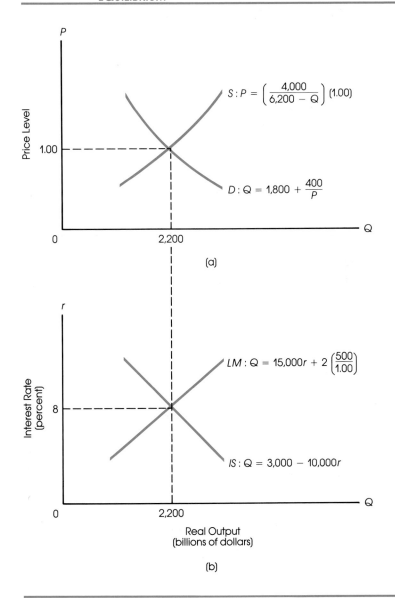

(a)

(b)

D–S equilibrium and *IS–LM* equilibrium occur at $P = 1.00$, $Q = \$2{,}200$ billion, and $r = 8\%$.

based:

$$(1.31) \qquad C = 0.8(Q - T + R)$$
$$C = 0.8(Q - 0.25Q + 250)$$
$$C = 0.8(2{,}200 - 550 + 250)$$
$$C = 1{,}520$$

$$(2.1) \qquad I = 700 - 4{,}000r$$
$$I = 700 - 4{,}000(0.08)$$
$$I = 380$$

AN INCREASE IN THE MONEY SUPPLY

Suppose that the economy is initially at the $D-S$ equilibrium in period 0 shown in Figure 3.13, based on an LM curve where the nominal money supply $M = \$500$ billion, as given by equation (3.1). If the nominal money supply increases to $M = \$600$ billion in period 1, then the D curve would shift to the right. We calculated earlier that the new aggregate demand curve with $M = \$600$ billion would be

$$(3.4) \qquad Q = 1{,}800 + \frac{480}{P}$$

Before we can find the intersection of the aggregate demand and aggregate supply curves in period 1, we must specify P^e in period 1. We will consider two alternatives:

I: $P^e = P_{-1}$. Here, we assume that the expected price in period 1 equals the actual price in period 0. This is the hypothesis of inertial expectations.

R: $P^e = P$. Here, we assume that the expected price in period 1 equals the actual price in period 1. This is the hypothesis of rational expectations (with perfect information and no long-term wage contract).

Let's consider the inertial expectations (I) hypothesis first. In this case, $P^e = 1.00$ in period 1. Hence, the S curve equation in period 1 is the same as it was in period 0. Thus, despite the rightward shift of the D curve due to the increase in the nominal money supply to $M = \$600$ billion, the S curve remains fixed, as shown in Figure 3.14. We can solve for equilibrium point (Q, P) in period 1 by repeating the steps outlined in the preceding section, employing the new D curve equation. Once again, the aggregate demand and short-run aggregate supply equations each contribute an expression for PQ:

$$PQ = 1{,}800P + 480$$
$$PQ = 6{,}200P - 4{,}000$$

FIGURE 3.14 AN INCREASE IN THE NOMINAL MONEY SUPPLY WITH INERTIAL EXPECTATIONS (*I*)

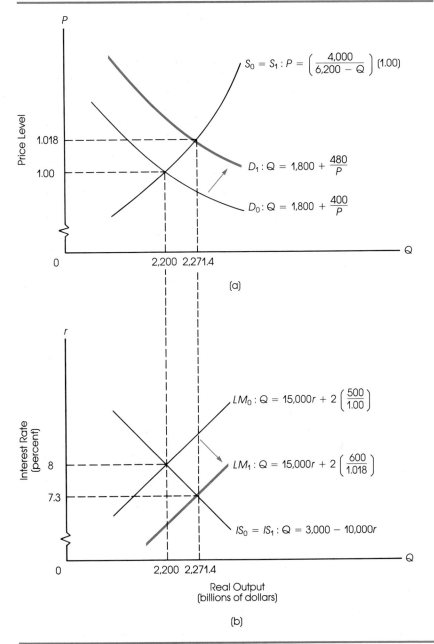

P

$S_0 = S_1 : P = \left(\dfrac{4{,}000}{6{,}200 - Q} \right)$ (1.00)

Price Level

1.018

1.00

$D_1 : Q = 1{,}800 + \dfrac{480}{P}$

$D_0 : Q = 1{,}800 + \dfrac{400}{P}$

Q

0   2,200 2,271.4

(a)

r

$LM_0 : Q = 15{,}000r + 2 \left(\dfrac{500}{1.00} \right)$

Interest Rate (percent)

8

$LM_1 : Q = 15{,}000r + 2 \left(\dfrac{600}{1.018} \right)$

7.3

$IS_0 = IS_1 : Q = 3{,}000 - 10{,}000r$

Q

0   2,200 2,271.4

Real Output
(billions of dollars)

(b)

When the nominal money supply increases from $500 billion to $600 billion, the *D* curve shifts to the right from D_0 to D_1 and, with inertial expectations, the *S* curve stays fixed ($S_0 = S_1$) in (a). The real money supply M/P increases, so the *LM* curve shifts to the right from LM_0 to LM_1 in (b). Hence, *P* rises from 1.00 to 1.018, *Q* increases from $2,200 billion to $2,271.4 billion, and *r* declines from 8% to 7.3%.

Thus

$$6,200P - 4,000 = 1,800P + 480$$
$$4,400P = 4,480$$
$$P = 1.018$$

From equation (3.4), we obtain $Q = \$2,271.4$ billion; nominal demand $Y = PQ$ then becomes $\$2,312.3$ billion. Hence, nominal demand Y increases by 5.1%, equilibrium output Q increases by 3.2%, and the equilibrium price level P increases by 1.8%.

Once again, we find the new interest rate r by using the associated IS or LM equation:

(2.2) IS: $Q = 3,000 - 10,000r$
$$2,271.4 = 3,000 - 10,000r$$
$$10,000r = 728.6$$
$$r = 7.3\%$$

(3.3) LM: $Q = 15,000r + 2\left(\dfrac{600}{P}\right)$

$$2,271.4 = 15,000r + 2\left(\dfrac{600}{1.018}\right)$$
$$2,271.4 = 15,000r + 2(589.39)$$
$$1,092.6 = 15,000r$$
$$r = 7.3\%$$

Note that although the nominal money supply M has increased from $\$500$ billion to $\$600$ billion, the real money supply M/P has increased from $\$500$ billion to $\$589.39$ billion because P has risen from 1.00 to 1.018. An increase in the nominal money supply M does raise the real money supply M/P—but not by as much as it would if P remained constant. An increase in the real money supply shifts the LM curve to the right and reduces the interest rate r. The $D-S$ equilibrium in period 1 is graphed in Figure 3.14.

Now let's turn to the rational expectations (R) hypothesis. In this case, P^e equals the P that results in period 1. This means that we can obtain Q from the S curve equation alone, without using the D curve equation:

(3.17) $P = \left(\dfrac{4,000}{6,200 - Q}\right)P^e$

If P^e is replaced with P, then

$$P = \left(\frac{4,000}{6,200 - Q}\right) P$$

Canceling the Ps

$$1 = \frac{4,000}{6,200 - Q}$$
$$6,200 - Q = 4,000$$
$$Q = 2,200$$

Hence, under the R hypothesis, the S curve will shift up from period 0 to 1 by exactly the upward shift in the D curve (as shown in Figure 3.15), so that the $D-S$ intersection remains at $Q = \$2,200$ billion. We can obtain P from the D curve equation:

(3.4)
$$Q = 1,800 + \frac{480}{P}$$

$$2,200 = 1,800 + \frac{480}{P}$$

$$400 = \frac{480}{P}$$

$$P = \frac{480}{400} = 1.20$$

Thus, in this case, when the nominal money supply M increases by 20%, P increases by 20%; the real money supply M/P remains constant at \$500 billion (600/1.20), the LM curve does not shift (as shown in Figure 3.15), and Q stays constant. Note that nominal demand Y therefore also increases by 20%.

We can confirm that both the S curve and the D curve have shifted up by 20% at the initial Q. We have just seen that at $Q = \$2,200$ billion, the new D curve implies a P of 1.20 instead of 1.00; hence, at that Q, the D curve has shifted up by 20%. From the S curve equation, in which P replaces P^e since the P on the right has increased by 20%, it follows that the P on the left will be 20% higher at the initial Q.

We have completed our presentation of the basic building blocks of macroeconomics. In Part 2, we will begin our analysis of inflation and unemployment.

SUMMARY

1. A decrease in the price level P shifts the LM curve to the right and raises equilibrium output Q in the $IS-LM$ diagram. This relationship between P and Q is the *aggregate demand D curve*.

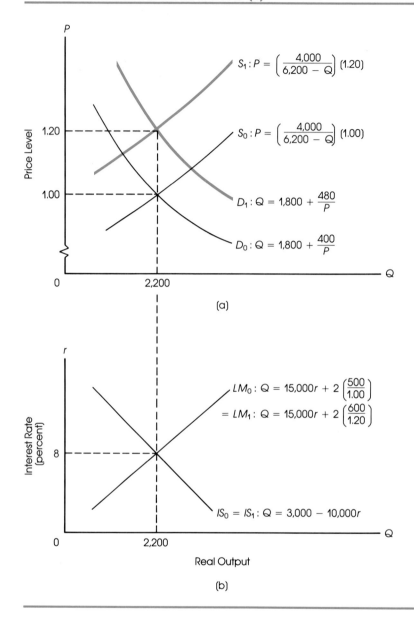

$$S_1 : P = \left(\frac{4{,}000}{6{,}200 - Q} \right) (1.20)$$

$$S_0 : P = \left(\frac{4{,}000}{6{,}200 - Q} \right) (1.00)$$

$$D_1 : Q = 1{,}800 + \frac{480}{P}$$

$$D_0 : Q = 1{,}800 + \frac{400}{P}$$

(a)

$$LM_0 : Q = 15{,}000r + 2 \left(\frac{500}{1.00} \right)$$

$$= LM_1 : Q = 15{,}000r + 2 \left(\frac{600}{1.20} \right)$$

$$IS_0 = IS_1 : Q = 3{,}000 - 10{,}000r$$

Real Output

(b)

When the nominal money supply increases from $500 billion to $600 billion, the *D* curve shifts up from D_0 to D_1 and, with rational expectations, the *S* curve shifts up by the same amount from S_0 to S_1 in (a). The real money supply M/P stays constant, so the *LM* curve remains constant. Hence, *P* rises from 1.00 to 1.20, *Q* stays constant at $2,200 billion, and *r* remains constant at 8%.

2. An expansion of fiscal policy (which shifts the *IS* curve to the right) or an expansion of monetary policy (which shifts the *LM* curve to the right) will also shift the aggregate demand *D* curve to the right.

3. Any change that raises consumption demand *C* or investment demand *I* at a given interest rate *r* and output *Q* on the *IS–LM* diagram will shift the *IS* curve to the right and therefore will shift the aggregate demand *D* curve to the right. Any change that decreases real money demand M^D/P at a given *IS–LM* diagram point (r, Q) and price level *P* will also shift the *LM* curve to the right and therefore will shift the aggregate demand *D* curve to the right.

4. The *long-run aggregate supply* S_{LR} *curve* is vertical. In the long run, only one value of *Q* will be supplied at any *P*. Q^* is the real output produced when factor markets are in long-run equilibrium (specifically, when labor employed is L^* and capital utilized is K^*). Regardless of the position of the *D* curve, $Q = Q^*$ in the long run.

5. The *long-run equilibrium level of labor* L^* is determined by the intersection of the *aggregate labor supply* L^S *curve* and the *aggregate labor demand* L^D *curve* (the *marginal product of labor* MPL *curve*).

6. The *short-run aggregate supply S curve* has a positive slope. When real output *Q* increases, the unemployment rate *U* decreases, the wage *W* increases, *unit labor cost* ULC increases, and the price level *P* increases.

7. The height of the short-run aggregate supply *S* curve at a given *Q* depends on the expected price level P^e. If P^e increases, then *W* increases (provided *W* is not constrained by a labor contract), unit labor cost ULC increases, and the price level *P* — the height of the *S* curve — increases.

8. When the aggregate demand *D* curve shifts, if the short-run aggregate supply *S* curve is fixed, then equilibrium output *Q* changes. But if the *S* curve shifts vertically by the same amount as the *D* curve, then there is no change in *Q*.

9. Under the *inertial expectations (I) hypothesis,* $P^e = P_{-1}$ and the *S* curve remains fixed when the *D* curve shifts; hence, equilibrium output *Q* changes. But under the *rational expectations (R) hypothesis,* $P^e = P$ and the *S* curve shifts vertically by the same amount as the *D* curve, so that there is no change in *Q*.

TERMS AND CONCEPTS

aggregate demand (*D*) curve
aggregate demand (*D*) curve equation
aggregate labor demand (*L^D*) curve

aggregate labor supply (*L^S*) curve
aggregate supply *S* curve equation
competition

diminishing returns

$D-S$ equilibrium

expected price level (P^e)

inertial expectations (I) hypothesis

labor demand–labor supply diagram

labor productivity (output per hour) (A)

long-run aggregate supply (S_{LR}) curve

long-run equilibrium level of capital (K^*)

long-run equilibrium level of labor (L^*)

long-run equilibrium level of output (Q^*)

long-run equilibrium real wage (W/P^*)

marginal analysis

marginal product of labor (MPL)

marginal revenue product of labor (MRPL)

nominal demand (Y)

nominal demand equation

nominal money supply (M)

nominal (money) wage (W)

percentage growth rate of nominal demand (y)

perfectly competitive labor market

price index

price–unit labor cost (P/ULC) ratio (K)

production function

profit maximization

rational expectations (R) hypothesis

real wage (W/P)

short-run aggregate supply (S) curve

transition path

unit labor cost (ULC)

QUESTIONS

3.1 In Question 2.1 at the end of Chapter 2, you obtained the equation for an IS curve. In Question 2.2, you obtained the equation for an LM curve when the real money supply $M/P = \$625$ billion. What is the LM equation if the nominal money supply $M = \$625$ billion?

3.2 Use the IS equation you obtained in Question 2.1 and the LM equation when $M = \$625$ billion to derive the aggregate demand D curve equation.

3.3 What will shift the D curve to the right?

3.4 If the nominal money supply M increases from $625 billion to $906.25 billion, what is the equation for the new LM curve? For the new D curve?

3.5 Find the nominal demand Y equation that corresponds to the D curve equation you obtained in Question 3.2 and the nominal demand Y equation that corresponds to the D curve equation you obtained in Question 3.4. From Question 3.2 to Question 3.4, M has increased by 45% (from $625 billion to $906.25 billion). If P also increases by 45%, what is the increase in nominal demand Y? If P

increases by less than 45%, what happens to Y? If P increases by more than 45%, what happens to Y?

3.6 Why is the long-run aggregate supply S_{LR} curve vertical?

3.7 Why does the short-run aggregate supply S curve have a positive slope? Why does the S curve shift up when P^e increases?

3.8 For each of the following, draw a D–S diagram directly above an IS–LM diagram. Show what happens if:
   a. The IS curve shifts to the right with inertial expectations.
   b. The IS curve shifts to the right with rational expectations.
   c. The LM curve shifts to the right (for a given P) with inertial expectations.
   d. The LM curve shifts to the right (for a given P) with rational expectations.

3.9 Suppose that the aggregate supply S curve equation is

$$P = \left(\frac{4{,}000}{6{,}500 - Q} \right) P^e$$

If $P^e = 1.00$ in period 0, use the D curve equation you obtained in Question 3.2 to find P and Q.

3.10 In period 1, suppose that the D curve equation shifts to the D curve equation you obtained in Question 3.4. Find P and Q with inertial expectations. With rational expectations.

APPENDIX 3A

THE ALGEBRA OF AGGREGATE DEMAND AND AGGREGATE SUPPLY

In Appendix 3A, we will develop the model of aggregate demand and aggregate supply algebraically. We have already examined the basic equations of this model using numerical illustrations. Here, more formal derivations will be presented.

3.A.1 The Aggregate Demand D Curve Equation

We begin with the reduced-form equation for equilibrium output Q from the IS–LM system that we derived in Appendix 2A:

(2.A.10)
$$Q = m \left[D_a + \left(\frac{j}{h} \right) \left(\frac{M}{P} - \frac{M_a}{P} \right) \right]$$

where $D_a \equiv C_a - cT_a + cR + I_a + G$

(2.A.11)
$$m \equiv \frac{1}{[1 - c(1 - t)] + (jk/h)}$$

In Appendix 2A, where we derived equation (2.A.10), we assumed that the price level P remained constant and examined how equilibrium output Q would change when other variables on the right side of the equation change, including M, G, R, T_a, and t. Now we will regard all other variables and parameters as given and observe how Q changes when P changes.

From equation (2.A.10), assuming $M > M_a$, as P declines, Q increases. Recall that m and D_a are independent of P. This *inverse* relationship between Q and P is represented by the aggregate demand D curve. When equation (2.A.10) is interpreted as a relationship between Q and P, it is the aggregate demand D curve equation.

What makes the aggregate demand D curve shift to the right? Anything that makes Q in equation (2.A.10) larger at each P causes a rightward shift in the D curve. Clearly, an increase in M will raise the output level Q that corresponds to each price level P; hence, an increase in the nominal money supply M shifts the D curve to the right.

Now let's consider fiscal policy. An increase in government purchases G or in government transfers R will increase D_a and therefore increase the Q that corresponds to each P. Thus, an increase in government spending $(G + R)$ will shift the D curve to the right.

Now let's consider taxes. Recall that the average tax rate ATR is defined as T/Q, and is equal to $(T_a/Q) + t$. If the ATR is cut by reducing autonomous tax revenue T_a, then clearly D_a increases, thereby raising the Q that corresponds to each P. If the ATR is cut by reducing the tax rate t, then the multiplier m will increase because $c(1 - t)$ will rise, causing the denominator $1 - c(1 - t)$ to decrease. A larger m will raise the Q that corresponds to each P. Thus, a cut in the average tax rate ATR via either T_a or t will shift the D curve to the right.

Monetary or fiscal policy is not the only source of a rightward shift in the aggregate demand D curve. For example, an increase in autonomous demand D_a due to an increase in autonomous consumption or investment C_a or I_a will shift the D curve to the right. Also, from equation (2.A.10), it is clear that a decrease in *autonomous nominal money demand* M_a has the same effect as an increase in the nominal money supply M; both shift the D curve to the right.

If we multiply equation (2.A.10) by P, we obtain nominal demand Y, which is defined as PQ:

(3.A.1) $$Y \equiv PQ = m\left[D_a P + \left(\frac{j}{h} \right) (M - M_a) \right]$$

If fiscal and monetary policy variables and other exogenous variables and parameters are set, all terms on the right will be fixed except P, so that Y will depend on P. We will see that the particular point (Q, P) that results depends on the aggregate supply S curve.

3.A.2 The Aggregate Supply S Curve Equation

We will hypothesize that the expected real wage W/P^e varies *inversely* with the unemployment rate U and, therefore, that W/P^e varies *directly* with real output Q. In particular, we will assume that

$$(3.A.2) \qquad \frac{W}{P^e} = \left(\frac{A}{K}\right)\left(\frac{\overline{Q} - Q^*}{\overline{Q} - Q}\right)$$

where $A \equiv \dfrac{Q}{H}$ = output per hour (labor productivity)

$\quad K =$ the price–unit labor cost (P/ULC) ratio

$\quad Q^* =$ the long-run equilibrium level of output Q

$\quad \overline{Q} =$ an amount of real output Q that exceeds the maximum feasible Q, so that both the numerator $\overline{Q} - Q^*$ and the denominator $\overline{Q} - Q$ are positive

Note that at a given Q, if P^e increases by $X\%$, then the nominal wage W will also increase by $X\%$. Also, if P^e is given and Q increases, then the denominator will be reduced; the right side of equation (3.A.2) will therefore become larger, and W will increase. Thus, equation (3.A.2) embodies the concepts we discussed in Chapter 3 concerning the behavior of the nominal wage W.

Multiplying equation (3.A.2) by P^e, gives us

$$(3.A.3) \qquad W = \left[\left(\frac{A}{K}\right)\left(\frac{\overline{Q} - Q^*}{\overline{Q} - Q}\right)\right] P^e$$

Given

$$(3.16) \qquad P \equiv K\left(\frac{W}{A}\right) \equiv W\left(\frac{K}{A}\right)$$

and substituting the expression for W from equation (3.A.3) into equation (3.16) yields the aggregate supply S curve equation

$$(3.A.4) \qquad P = \left(\frac{\overline{Q} - Q^*}{\overline{Q} - Q}\right) P^e$$

Equation (3.17) is obtained from equation (3.A.4) by setting $\overline{Q} =$ \$6,200 billion and $Q^* =$ \$2,200 billion, so that

$$P = \left(\frac{6,200 - 2,200}{6,200 - Q}\right) P^e$$

$$(3.17) \qquad P = \left(\frac{4{,}000}{6{,}200 - Q} \right) P^e$$

It should be noted that the value of $\overline{Q}$ will influence the slope of the aggregate supply S curve.

To obtain an expression for PQ from equation (3.A.4), we multiply both sides of the equation by $\overline{Q} - Q$:

$$P(\overline{Q} - Q) = (\overline{Q} - Q^*)P^e$$
$$P\overline{Q} - PQ = (\overline{Q} - Q^*)P^e$$

Isolating PQ, we obtain the *nominal supply equation*

$$(3.A.5) \qquad PQ = P\overline{Q} - (\overline{Q} - Q^*)P^e$$

3.A.3 Equilibrium *P* and *Q*

We now have two expressions for PQ:

$$(3.A.1) \qquad PQ = m \left[D_a P + \left(\frac{j}{h} \right) (M - M_a) \right] \quad \text{for nominal demand}$$

$$(3.A.5) \qquad PQ = P\overline{Q} - (\overline{Q} - Q^*)P^e \quad \text{for nominal supply}$$

Let's consider two alternative hypotheses. First, suppose that the **expected price level** P^e is exogenous to our model. This means that the **value of** P^e **does** not depend on P or Q as determined by our model; P^e is **determined** outside the model. For example, under the inertial expectations I assumption, P^e equals the price in the previous period P_{-1}. **Then** P^e **can be** treated as given in equation (3.A.5).

Note that only P (not Q) appears on the right side of equations **(3.A.1) and (3.A.5).** Hence, we can equate equations (3.A.1) and (3.A.5) **and** solve for P:

$$P\overline{Q} - (\overline{Q} - Q^*)P^e = mD_a P + m \left(\frac{j}{h} \right) (M - M_a)$$

$$P\overline{Q} - mD_a P = m \left(\frac{j}{h} \right) (M - M_a) + (\overline{Q} - Q^*)P^e$$

Factoring out P on the left, we obtain

$$P(\overline{Q} - mD_a) = m \left(\frac{j}{h} \right) (M - M_a) + (\overline{Q} - Q^*)P^e$$

Dividing by $(\overline{Q} - mD_a)$ gives us the reduced-form equation for P when P^e is *exogenous:*

$$(3.A.6) \qquad P = \frac{\left[m \left(\frac{j}{h} \right) (M - M_a) \right] + [(\overline{Q} - Q^*)P^e]}{\overline{Q} - mD_a}$$

Both m and D_a are defined at the beginning of this appendix, where equation (2.A.10) is presented. All terms on the right side of equation (3.A.6) are parameters or exogenous variables in our model. Once P is obtained, Q can be found from the aggregate demand D curve equation (2.A.10), from the aggregate supply S curve equation (3.A.4), from the nominal demand equation (3.A.1), or from the nominal supply equation (3.A.5).

If autonomous demand D_a increases, it is clear that the denominator of equation (3.A.6) will become smaller, thereby increasing P. If the nominal money supply M increases or if autonomous money demand M_a decreases, then P will increase. Finally, if P^e increases, then P will increase.

Now what if D_a increases? We know that D_a affects the aggregate demand D curve equation but not the aggregate supply S curve equation. We have just determined that P increases when D_a increases. Thus, looking at the aggregate supply S curve equation (3.A.4), Q will also increase, because a larger Q will reduce the denominator and result in a larger P. In Figure 3.6 (page 138) the D curve shifts to the right from D_0 to D_1 while the S curve remains fixed, so that Q and P change in the same direction.

Now suppose that P^e increases. We know that P^e affects the aggregate supply S curve equation but not the aggregate demand D curve equation. We have just determined that P increases when P^e increases. Thus, looking at the aggregate demand D curve equation (2.A.10), Q will decrease, because a larger P will reduce Q in the demand equation.

Now let's consider the second hypothesis concerning P^e. Suppose that the expected price P^e is *endogenous* to our model, meaning that P^e is dependent on either Q or P. In particular, let's consider the rational expectations hypothesis, which holds (in this context) that

$$(3.A.7) \qquad P^e = P$$

In this case, the supply S curve alone is sufficient to determine Q. To see this, we substitute P for P^e in equation (3.A.4) to obtain

$$(3.A.8) \qquad P = \frac{\overline{Q} - Q^*}{(\overline{Q} - Q)} P$$

P cancels, so that Q must clearly equal Q^*. Then P can be obtained by substituting Q^* for Q in equation (2.A.10). The endogenous adjustment of P^e to P always ensures that the supply S curve shifts vertically by the same amount as the demand D curve, so that the $D - S$ intersection remains at $Q = Q^*$.

2 Inflation and Unemployment

4

The Inflationary Process

How does inflation arise? In this chapter, we will use aggregate demand–aggregate supply $(D-S)$ analysis to help us answer this question. We will begin with an economy that is enjoying *price stability* (zero inflation) and then examine how inflation begins.

In our analysis, we will rely heavily on a new diagram — the *DG–SG (demand growth–supply growth) diagram*. Initially, we will show how inflation can be analyzed in the $D-S$ diagram we developed in Chapter 3. But we will quickly see that it is better to perform the analysis in the closely related $DG-SG$ diagram.

Like the $D-S$ diagram, the $DG-SG$ diagram plots real output Q on the horizontal axis. On the vertical axis, however, the $DG-SG$ diagram plots the inflation rate p instead of the price level P. The intersection of the DG and SG curves determines the real output Q and the inflation rate p for the period. The DG curve is closely related to the aggregate demand D curve, and the SG curve is closely related to the short-run aggregate supply S curve. Our new $DG-SG$ diagram is simply a new method of implementing the aggregate demand–aggregate supply analysis we began in Chapter 3.

4.1 Inflation in the Aggregate Demand–Aggregate Supply $(D-S)$ Diagram

In this section, we will focus on the $D-S$ diagram that employs the short-run aggregate supply S curve. The $D-S$ diagram yields the price level P and the level of real output Q in each period. Inflation is defined as a sustained rise in P over time. It follows, then, that inflation will occur when the $D-S$ intersection shifts upward over time.

Initially, suppose that the economy is enjoying price stability (zero inflation) and that Q is at its long-run equilibrium value Q^* (described in Chapter 3). Equivalently, the unemployment rate U is at its corresponding long-run equilibrium value U^*. Recall that Q^* is determined solely by the position of the vertical long-run aggregate supply S_{LR} curve.

Let's assume that the aggregate demand D curve and the short-run aggregate supply S curve also intersect at Q^* and that they have been in the same position for several periods, so that both P and Q have remained constant in the recent past.

Now suppose that a sustained monetary–fiscal expansion begins, so that the D curve shifts up by the same percentage in each period. What happens to the economy?

Suppose that expectations are *inertial*, so that the expected price level P^e does not respond immediately to the upward shift in the D curve. In the initial period, the upward shift of the D curve will raise real output Q above Q^* (reduce the unemployment rate U below U^*); the price level P will rise, but by a smaller magnitude than the upward shift in the D curve. As we explained at the end of Chapter 3, however, this is only the beginning — not the end — of the inflationary story. In subsequent periods, the S curve will shift up, reducing Q back toward Q^* (raising U back toward U^*) and further raising P.

If we performed a complete analysis of this inflationary process using the D–S diagram, the S curve would chase the D curve in its movements upward. In the long run, the D and S curves would intersect at Q^* in each period, and P would rise in each period by the same percentage as the upward shift in the D curve.

However, if we used the D–S diagram to analyze the inflationary process, then the D curve, the S curve, and the price level P would all soon shift up above the page. It is therefore more convenient to perform the analysis using the DG–SG diagram. With the inflation rate p instead of the price level P plotted on the vertical axis, a compact diagram can describe the entire inflationary process — including the long-run equilibrium that results.

In Sections 4.2 and 4.3, we will develop the DG curve and the SG curve, respectively. Neither curve alone can tell us the inflation rate p and the real output Q that will occur in a given period. The intersection of the DG and SG curves yields the combination of p and Q that will actually occur in that period.

First, we will analyze the inflationary process in a no-growth economy, in which both the labor force and labor productivity (output per hour) remain constant. In Section 4.6, we will find that it is easy to modify our analysis to incorporate the labor force and labor productivity growth.

Because we will ultimately apply our analysis to a growing economy, we will develop most of our relationships so that they will be correct in either a growing or a stationary economy. For example, we will assume that labor productivity growth a is not necessarily 0% when we consider how the *inflation rate* p is determined. We will therefore minimize the number of relationships that must be modified when we move from a no-growth economy to a growing economy.

4.2 The Demand Growth *DG* Curve

In Chapter 3, we defined nominal demand Y as the intended expenditure PQ of the buyers of output, so that

(3.5) $Y \equiv PQ$

If nominal demand Y increases by 6% during this period, then the intended expenditure PQ thereby increases by 6%. This increase may be due to a 6% growth in P while Q stays constant, or to a 6% growth in Q while P stays constant, or to percentage growth changes in P and Q that total 6%.

In this chapter, we are interested in the percentage growth rate of the price level P—the inflation rate p. However, equation (3.5) relates the level of P and Q to the level of Y. We will find it more useful to relate the growth rates of P and Q (p and q, respectively) to the growth rate of Y, denoted by y.

In a moment, we will see that the following equation holds *approximately:*

(4.1) $y \equiv p + q$

where y = the percentage growth rate of Y

p = the percentage growth rate of P

q = the percentage growth rate of Q

For example, if nominal demand Y increases by 6% per period, so that $y = 6\%$, then the sum of p and q must be (approximately) 6%. When $y = 6\%$, the following combinations of p and q are possible: $p = 6\%$, $q = 0\%$; $p = 0\%$, $q = 6\%$; $p = 4\%$, $q = 2\%$; $p = 9\%$, $q = -3\%$; and so on.

▶ In this chapter, a lower-case letter will generally indicate the percentage growth rate of the corresponding capital-letter variable.

Initially, suppose that $P = 1.00$ and $Q = 100$, so that $Y = PQ = 100$. If $y = 6\%$, then $Y = 106$ at the end of the period, so that $PQ = 106$. This might be due to $P = 1.06$ ($p = 6\%$) and $Q = 100$ ($q = 0\%$); or to $P = 1.00$ ($p = 0\%$) and $Q = 106$ ($q = 6\%$); or to $P = 1.04$ ($p = 4\%$) and $Q = 102$ approximately ($q = 2\%$ approximately); or to $P = 1.09$ ($p = 9\%$) and $Q = 97$ approximately ($q = -3\%$ approximately); and so on.

▶ For convenience, we will always assign the value of 100 to Q in the initial period. Hence, Q is really an index of the quantity of output and is not given in billions of dollars. For example, if the initial value of real output Q is, say, \$2,200 billion, we will call this value 100 in our DG–SG diagram. If actual real output Q increases by 1% (by, say, \$22 billion from \$2,200 billion to \$2,222 billion), then Q will increase from 100 to 101 in our DG–SG diagram.

The box on pages 170–71 on the *math growth-rate rule* explains why equation (3.5) implies equation (4.1). We will use the math growth-rate rule throughout the text.

Keeping equation (4.1) in mind, we will draw the *demand growth DG curve*. We want to plot the DG curve on a diagram with the level of real output Q (not its growth rate q) on the horizontal axis and the inflation rate p on the vertical axis, as shown in Figure 4.1. Let's see how the DG curve is constructed.

FIGURE 4.1 A DEMAND GROWTH DG CURVE

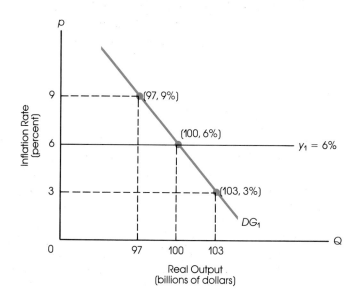

For last period (period 0), real output $Q_0 = 100$. For this period (period 1), the nominal demand growth rate y_1 is set at 6%; hence, the horizontal y_1 line is drawn with a height of 6%. If real output is again $Q_1 = 100$, so that the real output growth rate $q_1 = 0\%$, then $p_1 = 6\%$ since $y_1 = 6\% = p_1 + q_1$. Hence, the Q–p point (100, 6%) lies on the new DG_1 curve. If $Q_1 = 103$, so that $q_1 = 3\%$, then $p_1 = 3\%$. Thus, point (103, 3%) also lies on the DG_1 curve. Finally, if $Q_1 = 97$, so that $q_1 = -3\%$, then $p_1 = 9\%$; so point (97, 9%) also lies on the DG_1 curve. Note that the slope of the DG_1 curve is -1.

The Math Growth-Rate Rule

To state the *math growth-rate rule,* let a lower-case letter denote the *percentage growth rate* of the same capital-letter variable. (For example, z is the percentage growth rate of the variable Z.) Then the following is *approximately* true:

If $Z = XY$, then $z = x + y$.

If $Z = \dfrac{X}{Y}$, then $z = x - y$.

The math growth-rate rule is a mathematical (not an economic) relationship. Suppose that some variable Z equals the product of two variables X and Y, so that

$$Z = XY$$

If, for example, initially $X = 100$ and $Y = 100$, then $Z = 10,000$.

Now suppose that X increases by 2% to 102, so that the percentage growth rate of X is $x = 2\%$. Also suppose that Y increases by 4% to 104, so that the percentage growth rate of Y is $y = 4\%$. Since both X and Y increase, Z will obviously increase. Now, will the percentage growth rate of Z be approximately $z = 6\%$ or approximately $z = 8\%$? In other words, is $z = x + y$ or $z = xy$ approximately correct?

If $X = 102$ and $Y = 104$, multiplying them gives us $Z = 10,608$. So Z will increase by 608, or 6.08% (approximately 6%). Thus

If $Z = XY$, then $z = x + y$ (approximately).

Your sense of symmetry should tell you that the following is also true:

If $Z = \dfrac{X}{Y}$, then $z = x - y$.

You can check this by substituting a numerical example.

(continued)

▶ To simplify, we will assume that monetary policy is adjusted to achieve a targeted y for a given period. Under this assumption, we can specify y in advance, and the *DG* curve will turn out to be a straight line.

We will now prove algebraically that the rule is valid. When X increases by ΔX and Y increases by ΔY, Z will increase by ΔZ. Then

$$Z + \Delta Z \equiv (X + \Delta X)(Y + \Delta Y)$$

Multiplying out on the right side of this equation, we obtain

$$Z + \Delta Z = XY + X(\Delta Y) + (\Delta X)Y + (\Delta X)(\Delta Y)$$

But $Z = XY$. Subtracting Z from the left side and XY from the right side of the equation gives us

$$\Delta Z = X(\Delta Y) + Y(\Delta X) + (\Delta X)(\Delta Y)$$

The percentage growth rate of Z, z, is

$$z \equiv \frac{\Delta Z}{Z}$$

Dividing the left side by Z and each term on the right side by XY (which equals Z) gives us

$$\frac{\Delta Z}{Z} = \frac{\Delta Y}{Y} + \frac{\Delta X}{X} + \left(\frac{\Delta X}{X}\right)\left(\frac{\Delta Y}{Y}\right)$$
$$z \;\; = \;\; y \;\; + \;\; x \;\; + xy$$

But xy is the product of two percentages and will be small relative to x and y as long as the percentages are small. Thus, if we drop xy, it will be *approximately* true that

$$z = x + y$$

This completes our derivation in the case of a product. In the case of a quotient, where $Z = X/Y$, $ZY = X$. It follows immediately from the product case that $z + y = x$, so that $z = x - y$. This completes our derivation in the case of a quotient.

Suppose that the level of Q in period 0 is $Q_0 = 100$. This will be our reference point when we draw the DG_1 curve for period 1.

Suppose that $y = 6\%$ in period 1, so that Y_1 in equation (3.5) is 6% greater than Y_0. If $Q_1 = 100$ (the same value as Q_0), then $q = 0\%$ and, from equation (4.1), $p = 6\%$. Thus, we plot a point (Q, p) at $Q = 100$ and $p = 6\%$ in Figure 4.1.

Now suppose that $Q_1 = 103$, so that $q = 3\%$ and $p = 3\%$. Then we plot a second point at $Q = 103$ and $p = 3\%$. Finally, suppose that $Q_1 = 97$, so that $q = -3\%$ and $p = 9\%$. Then we plot a third point at $Q = 97$ and $p = 9\%$. Connecting these points yields the DG_1 curve for period 1.

Note that when y is assumed to be fixed, regardless of the Q–p combination, the slope of the DG curve is *constant*. With $Q_0 = 100$, a 1-unit (1%) reduction in Q leads to a 1% increase in p. Thus, whenever we analyze the path of the economy on the assumption that monetary and fiscal policy maintain a specific nominal demand growth y in a given period, the DG curve will be a straight line.

A RULE FOR PLOTTING THE DG CURVE

Suppose that y is again 6% in period 2, so that Y_2 in equation (3.5) is 6% greater than Y_1. This does not, in general, mean that the DG_2 curve in period 2 coincides with the DG_1 curve in period 1. DG_2 will coincide with DG_1 if and only if Q_1 is equal to Q_0 (in our example, 100). Why?

We will see that Q_1 is determined by the intersection of the SG_1 curve and the DG_1 curve. Suppose that $Q_1 = 103$ (not 100). Now when we plot the DG_2 curve, the real output of the previous period $Q_1 = 103$ is our reference point. With $Q_1 = 103$, a Q_2 of 103 would imply that $q = 0\%$ and $p = 6\%$. Thus, a point should be plotted at $Q = 103$ and $p = 6\%$; the DG_2 curve would go through this point. Note that this point does not lie on the DG_1 curve. Hence, DG_2 would not coincide with DG_1 in this case, but would lie above it.

If $Q_1 = 97$ (not 100), then a Q_2 of 97 would imply that $q = 0\%$ and $p = 6\%$. Thus, a point should be plotted at $Q = 97$ and $p = 6\%$; the DG_2 curve would go through this point. Note that this point does not lie on the DG_1 curve. Hence, DG_2 would not coincide with DG_1 in this case, but would lie below it.

We can now state the procedure for constructing the DG curve for a given period. First, it is convenient to draw a horizontal line at the height of y, the growth rate of nominal demand. We will call this line "the y line."

▶ To draw the DG curve for a given period, go to last period's DG–SG intersection point and move vertically until you reach the horizontal y line (in a no-growth economy). Through this point, draw the DG curve with a constant slope approximately equal to -1.

Note the use of the phrase "no-growth economy." As we will see in Section 4.6, the $\hat{y}$ line replaces the y line in a growing economy.

THE SLOPE OF THE *DG* CURVE

Why is the slope of the *DG* curve approximately -1? Each point on the *DG* curve must satisfy equation (4.1). The percentage growth in real output q is measured from the Q in the previous period. Suppose that $Q = 100$ in the previous period. Since 1% of 100 = 1, p increases by 1% for each 1-unit reduction in Q (1% of last period's Q). Thus, the slope is exactly -1.

Now suppose that $Q = 103$ in the previous period. Since 1% of 103 = 1.03, p increases by 1% for each reduction in Q by 1.03 (1% of last period's Q). Thus, if last period's $Q = 103$, then the constant slope of the *DG* curve will be slightly flatter than it will be if last period's $Q = 100$. Thus, the slope is slightly less negative than -1, or $1/-1.03 = -0.97$.

If Q changes from one period to the next, then even if y stays constant, the slope of the *DG* curve will change slightly from one period to the next. But if we assign the initial-period Q a value of 100, then as long as Q does not deviate too far from 100, the constant negative slope of the *DG* curve for each period will be approximately -1. A 1-unit decrease in Q (approximately) is accompanied by a 1% increase in p.

In this section, we have assumed that monetary policy will maintain a specific percentage growth rate of nominal demand y in a given period, regardless of the $q-p$ combination that actually occurs. It is instructive and convenient to analyze the path of the economy when y is specified for each period.

It should be pointed out, however, that monetary policy may have to be adjusted to achieve a particular y in a given period, depending on the particular $q-p$ combination that occurs. As we saw in Chapter 3, there is no guarantee that a particular *money-supply growth rate* m will achieve a y of, say, 6% regardless of the $q-p$ combination that occurs. The feasible $Q-P$ combinations for a given money supply depend on the slope of the aggregate demand D curve we analyzed in Chapter 3.

▶ If monetary policy does not adjust to achieve a targeted y for a given period, then the *DG* curve is a *curve*, not a straight line.

▶ To justify our *DG line*, imagine the following hypothetical policy process. Assume that monetary policymakers set a target value of y for each period. The money-supply growth rate is adjusted to achieve a particular level of y, regardless of the $q-p$ combination that emerges. Thus, the slope of the *DG* curve in a given period will always be constant (approximately -1). Moreover, we can speak of the value of y for a given period — even before the *DG–SG* intersection determines the particular q and p that will result.

4.3 The Supply Growth SG Curve

In this section, we will examine the behavior of the SG curve based on two assumptions: (1) that there is no "supply shock," and (2) that expectations are "inertial." (We will consider "rational" expectations in Chapter 6.)

In Section 4.8, we will consider *supply inflation* and *supply shocks*. There, we will see that a supply shock causes the *wage inflation rate w* and/or the *price inflation rate p* to temporarily diverge from the values predicted by the model we will develop in this section and apply in Sections 4.3–4.7. Such a supply shock temporarily suspends the rule for shifting the SG curve that we will derive here. At the outset, then, we must emphasize that

▶ The conclusions we will develop in Section 4.3 and apply in Sections 4.3–4.7 concerning the behavior of wage inflation *w* and price inflation *p* and the shifting of the SG curve are valid only in the absence of a supply shock and must be temporarily modified in response to such a shock (as described in Section 4.8).

In Chapter 3, we saw that the short-run aggregate supply S curve gives the price level P that producers will set at each level of real output Q for a given period. The SG curve gives the inflation rate p that producers will set at each Q for a given period.

Suppose that producers decide to set a price level of 1.06 at a particular level of Q for this period. At this Q, the height of the S curve will be 1.06. To plot the corresponding point on the SG curve, we must determine last period's price level P_{-1}. If $P_{-1} = 1.00$, then by choosing a price level of $P = 1.06$, producers are choosing an inflation rate of $p = 6\%$. Hence, at this particular Q, the height of the SG curve will be 6%.

Given this close link between the S and SG curves, our analysis of the slope and the position of the S curve is relevant to the SG curve. If the S curve is steeper, then the SG curve will be steeper. The same elements that influence the slope of the S curve also influence the slope of the SG curve: (1) the degree to which long-term wage contracts are prevalent, and (2) the responsiveness of relative bargaining strength — and, hence, of the wage — to a change in the unemployment rate.

Just as the position of the S curve depends on the expected price level P^e, the position of the SG curve depends on the *expected inflation rate* p^e. In this section, we will investigate the important case of *inertial (adaptive) price expectations*, in which the expected inflation rate p^e is equal to last period's inflation rate p_{-1}.

Under this simple form of inertial expectations, current economic events during this period do not influence the expected inflation rate p^e. Workers and managers simply expect the inflation rate in the current period to equal last period's rate and do not adjust their expectations promptly in response to current events during this period.

The word "inertial" is borrowed from physics and serves as a reminder of English mathematician and physicist Sir Isaac Newton's laws of motion. In particular, Newton contended that a body continues to maintain a constant velocity — to exhibit inertia — unless it is acted on by an outside force. Maintaining a constant velocity may therefore be regarded as normal and "to be expected." Under *inertial expectations*, people expect the inflation rate to remain constant.

THE HEIGHT OF THE *SG* CURVE

The height of the *SG* curve is the inflation rate p that producers set at each level of real output Q during each period. We begin our examination of the behavior of the *SG* curve by returning to equations (3.13) and (3.16):

(3.13)
$$P \equiv K(\text{ULC})$$

(3.16)
$$P \equiv K\left(\frac{W}{A}\right)$$

where ULC = unit labor cost
$\quad\quad A$ = labor productivity (output per hour)
$\quad\quad K$ = the price–unit labor cost (P–ULC) ratio

Because we are now interested in the inflation rate p (rather than the price level P), we apply the math growth-rate rule to equations (3.13) and (3.16) to obtain

(4.2)
$$p \equiv k + \text{ulc} \equiv k + w - a$$

where k = the percentage growth rate of the P–ULC ratio
$\quad\quad$ ulc = the percentage growth rate of the unit labor cost
$\quad\quad w$ = the percentage growth rate of the wage per hour
$\quad\quad a$ = the percentage growth rate of labor productivity

Note that, like equations (3.13) and (3.16), equation (4.2) must be true. K is defined as the ratio of price to unit labor cost (the ratio of P to ULC, or the ratio of P to W/A). Therefore, equations (3.13) and (3.16) are true by definition of K. Equation (4.2) must also be true because it is obtained from equations (3.13) and (3.16) by applying the math growth-rate rule.

Now suppose that we propose the hypothesis that the P–ULC ratio K changes very slowly (if at all) over time, so that k—the percentage growth rate of K—is normally close to 0%. Whether this hypothesis is true or false is an empirical issue that must be tested against actual data. We will do this shortly. If k can be taken as approximately 0%, then equation (4.2) becomes the *price equation*

(4.3) $p = \text{ulc} = w - a$

In contrast to equation (4.2), equation (4.3) is not true by definition. It will only be true if our hypothesis that k is normally approximately 0% turns out to be empirically accurate.

For example, suppose that the growth rate of output per hour (labor productivity) $a = 2\%$ per year. If the growth rate of the wage per hour (the *wage inflation rate*) $w = 2\%$ per year also, then $p = 0\%$ according to equation (4.3). If the average worker produces 2% more per hour and is also paid 2% more per hour, then the unit labor cost ULC stays constant. Thus, the growth rate of unit labor cost $\text{ulc} = 0\%$, and $p = 0\%$.

Now suppose that $w = 8\%$ when $a = 2\%$. Then $\text{ulc} = 6\%$ and $p = 6\%$. To reduce p from 6% to 0%, w must be reduced by 6% (from 8% to 2%), so that w is equal to a.

Is the assumption that the growth rate of the $P - \text{ULC}$ ratio k is close to 0% really valid empirically? For the United States over the past two decades, the answer is yes. The evidence presented in Table 4.1 justifies our use of price equation (4.3) as an approximation.

To simplify our model, we will also assume that productivity growth is constant. We must now distinguish between *actual* productivity growth and *normal* productivity growth. *Normal productivity growth* is simply average productivity growth over several periods. Actual productivity growth fluctuates from period to period; normal productivity growth is much more stable. Here, by a, we mean normal labor productivity growth.

By unit labor cost ULC, we mean *normal* unit labor cost. It can be argued that firms set prices based on normal unit labor costs because normal ULC is more predictable than actual ULC. Clearly, it is inaccurate to assume that actual labor productivity growth is constant over time, but it is tolerable to assume that normal a is roughly constant over time. This we will do.

If a is constant, then from equation (4.3), we know that if w stays constant, then p stays constant; if w changes by $X\%$, then p changes by $X\%$. Thus, assuming that a and k are constant, we have

(4.4) $$\Delta p = \Delta w$$

where $\Delta p =$ the change in the price inflation rate

$\Delta w =$ the change in the wage inflation rate

For example, suppose that $a = 2\%$ and that, initially, $w = 2\%$ and $p = 0\%$. If w increases by 6% ($\Delta w = 6\%$) to 8%, then from equation

TABLE 4.1

THE GROWTH RATE OF THE PRICE – UNIT
LABOR COST RATIO (all numbers are
percentages)

Year	p	$-$ ulc	$\equiv$ k
1965	1.6	0.3	1.3
1966	2.8	3.5	−0.7
1967	3.2	3.5	−0.3
1968	4.0	4.1	−0.1
1969	4.7	6.8	−2.1
1970	4.8	6.6	−1.8
1971	4.5	3.1	1.4
1972	3.0	2.8	0.2
1973	3.8	5.0	−1.2
1974	10.2	12.2	−2.0
1975	10.3	7.5	2.8
1976	5.1	4.7	0.4
1977	5.7	5.2	0.5
1978	7.1	8.0	−0.9
1979	8.8	10.7	−1.9
1980	10.0	11.1	−1.1
1981	9.8	8.0	1.8
1982	5.7	7.7	−2.0
1983	3.2	1.4	1.8
1984	3.1	1.5	1.6
Average			
1965–1969			−0.4
1970–1974			−0.7
1975–1979			0.2
1980–1984			0.4
1965–1984			−0.1

SOURCE: *Economic Report of the President 1985*,
Table B-41, p. 279; data on nonfarm business
sector for unit labor cost ulc and the implicit
price deflator p.

(4.3), p increases to 6% ($\Delta p = 6\%$). Thus, equation (4.4) holds: $\Delta p = \Delta w = 6\%$.

In equation (4.3), with a assumed constant, the spotlight now shines on w. In Chapter 3, we explained why the expected price level P^e should influence the nominal wage W. For the same reasons, the expected inflation rate p^e should influence the wage inflation rate w. If workers and managers raise p^e, then w should rise correspondingly. In fact, we will make the following simple assumption:

▶ At a given real output Q (equivalently, at a given unemployment rate U), if the expected inflation rate p^e increases (decreases) by $X\%$, then the wage inflation rate w normally increases (decreases) by $X\%$.

For example, suppose that $p^e = 0\%$ results in $w = 2\%$ at a particular level of Q. According to our simplifying assumption, if $p^e = 6\%$ at the same Q, then $w = 8\%$.

But if w increases (decreases) by $X\%$, then from equation (4.4), the actual inflation rate p will also increase (decrease) by $X\%$.

▶ At a given real output Q, if the expected inflation rate p^e increases (decreases) by $X\%$, then the height of the SG curve p normally increases (decreases) by $X\%$. Thus, an $X\%$ increase in p^e will shift the SG curve up by $X\%$.

For example, suppose that $p^e = 0\%$ results in $w = 2\%$ at a particular level of Q. Then if $p^e = 6\%$ at the same Q, then $w = 8\%$; with $a = 2\%$ in equation (4.3), $p = 6\%$. Therefore, if p^e increases by 6%, then p increases by 6%. Thus, the height of the SG curve p depends on the expected inflation rate p^e.

THE SLOPE OF THE SG CURVE

In Chapter 3, we explained why the nominal wage W (and therefore the wage inflation rate w) should be influenced by the unemployment rate U, which reflects the demand for labor relative to the supply of labor. If U declines, then labor demand increases relative to labor supply and w also increases for a given p^e. We therefore make the following assumption:

▶ Given the expected inflation rate p^e, the wage inflation rate w varies inversely with the unemployment rate U (as shown in Figure 4.2). Thus, for a given p^e, w increases as U decreases. Moreover, for a given p^e, a particular w results from a particular U.

This hypothesis is based on the premises that, given p^e, w is determined by the relative relationship of labor demand to labor supply and that the unemployment rate serves as an indicator (a "proxy") for this relationship. In Chapter 14, we will provide a more careful defense of the propositions that a decline in the unemployment rate U reflects an

FIGURE 4.2 *w* VARIES INVERSELY WITH *U* AND SHIFTS DIRECTLY WITH p^e

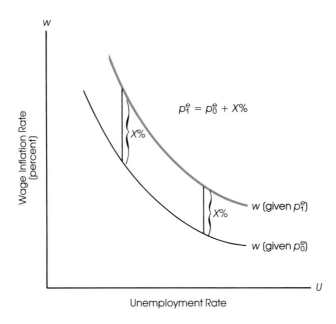

Given the expected inflation rate p_0^e, the *w* curve shows how the wage inflation rate declines as the unemployment rate *U* rises. As *U* rises, labor supply increases relative to labor demand. If p^e increases by *X*% to p_1^e, then the *w* curve will shift up by *X*%. At each level of *U*, *w* will now be *X*% higher. This occurs because employers and workers set the wage inflation rate *w* relative to the expected inflation rate p^e.

increase in labor demand relative to labor supply and that such an increase should raise the wage inflation rate *w*.

For a given p^e, *w* increases as *U* decreases. From the price equation (4.3), the price inflation rate *p* also increases.

▶ Given the expected inflation rate p^e, the actual inflation rate *p* varies inversely with the unemployment rate *U*. Thus, for a given p^e, *p* increases as *U* decreases. Moreover, for a given p^e, a particular *p* results from a particular *U*.

Since *Q* increases as *U* decreases, this hypothesis implies that

▶ Given the expected inflation rate p^e, the actual inflation rate *p* varies directly with real output *Q*. Thus, for a given p^e, *p* increases as *Q* increases; hence, the slope of the supply growth

SG curve is positive. Moreover, for a given p^e, a particular p results at a particular Q.

The supply growth *SG* curve is based on a specific p^e because, as we have seen, a specific p^e influences w, which in turn influences the p that firms set. As we emphasized at the beginning of this section, supply shocks can disrupt the normal relationships that usually link p^e to w to p. (We will consider such shocks in Section 4.8.)

Figure 4.3 graphs a positively sloped supply growth *SG* curve based on a particular p^e and shows a horizontal line with a height equal to that same p^e.

FIGURE 4.3 THE SUPPLY GROWTH *SG* CURVE HAS A POSITIVE SLOPE AND SHIFTS WITH p^e

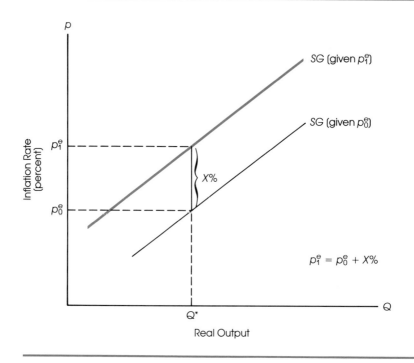

The *SG* curve has a positive slope. As the level of real output Q rises, the unemployment rate U declines, the wage inflation rate w increases, and the growth rate of the unit labor cost ulc increases, so p increases. If p^e increases by $X\%$ from p_0^e to p_1^e, then the *SG* curve will shift up by $X\%$. At each level of real output Q, the inflation rate p will be $X\%$ higher. This occurs because w will be $X\%$ higher, so that ulc and, hence, p will rise by $X\%$.

▶ The intersection of the supply growth SG curve and the horizontal expected inflation rate p^e line occurs at a particular level of real output Q, denoted by Q^*. At that Q^*, the actual inflation rate p that firms set equals p^e. At any Q less than Q^*, the actual p is less than p^e; at any Q greater than Q^*, the actual p is greater than p^e.

We will see in a moment that this special Q is the Q at which the long-run aggregate supply S_{LR} curve is vertical; hence, we are justified in reusing the symbol Q^*.

Now if p^e increases by $X\%$, then according to our earlier assumption, the SG curve will shift up by $X\%$. Figure 4.3 also shows the new SG curve, based on this higher expected inflation rate p_1^e and the new horizontal p^e line. It is clear that the new SG curve and the new p^e line intersect at the same Q^*. Thus:

▶ The supply growth SG curve generally shifts from one period to the next due to changes in the expected inflation rate p^e. However, in all periods, the same level of real output Q results in an actual inflation rate p that equals p^e. This level of Q is denoted by Q^*.

In Chapter 3, we used the symbol Q^* to designate the level of real output Q at which the long-run supply S_{LR} curve is vertical in Figure 3.2 (page 122). This Q^* results when the long-run equilibrium level of labor L^* is inserted into the production function given by equation (3.11), along with the long-run equilibrium level of capital K^*. L^* is given by the intersection of the labor demand L^D curve and the labor supply L^S curve in Figure 3.3 (page 124) in a frictionless economy.

Is the Q^* we are using here to define the Q at which p always equals p^e the same Q^* we used in Chapter 3 to define the Q at which the long-run supply S_{LR} curve is vertical? The answer is yes.

Imagine that the economy is in the long-run equilibrium condition shown in Figure 3.3, with labor L at L^* and the real wage at $(W/P)^*$, so that real output is at Q^*. Period after period, workers prefer to supply L^* in response to the real wage $(W/P)^*$ and firms prefer to employ L^* at the real wage $(W/P)^*$. Period after period, real output Q^* is supplied.

In such a long-run equilibrium, expectations must be correct. The expected price level P^e must equal the actual price level P; equivalently, the expected inflation rate p^e must equal the actual inflation rate p. If, instead, expectations turned out to be incorrect, then workers would want to readjust the supply of labor and firms would want to readjust the demand for labor. The level of real output Q would then change, instead of remaining constant period after period.

Thus, if Q^* is the long-run equilibrium level of output Q, then it is the Q that is produced when price expectations are correct. In this chapter, we define $Q*$ as the Q at which price expectations are correct ($p^e = p$). Thus, $Q*$ must be the same in both cases and we are justified in using the same symbol $Q*$.

We therefore arrive at the following rule for plotting the supply growth SG curve:

▶ The height of the SG curve at $Q*$ (the long-run equilibrium level of output Q) equals the expected inflation rate p^e (in the absence of a supply shock). To plot the SG curve in a given period, draw a horizontal line with a height of p^e and a vertical line at $Q*$. Through the intersection point $(Q*, p^e)$, draw the SG curve with a positive slope.

Under inertial expectations, $p^e = p_{-1}$, where p_{-1} denotes the inflation rate in the preceding period. Hence

▶ Under inertial expectations, the actual inflation rate p that firms set at real output $Q*$ equals p_{-1}. At any Q less than $Q*$, p is less than p_{-1}; at any Q greater than $Q*$, p is greater than p_{-1}.

▶ With inertial expectations ($p^e = p_{-1}$), $Q*$ is Q_c, the *constant inflation output*, and $U*$ is U_c, the *constant inflation rate of unemployment* (CIRU):

(4.5)   If $Q = Q_c$ $(U = U_c)$, then the inflation rate will stay constant $(p = p_{-1})$.

If $Q < Q_c$ $(U > U_c)$, then the inflation rate will decline $(p < p_{-1})$.

If $Q > Q_c$ $(U < U_c)$, then the inflation rate will rise $(p > p_{-1})$.

With inertial expectations, the economy possesses a CONSTANT INFLATION RATE OF UNEMPLOYMENT (CIRU) U_c and a CONSTANT INFLATION OUTPUT Q_c, where the subscript c denotes *constant inflation*.

▶ Q_c coincides with the *long-run equilibrium level of output $Q*$. U_c coincides with the associated *long-run equilibrium unemployment rate $U*$.

▶ Throughout the remainder of Chapter 4, Chapter 5, and Chapter 6 (except for Section 6.5 on rational expectations), we will assume that the economy is characterized by inertial expectations and will use the symbols Q_c (instead of $Q*$) and U_c (instead of $U*$).

It should be noted that U_c, the constant inflation rate of unemployment (CIRU), is sometimes called the *nonaccelerating inflation rate of unemployment* (NAIRU). We will use CIRU instead of NAIRU here because "constant" is a clearer concept than "nonaccelerating."

We have seen that the *SG* curve goes through point (Q^*, p^e). With inertial expectations, the *SG* curve goes through point (Q_c, p_{-1}). Last period's intersection point has a height of p_{-1}. Thus, with inertial expectations, our rule for plotting the supply growth *SG* curve becomes

▶ To plot this period's *SG* curve under inertial expectations, go to last period's $DG - SG$ intersection point and move horizontally until you reach the vertical Q_c line. Through this point (where $Q = Q_c$ and $p = p_{-1}$), draw this period's *SG* curve with a positive slope.

Note that the economy has a constant inflation rate of unemployment U_c and a constant inflation output Q_c if expectations are inertial. The inertial expectations assumption permits us to replace p^e with p_{-1}, and this substitution results in $p = p_{-1}$ at Q_c (and U_c). We will see that under rational expectations, the economy does not possess a U_c and Q_c; in other words, there is no value of the unemployment rate U and real output Q at which the price inflation rate p normally stays constant.

In Section 4.8, we will see that a supply shock can cause the inflation rate to rise or fall even if expectations are inertial and $Q = Q_c$ $(U = U_c)$. Hence

▶ When we assert that the inflation rate p will remain constant if $Q = Q_c$ $(U = U_c)$, we are assuming that there is no supply shock.

Relationship (4.5) may be contrasted with the *Phillips curve hypothesis*, which was believed by many economists in the 1960s. According to hypothesis (4.5)

▶ If U is a stable, low value (less than U_c), then p rises. If U is a stable, high value (greater than U_c), then p declines.

By contrast, according to the Phillips curve hypothesis

If U is a stable, low value, then p is a stable, high value.

If U is a stable, high value, then p is a stable, low value.

The Phillips curve hypothesis is often contradicted by the data and hypothesis (4.5) is generally consistent with the data. In Chapter 5, we will see that a recession generally does cause the inflation rate p to decline, as hypothesis (4.5) predicts. If the recession begins when the economy is at a high inflation rate, however, then the recession will witness a high unemployment rate U and an initially high (although declining) inflation rate p, contradicting the Phillips curve hypothesis.

Thus, the Phillips curve hypothesis, which claims that the economy cannot experience high unemployment and high inflation at the same time, has been discredited. Hypothesis (4.5), which claims that high unemployment should result in declining inflation, appears to be generally consistent with economic experience.

This completes our derivation of the supply growth SG curve under inertial expectations in the absence of supply shocks. In Section 4.8, we will examine the behavior of the SG curve when supply shocks do occur.

4.4 Demand Inflation

We are now ready to answer our original question: How does inflation arise? We will also trace the path that the economy follows before it arrives at long-run equilibrium. In this section, we will focus on *demand-generated inflation* or, more simply, *demand inflation*.

We will assume that the supply growth SG curve is normal (that there are no supply shocks), so that the normal relationships we traced in Section 4.3 all hold. Moreover, we will assume that the SG curve is based on inertial expectations.

To begin, we return the economy to its initial equilibrium point at $Q = Q_c$ ($U = U_c$) with price stability (zero inflation). The aggregate demand D curve and the short-run aggregate supply S curve have been fixed for several periods, so that the price level P has been constant; the D and S curves intersect at Q_c, and the nominal demand growth rate $y = 0\%$.

We will call this period 0. Our task is to construct the corresponding SG_0 and DG_0 curves illustrated in Figure 4.4.

At this point, it is convenient to restate the procedure for constructing the DG and SG curves in each period.

▶ To plot this period's DG and SG curves under inertial expectations, go to last period's $DG – SG$ intersection point and move vertically until you reach the horizontal y line (in a no-growth economy). Through this point, draw the DG curve. Return to last period's $DG – SG$ intersection point and move horizontally until you reach the vertical Q_c line. Through this point, draw the SG curve.

First, we will plot the DG_0 curve. We go to last period's $DG – SG$ intersection point, which is $(Q_c, 0\%)$. We then move *vertically* until we reach the horizontal $y = 0\%$ line and draw the DG_0 curve through this point. But we are already at the $y = 0\%$ line, so the DG_0 curve is drawn through the point $(Q_c, 0\%)$ with a negative slope equal to -1.

To plot the SG_0 curve, we go to last period's $DG – SG$ intersection point which is $(Q_c, 0\%)$. We then move *horizontally* until we reach the

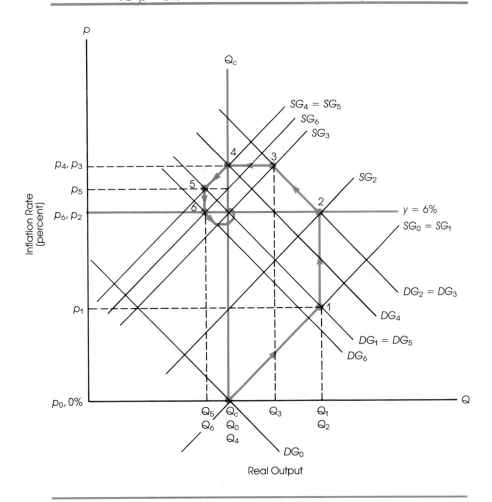

Initially, the nominal demand growth rate $y = 0\%$, the inflation rate $p = 0\%$, and real output $Q = Q_c$. In period 1, y is raised permanently to 6%, so that the y line is drawn with a height of 6%. Following our plotting rule, in period 1, SG_1 coincides with SG_0 but DG_1 lies 6% above DG_0; the economy therefore moves to the $DG_1 - SG_1$ intersection at point 1. In period 2, SG_2 lies above SG_1 and DG_2 lies above DG_1; the economy therefore moves to the $DG_2 - SG_2$ intersection at point 2. By continuing to follow the rule for plotting the DG and SG curves, we can see that the economy will eventually spiral into the long-run equilibrium point given by $p = y = 6\%$ and $Q = Q_c$. Thus, in the long run, the increase in the nominal demand growth rate to $y = 6\%$ raises the inflation rate p by 6% but has no effect on the level of real output Q or on the unemployment rate U.

vertical Q_c line and draw the SG_0 curve through that point. But we are already at the Q_c line, so the SG_0 curve is drawn through the point (Q_c, 0%) with a positive slope.

It follows that the SG_0 and DG_0 curves intersect at $Q = Q_c$ and $p = 0\%$ (point 0). This is the peaceful picture in period 0 that we will disturb forever—beginning in period 1.

We will suppose that nominal demand, propelled by a sustained monetary–expansion, grows by 6% ($y = 6\%$) in period 1 and in each subsequent period. Later, we will examine more carefully the role of monetary and fiscal policy in generating a sustained positive growth rate of nominal demand. Here, we will simply accept the assumption that $y = 6\%$ in all subsequent periods.

To obtain the DG_1 and SG_1 curves for period 1 (shown in Figure 4.4), we go to last period's DG-SG intersection point 0. From there, we move vertically until we reach the horizontal $y = 6\%$ line; through this point, we draw the DG_1 curve. We then return to point (Q_c, 0%) and move horizontally until we reach the vertical Q_c line (but we are already there). Through this point, we draw the SG_1 curve. SG_1 therefore coincides with SG_0.

Because DG_1 lies above DG_0 but SG_1 coincides with SG_0, the DG_1 and SG_1 curves intersect "northeast" of the equilibrium point ($Q = Q_c$, $p = 0\%$) for period 0. Thus, in period 1, demand growth raises both real output Q and the inflation rate p. The division between Q and p depends on the slope of the SG curve. Since the SG curve has a positive slope, it is certain that Q_1 exceeds $Q_0 = Q_c$ and that p_1 lies between 0% and $y = 6\%$. By equation (4.1), the sum of p_1 and q_1 must be 6% (the value of y).

Now what happens in period 2? We go to last period's DG-SG intersection point 1, shown in Figure 4.4. We then move vertically until we reach the horizontal $y = 6\%$ line; through this point, we draw the DG_2 curve. We then return to last period's intersection point 1 and move horizontally until we reach the vertical Q_c line; through this point, we draw the SG_2 curve.

How will the DG-SG intersection in period 2 (point 2) compare with the DG-SG intersection in period 1 (point 1)? In general, Q_2 may be greater than, equal to, or less than Q_1. You can see this if you experiment with alternative slopes for the SG curves. In our example, it is certain that p_2 must exceed p_1, because DG_2 lies above DG_1 and SG_2 lies above SG_1, so that the intersection must be higher. However, since p_1 is less than 6%, it is not certain whether p_2 is greater than, equal to, or less than 6%.

In Figure 4.4, it is convenient to draw the slope of the SG curve such that, in period 2, $p_2 = 6\%$ and $Q_2 = Q_1$. Then point 2 lies directly above point 1 at a point on the horizontal $y = 6\%$ line. Recall that

(4.1) $y \equiv p + q$

In period 2, $y = 6\%$, $p = 6\%$, and $q = 0\%$, so that $Q_2 = Q_1$. Thus, in period 2, the inflation rate equals the nominal demand growth rate ($p = y$) and output stays constant at a level greater than Q_c (U is less than U_c). What happens next?

THE SPIRAL PATH OF THE ECONOMY

If you suspect that the inflation rate p will equal y (6%) in the long run, you are right. But if you think that p_3 will stay at 6% (equal to p_2), you are wrong. To illustrate, let's construct the DG_3 and SG_3 curves in Figure 4.4. We go to $DG_2 - SG_2$ intersection point 2 and move vertically to the y line (but we are already there). Through this point, we draw the DG_3 curve, which coincides with the DG_2 curve. We then return to point 2 and move horizontally to the Q_c line; through this point, we draw the SG_3 curve. Two things are certain about the $DG - SG$ intersection point for period 3 (point 3), as shown in Figure 4.4. First, since DG_3 coincides with DG_2 but SG_3 lies above SG_2, p_3 must exceed p_2; hence, p_3 must exceed $y = 6\%$. Second, since DG_3 coincides with DG_2 but SG_3 lies to the left of SG_2, Q_3 must be less than Q_2.

A dramatic event has occurred in period 3. The inflation rate p (after a slow start) has risen above $y = 6\%$, and real output Q, which has been rising since demand growth began, has begun to decline. (Similarly, the unemployment rate U, which has been declining since demand growth began, has begun to rise.) Note that Q_3 still exceeds Q_c, so that U_3 is still less than U_c.

In period 4, we move vertically from $DG_3 - SG_3$ intersection point 3 to the y line; through this point, we draw the DG_4 curve. Returning to point 3, we then move horizontally to the Q_c line; through this point, we draw the SG_4 curve.

You can see in Figure 4.4 that another dramatic event has occurred: DG_4 lies below DG_3. For the first time since the start of this inflationary story, DG has shifted *downward* from one period to the next.

Since DG_4 lies below DG_3 but SG_4 lies above SG_3, p_4 may be greater than, equal to, or less than p_3. We will conveniently draw the slopes of the DG and SG curves such that $p_4 = p_3$, so that the $DG - SG$ intersection is at point 4. At last, the inflation rate has stopped rising. This means that the DG_4 and SG_4 curves intersect at $Q_4 = Q_c$, because the height of SG_4 at Q_c is p_3. At last, Q has returned to Q_c (and U to U_c).

▶ Note from Figure 4.4 that $Q_4 = Q_c$ ($U_4 = U_c$), and $p_4 = p_3$. Thus, in our model with inertial expectations, inflation stays constant when $Q = Q_c$ ($U = U_c$).

If you suspect that Q will converge to Q_c (and U to U_c) in the long run, you are right. But if you think that Q will stay at Q_c in period 5, you are wrong. In period 5, moving vertically from point 4 to the y line, we draw the DG_5 curve through this point. Then, moving horizontally from point 4 to the Q_c line (but we are already there), we draw the SG_5 curve, which coincides with the SG_4 curve, through this point.

Thus, since DG_5 lies below DG_4 but SG_5 coincides with SG_4, Q_5 is less than $Q_4 = Q_c$ and p_5 is less than p_4. Both of these events are dramatic. For the first time, real output Q has fallen below Q_c and the inflation rate p has peaked and started back toward $y = 6\%$.

To plot period 6, we move vertically from point 5 to the y line; through this point, we draw the DG_6 curve. Returning to point 5, we move horizontally to the Q_c line; through this point, we draw the SG_6 curve. Another dramatic event has now occurred. For the first time, the SG curve has shifted *downward*. With DG_6 lying below DG_5 and SG_6 lying below SG_5, p_6 is clearly less than p_5. Although Q_6 may be greater than, equal to, or less than Q_5, it is convenient to draw $Q_6 = Q_5$, so that $q_6 = 0\%$. Then p_6 must be 6%.

Instead of plotting the DG and SG curves for period 7, let's make an intuitive leap. You should sense that the path of the economy in Figure 4.4 will spiral inward until it converges to $Q = Q_c$ ($U = U_c$) and $p = y$ (6%) in the long run. For this is, in fact, the case:

▶ If y is held constant, then, in the long run, p will converge to y (in a no-growth economy), Q will converge to Q_c, and U will converge to U_c.

From Figure 4.4, it is easy to see that if the DG and SG curves eventually stop shifting, it must be at the intersection point of $Q = Q_c$ and $p = y$ (6%). Why? Suppose that in this period, the DG and SG curves intersect at $Q = Q_c$ and $p = y$. Will each curve remain in the same position next period, so that the $DG-SG$ intersection remains the same?

The answer is yes. To see why, we begin at this period's intersection point (Q_c, y) in Figure 4.4 and move vertically to the y line (but we are already there); through this point, we draw next period's DG curve, which coincides with this period's DG curve. Returning to point (Q_c, y), we then move horizontally to the Q_c line (but we are already there); through this point, we draw next period's SG curve, which coincides with this period's SG curve.

For any other point in the $Q-p$ diagram, at least one of the two curves will shift. If this period's p does not equal y, then next period's DG curve will not coincide with this period's DG curve. If this period's Q does not equal Q_c, then next period's SG curve will not coincide with this period's SG curve.

Our conclusions here focus on the point to which the inflationary process converges in Figure 4.4. Now we will concentrate on the *transi-*

tion path of the economy—the spiral path in Figure 4.4. When the nominal demand growth rate is raised from $y = 0\%$ to $y = 6\%$ in period 1, Q initially rises above Q_c (U initially falls below U_c). Then Q reaches a *peak* (U reaches a *trough*) and begins to move back toward its long-run equilibrium value Q_c.

▶ In an economy with inertial expectations, a permanent rise in the nominal demand growth rate y temporarily raises real output Q (reduces the unemployment rate U).

It is important to know more about the quantitative dimensions of the transition path. If y is raised from 0% to 6%, how much does the unemployment rate U decline before it reaches its trough? How long does it take the unemployment rate to reach its trough? To return to its long-run equilibrium?

These questions of magnitude are particularly crucial when the process is reversed (when *disinflation* is engineered through a permanent cut in the nominal demand growth rate y). We will postpone our analysis of the magnitudes of the transition path of the economy until Chapter 6.

4.5 The Consequence of Trying to Maintain $U < U_c$ $(Q > Q_c)$

Suppose that the economy is initially at $U = U_c$ $(Q = Q_c)$ and $p = 0\%$ in period 0; the DG and SG curves intersect at this point. Policymakers then decide to use *demand policy* (monetary and fiscal policy) to try to reduce the unemployment rate to U' (which is less than U_c) and to maintain the economy at $U = U'$. Equivalently, they wish to maintain real output at Q' (which is greater than Q_c). What happens? The answer is illustrated in Figure 4.5.

In this case, it is easier to construct the SG curve first. We begin at the intersection point for period 0 $(Q_c, 0\%)$ and move horizontally to the Q_c line (but we are already there); through this point, we draw the SG_1 curve, which coincides with SG_0. Policymakers want Q_1 to equal Q' (the value of Q that corresponds to U'), which exceeds Q_c. This requires the DG_1 curve to intersect SG_1 at point 1 where $Q = Q'$. What level of y_1 will yield this DG_1? From point 1, we follow the required DG_1 line northwest in Figure 4.5 until it reaches last period's Q (Q_c). The height of that point is the required y_1. Why?

To plot DG_1, we begin at last period's intersection (point 0) and move vertically to the y_1 line; through this point, we draw the DG_1 curve. This gives us the required DG_1 line—the DG line that intersects SG_1 at point 1. Thus, a monetary–fiscal expansion that raises y_1 to the indicated height yields $Q_1 = Q'$. Note that in period 1, y_1 exceeds p_1; this results in a positive q_1 and enables Q to increase from Q_c to Q'.

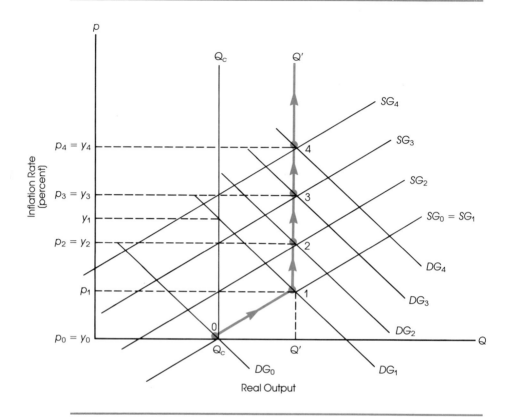

Real Output

Initially, the nominal demand growth rate $y = 0\%$, the inflation rate $p = 0\%$, and real output $Q = Q_c$ (hence, the unemployment rate $U = U_c$). Beginning in period 1, y is set in each period to achieve $Q = Q'$ (hence, $U = U'$), where $Q' > Q_c$ ($U' < U_c$). According to the rule for plotting the DG and SG curves, to move Q from Q_c to Q' in period 1 requires a rise in y from $y = 0\%$ to y_1. In period 2, y_2 is sufficient to hold Q at Q' (y_2 happens to be less than y_1). From this point on, however, y must rise in each period to sustain Q at Q'; since $p = y$ in each period, p must also rise steadily to sustain Q at Q'.

Now what happens in period 2? To draw SG_2, we go to point 1 and move horizontally until we reach the Q_c line; through this point , we draw the SG_2 curve, which lies above SG_1. If Q_2 is to equal Q' (so that U_2 will equal U'), then the DG_2 curve must be set above DG_1, so that SG_2 and DG_2 can intersect at point 2. But this means that p_2 will exceed p_1 (the inflation rate will rise).

What level of y_2 will yield the required DG_2? From point 2, we follow the required DG_2 line northwest in Figure 4.5 to last period's Q (Q'); but we are already there. If y_2 has this height, then DG_2 intersects SG_2 at point 2. Note that $p_2 = y_2$. This makes sense because, with $Q_2 = Q_1$, $q_2 = 0\%$.

In each subsequent period, the SG curve will be higher than in the previous period and the DG curve must be shifted up by an equal amount to keep Q at Q'. But this means that the inflation rate p will rise in each period and that the nominal demand growth rate y must be raised in each period. In fact, in each subsequent period, $p = y$ (and $q = 0\%$).

To summarize the conclusion from our diagram:

▶ To maintain the unemployment rate U at U', which is less than U_c, the inflation rate p must increase in each period.

We have now detected one possible reason why inflation arises. Policymakers may not be satisfied with an unemployment rate of U_c and may try to "stimulate" the economy to achieve and maintain a U that is less than U_c. But the attempt to maintain such a U' by demand expansion accelerates inflation.

Our analysis does not indicate that there is no policy capable of reducing the unemployment rate without accelerating inflation. Given the current U_c of the economy, however, an attempt to reduce U below this U_c by demand policy will result in accelerating inflation. In Chapter 7, we will consider how the constant inflation unemployment rate U_c may be reduced by supply-oriented policies.

4.6 Demand Inflation in a Growing Economy

Thus far, our examination of inflation has been based on a no-growth economy in which the labor force and labor productivity are held constant. This implies that if U stays constant, then Q remains constant. But in a growing economy, the Q_c that corresponds to a constant U_c increases in each period. A simple example will illustrate this point.

Suppose that in period 0, the labor force is 100 persons and labor productivity (output per worker) is 2. If U_c is 7% and $U = U_c$, then 93 persons will be employed and 7 persons will be unemployed. If labor productivity $A = 2$, real output Q will be 186. Therefore, $Q = 186$ is the output that occurs in period 0 when $U = U_c$, so that $Q_c = 186$.

Now suppose that the labor force grows to 101 in period 1, so that *labor-force growth f* = 1%, and labor productivity grows to 2.04, so that labor productivity growth a = 2%. If $U = U_c = 7\%$, then 93.93 persons (93% of 101) will be employed and output $Q = 191.6172$ (2.04 × 93.93). This is the output that occurs in period 1 when $U = U_c$, so that $Q_c = 191.6172$ in period 1.

To summarize, labor-force and labor productivity growth both cause Q_c to grow. In fact, Q_c grows by approximately 3%—the sum of labor-force growth (1%) and labor productivity growth (2%). (Confirm this by taking 3% of 186 and adding it to 186; you will obtain 191.58.)

The NORMAL REAL OUTPUT GROWTH RATE q_c (the growth rate of Q_c) equals the *labor-force growth rate f* plus the *labor productivity growth rate a*, or

(4.6) $q_c = f + a$

With Q_c growing at the rate of $q_c = a + f$, we have two choices. We can diagram the rightward movement of Q for each period, due to the growth of Q_c, as it fluctuates around Q_c. Or we can perform our analysis *relative* to Q_c, bearing in mind that Q_c is growing at the rate of $q_c = a + f$. We will adopt the second course.

Thus, our diagrams illustrating $DG-SG$ analysis (such as Figure 4.4) remain the same, but our interpretation must be modified. Earlier, we showed that at a constant nominal demand growth rate, the economy eventually converges to $Q = Q_c$ ($U = U_c$) after oscillating above and below Q_c. This conclusion is still correct for a growing economy. We must simply recognize that Q_c itself is growing at the rate of $q_c = a + f$ throughout the process.

For example, suppose that labor productivity $a = 1\%$ and labor-force growth $f = 2\%$, so that $q_c = 3\%$. In initial equilibrium, prior to nominal demand growth, Q is therefore not constant; it is growing by 3% in each period. Once the nominal demand growth rate is raised permanently, q (the growth rate of Q) initially rises above 3%, so that Q is growing at a faster rate than Q_c. When Q reaches its peak and begins to decline in our $DG-SG$ diagram, the decline is relative to Q_c, which is growing at a rate of q_c. Hence, the decline in Q relative to Q_c means that q has fallen below 3%. In final equilibrium, $q = 3\%$.

ADJUSTED NOMINAL DEMAND GROWTH ŷ

To adapt our $DG-SG$ analysis to a growing economy, the concept of adjusted nominal demand growth $\hat{y}$ replaces nominal demand growth y.

The ADJUSTED NOMINAL DEMAND GROWTH RATE $\hat{y}$ is the nominal demand growth rate y that is *in excess of* the normal real output growth rate q_c, or

(4.7) $\hat{y} \equiv y - q_c$

In a growing economy, we replace nominal demand growth y with adjusted nominal demand growth $\hat{y}$ and the horizontal y line with the horizontal $\hat{y}$ line.

Consider the initial, noninflationary equilibrium, at which $p = 0\%$. In a no-growth economy, with $q_c = 0\%$, a nominal demand growth rate of $y = 0\%$ will sustain this equilibrium ($y = p + q$). In a growing economy, with $q_c = 3\%$, an adjusted nominal demand growth rate of $\hat{y} = 0\%$ will sustain the initial equilibrium with $p = 0\%$. This implies that a nominal demand growth rate of $y = 3\%$ is required.

We have already seen what happens when y is raised from 0% to 6% in a no-growth economy. In a growing economy, the same analysis tells us what happens when $\hat{y}$ is raised from 0% to 6% (equivalently, when y is raised from 3% to 9%). In our no-growth economy, p converges to y (6%). In our growing economy, p converges to $\hat{y}$ (6%).

When we plot the DG curve for a growing economy, we again begin at last period's DG–SG intersection point, but now we move vertically to the horizontal $\hat{y}$ line. For example, in initial equilibrium with $p = 0\%$, the $\hat{y}$ line is at 0%; the DG and SG curves intersect at $Q = Q_c$ and $p = 0\%$; $y = 3\%$, and $q = 3\%$. In final equilibrium with $p = 6\%$, the $\hat{y}$ line is at 6%, the DG and SG curves intersect at $Q = Q_c$ and $p = 6\%$; $y = 9\%$, and $q = 3\%$.

▶ To draw the DG curve in a growing economy, we use the $\hat{y}$ line instead of the y line, where $\hat{y} \equiv y - q_c$.

Hence, our earlier rules for constructing the DG and SG curves in a no-growth economy can be modified to apply to a growing economy simply by replacing y with $\hat{y}$:

▶ To find this period's DG and SG curves, go to last period's DG–SG intersection point and move vertically until you reach the horizontal $\hat{y}$ line (in a growing economy); through this point, draw the DG curve. Return to last period's intersection and move horizontally until you reach the vertical Q_c line; through this point, draw the SG curve.

Because the $\hat{y}$ line (not the y line) plays the key role in the DG–SG diagram for a growing economy, it follows that the condition for long-run equilibrium must also be modified by replacing y with $\hat{y}$:

▶ If y is held constant, so that $\hat{y}$ is held constant, then, in the long run, p will converge to $\hat{y}$ (in a growing economy), Q will converge to Q_c, and U will converge to U_c.

Thus, if the normal real output growth rate $q_c = 3\%$ and the nominal demand growth rate is fixed at $y = 9\%$ (which implies that the adjusted nominal demand growth rate is fixed at $\hat{y} = 6\%$), then the inflation rate p will converge to 6% in the long run.

Of course, p will eventually converge to $\hat{y}$ even if $q_c = 0\%$; in this special case, $y = \hat{y}$. Thus, the rules for a growing economy are always valid, even in the special case of a normal real output growth rate of $q_c = 0\%$. We should always focus on $\hat{y}$ (not y) to determine the long-run inflation rate p.

Once the $\hat{y}$ line replaces the y line, our $DG-SG$ diagram remains exactly the same for a growing economy as it is for a no-growth economy. The Q for each period should be interpreted relative to the Q_c for that period. Thus, if $Q_c = 100$ in period 0, we keep Q_c fixed in our diagram. But for each period, the value of Q_c rises. (In period 1, Q_c may be, say, 103; in period 2, slightly above 106; and so on.)

RELATIVITY

An analogy may be helpful. A desperately bored traveler sits in the passenger car of a train. Beginning at the center of the car, our tragic hero walks to the front of the car, does an about-face, and walks back toward the middle of the car. After crossing the middle line of the car but before reaching the back of the car, he does another about-face even sooner than the last one and walks across the middle line again. As he continues in this way, his about-faces become more and more rapid and occur closer and closer to the middle line of the car. At last he "converges" to the center of the car, where, to the amazement of the other passengers, he collapses into his seat. The passenger's oscillations exactly mirror the oscillations of Q in Figure 4.4.

Now comes the key point. We have not yet said whether the car is at rest or in motion relative to the earth. Suppose that our goal is to map our traveler's behavior relative to the earth. If the car is in motion, his behavior relative to the earth may at first appear to be complex. But our strategy of analysis is simple. Analyze the passenger's motion relative to the car, observe the car's motion relative to the earth, and add the two together.

This is what we have done in this chapter. We began by analyzing the economy's motion relative to Q_c. Now, in this section, we recognize that Q_c is "in motion." The motion of the output of the economy Q is the sum of its motion relative to Q_c and the motion of Q_c itself.

In a no-growth economy, we saw that whenever Q increases in the $DG-SG$ diagram, U declines; whenever Q decreases in the $DG-SG$ diagram, U rises. This remains true in a growing economy. When we observe that Q is rising from one period to the next in the $DG-SG$ diagram, we can be sure that U is declining. But our interpretation must be modified.

When Q rises in the $DG-SG$ diagram, it means that Q is growing at a faster rate than Q_c; therefore, q exceeds q_c. The proper interpretation is that if q exceeds q_c, then U declines. Symmetrically, when Q decreases in the diagram, it means that Q is growing at a slower rate than Q_c;

therefore, q is less than q_c. The proper interpretation is that if q is less than q_c, then U rises.

(4.8)   If Q grows at the same rate as Q_c ($q = q_c$), then U stays constant.
If Q grows at a faster rate than Q_c ($q > q_c$), then U declines.
If Q grows at a slower rate than Q_c ($q < q_c$), then U rises.

For example, suppose that $q_c = 3\%$ (because labor-force growth $f = 1\%$ and labor productivity growth $a = 2\%$). If Q grows by 3%, then U will stay constant. Q must grow at a faster rate than 3% to reduce U. If Q grows at a slower rate than 3%, U will rise.

4.7   The Monetary View of Inflation

We have seen that the inflation rate p will converge to the adjusted nominal demand growth rate $\hat{y}$ in the long run. We have also referred to a monetary–fiscal policy expansion as the source of nominal demand growth y. Let's elaborate. We can now state the *monetary view of inflation*, which—in its flexible, "approximate" form—is held by many economists.

According to the MONETARY VIEW OF INFLATION, the money-supply growth rate m normally governs the nominal demand growth rate y. Therefore, in the long run, m largely controls the inflation rate p.

How does the monetary view of inflation relate to our $DG-SG$ analysis? According to that analysis, the inflation rate p will converge to the adjusted nominal demand growth rate $\hat{y} \equiv y - q_c$ in the long run. The monetary view of inflation is simply a hypothesis about the source of $\hat{y}$. If money-supply growth m controls $\hat{y}$, then it will control the long-run inflation rate p.

$DG-SG$ analysis is relevant for any source of nominal demand growth. The monetary view holds that money-supply growth is the dominant determinant of nominal demand growth and that fiscal policy and autonomous consumption and investment have a minor influence over the long run. $DG-SG$ analysis applies whether or not the monetary hypothesis is correct.

We can better understand the monetary view of inflation if we familiarize ourselves with the concept of the *velocity of money V*, which is defined as the ratio of nominal GNP to the money supply M:

(4.9) $$V \equiv \frac{PQ}{M}$$

This is simply a definition. Why the term "velocity"? Suppose that for a given money supply M, PQ rises; this means that each dollar of money must be circulating faster. More transactions are occurring, thereby generating a higher income PQ for the given money supply.

Multiplying both sides of definition (4.9) by M, we obtain

(4.10) $$MV \equiv PQ$$

Equation (4.10) is true simply due to definition (4.9). V automatically assumes the necessary value to make equation (4.10) hold.

Applying the math growth-rate rule to equation (4.10) gives us

(4.11) $$m + v \equiv p + q \equiv y$$

where v = the percentage growth rate of the velocity of money

Equation (4.11) is true due to definition (4.9) and the math growth-rate rule. v automatically takes on whatever value is needed to make equation (4.11) hold. Consider two examples. If $p = 0\%$, $q = 3\%$, and $m = 1\%$, then $v = 2\%$; if $p = 6\%$, $q = 3\%$, and $m = 7\%$, then $v = 2\%$.

Now consider the constant *velocity growth hypothesis:*

According to the constant VELOCITY GROWTH HYPOTHESIS, the normal value of the *growth rate of the velocity of money v* is roughly constant over time. Hence, money-supply growth m governs nominal demand growth y; specifically, $y = m + v$.

Note that the velocity growth hypothesis does not insist that v is constant from one year to the next. v may fluctuate, but its normal value over a period of several years is regarded as constant. Also note that the hypothesis does not assert that the velocity of money V is itself constant — only that its growth rate v is constant. For example, a constant v of 2% satisfies the hypothesis; on average, the velocity of money V will grow by 2% per year.

If the constant velocity growth hypothesis is correct, then m will normally govern $p + q$. For example, if v is constant at 2% and $m = 1\%$, then $p + q = 3\%$; but if m is raised by 6% to 7%, then $p + q$ will be raised by 6% to 9%. The change in m will equal the change in $p + q$. Thus

(4.12) If velocity growth v is constant, then $\Delta m = \Delta y = \Delta p + \Delta q$

Thus far, we have said that if m increases by 6%, then $p + q$ will increase by 6%. But we have not yet said anything about the division of Δm between Δp and Δq. In the short run, our DG–SG analysis tells us that if SG has a positive slope, then the upward shift of the DG curve, which is now due to the increase in m, will be divided between p and q.

But that same analysis also tells us that if the nominal demand growth rate y is held constant, then q will eventually return to q_c (Q will settle at Q_c) in the long run. For example, if Q_c grows by 3% per year, then Q will eventually grow by 3% per year. But this means that there will be no change in q in the long run. The growth rate of q begins at q_c and ends at q_c, so that $\Delta q = 0\%$ in hypothesis (4.12) in the long run. Hence, we see that

(4.13)   If velocity growth v is constant, then in the long run $\Delta p = \Delta m$.

According to the monetary view of inflation embodied in hypothesis (4.13), the inflation rate p will eventually rise permanently by $X\%$ if and only if the money-supply growth rate m is permanently increased by $X\%$. For example, with $v = 2\%$ and $q_c = 3\%$, p will increase permanently from 0% to 6% if and only if m increases permanently from 1% to 7%. ($X\% = 6\%$ in this example.)

What value of m will result in $p = 0\%$ in the long run? Call this value m_0. We can obtain an expression for m_0 by rewriting equation (4.11):

(4.11) $$m + v \equiv p + q$$

In the long run, q converges to q_c, so that

$$m_0 + v = 0\% + q_c$$

Subtracting v from both sides, we see that

(4.14)   If velocity growth v is constant, then the growth rate of money m_0 that will achieve zero inflation in the long run is given by $m_0 = q_c - v$.

For example, if $q_c = 3\%$ and $v = 2\%$, then $m_0 = 1\%$.

Stated verbally, equation (4.14) tells us that the money-supply growth rate m_0 that will achieve zero inflation in the long run is equal to the normal growth rate of real output q_c minus the normal growth rate of the velocity of money v.

In Chapter 5, we will review the history of inflation in the United States over the last few decades and assess the empirical validity of the monetary view of inflation over that period.

4.8 Supply Inflation

Thus far, inflation has been completely demand-generated. True, the SG curve did play an important role, shifting throughout the inflationary story shown in Figure 4.4. But if the DG curve had remained in its period 0 position, the *SG* curve would have stayed in its period 0 position. The *SG* curve shifts only in response to shifts in the *DG* curve when inflation is demand-generated.

It is now time to consider the *SG* curve in a leading — rather than merely a supporting — role. Can inflation be supply-generated? Can the *SG* curve shift up before the *DG* curve shifts up?

Suppose that the economy is initially in long-run equilibrium; the *SG* and *DG* curves have been constant for several periods, intersecting at $Q = Q_c$ and $p = 0\%$. Thus far, we have assumed that the *SG* curve never shifts up unless the *DG* curve shifts up first. Why?

Recall equation (4.2):

(4.2) $$p \equiv k + w - a$$

The *SG* curve indicates the p that firms would set at each Q. The *SG* curve does not shift unless one of the three terms on the right side of equation (4.2) changes at a given Q. We have assumed that k and a are constant. We have also assumed that at a particular Q (and the associated U), w depends on the inflation rate in the previous period p_{-1}. If p_{-1} is constant for several periods, then w will be constant.

Supply inflation occurs if k, a, or w increases at a given Q and p_{-1}. A change in any of these variables will raise p in equation (4.2). When firms set a higher p at any given Q, the *SG* curve shifts up.

Let's consider an increase in k. The data in Table 4.1 show that, on average, k — the growth rate of the price – unit labor cost ratio K — is close to 0%. But this does not mean that $k = 0\%$ in every year. If k rises from 0% to a positive value in a given year, this will raise p in that year.

Why may the P–ULC ratio K increase in a given year, so that k becomes positive in that year? Recall that K is the ratio of price to unit *labor* cost (not unit cost). Hence, one reason why K might increase is an increase in nonlabor cost. To cite an important example from the 1970s, if the world price of oil increases, then the P–ULC ratio K must increase to cover the higher price of oil. Similarly, an increase in the world price of raw materials will also raise the P–ULC ratio K.

Now let's consider an example of a permanent rise in the P–ULC ratio K. Suppose that the K ratio has been 1.50 but that it becomes 1.53 permanently beginning in period 1. In period 1, the percentage increase in K is 2%; hence, $k = 2\%$. But in each subsequent period, k returns to 0%, while K remains constant at 1.53.

In the *DG* – *SG* diagram for period 1, the *SG* curve shifts up; the p that producers set at each Q will increase due to the increase in k given by equation (4.2). What happens to Q and p? The answer, of course, depends on the *DG* curve. We will consider two cases.

In the first case, shown in Figure 4.6, policymakers choose to ignore the upward shift of the *SG* curve and to hold the *DG* curve constant.

FIGURE 4.6 NONACCOMMODATION OF A SUPPLY SHOCK

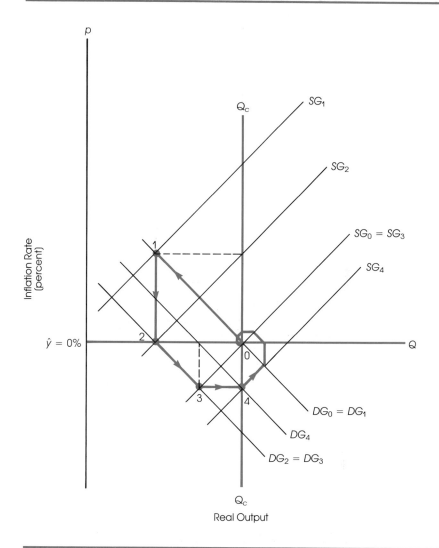

Initially, the adjusted nominal demand growth rate $\hat{y} = 0\%$, the inflation rate $p = 0\%$, and real output $Q = Q_c$. In period 1, a supply shock shifts the SG curve up to SG_1. A policy of "nonaccommodation" means that $\hat{y}$ is kept at 0%. From this point on, we follow the plotting rule to construct the DG and SG curves for each period. After a *transitional recession*, the economy will return to its initial equilibrium point ($Q = Q_c$, $p = 0\%$).

Thus, Q_1 is less than Q_c (U_1 is greater than U_c). Beginning in period 2, k has returned to its normal value of 0%. From then on, the SG curve is constructed according to our plotting rule, so that the SG curve shifts to the right. Eventually the SG and DG curves return to their period 0 positions; the inflation proves to be temporary.

In the second case, shown in Figure 4.7, policymakers are committed to setting a nominal demand growth rate y for each period, so that Q stays at Q_c (U stays at U_c). In period 1, a monetary–fiscal policy expansion shifts the DG curve up enough to keep the SG_1–DG_1 intersection at Q_c. Note that the inflation rate p_1 is positive. In period 2, even though k is now back to 0%, our rule for plotting the SG curve implies that it will remain constant; SG_2 coincides with SG_1. Hence, to keep $Q_2 = Q_c$,

FIGURE 4.7 ACCOMMODATION OF A SUPPLY SHOCK

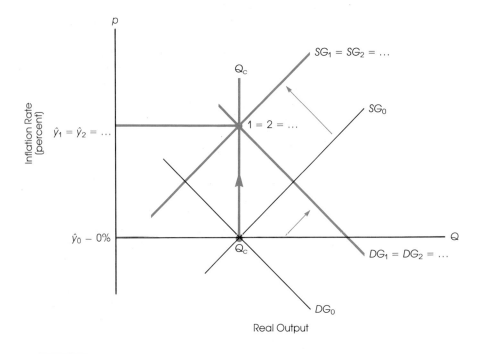

Initially, the adjusted nominal demand growth rate $\hat{y} = 0\%$, the inflation rate $p = 0\%$, and real output $Q = Q_c$. In period 1, a supply shock shifts the SG curve up to SG_1. A policy of "accommodation" means that $\hat{y}$ is raised immediately to keep Q at Q_c and is set in each period to maintain Q at Q_c. From this point on, we follow the rule for plotting the DG and SG curves to construct the DG and SG curves for each period. The DG and SG curves and the $\hat{y}$ line remain permanently at their period 1 values, and the inflation rate p is permanently raised to the new adjusted nominal demand growth rate $\hat{y}$.

policymakers must keep DG constant, so that DG_2 coincides with DG_1. But the DG curve must be kept in this position in every subsequent period to prevent Q from declining below Q_c. If this is done, then the inflation rate p will remain at its period 1 level permanently.

To summarize, in response to an increase in the price–unit labor cost ratio K — if policymakers are willing to accept a temporary decrease in Q to below Q_c (a temporary rise in U to above U_c) and to hold the DG curve constant at its period 0 level, then eventually the inflation rate will return to $p = 0\%$ and Q will return to Q_c (U will return to U_c). But if policymakers are committed to avoiding any rise in U to above U_c (any decrease in Q to below Q_c), then a permanent increase in the inflation rate p will result.

We describe the first case by saying that policymakers refuse to "ratify" or to "accommodate" the *supply shock* or "cost–push" pressure. In the second case, we say that policymakers ratify or accommodate the *supply inflation*. Without demand ratification, supply-generated inflation will prove temporary and will be eliminated by a recession; with demand ratification to avoid a recession, supply-generated inflation can prove permanent.

If the demand response is crucial to these results, then why do we refer to "supply" inflation and to "supply" shocks? First, even if DG is held constant, then the inflation rate p rises in period 1. Hence, without any change in the nominal demand growth rate y, the inflation rate p will rise in the short run.

Second, the supply shock presents policymakers with a dilemma. They can prevent a permanent rise in inflation only if they are willing to accept a temporary rise in unemployment. A demand-generated inflation presents no such dilemma. If policymakers keep the DG curve at DG_0, intersecting Q_c at $p = 0\%$, then U will remain at U_c. A supply shock, such as an increase in the P–ULC ratio K, makes it more difficult for policymakers to hold the DG curve at DG_0, because a temporary rise in U to above U_c will result.

Now let's consider labor productivity growth a. We can handle this case quickly. A temporary decline in a will have the same impact as the temporary increase in k that we just analyzed. Thus, if productivity growth declines temporarily, the SG curve will shift up. If the DG curve is held constant, the upward shift of the SG curve will produce a rise in the inflation rate p in the short run. Moreover, policymakers will face the same dilemma — the inability to prevent a permanent rise in inflation unless they accept a temporary rise in unemployment.

Now let's consider wage inflation w. Thus far, wage inflation has been "well behaved." The wage inflation rate w has been dependent on the unemployment rate U (a proxy for labor demand relative to labor supply) and on the expected inflation rate p^e. Under inertial (adaptive) expectations, the expected inflation rate is equal to last period's inflation rate ($p^e = p_{-1}$). Hence, w has been linked precisely—and reliably—to two economic variables, U and p_{-1}.

But suppose that w is occasionally rebellious. For example, let's assume that, at times, p^e becomes volatile and unpredictable. Not only does p^e vary significantly from p_{-1} in some periods, but it does not appear to be closely linked to any other economic variable. This doesn't mean that there are no causes of p^e—only that we cannot hope to detect them.*

Suppose, then, that at times, w rises exogenously, without any clearly detectable cause; otherwise, w behaves appropriately, as influenced by U and p_{-1}. The result is essentially the same as in the cases of k and a. In period 1, the SG curve will shift up. If DG is held constant, the inflation rate p will rise in the short run.

What happens next to the economy depends on how policymakers respond. If they refuse to ratify this *wage shock* and accept a rise in U above U_c, then eventually the inflation rate will return to $p = 0\%$ (and U will return to U_c). If they adjust demand to prevent U from rising above U_c, then the wage shock will result in a permanent increase in the inflation rate p.

If we compare supply-generated and demand-generated inflation, an important difference emerges:

▶ When an upward supply shock occurs, our rule for constructing an SG curve is temporarily suspended; the height of the SG curve at Q_c will exceed last period's inflation rate p_{-1}. It therefore follows that hypothesis (4.5) is also temporarily suspended; if the DG curve is held constant, then the inflation rate p will rise even though Q declines below Q_c (and U rises above U_c). Hence, in the period when a supply shock occurs, inflation will not stay constant if $Q = Q_c$ ($U = U_c$).

It should be emphasized, however, that our rule is suspended only in the period in which the supply shock occurs. Thereafter, it becomes valid again. As we will see in Chapter 5, supply shocks do not appear to occur frequently, so that these behavioral rules are valid for most years.

SUMMARY

1. The *demand growth DG curve* indicates the combinations of real output Q and the *(price) inflation rate p* (the percentage growth rate of the price level P) that are feasible, given monetary and fiscal policy. If the initial period Q is assigned a value of 100 and monetary

---

* The hypothesis of an exogenous w is set out by Sidney Weintraub in *Capitalism's Inflation and Unemployment Crisis* (Reading, Mass.: Addison-Wesley, 1978).

policy is adjusted to achieve a targeted *nominal demand growth rate* y, then the *DG* curve is a *straight line* with a slope of approximately -1.

2. To plot the *DG* curve for a given period, go to last period's *DG – SG* intersection point and move *vertically* until you reach the horizontal $\hat{y}$ line. Through this point, draw the *DG* curve with a constant slope approximately equal to -1. The *adjusted nominal demand growth rate* $\hat{y}$ is defined as $y - q_c$, where q_c is the *normal real output growth rate* (the sum of *normal labor-force growth* f and *normal labor productivity growth* a). For example, if $y = 9\%$ and $q_c = 3\%$, then $\hat{y} = 6\%$.

3. The *supply growth SG curve* gives the inflation rate p that firms will set at each level of real output Q. The *SG* curve has a positive slope, because if Q increases (and the associated unemployment rate U decreases), then the *wage inflation rate* w increases, the *growth rate of the unit labor cost* ulc increases, and the inflation rate p increases. The *SG* curve shifts up if the expected inflation rate p^e rises because, at a given Q (and U), a rise in p^e raises w and, hence, ulc and p.

4. Q^* is the value of Q (and U^* is the associated value of U) at which firms will set the inflation rate equal to the expected inflation rate ($p = p^e$). If expectations are inertial, so that $p^e = p_{-1}$, then at Q^* firms will set $p = p_{-1}$ (the inflation rate will stay constant). Hence, with inertial expectations, the economy possesses a constant inflation output Q_c and a corresponding constant inflation unemployment rate U_c. If the unemployment rate U rises above U_c (if Q falls below Q_c), then p is less than p_{-1} and the inflation rate p declines.

5. To plot the *SG* curve for a given period when expectations are inertial, go to last period's *DG – SG* intersection point and move *horizontally* until you reach the vertical Q_c line. Through this point, draw this period's *SG* curve with a positive slope.

6. If the adjusted nominal demand growth rate $\hat{y}$ is raised from 0% to 6%, then, in the short run (assuming inertial expectations), p will rise above 0% and Q will rise above Q_c (q will rise above q_c); in the long run, p will converge to $\hat{y}$ (6%) and Q will return to Q_c (q will return to q_c).

7. To maintain the unemployment rate U at a U' below U_c, the inflation rate p must increase in each period.

8. According to the *monetary view of inflation,* the *money-supply growth rate* m determines the nominal demand growth rate y, and hence the adjusted nominal demand growth rate $\hat{y}$. Thus, m determines the long-run inflation rate, which must equal $\hat{y}$.

9. *Supply inflation* occurs when the *SG* curve shifts up before the *DG* curve shifts up as a result of an increase in k or ulc at a given Q. If nominal demand growth is not raised, then the supply inflation

will prove temporary and will be eliminated by a recession. If nominal demand growth is raised to avoid a recession, then the rise in inflation will be permanent.

QUESTIONS

Assume inertial expectations in all of the following questions.

4.1 Assume that the normal real output growth rate $q_c = 3\%$ and that, for many periods, the nominal demand growth rate $y = 3\%$, so that the adjusted nominal demand growth rate $\hat{y} = 0\%$.

a. To what inflation rate p, real output growth rate q, and real output level Q has the economy converged? Call this the period 0 equilibrium, and draw the $\hat{y}$ line, the Q_c line, and the DG_0 and SG_0 curves.

b. If labor productivity growth $a = 2\%$, to what wage inflation rate w has the economy converged?

c. Assume that the nominal demand growth rate y is raised permanently from 3% to 12% beginning in period 1. Draw the new $\hat{y}$ line, and find the $DG_1 - SG_1$ intersection point.

d. Draw the DG and SG curves for periods 2–6.

e. To what inflation rate p, real output growth rate q, real output level Q, and wage inflation rate w will the economy converge?

4.2 Assume that $U_c = 7\%$ and that, initially, $p = 0\%$, $q = q_c$, and $Q = Q_c$. If demand policymakers try to hold the unemployment rate at a U' less than 7% (at a Q' greater than Q_c):
  a. Draw the SG_1 and DG_1 curves and the $\hat{y}_1$ line.
  b. Draw the SG and DG curves and the $\hat{y}$ lines for periods 2 and 3.
  c. What will happen to the inflation rate p if the unemployment rate U is held at U'?

4.3 Assume that the *"monetary view of inflation"* is correct and that the normal growth rate of the velocity of money $v = 2\%$.
  a. At the initial equilibrium in Question 4.1, where $p = 0\%$, what has the money-supply growth rate m been for many periods?
  b. In Question 4.1(c), to what value is m raised permanently?
  c. In Question 4.2, what has m been initially for many periods?
  d. In Question 4.2, what must happen to m to hold U at U'?

4.4 Suppose that the economy is initially at $p = 0\%$ and $Q = Q_c$. Then a supply shock shifts the SG curve up by 3% in period 1.
  a. If $\hat{y}$ is held at 0%, find the $DG - SG$ intersection points in periods $1-4$. To what will p and Q converge in the long run?
  b. Show how $\hat{y}$ can be set to keep Q at Q_c. If this is done, what will happen to p in subsequent periods?

4.5 Why does the SG curve have a positive slope? Why does a change in the expected inflation rate p^e shift the SG curve?

4.6 Why does the rule for shifting the SG curve depend on inertial expectations?

4.7 Contrast our inflation–unemployment relationship (4.5) with the Phillips curve hypothesis.

5 Inflation: History, Prevention, and Consequences

In this chapter, we will review the recent history of inflation in the United States, ask how inflation can be prevented, and examine the consequences of inflation.

5.1 Inflation in the United States Over the Past Two Decades

How did inflation arise in the United States during the 1960s and the 1970s? Why did inflation decline in the first half of the 1980s? Does the demand growth–supply growth model we developed in Chapter 4 help to explain the actual data of the U.S. economy? This chapter will focus on the rise of inflation in the 1960s and 1970s. Chapter 6 will analyze the decline of inflation in the first half of the 1980s.

In Table 5.1, two measures of inflation for 1960–1985 are given: the percentage growth rate of the GNP deflator p, and the percentage growth rate of the Consumer Price Index (cpi). In most years, these two measures are quite close. But they do differ significantly in several years (for example, 1974 and 1979). The broad pattern of inflation is the same, whichever measure is used.

The *GNP deflator* is the broadest measure of the price of all goods and services produced in the United States in a given year, because it includes all components of the GNP. By contrast, the *Consumer Price Index* (CPI) includes only goods that are consumed in the United States in a given year. In Table 5.1, the growth rate of the GNP deflator is denoted by p; the growth rate of the CPI is denoted by cpi. Both price indexes are discussed further in Appendix 1A.

It is important to recognize two other differences when interpreting economic data in the 1970s, which saw a large increase in the world price of oil by the Organization of Petroleum Exporting Countries (OPEC) and sharp swings in interest rates. First, the GNP deflator mea-

TABLE 5.1

U.S. DATA 1960–1985 (all numbers are percentages)

Year	p	cpi	q	U	y	m1	m2	r	Q_c surplus
1960	1.6	1.6	2.2	5.4	3.9	0.6	4.9	4.82	0.5
1961	1.0	1.0	2.6	6.5	3.6	3.3	7.4	4.50	0.3
1962	2.2	1.1	5.3	5.4	7.6	1.8	8.1	4.50	−0.9
1963	1.6	1.2	4.1	5.5	5.6	3.7	8.4	4.50	−0.1
1964	1.5	1.3	5.3	5.0	7.1	4.7	8.0	4.50	−1.2
1965	2.7	1.7	5.8	4.4	8.5	4.7	8.1	4.54	−1.2
1966	3.6	2.9	5.8	3.7	9.5	2.5	4.5	5.63	−2.3
1967	2.6	2.9	2.9	3.7	5.8	6.6	9.2	5.61	−3.8
1968	5.0	4.2	4.1	3.5	9.3	7.7	8.0	6.30	−3.1
1969	5.6	5.4	2.4	3.4	8.0	3.2	4.1	7.96	−1.7
1970	5.5	5.9	−0.3	4.8	5.4	5.2	6.6	7.91	−2.4
1971	5.7	4.3	2.8	5.8	8.6	6.6	13.5	5.72	−2.3
1972	4.7	3.3	5.0	5.5	10.0	9.2	13.0	5.25	−2.1
1973	6.5	6.2	5.2	4.8	12.1	5.5	6.9	8.03	−1.8
1974	9.1	11.0	−0.5	5.5	8.3	4.4	5.5	10.81	−1.6
1975	9.8	9.1	−1.3	8.3	8.5	4.9	12.6	7.86	−2.3
1976	6.4	5.8	4.9	7.6	11.5	6.6	13.7	6.84	−1.8
1977	6.7	6.5	4.7	6.9	11.7	8.1	10.6	6.83	−1.8
1978	7.3	7.7	5.3	6.0	13.0	8.3	8.0	9.06	−1.8
1979	8.9	11.3	2.5	5.8	11.5	7.2	7.8	12.67	−1.4
1980	9.0	13.5	−0.2	7.0	8.9	6.6	8.9	15.27	−1.8
1981	9.7	10.4	1.9	7.5	11.7	6.5	10.0	18.87	−1.3
1982	6.4	6.1	−2.5	9.5	3.7	8.8	8.9	14.86	−1.8
1983	3.8	3.2	3.5	9.5	7.4	9.8	12.0	10.79	−2.6
1984	4.1	4.3	6.5	7.4	11.0	5.8	8.4	12.04	−4.0
1985	3.3	3.6	2.3	7.1	5.8	11.9	8.1	9.93	−4.7

SOURCES: *Economic Report of the President 1986* for all variables except Q_c surplus. *p* is the percentage change in the implicit GNP deflator, cpi is the percentage change in the Consumer Price Index, *q* is the growth rate of real GNP, *U* is the unemployment rate, *y* is the growth rate of nominal GNP, and *r* is the prime interest rate charged by banks. Note that the sum of *p* and *q* approximately equals the nominal GNP growth rate *y*. *m1* is the growth rate of the narrowly defined money supply, and *m2* is the growth rate of the broadly defined money supply (see page 214). Q_c surplus (as a percentage of GNP) is estimated as follows: actual (federal) surplus and actual *U* are given in the *Report*. Based on Table 6.2 (page 258), we assume that the constant inflation unemployment rate U_c increases smoothly from 5.5% in 1960 to 6.9% in 1985. Based on Congressional Budget Office report *The Economic and Budget Outlook* (August 1985), Tables II–5 and II–6, we assume that a 1% rise in *U* implies a 1% reduction in the surplus–GNP ratio.

sures *only* the price of goods and services produced in the United States; it does not reflect the direct impact of import prices set on goods not produced in the United States. By contrast, the CPI includes the price of all consumer goods, whether the source is domestic or foreign. Second, many analysts believe that the CPI gave excessive weight to current mortgage interest rates prior to 1983 when this defect was corrected. As a result, the CPI overstated the impact of sharp fluctuations in interest rates.

Both oil price and interest rate increases were important in 1974 and 1979, when the CPI increased several points more than the GNP deflator. With the exception of these years, the pattern is quite similar under both measures of inflation. In the early 1960s, both measures show little inflation. By 1980, the inflation rate has risen to roughly 10% per year. How did this happen?

DG-SG ANALYSIS AND U.S. DATA

Our $DG-SG$ analysis tells us to look at the unemployment rate U. According to this analysis (if there is no supply shock), when the unemployment rate is at U_c, the inflation rate will stay constant; when the unemployment rate is less than U_c, the inflation rate will rise; when the unemployment rate is greater than U_c, the inflation rate will decline.

When we turn to the complex economy, common sense should warn us that we cannot expect this simple rule to hold perfectly in every year. In particular years, factors other than the unemployment rate may influence the inflation rate. Supply shocks do occur. We will discuss such factors more carefully later in this section.

Nevertheless, if our $DG-SG$ analysis is to be useful and basically valid and if supply shocks are relatively rare, then in most years when the unemployment rate is relatively high, the inflation rate should decline (or at least not rise) and in most years when the unemployment rate is relatively low, the inflation rate should rise. Is this in fact the case?

In the early 1960s, the unemployment rate averaged about 5.6%, as Table 5.1 shows. In those years, the inflation rate remained fairly constant (in the 1%–2% range). Based on this data, we can tentatively assume that the constant inflation unemployment rate U_c was roughly 5.6%. In Chapter 6, we will show how we estimate the value of U_c and will present evidence that U_c may have changed slowly over time. We should be alert to the likelihood that U_c increased slowly over the last two decades.

In the early 1960s, the unemployment rate moved slightly below 6%. By the mid-1960s, it moved significantly below 6%; in fact, from 1965–1969, the unemployment rate averaged 3.7%. According to our $DG-SG$ analysis, with the unemployment rate significantly below our estimate of U_c, we would expect the inflation rate to rise. This is in fact what occurred. The mid-1960s saw the beginning of the rise in the inflation rate. By the end of the decade, the inflation rate was above 5% — significantly above the 1% rate of the early 1960s.

In 1971, the unemployment rate moved up to almost 6%. Our DG – SG analysis would predict that with the unemployment rate close to U_c, the rise in the inflation rate should stop. Table 5.1 shows that inflation did stabilize. It should be noted, however, that in the last third of the year 1971, the economy was under a strict wage–price controls program. (We will discuss the controls program in Chapter 6.)

In 1972, the unemployment rate of 5.5% did not exceed our estimate of U_c, but the inflation rate still declined. However, 1972 was a year of wage and price controls. Controls were relaxed at the beginning of 1973. With the unemployment rate at 4.8%, still below U_c, it is not surprising that inflation resumed its rise.

Although in 1974 the unemployment rate of 5.5% was not much below our estimate of U_c, a large jump in the inflation rate occurred. The main reason for this was a supply shock from OPEC. During 1974, the Persian Gulf oil countries (joined by several other major oil exporters) *quadrupled* the world price of oil. As this enormous energy price increase of roughly 300% rippled through our economy, the CPI jumped; even the GNP deflator rose, as the price of domestically produced energy was pulled up by the rise in the world price.

In 1975, a severe recession occurred; the unemployment rate averaged 8.3%. Even after recovery began, the unemployment rate remained high at 7.6% in 1976. With the unemployment rate in the 8% range, our DG – SG model would predict a decline in the inflation rate. From 1975 to 1977, a significant decline did in fact occur. Two points should be noted, however.

First, it would not be correct to attribute the entire decline in the inflation rate to the high unemployment rate. From the beginning of 1975 through 1978, OPEC raised the world price of oil very modestly; hence, the end of the sharp rise in oil prices would in itself have caused the inflation rate to decline, even without a high unemployment rate. Second, there appears to have been a lag in the impact of the high unemployment rate on the inflation rate; the percentage change in the GNP deflator was actually slightly higher in 1975 than it was in 1974; the big decline did not occur until 1976.

The years 1977 and 1978 raise a troubling question. Over these two years, the inflation rate rose roughly 1%, but the unemployment rate averaged 6.5%. In any one- or even two-year period, deviations from our simple rule must be expected in a complex economy. Even if U_c is still close to 6%, a supply shock can cause a short-run rise in the inflation rate.

But it is quite possible that the U_c of the economy has risen to roughly 7%. (In Chapter 6 we will show how we can apply statistical techniques to the data to estimate U_c.) The possibility that U_c is now roughly 7% must be kept in mind when we consider how to prevent inflation in Section 5.2.

The rise in inflation in 1979 is easier to explain. Not only was the unemployment rate slightly below 6%, but the U.S. economy again received a supply shock from OPEC.

The data for 1980–1981 further support the view that U_c is now close to 7%. Despite an unemployment rate of just above 7%, there is a slight rise in the inflation rate. Not until 1982, when the unemployment rate rises above 9%, does a significant decline in the inflation rate finally take place. Once again, U_c appears to be roughly 7%.

A significant rise in the unemployment rate above our new U_c estimate of 7% did bring about a significant reduction in the inflation rate in 1982 and 1983. In 1984 and 1985, the unemployment rate averaged just above 7%, and the inflation rate stayed roughly constant near 4%.

Looking back on the past two decades, the unemployment rate has, with only a few exceptions, been a highly reliable guide to the *change* in the inflation rate. In low-unemployment years, the inflation rate has generally risen; in high-unemployment years, the inflation rate has generally declined. This basic implication of our *DG–SG* analysis proves generally consistent with U.S. economic data.

Note that the "old" Phillips curve does not pass the test. According to the "old" Phillips curve view, low-unemployment years should have a high inflation rate and high-unemployment years should have a low inflation rate. But consider the late 1960s when the unemployment rate dropped below 4% and the inflation rate averaged 3%–4%, and the 1975–1976 period when the unemployment rate was close to 8% and the inflation rate averaged 8%. Clearly, it is not true that a low unemployment rate implies a high inflation rate, or vise versa.

But it is true that a low unemployment rate implies a *rising* inflation rate; during the late 1960s, the inflation rate rose from 2% to 5%. And it is true that a high unemployment rate implies a *declining* inflation rate; in 1975–1976, the inflation rate dropped 3% (recall that part of that decline was due to the halt in the OPEC oil-price inflation).

INFLATION, UNEMPLOYMENT, AND NOMINAL DEMAND GROWTH

Now that we have established that the unemployment rate is a reasonably reliable guide to the *change* in the inflation rate, we can draw the following important conclusion:

▶ The inflation rate was much higher at the end of the 1970s than it was in the early 1960s, primarily because the average unemployment rate over these two decades was significantly below the constant inflation unemployment rate U_c. Oil-price supply shocks, however, also contributed significantly to the rise in the inflation rate during this period.

The average unemployment rate from 1960 to 1979 was 5.4%. We have tentatively estimated that constant inflation unemployment rate U_c averaged about 6.3% (5.6% in the early 1960s; 7% in the late 1970s). Why was the average unemployment rate less than U_c over these two decades?

Our model of demand inflation tells us that an increase in the nominal demand growth rate y will initially raise real output Q above Q_c (equivalently, reduce the unemployment rate U below U_c) and raise the inflation rate p. Eventually, Q will return to Q_c (U will return to U_c), and the inflation rate p will increase by the same percentage as the nominal demand growth rate y. During the transition from short-run to long-run equilibrium in the economy, U will spend most of its time below U_c, although the unemployment rate will oscillate as the economy approaches long-run equilibrium. The increase in the nominal demand growth rate y is what drives U below U_c and generates the rise in the inflation rate p.

Did the nominal demand growth rate $y = p + q$ increase over the two decades? Table 5.1 provides the answer. Nominal demand growth began the 1960s in the 4% range. By the late 1960s, it was in the 8% range. In the early 1970s, y jumped to roughly 10%, dropped back to 8% during the 1975 recession, and then rose to 12% in the late 1970s. If the growth rate of Q_c is assumed to be roughly $q_c = 3\%$, then the rise in the nominal demand growth rate from $y = 4\%$ to $y = 12\%$ should be expected to raise the inflation rate by roughly 8% from $p = 1\%$ to $p = 9\%$. This is in fact what happened and leads us to another important conclusion.

▶ The inflation rate was much higher at the end of the 1970s than it was in the early 1960s, primarily because the nominal demand growth rate y rose significantly over these two decades.

But what caused this rise in the nominal demand growth rate? Our demand inflation model tells us that monetary and fiscal expansions fuel nominal demand growth. Let's examine monetary and fiscal policy, beginning in the mid-1960s with fiscal policy.

FISCAL POLICY AND U.S. INFLATION

In Part 1, we learned that a fiscal expansion results from either an increase in government spending $G + R$ or a decrease in the tax rate t. Such an expansion shifts up the aggregate demand D line in the 45° diagram in Figure 1.3 (page 24), shifts the IS curve to the right to IS' in the $IS-LM$ diagram in Figure 2.5 (page 67), and shifts the aggregate demand D_0 curve to the right to D_1 in the $D-S$ diagram in Figure 3.6 (page 138).

We also learned that tax revenues and certain government expenditures (like unemployment compensation and welfare) vary automatically with the GNP. For example, if the GNP declines, tax revenues T automatically decrease and government transfers R to the unemployed automatically increase; the government budget moves toward deficit.

To discern whether a fiscal expansion has occurred, we must not be confused by changes in the deficit that follow automatically from changes in the GNP. We are interested in detecting whether—at a fixed level of GNP—the deficit would increase due to a tax rate cut or an increase in government spending. If so, then there has been a fiscal expansion.

Although any level of GNP will do, it seems natural to use the constant inflation output Q_c—the level of real GNP that results in an unemployment rate U equal to the constant inflation unemployment rate U_c. We will call this the Q_c *budget surplus* or *deficit,* or the *normal output budget surplus* or *deficit:* the budget surplus or deficit that would occur in a given year if $Q = Q_c$ (if $U = U_c$).

Clearly, if U exceeds U_c (if Q is less than Q_c) in a given year, then the actual deficit will be greater than the Q_c deficit. At a higher U (lower Q), tax revenues are automatically lower and certain government expenditures are automatically higher.

The key point is that the change in the actual deficit from one year to the next is partly due to a change in Q (and U); hence, the change in the actual deficit is a misleading indicator of fiscal expansion or contraction. But the change in the Q_c deficit is solely due to changes in tax rates and government-expenditure rates at U_c; it is independent of the actual movement of the GNP. Hence, an increase in the Q_c deficit is an accurate signal of fiscal expansion.

Note that the level of the Q_c surplus or deficit depends on the estimate of U_c and Q_c, but the *change* in the Q_c surplus or deficit will be largely independent of these estimates. Only the change in (not the level of) the Q_c surplus or deficit from one year to the next counts in our analysis. Because the constant inflation output Q_c of the economy grows each year, it is more useful to present the Q_c budget surplus or deficit as a percentage of Q_c, as shown in the last column of Table 5.1.

Table 5.1 illustrates the dramatic change in the Q_c surplus position beginning in the mid-1960s. From a Q_c surplus of 0.3% of Q_c in 1961, the Q_c budget moved toward deficit, reaching a Q_c deficit of 3.8% in 1967 and 3.1% in 1968. There was nothing subtle about the behavior of fiscal policy in the mid-1960s; it was strongly expansionary.

Only the motives remain. There were two. In the early 1960s, the

Kennedy Administration set a goal of 4% unemployment and proposed a tax cut to stimulate demand to achieve it. How could the Administration set a 4% unemployment target with U_c in the 5.6% range?

Economists did not realize that U_c was about 5.6%. In fact, economists generally (there were some exceptions) did not recognize that the economy possessed a constant inflation unemployment rate U_c. The prevailing view then was what we now call the "old" Phillips curve view. In the early 1960s, economists believed that a lower unemployment rate would result in a moderately higher but stable inflation rate.

Kennedy Administration economists believed that the worst economic effect of reducing the unemployment rate to 4% would be to raise the inflation rate a few percentage points. They proposed a voluntary *wage–price control program* to try to limit the inflation. But even if their wage–price program failed, they believed the risk of inflation was limited. Based on this thinking, a large tax cut was enacted in 1964 and, together with a reinforcing monetary expansion (we will side-step the debate over which was more important), the unemployment rate was driven below 5%.

If Kennedy Administration economists had believed in our $DG-SG$ model with a U_c of roughly 5.5% to 6% (as most economists now do, although U_c appears to be closer to 7% today), they presumably would not have advocated demand stimulus as a method of reducing the unemployment rate to 4%. As we will see in Chapter 7, supply-oriented policies can be implemented to reduce U_c itself. Most economists now agree that such policies, rather than nominal demand growth, are the tools that should be used in attempting to reduce the permanent unemployment rate.

The second motive concerns the Vietnam War, which began in the mid-1960s. The Johnson Administration wanted to believe—and to have everyone else believe—that the War would be over quickly. The Administration therefore repeatedly underestimated the rise in military expenditures that would be required. Fiscal responsibility called for a large tax increase to match the large expenditure increase in order to avoid excessive fiscal stimulus. But political pragmatism told the Johnson Administration that to propose such a tax increase would only intensify the growing opposition to the War.

To their credit, the Council of Economic Advisers, under Gardner Ackley, tried to warn the Administration that unless a large tax increase was enacted to match the expenditure increase, the economy would become overheated and inflation would result. But their warning went unheeded. The column on the Q_c budget in Table 5.1 tells the story. The Q_c budget was permitted to move from a small Q_c deficit to a large Q_c deficit during this period.

For the record, we should note that in 1968 the Johnson Administration did finally enact a tax increase (surcharge), which contributed to a significant reduction in the Q_c deficit in 1969. But much inflationary damage had already been done.

MONETARY POLICY AND U.S. INFLATION

The time has now come to turn to monetary policy. Table 5.1 (page 207) shows the rate of money growth, where money is defined in two ways. M1 is the narrowest and most traditional definition of money: it denotes the sum of currency and demand (checking) deposits in commercial banks. M2 is a broader definition of money than M1; it includes M1 plus savings accounts and small time deposits in banks.

If the two money-supply growth rates $m1$ and $m2$ always changed by the same percentage, there would be no practical problem. However, a glance at Table 5.1 shows that $m1$ and $m2$ do not always do this. For example, from 1979 to 1980 $m1$ declined from 7.2% to 6.6% but $m2$ increased from 7.8% to 8.9%. If you peruse the two columns, you will see that this divergence is not unique.

Some sympathy for the Federal Reserve is clearly in order. Suppose that the Fed accepts the monetary view of inflation and believes that a low money-supply growth rate is essential to achieving a low inflation rate. Which measure ($m1$ or $m2$) should it watch? From 1979 to 1980, $m1$ shows a decline (from 7.2% to 6.6%), but $m2$ shows an increase (from 7.8% to 8.9%).

Perhaps a more careful, detailed understanding of each specific episode would reveal special factors that would enable the Fed to determine the more appropriate measure for that period. The point here is that simply watching $m1$ and $m2$ can lead to divergent signals in the short run. The Fed's job is not easy.

Such short-run divergences, however, should not obscure the important, constructive message that still emerges from Table 5.1. Whichever measure of money-supply growth is used, there is no ambiguity about the following key point:

▶ The money-supply growth rate m rose significantly from the early 1960s to the later 1970s. Moreover, the increase in the money-supply growth rate was only somewhat less than the increase in the inflation rate.

The data are consistent with a flexible version of the monetary view of inflation, although the inflation rate seems to have risen somewhat more than the money-supply growth rate.

The question of motive remains. Why did the Fed let money-supply growth rise over these two decades? Even if an economist believes that the money-supply growth rate controls the inflation rate, regardless of fiscal policy, the history of this period shows that fiscal expansion can place pressure on the Fed to expand the money supply.

Let's return to the mid-1960s. We reported earlier that there were two motives for fiscal expansion: the Kennedy Administration's goal of reaching a 4% unemployment rate by demand stimulus, and the Johnson Administration's reactions to the Vietnam War dilemma. The Fed did not appear to share either motive. The seven members of the Board of Governors of the Federal Reserve System and the twelve members of the Federal Open Market Committee (it includes the seven governors and five branch bank presidents) on the whole came from a "sound money" tradition. Their public statements strongly suggest that price stability (a "sound" dollar) was their first priority, not reducing unemployment. The fiscal problem raised by the Vietnam War was the Administration's — not theirs.

To explain the monetary expansion, we must ask: what happens if monetary policy holds firm in the face of a large fiscal expansion? The answer is given by our trusty $IS-LM$ diagram (introduced in Chapter 2). The IS curve shifts to the right; if the LM curve does not also shift right, then the interest rate rises sharply. A moderate increase in the money supply will shift the LM curve to the right and reduce the rise in the interest rate. An even larger increase in the money supply will prevent any rise in the interest rate.

In Table 5.1 (page 207), r is the *prime rate* — the interest rate that banks charge their most reliable customers. There are many other interest rates (on Treasury bonds, corporate bonds of varying degrees of risk and maturity, and so on). Although these rates do not all move identically, they normally move in the same direction. Movements in the prime rate generally reflect the movement of all other interest rates.

In Table 5.1, the prime rate, which had remained steady at roughly 4.50% through 1965, rose significantly beginning in 1966. It is important to recognize that, without the increase in the money-supply growth rate in 1967 and 1968, the rise in interest rates would have been even sharper in those years. But why didn't the Fed keep money-supply growth constant and accept a larger rise in interest rates?

Rising interest rates generate a political reaction. Both businesses and households complain that they cannot afford to borrow for all kinds of worthwhile purposes. The chairman of the Fed tried to blame government deficits for the rise in interest rates in the mid-1960s. But President Johnson fought back, accusing the Fed of holding back the economy. (Recall that Johnson had won the presidential election by a landslide in 1964; few people even knew the name of Fed Chairman William McChesney Martin.) A large Democratic majority controlled Congress at this time, swept into office by the 1964 landslide; such key leaders as "populist" Congressman Wright Patman, argued that the Fed was the source of high interest rates and that perhaps its power and independence needed to be reviewed.

The Fed also faced a "disintermediation" problem. With legal ceilings placed on the interest rates that certain financial institutions could charge, a rise in market interest rates would cause savers to withdraw funds from the regulated institutions, placing these institutions in jeopardy. It should be noted that the phasing out of such ceilings in the 1980s has increased the Fed's ability to engineer a tight money policy.

The Fed did not succumb instantly. The money-supply growth rate declined significantly in 1966. A "credit crunch" and a serious "disintermediation" problem occurred in 1967, as the Fed tried to combat the fiscal expansion. But despite these efforts, the Fed allowed the money-supply growth rate to be significantly higher in 1967 and 1968 than it had been at the beginning of the decade or in 1966.

U.S. INFLATION IN THE 1970s

The decade of the 1970s began on a note of resolve. The Nixon Administration had come into office in 1969, pledging to bring down inflation; Arthur Burns was appointed chairman of the Fed. The Q_c budget deficit was significantly reduced from 1968 to 1969 (partly due to the tax surcharge enacted in 1968), and the money-supply growth rate was cut by several percentage points. From 1968 to 1970, the nominal demand growth rate y fell significantly. In 1970, a recession began and the unemployment rate began to rise; by 1971, it approached 6%.

Our $DG-SG$ analysis predicts that, with U_c in the 6% range (and perhaps a bit higher by this point), the rise in inflation should stop; but there is no reason to expect the inflation rate to decline. For it to decline, the unemployment rate would have to increase significantly above 6% through a further reduction in the nominal demand growth rate y.

The data are consistent with our prediction. The inflation rate stabilized; it stopped rising, but it did not decline. In retrospect, this result seems perfectly understandable. But at the time, the failure of the 1970 recession to "subdue" the inflation generated great frustration and puzzlement. Why?

Economists were just beginning to reject the "old" Phillips curve view and to accept the new view that the economy possesses a constant inflation unemployment rate U_c. But few had begun to suspect the possibility that U_c was as high as 6%. The goal of 4% unemployment was still in the minds of many economists; perhaps a retreat to 5% could be considered. But the notion that the inflation rate would rise if the unemployment rate were less than 6% was not yet envisioned by most economists. Although the 1970 recession now appears to have been fairly mild, it was considered a very respectable recession at the time.

After all, the unemployment rate had risen from below 4% to 6%, and a 4% unemployment rate was still considered "normal" by many.

Today, many observers might argue that further fiscal and monetary tightening was necessary; a further reduction in nominal demand growth would have raised the unemployment rate above 6% and would have begun to reduce the inflation rate. So why wasn't this policy pursued?

First, the Vietnam War continued; so did pressure on the budget from military expenditures. Proposing a tax increase to pay for the War remained politically unappealing. After a one-year reduction in 1969, the Q_c deficit rose again in 1970 and stayed high in 1971.

In mid-summer 1971, a reelection campaign loomed on the horizon. The President and his advisers regarded the high unemployment rate (today, 6% would be considered low) as an obstacle to reelection. Monetary and fiscal expansion could bring the unemployment rate down and generate a prosperous business climate — but at the risk of increased inflation.

On the weekend of August 15, 1971, President Nixon huddled with his advisers at Camp David. Then, in a dramatic television address, he announced he was freezing all wages and prices. (We will return to the Nixon wage–price control program in Chapter 6.) Although the President's decision to institute controls dominated the headlines, just as important — but less noticed — was the Fed's decision to implement an expansionary monetary policy.

In 1971 and 1972, the money-supply growth rate rose sharply relative to 1970. As a result, the unemployment rate declined to approximately 5% by the end of 1972, producing a climate of prosperity. The wage–price controls temporarily held down inflation, and the performance of the economy contributed to Nixon's landslide reelection.

President Nixon always viewed his wage–price controls as a temporary expedient; they were relaxed at the beginning of 1973. But our $DG – SG$ analysis immediately posts a warning. Without controls, an unemployment rate below 6% should mean trouble on the inflation front. It did. With the unemployment rate close to 5%, the inflation rate rose in 1973. Then, in 1974, the economy received a supply shock from OPEC.

Nixon threatened "impoundment" (refusal to spend what Congress had appropriated), but he was weakened by the Watergate investigation and eventually resigned in 1974 to avoid impeachment. It was now up to Chairman Burns and the Fed to stop the inflation. At last, the Fed stepped hard on the monetary brake. Interest rates soared in early 1974, as the money-supply growth rate declined. The result was the most severe recession since the 1930s and a reduction in the inflation rate.

President Carter pledged to reduce the unemployment rate. Few economists suspected that the U_c of the economy might have risen to

7%. Together, monetary and fiscal policy were sufficiently expansionary to reduce the unemployment rate to below 6% by 1979. Now that we clearly recognize the possibility of a constant inflation unemployment rate of $U_c = 7\%$, what happened is understandable. The inflation rate rose. In 1979, the economy received another supply shock from OPEC. It should be noted (as we will see in Chapter 6) that Carter's voluntary wage–price policy probably had little effect in containing inflation.

Then came a turning point. In 1979, Carter appointed Paul Volcker to be the new chairman of the Fed. Under Volcker, the Fed proved willing to tighten monetary policy and to generate historically high interest rates in order to reduce nominal demand growth and inflation, even though this tightening might subject the economy to a severe recession. By the early 1980s, the Fed had succeeded in engineering a significant disinflation.

DEMAND VS. SUPPLY INFLATION

Looking back on the two decades, it seems clear that the rise in inflation was primarily demand-generated, although several years witnessed important supply shocks. Let's review the distinction between demand-generated and supply-generated inflation, using our DG–SG diagram.

We begin with the DG and SG curves intersecting at a real output level of $Q = Q_c$ and an inflation rate of $p = 0\%$. The economy in the early 1960s was not far from this position, with an inflation rate of $p = 1\%$ and an unemployment rate of about 5.6%. If inflation is demand-generated, then the DG curve shifts up first and the SG curve initially stays put. As a result, Q rises above Q_c (U declines below U_c); at the same time, the inflation rate p begins to increase. Thereafter, the picture gets more complicated as the SG curve starts to shift up. But the key point is that, in the beginning, the unemployment rate declines as the inflation rate begins to rise.

In contrast, if inflation is supply-generated, the SG curve shifts up first. Policymakers must then decide what to do to the DG curve. If the DG curve is held firm (the nominal demand growth rate y is held constant), then Q will decline below Q_c (U will rise above U_c) while the inflation rate begins to rise. If policymakers do not want the unemployment rate to rise above U_c, then they will raise the nominal demand growth rate y via monetary or fiscal expansion, shifting up the DG curve, and Q will remain at Q_c (U will remain at U_c). In neither case should Q rise above Q_c (U decline below U_c) as the inflation rate begins to rise.

But in the mid-1960s, the unemployment rate did decline significantly below U_c, dropping into the 3%–4% range, while inflation began to rise. The pattern fits the picture of a demand-generated inflation.

Similarly, in 1973, the unemployment rate was reduced to just under 5% as the inflation rate rose. In 1978 (a closer call), the unemployment rate was reduced to 6% as the inflation rate rose again. If our assumption that $U_c = 7\%$ is correct, then 1978 illustrates demand-generated inflation. But if U_c is really still 6%, then 1978 might illustrate supply-generated inflation, when demand policy "accommodates" or "ratifies" an *exogenous* rise in supply inflation, keeping U constant near U_c.

Two clear rounds of supply inflation occurred in 1974 and 1979–1980. The origin was OPEC: the energy price increase shifted the SG curve up. In both instances, policymakers did not shift the DG curve as much as the shift up in the SG curve. As a result, while the inflation rate increased, real output Q fell below Q_c and the unemployment rate U rose above U_c. Recession occurred (severe in 1975, mild in 1980) while inflation increased.

▶ Thus, supply inflation did contribute to the overall rise in the inflation rate during the 1960s and 1970s. But the evidence is clear that, prior to 1974, virtually the entire rise in the inflation rate was demand-generated; some of the inflationary rise in the late 1970s was probably also demand-generated. It seems safe to conclude that although supply shocks played an important role, the primary driving force behind most of the rise in the inflation rate during the 1960s and 1970s was excessive nominal demand growth generated by expansionary monetary and fiscal policy.

5.2   The Prevention of Inflation

If the economy is currently enjoying price stability (near zero inflation), how can we prevent the occurrence of inflation?

Our $DG-SG$ theory tells us that if the unemployment rate U stays at U_c, then the inflation rate will remain constant (in the absence of a supply shock); hence, if the inflation rate is initially $p = 0\%$, it will remain at 0%. But the inflation rate will rise if the unemployment rate U is driven below U_c. Therefore, our first rule for the prevention of inflation is

▶ Do not attempt to reduce the unemployment rate U below U_c by expansionary monetary or fiscal policy.

At present, U_c appears to be in the 7% range. But in Chapter 7, we will examine policies that should be able to reduce the constant inflation unemployment rate. If U_c were reduced to, say, 5%, then it would be safe to let nominal demand growth reduce the actual unemployment rate to the new U_c of 5%. However, the nominal demand growth rate does not alter U_c. At any moment in time, the economy has a U_c, and monetary and fiscal policy should heed it.

Care should be exercised not to misinterpret this conclusion. The current apparent value of U_c (roughly 7%) should not be accepted as an unemployment-rate goal. The supply-oriented policies we will review in Chapter 7 should be able to reduce the U_c of the economy below 7% and therefore deserve serious consideration.

But the lesson of the last two decades is that accelerating nominal demand growth by implementing fiscal and monetary expansion to reduce the unemployment rate below U_c is counterproductive. It achieves a temporary reduction in the unemployment rate that cannot be sustained without accelerating inflation. The historical evidence is consistent with the prediction of our $DG - SG$ model that as long as the unemployment rate is kept below U_c, inflation will rise indefinitely.

But how do we keep the unemployment rate from moving below U_c? The adjusted nominal demand growth rate must remain at $\hat{y} = 0\%$, so that the DG curve goes through the point ($Q = Q_c$, $p = 0\%$). This means the unadjusted nominal demand growth rate y must be kept equal to q_c, the *normal real output growth rate*. According to equation (4.6), $q_c = f + a$, where f is the labor-force growth rate and a is the labor productivity growth rate. A rough estimate is that $f = 1\%$ and $a = 2\%$, then $q_c = 3\%$. The nominal demand growth rate must therefore be kept near $y = 3\%$. If nominal GNP increases by 3%, then the real output (real GNP) growth rate therefore should be $q = 3\%$ and the inflation rate should be $p = 0\%$.

Thus, our second rule for the prevention of inflation is

▶ The nominal demand growth rate y should, on average, be kept equal to the normal real output growth rate q_c or, equivalently, equal to the sum of the *normal labor-force growth rate f* and the *normal labor productivity growth rate a*. If estimates of f and a are 1% and 2%, respectively, then the nominal demand growth rate should, on average, be kept near $y = 3\%$.

Hence, the normal target for nominal GNP growth should be q_c. But how is this target achieved? Even if an expansionary fiscal policy is implemented, a determined Federal Reserve has the power to tighten monetary policy sufficiently to achieve the targeted nominal demand growth rate and prevent inflation. In the last few years, the Fed has demonstrated the ability to do just this, as we shall see in Chapter 6. Thus, it is correct to focus the spotlight on the Fed.

MONETARY POLICY TO PREVENT INFLATION

Although the Fed can achieve the targeted nominal demand growth rate despite an expansionary fiscal policy, a tight fiscal policy makes the Fed's job easier. An expansionary fiscal policy would shift the IS curve to the right and raise nominal demand growth, unless the Fed counters this rightward shift of the *IS* curve with a tight money policy that causes a comparable leftward shift of the *LM* curve. Such a shift of the *LM* curve would raise interest rates and hence be unpopular. The Fed has recently been willing to raise interest rates enough to reduce inflation, but this has not always been the case (witness the mid-1960s). Therefore, it is helpful if fiscal policy does not turn expansionary in the first place.

Monetary policy must maintain a low money-supply growth rate. How low? The target for money growth can be obtained by observing the behavior of the growth rate of the velocity of money v over the past few years. Suppose that v has averaged 2% and that $q_c = 3\%$. Then according to equation (4.14), the money-supply growth rate m should be kept near 1% on average. If v averages 2%, then the nominal demand growth rate will average $y = 3\%$, enough to "support" a q of 3% and a p of 0%.

As we will see in Part 3, economists differ as to the method of managing monetary policy to achieve the right rate of nominal demand growth. Some economists believe the Fed should try to keep the money-supply growth rate m right on target and ignore fluctuations in the growth rate of the velocity of money v and, hence, fluctuations in the nominal demand growth rate y away from its target. According to this view, it would be counterproductive to try to adjust m to reflect every fluctuation in v. The best monetary policy is a steady m. Although v (and, hence, the nominal demand growth rate y) will fluctuate, they will be on target on average.

Other economists believe that m should be frequently adjusted to offset fluctuations in v, in an attempt to keep nominal demand growth and nominal GNP growth on target. According to this view, fluctuations in v—and perhaps even a change in the normal growth rate of the velocity of money v over time—make it necessary for monetary policy to address nominal GNP growth directly and not be satisfied with keeping m steady.

This disagreement among economists is important, but it should not obscure their basic agreement on the more fundamental point:

▶ The money-supply growth rate m must, on average, be kept low to maintain a low inflation rate. More specifically, to maintain a 0% inflation rate, the money-supply growth rate should equal $q_c - v$ on average.

For example, if $q_c = 3\%$ and v is normally estimated to be 2%, then m should be set at 1% on average.

If the inflation is primarily demand-generated, as most economists believe, then the policy rules just described would prevent inflation from arising by keeping the average unemployment rate near U_c. Suppose, however, that inflationary pressure is generated from the supply side of our model, which we analyzed in Section 4.8. From time to time, for example, suppose that world oil-price shocks occur or that wage growth jumps upward for no apparent reason, shifting the SG curve up. A firm grip on nominal demand growth will make such supply-generated inflation temporary. But it should be recognized that in the process of returning the inflation rate to 0%, the unemployment rate would rise above U_c temporarily.

If major supply shocks are infrequent, then accepting an occasional rise in the unemployment rate above U_c should be tolerable. Most economists probably believe that this would in fact be the case. As our review of recent economic history in Section 5.1 showed, not until 1974 was there clear evidence of an important supply shock—the OPEC oil-price increase—which was repeated again in 1979. There is no clear evidence of an exogenous wage hike, although a minor one may have contributed to an inflationary rise in the late 1970s when the unemployment rate was roughly 6%.

These supply-shock episodes require accepting a rise in the unemployment rate to above U_c to prevent the inflation from becoming permanent, if the method of containment is to hold the DG curve firm. Some economists fear that supply-generated inflation is not a minor phenomenon but a frequent occurrence. In their view, even if the DG curve is properly managed, supply-side inflation will frequently break out; if this inflation is not ratified, then the economy will spend much of its time with the unemployment rate above U_c during the transition necessary to eliminate the inflation.

In Chapter 6, we will see that some of these economists advocate a wage–price policy as a means of preventing supply inflation or limiting its harmful effects. Basically, such policies try to keep a lid on the SG curve in an effort to prevent it from shifting up.

To summarize:

▶ Most economists believe that the policy rules just described will prevent significant inflation. Few economists would deny that, from time to time, an episode of supply inflation will still occur, generating some temporary inflation. But despite these occasional episodes, most economists conclude that theory and evidence support the view that the economy can be kept at a low inflation rate if demand policy tries to keep $U = U_c$, and if monetary and fiscal policy are set to achieve the proper nominal demand growth rate y.

THE GAME OF STRATEGY

Now let's consider the prevention of inflation from another perspective—what has been called the "game of strategy." Initially, suppose that the Fed is committed to holding the adjusted nominal demand growth rate at $\hat{y} = 0\%$ (the rate consistent with a long-run inflation rate of $p = 0\%$). In particular, in our DG–SG diagram, the Fed is publicly committed to holding the DG curve constant even if a supply shock shifts the SG curve up. Such a shift of the SG curve would then reduce real output Q below Q_c and raise the unemployment rate above U_c. But the Fed is prepared to accept temporary recessions due to supply shocks to keep $\hat{y}$ at 0%.

Suppose that the Fed reaffirms its intent with action. Several times, when wage increases are raised above labor productivity growth, so that the SG curve shifts up, the Fed holds $\hat{y}$ at 0% and accepts the temporary recession. Assume that workers and managers become aware of this policy stance after these episodes.

Now suppose that when the workers (perhaps through unions) and the managers at a representative firm bargain over wage increases, both sides reason that if the money wage is raised above the labor productivity growth rate (so that unit labor cost and price rise), it will probably result in layoffs and a decline in sales and profits at that firm. Moreover, each worker–manager unit suspects that other units in the economy are reasoning the same way. Each unit may therefore guess that others will settle for a wage increase equal to the labor productivity growth rate because they expect inflation to stay at 0%. Each unit may judge that others, aware of the tough monetary policy, will not risk wage increases in excess of the labor productivity growth rate and the resulting price increases.

If most worker–manager units reason and behave in this way, then the SG curve will remain stable and avoid an upward supply shock due to excessive wage increases. The tough, credible stance of the Fed—the publicly announced and previously demonstrated willingness to accept a temporary recession rather than to give in—may deter the supply shock and prevent the recession while maintaining 0% inflation.

Now suppose that the Fed changes its stance and lets it be known that it will not tolerate any rise in the unemployment rate—however small or temporary—above the initial U_c. The Fed is prepared to act quickly to return U to U_c. In particular, it will adjust the nominal demand growth rate y to whatever level necessary to return U to U_c.

For example, suppose that the two curves in our DG–SG diagram initially intersect at $Q = Q_0$ ($U = U_0$) and $p = 0\%$ (where $Q_0 = Q_c$ and $U_0 = U_c$, under the former tough-demand policy). Then a supply shock due to the money wage increase w shifts the SG curve up. The Fed is now committed to implementing an expansionary monetary policy to raise the DG curve immediately, so that the DG and SG curves continue to intersect at $Q = Q_0$ but at a higher inflation rate p.

Let us assume that workers—especially union representatives—and managers become aware of this new, "accommodating" policy stance. Each worker–manager unit—reasoning that others may no longer fear layoffs and declines in sales and profits — now is no longer confident that other units will restrain their wage and price increases. Each group of workers does not want to fall behind wage and price increases in the economy, and each management group now believes it may not suffer a sales and profit decline by granting a wage increase in excess of labor productivity, thereby requiring a price increase.

It seems quite possible, then, that the typical worker–manager unit will push up its wage and price increase in the expectation that others will do the same and that no negative consequences (layoffs; declines in sales and profits) will follow. In response to this upward shift in the SG curve, the Fed will expand the money supply, raise the DG curve, and increase the nominal demand growth rate y, so that Q remains at Q_0 and U remains at U_0. But in each subsequent period, the DG–SG intersection will occur at a higher point, and inflation will accelerate.

But note that Q_0 is no longer the constant inflation output and that U_0 is no longer the constant inflation unemployment rate under the new, "accommodating" demand policy, because the inflation rate will rise (not stay constant) if the economy is at U_0 and Q_0. A higher unemployment rate U and a lower level of real output Q will be required to keep inflation constant under the new demand policy.

Are workers and managers sufficiently aware of the strategy of the demand-oriented policymakers to respond to alternative strategies? Some economists are skeptical. Others believe that workers, managers, and the Fed are engaged in a "game of strategy" that — if publicly and genuinely adopted by the Fed — can affect the constant inflation unemployment rate U_c of the economy.

▶ According to the "game of strategy" model, if the Federal Reserve Board genuinely shifts from an "accommodating" to a "nonaccommodating" demand policy and educates the public about the meaning of this shift, then the constant inflation unemployment rate U_c of the economy would decline and the incidence of supply inflation would be reduced.

THE LESSON FOR DEMAND POLICY

How should the analysis of the "game of strategy" influence policy to prevent inflation? If workers and managers can be made aware that the Fed will discipline the economy — and, in particular, those firms that raise their own wage and price increases w and p, so that an "inflationary" firm will be penalized — then it may be possible to deter such inflationary behavior. Moreover, as a result of disciplinary policy, the U_c of the economy may be lower than it would be under an accommodating monetary policy.

The Fed is faced with two problems. First, it must communicate to workers and managers that it has the power to discipline inflationary behavior — the power to assure that an inflationary firm is penalized. Second, it must convince workers and managers that it will enforce such a disciplinary policy.

An advocate of disciplinary policy might propose the following technique. The President announces that he will address the nation on prime-time television and that his special guest will be the chairman of the Federal Reserve System. The speech is billed as a major economic policy announcement.

The President introduces the chairman and explains that the Fed has made a decision that concerns everyone. The Fed chairman then explains the decision:

> We at the Fed will provide a noninflationary amount of money and credit to the economy. That amount will be enough to maintain prosperity, provided that firms do not raise prices or raise wages more than they increase productivity. But no matter what wages and prices are set by firms, the Fed cannot further raise the amount of money and credit, because to do so would be inflationary.
>
> If your firm increases wages more than average productivity growth in the economy — currently about 2% per year — and then raises prices, you may be priced out of the market. There may not be enough money and credit in the economy to maintain your sales and employment. We at the Fed will greatly regret your hardship. But we will be unable to help you, because to do so would launch an inflation that would eventually cause even more economic hardship. Please keep this in mind as you set your wages and prices.

Such a national address might launch an educational campaign. Perhaps other communication and educational techniques would be preferable. The example, however, illustrates the main point. In the "game of strategy," the Fed cannot assume that each player understands the consequences of her own moves. Undesirable behavior cannot be deterred unless warnings are comprehended.

Some economists believe that workers and managers would quickly grasp the implications of a disciplinary stance by the Fed without the benefit of special communication and educational devices. The key step is getting the Fed to make a genuine commitment to hold down nominal demand growth.

Other economists disagree. They emphasize that workers and managers are not economists and often have little understanding of the game we have been describing. They may not easily grasp the fact that under a new, tough policy stance, they could "price themselves out of the market" by raising their wages and prices.

These skeptical economists concede that even without special communication and educational techniques, workers and managers—after several costly mistakes—may eventually recognize the connection between their inflationary wage and price setting and their decline in sales and employment. But these economists also fear that the learning process would be long and costly.

To summarize the practical lesson of our "game of strategy" analysis:

▶ The Fed cannot assume that workers and managers know how to play the "game of strategy." Imaginative communication and educational techniques might expedite the learning process and minimize the potential for costly mistakes on the part of individual firms. Economists might find it worthwhile to devote more attention to the design of such techniques.

Another very important lesson follows from an awareness of the "game of strategy" and the need to discipline the economy. Our DG–SG diagram will help to make this point. We will assume that the SG and DG curves initially intersect at $Q = Q_c$ ($U = U_c$) and $p = 0\%$.

If the SG curve remains fixed (if no wage–price supply shock occurs) and if real output Q then diverges from constant inflation output Q_c (if U then diverges from U_c), it is only because the DG curve has shifted. In other words, the divergence of the nominal demand growth rate y from the normal real output (real GNP) growth rate q_c instigates the movement away from Q_c. Clearly, the Fed would want to implement policy to minimize the divergence of the nominal demand growth rate from its target, q_c.

Now, instead, suppose that the DG curve remains fixed (that nominal GNP growth is held on target, equal to q_c) but that the wage–price supply shock in our "game of strategy" shifts the SG curve up. This causes Q to fall below Q_c (U to rise above U_c). However, if the goal is to reduce the incidence of supply inflation in the future, then policymakers must accept this rise in the unemployment rate in order to discipline workers and managers.

This means that the Fed should not focus on whether real output Q diverges from the constant inflation output Q_c or on whether the unemployment rate U diverges from the constant inflation unemployment rate U_c. Instead, the Fed should focus on whether nominal GNP growth is on target—that is, on whether the DG curve has been held fixed. It should pledge only to keep the nominal GNP growth rate on target—not to prevent any rise in the unemployment rate.

There is one complication, however. A wage–price push in the "game of strategy" is not the only supply shock that can shift the SG curve up. The major oil-price supply shocks in 1974 and 1979 also pushed up the SG curve. Such supply shocks present the Fed with a dilemma.

If the Fed keeps the *DG* curve fixed (keeps nominal GNP growth at the normal level), then real output Q will fall below Q_c and a recession will occur. But if it raises the *DG* curve (temporarily raises nominal GNP growth above the normal level), then wage and price inflation will be greater. Economists disagree over which response is preferable.

Keeping this complication in mind, we will frame our conclusion:

▶ If the "game of strategy" model is accepted and if the primary policy goal is to prevent inflation, then demand-oriented management policy should focus on nominal GNP growth — not on real GNP growth or on the unemployment rate per se. Policymakers should try to keep nominal GNP growth on target. On average, the target should be q_c, although temporary modifications of the target may be desirable.

5.3   The Consequences of Inflation

In Section 5.2, we examined ways of keeping inflation from occurring in the first place. In Chapter 6, we will analyze how to reduce inflation ("disinflate") when the economy is already experiencing inflation. But how important is it to avoid inflation? What are the consequences of inflation?

It is important to distinguish three types of inflation:

1. Steady inflation with perfect anticipation and adaptation.
2. Unsteady inflation with imperfect anticipation and adaptation.
3. Hyperinflation (rapidly accelerating inflation).

We will consider each type of inflation in turn.

STEADY INFLATION WITH PERFECT ANTICIPATION AND ADAPTATION

Suppose that the economy is initially in equilibrium, with zero inflation. If the adjusted nominal demand growth rate $\hat{y}$ were raised permanently by 10%, then the economy would eventually settle into a 10% inflation equilibrium. Moreover, if the inflation rate remained steady at $p = 10\%$, everyone would eventually come to expect or anticipate it. Labor contracts and the tax system might eventually fully adapt to a 10% inflation rate.

Of course, in real economies, the inflation rate seldom remains steady over several years, and people are frequently surprised by unanticipated changes in the inflation rate. We will examine the consequences of unanticipated inflation shortly. However, economists find it instructive to first consider the consequences of a steady, fully anticipated inflation to which behavior has been fully adapted. So let's compare the 10% inflation economy with the 0% inflation economy.

Suppose that the labor productivity growth rate is the same in both economies (for example, $a = 2\%$). We know that the price inflation rate p must equal the unit labor cost growth rate ulc, so that

(4.3) $p = \text{ulc} = w - a$

With $a = 2\%$, if $p = 0\%$, then the wage inflation rate (nominal wage increase) must be $w = 2\%$; if $p = 10\%$, then $w = 12\%$. In either case, the *real wage increase* $w - p = 2\%$.

The REAL WAGE INCREASE $w - p$ equals the real labor productivity growth rate a, regardless of the inflation rate p. The average worker's standard of living advances at the labor productivity growth rate a.

(5.1) $w - p = a$

A sensible worker who understands this economic analysis should be equally satisfied whether the inflation rate is $p = 0\%$ or $p = 10\%$. But it is interesting to note that many workers in a 10% inflation economy may incorrectly reason: "My w is 12%; if p were 0%, I would enjoy a real wage increase of 12%; I've been 'robbed' 10% by the 10% inflation rate."

Price equation (4.3) shows why this reasoning is wrong. With $a = 2\%$, firms cannot afford to cut p from 10% to 0% unless w is cut from 12% to 2%. The average worker would receive a w of only 2% (not a w of 12%) if p were 0%.

In a 10% inflation economy, these workers would be frustrated because they would misunderstand the link between p and w. If they understood the link, they would realize that the real wage increase must equal the labor productivity growth rate $a = 2\%$, regardless of the inflation rate. Unfortunately, in practice, many workers do feel "robbed" in an inflationary economy. Until economic education does its work, this frustration must be considered an argument for a 0% inflation rate.

We will now turn to the interest rate. Suppose that the interest rate is initially $r = 3\%$ in the 0% inflation economy. What happens if the inflation rate is raised to $p = 10\%$? A lender of $100 will require $110 next year just to buy the same goods and services; to gain 3%, the lender will require a 13% interest rate—a repayment of $113 on a loan of $100. With wages and prices 10% higher, the average borrower will be able to afford a repayment that is 10% greater ($113 instead of $103). This reasoning suggests that if the inflation rate increases by 10%, then the nominal interest rate r should also rise 10% (in our example, from 3% to 13%).

This hypothesis was first proposed by American economist Irving Fisher in the early 1900s.

According to FISHER'S HYPOTHESIS, if the inflation rate p rises by X%, then the nominal interest rate r will eventually also rise by X%.

In an inflationary economy, it is useful to distinguish between the *nominal interest rate* r and the *real interest rate* i:

The REAL INTEREST RATE i is defined as the nominal interest rate r minus the inflation rate p, or

(5.2) $i \equiv r - p$

Rational potential borrowers and lenders compare the nominal interest rate r to the expected inflation rate p^e:

The EXPECTED REAL INTEREST RATE i^e is defined as the nominal interest rate r minus the expected inflation rate p^e, or

(5.3) $i^e \equiv r - p^e$

It is easy to calculate the real interest rate i at any time simply by subtracting the inflation rate p from the nominal interest rate r. It is more difficult to discern the expected real interest rate i^e, because the expected inflation rate p^e is not directly observable. Yet i^e (not i) motivates the behavior of rational borrowers and lenders.

Because we are considering an economy in which the anticipation of and the adaptation to inflation are perfect, the expected inflation rate would equal the actual inflation rate ($p^e = p$) in long-run equilibrium.

▶ Given steady inflation with perfect anticipation and adaptation, the expected real interest rate i^e equals the actual real interest rate i when the economy is in long-run equilibrium.

In our analysis of the long-run equilibrium of an economy with perfect anticipation and adaptation, we will therefore assume that i^e and i are equal.

In our example, when the inflation rate p increases by 10%, the nominal interest rate r also increases by 10% (from 3% to 13%), which illustrates Fisher's hypothesis. However, the real interest rate i remains constant at 3% (13% − 10% = 3%). Hence, another way of stating Fisher's hypothesis is

According to FISHER'S HYPOTHESIS, the real interest rate i in long-run equilibrium is independent of the inflation rate p.

Note the similarity between the adjustments of the nominal interest rate r and the nominal wage increase w. Both rise X% when the inflation rate p rises X%, so that both the real wage increase and the real interest rate remain constant (independent of the inflation rate).

In the *IS–LM* model we developed in Chapter 2, we implicitly assumed 0% inflation. Our *IS–LM* system determines the nominal interest rate r. If a rise in the inflation rate from 0% to X% really raises the nominal interest rate by X%, then it must shift the *IS* and *LM* curves up by X%. Does it?

First, consider the *IS* curve. Recall that it is based on the investment curve, which shows investment demand I increasing when the interest rate r decreases. In Chapter 2, we wrote the investment equation

(2.1) $\qquad I = I_a - jr$

where I_a = the autonomous component of investment demand

$\qquad\quad j$ = the investment responsiveness parameter

Because we were implicitly assuming zero inflation, we could avoid indicating whether investment demand I depends on the nominal interest rate r or on the expected real interest rate i^e. In Chapter 12, where we analyze investment in greater depth, we will explain why investment demand I depends on the expected real interest rate i^e given by equation (5.3), so that the r in investment equation (2.1) should be converted to i^e.

Returning to our example illustrating Fisher's hypothesis, if investment demand depends on the expected real interest rate $i^e = 3$%, then the investment I curve and the *IS* curve, which are plotted on the basis of the nominal interest rate r on the vertical axis, will each shift up X% when the inflation rate rises from 0% to X%, as shown in Figure 5.1. Why?

Consider the I curve with a 0% inflation rate in Figure 5.1(a). Suppose that $I = 100$ would be forthcoming at $r = 3$%, because $I = 100$ when the expected real interest rate $i^e = 3$%. Now if the inflation rate rises from $p = 0$% to $p = 10$%, so that the expected inflation rate eventually also rises to $p^e = 10$%, then the nominal interest rate r would have to rise to 13% to keep the expected real interest rate at 3% and investment demand at 100. But this means that $I = 100$ at a nominal interest rate of $r = 13$%. Thus, the I curve shifts up by 10% to I', as shown in Figure 5.1(a). Since the *IS* curve is derived from the I curve, it also shifts up by 10% to *IS'*, as shown in Figure 5.1(b). The equilibrium output Q associated with $I = 100$ now occurs at a nominal interest rate of $r = 13$%, instead of $r = 3$%.

If the inflation rate is to remain constant in the long run, Q must be kept at Q_c. Thus, in the *IS–LM* diagram, when the *IS* curve shifts up by X%, the Fed must shift the *LM* curve up by X% to keep the *IS–LM* intersection at the original $Q = Q_c$, as shown in Figure 5.1. This means that the nominal interest rate r will rise by X%.

▶ In long-run equilibrium, nominal money growth m and nominal demand growth y are each X% higher, the inflation rate p is X%

FIGURE 5.1 FISHER'S HYPOTHESIS

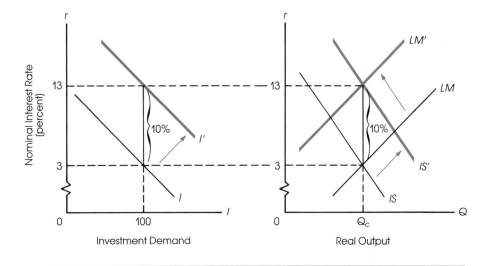

Given an inflation rate of $p = 0\%$, the IS and LM curves intersect at a nominal interest rate of $r = 3\%$, real output $Q = Q_c$, and investment demand $I = \$100$ billion. When the inflation rate rises by 10%, the I curve shifts up by 10% to I' because $I = \$100$ billion is now forthcoming if $r = 13\%$. The IS curve, based on the I curve, also shifts up by 10%. To keep long-run equilibrium output Q at Q_c, monetary policy must reduce the real money supply and thereby shift the LM curve upward by 10% to LM'. Therefore, the 10% rise in the inflation rate results in a 10% rise in the nominal interest rate from $r = 3\%$ to $r = 13\%$.

higher, and the real money-supply is constant at a level less than its original amount, so that the LM curve lies to the left of its original position.

Thus, $IS - LM$ analysis provides support for Fisher's hypothesis. In long-run equilibrium, a rise in the inflation rate from $p = 0\%$ to $p = X\%$ should raise the nominal interest rate r by $X\%$.

It should be pointed out that Fisher's hypothesis can only hold if nominal interest rates are unregulated and free to rise. Thus, it is important that the government permit the upward adjustment of nominal interest rates.

Also, Fisher's hypothesis depends on the full adaptation of the tax system to inflation. We have ignored taxation thus far, but we will see in the next section that tax systems are often poorly adapted to inflation. In particular, real capital income is often mismeasured, so that nominal capital income is taxed instead. In this section, we will assume that the tax system is fully adapted to inflation and that a tax on capital income correctly measures genuine real capital income.

Given these adjustments that preserve the real wage increase and the real interest rate (and assuming the tax system is fully adapted to the inflation), is there any basis for preferring the 0% inflation economy to the 10% inflation economy? The question — perhaps surprisingly — is difficult. We will briefly sketch the answer most economists give, without attempting a full explanation.

Real money — like any real good or service — yields a benefit to its holder. Inflation artificially raises the *price of holding money* (the nominal interest rate) and thereby overly discourages the use of money as people are compelled to hold less real money. Just as any tax on a good overly discourages its use, this *inflation tax* on real money overly discourages its use.

Efficiency requires that the price of any good or service equal its marginal cost. Because the marginal cost of producing real money is virtually 0, its price — the nominal interest rate — should be 0. The nominal interest rate will be 0% if the economy has a *deflation rate* (a *negative inflation rate*) equal to the marginal real return on investment — the productivity of additional machinery (see Chapter 12 for a further explanation). For example, if the real rate of return on investment is 3%, then a deflation rate of 3% will result in a nominal interest rate of 0%.

The conclusion often given to this argument is that this deflation rate would be optimal. But at least two complications must be considered. First, there is a trade-off between the inflation tax and other taxes (or government expenditures). Suppose that the economy is initially characterized by budget deficits financed by money growth and a positive inflation rate. To achieve the target deflation rate, taxes must be raised (or government expenditures must be cut) to convert the budget deficit to a budget surplus and money growth to money contraction. But if other taxes must be raised (or government expenditures must be cut) to eliminate the inflation tax, it is not clear whether total economic inefficiency is reduced.

The second complication is that the inflation rate — and the money-growth rate that generates it — may affect the capital–labor ratio of the economy.

▶ Thus, it is not easy to ascertain the optimal inflation (deflation) rate for the economy when inflation (deflation) is steady and when anticipation and adaptation are perfect.

UNSTEADY INFLATION WITH IMPERFECT ANTICIPATION AND ADAPTATION

The analysis of steady inflation with perfect anticipation and adaptation intrigues professional economists. But in practice, the inflation rate rarely remains constant. An unsteady inflation rate will inevitably be imperfectly anticipated. Individuals often forecast it incorrectly; institutions, such as the tax system, may not fully adapt to it. Let's examine the consequences of imperfect anticipation and adaptation.

Unexpected redistributions of real purchasing power do occur. Workers and management at firm A may agree to a 20% pay increase in anticipation of an 18% inflation rate. Both sides are prepared to accept a 2% real wage increase. But if the inflation rate turns out to be 22%, then the real wage "increase" will actually be -2%; if the inflation rate turns out to be 14%, then the real wage increase will be 6%. In either case, there is an unintended redistribution of real purchasing power from one party to the other.

Similarly, a firm may issue a bond at a nominal interest rate of 24% in anticipation of an 18% inflation rate; a lender may buy the bond, also expecting an 18% inflation rate. Both parties are prepared to accept a 6% real interest rate. But if the inflation rate turns out to be 22%, then the real interest rate will be only 2%; if the inflation rate turns out to be 14%, then the real interest rate will be 10%. Again, there is an unintended redistribution of real purchasing power from one party to the other.

Of course, an economy that normally sets an inflation rate of 2% will, in practice, vary its inflation rate to some degree. Hence, some unintended redistribution of real purchasing power will occur in a *low-inflation economy* as well as in a *high-inflation economy*. But the experience of various countries in various periods suggests that the variation in the inflation rate is greater at a higher inflation rate. In a 2% inflation economy, for example, the typical deviation might be 1%, so that inflation is sometimes 1% and sometimes 3%; in an 18% inflation economy, the typical deviation might be 4%, so that inflation is sometimes 22% and sometimes 14%. The evidence appears to suggest that unintended redistributions of real purchasing power are greater at a higher normal inflation rate.

It is true, of course, that "redistribution" means that there is as much winning as losing. But this does not mean that it is unimportant. After all, robbery is also "merely a redistribution," with as much winning as losing. But this does not mean that a high-robbery society is no worse than a low-robbery society.

The comparison is worth carrying a step further. In a high-robbery society, people live in fear of "redistribution"; they also must begin to devote time and energy to trying to protect themselves against adverse redistributions. The same is true in a high-inflation society. People fear redistributions of real purchasing power and devote time and energy trying to protect themselves from adverse redistributions. Protective responses to the threat of redistribution are clearly a loss for society as a whole.

In Section 5.2, we examined an economy in which institutions are fully adapted to a steady inflation rate. In actual economies, such adaptation is rarely complete. Economies with long histories of high inflation often adapt by the mechanism of *indexing;* even in these economies, however, indexing is often incomplete. What is indexing?

Labor contracts are "indexed" for inflation by the inclusion of automatic *cost-of-living adjustments* (COLAs). For example, a labor contract may specify a nominal wage increase of 2% if the inflation rate is 0%, but specify an automatic adjustment equal to the price inflation rate. Thus, if the price inflation rate is 18%, then the nominal wage would automatically increase to 20%.

In this example, indexing is complete; for each 1% increase in the inflation rate, the nominal wage increase will automatically rise by 1%. In practice in the United States, many negotiated labor contracts have only partial cost-of-living adjustments. Moreover, many workers receive nominal wage increases with no cost-of-living adjustment.

Retirement pensions are indexed if the payments are automatically adjusted according to the inflation rate. In the United States, few private pensions are fully indexed; many are completely unindexed. In contrast, however, the U.S. public pension program — Social Security — is indexed. Social Security benefits automatically increase with the inflation rate. Many government transfer programs for the poor are also indexed.

The lack of full adaptation of the U.S. tax system to inflation is one important reason why, in practice, inflation causes inequity and inefficiency. Two separate problems must be distinguished: (1) the mismeasurement of *real* capital income, and (2) the failure to index tax brackets, which results in "bracket creep." Let's consider each in turn.

The Mismeasurement of Real Capital Income

Suppose that a person buys corporate stock for $100 and sells it a year later for $110. During that year, the inflation rate is 10%. Then there is a *nominal capital gain* of $10; but there is no *real capital gain,* because the $110 at the end of the year has the same real purchasing power as the $100 at the beginning of the year. Yet under the U.S. tax system, the seller of the stock will be taxed on nominal (not real) capital income of $10.

Similarly, suppose that a person saves $100 and earns $10 of nominal interest in a year, totaling $110 at year's end. If the inflation rate remains at 10% throughout the year, then the nominal interest of $10 merely maintains real purchasing power. There is no real gain. Yet under the U.S. tax system, the saver will be taxed on nominal (not real) capital income of $10.

Consider what can happen when nominal capital income is taxed in place of real capital income. Suppose that an individual in the 33% tax bracket can, with no inflation, earn an interest rate of 3% on savings. Thus, the after-tax *real return on savings* is 2%. Now suppose that the inflation rate rises to 9%. According to Fisher's hypothesis, this should raise the nominal interest rate by 9% (from 3% to 12%). Although, in theory, Fisher's hypothesis requires modification for the presence of taxes, we did observe, in practice, a rise in nominal interest rates as inflation rose by roughly 9% from the 1960s to the 1970s in the United States (see Table 5.1).

If the nominal interest rate is 12%, with a 33% tax rate, then the after-tax *nominal return on savings* is 8%. But with an inflation rate of 9%, the after-tax "real" return is actually −1%. Thus, a 9% rise in the inflation rate will reduce the after-tax real return on savings from 2% to −1%.

When the U.S. inflation rate rose to about 9% back in the late 1970s, many households faced a negative after-tax real return on savings. It seems quite possible (although more careful analysis is required to confirm it) that the reduction in the real after-tax return on savings contributed to the decline in the personal savings rate from 8% to 6% during the 1970s in the United States.

What is certain is that the taxation of nominal capital income in a period of inflation causes the after-tax real return on savings to fall significantly below the *real return on investment* (see Chapter 12). Potential savers are given an inaccurate signal; the return they face understates the true productivity of saving (investment). The saving decision is "distorted"; it differs from what it would be if the signal were accurate. Using microeconomic theory, economists can show that the result is an *inefficiency*—that the well-being of the representative person is reduced by the inaccurate signal.

How could this problem be corrected? First, if there were no tax on nominal *or* real capital income, the problem would vanish. If the income tax were converted to a tax on labor income or to a tax on personal consumption, the problem would also disappear. But even if the income tax is retained, the problem could be solved by taxing *real* (not nominal) capital income.

Let's reconsider our two earlier examples. If stock is bought for $100 and price inflation is 10%, then the taxpayer will be instructed to inflate the purchase price by 10% (from $100 to $110). Only a sale price above $110 would result in a taxable capital gain. Similarly, if $100 is saved and price inflation is 10%, then the taxpayer will be instructed to inflate the amount saved by 10% (from $100 to $110). Only interest in excess of this $10 ($110 − $100) would be taxable.

Although it is therefore possible to correct the mismeasurement problem, it has not been corrected despite more than two decades of inflation in the United States. Why? The adjustment does raise certain practical problems. Also, some critics object that such an adjustment will "favor the rich" because they receive a disproportionate share of capital income. Finally, inertia always stands in the way of reform.

A similar problem concerns *depreciation* and the real value of a firm's debt. Under the U.S. income-tax system, a firm can deduct the depreciation of its real capital as a *cost* when computing its income. But the firm's total depreciation must equal the *historical cost* of its capital, even though the *replacement cost* is much higher due to inflation. Thus, the firm is not permitted sufficient depreciation, which raises its taxable profit and tax.

On the other hand, the real value of the firm's outstanding debt declines when inflation rises. This is a gain to the firm, but the gain is excluded from taxable profit. For some firms, the depreciation and debt distortions simply offset one another. For many firms, however, one or the other dominates, and the firm's genuine real capital income is mismeasured for tax purposes.

Again, adjustments could eliminate these problems. But as in the case of capital gains and interest, these adjustments have not been made in the United States.

Even without inflation, the differential taxation of capital income earned in different economic sectors tends to result in inefficient capital allocation. But a rise in inflation, given the mismeasurement problem, tends to make the inefficiency worse.

▶ Thus, when the tax system fails to adapt to inflation and continues to mismeasure real capital income, a rise in inflation generally reduces the efficiency of the economy by distorting savings and investment decisions and intensifying the misallocation of capital.

Bracket Creep

Now let's turn to the second tax problem — the failure to index tax brackets, which results in *bracket creep*. Under the progressive rate schedule of the U.S. income tax, as a household's income increases, its ratio of tax to income increases. The intent is to raise the *tax–income ratio* if the household's real income rises and enables it to afford a higher ratio.

But, in practice, the tax–income ratio rises whenever the household's nominal income increases, whether that increase is due to a rise in real income or to a rise in inflation. Thus, if a household's nominal income increases by 10% when inflation is 10%, then that household's real income remains unchanged but its tax–income ratio rises.

This process is called "bracket creep" for the following reason. Under the U.S. income tax system, a household's income is taxed by brackets, and the tax rate rises for each successive bracket. Rising bracket rates cause a household's tax–income ratio to rise when its nominal income increases. Hence, when inflation raises a household's nominal income, it is "pushed into a higher tax bracket."

The solution to bracket creep is to *index* the brackets. When inflation rises by 10%, the two dollar sums that define the bottom and the top of a bracket should each be raised by 10%. This "indexing of the tax system" would ensure that a household's tax–income ratio rises only when its real income increases. Indexing was enacted in 1981 and went into effect in 1985. For a decade and a half, however, the U.S. tax system was not adjusted to handle the problem of bracket creep caused by inflation.

▶ To summarize, inflation is never perfectly anticipated in actual economies. Moreover, economic institutions tend to adapt slowly — and imperfectly — to inflation. As a result, a high-inflation economy is, in practice, almost always characterized by more unexpected redistributions of real purchasing power and inequities and inefficiencies than a low-inflation economy.

HYPERINFLATION

A *hyperinflation* — an inflation that accelerates out of control — is an economic disaster. Hyperinflations have occurred. For example, Germany and several other European countries suffered hyperinflations in the early 1920s.

Historically, the cause of a hyperinflation has almost always been a rapid increase in the money supply to finance government budget deficits. The government is usually unable to collect taxes to match its expenditures due to political resistance. Therefore, the only way the government can finance its expenditures is to print money. During each period that expenditures exceed tax revenues, new money is injected into the economy. Thus, the government budget deficit becomes the catalyst for money-supply growth, nominal demand growth, and inflation.

The sharp monetary–fiscal expansion overheats the economy, and inflation begins to accelerate, according to our *DG – SG* analysis. If the government now held the money-supply growth rate constant, then the inflation rate would stop accelerating and converge to the rate that is consistent with this constant rate of money-supply growth. But in a hyperinflation, the government is almost always determined to maintain its real (inflation-adjusted) expenditure. If it tries to hold real expenditure constant as inflation rises, what happens?

With inflation accelerating, the government must accelerate its nominal expenditure to keep its real expenditure constant. Hence, the nominal government budget deficit must accelerate, which requires an accelerating money-supply growth rate. Thus, the attempt by the government to maintain real expenditure despite accelerating inflation ironically ensures that money-supply growth and inflation continue to accelerate.

As inflation accelerates, the public tries to shift out of currency and into goods, because currency declines in value at the rate of inflation. Checking deposits might, in theory, compensate owners for inflation by raising the nominal interest rate, but, in practice, interest on deposits is often regulated. With such regulation, inflation in effect imposes a tax on holders of money in the form of currency or checkable deposits, and the public tries to shift out of money to avoid the tax. This inflation tax reduces the public's wealth and consumption, releasing resources to the government.

Accelerating inflation begins to interfere with production. A worker paid on Friday finds that the purchasing power of a paycheck has declined significantly by the following week. It becomes essential to spend money as quickly as it is earned. Workers request shorter pay intervals.

The inefficient system of barter begins to revive, as sellers seek to be paid in goods and services instead of money. Of course, barter is much less efficient than the use of a stable currency. It is very time-consuming for employers to arrange to pay each worker a particular mix of products. Employers, in turn, must spend time obtaining these products from other producers who are willing to trade products. The inconvenience of barter quickly teaches us why money was invented in the first place. But with accelerating inflation, barter must be attempted.

Clearly, a hyperinflation drastically impairs the efficiency of the economy. It results in large, undeserved redistributions of income. It demoralizes a society, as skill at the inflation game becomes more important than hard work and thrift.

SUMMARY

1. The U.S. inflation rate was much higher at the end of the 1970s (approximately 10%) than it was in the early 1960s (approximately 1%), primarily because the average unemployment rate over these two decades was significantly below the constant inflation unemployment rate U_c. Oil-price supply shocks, however, also contributed significantly to the rise in the U.S. inflation rate during this period.

2. The U.S. inflation rate was much higher at the end of the 1970s than it was in the early 1960s, primarily because the nominal demand growth rate y rose significantly over these two decades.

3. The U.S. money-supply growth rate m rose significantly from the early 1960s to the later 1970s. Moreover, the rise in the money-supply growth rate was only somewhat less than the increase in the inflation rate. Expansionary fiscal policy raised the nominal de-

mand growth rate in the second half of the 1960s and may have induced the Federal Reserve to raise the money-supply growth rate.

4. To prevent inflation:
   a. Do not attempt to reduce the unemployment rate U below U_c by expansionary monetary or fiscal policy.
   b. Keep the nominal demand growth rate y—hence, the nominal GNP growth rate—approximately equal to the normal real output growth rate q_c or, equivalently, equal to the sum of the *normal labor-force growth rate f* and the *normal labor productivity growth rate a*. For example, if $f = 1\%$ and $a = 2\%$, then the nominal demand growth rate should, on average, be kept near $y = 3\%$.
   c. Keep the money-supply growth rate m low to maintain a low inflation rate. More specifically, to maintain a 0% inflation rate, the money-supply growth rate should equal $q_c - v$ on average. For example, if $q_c = 3\%$ and v is normally estimated to be 2%, then m should be set at 1% on average.

5. According to the "game of strategy" model, if the Federal Reserve Board genuinely shifts from an "accommodating" to a "nonaccommodating" demand policy and educates the public about the meaning of this shift, then the constant inflation unemployment rate U_c of the economy would decline and the incidence of supply inflation would be reduced. If the "game of strategy" model is accepted and if the primary policy goal is to prevent inflation, then demand management policy should primarily focus on nominal GNP growth—not on real GNP growth or on the unemployment rate per se. Policymakers should try to keep nominal GNP growth on target. On average, the target should be q_c, although temporary modifications of the target may be desirable.

6. The *real wage increase* equals the real labor productivity growth rate a, regardless of the inflation rate ($w - p = a$). Hence, the average worker's standard of living advances at the labor productivity growth rate, whether the inflation rate is high or low.

7. According to *Fisher's hypothesis*, if the inflation rate p rises by $X\%$, then the *nominal interest rate r* will eventually also rise by $X\%$.

8. It's not easy to determine the optimal inflation or *deflation* (a negative inflation rate) rate for the economy when inflation or deflation is steady and when anticipation and adaptation are perfect.

9. In actual economies, inflation is never perfectly anticipated. Moreover, economic institutions such as labor contracts and the tax system tend to adapt slowly—and imperfectly—to inflation. As a result, a *high-inflation economy* is, in practice, almost always char-

acterized by more *unintended redistributions of real purchasing power* and inequities and *inefficiencies* than a *low-inflation economy*. Thus, when the tax system fails to adapt to inflation and continues to mismeasure real capital income, a rise in inflation generally reduces the efficiency of the economy by distorting savings and investment decisions and intensifying the misallocation of capital.

10. A *hyperinflation*—an inflation that accelerates out of control—has historically almost always been caused by a rapid increase in the money supply to finance government budget deficits. A hyperinflation drastically impairs the efficiency of the economy, results in large, undeserved redistributions of income, and demoralizes a society.

TERMS AND CONCEPTS

"accommodating" demand policy
bracket creep
capital income mismeasurement
capital misallocation
Consumer Price Index (CPI)
cost-of-living adjustment (COLA)
deflation rate (negative inflation rate)
expected real interest rate (i^e)
Fisher's hypothesis
"game of strategy" model
GNP deflator
historical cost
hyperinflation
indexing
inflation tax
M1 definition of money
M2 definition of money
nominal capital gain
nominal capital income
nominal interest rate (r)
nominal return on savings

"nonaccommodating" demand policy
normal labor-force growth rate (f)
normal labor-productivity growth rate (a)
normal real output growth rate (q_c)
perfect/imperfect anticipation and adaptation
prime rate
Q_c (normal output) deficit
Q_c (normal output) surplus
real capital gain
real capital income
real interest rate (i)
real return on investment
real return on savings
real wage increase or gain ($w - p$)
replacement cost
tax–income ratio
wage–price control program

QUESTIONS

5.1 Explain why the U.S. inflation rate rose from approximately 1% in the early 1960s to approximately 10% at the end of the 1970s. Make sure your explanation is consistent with the data given in Table 5.1

(page 207). Your explanation should be based on important historical events as well as on $DG-SG$ analysis.

5.2 How should monetary–fiscal policy be conducted to prevent inflation? Refer to the unemployment rate, the nominal demand growth rate, the money-supply growth rate, and the "game of strategy" model in your answer.

5.3 Use an $IS-LM$ diagram to defend *Fisher's hypothesis*.

5.4 Suppose that the inflation rate is raised permanently from 0% to 10%; moreover, assume that there is perfect anticipation and adaptation to this steady inflation rate.

    a. If productivity growth a is not altered, what happens to the *real wage increase* $w-p$? Is the average worker's standard of living reduced by the higher inflation rate?

    b. What happens to the *nominal interest rate* r and to the *real interest rate* i?

    c. Does any genuine economic harm result from the higher inflation rate?

5.5 Give some examples of imperfect adaptation to inflation in the United States. What economic harm occurs when anticipation and adaptation are imperfect?

5.6 What is *hyperinflation* and why is it so harmful?

CHAPTER

6

Disinflation and Transitional Recession

In Chapter 4, we analyzed how inflation arises. In this chapter, we ask: If the economy is already experiencing inflation, how can we reduce it — that is, how can we "disinflate"? We will see that a permanent reduction in nominal demand growth is necessary to reduce inflation. To achieve *disinflation,* monetary and fiscal policy must be adjusted so that its net impact is to reduce nominal demand growth.

The analysis presented in this chapter, as in Chapter 4, relies primarily on the $DG - SG$ diagram. The same analysis can be performed and the same conclusions can be reached by using a simple algebraic model. Such a model is presented in Appendix 6A.

6.1   Abrupt Demand Deceleration: The "Cold Turkey" Policy

In Sections 6.1 – 6.3, we will assume that expectations are *inertial;* people expect the inflation rate in the current period to equal the actual inflation rate in the last period. (We assumed inertial expectations throughout our analysis in Chapter 4.) In Section 6.5, we will consider the alternative hypothesis of rational expectations.

In Chapter 4, we saw that if adjusted nominal demand growth $\hat{y}$ is raised from 0% to 6%, then the inflation rate p will rise from 0% and, in the long run, converge to $p = 6\%$; real output Q will return to Q_c; and the unemployment rate U will return to U_c. Now suppose that the economy is initially in an inflationary equilibrium, with adjusted nominal demand growth $\hat{y} = 6\%$, resulting in $p = 6\%$ and $Q = Q_c$ ($U = U_c$). What happens if $\hat{y}$ is reduced, immediately and permanently, to 0%? We call this a *"cold-turkey" policy* because, instead of gradually reducing $\hat{y}$ in stages from 6% to 0%, $\hat{y}$ is immediately cut to 0%.

Your sense of symmetry should guide you. In the short run, Q will drop below Q_c (U will rise above U_c) and p will begin to decline. In the long run, p will converge to 0% and Q will return to Q_c (and U will return to U_c). Let's go through the steps, period by period, to show that this is so. The *disinflation transition path* is shown in Figure 6.1.

At this point, it is convenient to restate the rule for shifting the DG and SG curves in a growing economy with inertial expectations:

▶ To plot this period's DG and SG curves under inertial expectations, go to last period's intersection point and move vertically until you reach the horizontal $\hat{y}$ line (in a growing economy). Through this point, draw this period's DG curve. Then return to last period's intersection point and move horizontally until you reach the vertical Q_c line. Through this point, draw this period's SG curve.

Recall that in a growing economy, the $\hat{y}$ line replaces the y line in the $DG-SG$ diagram; $\hat{y}$ is defined as the nominal demand growth rate minus the normal real output growth rate ($y - q_c$).

In period 0, the DG and SG curves intersect at $Q = Q_c$ and $p = 6\%$ in Figure 6.1. In period 1, adjusted nominal demand growth $\hat{y}$ is set at 0%. What happens? Go to last period's intersection point 0, and move vertically to the new $\hat{y} = 0\%$ line; through this point, draw DG_1. Then return to point 0 and move horizontally to the Q_c line (but you are already there); through this point, draw SG_1, which coincides with SG_0. DG_1 and SG_1 therefore intersect "southwest" of $Q = Q_c$ and $p = 6\%$. Thus, in period 1, *demand deceleration* reduces both output and the inflation rate. The division between q and p depends on the slope of the SG curve. Since the SG curve has a positive slope, it is certain that Q_1 is less than $Q_0 = Q_c$ and p_1 must lie between 0% and 6%.

This result deserves emphasis. Recall

(4.1) $y \equiv p + q$

Assume that $q_c = 3\%$ and our economy is initially at $\hat{y} = 6\%$ and $y = 9\%$ (6% + 3%). Recall from equation (4.7) that $\hat{y} \equiv y - q_c$.

If $\hat{y}$ is cut by 6% to 0% in period 1, then y is cut from 9% to 3%, so that $p_1 + q_1 = 3\%$.

The sum of p and q must decline by 6% from period 0 to period 1. Do both p and q share the decline? The $DG-SG$ diagram in Figure 6.1 shows that the answer is yes; p_1 is clearly less than 6% but greater than 0%. Thus, we have a crucial result:

▶ Assuming inertial expectations, when nominal demand growth y is cut, both the inflation rate p and the real output growth rate q share the decline in the short run. Inflation is reduced, but real output growth drops below the normal q_c and the unem-

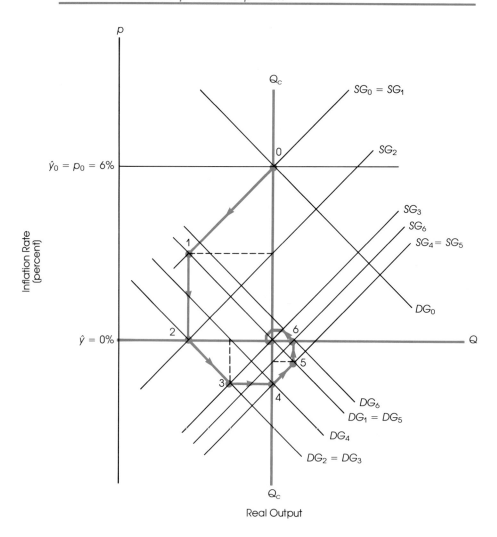

Real Output

Initially, adjusted nominal demand growth $\hat{y} = 6\%$, the inflation rate $p = 6\%$,
and real output $Q = Q_c$. In period 1, $\hat{y}$ is cut permanently to 0%, so that the $\hat{y}$ line
coincides with the horizontal axis. In period 1, SG_1 coincides with SG_0 but DG_1
lies 6% below DG_0. The economy moves to the $DG_1 - SG_1$ intersection at point 1.
In period 2, SG_2 lies below SG_1 and DG_2 lies below DG_1. The economy moves to
the $DG_2 - SG_2$ intersection at point 2. We can see that the economy eventually
spirals into its long-run equilibrium point ($p = \hat{y} = 0\%$, $Q = Q_c$). Thus, in the
long run, the decrease in $\hat{y}$ of 6% reduces the inflation rate p by 6% but has no
effect on the level of real output Q. A transitional recession occurs.

ployment rate rises above the normal U_c. The economy goes into recession.

Although it is certain that p and q share the decline in y, this does not mean that they share it equally. The $DG-SG$ diagram in Figure 6.1 shows clearly that the slope of the SG curve is the key to how the decline in y is shared. When y is cut by 6%, DG_1 shifts down 6% below DG_0, maintaining its standard slope. Thus

▶ If the SG curve is flatter, then the reduction in the inflation rate p is smaller and the reduction in the real output growth rate q is greater.

Later, we will discuss the determinants of the slope of the SG curve in more detail.

Returning to our $DG-SG$ diagram analysis, what happens in period 2? Go to last period's intersection point 1 in Figure 6.1, and move vertically to the $\hat{y} = 0\%$ line; through this point, draw DG_2. Then return to last period's intersection point 1, and move horizontally to the Q_c line; through this point, draw SG_2.

How does the period 2 intersection point compare to the period 1 intersection point? In general, Q_2 may appear less than, equal to, or greater than Q_1 in the diagram. You can see this if you experiment with alternative slopes for the SG curves. What is certain is that p_2 must be less than p_1, because DG_2 lies below DG_1 and SG_2 lies below SG_1, so that the $DG-SG$ intersection must be lower in period 2 than in period 1.

It is convenient to consider the case in which the slope of the SG curve is such that $p_2 = 0\%$, so that in period 2, point 2 lies directly below the $DG-SG$ intersection in period 1 at a point on the $\hat{y} = 0\%$ line. Again, recall equation (4.1): $y \equiv p + q$. In period 2, $y = 3\%$, $p = 0\%$, and $q = 3\%$.

If you suspect that in the long run, the inflation rate p will equal $\hat{y}(0\%)$, then you are right. But if you think that in period 3, p_3 will stay at 0%, like p_2, then you are wrong.

Go to last period's intersection point 2 in Figure 6.1, and move vertically to the $\hat{y} = 0\%$ line (but you are already there). Through this point, draw DG_3, which coincides with DG_2. Then return to last period's intersection point 2, and move horizontally to the Q_c line; through this point, draw SG_3.

Two things are certain about the period 3 intersection point 3. Since SG_3 lies below SG_2 but DG_3 coincides with DG_2, p_3 must be less than p_2. Hence, p_3 must be less than 0%; that is, the inflation rate is negative, and the price level declines. Second, since SG_3 lies to the right of SG_2 but DG_3 coincides with DG_2, Q_3 has moved back toward Q_c.

A dramatic event occurs in period 3. The inflation rate (after a slow start at disinflation) declines below $\hat{y} = 0\%$, and real output, which has been declining relative to Q_c since adjusted nominal demand growth was reduced to $\hat{y} = 0\%$, begins to rise relative to Q_c. Hence, the real output growth rate q, which has been continuously below $q_c = 3\%$ since adjusted nominal demand growth was reduced to $\hat{y} = 0\%$, now rises above 3% in period 3. The unemployment rate U, which has been rising since adjusted nominal demand growth was reduced to $\hat{y} = 0\%$, now begins to decline. Note that since Q_3 still is less than Q_c, U_3 is still greater than U_c. But recovery from the recession has begun.

Intuitively, why does recovery begin? Why does Q begin to move back up toward Q_c? Our result depends on a crucial assumption:

▶ We assume that $\hat{y}$ is held constant at 0% and, equivalently, that y is held constant at q_c (3%).

Why does this assumption assure an automatic recovery? With Q less than Q_c (and U greater than U_c), the inflation rate p will continue to decline, according to hypothesis (4.5). As p declines below 0% and becomes negative, q rises above q_c (3%), because $p + q = y = 3\%$; for example, when p reaches -1%, q rises to 4%. When q rises above q_c (3%), Q begins to move back up toward Q_c and recovery begins.

Note that we have not specified the monetary policy that would keep $\hat{y}$ constant at 0% and y constant at q_c (3%). Some economists would argue that, based on equation (4.14), a steady money-supply growth rate m equal to $q_c - v$ would keep $\hat{y}$ constant at 0%. Other economists would contend that, during the transitional recession, the money-supply growth rate might need to be raised temporarily to reduce interest rates enough to counter the pessimism that would otherwise depress consumption and investment demand in a recession.

We will return to this debate in our discussion of the conduct of monetary policy in Chapter 9. Here, our model assumes that monetary policy does whatever is necessary to keep $\hat{y}$ constant at 0% and to prevent it from becoming negative. If a collapse of consumer and business confidence is not effectively offset by monetary policy, then $\hat{y}$ will become more negative and recovery may not occur.

Let us return to our disinflation story, with $\hat{y}$ held constant at 0%. What happens in period 4? Go to intersection point 3 in Figure 6.1, and move vertically to the $\hat{y} = 0\%$ line; through this point, draw DG_4. Then return to intersection point 3, and move horizontally to the Q_c line; through this point, draw SG_4.

Another dramatic event occurs in period 4: DG_4 lies above DG_3. For the first time since the start of this disinflation story, DG shifts up from one period to the next. Since SG_4 lies below SG_3 but DG_4 lies above DG_3, p_4 may be less than, equal to, or greater than p_3. We will consider the convenient case in which the slopes are such that p_4 is equal to p_3, so that the DG – SG intersection is at point 4. At last, the inflation rate (still negative) has stopped declining. This means that DG_4 and SG_4 intersect at $Q_4 = Q_c$, because the height of SG_4 equals last period's inflation rate p_3 at Q_c.

▶ Note from Figure 6.1 that $Q_4 = Q_c$ ($U_4 = U_c$) and $p_4 = p_3$. Thus, in our model with inertial expectations, inflation stays constant when $Q = Q_c$ ($U = U_c$).

If you suspect that in the long run, Q will settle at Q_c (U at U_c), you are right. But if you think that Q will remain at Q_c from now on, you are wrong.

To see what happens in period 5, go to intersection point 4 in Figure 6.1, and move vertically to the $\hat{y} = 0\%$ line; through this point, draw DG_5. Then return to intersection point 4, and move horizontally to the Q_c line (but you are already there); through this point, draw SG_5, which coincides with SG_4.

Since DG_5 lies above DG_4 but SG_5 coincides with SG_4, Q_5 has moved above Q_c, and p_5 is greater than p_4. Both events are significant. For the first time, Q rises above Q_c; the inflation rate starts back up toward $\hat{y} = 0\%$.

Now let your intuition make an imaginative leap. You should sense that the path of the economy will spiral inward in Figure 6.1 until, in the long run, it converges to $Q = Q_c$ ($U = U_c$) and $p = \hat{y} = 0\%$. This is in fact the case.

It is easy to see that for the DG and SG curves to stabilize, they must intersect at $Q = Q_c$ and $p = \hat{y} = 0\%$. First, suppose that DG and SG intersect at $Q = Q_c$ and $p = \hat{y}$ in the last period. Will each curve remain in the same position in the current period, so that the $DG - SG$ intersection point remains the same? The answer is yes.

Go to last period's intersection point (Q_c, 0%), and move vertically to the $\hat{y} = 0\%$ line (but you are already there); through this point, draw this period's DG curve, which coincides with last period's DG curve. Then return to point (Q_c, 0%), and move horizontally to the Q_c line (but you are already there); through this point, draw this period's SG curve, which coincides with last period's SG curve. Hence, the $DG - SG$ intersection points for this period and last period are the same.

For any other point in the $Q-p$ diagram, at least one of the two curves will not remain stable. The DG curve will remain stable if and only if last period's $p = \hat{y}$. The SG curve will remain stable if and only if last period's $Q = Q_c$.

To summarize:

▶ We began with our economy experiencing an inflation rate of $p = 6\%$, generated by adjusted nominal demand growth of $\hat{y} = 6\%$. (With $q_c = 3\%$, this implies a nominal demand growth of $y = 9\%$.) Initially, the economy was at $Q = Q_c$ ($U = U_c$).

The Behavior of the Interest Rate During Disinflation Generated by a Reduction in Money Growth

It is worth connecting our $DG-SG$ analysis of disinflation with our $IS-LM$ analysis in Chapters 2 and 5, so that the behavior of the nominal interest rate r and the real interest rate i ($i \equiv r - p$) during disinflation can be noted. You may find it helpful to review the discussion of Fisher's hypothesis in Section 5.3 (pages 228–31) before you proceed.

Let's consider the important case in which the reduction in nominal demand growth y is engineered by monetary policy—by decreasing the money-supply growth rate m.

Initially, in period 1 of our disinflation story, the nominal money-supply growth rate m is cut more than the inflation rate p, so that the real money supply M/P declines; thus, the LM curve shifts to the left. With the IS curve initially fixed, the economy moves in a "northwest" direction up the fixed IS curve to a new $IS-LM$ intersection point at a higher interest rate r and a lower level of real output Q.

Soon, however, the interest rate r reaches a peak and then begins to decline. Why? As the inflation rate p declines, the reduction in p "catches up" to the reduction in money growth and the real money supply M/P begins to increase; hence, the LM curve shifts back to the right (downward).

Also, the investment demand I curve—and hence the IS curve—shift downward for two distinct reasons. First, as recession occurs, investment demand decreases at any given interest rate r due to pessimism and idle plant capacity; thus, the IS curve shifts to the left (downward). Second, as we said in Chapter 5 in our discussion of Fisher's hypothesis, investment demand I depends on the expected real interest rate i^e ($i^e \equiv r - p^e$); a full explanation will be given in Chapter 12. As the inflation rate p declines, the I curve shifts downward, because a lower nominal interest rate r corresponds to the same expected real interest rate i^e; hence, the IS curve shifts downward.

As disinflation continues, the nominal interest rate r eventually becomes lower than its initial value. In fact, in the long run, the reduction in r should roughly equal the reduction in p, according to Fisher's hypothesis (5.2). For example, if $r = 10\%$ and $p = 6\%$ initially and if p is reduced from 6% to 0% in the long run, then r should also be reduced by approximately 6% (to 4%). The real interest rate i would then be 4% at the end, just as it was at the beginning.

Let's summarize what happens to the interest rate r when disinflation is engineered by slowing the nominal money-supply growth rate. Initially, r rises; the higher interest rate reduces borrowing and investment demand, thereby generating recession. But then r peaks, begins to decline, and eventually becomes permanently lower than its original level. From beginning to end, the reduction in the interest rate r should roughly equal the reduction in the inflation rate p.

Adjusted nominal demand growth was then reduced immediately and permanently to $\hat{y} = 0\%$; nominal demand growth was reduced to $y = 3\%$. In the long run, this reduction in $\hat{y}$ from 6% to 0% succeeds in reducing the inflation rate p from 6% to 0%. Moreover, in the long run, real output Q returns to Q_c (and the unemployment rate U returns to U_c). But in the short run, a transitional recession—a transitional rise in the unemployment rate and decline in real output relative to Q_c—is generated.

INERTIA AS THE CAUSE OF THE RECESSION

Our $DG - SG$ diagram tells us that the reduction in the nominal demand growth rate y must generate a transitional decline in real output Q and a rise in the unemployment rate U. Intuitively, why is this so?

The answer lies in remembering what determines the position and slope of the SG curve. The reduction in the nominal demand growth rate y shifts the DG curve downward in period 1 in Figure 6.1. Because SG_1 coincides with SG_0, DG_1 intersects it at point 1 to the left of Q_c, so that a recession occurs.

Now suppose that SG_1 does not coincide with SG_0, but instead lies 6% below it (just as DG_1 lies 6% below DG_0 in Figure 6.1). Then DG_1 would intersect SG_1 at Q_c, and no transitional rise in the unemployment rate would occur. In Section 6.5, we will present the rational expectations hypothesis that would yield this happy result exactly.

Why does SG_1 coincide with the SG_0 in Figure 6.1? Let's review some of the important points in Chapter 4 regarding the determinants of the SG curve. For each period, the SG curve indicates the inflation rate p that producers will set at each level of real output Q (at each unemployment rate U). If the "normal" relationship holds in a given year and producers maintain a constant price–unit labor cost $(P-\text{ULC})$ ratio, then the inflation rate p will equal the unit labor cost growth rate (ulc), which is equal to the wage increase w minus labor productivity growth a, or

(4.3) $p = \text{ulc} = w - a$

For example, if $w = 8\%$ and $a = 2\%$ initially, then ulc $= 6\%$ and producers will set $p = 6\%$. If w is cut by 6% (to 2%), then, with labor productivity growth a held constant at 2%, p will also be reduced by 6% (to 0%). More generally, assuming that a remains constant

(4.4) $\Delta p = \Delta w$

Will the wage inflation rate w set in period 1 respond to the reduction in nominal demand growth y if U remains at U_c? The answer depends on whether the expected inflation rate p^e responds to the reduction in y. As we noted in Section 4.3:

▶ At a given real output Q (equivalently, at a given unemployment rate U), if the expected inflation rate p^e increases (decreases) by $X\%$, then the wage inflation rate w normally increases (decreases) by $X\%$.

If the expected inflation rate p^e immediately declines by 6% in response to a 6% cut in the nominal demand growth rate y, then the wage inflation rate w will be reduced by 6% and, from equation (4.3), so will the inflation rate p; hence, SG_1 will lie 6% below SG_0. But if p^e is unaffected by the cut in y, then w and p will be unaffected and SG_1 will coincide with SG_0.

At last, we arrive at our crucial assumption of inertial expectations:

▶ The expected inflation rate p^e is equal to last period's inflation rate p_{-1}.

Under inertial expectations, the expected inflation rate p^e in period 1 equals the actual inflation rate p in period 0 and therefore will be unaffected by any change in the nominal demand growth rate y in period 1. Thus, at any given Q (and U), a reduction in y will have no immediate effect on p^e or w—and, therefore, on p (the height of the SG curve at that level of Q). The position of SG_1 is independent of the change in y in period 1.

▶ The "refusal" of SG_1 to shift downward when the nominal demand growth rate y is cut results in a decrease in real output Q (since DG_1 does shift downward when y is cut). The source of this "refusal"—inertial expectations—keeps the wage increase w, and therefore the inflation rate p, at any level of Q independent of the cut in y.

This does not mean that this period's nominal demand growth rate y has no effect on the wage increase w. If reducing this period's y should raise the unemployment rate U, then w would decline for a given p^e. But that is just the point:

▶ Because a cut in the nominal demand growth rate y does not affect the expected inflation rate p^e, which equals last period's inflation rate p_{-1}, a reduction in y can reduce the wage inflation rate w only by raising the unemployment rate U. This is exactly what happens when y is cut in period 1.

Under inertial expectations, unless the unemployment rate U is raised, w, ulc, and p, through equation (4.3), will "refuse" to come down. Thus, the reduction in the nominal demand growth rate y brings down the inflation rate p only by first raising the unemployment rate U. The rise in U is necessary to reduce w, ulc, and p.

▶ Under inertial expectations, a reduction in the nominal demand growth rate y must generate a transitional rise in the unemployment rate U—a *transitional recession*—in the process of reducing the inflation rate p.

This sobering conclusion immediately causes us to ask: How much transitional unemployment? How severe a recession?

Once inertial expectations assures that SG_1 coincides with SG_0, the slope of this SG_1 curve becomes the determining factor. If the SG curve is flatter, then the reduction in p will be smaller and the reduction in Q will be greater when DG shifts downward.

What determines the slope of the SG curve? When Q declines (or U rises), by how much will firms cut the inflation rate p? The answer is crucially dependent on how the wage inflation rate w responds to the rise in the unemployment rate U. From equation (4.3), we know that if the cut in w is greater for a given rise in U, then the cut in the unit labor cost growth rate ulc—and, therefore, in p—will be greater and the SG curve will be steeper. If the SG curve is steeper, then the reduction in p will be greater and the reduction in Q will be smaller when the DG curve shifts downward.

▶ Thus, the steepness of the SG curve is crucially dependent on the responsiveness of the wage inflation rate w to a rise in the unemployment rate U.

We have now isolated the key element that determines how a decline in the nominal demand growth rate y is shared between the inflation rate p and the real output growth rate q. Can we actually provide a quantitative estimate of this relationship? We will now turn to this important task.

6.2 How Responsive Is Disinflation to a Rise in Unemployment?

Returning to an important conclusion we drew in Chapter 4, under inertial expectations (in the absence of supply shocks)

(4.5)   If $U = U_c$, then the inflation rate will stay constant
           ($\Delta p = \Delta w = 0\%$).
           If $U < U_c$, then the inflation rate will rise ($\Delta p = \Delta w > 0\%$).
           If $U > U_c$, then the inflation rate will decline ($\Delta p = \Delta w < 0\%$).

Note that these relations rely on equation (4.4). If the growth rate of the price–unit labor cost ratio k and labor productivity growth a are constant, then

(4.4) $\Delta p = \Delta w$

If equation (4.4) holds, it means that when we say "inflation" will decline by X%, we mean that both *price* and *wage* inflation will decline by X%.

Suppose that we adopt the hypothesis that the economy is characterized by inertial expectations, so that hypothesis (4.5) is valid. How can we quantify the magnitude of the responsiveness of disinflation to a rise in the unemployment rate?

We can write an equation that embodies hypothesis (4.5) and try to estimate the key parameters in the equation by "fitting the equation to the data" using statistical techniques. Let's assume that the relationship between Δw or Δp and U described in hypothesis (4.5) is governed by

(6.1) $$\Delta p = \Delta w = \frac{h(U_c - U)}{U} \qquad h > 0$$

where h = the responsiveness parameter

For example, if $U_c = 7\%$, then

$$\Delta p = \Delta w = \frac{h(7\% - U)}{U} \qquad h > 0$$

If the unemployment rate in a given period $U = 7\%$, then we simply substitute 7% for U to obtain

$$\Delta p = \Delta w = \frac{h(7\% - 7\%)}{7\%} = 0\%$$

Thus, $\Delta p = \Delta w = 0\%$. Hence, inflation will remain constant.

If the unemployment rate in a given period is less than 7% ($U < 7\%$), then the numerator $h(7\% - U)$ in equation (6.1) will be positive, so that Δw (and Δp) will be positive; hence, inflation will increase. If the unemployment rate in a given period is greater than 7% ($U > 7\%$), then the numerator $h(7\% - U)$ in equation (6.1) will be negative, so that Δw (and Δp) will be negative; hence, inflation will decrease.

Note that if this period's unemployment rate $U = U_c$, inflation stays constant ($\Delta p = 0\%$), so that U_c in equation (6.1) is really the constant inflation unemployment rate.

By how much does the wage inflation rate w respond to a given U? The numerical value of the responsiveness parameter h determines the answer. The value of h depends on the calendar length of a "period." Thus

▶ From this point on, we will consider the calendar length of a "period" to be one year.

For example, if $h = 0.09$ and $U = 9\%$, then

$$\Delta p = \Delta w = \frac{h(U_c - U)}{U}$$

$$= \frac{0.09(7\% - 9\%)}{9\%}$$

$$= \frac{0.09(-2\%)}{9\%}$$

$$= -2\%$$

In other words, if the unemployment rate U is raised 2% above U_c for one year, then the inflation rate p will decline by 2% over that year. If, instead, $h = 0.18$ (twice as large), then the inflation rate will decline by twice as much (4%).

Now let's relate the magnitude of h to the steepness of the SG curve. If h is larger, then the decline in w is greater for a given rise in U (or decline in Q); hence, the decline in p is greater. But if a larger h means that p declines more for a given decline in Q, then a larger h means that the SG curve will be steeper.

▶ If the responsiveness parameter h is larger, then the SG curve is steeper. Thus, the decline in the inflation rate p is greater and the decline in the real output growth rate q (and the rise in U) are smaller in response to a decline in the nominal demand growth rate y.

Returning to our example with $h = 0.09$ and $U_c = 7\%$, we saw that if the unemployment rate is held at $U = 9\%$ for one year, then the inflation rate p will consequently decline by 2%. In other words, if U is held 2 percentage points above the constant inflation unemployment rate of the economy ($U_c = 7\%$) for one year, then the inflation rate p will decline by 2%.

Now suppose that U is held only 1 percentage point above the U_c of the economy ($U_c = 7\%$) for two years. By how much will the inflation rate p decline over the two years? In one year, with $U = 8\%$, the inflation rate will decline by

$$\Delta p = \Delta w = \frac{0.09(7\% - 8\%)}{8\%}$$

$$= \frac{0.09(-1\%)}{8\%}$$

$$= -1\% \text{ (approximately)}$$

Thus, in two years, the inflation rate will decline by approximately 2%.

▶ The same reduction (approximately) in the inflation rate p is achieved if the unemployment rate U is held 2% above the constant inflation unemployment rate U_c for one year, or 1% above U_c for two years.

Due to this observation, it is useful to define a new concept:

1 POINT-YEAR OF EXCESS UNEMPLOYMENT occurs when the unemployment rate U is held 1 percentage point above the constant inflation unemployment rate U_c for one year; or 0.5 percentage points above U_c for two years; or 2 percentage points above U_c for one-half year; or any other combination of excess unemployment and the number of years it is sustained that yields a product that equals 1.

We can now summarize the example in which $h = 0.09$:

▶ When $h = 0.09$, 2 point-years (approximately) of excess unemployment (above 7%) will reduce the inflation rate p by 2%. The 2 point-years may be achieved by holding the unemployment rate at $U = 9\%$ for one year (so that excess unemployment is 2%), or by holding U at 8% for two years (so that excess unemployment is 1%), or by any combination of excess unemployment and the number of years it is sustained that has a product that equals 2. Thus, in this example, to reduce the inflation rate by 1% requires (approximately) 1 point-year of excess unemployment (above 7%).

ECONOMETRIC ESTIMATES

If our hypothesis is correct and equation (6.1) is a valid approximation of the true, normal relationship between Δw (and Δp) and U, then our problem is to find the numerical values of h and U_c that best fit the data for the United States. We seek econometric estimates for h and U_c—estimates that are based on statistical analysis of the data. How should we proceed?

We assume that the values of h and U_c have remained constant over our sample period. Our problem then is to find one value of h—and one value of U_c—that best fits the data for the sample period. Of course, in the real, complex economy, we should not expect a simple equation like equation (6.1) to fit the data perfectly for any values of h and U_c.

Let's illustrate. Suppose that we estimate that the "correct" value of h is 0.09 and that the "correct" value of U_c is 7.0%. Now take any year. If $U = 9\%$, then, given our numerical values for h and U_c, equation (6.1) predicts that $\Delta w = -2\%$. If, in fact, $\Delta w = -3\%$ for that year, then our prediction that year is "off" by 1%. We will call this the "error" for that year. For these values of h and U_c, we can compute the error for each year in our 20-year sample.

Now suppose that we estimate that the "correct" value of h is 0.045 (half as large as 0.09), and that the "correct" value of U_c is 7.0%. Then in the year when $U = 9\%$, our equation will now predict a Δw that is half as large (-1%). Since Δw in that year is actually -3%, our prediction will be off by 2%. For that year, our estimate of $h = 0.09$ fits the data better than our estimate of $h = 0.045$. In other years, however, the reverse may be true. Some other values of h and U_c may normally produce even smaller errors in most years.

Intuitively, we seek the values of h and U_c that will minimize error over the sample period. To be more precise, it might seem natural to try to find the values of h and U_c that will minimize the sum of the annual errors, but this might allow large positive and negative errors to cancel one another out, resulting in a small sum but a poor fit. To solve the "sign canceling" problem, we could minimize the sum of the squares of the errors. The estimates of h and U_c that achieve this are called the *ordinary least squares* (OLS) *estimates.* Standard computer programs will calculate the OLS estimates, given the actual data over the sample and the equation being fitted.

Before trying to obtain the OLS estimates for h and U_c, it will be useful to refer to Table 6.1 to determine if equation (6.1) appears to be valid for most years. Let's consider the high unemployment years 1975 and 1976. In 1975, despite a U of 8.3%, Δw is not negative; its small, positive value is 0.2%. In 1976, however, with a U of 7.6%, $\Delta w = -1.5\%$. If we combine the two years, U averages 8.0% and Δw averages -0.7%.

Next, consider the high unemployment years 1982 and 1983. In 1982, with a U of 9.5%, $\Delta w = -1.6\%$. In 1983, with a U of 9.5%, $\Delta w = -3.1\%$. If we combine the two years, U averages 9.5% and Δw averages -2.4%.

By contrast, let's consider some low unemployment years. From 1966 to 1969, U averages 3.6% and Δw averages 0.8%. However, in 1969, with a U of 3.4% Δw is nevertheless negative (-1.0%).

To summarize, a casual glance at the data suggests that although equation (6.1) with a positive h does not fit the data perfectly, it appears to be consistent with most years.

We now want to calculate the values of h and U_c that will minimize the sum of the squared errors over our sample period. Standard com-

TABLE 6.1

U.S. INFLATION AND UNEMPLOYMENT DATA

Year	U	w	Δw	p	Δp
1965	4.4%	3.4%	−1.1%	1.6%	0.4%
1966	3.7%	6.0%	2.6%	2.8%	1.2%
1967	3.7%	5.5%	−0.5%	3.2%	0.4%
1968	3.5%	7.5%	2.0%	4.0%	0.8%
1969	3.4%	6.5%	−1.0%	4.7%	0.7%
1970	4.8%	7.0%	0.5%	4.8%	0.1%
1971	5.8%	6.6%	−0.4%	4.5%	−0.3%
1972	5.5%	6.7%	0.1%	3.0%	−1.5%
1973	4.8%	7.6%	0.9%	3.8%	0.8%
1974	5.5%	9.4%	1.8%	10.2%	6.4%
1975	8.3%	9.6%	0.2%	10.3%	0.1%
1976	7.6%	8.1%	−1.5%	5.1%	−5.2%
1977	6.9%	7.5%	−0.6%	5.7%	0.6%
1978	6.0%	8.6%	1.1%	7.1%	1.4%
1979	5.8%	9.0%	0.4%	8.8%	1.7%
1980	7.0%	10.3%	1.3%	10.0%	1.2%
1981	7.5%	9.6%	−0.7%	9.8%	−0.2%
1982	9.5%	8.0%	−1.6%	5.7%	−4.1%
1983	9.5%	4.9%	−3.1%	3.2%	−2.5%
1984	7.4%	4.6%	−0.3%	3.1%	−0.1%

SOURCE: *Economic Report of the President 1985*, Tables B-33 and B-41, pp. 271, 279; data obtained by the U.S. Bureau of Labor Statistics. *U* is the unemployment rate of all workers, *w* is the percentage change in compensation per hour in the nonfarm business sector (includes fringe benefits as well as cash wages or salaries), and *p* is the percentage change in the implicit price deflator for the nonfarm business sector.

puter programs are available to do this. These programs usually require that the equation be of the form

(6.2) $Z = b_0 + b_1 X$

where X is the independent variable and Z is the dependent variable. If the computer is given the values for X and Z in each year of the sample, it will compute the value of b_0 and the value of b_1 that will minimize the sum of the squared errors. To obtain the OLS estimates for h and U_c, we must adapt equation (6.1) to the form of equation (6.2). First, we multiply out the numerator of the right side of equation (6.1):

$$\Delta p = \Delta w = \frac{hU_c - hU}{U}$$

Then we separate the right side of equation (6.1) into two terms:

$$\Delta p = \Delta w = \frac{hU_c}{U} - \frac{hU}{U} = hU_c \left(\frac{1}{U}\right) - h$$

$$\Delta p = \Delta w = -h + hU_c \left(\frac{1}{U}\right)$$

$$Z = b_0 + b_1 \quad X$$

Thus

$$Z = \Delta p = \Delta w$$

$$X = \frac{1}{U}$$

(6.3) $b_0 = -h$

(6.4) $b_1 = hU_c$

Hence, our independent variable is $1/U$, the reciprocal of the unemployment rate; our dependent variable is either Δw or Δp. The computer will supply the values of b_0 and b_1 that minimize the sum of the squared errors. From b_0 and b_1 we can easily obtain our estimates of h and U_c, since, from equations (6.3) and (6.4)

(6.5) $h = -b_0$

(6.6) $U_c = \dfrac{b_1}{h} = \dfrac{b_1}{-b_0}$

The data needed to obtain estimates of h and U_c were presented in Table 6.1. Table 6.2 shows the results for each dependent variable Δw and Δp for three sample periods: 1965–1984, 1970–1984, and 1975–1984. We can draw several conclusions from these data:

1. For a given sample period, the estimate of U_c is approximately the same for both dependent variables.
2. For a given sample period, the estimate of h is larger for Δp than for Δw. Price inflation appears to be more responsive than wage inflation to unemployment in the short run.
3. As the sample becomes more recent, the estimate of U_c rises.
4. As the sample becomes more recent, the estimate of h rises.

TABLE 6.2

THE RESPONSIVENESS OF INFLATION TO UNEMPLOYMENT

	1965–1984	1970–1984	1975–1984
Dependent Variable: Δw			
h	0.019	0.042	0.065
U_c	5.5%	6.3%	6.8%
Dependent Variable: Δp			
h	0.026	0.065	0.109
U_c	5.7%	6.4%	6.9%

Let's consider the two equations from the most recent sample period (1975–1984) more carefully. In both equations, the t statistics for b_0 and b_1 are approximately 3, indicating "statistical significance" (a t value greater than 2 suffices for "significance"). Thus, variations in the inflation rate are associated with variations in the unemployment rate. The adjusted R^2 statistic is near 0.5 for both equations, indicating that variations in the unemployment rate explain roughly 50% of the variation in the inflation rate.

For the 1975–1984 sample, the average value of U_c is 6.9% and the average value of h is 0.087. In drawing conclusions and providing examples, we will therefore assume that U_c is approximately 7% and that h is approximately 0.09.

We have intentionally used a simple equation with only one independent variable—the unemployment rate—to illustrate how economists attempt to obtain quantitative estimates. Our results, however, are similar to the results obtained in more sophisticated studies that consider several variables and employ more precise statistical techniques.*

We must emphasize that our estimates $U_c = 7\%$ and $h = 0.09$ should be expected to contain error. U_c could well be 6.5% or 7.5%; h could well be 0.06 or 0.12. Our estimates—and the conclusions they imply— should be viewed as rough approximations.

---

* For example, see Robert J. Gordon, "Understanding Inflation in the 1980s," *Brookings Papers on Economic Activity* 1(1985): 263–99.

We can draw a useful rule of thumb from our analysis. If we assume that the 1975–1984 period yields the most relevant estimates for the current values of U_c and h, then U_c appears to be roughly 7% and h appears to be roughly 0.09. But $U_c = 7\%$ and $h = 0.09$ are the values we used in our earlier example. We saw that an h of 0.09 implies that 1 point-year of excess unemployment (above 7%) is required to reduce the inflation rate by 1%.

▶ According to econometric analysis of the 1975–1984 data, it appears that an unemployment rate above 7% might be required to reduce the inflation rate. It is estimated that 1 point-year of excess unemployment (above 7%) would be required to reduce the inflation rate by 1%. As examples, an unemployment rate of 8% (so that excess unemployment is 1%), sustained for one year, should reduce the inflation rate by 1%; an unemployment rate of 9% (so that excess unemployment is 2%), sustained for one-half year, should reduce the inflation rate by 1%.

Some economists believe that such analysis of past data results in an inaccurate estimate of what would happen if the monetary authorities were to adopt a clear, well publicized policy of demand deceleration. We will examine this argument in Section 6.5.

Thus far, our quantitative analysis has focused on the unemployment rate. It is also important to know how much real output is lost when the unemployment rate rises above U_c during the disinflation process. Your first impression might be that each additional 1% of unemployment should correspond to an approximate 1% reduction in real output. Consider an example.

Suppose that out of an initial labor force of 100 persons with $U = 7\%$, 93 are employed and 7 are unemployed. The 93 employed persons produce a given output, which we will call Q_{93}. Now suppose that the unemployment rate rises by 1% to 8%. If the labor force remains at 100, then the number of employed persons will decrease to 92, and Q will decrease to Q_{92}.

It may seem that Q_{92} is about 1% less than Q_{93}. But analysis of actual data shows that a 1% rise in the unemployment rate normally is associated with at least a 2% decline in real output — not a 1% decline, as the example seems to imply. Why? There are several reasons.

First, when demand decelerates and real output begins to decline, firms initially try to minimize layoffs because they do not know whether the decline will be brief or sustained. If the decline in real output turns out to be brief, then the firms that minimize layoffs thereby minimize the cost of hiring and training new workers. Thus, initially, firms cut output by reducing the hours worked per employee and the intensity of effort required per worker. Hence, labor productivity (output per worker) begins to decline. In the extreme, if no employment reductions occurred at all, we would observe no rise in the unemployment rate but real output would decline nevertheless. In reality, some employment reductions will occur, but the unemployment rate will rise by a smaller percentage than real output will decline.

Second, as the unemployment rate rises, some persons become discouraged about finding work and drop out of the labor force. To be counted in the labor force — or to be counted as officially unemployed — a person must be actively looking for work. In our example, suppose that when the unemployment rate rises to 8%, 1 person out of 100 drops out of the labor force. Hence, an 8% unemployment rate corresponds to a labor force of 99 persons, with 8 unemployed and 91 employed. Thus, the 1% rise in the unemployment rate (from 7% to 8%) corresponds to a decline in real output from Q_{93} to Q_{91}; we may therefore suspect that a 2% (not a 1%) decline in real output Q occurs, because employment has declined roughly 2%.

This empirical relationship between the rise in the unemployment rate and the associated decline in real output is called *Okun's Law,* after the late Arthur Okun who first investigated it back in the early 1960s. Okun originally found a 3:1 relationship (a 1% rise in U corresponding to a 3% decline in Q). In recent years, other economists have estimated a relationship closer to 2:1. In Appendix 6A, we present a simple econometric analysis to support this basic 2:1 estimate.

According to OKUN'S LAW, a 1% rise in the unemployment rate U corresponds to roughly a 2% decline in real output Q.

For example, in 1982, current-dollar GNP was roughly $3 trillion. For each 1% increase in the unemployment rate that year, at least $60 billion of GNP (2% of $3 trillion) was lost. In 1982, the unemployment rate was 9.5%. If U_c is estimated at 7%, then the 2.5% rise in the unemployment rate above U_c corresponds to a loss of at least $150 billion (at least 5% of GNP) in that year, according to Okun's Law.

Let's compare the impact of two situations: (1) a 9% unemployment rate (2% excess unemployment) sustained for one year, and (2) an 8% unemployment rate (1% excess unemployment) sustained for two years. In both cases, there are 2 point-years of excess unemployment and there should be roughly a 2% reduction in the inflation rate. Will the real output loss be approximately the same in both cases?

The answer is yes. Excess unemployment of 2%, sustained for one year, will result in a 4% loss of annual GNP. Excess unemployment of 1%, sustained for one year, will result in a 2% loss of annual GNP; sustained for two years, 1% excess unemployment will result in a 4% loss of annual GNP. Thus, we can restate Okun's Law as follows:

According to OKUN'S LAW, each point-year of excess unemployment corresponds to a loss of roughly 2% of annual GNP.

Since each 1% reduction in the inflation rate requires 1 point-year of excess unemployment, and 1 point-year of excess unemployment corresponds to a loss of 2% of annual GNP, then:

▶ According to econometric analysis of the 1975–1984 data, each 1% reduction in the inflation rate requires a sacrifice of roughly 2% of annual GNP under a policy of demand deceleration.

Let's apply our quantitative rules to the 1982 recession. Based on the data presented in Table 6.1, the unemployment rate averaged 9.5% in 1982 and 1983. Over these two years, there were 5 point-years of excess unemployment. According to our rule of thumb, the wage and price inflation rates should have declined by roughly 5% over the two years. In fact, w fell 4.7% and p fell 6.6%. According to Okun's Law, approximately 10% of annual GNP was sacrificed over these two years.

WHY RESPONSIVENESS IS LIMITED

Thus far in this section, we have reviewed the empirical evidence concerning the responsiveness of disinflation to a rise in the unemployment rate. It appears that wage and price inflation do not respond quickly enough to a rise in the unemployment rate to avoid a significant recession during the disinflation process. The SG curve is too flat.

Why isn't the SG curve steeper? Why aren't wage inflation and price inflation more responsive? Why doesn't even a small rise in the unemployment rate above U_c cause a prompt, sharp drop in w and p, so that only a mild, short recession is needed to eliminate inflation? Several reasons have been offered by economists.

First, long-term wage contracts constrain wage responsiveness in important sectors of the economy. A rise in the unemployment rate generally cannot affect the scheduled wage increase in these sectors until the contract (often three years in length) expires. Because unit labor costs continue to rise according to the previously negotiated schedule, firms must cover these cost increases with price increases, despite the onset of recession.

Second, even when firms are free to change wages, they may be constrained from doing so by *implicit contracts*. Unlike an explicit wage contract, an implicit contract is unwritten and often involves a tacit understanding between management and workers. Arthur Okun calls an implicit contract an "invisible handshake" between the two parties. Management agrees not to take advantage of a rise in unemployment to sharply cut wage increases; workers pledge loyalty and effort.

Why might management adopt a wage policy that differs so dramatically from the behavior that should characterize a competitive labor market according to the traditional view? A rise in the unemployment rate should cause the typical employer to implement a sharp cut in the wage increase immediately and to replace any employee who would not accept a substantially reduced wage increase with an unemployed worker, according to traditional theory.

But according to the new *efficiency wage hypothesis,* this ruthless personnel policy may actually hurt the long-term profits of the firm. Employers who appear eager to use the unemployed to threaten their own workers may lose the loyalty of their workforce. The more valuable employees may quit as soon as economic recovery returns; even those who stay may reduce their effort and productivity.

Thus, firms may find it profitable in the long run to treat employees fairly. One element of such a policy would be not to take advantage of a rise in the unemployment rate. This does not mean that the wage increase might not be somewhat moderated in recession; indeed, our analysis of the data shows that some moderation clearly occurs. But the wage increase should be much less responsive to recession than the traditional view assumes.

This raises another question. When a firm tacitly agrees to exhibit inertia in w, it is forced to lay off workers when product demand declines. A cut in w might enable the firm to avoid the layoffs. Why, in the U.S. economy, do most firms hold w relatively steady and opt to lay off employees?

One reason may be the preference of unions. Junior workers are generally laid off first; workers with seniority are usually retained. If workers are ranked by seniority at a given firm, the most senior 70% (excluding exceptional cases) can feel confident that they will remain employed if w is not cut. These 70% may control union policy. The union, reflecting this majority, may press management to choose layoffs, rather than a cut in w, to reduce labor costs in response to a decline in revenues.

Even if there is no union, management may consider the senior 70% of the workforce to be more valuable than the junior 30%. A general cut in w hurts senior as well as junior workers and may, when economic prosperity returns, provoke some senior workers to leave. Firms may prefer to avoid this risk. It may pay for a firm to develop a reputation for protecting the wage increase of the senior majority rather than the jobs of the junior minority.

Finally, many workers may perceive a cut in w as more "exploitive" than layoffs. If management sharply cuts w ostensibly to avoid layoffs, then employees can never be sure whether layoffs actually would have occurred without the cut in w. The suspicion of management that this uncertainty may generate could produce lower morale and productivity and a higher rate of attrition. A layoff is usually harsh to the employee experiencing it, but at least the firm cannot continue to profit from the laid-off worker's labor. If most workers consider layoffs to be less exploitive than a cut in w, then management may layoff employees and avoid cutting w.

In recent years, macroeconomists have analyzed implicit contracts in an attempt to account for the limited responsiveness of wage and price inflation that we observe in a recessionary period. Progress has been made in showing why the traditional view, which assumes a very high responsiveness, is not likely to characterize much of the labor market. Thus, recognition of the "invisible handshake" provides an explanation of the limited responsiveness of wage and price inflation that we observe in the actual economy.

6.3 Gradual Demand Deceleration Versus "Cold Turkey"

In Section 6.1, we assumed that adjusted nominal demand growth $\hat{y}$ is cut abruptly from 6% to 0% (the rate required to eliminate inflation in the long run) and used the $DG-SG$ diagram to trace the disinflation path. With the economy at Q_c in period 0, we saw that the abrupt downward shift of the DG curve in period 1 results in a real output level of Q_1, which is less than Q_c.

If adjusted nominal demand growth $\hat{y}$ is reduced *gradually* (instead of abruptly) to 0%, then a smaller downward shift of the DG curve will clearly occur in period 1. Thus, Q_1 will not fall as far below Q_c (equivalently, U_1 will not rise as much above U_c). Can gradual demand deceleration reduce the cost of disinflation?

The answer lies in focusing on our basic equation

(6.1) $$\Delta w = \Delta p = \frac{h(U_c - U)}{U}$$

Suppose that gradual demand deceleration prevents Q from falling as far below Q_c (equivalently, U from rising as far above U_c) during the disinflation process. Then, clearly, the economy must spend more years with U above U_c (Q below Q_c) to achieve the desired total reduction in the inflation rate (in our example, a 6% reduction).

Suppose that we begin with a 6% inflation rate and our goal is 0% inflation. A *cold-turkey policy* will raise U sharply above U_c and cause a more rapid disinflation. A *gradualist policy* will raise U above U_c by a smaller amount, but U will have to stay above U_c longer to achieve a 6% reduction in the inflation rate.

Figure 6.2 shows the cold-turkey and the gradualist disinflation paths. These paths were obtained by shifting the DG and SG curves, as shown in Figure 6.1. The difference is that for the cold-turkey path, DG_1 reflects the abrupt cut of $\hat{y}$ from 6% to 0%. For the gradualist path, $\hat{y}$ is

FIGURE 6.2 GRADUALIST VERSUS COLD-TURKEY DISINFLATION

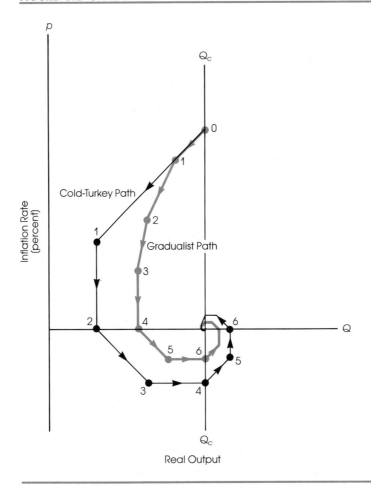

The cold-turkey path, which is identical to the disinflation path in Figure 6.1, is generated by reducing $\hat{y}$ immediately to 0% in period 1. The gradualist path is generated by reducing $\hat{y}$ to 0% over several periods. The DG and SG curves generate both paths but are not shown here to simplify the diagram. The cold-turkey path achieves a more rapid disinflation (p declines faster). On the cold-turkey path, the recession is shorter; by period 4, Q has returned to Q_c. On the gradualist path, Q still lies below Q_c in period 4. But the cold-turkey path causes a deeper recession; the lowest Q on the cold-turkey path is less than the lowest Q on the gradualist path.

reduced in several stages from 6% to 0%, so that the DG curves reflect this gradual reduction in $\hat{y}$.

It should be no surprise that in year 1, the cold-turkey path causes a bigger decline in both p and Q than the gradualist path. Earlier, we established that a reduction in nominal demand growth y is shared by both p and q; hence, if the decline in y is larger, then the decline in p and in q will be larger.

From Figure 6.2, it is evident that the minimum level of real output Q along this transition path is less under the cold-turkey policy, implying that the peak unemployment rate is higher. But it is also evident that the economy must spend more time at a level of real output Q less than Q_c (a U greater than U_c) under the gradualist policy before converging to a 0% inflation rate.

▶ Under inertial expectations, the cost of disinflation cannot be avoided by gradualism. The speed of demand deceleration entails a trade-off, and the preferable strategy is not immediately obvious. Under the cold-turkey policy, we "get it over with" relatively quickly but incur a sudden, steep cost. Under gradualism, we "drag it out." The worst year under gradualism is not as bad as the worst year under cold-turkey policy, but gradualism entails more above-normal unemployment years than cold-turkey policy.

▶ Because a cold-turkey policy may cause the collapse of confidence, make $\hat{y} < 0$, and trigger a depression, a gradualist policy is less risky.

6.4 The Disinflation of the Early 1980s

Table 6.1 shows that the unemployment rate rose to 9.5% in 1982 and remained at 9.5% in 1983. It is therefore no surprise that significant disinflation was achieved. The inflation rate was cut from nearly 10% in 1981 to less than 4% in 1985.

To examine this important disinflation episode more carefully, we need to glance back at Table 5.1 (page 207). By the end of the 1970s, the GNP deflator measured an inflation rate of nearly 10%. In response to the steady rise in inflation during the late 1970s, the Federal Reserve, under the leadership of Chairman Paul Volcker (appointed by President Carter in 1979), committed itself to engineering disinflation.

In October 1979, the Fed announced that it would place more emphasis on money-growth targets than on interest-rate targets, and that it would seek to steadily reduce the money-supply growth rate to achieve disinflation. Many observers concluded that the Fed had become "monetarist" and fully accepted the monetary view of inflation, which holds that a reduction in inflation requires a reduction in money growth.

As Table 5.1 shows, the Fed reduced $m1$ from 8.3% in 1978 to 7.2% in 1979, 6.6% in 1980, and 6.5% in 1981. However, Table 5.1 also shows that $m2$ did not decline; starting at 8.0% in 1978, it fell to 7.8% in 1979, then rose to 8.9% in 1980, and 10.0% in 1981. Thus, unless we are confident that $m1$ is more important than $m2$, it is not clear that the Fed achieved *monetary deceleration*. Moreover, $m1$ increased to 8.8% in 1982 and to 9.8% in 1983; $m2$ declined to 8.9% in 1982 but jumped back up to 12.0% in 1983.

Some economists have inferred from this data that the Fed did not play an important role in achieving the disinflation shown in the p column of Table 5.1. Such an inference is unwarranted. The crucial role of the Fed is evident in the behavior of the prime interest rate charged by banks to their most reliable customers. As the r column in Table 5.1 shows, beginning at 6.83% in 1977, the prime rate rose to 9.06% in 1978, to 12.67% in 1979, to 15.27% in 1980, and to 18.87% in 1981. Like the prime rate, other interest rates generally rose sharply during this period.

Let's offer one interpretation of this steady rise in interest rates to record heights in 1981. Policymakers at the Fed recognized that they must achieve a significant reduction in nominal demand growth y to achieve disinflation. They knew that a rise in interest rates would reduce business and consumer borrowing and spending at some point enough to achieve the desired reduction in y. Fed policymakers decided to adjust monetary policy through open-market operations (which we will explain in detail in Chapter 13) so that interest rates would keep rising until y declined significantly. The break finally came in 1982, when y fell from 11.7% in 1981 to 3.7% in 1982.

It is true that Fed policymakers stated that they were focusing primarily on money-growth targets rather than on interest-rate targets. Perhaps this was their sincere intention. But it is significant that this declaration made it easier for the Fed to let interest rates climb to record heights. The Fed might have precipitated a political reaction in Congress if it had declared that it would adjust its open-market operations in an attempt to double the prime interest rate. (Such a doubling in fact occurred from 1978 to 1981.)

The Fed defended its open-market operations, insisting they were focused on money growth, not interest rates. The fact is that interest rates did climb steadily to record heights. If the Fed had chosen to raise its open-market purchases and to raise the money-supply growth rate further, it could have prevented this steady rise.

This account of disinflation in the early 1980s does not discount that other forces in the economy—fiscal policy, autonomous consumption and investment, net export demand—all influence nominal demand growth. For example, fiscal policy appears to have helped the Fed by moving in a contractionary direction in 1981. The Q_c deficit fell from -1.8% in 1980 to -1.3% in 1981. Why, then, do we assign primary responsibility to the Fed?

▶ The Federal Reserve normally has the power to offset other forces in the economy and is committed to adjusting monetary policy continuously to offset these forces and to achieve its disinflation objective.

When Fed policymakers resolved to slow the nominal demand growth rate and to reduce the inflation rate, they, in effect, resolved to offset other forces in the economy in order to reduce y. If the economy weakened on its own — due to contractionary fiscal policy or a decline in autonomous investment, consumption, or net export demand — then less monetary "tightening" by the Fed would be required to achieve disinflation. But if the economy remained strong, then substantial monetary tightening by the Fed would be necessary. As it turned out, a doubling of the prime interest rate was needed to generate the severe recession and to achieve disinflation.

We end this account of the disinflation of the early 1980s by noting how the recovery of 1983–1984 occurred. Although autonomous consumption and investment may have played a role, there is no question that both fiscal and monetary policy turned strongly expansionary in 1982.

The fiscal policy expansion was unintentional. In 1981, prior to the recession, the Reagan Administration and its supporters in Congress succeeded in enacting a major tax cut. The rationale for the tax cut was to encourage work effort and saving (*supply-side economics*, which we will discuss in Chapters 10 and 15) — not to stimulate demand to counter a recession. The Reagan Administration and its supporters also succeeded in raising the growth rate of military expenditures. As a result, the Q_c deficit rose from -1.3% in 1981 to -1.8% in 1982. The unintended fiscal expansion was just what the economy needed in mid-1982.

By contrast, the monetary expansion was intentional. In mid-1982, Fed policymakers saw that nominal demand growth y had collapsed, disinflation was underway, and the recession was deepening. It was now time to shift from brake to accelerator to prevent the recession from becoming a depression. The Fed eased its monetary policy and permitted the prime interest rate to decline from 18.87% in 1981 to 14.86 in 1982, to 10.79% in 1983. This turnaround in Fed policy in mid-1982 played a key role in launching the strong economic recovery of 1983–1984.

6.5 Rational Expectations and "Credible" Demand Deceleration Policy

We now turn to a fundamental challenge that some macroeconomists have posed in recent years. Thus far, our analysis has suggested that demand deceleration must generate a transitional rise in unemployment. Such deceleration will eventually subdue inflation, but the economy will incur a significant transitional cost along the disinflation path. But is this conclusion really correct?

How did we arrive at our conclusion? First, our DG–SG diagram traced out the disinflation path in Figure 6.1. But the behavior of the SG curve was based on the hypothesis of inertial expectations, which states that the expected inflation rate p^e equals last period's actual inflation rate p_{-1}. This hypothesis implies that the height of the SG curve at Q_c equals last period's inflation rate and is therefore unaffected by this period's reduction in nominal demand growth y. But what if expectations are not inertial?

Second, we performed an econometric analysis of past data for the United States, but we did not observe a high responsiveness of wage and price inflation to a rise in the unemployment rate — certainly not a high enough responsiveness to avoid significant cost during disinflation. Is it possible that such limited responsiveness of w and p to U is not inevitable but depends crucially on the way demand deceleration policy is implemented?

Suppose that expectations are not inertial, but "rational." Expectations are "rational" if they are based on the efficient processing of all available information using a correct model of the economy. Instead of simply looking at last period's inflation rate and assuming it will occur in the current period, people are assumed to observe current economic policy and the current behavior of the economy and to forecast the inflation rate by efficiently processing up-to-date information using a correct economic model.

According to the rational expectations hypothesis, the actual inflation rate p should, on average, equal the expected inflation rate p^e. By processing up-to-date information efficiently using a correct model of the economy, people should, on average, formulate accurate expectations. This does not mean that expectations will always turn out to be perfectly accurate. But it does mean that there should be no *systematic* tendency to overestimate or underestimate a variable like the inflation rate.

According to the RATIONAL EXPECTATIONS HYPOTHESIS, if people have perfect information, then the expected inflation rate will, on average, equal the actual inflation rate ($p^e = p$).

Here, we will assume that information is perfect, so that the rational expectations hypothesis implies that $p^e = p$. (In the subsequent discussion of new classical macroeconomics, we will consider the possibility of rational expectations with imperfect information.) We will also assume that long-term wage contracts do not prevent prompt adjustment of w and p.

We should now recognize the contrast between rational and inertial expectations. Under inertial expectations, what people expect turns out to be systematically incorrect when disinflation is occurring. In the first stages of disinflation, people keep overestimating the inflation that will actually occur in each period. For example, in period 1 people expect the inflation rate to be 6% (its value in period 0), but p_1 turns out to be less than 6% in Figure 6.1. Only when the economy is in long-run equilibrium and inflation is constant do inertial expectations prove accurate.

According to the rational expectations hypothesis, what p^e will people set in period 1 when the authorities pledge to reduce $\hat{y}$ from 6% to 0%, thereby shifting the DG curve downward by 6% from DG_0 to DG_1 as shown in Figure 6.3?

FIGURE 6.3 DISINFLATION WITH RATIONAL EXPECTATIONS

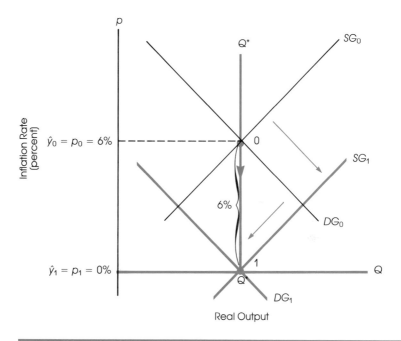

Initially, adjusted nominal demand growth $\hat{y} = 6\%$, the inflation rate $p = 6\%$, and real output $Q = Q^*$. In period 1, $\hat{y}$ is cut permanently to 0%, so that the $\hat{y}$ line coincides with the horizontal axis. In Figure 6.1, with inertial expectations, SG_1 coincides with SG_0. Here, with rational expectations, the SG curve shifts downward immediately to match the downward shift of the DG curve. SG_1 lies 6% below SG_0, just as DG_1 lies 6% below DG_0. Because the expected inflation rate p^e is cut immediately by 6% to 0%, the SG curve shifts downward by 6%. p^e proves accurate ("rational"); p turns out to be 0% in period 1 (and all subsequent periods). The economy disinflates immediately (without any transitional recession) in response to the cut in the nominal demand growth rate y.

They will set $p^e = 0\%$. Why? If $p^e = 0\%$ in period 1, then we know that SG_1 will go through the point ($Q^*, 0\%$), because the height of the SG curve at Q^* must equal p^e. Thus, under rational expectations, the SG curve will shift down by 6%; SG_1 will lie 6% below SG_0, which goes through point ($Q^*, 6\%$), as shown in Figure 6.3. (Note that under inertial expectations, SG_1 coincides with SG_0; see Figure 6.1.)

Thus, the SG curve shifts downward by exactly the same percentage as the DG curve (6%).

▶ Under rational expectations in the absence of long-term wage contracts, any shift in the DG curve is simultaneously matched by an equal vertical shift in the SG curve, so that the DG–SG intersection remains at Q^* (and U remains at U^*). The inflation rate p will change by the same percentage as the vertical shift in the DG and SG curves. The expected inflation rate p^e will equal the actual inflation rate p.

▶ Under rational expectations, the inflation rate p does not generally stay constant when $Q = Q^*$ ($U = U^*$), as the example in Figure 6.3 confirms. The economy does not possess a constant inflation output Q_c or unemployment rate U_c. We therefore use the symbols Q^* (not Q_c) and U^* (not U_c) to denote equilibrium output (and unemployment) in a rational expectations economy.

But how will people know to set $p^e = 0\%$ in this case? People may be able to forecast the adjusted nominal demand growth rate $\hat{y}$ that Fed policymakers will set. If the authorities pledge to cut $\hat{y}$ by 6% (from 6% to 0%) and if they are likely to keep their word, then people can immediately cut p^e by 6% (from 6% to 0%). If people behave in this way, then p^e will, on average, equal p (expectations will be rational).

CREDIBILITY

What about the econometric analysis of past data, which appears to support the inertial hypothesis? Suppose that past data was generated by demand deceleration policy that was not announced clearly in advance and was pursued with hesitation by Fed policymakers. If people are surprised by a deceleration or have a valid reason to suspect that the monetary authorities may back off if a recession begins to occur, then the disinflation without recession depicted in Figure 6.3 should not be expected to occur.

It can be argued that demand deceleration policy was often a surprise in the past. Even when it was announced in advance, it was not "credible"—that is, it was not believable because the authorities were not fully committed to going through with the deceleration. Past data, then, cannot tell us what will happen if the authorities really are fully committed to completing the deceleration policy.

According to this view, the public does not receive clear signals of an impending demand deceleration. Fiscal policy is usually erratic, representing the outcome of a complex interaction of rival parties in Congress and the White House. But even monetary policy, which has a greater potential for clarity, seldom generated a clear signal of demand deceleration.

Consider this interpretation. In the past, in response to inflation, the Federal Reserve Board would begin a monetary deceleration. But Fed policymakers were not committed to continuing the deceleration if it generated a significant rise in unemployment. Fed policymakers were tentative, hesitant, and ready to reverse deceleration if a significant recession occurred. In turn, the public sensed this equivocation by Fed policymakers. Quite sensibly, workers and managers did not believe that the demand deceleration would be carried through to its ultimate noninflationary target.

Past data, then, cannot tell us what would happen if the authorities really are fully committed to deceleration and announce and explain this commitment in advance. Econometric analysis of such data would underestimate the responsiveness that would occur under such a "credible" policy. The key, then, is "credibility." First, if necessary, the Fed must really be ready to face a severe, prolonged recession. Second, the Fed must convince the public of its readiness.

What does it take to be credible? One view holds that credibility can be achieved within our current institutional structure. What is necessary and sufficient is that the members of the Federal Reserve Board's Open Market Committee be fully committed to tightening monetary policy to whatever degree necessary — given fiscal policy — to steadily reduce the adjusted nominal demand growth rate to $\hat{y} = 0\%$ and keep it there permanently.

Another view is that appointing dedicated individuals to the Federal Reserve Board is not sufficient. The public will always suspect that a recession will initiate a policy reversal. What is necessary is the removal of *discretion*. For example, if a constitutional amendment stated that the Fed must tighten monetary policy to the degree necessary to achieve price stability, then tight monetary policy might be credible, because it would be more insulated from the pressures that would arise should a recession occur. But if people behaved "rationally" in response to credible monetary policy, there would be no transitional recession, as Figure 6.3 shows (ignoring long-term wage contracts).

Beginning in 1979, the Fed publicly committed itself to tightening monetary policy for as long as necessary to achieve significant disinflation. Effort was made to publicize this disinflation strategy and to encourage the public to adjust inflationary expectations in accordance with it.

Nevertheless, the 1982 recession was still severe. Of course, the recession may have occurred despite some downward adjustment of inflationary expectations. Perhaps without publication of the Fed's policy, an even worse recession would have been necessary to achieve the same reduction in inflation. What is clear is that the effort made by the Fed in the early 1980s was not sufficient to achieve disinflation without a severe recession.

Leadership by the President may also be important. Obviously, the public is much more familiar with the President than with the Chairman of the Federal Reserve Board. The President, through press coverage, is far more able to communicate the disinflation plan to the public.

If the Fed really plans to decelerate nominal demand growth, then the President should try to persuade the public that the Fed is prepared to accept a recession, if necessary, to reduce inflation and, moreover, that the recession will last longer if workers and managers delay reductions in wage and price increases.

It is counterproductive for the President to give the public the impression that there is no risk of pain in the disinflation process. If the public believes that the economy will remain prosperous during disinflation, there will be little pressure to reduce wage and price increases and the Fed's deceleration will in fact generate a recession.

It can be argued that Presidential communication on the economy in the past has virtually always been counterproductive. Each President has promised a painless reduction in inflation; each has denied that recession and unemployment might be necessary to achieve disinflation. Each has therefore helped to foster inertia by removing the threat of recession and unemployment.

In this section, we have presented the two pure cases of inertial expectations and rational expectations. There is, of course, a continuum. People may base their expectations partly on last year's inflation rate and partly on efficient processing of the latest information about current monetary policy. Macroeconomists differ as to the relative importance of these two methods of forming expectations.

Suppose that people's inflation expectations are partly inertial and partly rational. Then in the $DG-SG$ diagram, when the nominal demand growth rate y is cut, shifting the DG curve downward, the SG curve will also shift downward — but not by as much as the DG curve. This makes sense, because under pure inertial expectations, the SG curve would not shift down at all and under pure rational expectations, the SG curve would shift down as much as the DG curve. Thus, the cut in y would still be shared by p and q. But in comparison with pure inertial expectations, p would now decline more and q would decline less.

Similarly, just as the degree to which inflation expectations are inertial rather than rational is important, the degree of credibility is also an issue. If credibility is greater, then the cost of demand deceleration will be less.

Every citizen should want the economy to behave as if people formed expectations rationally and found demand deceleration policy fully credible. The controversial issue is whether the economy does, in fact, behave that way—or can be made to behave that way—by improving the implementation of deceleration policy.

THE NEW CLASSICAL MACROECONOMICS

We have analyzed rational expectations in our DG–SG model. It should be pointed out that some advocates of rational expectations, including Robert Lucas, Thomas Sargent, and Robert Barro, believe that a fundamentally new approach to macroeconomics is warranted.

This new approach, which is called *new classical macroeconomics,* postulates that all markets are always in competitive equilibrium. All economic agents are perfect *optimizers;* they process information efficiently and form expectations rationally.

Most economists are intellectually intrigued by the new classical economics. Ultimately, however, it must be asked: How accurate are the predictions of the new classical model?

Let's compare the predictions of our "mainstream" model and the new classical model in terms of the impact of a sustained tight monetary policy, such as the one conducted by the Federal Reserve in the early 1980s. The mainstream model with inertial expectations predicts disinflation with a transitional recession (as shown in Figure 6.1), just as actually occurred.

The prediction of the new classical model depends on the assumptions concerning information and wage contracts. If information is assumed to be perfect, then the rational expectations hypothesis implies that $p^e = p$; if wages are assumed to be flexible, then the new classical model predicts disinflation without any transitional recession (as shown in Figure 6.3). Such a prediction is contradicted by the data.

If information is imperfect, then the rational expectations hypothesis does not imply that $p^e = p$ and the new classical model predicts a recession until accurate information is acquired. With imperfect information, the new classical theorist can postulate (1) a long information lag, (2) a short information lag with long-term wage contracts, or (3) a short information lag with flexible wages. Let's consider each option.

Under option (1), the theorist postulates that accurate information may take several years to acquire. According to this hypothesis, a transitional recession may last for several years. The virtue of this hypothesis is that the new classical prediction is then consistent with experiences like the 1975 and 1982 recessions, although the Great Depression of the 1930s still remains a puzzle.

But there are two objections to option (1). First, is it plausible that rational economic agents will take several years to acquire accurate information? After all, all of the necessary economic data are published monthly or quarterly and reported by the financial press. Second, how does the new classical model with a long information lag improve on the mainstream model? Their predictions are the same.

Under option (2), the new classical theorist postulates that accurate information can be acquired rapidly (certainly within six months) by rational economic agents. But with long-term wage contracts, a significant transitional recession accompanies disinflation. The objection again is: How does the new classical model with a short information lag and long-term wage contracts improve on the mainstream model? Their predictions are the same.

Finally, under option (3), the new classical theorist postulates that accurate information can be acquired rapidly and that wages are flexible; thus, a short transitional recession will last only until accurate information is acquired. The basic objection to this option is that it is inconsistent with the experience of the recessions of 1975 and 1982 and with the Great Depression of the 1930s.

▶ If the new classical model assumes either a long information lag or long-term wage contracts, its predictions are the same as the mainstream model with inertial expectations. If the new classical model assumes a short information lag and flexible wages, its predictions are at variance with economic experience.

The new classical macroeconomics has stimulated improvements in the mainstream model. Macroeconomics should try to incorporate the best insights of any new challenge. But the new classical model, depending on the information and wage contract assumptions it utilizes, either generates the same prediction as the mainstream model or a less accurate prediction. The case for replacing the mainstream model with the new classical model is therefore weak.

6.6 Complementary Disinflation Policies

The disinflation policies introduced in this section are proposed as complements to (not as substitutes for) demand deceleration. These policies are supply-oriented in that they attempt to directly influence the position or slope of the SG curve. Macroeconomists agree that disinflation requires demand deceleration. They disagree about whether a disinflation strategy should also include one of the complementary, supply-oriented policies we will consider here.

We will analyze two strategies:

1. *Price policy* (sometimes called *wage–price policy* or *incomes policy*).
2. *Flexible compensation contracts (gain-sharing* or *profit-sharing).*

We will also briefly consider several other disinflation proposals. We will begin with price policy.

PRICE POLICY

To understand the aim of a price policy, we will return to our $DG-SG$ diagram in Figure 6.1 (page 244) and once again assume inertial expectations. Recall that when demand deceleration shifts the DG curve downward, the SG curve does not immediately shift downward as well, so that the period 1 $DG-SG$ intersection is at a Q_1 less than Q_c. If expectations were rational, instead of inertial, then the SG curve would respond immediately to a downward shift of the DG curve, SG_1 would shift downward by as much as DG_1, so Q_1 would equal Q_c, and there would be no recession — only disinflation.

A PRICE POLICY is intended to complement demand deceleration policy. Its aim is to shift the SG curve downward. Under rational expectations, the SG curve automatically shifts downward in response to a downward shift of the DG curve. A price policy is designed to shift the SG curve downward in an economy characterized by inertial expectations.

As shown in Figure 6.4, we will suppose that the economy is initially at $Q = Q_c$ ($U = U_c$) with an inflation rate of $p = 6\%$ (so that the adjusted nominal demand growth rate in period 0 is $\hat{y}_0 = 6\%$). If $\hat{y}$ is reduced by 3% in period 1, then DG_1 will lie 3% below DG_0. Under rational expectations, SG_1 would also lie 3% below SG_0, so that Q_1 would equal Q_c ($U_1 = U_c$). But under inertial expectations with no price policy, SG_1 will coincide with SG_0, so that Q_1 will be less than Q_c (U_1 will be greater than U_c).

The aim of a price policy is to shift down the SG curve so that SG_1 will intersect DG_1 at $Q = Q_c$, as in the case of rational expectations. A price policy can affect the $DG-SG$ diagram in one of two ways. The first effect, illustrated in Figure 6.4, is to make the SG_1 curve horizontal. A flat SG curve would result from a price control or a "market anti-inflation plan" (MAP). The second effect, illustrated in Figure 6.5, is to keep the same slope for the SG_1 curve as the SG_0 curve. A sloped SG curve would result from a "tax incentive inflation policy" (TIP).

Whether the SG curve becomes flat or retains its positive slope, the result is the same in our example in period 1. In both Figures 6.4 and

FIGURE 6.4 DISINFLATION WITH A MAP PRICE POLICY

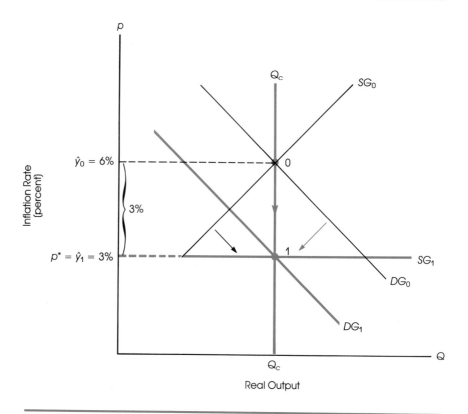

Real Output

Initially, adjusted nominal demand growth $\hat{y} = 6\%$, the inflation rate $p = 6\%$, and real output $Q = Q_c$. In period 1, $\hat{y}$ is cut by 3% to 3%. A price policy attempts to shift the SG curve downward at Q_c. Under a MAP price policy, the SG curve becomes horizontal at the targeted inflation rate p^* (for any Q, p would be $p^* = 3\%$). In this example, with the targeted $p^* = 3\%$, the economy moves from point 0 to point 1, p declines by 3% (from 6% to 3%), and Q remains at Q_c.

6.5, the inflation rate p declines by 3% (from 6% to 3%) and real output Q remains at Q_c (U remains at U_c).

To generalize, let's define the "strength" of a price policy:

The STRENGTH OF A PRICE POLICY is defined as the magnitude of the downward shift of the SG curve at Q_c.

Thus

▶ If an economy characterized by inertial expectations is initially at $Q = Q_c$ and the nominal demand growth rate y is cut by

FIGURE 6.5 DISINFLATION WITH A TIP PRICE POLICY

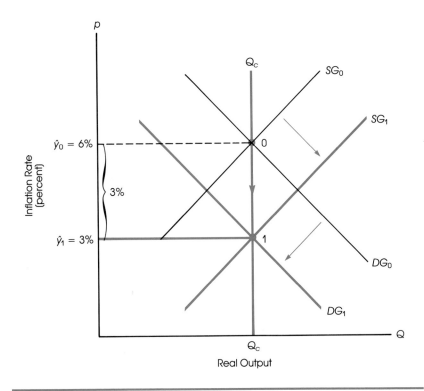

Initially, adjusted nominal demand growth $\hat{y} = 6\%$, the inflation rate $p = 6\%$, and real output $Q = Q_c$. In period 1, $\hat{y}$ is cut by 3% to 3%. A price policy attempts to shift the SG curve downward at Q_c. Under a TIP price policy, the SG curve retains its positive slope. In this example, the strength of TIP is 3%. Hence, the economy moves from point 0 to point 1, p declines by 3% (from 6% to 3%), and Q remains at Q_c.

$X\%$ — complemented by a price policy with a *strength* of $X\%$ — then the inflation rate p will decline by $X\%$ and real output Q will remain at Q_c (U will remain at U_c).

As we will see, some critics doubt that any price policy has the strength to shift the SG curve downward. Other critics point out the harmful side effects of a price policy, even if it is strong enough to shift the SG curve downward. We will return to these criticisms shortly.

Traditionally, price policy has taken one of two forms: (1) voluntary guidelines, or (2) mandatory controls. Recently, however, a new approach to price policy—financial incentives to induce firms to set smaller price increases—has been proposed. Two methods of implementing this new "incentive" price policy have been offered: a *tax-incentive inflation policy* (TIP), based on a tax incentive, and a *market anti-inflation plan* (MAP), based on a marketable permit incentive.

The United States and most other economically advanced countries have experimented with the two traditional kinds of price policy—guidelines and controls. We will review the recent history of such experiments in the United States and then briefly describe the new incentive price policies.

Wage–Price Guidelines and Controls Since 1960

During World War II and the Korean War, comprehensive, mandatory wage–price controls were imposed in the United States. These controls were removed when peace returned. In the early 1960s, the Kennedy Administration introduced voluntary wage–price guideposts. At the time, the inflation rate was approximately 1%, but because the unemployment rate was regarded as high—roughly 6%—the Administration planned a monetary and fiscal expansion. To counter any inflationary tendencies that might develop, the guideposts were introduced. The government requested that wage increases not exceed average productivity growth in the economy (estimated at 3.2%), because only then would average unit labor cost remain constant, permitting a 0% inflation rate.

Whether these wage–price guideposts achieved a positive, temporary effect has been debated. It is generally agreed, however, that the guideposts were no match for the inflationary pressures generated by government expenditures on the Vietnam War. In the mid-1960s, the Johnson Administration escalated military spending but was reluctant to ask Congress to enact a comparable tax increase to finance it to prevent an excessive fiscal expansion.

As a result, in the *IS – LM* diagram we developed in Chapter 2, the *IS* curve shifted sharply to the right. Although at times the Fed tried to counter the fiscal expansion (letting interest rates rise in the *IS – LM* diagram), the Fed eventually gave in and reinforced the fiscal expansion with a monetary expansion, which brought down interest rates and further raised aggregate demand. The unemployment rate fell below 4% in 1966 and remained there through 1969. It is little wonder that the inflation rate rose in the second half of the 1960s to more than 5%—overpowering the guideposts and causing their termination.

When the Nixon Administration came into office in 1969, fiscal and monetary restraint was adopted as the anti-inflation strategy and wage–price policy was initially rejected. In 1970, restraint resulted in a recession; by 1971, the unemployment rate had reached 6%. In 1970, the Democratic Congress had passed a bill granting the President the authority to impose wage and price controls. Ironically, President

Nixon threatened to veto the bill because, he said, he was philosophically opposed to controls. But because the bill was attached to a military bill, Nixon signed it into law, vowing never to use it.

In August 1971, however, it seemed to many that the recession was causing little reduction in inflation. With a Presidential election approaching, the Administration faced a dilemma. If it decided to fight the recession with expansionary fiscal and monetary policy, inflation would surely rise. But if it continued to fight inflation with restraint, the recession would continue. Neither prospect looked attractive in an election year.

On a weekend in mid-August, Nixon met with his economic advisors at Camp David. On Sunday night, he went on television and dramatically announced that he was immediately imposing a wage–price freeze, to be called Phase I, on the economy for three months. Phase I would be followed by Phase II—a mandatory controls program that would permit moderate wage and price increases up to a ceiling. Only the Democratic bill in the 1970 Congress enabled Nixon to act in mid-1971.

Phase II lasted just over a year; 1972 was a year of wage and price controls. A Pay Board was established for wage increases; a Price Commission, for price increases. The Pay Board, consisting of representatives of labor, business, and the public, set a wage increase ceiling of 5.5%. The Price Commission, consisting of representatives of the public, set a goal of 2.5% for price increases; it was estimated that productivity growth would average 3%. In the $DG-SG$ diagram, the goal was a horizontal SG_1 curve (as shown in Figure 6.4) at a height of 2.5%. The Commission attempted to reach its goal by establishing regulations limiting price increases to the minimum necessary to pass on a 5.5% pay increase and to maintain a normal profit margin.

The controls enabled monetary and fiscal policy to focus on fighting the recession. From 1971 to 1972, the unemployment rate fell from 6.1% in August 1971 to 5.1% in December of 1972. At the same time, the controls helped to reduce the inflation rate from 5.7% in 1971 to 4.7% in 1972. Simultaneous progress on both inflation and recession helped contribute to Nixon's easy re-election win.

In early 1973, however, the Nixon Administration's wage–price controls were converted, in effect, into a voluntary program as Phase III replaced Phase II. Why was this done? True, the controls had helped reduce inflation and unemployment simultaneously. But they had a minus side—as well as a plus side—which now must be reviewed.

According to microeconomic theory, flexible wages and prices promote consumer welfare. For example, suppose that industry E enjoys an expansion in consumer demand, while industry C suffers a contraction in consumer demand. In effect, consumers are indicating that they would prefer resources—labor, capital, and raw materials—

to move from industry C to industry E. As Adam Smith first emphasized in his *Wealth of Nations* in 1776, a market system with flexible prices and wages would move the resources from industry C to industry E, even though producers are motivated by self-interest. How does this happen?

The expansion in demand for product E bids up its price relative to the price of product C, causing a short-run rise in industry E's profit. This attracts new capital to industry E and helps to finance its expansion. To attract the necessary labor to produce more of product E, industry E will find it worthwhile to grant a larger wage increase to its workers than industry C grants. Hence, the rise in the *relative* price and wage of E (relative to C) will move labor and capital into E, so E's output increases relative to C's, just as consumers desire.

A rigid wage–price controls program would prevent this desirable movement of resources from C to E, because it would not permit E to exceed the legal price and wage ceilings. A shortage of E's product would develop, as consumer demand exceeded supply at the ceiling price; a shortage of E's labor would also develop, as E sought to hire more workers than were available at the ceiling wage.

Of course, every controls program intends flexibility. Phase II of the Nixon Administration's wage–price control program was no exception. The main function of the Pay Board and the Price Commission was to consider exceptions. In terms of our example, the intent was to permit a genuine E firm to exceed the legal ceiling in order to reduce or to eliminate shortages.

But the practical question is: Can a controls agency process information quickly and efficiently? Even if the controls program is limited to large corporations, hundreds of firms can be expected to appeal for an exception. In each case, the firm knows more about its own situation than the controls agency. The agency would need a large, highly competent staff to evaluate each appeal fairly and promptly.

In fact, during Phase II, the staffs of the Pay Board and the Price Commission were very small, much smaller than they were during World War II or the Korean War. It is not surprising that backlogs developed, and frustration spread among firms and unions seeking appeal. Shortages began to develop.

Some supporters of controls argue that by limiting coverage to large corporations, employing a large and competent staff, and appointing administrators who really believe in controls, the information processing could be handled satisfactorily and shortages could be limited. Opponents believe that, even then, the information overload would be too severe, and serious shortages and inefficiencies would be inevitable.

In any case, it is certainly true that the Nixon Administration always intended to end wage–price controls as soon as feasible. It is also true that only a small staff was established to regulate these controls.

Phase III began, however, with monetary and fiscal expansion propelling the economy out of recession, pushing the unemployment rate below 5%. Not surprisingly, this demand acceleration generated inflationary pressure, which burst forth later in Phase III. After several months, a new freeze was imposed, followed by Phase IV controls that were finally abolished in early 1974. 1974 saw the quadrupling of oil prices by OPEC, a jump in the cpi inflation rate to over 10%, and the Fed's decision to fight inflation by letting interest rates rise to record heights. The result was the deep recession of 1974–1975, which saw the unemployment rate reach 9% but did reduce the inflation rate to 5%.

In 1975, the Fed eased, letting interest rates decline. With the help of a tax cut, the economy emerged into recovery in 1976; but inflation had only been reduced to 6%. When the Carter Administration took office in 1977, it sought to continue recovery and to reduce the unemployment rate, which was still above 7%. It opted for voluntary wage–price guidelines to try to hold the lid on inflation while promoting recovery.

The voluntary method did not succeed. The Council on Wage and Price Stability (COWPS) did require large firms to report wage and price increases, but no penalties were incurred for violating the guidelines — other than occasional bad publicity or the hint that a government contract might not be forthcoming. The unemployment rate was reduced to 5.8% in 1979. That year also saw another round of large oil-price increases, and the inflation rate jumped back to roughly 10%.

In response, the Fed — led by its new chairman Paul Volcker, appointed by President Carter in 1979 — committed itself to bring down inflation by implementing a tight monetary policy; it pursued this policy for the next three years. When the Reagan Administration took office in 1981, it immediately abolished COWPS, rejected wage–price policy, and generally supported the Fed's disinflation policy. By late 1981, the Fed's tight monetary policy had taken interest rates to new record heights and generated a severe recession; in late 1982, the unemployment rate rose above 10%. In both 1982 and 1983, the unemployment rate averaged 9.5%. In 1982, the inflation rate declined to 6%; in 1983 and 1984, it declined to 4%.

In mid-1982, the Fed responded to the deepening recession by easing monetary policy, permitting interest rates to drop significantly. At the same time, an unintentional fiscal expansion stimulated the economy. The Reagan Administration's tax cut — enacted in 1981, prior to the recession — went into effect. But government spending increased as a percentage of GNP, because the rise in military expenditures outweighed some cuts in domestic spending. The combined monetary and fiscal expansion produced a strong recovery in 1983 and 1984. But with the unemployment rate remaining above 7% through most of 1984, the inflation rate stayed near 4%.

Incentive Price Policies

We will now consider *incentive price policies*. These policies were first proposed in the 1970s but have not yet been tried. Under an incentive price policy, a covered firm would be given a financial incentive to hold down its price increase. Two methods have been suggested: a tax incentive (TIP), first proposed by Sidney Weintraub and Henry Wallich in 1971,* and a marketable permit incentive (MAP), first proposed by Abba Lerner and David Colander in 1980.†

To reduce administrative and compliance costs, some advocates propose that coverage of the incentive price policy be limited to large corporations — perhaps to the largest 2,000, which contribute roughly half of the GNP of the economy. Others advocate a broader coverage that includes most firms in the economy.

According to advocates, the rationale for an incentive price policy can be understood by noting a similarity between the inflation problem and the environmental pollution problem. Economists regard pollution as a "market failure"; the market fails because polluters bear no private cost when they impose a *social cost* — pollution. Most economists believe that the proper solution is to give firms a financial incentive to reduce pollution — to make firms confront the cost they impose on society when they pollute.

To reduce environmental pollution, economists have suggested two incentive price policies: a tax incentive and a permit incentive. Under the tax incentive, a firm is taxed on each unit of pollution it emits; each firm is subject to the same tax per unit of a given pollutant. Under the permit incentive, a firm is legally required to buy a permit for each unit of pollution it emits; each firm is subject to the same permit price per unit of a given pollutant. In both cases, the firm is offered a financial incentive to reduce pollution.

Similarly, when firms "inflate" (instead of pollute), they impose a social cost but bear no private cost for doing so. To "internalize the externality," firms should be given a financial incentive to reduce price increases. As in the environmental case, to reduce inflation, economists have suggested two incentive price policies: a tax incentive (TIP), and a permit incentive (MAP).

---

* Henry Wallich and Sidney Weintraub, "A Tax-Based Incomes Policy," *Journal of Economic Issues* 5(1971): 1–19.
† Abba Lerner and David Colander, *A Market Anti-Inflation Plan* (New York: Harcourt Brace Jovanovich, 1980).

Under TIP, each covered firm suffers a tax increase if it raises its own p above $p*$ and enjoys a tax cut if it lowers its own p below $p*$. Congress establishes the magnitude of the tax penalty or reward—and, hence, the strength of the financial incentive—and the target $p*$.

Under MAP, a covered firm is required to buy permits if it raises its own p above $p*$ and to sell permits if it lowers its own p below $p*$. A price-raising firm ($p > p*$) can only obtain permits from a price-cutting firm ($p < p*$). A firm can only raise its own p if another firm is cutting its own p. Hence, price raising is matched by price cutting, and the average price increase p in the economy should be roughly equal to $p*$.

An advantage of MAP over TIP is that the price of a permit (the "permit rate") is set automatically by supply and demand in the permit market. The permit rate rises until the permits supplied by price cutters match the permits demanded by price raisers. By contrast, Congress must estimate the TIP tax rate that provides the desired incentive strength. An advantage of TIP over MAP is that there is more experience and familiarity with the tax incentive method than with the marketable permit method.

It is important to understand how TIP and MAP would affect the $DG-SG$ diagram and equation (6.1). The impact of TIP on the $DG-SG$ diagram is illustrated in Figure 6.5 (page 277). In this example, TIP has a strength of 3%. The TIP tax rate provides an incentive that would cause the average firm to set its price increase p at 3% below what it otherwise would be. Hence, the SG curve shifts down by 3% from SG_0 to SG_1 and retains its positive slope.

TIP would cause equation (6.1) to be modified to

(6.7) $$\Delta p = \Delta w = \frac{h(U_c - U)}{U} - X$$

where X = the strength of TIP

For example, suppose if $h = 0.09$, $U_c = 7\%$, and $X = 3\%$, then

$$\Delta p = \Delta w = \frac{0.09(7\% - U)}{U} - 3\%$$

If U remains at 7%, then the direct pressure of TIP would cause $\Delta p = \Delta w = -3\%$. The consequences of this modification of equation (6.1) by TIP is explored in Appendix 6A, Section 6.A.4.

The impact of MAP on the $DG-SG$ diagram is illustrated in Figure 6.4 (page 276). In this example, the targeted inflation rate $p* = 3\%$. MAP ensures that the actual average inflation rate p of the economy is 3% at any level of real output Q. Hence, SG_1 is horizontal at $p = 3\%$. Note that a traditional price control with the targeted inflation rate of $p* = 3\%$ would have the same effect on the diagram.

MAP suspends the validity of equation (6.1). For any unemployment rate U, $\Delta p = -3\%$ in period 1. Note that a traditional price control with the targeted inflation rate of $p^* = 3\%$ would also suspend the validity of equation (6.1).

TIP and MAP are discussed further in Appendix 6B.

According to its advocates, an incentive price policy should produce less inefficiency than mandatory controls, because it relies on incentives and has built-in flexibility. Let's review this argument.

According to microeconomic theory, changes in relative prices and wages in response to market forces cause resources to be allocated in a way that promotes consumer welfare. Wage–price controls tend to prevent such relative price and wage changes. An incentive price policy might slow the response of wages and prices to market forces, but such a response should continue to occur.

Consider an example. If industry E experiences an expansion in consumer demand for its product and industry C suffers a contraction in such demand, what happens in a market economy with no incentive price policy? The relative rise in the demand for E's product causes a short-run rise in price and profit, which encourages industry E to expand its output. The relative labor shortage in industry E causes firms in E to raise the industry wage relative to other industry wages to attract labor. The reverse occurs in industry C. As a result, labor and capital move from C to E, and E's output rises relative to C's output, exactly as consumers desire. Adam Smith's "invisible hand" is at work, leading firms that seek only their own profit to promote consumer welfare.

Under an incentive price policy, both E and C would set smaller wage and price increases due to the financial incentive provided by the tax (TIP) or the permit price (MAP). But E would continue to set larger wage and price increases than C, because both firms continue to feel the pressure of market forces and are free to respond to them. Thus, relative wages and prices should still change in the right direction.

Even advocates concede that an incentive price policy and price controls have at least one serious problem in common. Under each, a covered firm must perform certain measurements to determine its price (or wage) increase. This means that a government agency must issue instructions concerning how to make these measurements. At least a sample of firms must be carefully audited in an effort to induce most firms to perform reasonably accurate measurements. As in other tax and regulatory programs, this represents both an administrative cost to the government and a compliance cost to firms. Moreover, given the rules concerning how the measurements are to be made, firms may not behave in the intended manner, and significant economic inefficiency may result.

To minimize administrative and compliance costs, some advocates propose that coverage of the incentive price policy be limited to large corporations—perhaps to the largest 2,000 firms, which contribute roughly half of the GNP of the economy. They argue that effective auditing of 2,000 large corporations would be feasible, that the large corporations and their unions possess the most discretion over wage and price increases, and that their wage–price decisions set the pattern for much of the economy. Other advocates disagree, arguing that the benefits of a broader coverage that includes most firms in the economy —equity and uniformity—outweigh the costs.

An incentive price policy shares another potential problem with traditional price controls: the *"pass through" cost*. If a firm is to be judged on the actual price increase of its product, firm managers will probably offer the objection that the rising prices of inputs purchased from other firms have forced their firm to raise the price of its product.

▶ It can be argued that this objection has merit and that any incentive price policy should judge a firm only on the price increase of its product in excess of the *input price increase* (inputs purchased from other firms) that is merely passed on by the firm. A firm should be allowed to subtract this *"pass through" cost* increase from the price increase of its product for the purpose of assessment under an incentive price policy.

If this argument is accepted, then the firm should not be judged on the *product price increase* p_q. Instead, the firm should be judged on its *value-added price increase* p_v, which adjusts p_q for the "pass through" cost. The relation of p_v to p_q and to the *input price increase* p_i is given in Appendix 6B.

▶ A case can be made for using the *value-added price increase* p_v, rather than the unadjusted *product price increase* p_q, in any incentive price policy.

Even advocates acknowledge that the practical problems of implementing an incentive price policy (TIP or MAP) have yet to be carefully addressed. This suggests the following strategy. Suppose that a gradual disinflation is planned. In the initial year, the slowing of nominal demand growth would be accompanied by a traditional price control. During that year, a task force would prepare the conversion of the price-control policy into either TIP or MAP. Beginning in the second year, TIP or MAP would replace the price control for the remainder of the disinflation.

We will now turn to the criticisms of incentive price policies. Critics contend that the problem of regulating the measurement of wage and price increases by firms would be extremely severe for any incentive price policy, even if coverage were limited to large corporations. The fundamental problem, they argue, is the difficulty of distinguishing between a genuine *price* change and a *quality* change. Inflation is a rise in the price of products of a given quality; it is this genuine price increase that an incentive price policy is designed to deter. Although the policy is not intended to deter apparent price increases that reflect quality improvements, critics believe that it will be impossible to distinguish between the two sources of an apparent price change.

Any incentive price policy would therefore result in a significant compliance cost for firms, in an administrative (auditing) cost for the government, in litigation costs for both parties, and in important inequities. Critics also argue that firms — in an effort to avoid the TIP tax or the MAP permit expenditure — might engage in behavior that results in significant economic inefficiency, such as the reduction of product quality, innovation, or productivity, or the distortion of the input or output mix.

Critics believe that relative wage and price changes would still be significantly impeded and that a serious misallocation of resources would occur. Although the incentive price policy is more flexible than mandatory controls, it would still generate shortages and gluts in particular markets — and the inefficiencies and inequities that accompany sectoral excess demand and supply.

Critics also make several other points. The incentive price policy might divert energy from the main task: demand deceleration. Lobbying by special-interest groups during the legislative process could distort and undermine the policy. The incentive price policy could eventually be converted into rigid controls that would intrude on economic freedom. Therefore, critics argue, the government should not try to directly influence the prices that private firms set.*

FLEXIBLE COMPENSATION CONTRACTS ("GAIN-SHARING" OR "PROFIT-SHARING")

Now let's consider the flexible compensation strategy recently proposed by Martin Weitzman and Daniel Mitchell.[†]

The purpose of the FLEXIBLE COMPENSATION STRATEGY is to *steepen* the *SG* curve (as shown in Figure 6.6). If the *SG* curve is steeper, then the

---

* For a discussion of the pros and cons of incentive price policies, see Arthur Okun and George Perry (eds.), *Curing Chronic Inflation* (Washington D.C.: The Brookings Institution, 1978); these articles originally appeared in *Brookings Papers on Economic Activity*, 2(1978). See also David Colander (ed.), *Incentive Based Incomes Policies: Advances in TIP and MAP* (Cambridge, MA: Ballinger, 1986).

[†] Martin Weitzman, *The Share Economy* (Cambridge, MA: Harvard University Press, 1984); Daniel Mitchell, "Gain-Sharing: An Anti-Inflation Reform," *Challenge*, 25 (July/August 1982): 18–25.

FIGURE 6.6 FLEXIBLE COMPENSATION CONTRACTS STEEPEN THE SG CURVE

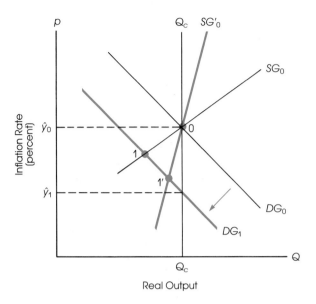

SG_0 is the SG curve with fixed compensation contracts. SG'_0 is the SG curve with flexible compensation contracts. A reduction in the adjusted nominal demand growth rate from $\hat{y}_0$ to $\hat{y}_1$ shifts the DG curve down from DG_0 to DG_1. With flexible compensation contracts, the economy moves to point 1'. Compared to point 1, point 1' has a larger Q_1 (implying a smaller U_1) and a smaller p_1.

downward shift in the DG curve would cause a smaller decline in Q and a larger decline in p.

The goal of the flexible compensation strategy is to achieve a fundamental change in the form of labor contracts. Under most current labor contracts, a worker's compensation is independent of a firm's *gain* (revenue or profit). Under the flexible compensation strategy, labor contracts would vary compensation automatically with the firm's gain.

Why do flexible compensation contracts steepen the SG curve? Even with fixed compensation contracts, the SG curve has a positive slope, because a decline in Q (a rise in U) shifts relative bargaining strength from workers to management and reduces the wage (compensation) increase w under *new* labor contracts. But a firm's compensation increase w remains fixed until its labor contract expires, even if the firm's revenue and profit decrease. Hence, a decline in the average compensation increase w of all firms is inhibited by fixed compensation contracts. As Q drops, the decline in the average compensation increase w — and, therefore, in the inflation rate p — is modest, so that the SG curve is relatively flat, as shown in Figure 6.6.

Under a flexible compensation contract, a worker's w has two components: a *fixed component* $\overline{w}$, and a *flexible share component* w_s:

$$(6.8) \qquad w = \overline{w} + w_s$$

Under this contract, w_s is adjusted automatically with the gain of the firm.

Consider what happens under flexible compensation contracts in response to demand deceleration that shifts the DG curve downward, as shown in Figure 6.6. A reduction in the adjusted nominal demand growth rate $\hat{y}$ reduces the revenue and profit of the average firm. As Q drops, the compensation increase w declines automatically due to the decline in w_s. Hence, p declines more sharply as Q drops, and the SG curve becomes steeper. Compared to the outcome with fixed compensation contracts, the decline in Q is smaller (the rise in U is smaller) and the decline in w (and p) is larger (point $1'$ instead of point 1).

One advantage of the flexible compensation strategy is that it can be effective even in the presence of long-term labor contracts. Such contracts are attractive to many firms and unions because they reduce the frequency of labor – management negotiations and strikes. Even before the contract expires, w is automatically adjusted by the variation of w_s.

Despite the apparent desirable effects of flexible compensation, this form of worker compensation is currently the exception, not the rule, in the U.S. economy. One possible explanation is that the labor contract may reflect the preferences of the worker with average seniority at the workplace, rather than the preferences of the low-seniority worker. The worker with average seniority faces little risk of being laid off in a recession. Workers are generally retained according to seniority. In a typical recession, almost all persons laid off are low-seniority workers.

Hence, the worker with average seniority may not find a flexible compensation contract attractive. A risk-averse worker will prefer a fixed, virtually guaranteed income to the same expected income from a flexible compensation contract.

By contrast, a flexible compensation contract will reduce the possibility that low-seniority workers will be laid off, although they may not recognize this fact. A flexible compensation contract does not specifically guarantee that there will be no layoffs. Moreover, the firm will probably find it more profitable to respond to the preferences of average-seniority workers, rather than low-seniority workers, in any case.

The social insurance and welfare system may reinforce this choice. If low-seniority workers received no assistance during unemployment, their plight might exert more pressure on managements and unions to accept flexible compensation contracts. The current "safety net" of unemployment compensation and welfare reduces this pressure.

According to this explanation, those who choose the form of the labor contract have no incentive to weigh the cost of lost output and employment that results under demand deceleration. Hence, an important externality is present.

The proper response is to "internalize the externality." Managements and/or workers should be given an incentive to weigh this cost of the current fixed wage system. This incentive could be implemented through the tax system. Share compensation w_s could be taxed at a lower rate than fixed compensation $\overline{w}$. The differential taxation of the two forms of compensation would induce firms and workers to shift toward flexible compensation.

The U.S. tax system currently favors certain forms of profit-sharing. But it does not fully encourage gain-sharing so that w varies cyclically. First, to receive favorable tax treatment, the share compensation must be a contribution to a pension. But many workers may want to use most of their compensation for current needs. Second, tax treatment is only favorable if profit is the measure of gain. But some firms and workers may prefer revenue (or some other measure of gain) to profit. Finally, tax treatment is favorable even if the bonus does not vary with the gain. But the aim should be to encourage such variation, because this is what makes the compensation increase w responsive to cyclical fluctuations.

Although flexible compensation contracts are the exception in the United States, they are common in several other economies, including Japan. Some argue that the Japanese economy does appear to exhibit smaller fluctuations in output and employment. Perhaps flexible compensation is partly responsible for this greater economic stability.

The flexible compensation strategy does entail practical problems. Exactly what measures of "gain" qualify for favorable tax treatment? How favorable should the tax treatment be? Would all firms and workers in the economy be eligible for such treatment? These and other practical aspects would need to be addressed.

Although it seems likely that flexible compensation makes disinflation less costly, it is more difficult to assess the long-run properties of a "share economy." Economists are only beginning to provide the required analysis.

Other Disinflation Policies

Here, we will briefly consider several other disinflation policies. One has been offered by James Meade—a Nobel Prize winner in economics. Meade suggests "not quite compulsory arbitration" as a method of inducing noninflationary wage settlements. Either party to a wage negotiation — management or the union — would be given the legal right to send the dispute to an arbitrator, whose recommendation would be binding. The arbitrator would be guided by the noninflationary wage standard of the government.

Meade contends that this system would avoid the risk of arbitration by pressuring both parties to voluntarily agree to a settlement that is close to the government standard. The small number of cases that would actually go to arbitration would not be too costly to administer.

One possible problem is that such a wage-only policy may not be acceptable to unions and workers. It might be necessary to combine Meade's proposal with a price TIP or some kind of profit-margin control to balance the package.

Another disinflation policy focuses on raising the responsiveness of wage increases to recession by making multi-year wage contracts illegal. It seems plausible that multi-year contracts lock in firms to wage increases despite recession. One-year contracts would keep wage settlements in tune with economic conditions. But some labor economists emphasize the advantages of multi-year contracts in terms of improved stability and planning and reduced negotiation and strike costs. The cons as well as the pros must be weighed.

Another policy requires simultaneous wage-setting. When major wage-setting is "staggered," rather than simultaneous, each settlement may be influenced by recent wage settlements, thereby fostering inertia. If major settlements occur simultaneously, then the reduction of each settlement is matched by others, so that relative positions are not altered.

Institutionally, how would this work? A single wage negotiation is complex. Could a large number of unions bargain jointly with a large number of employers, with tentative wage settlements causing others to be reopened, until all parties are satisfied? What exactly does "simultaneous" mean in practice? Moreover, is inertia due to relative wage comparisons or real wage expectations (expectations of price inflation)? If the latter is more important, then would prices also have to be set simultaneously? Is this feasible?

To raise these questions is not to imply that they cannot be given satisfactory answers. The point is that these complementary disinflation policies may have disadvantages as well as advantages that must be carefully examined and weighed.

SUMMARY

1. If expectations are inertial, so that $p^e = p_{-1}$, then when the nominal demand growth rate y is cut, both the inflation rate p and the real output growth rate q share the decline in the short run. If the SG

curve is flatter, then the reduction in p is smaller and the reduction in q is greater.

2. In the long run, a reduction in adjusted nominal demand growth $\hat{y}$ from 6% to 0% reduces the inflation rate p from 6% to 0% and returns real output Q to Q_c (and q to q_c). But in the short run, if expectations are inertial, then Q will fall below Q_c.

3. With inertial expectations, a reduction in the nominal demand growth rate y must generate a transitional rise in the unemployment rate U — a *transitional recession* — in the process of reducing the inflation rate p.

4. The "refusal" of SG_1 to shift downward when the nominal demand growth rate y is cut results in a decrease in real output Q (since DG_1 does shift downward when y is cut). The source of this "refusal" — inertial expectations — keeps the wage inflation rate w, and therefore the inflation rate p, at any level of Q, independent of the cut in y. Because the cut in y does not affect the expected inflation rate p^e, which equals last period's inflation rate p_{-1}, a reduction in y can reduce w only by raising U.

5. According to econometric analysis of U.S. data for 1975 – 1984, it appears that an unemployment rate above 7% might be required to reduce the inflation rate. It is estimated that roughly 1 *point-year of excess unemployment* (above 7%) would be required to reduce the inflation rate by 1%. For example, an unemployment rate of 8% (so that excess unemployment is 1%), sustained for one year, should reduce the inflation rate by roughly 1%.

6. According to *Okun's Law*, each point-year of excess unemployment corresponds to a loss of roughly 2% of annual GNP. Together with the econometric analysis just reported, this implies that a 1% reduction in the inflation rate requires a sacrifice of roughly 2% of annual GNP under a policy of *demand deceleration*.

7. Under inertial expectations, the cost of *disinflation* cannot be avoided by *gradualism*. The speed of demand deceleration entails a trade-off. Under the *cold-turkey policy*, we "get it over with" relatively quickly but incur a sudden, steep cost. Under gradualism, we "drag it out." The worst year under gradualism is not as bad as the worst year under cold-turkey policy, but gradualism entails more above-normal unemployment years than cold-turkey policy.

8. If expectations are rational, and long-term wage contracts are uncommon, then a clearly announced, "credible" demand deceleration policy would achieve disinflation without recession. In our $DG - SG$ diagram, the SG curve shifts downward immediately by the same amount as the DG curve; p declines, and the $DG - SG$ intersection remains at Q^*.

9. A *price policy* is designed to exert direct, downward pressure on price increases to reduce the level of p that firms will set at any level of Q (and U). Its aim is to shift the SG curve downward. A price policy is intended to complement demand deceleration policy. Price policy has traditionally been implemented by voluntary guidelines or mandatory controls. Recently, incentive price policies—a tax-incentive inflation policy (TIP) and a market anti-inflation plan (MAP)—have been proposed.

10. A flexible compensation strategy steepens the SG curve, and thereby reduces the cost of disinflation. This strategy urges the adoption of labor contracts that vary compensation automatically with the firm's gain (revenue or profit).

TERMS AND CONCEPTS

cold-turkey policy
credibility
demand deceleration (policy)
disinflation
disinflation transition path
econometric analysis
efficiency wage hypothesis
fixed compensation ($\overline{w}$)
flexible compensation strategy
gradualist policy
imperfect information
implicit contract
incentive price policy
inertial expectations
input price increase (p_i)
invisible handshake
market anti-inflation plan (MAP)
new classical macroeconomics
Okun's Law

ordinary least-squares (OLS)
   estimates
"pass through" cost
point-year of excess
   unemployment
price change versus quality
   change
price policy
product price increase (p_q)
rational expectations
share compensation (w_s)
share economy
social cost
strength of a price policy
tax-incentive inflation policy
   (TIP)
transitional recession
value-added price increase (p_v)

QUESTIONS

Assume that the economy is characterized by inertial expectations unless rational expectations are specified.

6.1 Assume that the normal real output growth rate $q_c = 3\%$ and that, for many periods, the nominal demand growth rate has been $y = 12\%$, so that adjusted nominal demand growth $\hat{y} = 9\%$.
   a. To what inflation rate p, real output growth rate q, and level of real output Q has the economy converged? Construct a $DG - SG$ diagram, label this the "period 0 equilibrium," and draw the $\hat{y}$ line, the Q_c line, and the DG_0 and SG_0 curves.

292   DISINFLATION AND TRANSITIONAL RECESSION

b. If the labor productivity growth rate $a = 2\%$, to what wage inflation rate w has the economy converged?

c. If the nominal demand growth rate y is cut permanently from 12% to 3% beginning in period 1, draw the new $\hat{y}$ line. Then find the $DG_1 - SG_1$ intersection point.

d. In words, explain why a recession has occurred in period 1.

e. Draw the DG and SG curves for periods 2–6.

f. To what inflation rate p, real output growth rate q, level of real output Q, and wage inflation rate w will the economy converge in the long run?

6.2 Assume the period 0 equilibrium in Question 6.1. Now a gradual demand deceleration policy is implemented, so that y is cut from 12% to 3% over three years (instead of in one year). Hence, in period 1, $y_1 = 9\%$.

a. Find the $DG_1 - SG_1$ intersection point. How does it compare to the $DG_1 - SG_1$ intersection point in Question 6.1(c)?

b. Construct a $DG - SG$ diagram to show how the *gradualist path* compares with the *cold-turkey path*.

c. What is the advantage of the gradualist path? Of the cold-turkey path?

6.3 Based on *Okun's Law* and on our econometric estimates in this chapter, how many *point-years of excess unemployment* and how much sacrifice in real output would be required to reduce the inflation rate from 9% to 0% by demand deceleration?

6.4 Why doesn't the wage inflation rate w decline more quickly when the unemployment rate rises above U_c?

6.5 Suppose that in Question 6.1, expectations are rational, information is perfect, and long-term wage contracts are uncommon.

a. Construct a $DG - SG$ diagram, and reanswer Question 6.1(c).

b. Explain (a) in words.

6.6 Present an argument to support making a demand deceleration policy "credible." How could this be done? Do you think such techniques would enable the *disinflation path* to be closer to the rational expectations path in Question 6.5 than to the inertial expectations path in Question 6.1? Explain your answer.

6.7 Suppose that expectations are inertial and that the gradual demand deceleration policy in Question 6.2 is complemented by a price policy with a strength of 3%.

a. Locate the $DG_1 - SG_1$ intersection point. How does it compare to the $DG_1 - SG_1$ intersection point in Question 6.2(a)? Explain this result in words.

b. What criticisms have been made of *price controls?*

c. Explain the *incentive price policies* TIP and MAP.

d. What criticisms have been made of TIP and MAP?

THE ALGEBRA OF THE *DG–SG* MODEL

In Chapters 4 and 6, we have relied primarily on the *DG–SG* diagram to analyze inflation and disinflation. A diagram can tell us the *qualitative* pattern, but it cannot provide precise, *quantitative* results. In this appendix, we will perform the same analysis using algebra. We will then be able to calculate numerical values of the key variables when nominal demand growth is altered.

6.A.1 A Model of an Economy with Inertial Expectations

Our model consists of three equations:

(6.A.1)   *The demand growth (inflation–output growth) equation*

$$y \equiv p + q$$

(6.A.2)   *The inflation–unemployment equation*

$$\Delta p \equiv p - p_{-1} = \frac{h(U_c - U)}{U} \qquad h > 0$$

(6.A.3)   *The Okun's Law (unemployment–output growth) equation*

$$\Delta U \equiv U - U_{-1} = j(q_c - q) \qquad j > 0$$

Equations (6.A.1) and (6.A.2) are discussed explicitly in the text. It is important to emphasize that equation (6.A.2) is the "normal" relationship between the inflation rate p and the unemployment rate U in the absence of supply shocks. A supply shock would cause p to differ from the value predicted by equation (6.A.2). Thus, the analysis will focus on how the economy responds to changes in nominal demand growth, ignoring supply shocks.

Because equation (6.A.2) depends on inertial expectations, our three-equation model describes an economy characterized by inertial expectations. (In Section 6.A.2, we will explain why equation (6.A.2) is based on inertial expectations.)

Equation (6.A.3) expresses relation (4.8), which we now restate:

(4.8)   If Q grows at the same rate as Q_c ($q = q_c$), then U stays constant.

If Q grows at a faster rate than Q_c ($q > q_c$), then U declines.

If Q grows at a slower rate than Q_c ($q < q_c$), then U rises.

In equation (6.A.3), if the real output growth rate q is normal (q_c), then the unemployment rate U will stay constant ($\Delta U = 0\%$); if the real output growth rate q is above normal ($q > q_c$), then the unemployment rate U will decline ($\Delta U < 0\%$); and if the real output growth rate q is below normal ($q < q_c$), then the unemployment rate U will rise ($\Delta U > 0\%$). The parameter j determines the magnitude of the rise or fall in U. In Section 6.A.5, we will further analyze Okun's Law equation (6.A.3) and see how econometric technique can provide an estimate for j.

Once the value of the nominal demand growth rate y is given for the period, the three equations have three unknowns: the inflation rate p, the unemployment rate U, and the real output growth rate q. In Section 6.A.6, we will learn how to solve for the values of these three unknowns. The values of p, q, and U, period by period, provide the path of the economy in response to the specified path of the nominal demand growth rate y.

Let's see how our model works. To illustrate, we will assume that $h = 0.07$ and $j = 0.5$. (These values are roughly consistent with econometric analysis of U.S. data.) We will examine disinflation, beginning in the initial period equilibrium with $p = 6\%$, $q = q_c = 3\%$, $U = U_c = 7\%$, and $y = 9\%$.

Note that adjusted nominal demand growth $\hat{y} \equiv y - q_c = 9\% - 3\% = 6\%$, so that $\hat{y} = p$ in the initial period equilibrium. We saw that in a growing economy, $\hat{y}$ (not y) plays the key role; the horizontal line in the $DG - SG$ diagram is drawn at $\hat{y}$. Moreover, in the long run, once y is fixed, the inflation rate p eventually converges to $\hat{y}$.

First, let's check to make sure that if y remains at 9%, then p, U, and q will stay constant. Our three equations become

(6.A.1) $\qquad 9\% = p + q$

(6.A.2) $\qquad p - 6\% = \dfrac{0.07(7\% - U)}{U}$

(6.A.3) $\qquad U - 7\% = 0.5(3\% - q)$

We can easily see that the values $p = 6\%$, $q = 3\%$, and $U = 7\%$ "work" in all three equations; just plug them in:

(6.A.1) $\qquad 9\% = 6\% + 3\%$

(6.A.2) $\qquad 6\% - 6\% = \dfrac{0.07(7\% - 7\%)}{7\%}$

(6.A.3) $\qquad 7\% - 7\% = 0.5(3\% - 3\%)$

In Section 6.A.6, we will prove that there is only one economically relevant solution; hence, the above values are the solution if $y = 9\%$. As long as y remains at 9%, the values of p, q, and U will stay constant.

Now, consider a *gradualist deceleration policy*. Suppose that y is cut by 1.5% to 7.5% in period 1, so that $\hat{y}$ is also cut by 1.5% to 4.5%. y is then cut by 1.5% in each of the next three periods and is then permanently set at 3%, so that $\hat{y}$ is permanently set at 0%. What happens in period 1?

In period 1, with $y = 7.5\%$, we have

(6.A.1) $7.5\% = p + q$

(6.A.2) $p - 6\% = \dfrac{0.07(7\% - U)}{U}$

(6.A.3) $U - 7\% = 0.5(3\% - q)$

To obtain the numerical values for p, q, and U, we must solve our three equations for these three unknowns (see Section 6.A.6). But even without obtaining the precise solution, we can draw some important qualitative conclusions.

AN ITERATIVE APPROACH TO THE SOLUTION

In equation (6.A.1), y is reduced by 1.5% (from 9% to 7.5%). Hence, the sum $p + q$ must decline by 1.5%. Will both p and q be reduced, thereby sharing the 1.5% decline? Or will one bear the entire burden, declining 1.5%, while the other stays constant? Or will one actually rise while the other declines more than 1.5%? Our $DG - SG$ diagram tells us that when the DG curve shifts downward and the SG curve remains fixed, both q and p decline; in other words, the decline in y is shared.

The relevant $DG - SG$ diagram is shown in Figure 6.A.1. In period 0, the $\hat{y}_0$ line is at 6%; in period 1, it shifts down to $\hat{y}_1 = 4.5\%$. In period 0, the DG_0 line passes through the intersection of the $\hat{y}_0 = 6\%$ line and the Q_c pole. In period 1, the DG line shifts downward by 1.5% to DG_1 and passes through the intersection of the $\hat{y}_0 = 4.5\%$ line and the Q_c pole. Since $SG_1 = SG_0$, it is clear that p_1 must lie between 4.5% and 6%, so that

$4.5\% < p_1 < 6\%$

But since $y_1 = 7.5\%$, it is easy to find the range for q_1. A p_1 of 4.5% implies a q_1 of 3%; a p_1 of 6% implies a q_1 of 1.5%. Hence

$1.5\% < q_1 < 3\%$

Finally, from equation (6.A.2), it is clear that for p_1 to decline below 6%, U_1 must rise above 7%, so that

$7\% < U_1$

We know that p_1 will be between 4.5% and 6%. If h is larger, then the SG curve is steeper and p_1 is smaller (closer to 4.5%). Thus, q_1 will be larger (closer to 3%), and U_1 will be smaller (closer to 7%).

FIGURE 6.A.1 p AND q "SHARE" A REDUCTION IN DEMAND GROWTH

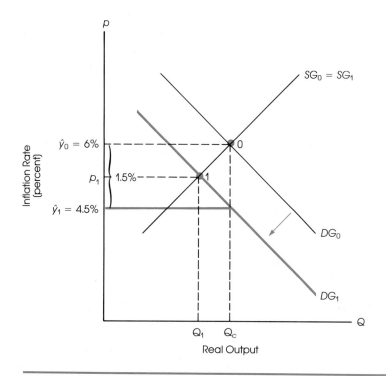

Real Output

Initially, in period 0, the adjusted nominal demand growth rate $\hat{y}_0 = 6\%$ (the normal real output growth rate $q_c = 3\%$, so that $y_0 = 9\%$), the inflation rate $p = 6\%$, real output $Q = Q_c$, and the real output growth rate $q_0 = q_c = 3\%$. Then $\hat{y}$ is cut by 1.5% in period 1, so that $\hat{y}_1 = 4.5\%$ ($y_1 = 7.5\%$). The economy moves from point 0 to point 1. SG_1 coincides with SG_0, but DG_1 lies 1.5% below DG_0. Clearly, the inflation rate in period 1 p_1 must lie between 6% and 4.5%. Hence, p declines, but by a lesser amount than 1.5%. Since $p + q = y$ and since y declines by 1.5%, q must "share" some of this decline. Q_1 does indeed lie below Q_c, implying that q_1 is less than q_c (3%).

Can we confirm this sharing result by examining the three equations, without referring to the $DG - SG$ diagram? The answer is yes. We will now show that the sharing outcome is consistent with all three equations and that the nonsharing outcomes will lead to a contradiction.

First, is the sharing outcome consistent with all three equations? We begin with equation (6.A.2). For p to decline below 6%, U must rise above 7%. Now, turning to equation (6.A.3), if U rises above 7%, then q must fall below 3%. Thus, the shared decline in both p and q is consistent with all three equations.

Now let's show that a nonsharing outcome will lead to a contradiction. For example, is it possible for p to decline 1.5% while q stays constant at 3%? From equation (6.A.2), for p to decline by 1.5% (from 6% to 4.5%), U must clearly rise above 7%. From equation (6.A.3), if U rises above 7%, then q must clearly fall below 3%. But this contradicts our initial assumption that q remains constant at 3%. Any other nonsharing outcome will lead to a similar contradiction; try it out to convince yourself.

▶ Thus, in our model, a reduction in the nominal demand growth rate y will immediately generate a recession—a rise in the unemployment rate U and a decline in the real output growth rate q below q_c—but will also immediately reduce the inflation rate.

NARROWING THE SOLUTION RANGE

The ranges for p_1, q_1, and U_1 that we have established are sufficient to guarantee that p and q share the decline in y, but we can narrow these ranges even further. We have not yet made use of the value of the responsiveness parameter h in equation (6.A.2) or the value of the parameter j in equation (6.A.3). In the $DG-SG$ diagram in Figure 6.A.1, we can immediately see that p_1 must lie between 4.5% and 6%, simply because the slope of the SG curve is positive. But the particular values of h (0.07) and j (0.5), taken together, determine the slope of the SG curve. Information about the slope of the SG curve should enable us to narrow the range for p_1 still further. Here's how we can use this information. We have already established this range for q_1:

$$1.5\% < q_1 < 3\%$$

Let's insert these values for q_1 into equation (6.A.3), using the information that $j = 0.5$:

$$U_1 - 7\% = 0.5(3\% - q_1)$$

A q_1 of 3% implies a U_1 of 7%. A q_1 of 1.5% implies a U_1 of

$$U_1 - 7\% = 0.5(3\% - 1.5\%) = 0.75\%$$
$$U_1 = 7.75\%$$

Thus, we can narrow our range for U_1 to

$$7\% < U_1 < 7.75\%$$

Now if we insert these values for U_1 into equation (6.A.2), using the information that $h = 0.07$, we can narrow our range for p_1:

$$p_1 - 6\% = \frac{0.07(7\% - U_1)}{U_1}$$

If $U_1 = 7.75\%$, then

$$p_1 = 6\% + \frac{0.07(7\% - 7.75\%)}{7.75\%}$$
$$= 6\% - 0.7\% = 5.3\%$$

Thus, the range for p_1 is narrowed to

$$5.3\% < p_1 < 6\%$$

But from equation (6.A.1), this range for p_1 implies a narrower range for q_1 of

$$1.5\% < q_1 < 2.2\%$$

Clearly, we can continue this process of narrowing the ranges for p_1, q_1, and U_1 indefinitely. Eventually, we will converge on the actual solutions for p_1, q_1, and U_1. But if we want to obtain the exact solution, we may as well solve the three equations directly, using the method given in Section 6.A.6 to obtain $p_1 = 5.5\%$, $q_1 = 2.0\%$, and $U_1 = 7.5\%$. These values for p_1 and U_1 appear in Table 6.A.1 for year (period) 1 under the gradualist path.

THE LONG-RUN EQUILIBRIUM

What happens in the long run? We can generate the path of the economy by solving our three-equation model period by period. Using the formula derived in Section 6.A.6 to solve the model, we obtain the solution for period 1 just given. Now we are ready to solve for the period 2 values p_2, q_2, and U_2. Let's rewrite our three equations:

(6.A.1) $$y = p + q$$

(6.A.2) $$p - p_{-1} = \frac{0.07(7\% - U)}{U}$$

(6.A.3) $$U - U_{-1} = 0.5(3\% - q)$$

In period 2, the "last period" is period 1. Thus, $p_{-1} = p_1 = 5.5\%$,

TABLE 6.A.1

GRADUALIST AND COLD-TURKEY PATHS

	Gradualist Path			Cold-Turkey Path		
Year	$\hat{y}$	U	p	$\hat{y}$	U	p
0	6.0%	7.00%	6.00%	6.0%	7.00%	6.00%
1	4.5	7.51	5.52	0.0	9.17	4.34
2	3.0	8.24	4.47	0.0	10.24	2.13
3	1.5	8.96	2.93	0.0	10.20	−0.07
4	0.0	9.51	1.09	0.0	9.30	−1.80
5	0.0	9.21	−0.59	0.0	7.97	−2.66
6	0.0	8.35	−1.72	0.0	6.77	−2.41
7	0.0	7.33	−2.04	0.0	6.09	−1.36
8	0.0	6.55	−1.56	0.0	5.99	−0.19
9	0.0	6.21	−0.67	0.0	6.29	0.60
10	0.0	6.28	0.13	0.0	6.73	0.88
11	0.0	6.57	0.59	0.0	7.12	0.77
12	0.0	6.91	0.68	0.0	7.34	0.44
13	0.0	7.17	0.51	0.0	7.38	0.08
14	0.0	7.29	0.24	0.0	7.28	−0.19
15	0.0	7.27	−0.03	0.0	7.13	−0.31
16	0.0	7.18	−0.20	0.0	6.98	−0.29
17	0.0	7.05	−0.25	0.0	6.89	−0.18
18	0.0	6.95	−0.20	0.0	6.87	−0.05
19	0.0	6.90	−0.10	0.0	6.90	0.06
20	0.0	6.90	−0.00	0.0	6.95	0.11
21	0.0	6.93	0.07	0.0	7.00	0.11
22	0.0	6.98	0.09	0.0	7.04	0.07
23	0.0	7.01	0.07	0.0	7.05	0.02
24	0.0	7.03	0.04	0.0	7.04	−0.02
25	0.0	7.04	0.00	0.0	7.02	−0.04
26	0.0	7.02	−0.02	0.0	7.00	−0.04
27	0.0	7.01	−0.03	0.0	6.99	−0.03
28	0.0	7.00	−0.03	0.0	6.98	−0.01
29	0.0	6.99	−0.02	0.0	6.99	0.01
30	0.0	6.99	−0.00	0.0	6.99	0.01
31	0.0	6.99	0.01	0.0	7.00	0.01
32	0.0	7.00	0.01	0.0	7.00	0.01
33	0.0	7.00	0.01	0.0	7.01	0.00
34	0.0	7.00	0.01	0.0	7.01	−0.00
35	0.0	7.00	0.00	0.0	7.00	−0.00
36	0.0	7.00	−0.00	0.0	7.00	−0.01
37	0.0	7.00	−0.00	0.0	7.00	−0.00
38	0.0	7.00	−0.00	0.0	7.00	−0.00
39	0.0	7.00	−0.00	0.0	7.00	0.00

$U_{-1} = U_1 = 7.5\%$, and $y_2 = 6\%$, giving us

(6.A.1) $$6\% = p_2 + q_2$$

(6.A.2) $$p_2 - 5.5\% = \frac{0.07(7\% - U_2)}{U_2}$$

(6.A.3) $$U_2 - 7.5\% = 0.5(3\% - q_2)$$

Therefore, in period 2, we have three equations and three unknowns. Using the formula derived in Section 6.A.6, we can obtain the values of p_2, q_2, and U_2. By the same procedure, we can obtain the values of p_3, q_3, and U_3 for period 3, and so on. Of course, it is only sensible to write a computer program to perform these calculations.

The gradualist path is presented in Table 6.A.1. We can see that, in the long run, the economy converges to $p = \hat{y} = y - q_c = 3\% - 3\% = 0\%$, $q = q_c = 3\%$, and $U = U_c = 7\%$. It is instructive to compare the gradualist path with a cold-turkey path where y is reduced to 3% in period 1. The cold-turkey path shown in Table 6.A.1 is obtained by the same method; beginning in period 1, $y = 3\%$ ($\hat{y} = 0\%$) in all subsequent periods. The cold-turkey path converges to the same values as the gradualist path. This should not be surprising, because $y = 3\%$ ($\hat{y} = 0\%$) in both cases from period 4 onward.

Only by solving the model, period by period, do we confirm that the economy does converge to stable values of p, q, and U. But if we are told that the economy does, in fact, converge to stable values of p, q, and U, then we can easily determine those values by inspecting our equations. Look at equation (6.A.2):

(6.A.2) $$p - p_{-1} = \frac{h(U_c - U)}{U}$$
$$= \frac{0.07(7\% - U)}{U}$$

If the economy converges so that p becomes stable, then $p = p_{-1}$. But this will happen only if U has converged to U_c (7%).

Next, look at equation (6.A.3):

(6.A.3) $$U - U_{-1} = j(q_c - q)$$
$$= 0.5(3\% - q)$$

If the economy converges so that U becomes stable, then $U = U_{-1}$. But this will happen only if q has converged to q_c (3%).

Finally, look at equation (6.A.1):

(6.A.1) $$y = 3\% = p + q$$

If q converges to $q_c = 3\%$, then p must converge to $y - q_c = \hat{y} = 3\% - 3\% = 0\%$.

▶ Thus, we have easily seen that if the economy converges to stable values of p, q, and U when y is set permanently equal to q_c (so that $\hat{y} = y - q_c$ is set permanently at 0%), then those stable values must be $p = \hat{y} = y - q_c = 0\%$, $U = U_c = 7\%$, and $q = q_c = 3\%$.

WHY THE RECOVERY OCCURS

Why does the unemployment rate reach a peak and then decline? We have already seen why demand deceleration must generate a recession in our model; we are now asking why the recession will not be permanent. We know that the unemployment rate U will immediately rise above U_c; from equation (6.A.2), we also know that this will begin to reduce the inflation rate p. As long as U remains above U_c, p will continue to decline. At some point in time, p will reach 0%. Since the nominal demand growth rate is never below $y = 3\%$, when p reaches 0%, given equation (6.A.1), q will be 3% (q_c). Thus, from equation (6.A.3), $U = U_{-1}$; the unemployment rate will stop rising and will stay constant in that period.

But since U is still above U_c, given equation (6.A.2), p will keep falling and become negative. From equation (6.A.1), if p is negative, then q will exceed 3% (q_c). Thus, from equation (6.A.3), $U < U_{-1}$; the unemployment rate will begin to decline.

▶ Once the nominal demand growth rate y is fixed at its new, permanent level, the unemployment rate U will reach a peak and then begin to decline; the recession will not be permanent.

We will now examine how the value of the parameter h affects the path of the economy. Table 6.A.1 shows the gradualist path of the economy with $h = 0.07$. Suppose, instead, that $h = 0.035$, so that the inflation rate p is 50% as responsive to a rise in the unemployment rate U. In this case, we know that the SG curve is flatter, so that a downward shift in the DG curve causes a larger reduction in Q (rise in U) and a smaller decline in p. Table 6.A.2 shows the gradualist path of the economy with $h = 0.035$. Since h is smaller, the economy takes longer to converge to its equilibrium values ($U = 7\%$, $p = 0\%$); some oscillation continues past period 39. A comparison with the gradualist path shown in Table 6.A.1, where $h = 0.07$, yields the following conclusion:

▶ With a smaller h, disinflation occurs more slowly, the peak unemployment rate is higher, and the economy stays longer at an unemployment rate above U_c (7%).

TABLE 6.A.2

GRADUALIST PATH WITH $h = 0.035$

Year	$\hat{y}$	U	p
0	6.0%	7.00%	6.00%
1	4.5	7.61	5.72
2	3.0	8.64	5.06
3	1:5	9.90	4.03
4	0.0	11.26	2.71
5	0.0	11.89	1.27
6	0.0	11.81	−0.16
7	0.0	11.09	−1.45
8	0.0	9.86	−2.46
9	0.0	8.34	−3.03
10	0.0	6.86	−2.96
11	0.0	5.76	−2.20
12	0.0	5.25	−1.03
13	0.0	5.29	0.10
14	0.0	5.73	0.87
15	0.0	6.35	1.23
16	0.0	6.97	1.25
17	0.0	7.48	1.02
18	0.0	7.81	0.66
19	0.0	7.93	0.25
20	0.0	7.87	−0.14
21	0.0	7.65	−0.43
22	0.0	7.35	−0.60
23	0.0	7.04	−0.62
24	0.0	6.78	−0.51
25	0.0	6.63	−0.31
26	0.0	6.58	−0.09
27	0.0	6.63	0.10
28	0.0	6.75	0.23
29	0.0	6.89	0.29
30	0.0	7.03	0.27
31	0.0	7.13	0.21
32	0.0	7.19	0.11
33	0.0	7.20	0.02
34	0.0	7.17	−0.06
35	0.0	7.11	−0.12
36	0.0	7.04	−0.14
37	0.0	6.98	−0.13
38	0.0	6.93	−0.09
39	0.0	6.91	−0.04

Note how the monetary view of inflation relates to our model. By the definition of velocity

(4.11) $m + v = y = p + q$

According to the monetary view, the normal growth rate of velocity v can be taken as roughly constant. It therefore follows that the money-supply growth rate m will control the nominal demand growth rate y. If, for example, v is normally 2%, then $m = 7\%$ in our initial equilibrium with $y = 9\%$. To reduce y by 6% (to 3%), the Fed must cut m by 6% (to 1%). Thus, the key policy variable is m. Once m is set, y is simply equal to $m + v$; then our three-equation model governs the behavior of the economy under the specified path for m (and, hence, y).

ADJUSTED NOMINAL DEMAND GROWTH $\hat{y}$ DETERMINES THE PATH

At this point, we will state and then demonstrate an important property of our model:

▶ The unemployment rate U and the inflation rate p depend on the adjusted nominal demand growth rate $\hat{y}$ which, by definition (4.7), is $y - q_c$. What affects U and p is not the nominal demand growth rate y or the normal real output growth rate q_c per se, but the difference between y and q_c—namely $\hat{y}$.

For example, U and p would be the same for $y = 6\%$ and $q_c = 0\%$ as for $y = 9\%$ and $q_c = 3\%$. In both cases, $\hat{y} = 6\%$.

Now, we will show that this property is true in our model. Returning to our basic three-equation model, we subtract q_c from both sides of equation (6.A.1) to obtain

(6.A.4) $y - q_c = p + q - q_c$

If we define g, the q "gap," as

(6.A.5) $g \equiv q - q_c$

then equation (6.A.4) becomes

(6.A.6) $\hat{y} = p + g$

Using the definition of the q "gap" g in equation (6.A.5), we can rewrite equation (6.A.3) as

(6.A.7) $\Delta U = U - U_{-1} = j(-g)$

We can now rewrite our basic three-equation model as

(6.A.6) $\qquad \hat{y} = p + g$

(6.A.2) $\qquad \Delta p = p - p_{-1} = \dfrac{h(U_c - U)}{U}$

(6.A.7) $\qquad \Delta U = U - U_{-1} = j(-g)$

Our three unknowns are now p, g, and U. Once the value of the adjusted nominal demand growth rate $\hat{y}$ is given, we can solve for these three unknowns (see Section 6.A.6). Thus, p and U depend on $\hat{y}$.

▶ In tables showing the paths of the inflation rate p and the unemployment rate U that result from a particular path of the nominal demand growth rate y, we will show the path of the adjusted nominal demand growth rate $\hat{y}$, because this is the key variable.

If $\hat{y}$ is reduced, say, from 6%, to 4.5%, 3%, 1.5%, 0% (as in Table 6.A.1), then p and U will follow the same path, regardless of the values of y and q_c. For example, the paths of p and U will be identical in these two cases: $q_c = 0\%$ and y declines from 6%, to 4.5%, 3%, 1.5%, 0%; $q_c = 3\%$ and y declines from 9%, to 7.5%, 6%, 4.5%, 3%.

6.A.2 The Inflation–Unemployment Equation

The *inflation–unemployment equation*

(6.A.2) $\qquad \Delta p \equiv p - p_{-1} = \dfrac{h(U_c - U)}{U}$

states the "normal" relationship between Δp and U in the absence of a supply shock.

We will now show that equation (6.A.2) can be derived by combining a "wage equation," a "price equation," and inertial expectations. Our *wage equation* simply reflects two hypotheses about wage behavior that were stated in Chapter 4:

▶ At a given unemployment rate U, if the expected inflation rate p^e is $X\%$ higher (or lower), then the wage inflation rate w will be $X\%$ higher (or lower).

▶ Given p^e, w varies inversely with U. Thus, for a given p^e, w increases as U decreases.

An equation that embodies these hypotheses is

$$(6.A.8) \qquad w = a + p^e + \frac{h(U^* - U)}{U} \qquad h > 0$$

Note that in equation (6.A.8) we use the symbol U^* instead of U_c because this hypothesis is assumed to be valid whether or not expectations are inertial. Note also that this hypothesis assumes that w can respond immediately to a change in p^e. Hence, it ignores long-term wage contracts that impede this response in the short run. Clearly, in equation (6.A.8), if p^e is X% higher, then w is X% higher. For example, if $a = 2\%$, $p^e = 0\%$, initially $U = U^* = 7\%$, and $h = 0.07$, then initially

$$w = 2\% + 0\% + \frac{0.07(7\% - 7\%)}{7\%} = 2\%$$

But if $p^e = 6\%$ (6% higher), then

$$w = 2\% + 6\% + \frac{0.07(7\% - 7\%)}{7\%} = 8\%$$

so that w is actually 6% higher.

Similarly, in equation (6.A.8), w increases as U decreases. For example, with $p^e = 0\%$, if $U = 7\%$, then

$$w = 2\% + 0\% + \frac{0.07(7\% - 7\%)}{7\%} = 2\%$$

But if U decreases to 6%, then

$$w = 2\% + 0\% + \frac{0.07(7\% - 6\%)}{6\%} \approx 3\%$$

so that w increases.

Our *price equation* is equation (4.3):

$$(4.3) \qquad p = w - a$$

Now let's combine equations (6.A.8) and (4.3). In equation (6.A.8), we subtract a from both sides to obtain

$$(6.A.9) \qquad w - a = p^e + \frac{h(U^* - U)}{U}$$

According to equation (4.3), we can replace $w - a$ in equation (6.A.9) with p, so that

(6.A.10) $$p = p^e + \frac{h(U^* - U)}{U}$$

Subtracting p^e from both sides of equation (6.A.10) yields

(6.A.11) $$p - p^e = \frac{h(U^* - U)}{U}$$

▶ The actual inflation rate p will equal the expected inflation rate p^e if and only if the unemployment rate U equals the long-run equilibrium unemployment rate U^*. Equation (6.A.11) holds for any hypothesis concerning expectations.
Under inertial expectations

$$p^e = p_{-1}$$

Substituting this equation into equation (6.A.11) yields

(6.A.2) $$\Delta p = p - p_{-1} = \frac{h(U_c - U)}{U}$$

Note that with inertial expectations we replace U^* with U_c.
It is clear from equation (6.A.2) that if $U = U_c$, then the inflation rate p will normally (in the absence of a supply shock) stay constant. In other words, in the absence of a supply shock, the economy will possess a constant inflation unemployment rate U_c. Note that this result is crucially dependent on the inertial expectations condition that $p^e = p_{-1}$. This hypothesis converts equation (6.A.11) to equation (6.A.2).
By contrast, both the wage equation (6.A.8) and equation (6.A.11) are valid for any expectations hypothesis. We will use them in our discussion of rational expectations in Section 6.A.3.

6.A.3 Rational Expectations

In a rational expectations economy, we use the symbols U^*, q^*, and Q^* in place of U_c, q_c, and Q_c. We begin with equation (6.A.11), which is derived from equation (6.A.8):

(6.A.11) $$p - p^e = \frac{h(U^* - U)}{U}$$

Under inertial expectations, $p^e = p_{-1}$. By contrast, under rational expectations with perfect information:

$$p^e = p$$

The rational expectations hypothesis asserts that if economic agents have perfect information, expectations will normally be correct. (Errors can occur, but they are random, not systematic; on average, they will be zero.) If p^e is replaced with p in equation (6.A.11), then the left side of the equation becomes 0

(6.A.12) $$p - p = 0 = \frac{h(U^* - U)}{U}$$

Therefore, U must normally equal U^* (implying that Q must equal the corresponding Q^*). This is true in all periods, not merely in the long run. From equation (6.A.3) (replacing q_c by q^*), it follows that

(6.A.13) $$U - U_{-1} = U^* - U^* = 0\% = j(q^* - q)$$

Hence, q must equal q^* in all periods. Then from (6.A.1), it follows that

(6.A.14)
$$y = p + q = p + q^*$$
$$p = y - q^* \equiv \hat{y}$$

Hence, the inflation rate p must equal the adjusted nominal demand growth rate $\hat{y}$ in all periods, not merely in the long run. For example, suppose that the economy is at its initial equilibrium point, with $p = 6\%$ and $y = 9\%$. Then under the cold-turkey policy in period 1, y is cut by 6% (from 9% to 3%), so that $\hat{y}$ is cut by 6% (from 6% to 0%). Then under rational expectations, p in period 1 is also cut by 6% (from 6% to 0%), U remains at U^* (7%), Q stays at Q^*, and q remains at q^* (3%).

In the DG–SG diagram, the SG_1 curve shifts downward by 6%, just like the DG_1 curve, so that Q remains at Q^* (and U remains at U^*), while p declines by 6%. We saw that the SG curve behaves this way under rational expectations in Figure 6.3 (page 269). Note that this result — a fall in p while U remains equal to U^* — depends on the assumption that long-term wage contracts do not impede the response of w to p^e in equation (6.A.8).

It should now be clear why, under rational expectations, the economy does not possess a constant inflation unemployment rate U_c (or a constant inflation output Q_c). While U remains at U^* (and Q remains at Q^*), the reduction in $\hat{y}$ causes p to decline. It is simply not true that when $U = U^*$, p will remain constant under rational expectations.

6.A.4   A Tax-Incentive Inflation Policy (TIP)

Recall that TIP is an incentive price policy based on a tax incentive that would induce a firm to reduce its price increase p to less than it would otherwise be at any unemployment rate U.

Here, we will once again assume inertial expectations, so that $p^e = p_{-1}$ and assume that equation (6.A.2) will hold without TIP. If TIP were to succeed, it would shift the right side of equation (6.A.2) downward by X, where X is defined as the "strength" of the policy, so that

(6.A.15) $$\Delta p = p - p_{-1} = \frac{h(U_c - U)}{U} - X$$

Thus, an effective TIP would make one change in our three-equation model — the addition of TIP strength $(-X)$ to the right side of equation (6.A.2).

For example, if TIP has the strength to make p 2% less than it otherwise would be at any U, then $X = 2\%$. Suppose that $U_c = 7\%$, $p_{-1} = 6\%$, and $h = 0.07$. If $U = 7\%$, then $p = 6\%$ without TIP; with a TIP of strength 2%, $p = 4\%$.

How will the introduction of TIP affect the $DG - SG$ diagram? The answer lies in equation (6.A.15). If TIP is effective, then according to our equation, at any U (and, hence, at any Q), firms will set p at a lesser value than they would otherwise set — specifically, X less. For example, if $X = 2\%$, then firms will set p 2% lower than the value they would otherwise set. The SG curve determines the value of p that firms will set at each level of Q. Thus, TIP will shift the SG curve downward by X; for example, if $X = 2\%$, then the SG curve will shift downward by 2% at each level of Q. We have already pursued the implications of this downward shift in the SG curve by TIP in Figure 6.5 (page 277).

In the absence of X, equation (6.A.2) embodies the sober conclusion that inflation can only be reduced if the unemployment rate is raised above U_c. Without X, if $U = U_c$, then the inflation rate will stay constant; therefore, without a tax-incentive policy, the constant inflation unemployment rate of the economy is equal to U_c. But with X in equation (6.A.15), this is no longer the case. With X, if $U = U_c$, then the inflation rate will be reduced by X; for example, if $X = 2\%$, then p will decline by 2%. Hence, the constant inflation unemployment rate is no longer equal to the initial U_c, but is now equal to U'_c.

What is the common-sense reason for this result? Without TIP, a rise in the unemployment rate above U_c is necessary to reduce labor demand relative to labor supply and, thereby, to induce workers to accept a reduction in the wage inflation rate w. But if TIP works, its downward pressure on w is a substitute for an above-normal unemployment rate. The pressure of TIP will reduce w, even with no change in the state of labor demand relative to labor supply (no change in the unemployment rate).

With X in equation (6.A.15), it is possible for the inflation rate to decline even if the unemployment rate is below U_c. If U is below U_c, then the first term in equation (6.A.15), $h(U_c - U)/U$, will be positive and will, in itself, tend to raise inflation. But as long as $-X$ outweighs this first term, the inflation rate will still decline. In other words, as long as the downward pressure of TIP outweighs the upward pressure of the below-U_c unemployment rate, p will still decline.

THE IMPACT ON THE CONSTANT INFLATION UNEMPLOYMENT RATE

The two forces will be in balance—permitting the inflation rate to remain constant—at the value of U that is the new constant inflation unemployment rate U_c' of the economy under TIP. Let's find the value of U_c' in a specific example. Suppose that $X = 2\%$, $h = 0.07$, and $U_c = 7\%$. We want to find the value of U, which we will call U_c', that will make the left side of equation (6.A.15) equal 0%:

(6.A.15)
$$\Delta p = \frac{h(U_c - U)}{U} - X$$

$$0\% = \frac{0.07(7\% - U_c')}{U_c'} - 2\%$$

To find U_c', we multiply every term by U_c' and set $2\% = 0.02$, so that

$$0\% = 0.07(7\% - U_c') - 0.02U_c'$$

Multiplying both sides of this equation by 100 (moving the decimal point two places to the right), we obtain

$$0\% = 7(7\% - U_c') - 2U_c'$$

Thus

$$0\% = 49\% - 7U_c' - 2U_c'$$
$$9U_c' = 49\%$$
$$U_c' \approx 5.44\%$$

Thus, without TIP, the constant inflation unemployment rate $U_c = 7\%$; with a TIP that has a strength of 2%, the new $U_c' \approx 5.4\%$, if $h = 0.07$. Now let's repeat the same steps for any values of U_c, h, and X:

(6.A.15)
$$\Delta p = \frac{h(U_c - U)}{U} - X$$

$$0\% = \frac{h(U_c - U_c')}{U_c'} - X$$
$$0\% = h(U_c - U_c') - XU_c'$$

$$0\% = hU_c - hU'_c - XU'_c$$
$$hU'_c + XU'_c = hU_c$$

Factoring out U'_c on the left gives us

$$U'_c(h + X) = hU_c$$

Dividing through by $h + X$ yields

(6.A.16) $\qquad U'_c = \dfrac{hU_c}{h + X} = \left(\dfrac{h}{h + X}\right) U_c$

Since $h/(h + X)$ is clearly a fraction less than 1, the new U'_c is less than the initial U_c. If X is larger, then TIP is stronger and U'_c is lower.

▶ When TIP is introduced, even if U is reduced below the initial U_c, as long as U is greater than the value of U'_c given by equation (6.A.16), p will decline. If, however, U is reduced below that value of U'_c, then p will rise despite TIP.

Now, let's return to our initial equilibrium condition, with $p = 6\%$ and $y = 9\%$. Suppose that in period 1, a TIP with a strength of $X = 2\%$ is implemented and that the nominal demand growth rate y is cut by 2% (from 9% to 7%); thus, the adjusted nominal demand growth rate $\hat{y}$ is also cut by 2% (from 6% to 4%). What happens in period 1?

Recall from Figure 6.5 (page 277) that if the strength of the price policy (TIP) happens to be equal to the cut in $\hat{y}$, so that the SG and DG curves shift downward by the same percentage, then p will shift downward by that same percentage and Q will stay at Q_c (U will stay at U_c). We can confirm this result by writing our three basic equations:

(6.A.1) $\qquad 7\% = p + q$

(6.A.15) $\qquad p - 6\% = \dfrac{0.07(7\% - U)}{U} - 2\%$

(6.A.3) $\qquad U - 7\% = 0.5(3\% - q)$

We can easily verify that the values $p = 4\%$, $q = 3\%$, and $U = 7\%$ will "work" in these three equations:

(6.A.1) $\qquad 7\% = 4\% + 3\%$

(6.A.15) $\qquad 4\% - 6\% = \dfrac{0.07(7\% - 7\%)}{7\%} - 2\%$

(6.A.3) $\qquad 7\% - 7\% = 0.5(3\% - 3\%)$

Because the cut in $\hat{y}$ of 2% is equal to X, p is also cut by 2% (from 6% to 4%), while U is held constant at 7% and q remains at 3%. Without TIP, we know that a decline in y must be shared by p and q. But with TIP, this is no longer necessarily so. In this particular case, q bears none of the decline and p bears all of it.

THE GRADUALIST PATH WITH TIP

Now we will reconsider the gradualist policy we examined in Section 6.A.1. In our example, y is cut by 1.5% in each of four periods and is then set permanently at 3%. This time, however, a TIP is implemented simultaneously, with $X = 2\%$. What happens in period 1?

The outcome is shown in Figure 6.A.2. When the strength X of a TIP exceeds the cut in the adjusted nominal demand growth rate $\hat{y}$, the SG curve shifts downward more than the DG curve does, so that the new $DG - SG$ intersection point is at a level of Q greater than Q_c (at a level of U less than U_c) and p declines more than $\hat{y}$ but less than X. Thus, both p and U decline, and q exceeds the normal real output growth rate q_c.

Our three equations are then

(6.A.1) $\qquad 7.5\% = p + q$

(6.A.15) $\qquad p - 6\% = \dfrac{0.07(7\% - U)}{U} - 2\%$

(6.A.3) $\qquad U - 7\% = 0.5(3\% - q)$

To find the precise period 1 solution, we must use the formula derived in Section 6.A.6. This solution turns out to be $p_1 = 4.2\%$, $q_1 = 3.3\%$, and $U_1 = 6.8\%$. Note the consistency with the $DG - SG$ diagram in Figure 6.A.2. When $\hat{y}$ declines by 1.5% and $X = 2\%$, p declines by 1.8% (from $p_0 = 6\%$ to $p_1 = 4.2\%$). Since q exceeds $q_c = 3\%$, Q_1 exceeds Q_c and U_1 is less than U_c (7%).

What happens in the long run? We can find out by solving the model period by period, thereby generating the path of the economy. Using the formula derived in Section 6.A.6 to solve the model, we can obtain the period 1 solution just given. Now, we are ready to solve for the period 2 values p_2, q_2, and U_2. Let's rewrite our three basic equations:

(6.A.1) $\qquad y = p + q$

(6.A.15) $\qquad p - p_{-1} = \dfrac{0.07(7\% - U)}{U} - 2\%$

(6.A.3) $\qquad U - U_{-1} = 0.5(3\% - q)$

In period 2, "last period" is period 1, so that $p_{-1} = p_1 = 4.2\%$, $U_{-1} = U_1 = 6.8\%$, and $y_2 = 6\%$. Thus

FIGURE 6.A.2 THE GRADUALIST PATH WITH TIP

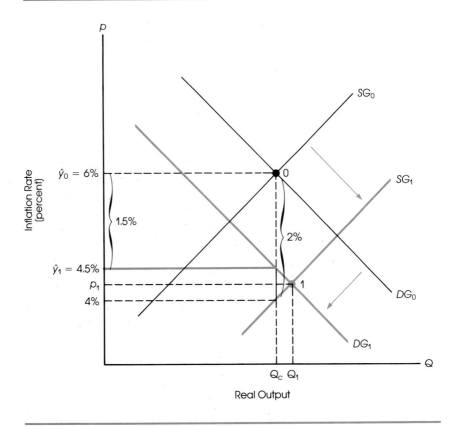

Real Output

Initially, in period 0, the adjusted nominal demand growth rate $\hat{y}_0 = 6\%$, the inflation rate $p = 6\%$, and real output $Q = Q_c$. In period 1, $\hat{y}$ is cut by 1.5%, so that $\hat{y}_1 = 4.5\%$, and a TIP with a strength of $X = 2\%$ is introduced. The cut in $\hat{y}$ shifts the DG curve downward by 1.5% (6% to 4.5% at Q_c). The introduction of a TIP shifts the SG curve downward by 2% (6% to 4% at Q_c). The economy moves from point 0 to point 1. p_1 lies between 4.5% and 4%, so p has declined between 1.5% and 2%. Because Q_1 exceeds Q_c, U_1 is less than U_c; hence, the unemployment rate has also declined.

(6.A.1) $$6\% = p_2 + q_2$$

(6.A.15) $$p_2 - 4.2\% = \frac{0.07(7\% - U_2)}{U_2} - 2\%$$

(6.A.3) $$U_2 - 6.8\% = 0.5(3\% - q_2)$$

Thus, in period 2, we have three equations and three unknowns. Using the formula derived in Section 6.A.6, we can obtain the values of p_2, q_2, and U_2. By the same procedure, we can obtain the values of p_3, q_3, and U_3 for period 3, and so on. A computer program performs the calculations for us. The path of the economy is presented in Table 6.A.3.

Compare this gradualist path with TIP to the gradualist path without TIP shown in Table 6.A.1 (page 300). With TIP, in the long run, the economy converges to $p = \hat{y} = y - q_c = 3\% - 3\% = 0\%$, $U = U'_c = 5.4\%$, and $q = q_c = 3\%$. The long-run values of p and q are the same, with or without TIP. What differs is the constant inflation unemployment rate. Without TIP, $U_c = 7\%$. With TIP, $U'_c = [h/(h + X)]U_c = 5.4\%$, which is less than U_c (7%).

TABLE 6.A.3

GRADUALIST PATH WITH TIP

Year	$\hat{y}$	U	p
0	6.0%	7.00%	6.00%
1	4.5	6.83	4.17
2	3.0	6.62	2.57
3	1.5	6.45	1.16
4	0.0	6.38	−0.15
5	0.0	5.93	−0.89
6	0.0	5.47	−0.93
7	0.0	5.21	−0.52
8	0.0	5.18	−0.06
9	0.0	5.29	0.21
10	0.0	5.42	0.26
11	0.0	5.50	0.17
12	0.0	5.52	0.04
13	0.0	5.50	−0.05
14	0.0	5.46	−0.07
15	0.0	5.43	−0.06
16	0.0	5.42	−0.02
17	0.0	5.43	0.01
18	0.0	5.44	0.02
19	0.0	5.45	0.02
20	0.0	5.45	0.01
21	0.0	5.45	−0.00
22	0.0	5.45	−0.01
23	0.0	5.44	−0.01
24	0.0	5.44	−0.00
25	0.0	5.44	−0.00
26	0.0	5.44	0.00

As before, only by solving the model, period by period, do we confirm that the economy does converge to stable values of p, q, and U. But if we are told that the economy does, in fact, converge to stable values of p, q, and U, then we can easily determine those values by inspecting our equations. Look at equation (6.A.15):

(6.A.15) $$p - p_{-1} = \frac{h(U_c - U)}{U} - X$$

If the economy converges so that p becomes stable, then $p = p_{-1}$. But this will happen only if U has converged to U'_c—the value of U that makes the right side of equation (6.A.15) equal to 0. We have already solved for this U'_c and obtained

$$U'_c = \frac{h}{h + X} U_c$$

Next, look at equation (6.A.3):

(6.A.3) $$U - U_{-1} = j(q_c - q)$$

If the economy converges so that U becomes stable, then $U = U_{-1}$. But this will happen only if q has converged to the normal real output growth rate q_c.

Finally, look at equation (6.A.1):

(6.A.1) $$y = p + q$$

If q has converged to q_c, then p must converge to $y - q_c = \hat{y}$.

▶ Thus, we have seen that if the economy converges to stable values of p, q, and U when y is set permanently equal to q_c in the presence of a TIP with a strength of X, then those stable values must be $U = U'_c = [h/(h + X)]U_c$, $p = \hat{y} = 0\%$, and $q = q_c$.

It must be emphasized that the gradualist path of the economy just shown depends on the ability of TIP to shift the right side of equation (6.A.2) downward by X so that it becomes equation (6.A.15) with the $-X$ term. Why TIP might possess this ability is explained in Appendix 6B. Critics of TIP who challenge its ability to reduce the wage increase w and the price increase p that firms set would deny that TIP can transform equation (6.A.2) into equation (6.A.15).

6.A.5 The Okun's Law (Unemployment – Output Growth) Equation

The *Okun's Law equation* is

(6.A.3) $$\Delta U = U - U_{-1} = j(q_c - q) \qquad j > 0$$

In this section, we will (1) present econometric evidence on the numerical values of j and q_c, and (2) show that relation (4.8), which states the relation between U and q expressed in equation (6.A.3), is true.

We will employ the same econometric method that we used to estimate the values of h and U_c in equation (6.1) in Section 6.2. (You should review the text discussion on pages 254–58, beginning with equation (6.1), at this time.) We must convert equation (6.A.3) to the form

(6.2) $$Y = a + bX$$

This is easily done. Multiplying out the right side of equation (6.A.3) gives us

(6.A.3) $$\Delta U = jq_c - jq$$
$$Y = a + bX$$

Thus

$$Y = \Delta U$$
$$X = q$$
(6.A.17) $$a = jq_c$$
(6.A.18) $$b = -j$$

Hence, the independent variable is q, the real output (real GNP) growth rate, and the dependent variable is ΔU, the change in the unemployment rate. The computer will give us the values of a and b that minimize the sum of the squared errors over the sample. From a and b, we can easily obtain estimates of j and q_c, since, from equations (6.A.18) and (6.A.17)

(6.A.19) $$j = -b$$

(6.A.20) $$q_c = \frac{a}{j} = -\frac{a}{b}$$

Table 6.A.4 shows the results of a regression run on the sample years 1975–1984. Based on this result, we have used the values $j = 0.5$

TABLE 6.A.4

AN EMPIRICAL ESTIMATE
OF OKUN'S LAW

	1975–1984
j	0.46
q_c	3.1%

and $q_c = 3\%$. A j of 0.5 implies an Okun's Law rule of 2 to 1 (since $1/0.5 = 2$); a 1% rise in the unemployment rate corresponds to a 2% loss in real GNP.

THE DERIVATION OF THE OUTPUT–UNEMPLOYMENT RELATIONSHIP

We will now turn to a derivation of (4.8) which states the underlying concept of equation (6.A.3). Recall from equation (4.6) that q_c is defined as the sum of the labor-force growth rate f and the labor productivity growth rate a. Then

(4.8)   If $q = q_c$, then U stays constant ($\Delta U = 0\%$)

If $q > q_c$, then U declines ($\Delta U < 0\%$)

If $q < q_c$, then U rises ($\Delta U > 0\%$)

We will now show that if the unemployment rate is to stay constant, the real output growth rate q must equal the sum of the growth rates of labor productivity a and the labor force f; hence, q must equal q_c. We begin with the definition of labor productivity A:

(6.A.21) $$A \equiv \frac{Q}{N}$$

where A = labor productivity (output per worker)

Q = real output

N = employment

Multiplying both sides by N gives us

$$Q \equiv AN$$

Applying the math growth-rate rule (pages 170–71), we obtain

(6.A.22) $$q \equiv a + n$$

where n = the growth rate of employment

Letting f denote the labor-force growth rate, we subtract f from both sides of equation (6.A.22) and move a to the left side, so that

(6.A.23) $\quad q - a - f \equiv n - f$

We will now show that

(6.A.24) $\quad e \equiv n - f$

where e = the growth rate of the employment rate

To see that equation (6.A.24) is so, consider

(6.A.25) $\quad E \equiv N/F$

where E = the employment rate

N = employment

F = the labor force

For example, if $F = 100$ and $N = 93$, then $E = 93\%$ and the unemployment rate $U = 7\%$. Applying the math growth-rate rule to equation (6.A.25) yields equation (6.A.24).

Substituting equation (6.A.24) into equation (6.A.23) yields

(6.A.26) $\quad q - a - f \equiv e$

If $e = 0\%$, then E is constant and U is constant. Thus, to keep U constant

(6.A.27) $\quad q = a + f$

From equation (6.A.26), we know that if q is greater than $a + f$, then e will be positive; the employment rate E will rise, and the unemployment rate U will decline. Symmetrically, if q is less than $a + f$, then e will be negative; the employment rate E will decline, and the unemployment rate U will rise. Because q_c is defined as $(a + f)$, we have shown that relation (4.8) is correct.

6.A.6 Solving the Three-Equation Model of an Economy with Inertial Expectations

We will now solve our basic three-equation model with inertial expectations (allowing for the possible impact of a TIP policy, as explained in Section 6.A.4). First we rewrite equation (6.A.1) and equation (6.A.15) to obtain

(6.A.28) $q = y - p$

(6.A.29) $p = p_{-1} + \dfrac{h(U_c - U)}{U} - X$

Note that $X = 0$ in the absence of TIP.
Substituting equation (6.A.29) into equation (6.A.28) gives us

(6.A.30) $q = y - p_{-1} - \dfrac{h(U_c - U)}{U} + X$

Substituting equation (6.A.30) into equation (6.A.3) yields

(6.A.31) $U - U_{-1} = j \left\{ q_c - \left[y - p_{-1} - \dfrac{h(U_c - U)}{U} + X \right] \right\}$

U is the only unknown in equation (6.A.31), which can be rewritten
as

$$U = U_{-1} + j \left[q_c - y + p_{-1} + \dfrac{h(U_c - U)}{U} - X \right]$$

Multiplying every term on both sides by U gives us

$$U^2 = U\{U_{-1} + j[q_c - y + p_{-1} - X]\} + jhU_c - jhU$$

Moving every term to the left side yields

(6.A.32) $U^2 + \{j[h - q_c + y - p_{-1} + X] - U_{-1}\}U + (-jhU_c) = 0$

Let's compare equation (6.A.32) to the general form of a quadratic
equation in which Y is the unknown:

(6.A.33) $AY^2 + BY + C = 0$

Equation (6.A.32) is a quadratic equation with the unknown U; all
other terms in this equation are known, and p and q have been eliminated. The quadratic formula can be used to obtain U. Once U is known,
p is easily obtained from equation (6.A.15); q is then easily obtained
from equation (6.A.1). Recall from basic algebra that if a quadratic
equation is written in the form of equation (6.A.33), then the quadratic
formula for Y is given by

(6.A.34) $Y = \dfrac{-B +/- \sqrt{B^2 - 4AC}}{2A}$

We have written equation (6.A.32) in this form, so that

$$Y = U$$
$$A = 1$$
$$B = j(h - q_c + y - p_{-1} + X) - U_{-1}$$
$$C = -jhU_c$$

If we insert these values for A, B, and C into the quadratic formula (6.A.34), then we will obtain the solution.

Note that since the adjusted nominal demand growth rate $\hat{y} = y - q_c$, we can rewrite B as

$$B = j(h + \hat{y} - p_{-1} + X) - U_{-1}$$

Thus, the value of U depends on the difference $y - q_c$, which is equal to $\hat{y}$. For example, U will be the same in these two cases: $y = 6\%$ and $q_c = 0\%$; $y = 9\%$ and $q_c = 3\%$. This confirms the important property of our three-equation model, stated earlier, that U and p are dependent on $\hat{y}$.

As the $+/-$ in quadratic formula (6.A.34) indicates, two values of U actually satisfy the equation. We will now prove that one and only one solution for U will be positive in equation (6.A.32) (the value obtained using the $+$ in the quadratic formula). This is the economically relevant solution, because the unemployment rate must be positive.

From the quadratic formula, it is evident that the two roots will be "real" as long as the term under the square-root sign $(B^2 - 4AC)$ is positive. (If this term were negative, then the roots would be "imaginary".) If AC is negative, then $-4AC$ will be positive; since B^2 must be positive, $B^2 - 4AC$ will be positive. In equation (6.A.32), $A = 1$ and $C = -jhU_c$; C is clearly negative (recall that h and j are both positive). Thus, AC is negative, so the two solutions for U are real.

It is also true that C/A is equal to the product of the roots. To prove this, if r_1 and r_2 are the two roots, then it follows that

(6.A.35) $$(Y - r_1)(Y - r_2) = AY^2 + BY + C = 0$$

Multiplying out the left side gives us

$$Y^2 - (r_1 + r_2)Y + r_1 r_2 = Y^2 + (B/A)Y + \frac{C}{A} = 0$$

Clearly, C/A equals the product of the roots, $r_1 r_2$. In equation (6.A.32), C is negative and $A = 1$, so the product AC is negative. It follows that one root must be positive and the other root must be negative. We have therefore proved that one and only one solution for U in equation (6.A.32) is positive; this is the economically relevant root. Because the root obtained using the $+$ must be greater than the root obtained using the $-$, the $+$ yields the economically relevant value of U.

APPENDIX 6B

INCENTIVE PRICE POLICIES

In this appendix, we will further analyze incentive price policies. The two policies we will consider are the tax incentive inflation policy (TIP) and the market anti-inflation plan (MAP). TIP employs a tax incentive, and MAP employs a marketable permit incentive. Let's begin with the tax incentive.

THE TAX INCENTIVE INFLATION POLICY (TIP)

The original TIP proposal was offered in 1971 by Sidney Weintraub and Henry Wallich. Alternate versions of TIP have been developed by Arthur Okun and others. For the purposes of illustration, we will describe one particular version of TIP that limits coverage to large corporations (perhaps the largest 2,000, which contribute roughly 50% of the GNP). We will call the *targeted inflation rate p^**. Although p^* will eventually be set near 0%, it may be set at a larger value during the first stage of a disinflation.

Any large corporation will incur a tax increase if it raises its price increase p above the targeted inflation rate p^* and will enjoy a tax cut if it lowers its p below p^*. Each covered corporation is free to set any price increase but now has a financial incentive to reduce its p.

In practical terms, how would this version of TIP work? Each covered corporation would be subject to the following TIP tax:

(6.B.1) $T = tB$

where $T =$ the TIP tax

$t =$ the TIP rate

$B =$ the TIP base

The TIP base B would be 0 if the firm sets p equal to p^*, positive if the firm sets p above p^*, and negative if the firm sets p below p^*. In the case of $p < p^*$, the firm's TIP "tax" would be negative; the total tax liability of the firm would be reduced.

The TIP base could be measured as follows:

(6.B.2) $B = R - R^*$

INCENTIVE PRICE POLICIES   321

Actual net revenue R (nominal value-added) is equal to the firm's sales revenue minus purchases from other firms; hence, net revenue is the firm's employee compensation plus interest, rent, and profit. R^* is the net revenue that the firm would earn on its current real output if its p were equal to the target p^*.

Thus, the TIP base B would be "excess" net revenue. The "excess" would be positive if $p > p^*$ and negative if $p < p^*$.

An example will illustrate this point. Suppose that if a corporation calculates the net revenue it would earn if $p = p^*$, then its net revenue $R^* = \$500$ million. Let the TIP tax rate $t = 50\%$. If the corporation's actual net revenue $R = \$520$ million, its "excess" net revenue $B = \$20$ million ($\$520 - \$500$) and its TIP tax $T = \$10$ million (50% of its base of $20 million). On the other hand, if the corporation's actual net revenue $R = \$480$ million, its "excess" net revenue $B = -\$20$ million and its TIP tax $T = -\$10$ million, so that the corporation's total tax liability would decline by $10 million.

Although this version of TIP focuses on the price increase p, not on the wage increase w, it should be recognized that TIP would indirectly exert pressure on w. In general, each 1% cut in p would require a 1% cut in w to preserve the original price – unit labor cost (P – ULC) ratio. Thus, TIP should cause managements to intensify their efforts to hold w down in order to hold p down.

Let's consider more carefully the impact of TIP on *collective bargaining* and the *wage settlement*. In the model illustrated in Figure 6.B.1, it is assumed that the wage increase w that results from collective bargaining is due to the interaction of *union push UP* and *management resistance MR*. We will examine the *MR* and *UP* curves in turn.

Why does the *MR* curve slope upward? Management resistance to a 1% increase in w from, say, 2% to 3%, is less than it is from, say, 7% to 8%. As the level of w increases, the firm's *net* (after-tax) *profit* $n\pi$ declines. It seems reasonable to assume that as $n\pi$ gets lower, management will resist further reductions in $n\pi$ more intensely, perhaps because managers may fear replacement by the board of directors if the firm's net profit becomes unusually low.

Why does the *UP* curve slope downward? Clearly, labor would push more intensely to raise w from 2% to 3% than to raise it from 7% to 8%. If a higher w is achieved, a further increase is less crucial.

The vertical axis of Figure 6.B.1 measures "resistance" and "push" in terms of "bargaining pressure." To make this concept operational, it should be regarded as a reflection of the length of a strike that the party would be willing to incur rather than accept a 1% increase (management) or a 1% decrease (union) in w. We will postulate that agreement results when push is equal to resistance—in this case, at $w = 5\%$ prior to TIP.

Now, suppose that TIP is introduced with a targeted inflation rate of

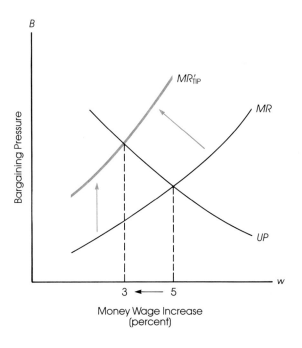

The collective bargaining model hypothesizes that the wage increase w occurs where union push UP equals management resistance MR. Here, without TIP, $w = 5\%$. With TIP, which provides a tax incentive to the firm to reduce its price increase p (and, hence, w), the MR curve shifts up to MR'_{TIP}, thereby reducing the wage settlement. Here, TIP reduces w from 5% to 3%; hence, this TIP is said to have a "strength" of 2%.

$p^* = 0\%$. Given a labor productivity growth rate of $a = 2\%$, this implies a targeted wage inflation rate of $w^* = 2\%$. For each 1% that w exceeds 2% and p exceeds 0%, the firm's tax will be raised; for each 1% that w is below 2% and p is below 0%, the firm's tax will be lowered.

In response to TIP, the management resistance MR curve will shift up. Why? An increase in w from 2% to 3% will still presumably reduce the *gross* (before-tax) *profit* $g\pi$ by the same amount. However, now an increase in w will reduce the net (after-tax) profit $n\pi$ by a larger amount than it would without TIP, because the 1% increase in w will raise the firm's tax. Thus, at each w above 2%, the reduction in $n\pi$ due to a 1% rise in w will be greater, giving management a greater incentive to resist each 1% increase. Even an increase in w from 1% to 2% will be resisted more, because it will now cause the firm to forego a tax cut.

The higher MR'_{TIP} curve will intersect the same UP curve at a lower w (for example, 3%); hence, p will be 2% lower (1% instead of 3%). If the average firm responds in this way, then the SG curve will shift downward by 2%.

Note that the reduction in w and p is due solely to the shift in MR; we assume that the union's bargaining posture, reflected in the UP curve, is not initially altered by TIP.

To summarize, although the TIP incentive may apply directly to a firm's price increase p, it must indirectly influence the firm's wage increase w to succeed. This collective bargaining model is one way to analyze the impact of TIP on the wage inflation rate w.

The use of a tax to implement the financial incentive — in the case of pollution or inflation — has one important shortcoming. The aim is to achieve a particular reduction in total pollution or inflation. However, it is not possible to know in advance precisely what tax rate t will induce the desired reduction. In our example, we used a tax rate of $t = 50\%$. But how can we know in advance that this tax rate will provide just the right incentive to achieve the inflation target $p*$?

Under the tax method, the government must set an initial tax rate. If the response of firms proves too small, it can raise the tax rate; if the response proves too great, it can reduce the tax rate. Frequent (perhaps annual) readjustment of the tax rate might be necessary to keep pollution or inflation near its target. But it may be politically difficult to obtain such frequent readjustment or to ensure that the readjustment is based on objective estimates. For example, would Congress be satisfied to set the pollution or inflation target but delegate the task of readjusting the tax rate to hit the target to an independent commission, staffed by professionals?

Even with annual readjustment of the tax rate based on objective procedures, however, it is not clear how effective the government would be in approaching its targeted pollution or inflation rate. In a dynamic economy, the tax rate that would have been appropriate last year may not be appropriate this year. In the case of pollution, changes in technology and product demand occur continuously; hence, the tax rate necessary to hit the target changes continuously. In the case of inflation, changes in inflationary pressure in the economy occur continuously; hence, the tax rate necessary to hit the target changes continuously.

In the case of pollution, this has led some economists to favor the permit approach. With permits, the government could effectively control total pollution. If the government issues a total of X permits, then total pollution will be approximately X units. The market price of a permit would be governed by the interaction of demand and supply, and demand would change continuously. Experiments with "transferable" or "marketable" permits have recently begun to occur.

In the case of inflation, the same reasoning has led some economists to advocate the marketable permit approach, called a *market anti-inflation plan* (MAP) by its original proponents, Abba Lerner and David Colander in 1980. To maintain symmetry with our description of TIP, we will envision a MAP that applies only to large corporations (perhaps the largest 2,000).

It is convenient to define a MAP permit as entitling the holder to $1 of net revenue. Under MAP, each covered firm would annually receive a quantity of free permits from the government equal to the net revenue R^* that the firm would earn on its current real output if its price increase p were equal to the targeted inflation rate p^*. But each firm would be legally required to hold a quantity of permits equal to its actual net revenue R.

It follows that any firm willing to set its p less than p^* (so that R is less than R^*) would be required to sell its excess permits $R^* - R$. Any firm willing to set its p greater than p^* (so that R is greater than R^*) would be legally required to buy $R - R^*$ permits to eliminate its permit deficiency.

The expenditure that a firm must make to buy its required MAP permits — or the revenue that it would receive from selling its MAP permits — equals the price — the permit rate — multiplied by the quantity of permits. Then

(6.B.3)
$$T = tB$$

where T = the MAP permit expenditure (revenue)

t = the MAP permit rate (percent)

B = the MAP permit base

(6.B.4)
$$B = R - R^*$$

As before, R is the actual net revenue; R^* is the net revenue that the firm would earn on its current real output if its price increase p were equal to the targeted inflation rate p^*. If $R < R^*$, then $B < 0$ and $T < 0$.

The symmetry or duality between MAP and TIP should be evident. Equations (6.B.1) and (6.B.2) for TIP are identical to equations (6.B.3) and (6.B.4) for MAP.

▶ An advantage of MAP is that the permit market would continuously adjust the value of the MAP permit rate t so that the demand for *price raising* (setting p above p^*) would equal the supply of *price cutting* (setting p below p^*).

A PRICE RAISER sets a price increase p above the targeted inflation rate p^*; a PRICE CUTTER sets p below p^*.

Firms could obtain marketable permits and set p above p^* only to the extent that other firms would be able to supply permits because they set p below p^*. Thus, the average p among covered firms would have to remain roughly equal to p^*. This is an accounting identity, which simply says that permits bought must equal permits sold. It is true whether or not the demand for permits at the market permit rate equals the supply of permits at that rate. If demand and supply are unequal at any moment, permits bought and sold would equal the smaller of the two.

▶ Thus, the claim that the average p will equal the targeted inflation rate p^* under MAP does not depend on "equilibrium" —the equality of demand and supply—being achieved in the MAP permit market. The claim that $p = p^*$ depends only on the accounting identity that permits bought must equal permits sold.

But it is important that the MAP permit market tend toward an equilibrium condition in which the permit price equates demand and supply. Why? Suppose that the permit rate t is too low, so that demand exceeds supply. Permits bought and sold would equal the limited supply; the average p would equal p^*. But the desirable pattern of price cutting and price raising across firms would not emerge. For example, one firm enjoying a sudden boom in consumer demand might obtain no permits; another firm experiencing only a small increase in consumer demand might obtain all of the permits it desires. This is the standard misallocation that occurs when there is excess demand (a "shortage") in any market.

However, the market-determined MAP permit rate t would be adjusted continuously, so that the demand for permits by price raisers would normally be equal to the supply of permits by price cutters. For example, suppose that initially $p = p^*$, but suddenly there is a rise in inflationary pressure in the economy. Most covered firms would want to raise p above p^*, but few firms would want to cut p below p^*. Most firms would demand more permits, and few firms would be willing to supply them.

Immediately, the excess demand for permits would drive up the permit rate t. A rising permit rate would encourage firms to switch from being permit demanders to being permit suppliers—from being price raisers to being price cutters. The firm facing only a small increase in consumer demand might shift to being a permit supplier (a price cutter); the firm enjoying a boom in consumer demand might reduce its price increase but still remain a permit demander (a price raiser). Very quickly, the permit rate t would rise until demand is equal to supply. At the equilibrium rate, each firm would be able to buy or sell as many permits as it desired.

The MAP permit, like the TIP tax, would provide a financial incentive against price increases. Like TIP, MAP would leave wage and price setting up to each firm, and market forces would continue to influence relative wages and prices.

TIP would shift the SG curve downward but retain its positive slope (see Figure 6.5, page 277). MAP would not only shift the SG curve downward; it would also make it horizontal at the targeted inflation rate p^* (see Figure 6.4, page 276). At any Q (and any U), regardless of the inflationary pressure, MAP would keep the average price increase p equal to the targeted inflation rate p^*. The difference between TIP and MAP is that TIP does not automatically adjust t; MAP does.

Unlike TIP, MAP requires the establishment of a permit market. How would such a market behave, and by what rules would transactions be governed? For example, would speculation occur in the permit market, and would it be destabilizing? Would futures contracts be allowed? The practical details of the operation of the permit market must be developed.

A VALUE-ADDED PRICE INCREASE

In these net-revenue versions of TIP and MAP, the measurement of R would be relatively straightforward. The measurement of R^* would pose greater difficulty. Advocates have suggested possible methods for computing R^* and contend that the difficulties would be tolerable.

Critics argue, however, that the "measurement problem" would be extremely severe for any version of TIP or MAP. The criticisms of TIP and MAP were examined in Chapter 6 (pages 285–86).

The case for using a value-added price increase p_v in any price policy was presented in Chapter 6.

▶ Recall that the *value-added price increase* p_v adjusts the *product price increase* p_q to allow for a cost "pass through" of the *input price increase* p_i of inputs purchased from other firms. Thus, in our discussion of TIP and MAP, p should always be interpreted as p_v, not as p_q.

Shortly, we will derive the following relation between p_q, p_i, and p_v:

(6.B.5) $$p_q \equiv sp_i + (1 - s)p_v$$

where p_q = the average percentage increase of the price of products sold by the firm

p_i = the average percentage increase of the price of inputs purchased from other firms

s = the ratio of input expenditure to sales revenue

$1 - s$ = the ratio of value-added to sales revenue

Equation (6.B.5) states that the product price increase p_q is a *weighted average* of the input price increase p_i and the value-added price increase p_v. The weights are the share of input expenditure in total revenue s and the share of value-added in total revenue $1 - s$. Hence

▶ A firm's product price increase p_q must lie between its input price increase p_i and its value-added price increase p_v.

From equation (6.B.5), it is immediately clear that to achieve a p_v of 0%, the firm must set p_q equal to sp_i.

From equation (6.B.5), we can isolate p_v by moving sp_i to the left side and dividing through by $1 - s$ to obtain

(6.B.6)
$$p_v \equiv \frac{p_q - sp_i}{1 - s}$$

Under any price policy using p_v, the firm would obtain its p_q, p_i, and s and use equation (6.B.6) to compute its p_v.

Note that if p_q is larger, given p_i, then p_v is larger. But if p_i is larger, given p_q, then p_v is smaller.

Suppose that the firm sets p_q equal to p_i. Substituting p_q for p_i gives us

$$p_v = \frac{p_q - sp_q}{1 - s}$$

$$p_v = \frac{(1 - s)p_q}{1 - s}$$

$$p_v = p_q$$

In this case, the firm's p_v would equal its p_q.

The derivation of equation (6.B.5) follows. We begin with the accounting identity that *total sales revenue* equals *total input expenditure* plus *total nominal value-added,* or

(6.B.7)
$$P_Q Q \equiv P_I I + P_V V$$

where $P_Q Q$ = sales revenue

P_Q = the product price

Q = real output sold

$P_I I$ = expenditure on inputs purchased from other firms

$$P_I = \text{the input price}$$
$$I = \text{real input purchased from other firms}$$
$$P_V V = \text{nominal value-added}$$
$$P_V = \text{the value-added price}$$
$$V = \text{real value-added}$$

With Q, I, and V fixed, suppose that P_I increases by ΔP_I and that P_V increases by ΔP_V. Let the resulting increase in P_Q be ΔP_Q. Then substituting into equation (6.B.7), we obtain

(6.B.8) $$(P_Q + \Delta P_Q)Q = (P_I + \Delta P_I)I + (P_V + \Delta P_V)V$$

Subtracting equation (6.B.7) from equation (6.B.8) yields

(6.B.9) $$(\Delta P_Q)Q = (\Delta P_I)I + (\Delta P_V)V$$

We divide both sides of equation (6.B.9) by $P_Q Q$, and then multiply the numerator and denominator of the first term on the right side by P_I and the numerator and denominator of the second term on the right side by P_V. The result is

(6.B.5) $$p_q = s p_i + (1 - s) p_v$$

where $$p_q = \frac{\Delta P_Q}{P_Q}$$

$$p_i = \frac{\Delta P_I}{P_I}$$

$$p_v = \frac{\Delta P_V}{P_V}$$

$$s = \frac{P_I I}{P_Q Q}$$

$$1 - s = \frac{P_V V}{P_Q Q}$$

This completes the derivation of equation (6.B.5).

As explained earlier in this appendix, to compute the TIP or MAP base B, first R^* must be computed. R^* is the nominal value-added that the firm would have if its real value-added V remains the same but its value-added price increase p_v were equal to p_v^*, the *targeted value-added price increase* set by the government. With V held constant, so that R^* differs from R solely due to the difference between p_v^* and p_v, then R^* is given by

(6.B.10) $R^* = [(1 + p_v^*)/(1 + p_v)]R$

From equation (6.B.10), if $p_v = p_v^*$, then $R^* = R$ and $B = 0$. If $p_v >$ p_v^*, then $R^* < R$ and B is positive. If $p_v < p_v^*$, then $R^* > R$ and B is negative.

Once the firm's managers compute p_v, using equation (6.B.6), they can obtain R^* from equation (6.B.10).

7 Unemployment

The unemployment rate has played a central role in our analysis in Part 2. We have seen that the economy appears to possess a constant inflation rate of unemployment (CIRU), denoted by U_c. Moreover, the CIRU currently appears to be roughly 7%, although there is considerable uncertainty about this estimate. If an expansion in nominal demand growth pushes the unemployment rate below U_c, then wage and price inflation normally rise; if a reduction in nominal demand growth raises the unemployment rate above U_c, then wage and price inflation normally decline.

In this chapter, we will examine the important facts about unemployment and the recent controversy over the interpretation of these facts. We will then consider "supply-oriented" policies designed to reduce the U_c of the economy.

In Chapter 14, we will construct a labor-market model of unemployment, vacancies, and inflation. This model, which is fully consistent with our $DG - SG$ analysis, will permit a more precise description of the labor-market behavior that accompanies the output and price-inflation movements in the $DG - SG$ model. The model will be used to analyze the impact of "supply-oriented" policies on the U_c of the economy.

7.1 How Is the Unemployment Rate Measured?

The unemployment rate is defined as the percentage of the labor force that is "unemployed." The labor force consists of the employed plus the unemployed. An "unemployed" person must be actively seeking employment. A person who is not working and who is not seeking work is officially counted "out of the labor force."

Table 7.1 presents the unemployment rate in the United States over the past three decades. We can see that this unemployment rate has

TABLE 7.1

THE UNEMPLOYMENT RATE (1955 – 1985)

1955	4.3%	**1971**	5.8%
56	4.0	**72**	5.5
57	4.2	**73**	4.8
58	6.6	**74**	5.5
59	5.3	**75**	8.3
60	5.4	**76**	7.6
61	6.5	**77**	6.9
62	5.4	**78**	6.0
63	5.5	**79**	5.8
64	5.0	**80**	7.0
65	4.4	**81**	7.5
66	3.7	**82**	9.5
67	3.7	**83**	9.5
68	3.5	**84**	7.4
69	3.4	**85**	7.1
70	4.8		

fluctuated significantly during this period. It dropped to 3.4% in the late 1960s, and rose to 8.3% in 1975. It fell to 5.8% in 1979, but then rose to 9.5% in 1982 and 1983, before falling to 7.4% in 1984 and to 7.1% in 1985.

How are the data presented in Table 7.1 obtained? The Bureau of Labor Statistics (BLS) of the U.S. Department of Labor is the government agency responsible for analyzing and publishing the official labor-market data. The BLS obtains its data from the monthly *Current Population Survey* (CPS) performed by the U.S. Bureau of the Census. The CPS interviews a scientifically selected sample of 60,000 households; only 1 household out of every 1,500 in the United States is represented in the sample. Thus, the unemployment rate presented in Table 7.1 for a given year is an estimate based on a sample of households.

▶ The true unemployment rate for the whole population may differ from the official rate reported by the BLS. It may be useful to think of the data in Table 7.1 as *estimated* unemployment rates for the entire United States based on the analysis of a sample of households.

According to the BLS, statistical theory implies that we can be 90% confident that when a 7.0% unemployment rate is estimated, the true unemployment rate is somewhere between 6.8% and 7.2%. In other words, the chances are 9 out of 10 that the error will be no more than ±0.2%.

Each month, trained interviewers from the U.S. Census Bureau contact each of the 60,000 households in the sample. The interviewer asks each household member 16 years or older a standard set of questions about labor-market activity during the preceding "reference" week.

To be considered "employed" during the reference week, a person must have worked at least 1 hour for pay or profit; or at least 15 hours without pay in a family enterprise; or be temporarily absent from his job due to illness, bad weather, vacation, a labor–management dispute, or personal reasons. Note that an "employed" person may be working only part time. Persons who are "underemployed"—employed part time although they seek full-time work—are counted as "employed."

To be considered "unemployed" during the reference week, a person must be without a job that week and must have taken some specific step in the preceding four weeks to try to find a job (by applying directly to an employer or checking with an employment agency); or be expecting to be recalled from a layoff; or be waiting to begin a new job within 30 days. People who say they want a job but who have taken no concrete steps to find one during the past four weeks (and who are not awaiting recall or beginning a new job) are counted as "out of the labor force."

Consider a person who has no job, says he wants one now, but says he is so discouraged about finding a job that he has not taken any step to do so in the last four weeks. This person believes that no work in his line is available; he has looked and cannot find work. In addition, he lacks necessary training, skills, or experience. Employers think he is too young or too old; he feels he is barred by discrimination.

Most citizens would regard this person as unemployed, but he would not be officially counted as "unemployed" by the BLS. This "discouraged worker" would not be included in the official unemployment rate. The BLS reports that about 1 out of every 10 persons that it excludes from the labor force reports a desire to hold a job at the time of the survey.

Why doesn't BLS count "discouraged workers" as "unemployed"? It can be argued that it is better to place persons in categories based on actual behavior, rather than a statement of intent. How can we be sure that our discouraged worker really wants a job unless he actually searches for one? Also, potential workers who do not search for jobs exert no downward pressure on wage increases in the labor market. Thus, it can be argued that the unemployment rate (excluding discouraged workers) is a more reliable measure of the pressure on wage increases.

On the other hand, many discouraged workers do want a job and are genuinely discouraged. By excluding them from unemployment measurements, the BLS reports an unemployment rate that does not include a significant number of persons many citizens regard as "unemployed."

On the other hand, the unemployment rate includes persons who are not suffering serious economic hardship. Some are second earners seeking part-time work (cases in which the primary earner already provides a secure income for the household); some are teen-agers from affluent homes. Even here, however, unemployment may involve frustration for the job seeker, although economic hardship is minor.

Another aspect of the unemployment rate is often misunderstood. Suppose that the unemployment rate in a given year is 7%. Does this mean that only 7% of the work force experiences unemployment during that year? No. In any one week, some of the unemployed leave unemployment and others take their place. The CPS annually asks a question that reveals that the number of persons who are unemployed at some time during the year is usually 2.5–3.5 times greater than the number of persons unemployed at any moment. For example, in 1981, the unemployment rate was 7.5%, but the percentage of the labor force experiencing unemployment sometime in 1981 was 2.8 times greater, or 21.3%.

7.2 The Composition of Structural and Cyclical Unemployment

It is useful to distinguish between *structural* and *cyclical* unemployment.

STRUCTURAL UNEMPLOYMENT is the U_c level of unemployment.

CYCLICAL UNEMPLOYMENT is unemployment in excess of the U_c level.

Why is it useful to distinguish between cyclical and structural unemployment? Minimizing cyclical unemployment — unemployment in excess of U_c — is a task for demand policy (monetary and fiscal policy). Once disinflation is achieved, demand policy should attempt to limit cyclical unemployment.

By contrast, structural unemployment must be approached by *supply-oriented policy*. In Chapter 4, we learned the important lesson that demand policy should not try to push the unemployment rate below the U_c of the economy (below the prevailing level of structural unemployment) because accelerating inflation would result. In Section 7.4, we will consider supply-oriented policies that are designed to reduce structural unemployment (the U_c of the economy).

Let's contrast two years — one in which the unemployment rate is near U_c, and one in which the unemployment rate is significantly above U_c. In 1978, the unemployment rate was 6.0% (perhaps slightly below U_c); in 1982, it was 9.5%. Let's compare the compositions of unemployment in 1978, when unemployment was structural, and unemployment in 1982, when an important fraction of it was cyclical.

Figure 7.1 shows the composition of unemployment by age and sex for 1978 and 1982.* Young people under age 24 constitute 49% of structural unemployment in 1978. But when the economy goes into a recession, this percentage declines to 41% in 1982 as older workers are laid off. Still, even in a weak economy, roughly 40% of the unemployed are young. Table 7.2 shows that the unemployment rate varies sharply across demographic groups.

Figure 7.2 shows the composition of unemployment by family status. Normally, the most serious hardship occurs when the sole supporter ("without working spouse") of the family is unemployed. In 1978, 20% of the unemployed were "sole supporters." Recession raises the share of sole supporters to 24% in 1982. Figure 7.3 shows the distribution of unemployment by race. In 1978, 24.3% of the unemployed were blacks and other nonwhites. This figure declined slightly to 22.8% in 1982 in a recession.

FIGURE 7.1 DISTRIBUTION OF UNEMPLOYMENT BY AGE AND SEX

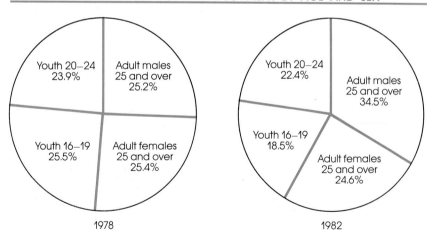

Note: Data relate to persons 16 years and over.
SOURCE: U.S. Department of Labor, Bureau of Labor Statistics.

* Data in figures and table from *Economic Report of the President 1983*

TABLE 7.2

UNEMPLOYMENT RATES OF DEMOGRAPHIC
GROUPS IN 1978

Married men with spouse present	2.8%
Males 20 and over	4.3%
Females 20 and over	6.0%
Teen-agers 16–19	16.4%
Whites	5.2%
Blacks and other nonwhites	11.9%
Black male teen-agers, 16–19	34.0%
Black female teen-agers, 16–19	38.1%

Figure 7.4 shows the distribution of unemployment by reason. In 1978, job losers plus job losers on layoff constituted 41.7% of the unemployed. Nearly 60% of the unemployed were job leavers (persons who voluntarily quit their jobs), new entrants into the labor force, and reentrants into the labor force. But in a serious recession, job losers plus job

FIGURE 7.2   DISTRIBUTION OF UNEMPLOYMENT BY FAMILY STATUS

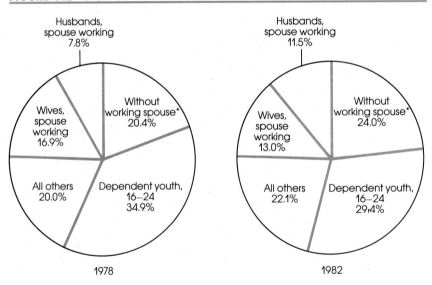

*Husbands and wives whose spouse does not work and persons who maintain families.

Note: Data relate to persons 16 years and over.

SOURCE: U.S. Department of Labor, Bureau of Labor Statistics.

FIGURE 7.3 DISTRIBUTION OF UNEMPLOYMENT BY RACE

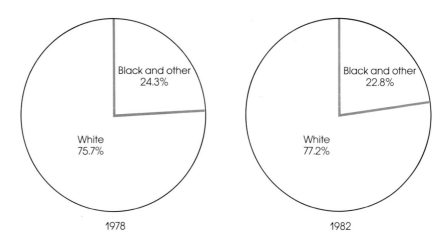

Black and other
24.3%

White
75.7%

1978

Black and other
22.8%

White
77.2%

1982

Note: Data relate to persons 16 years and over.
SOURCE: U.S. Department of Labor, Bureau of Labor Statistics.

FIGURE 7.4 DISTRIBUTION OF UNEMPLOYMENT BY REASON

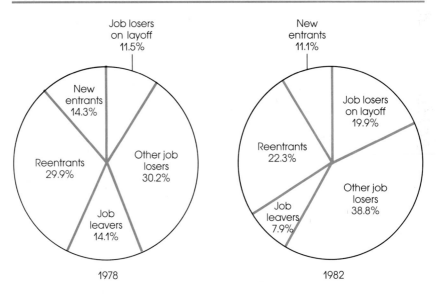

Job losers
on layoff
11.5%

New
entrants
14.3%

Reentrants
29.9%

Other job
losers
30.2%

Job
leavers
14.1%

1978

New
entrants
11.1%

Job losers
on layoff
19.9%

Reentrants
22.3%

Other job
losers
38.8%

Job
leavers
7.9%

1982

Note: Data relate to persons 16 years and over.
SOURCE: U.S. Department of Labor, Bureau of Labor Statistics.

losers on layoff rose dramatically to 58.7% in 1982. Thus, in a strong economy, job losers constitute a minority of the unemployed; in a weak economy, job losers constitute a majority.

Figure 7.5 shows the distribution of unemployment by duration. *Duration* is measured by asking persons who are unemployed in the survey week how long they have been out of work. Even in the strong economy of 1978, 53.8% of the unemployed had already been out of work for more than five weeks and 22.8% of the unemployed had already been out of work for more than 15 weeks.

When people report that they have "already" been out of work for five weeks, their spell of unemployment will probably last longer than five weeks. The duration data show that—even in a strong economy—more than 50% of those unemployed in a given week are in the midst of a spell of unemployment that will last more than five weeks. Nearly 25% of those unemployed in a given week are in the midst of a spell of unemployment that will last more than 15 weeks.

When the economy goes into a recession, the duration of unemployment increases. From 1978 to 1982, the fraction of the unemployed already out of work more than five weeks rose from one-half to two-thirds; the fraction of the unemployed already out of work more than 15 weeks rose from one-fourth to one-third.

FIGURE 7.5 DISTRIBUTION OF UNEMPLOYMENT BY DURATION

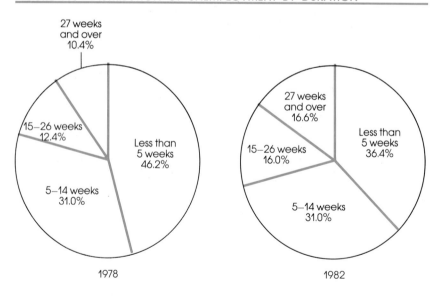

Note: Data relate to persons 16 years and over.
SOURCE: U.S. Department of Labor, Bureau of Labor Statistics

7.3 The Unemployment Controversy

The data regarding the duration of unemployment cited in Figure 7.5 show that even when the economy is strong, the majority of those unemployed at any moment are in the midst of a serious unemployment experience — a rather lengthy spell of unemployment of more than five weeks. In the 1970s, however, researchers began to focus on data on unemployment spells that appear, at first glance, to present unemployment in a different light. What is a *spell of unemployment?* When a person becomes unemployed, a spell begins; when that person leaves unemployment, the spell ends.

Note that the duration data do not tell us the length of a spell of unemployment. Each person who is unemployed during the survey week is in the midst of a spell. We know that the length of the spell is at least as great as the duration thus far, but we don't know the length of the spell from beginning to end. For example, we know that the majority have already experienced at least five weeks of unemployment, but we don't know how much longer than five weeks these persons will remain unemployed.

You can see that it is easier to obtain data related to the duration of unemployment than it is to obtain data related to the length of an unemployment spell. To obtain duration data, the researcher questions an unemployed person only once. But a person who is unemployed this week cannot provide information on the length of a completed unemployment spell; no one knows when a spell will end. Nevertheless, with ingenuity, researchers have been able to use CPS data to estimate the length of completed unemployment spells.

What fraction of spells have a length of less than one month? In the 1970s, researchers discovered that most spells last less than one month in a strong economy. One study* estimates that nearly 80% of all spells end in less than one month; even in a weak economy, more than 50% of all spells end in less than one month.

The discovery that most spells of unemployment are brief led some economists to proclaim a "new view of unemployment" in the 1970s, thereby launching the unemployment controversy. According to this "new view," unemployment is not a serious social problem when an economy is operating near its constant inflation unemployment rate U_c, because most persons experience a brief unemployment spell and limited hardship.

The "new view" conveyed the impression that if the unemployment rate is, say, 7%, most of the 7% unemployed are in the midst of a brief spell. Although some advocates of the "new view" did not make such a

---

* See Kim Clark and Lawrence Summers, "Labor Market Dynamics and Unemployment: A Reconsideration," *Brookings Papers on Economic Activity* 1 (1979): 13–60.

claim, it is fair to say that many drew such an inference. Yet, as we have already seen, duration data show that this is not so; most of the 7% unemployed are in the midst of a spell that will last more than five weeks.

How can most spells be brief but most of those unemployed at any moment be in the midst of a rather lengthy spell? An example will illustrate.

Suppose that the labor force consists of 100 persons; at any moment, 7 are unemployed, so that the unemployment rate is 7%. If 90% of all unemployment spells last one month, does this imply that most of the 7% unemployed are in the midst of a spell that will last one month or less? Not necessarily. Let's consider how the data might be generated.

Suppose that four persons out of the 100 — call them W, X, Y, and Z — will be unemployed for the entire year; each will experience a 12-month spell. The other three unemployment slots will rotate each month. On January 1, W, X, Y, and Z become unemployed. They are joined by A, B, and C. On February 1, A, B, and C find jobs and are replaced by D, E, and F. On March 1, D, E, and F find jobs and are replaced by G, H, I, and so on. At any moment in time, seven persons are unemployed, and four of them — W, X, Y, and Z (the majority of the unemployed at that moment) — are in the midst of a 12-month unemployment spell.

If three new persons become unemployed each month, then there are 36 spells of unemployment, each lasting one month. W, X, Y, and Z each have a 12-month unemployment spell. Thus, out of 40 spells of unemployment that occur during the year, 36 (90%) last only one month. Yet the majority of those unemployed at any moment are in the midst of a 12-month spell.

At the end of the 1970s, several economists* sharply criticized the "new view." Perhaps their critique should be called "the new, new view of unemployment." The "new, new view" does not dispute the fact that most spells are short, but it makes two additional basic points.

First, even though most spells are short, the data show that the majority of those unemployed at any moment, even in a strong economy, are in the midst of a rather lengthy spell. When the unemployment rate is 7%, most of the 7% unemployed at any moment are in the midst of a fairly lengthy spell, contrary to the impression created by the "new view."

Second, many spells are short not because the unemployed find jobs but because they drop out of the labor force. In the data, an unemployment spell is counted as "completed" when a person stops search-

---

* See Clark and Summers, "Labor Market Dynamics"; and George Akerlof and Brian Main, "Unemployment Spells and Unemployment Experience," *American Economic Review* 70 (December, 1980): 885–893.

ing for a job and is therefore no longer officially in the labor force. One study* estimates that almost 50% of all unemployment spells end when persons leave the labor force—not when they find jobs. Thus, the fact that most spells are short does not mean that most persons who become unemployed find jobs quickly. It means that they either find jobs quickly or they stop searching.

The "new, new view" tends to restore the more traditional view of unemployment as a serious social problem, even in a strong economy. The unemployment controversy certainly shows that the "facts" do not always "speak for themselves." Proper interpretation is essential.

7.4 Policies to Reduce the Constant Inflation Rate of Unemployment (CIRU)

Any discussion of unemployment policies must distinguish between cyclical and structural unemployment. Recall that structural unemployment is the U_c level of unemployment; cyclical unemployment is unemployment in excess of the U_c level.

As we saw in Chapter 6, cyclical unemployment is sometimes the intentional result of a disinflation strategy. We will see in Part 3 that cyclical unemployment can, of course, be unintentional as well. Even if monetary and fiscal policy is implemented to avoid such unemployment, it is difficult to stabilize the economy at its constant inflation unemployment rate U_c. We will discuss alternative strategies for limiting unintentional cyclical unemployment in Part 3.

As we saw in Chapter 4, it is always possible to reduce the unemployment rate by raising the nominal demand growth rate y through monetary and/or fiscal expansion. But when a rise in nominal demand growth pushes the unemployment rate below U_c, the inflation rate p rises. As long as the demand authorities try to hold the unemployment rate below U_c, the inflation rate will keep rising. Thus, this method of reducing the unemployment rate is clearly not sustainable.

In this section, we will focus on *supply-oriented policies* designed to reduce the constant inflation unemployment rate, hereafter referred to as CIRU. If a policy achieves a reduction in the CIRU, then the Fed can move the economy to this lower unemployment rate without causing the inflation rate to rise. Such a reduction in the unemployment rate would be sustainable.

To show that a supply-oriented policy could reduce the CIRU of the economy, we must develop a labor-market model and analyze the impact of the policy in the model. This will be done in Chapter 14. Here, we will present each policy and provide some intuition concerning its impact on the CIRU.

---

* Clark and Summers, "Labor Market Dynamics," 16.

At the outset, the following point deserves emphasis:

▶ A citizen need not regard a policy as socially desirable simply because it may reduce the CIRU of the economy. Other consequences of the policy should be considered as well.

As we review each of the following policies to reduce the CIRU, we will note relevant trade-offs. Policies that may achieve a reduction in the CIRU include:

1. Weakening unions
2. Reducing unemployment compensation
3. Providing job training and retraining
4. Instituting a wage subsidy for low-skilled workers
5. Lowering the legal minimum wage
6. Reducing discrimination
7. Improving the Employment Service
8. Implementing a TIP policy
9. Implementing a MAP policy

Let's consider each policy in turn.

WEAKENING UNIONS

Unemployment tends to exert a downward pressure on wage increases. In the absence of a union, an employer can replace an individual worker with an unemployed person if the worker fails to accept a smaller wage increase. One purpose of a union is to resist such pressure. The union may strike if the employer tries to coerce workers into accepting smaller wage increases. Although an employer may be able to replace a small number of workers with unemployed people during a strike, it is usually impossible for a firm to replace the whole work force.

Thus, a strong union reduces the downward pressure on wage increases that results from a given unemployment rate. This implies that a higher unemployment rate results in constant wage and price inflation rates. Hence, unionization should raise the CIRU of the economy. It therefore follows that weakening unions should reduce the CIRU.

Unions might be weakened by a repeal of the legislation that protects them. Beginning with the National Labor Relations Act, passed in the 1930s, legislation has provided protection for unions and has encouraged collective bargaining between management and unions.

Obviously, many citizens would object to an attempt to weaken unions. Unionization helps to protect workers from arbitrary and unfair treatment by employers. Unions resist the intimidation of workers by management, obtain grievance procedures for workers, and perform many other positive services.

Of course, some unions have abused their power. Moreover, citizens are divided over the proper degree of power to designate to unions. Nevertheless, it is doubtful that a majority of citizens would favor an attempt to significantly weaken the power of unions. Such an attempt would surely be divisive and might return the nation to the bitter labor–management disputes and climate of class warfare that existed prior to the legislation encouraging and protecting unionization.

REDUCING UNEMPLOYMENT COMPENSATION

Under the unemployment compensation program, workers who lose their jobs receive cash benefits while they remain unemployed. Each state administers its own program, subject to federal guidelines. The typical cash benefit is roughly 50% of the previous pre-tax wage, up to some maximum. Benefits are normally paid up to 26 weeks, though an extension is often enacted during a severe recession. In most states, new entrants to the labor force and persons who quit their jobs are not eligible.

The cash benefit reduces the economic hardship that results from unemployment. Making the period of unemployment more bearable, however, may reduce the intensity with which some unemployed people search for a new job and may enable some of the unemployed to be more selective about the job they accept.

Reducing the cash benefit per unemployed person would increase the urgency of obtaining a new job. As a consequence, the duration of unemployment should be reduced and the CIRU should be lowered.

Obviously, citizens will disagree over the optimum level of benefit per unemployed person. Some citizens are most concerned about the abuse of unemployment compensation programs by unemployed persons who prefer not to work; other citizens are more concerned with helping people who genuinely cannot find a job.

PROVIDING JOB TRAINING AND RETRAINING

When workers are unsuited for available jobs, the jobs remain vacant and the workers remain unemployed. This mismatch of workers and jobs can be reduced by providing job training and retraining. Such training occurs continuously in the economy, but the government can speed the process by providing the training or by subsidizing private firms to provide it.

Training absorbs resources. The time and energy of supervisors and trainees, at least in part, must be diverted from production. Training therefore entails a real cost to the economy. If the government finances the training, then taxpayers bear part of this cost. Thus, the benefit of training must be weighed against its cost.

One argument against the government subsidization of training programs is that the private sector, without subsidies, is already providing the proper degree of training to the work force. Whenever productivity will be raised by more than the cost of a training program, it is profitable for the private sector to undertake the training. Government intervention is undesirable; it will only encourage unnecessary overtraining that will yield a benefit that is less than the cost.

In reply, it can be argued that the social benefit of training exceeds the private benefit that can be captured by the firm or the worker. Workers who are unequipped for jobs may burden the welfare system or engage in crime — perhaps transmitting their alienation and disadvantages to the next generation. Private firms cannot be expected to account for these social consequences in their profit calculations. Thus, the government plays a legitimate and important role in the training of persons the private sector would ordinarily find it unprofitable to train.

The most recent federal training initiative is the Job Training Partnership Act (JTPA), enacted in 1982. JTPA uses federal funds to involve private firms and vocational training institutions in the training of persons most in need: disadvantaged youths, low-skilled and chronically unemployed adults, and skilled workers who have lost jobs in declining industries and regions.

INSTITUTING A WAGE SUBSIDY FOR LOW-SKILLED WORKERS

Low-skilled workers have low productivity and are profitable to hire only at a correspondingly low wage. Given the apparent excess supply of low-skilled labor at the current real wage, why doesn't the wage decline until the demand for labor matches the available supply of labor? We will see shortly that a minimum-wage law may prevent such a decline. But even in the absence of a minimum-wage law, important obstacles to the hiring of low-skilled workers would remain.

First, many employers might be reluctant to offer a very low wage to adult workers — particularly to heads of households. Some employers would regard such a policy as unethical; others might fear that it would create poor public relations that would hurt the long-run profitability of the firm. Better paid employees might even resent the "exploitation" of these low-skilled workers, and worker morale and productivity might suffer. Hostility toward management might make strikes more likely. Hence, many employers might decide it is better to offer jobs only to workers who are sufficiently productive to earn a "decent" wage.

Second, even if employers were to offer jobs at a very low wage, some low-skilled workers might reject them, preferring to seek welfare or risk crime rather than work for so little. If the wage were cut, the effective supply of labor might become less than the demand for labor.

From the social point of view, it would be better if employers could be induced to offer more jobs to low-skilled workers at a "decent" wage. Under a *wage subsidy* for low-skilled workers, an employer would be reimbursed by the government for a fraction of its wage cost. For example, if a firm paid a low-skilled worker $5 per hour, then the firm might be reimbursed $2 per hour, so that its wage cost would be only $3 per hour.

A wage-subsidy program has costs and entails administrative problems. Taxpayers must finance the subsidy payments to employers. Various administrative questions must be addressed: Which workers are eligible? Which firms are eligible? How can the government ensure that subsidized workers do not simply replace unsubsidized workers? Can firms be effectively monitored to prevent significant fraud?

Despite these problems, a wage subsidy for low-skilled workers is currently being implemented. Under the *targeted jobs tax credit,* firms are given a tax credit for hiring persons with certain characteristics, including disadvantaged young workers aged 18–24, welfare recipients, handicapped persons, and ex-convicts. The tax credit lasts for up to two years. In the first year, it is equal to 50% of the worker's earnings, up to a maximum credit of $3,000. In the second year it is equal to 25% of the worker's earnings, up to a maximum credit of $1,500. Recently, a special tax credit for employing disadvantaged youths (aged 16–17) during the summer has been added.

A wage subsidy may be part of the *enterprise-zone strategy.* It has been proposed that poverty areas be designated as "enterprise zones." Firms that locate in these zones would enjoy a lower tax rate on capital income. In one version, firms would also be given a wage subsidy to hire low-skilled workers who live in the enterprise zones.

LOWERING THE LEGAL MINIMUM WAGE

We have just noted that one reason employers do not offer very low wages to low-skilled workers is that they must abide by a legally established minimum wage (currently $3.35 per hour). Even without this legal barrier, employers might hesitate to offer such low wages to adult workers and adult workers might refuse to accept jobs at such low wages. But some analysts believe that the legal minimum wage is a major barrier to teen-age employment. Few employers would be reluctant to pay lower-than-minimum wages to teen-agers, and many teen-agers would be willing to take full-time, part-time, or part-year jobs at such low wages.

Reducing the legal minimum wage for *all* workers should reduce the CIRU of the economy. But a trade-off must be acknowledged and weighed. Many workers currently employed at the minimum wage would suffer a wage cut — a reduction in earnings. Such an earnings cut would be especially undesirable when the worker is the head of a household. This reduction in earnings for low-wage workers must be balanced against the gain in employment that it would undoubtedly generate.

In response to concern about the earnings of adult workers, it has been proposed that the legal minimum wage be cut only for teen-agers. This would prevent a cut in the legal minimum wage of adult workers who remain employed. However, a dual minimum wage creates another problem in that it offers employers the incentive to replace adult workers with cheaper teen-age workers.

Supporters of the subminimum wage for teen-agers point out that many employers would not find it worth making such a substitution. They argue that some jobs require more permanent, reliable, adult workers and that other jobs are suited to teen-agers who are not expected to work for a long period. One version would limit the subminimum wage to the summer of each year; such a restriction should further reduce substitution. Finally, the legislation would be designed to prohibit employers from making substitutions.

Opponents of the subminimum wage argue that teen-agers are often suitable substitutes for low-skilled adult workers. Employers in the low-skilled labor market expect a high turnover from employees. Adult women who work at the minimum wage may be particularly vulnerable to replacement. Legislative prohibitions against substitution are likely to prove ineffective, because employers can always argue that discharges occurred for other reasons.

One compromise might be the following package. Adult low-skilled workers might have their earnings protected by a "decent" minimum wage, but employers could be induced to hire them by a generous wage subsidy, implemented by targeted tax credits. Generously financed training programs would also be targeted at these adult workers, giving them an opportunity to raise their productivity. Given these incentives for hiring adult low-skilled workers, a subminimum wage for teen-agers might then be used to induce an increase in teen-age employment. A wage subsidy and training program for adult workers and a subminimum wage for teen-agers should raise the employment of both adult and teen-age low-skilled workers, while protecting the earnings of the adult low-skilled workers currently employed.

REDUCING DISCRIMINATION

In Table 7.2, we saw that particular demographic groups have widely varying unemployment rates. In particular, the black unemployment rate is often almost twice as great as the white unemployment rate. The female unemployment rate is often one-and-a-half times the male unemployment rate.

How much of each disparity is due to "discrimination" by race or by sex? *Discrimination* means that an employer does not judge an applicant solely by the person's job-related characteristics but is influenced by racial, religious, or other personal characteristics (in this example, whether the person is white or nonwhite, male or female).

Blacks, on average, have less education than whites; females, on average, have fewer years of job experience than men. If employers choose individuals based on education and job experience, without regard for race or sex, then it is likely that blacks will have a higher unemployment rate than whites and females will have a higher unemployment rate than males. Some analysts therefore believe that discrimination plays only a minor role in the labor market.

There is evidence, however, to suggest that race or sex are often considered in hiring decisions. Some discriminatory employers may view an applicant as less desirable simply because he or she is nonwhite. Others may believe that a female applicant is less likely than a male to remain with the firm for many years, because she will probably leave to raise children. Some employers may believe that males should hold top managerial and professional positions.

Under Title VII of the Civil Rights Act of 1964, employers are prohibited from discriminating against persons on the basis of race or sex. The law proclaims a "color-blind, sex-blind" standard for employers; each job applicant is to be judged on individual merit alone. The Equal Employment Opportunity Commission (EEOC) is responsible for implementing Title VII. If all employers could be compelled to adhere to this standard, it is likely that the disparity between black–white and male–female unemployment rates would be reduced and that the CIRU of the economy would be lower.

Although many people accept the "color-blind, sex-blind" standard as the proper ideal, a practical problem arises. Suppose that a firm is observed to have few minorities or women. The firm claims that this resulted from judging applicants on the basis of individual merit. Ideally, particular job applications to this firm should be reviewed to determine whether nonwhites or females were denied jobs in favor of whites or males with no better individual qualifications. The recruitment practices of the firm should also be scrutinized to determine whether the firm sought white male applicants in preference to minorities or women.

But this is a difficult, time-consuming process. It is much simpler to require firms to have a numerical balance by race and sex. This approach compels employers to judge persons partly on the basis of their race and sex—instead of solely on the basis of individual job-related characteristics — to ensure that a balance results. It has been suggested that preferential treatment is warranted to compensate for past discrimination, but some people object to this approach as "reverse discrimination." Antidiscrimination policy therefore remains controversial.

IMPROVING THE EMPLOYMENT SERVICE

The U.S. Employment Service tries to bring vacant jobs and unemployed workers together. The efficiency with which workers search for jobs and employers search for workers can be raised by an effective Employment Service. Computerized job banks, improved techniques of matching workers and jobs, and assistance during nonwork hours should all help to reduce the CIRU of the economy.

IMPLEMENTING A TIP POLICY

Recall from Chapter 6 that TIP is an incentive price policy. TIP would give a covered corporation a tax incentive to hold down its average price increase. Why might a TIP policy reduce the CIRU of the economy?

At the CIRU, the upward pressure on wage increases from vacancies is just balanced by the downward pressure on wage increases from unemployment. When firms compete to fill vacancies, they tend to bid up wage increases; when unemployed workers compete for jobs, they tend to push down wage increases. When these two forces balance, wage increases stay constant — and so does price inflation.

Suppose that at a 7% unemployment rate, the upward and downward pressures on wage increases balance, so that the CIRU is initially 7%. Now, assume that a TIP is introduced. At the 7% unemployment rate and the associated level of vacancies, employers will now exert less upward pressure on wage increases, because TIP discourages price and wage increases. Thus, at a 7% unemployment rate, the downward pressure from unemployment will exceed the upward pressure from vacancies, and both wage and price inflation will decline.

This means that there is some lower unemployment rate at which the downward and upward pressures on wage increases will now balance. As the unemployment rate is reduced below 7%, the downward pressure from unemployment is reduced. Vacancies increase as the unemployment rate declines, so that the upward pressure from vacancies rises. At some unemployment rate below 7%, despite the downward pressure of TIP, wage increases should remain constant. This unemployment rate will be the new CIRU of the economy under TIP. If the financial incentive of TIP becomes stronger, the new CIRU should become lower.

Several points should be made concerning this argument. First, even if TIP could reduce the CIRU, the costs and disadvantages of TIP must be weighed against the lower CIRU. (The possible shortcomings of TIP were noted on pages 285–86.) Second, even if the TIP policy were implemented, it can be argued that, in practice, firms would be able to circumvent TIP and therefore prove largely immune to its incentive.

Third, many economists doubt that even an effective TIP would reduce the CIRU. They do not believe that a realistic model of the labor market would imply such a conclusion. They reject the argument given in this section. The construction of the labor-market model is one of the most controversial and challenging tasks in macroeconomics. For the purposes of illustration, we develop one such model in Chapter 14. Conclusions that depend on the labor-market model chosen should generally be regarded as tentative.

IMPLEMENTING A MAP POLICY

Recall from Chapter 6 that MAP is an incentive price policy. MAP would use marketable permits to hold the average price increase p constant at p^*. Under MAP, a covered firm that wished to raise its p above p^* would be required to buy permits from a covered firm that was willing to cut its p below p^*, thereby entitling it to sell permits. If MAP were administered successfully, then the average p of MAP-covered firms would remain constant; the inflation rate in the MAP-covered sector would be the targeted p^*.

If MAP holds the inflation rate at p^*, then any sustainable unemployment rate would be a CIRU. Beginning at the CIRU prior to MAP (for example, 7%), an increase in nominal demand growth should raise real output and reduce the unemployment rate; MAP should keep the inflation rate roughly at the targeted p^*.

Note that the same argument can be made for a price-control program. If the inflation target is p^* and the controls are effective, then any sustainable unemployment rate would be a CIRU. The advantage of MAP over price control is that its automatic flexibility allows some firms to raise their p as long as others lower their p. With respect to the CIRU of the economy, MAP and price controls ought to have a similar impact.

As with TIP, several points should be made in response to this argument. First, even if MAP could reduce the sustainable CIRU, the costs and disadvantages of MAP must be weighed against the lower CIRU. (The possible shortcomings of MAP were noted on pages 285–86.) Second, even if the MAP policy were implemented, it can be argued that, in practice, firms would be able to circumvent MAP and undermine its effectiveness.

Third, as with TIP, many economists doubt that even an effective MAP would reduce the CIRU. They do not believe that a realistic labor-market model would imply that a lower unemployment rate would be sustainable under MAP. Once again, the model of the labor market is clearly at issue. Until economists develop a strong consensus regarding the correct labor-market model for the economy, conclusions based on how the labor market functions must be regarded as tentative.

SUMMARY

1. To be counted by the U.S. Bureau of Labor Statistics (BLS) as "un-employed," a person must be actively seeking employment and must have taken some specific step in the preceding four weeks to try to find a job. A person who is not working and who has not taken concrete steps in the preceding month to find work is officially counted by the BLS as "out of the labor force."

2. The official unemployment rate is an estimate based on a sample of 60,000 households. There is a 90% probability that the official esti-mate is within 0.2% of the true unemployment rate.

3. The unemployment rate overstates hardship by including teen-agers from affluent households who are seeking part-time work. But the unemployment rate understates hardship by excluding heads of households who are so discouraged that they have taken no concrete steps to find work in the preceding month.

4. The percentage of the work force that experiences unemployment at some given point during the year is usually about three times greater than the average unemployment rate. For example, in 1981, the unemployment rate was 7.5%, but the percentage of the work force experiencing unemployment at some time during that year was 21.3%.

5. *Structural unemployment* is the U_c level of unemployment. *Cyclical unemployment* is unemployment in excess of U_c. Reducing cyclical unemployment is a task for demand policy (monetary and fiscal policy). Reducing structural unemployment is a task for *supply-oriented policy.*

6. Although most spells of unemployment are short (a month or less), the majority of those unemployed at any moment are in the midst of a lengthy *unemployment spell.* Also, many spells are short because the unemployed drop out of the labor force — not because they find jobs.

7. A citizen need not regard a policy as socially desirable simply be-cause it may reduce the constant inflation rate of unemployment (CIRU) of the economy. Other consequences of the policy should be considered as well.

8. The following supply-oriented policies may reduce the CIRU of the economy: weakening unions; reducing unemployment compensation; providing job training and retraining; instituting a wage subsidy for low-skilled workers; lowering the legal minimum wage; reducing discrimination; improving the Employment Service; implementing a TIP policy; and implementing a MAP policy.

TERMS AND CONCEPTS

cyclical unemployment	out of the labor force
demographic group	structural unemployment
discouraged worker	supply-oriented policy
duration of unemployment	targeted jobs tax credit
employed	Title VII of Civil Rights Act of 1964
employer discrimination	unemployed
enterprise-zone strategy	unemployment controversy
labor force (work force)	unemployment rate
legal minimum wage	unemployment spell
"new, new view" of	U.S. Employment Service
unemployment	wage subsidy
"new view" of unemployment	

QUESTIONS

7.1 Suppose that the labor force consists of 100 persons and that, at any moment, seven are unemployed, so that the unemployment rate is 7%. Suppose that five persons out of the 100 (call them V, W, X, Y, and Z) are unemployed for the entire year; each experiences a 12-month unemployment spell. But the other two unemployment slots rotate each month. On January 1, V, W, X, Y, and Z become unemployed; they are joined by persons A and B. On February 1, A and B find jobs and are replaced by persons C and D, and so on. At any moment in time, seven persons are unemployed.
a. How many unemployment spells occur during the year?
b. What percentage of these spells lasts for one month?
c. At any moment, what percentage of the unemployed is in the midst of a 12-month spell?
d. What conclusion can you draw from this example?

7.2 Give an intuitive explanation of why each of the following supply-oriented policies may reduce the CIRU of the economy:
a. Weakening unions
b. Reducing unemployment compensation
c. Providing job training and retraining

d. Instituting a wage subsidy for low-skilled workers
e. Lowering the legal minimum wage
f. Reducing discrimination
g. Improving the Employment Service
h. Implementing a TIP policy
i. Implementing a MAP policy

PART

3 Stabilization

8 Stabilization Policy

In the early 1980s, as we have seen, the U.S. economy embarked on a period of disinflation engineered by a reduction in nominal demand growth due to a tight monetary policy. Suppose that this disinflation strategy eventually succeeds, so that the economy reaches its targeted inflation rate of $p^* = 0\%$ (or some positive rate that citizens are content to accept) and returns to its constant inflation rate of unemployment (CIRU) of U_c.

As we saw in Chapter 7, we might still wish to implement supply-oriented policies to reduce the U_c of the economy. But whether such policies are implemented or not, we would want monetary and fiscal policy to keep the economy as close to the current U_c as possible.

Ideally, we would like the economy to remain at the current U_c and the targeted inflation rate (presumably near 0%). If fluctuations in the unemployment and inflation rates U and p must occur, we would like them to be as small as possible. In particular, we would want to avoid a serious recession or a serious inflation. The task of keeping the economy near its U_c and p^* is called *stabilization*. Stabilization policy is the subject of this chapter. In Chapter 9, we will examine the role of fiscal and monetary policy in implementing stabilization policy.

First, we will set out some fundamental obstacles that stabilization policy must confront. The model and examples developed in Part 1 may have given you the impression that it is easy to adjust monetary and fiscal policy to achieve the targeted output. Unfortunately, in the real economy, it is difficult to achieve the targeted output for several reasons.

There is uncertainty about what the equilibrium level of output would be if policy were unaltered. Lags impede the implementation of policy. There is uncertainty about the impact of a change in a policy instrument and its impact on the economy. The degree of inherent instability of the private economy must be assessed to determine the best stabilization policy. Institutional and political constraints must be considered.

Thus, the best way to conduct stabilization policy is far from obvious. We will see that the *Keynesian legacy* supports active, "countercyclical" monetary and fiscal policy, especially in the face of a severe fluctuation of the economy. A *countercyclical (activist) policy* varies a policy instrument—such as the money supply or the tax rate—in an attempt to limit the fluctuation and keep the economy near its targeted U_c and p^*. A countercyclical policy may be implemented automatically, according to a rule, or may be subject to the discretion of policymakers.

By contrast, the *classical legacy* supports "constant" monetary and fiscal policy that does not attempt to offset fluctuations but provides a stable environment for the private economy.

8.1 Stabilization Policy Under Uncertainty

Recall the simple model introduced in Chapter 1:

(1.30) $\qquad Q = C + I + G$

(1.31) $\qquad C = C_a + c(Q - T + R)$

(1.32) $\qquad T = tQ$

Assume that the following values are known with certainty for the year about to begin: $G = \$300$ billion, $C_a = 0$, $c = 0.8$, and $R = \$250$ billion. Thus

(1.30) $\qquad Q = C + I + 300$

(1.31) $\qquad C = 0.8(Q - T + 250)$

(1.32) $\qquad T = tQ$

Suppose that this year a total output level of $Q = \$2,200$ billion will keep $U = U_c$, so that $Q_c = \$2,200$ billion; therefore, the targeted value of Q is $\$2,200$ billion. (Here, we will ignore the goal of balancing the budget.) Our task is simply to adjust the tax rate t to achieve $Q = \$2,200$ billion.

If investment I were known with certainty, then it would be easy to select the tax rate t that would achieve the targeted value of Q. For example, if we knew with certainty that $I = \$380$ billion this year, then we could find the value of t that would make $Q = \$2,200$ billion. First, we would find the required tax revenue T by substituting equation (1.31) into equation (1.30) and setting $Q = \$2,200$ billion, so that

$$Q = 0.8(Q - T + 250) + 680$$
$$2,200 = 0.8(2,200 - T + 250) + 680$$
$$2,200 = 1,760 - 0.8T + 200 + 680$$
$$0.8T = 440$$
$$T = 550$$

Then the required tax rate t is

$$t = \frac{T}{Q} = \frac{550}{2,200} = 25\%$$

Recall that when we were given $t = 25\%$ in Chapter 1, we calculated that $Q = \$2,200$ billion.

If, instead, we knew with certainty that $I = \$300$ billion (\$80 billion less) in this year, then the tax rate t required to achieve $Q = \$2,200$ billion would be found in the same way:

$$Q = 0.8(Q - T + 250) + 600$$
$$2,200 = 0.8(2,200 - T + 250) + 600$$
$$T = 450$$
$$t = \frac{T}{Q} = \frac{450}{2,200} = 20.5\%$$

Note that in the examples in this chapter, many answers are rounded off.

If, instead, we knew with certainty that $I = \$460$ billion (\$80 billion more than our original value), then by the same method

$$T = 650$$
$$t = \frac{T}{Q} = 29.5\%$$

If I could be known with certainty, then it would be desirable to set t at the value required to make $Q = \$2,200$ billion (once again, ignoring the goal of balancing the budget).

But suppose that I is not known with certainty; this is, of course, the actual situation facing policymakers. To simplify this example, however, assume that we know that I can take on only the three values of \$380 billion, \$300 billion, or \$460 billion and, moreover, that each value of I has occurred one-third of the time in past years.

Two basic stabilization strategies are available: *constant policy*, and *countercyclical policy:*

Under CONSTANT POLICY, the policy instrument is kept at a *constant value*. Under COUNTERCYCLICAL (ACTIVIST) POLICY, the policy instrument is adjusted each year in an attempt to keep the economy at its targeted values.

▶ Countercyclical policy may be implemented automatically according to a rule or may be subject to the discretion of policymakers. In this section, we will consider a countercyclical rule.

A CASE FAVORING CONSTANT POLICY

With perfect certainty, a countercyclical policy always achieves the targeted output and is clearly preferable to a constant policy. We will now consider a case in which constant policy is superior to countercyclical policy.

We begin with the constant policy. Under this strategy, the tax rate t is kept at the same value every year. Naturally, the particular value of t will prove important. We will consider the case that will prove most favorable to constant policy in our example: $t = 25\%$.

With t always set at 25%, since I can take on three different values, so can Q. For $I = \$300$ billion, with $t = 25\%$, we obtain

$$Q = 0.8(Q - 0.25Q + 250) + 300 + 300$$
$$Q = 2,000$$

For $I = \$460$ billion, with $t = 25\%$, we obtain

$$Q = 0.8(Q - 0.25Q + 250) + 460 + 300$$
$$Q = 2,400$$

Thus, with $t = 25\%$

$t = 25\%$	Probability	1/3	1/3	1/3
	I	300	380	460
	Q	2,000	2,200	2,400

Now let's examine countercyclical policy. Under this strategy, the tax rate t is adjusted each year in an attempt to achieve $Q = \$2,200$ billion (in our example).

▶ We will make the realistic assumption that this year's value of the tax rate t must be selected last year. At the time of the decision, last year's investment I is known but this year's I is not known. Let's consider the following countercyclical rule: I is forecast to remain constant, and t is set so that, according to the model, total output Q will achieve its targeted level of $2,200 billion.

Thus, if last year's $I = \$380$ billion, then this year's $t = 25\%$; if last year's $I = \$300$ billion, then this year's $t = 20.5\%$; and if last year's $I = \$460$ billion, then this year's $t = 29.5\%$. These values were calculated earlier in this section.

▶ Note that under this countercyclical rule, policymakers have *no discretion*. The required tax rate t follows automatically from the forecast of a constant level of investment I and our three-equation model (1.30), (1.31), (1.32). Hence, countercyclical (activist) policy need not be discretionary.

We will now consider the impact of countercyclical policy under an assumption that proves unfavorable to such policy:

▶ We will assume that this year's I is *completely independent* of last year's I.

If last year's I was $300 billion, then policymakers will assume that this year's I will also be $300 billion, so that this year's t is set at 20.5%. But this year, each of the three values of I has a one-third chance of occurring. If I does turn out to be $300 billion, then Q will be $2,200 billion. But if I turns out to be $380 billion, then with $t = 20.5\%$

$$Q = 0.8(Q - 0.205Q + 250) + 680$$
$$Q = 2,418$$

If I turns out to be $460 billion, then with $t = 20.5\%$

$$Q = 0.8(Q - 0.205Q + 250) + 760$$
$$Q = 2,637$$

To summarize, if last year's $I = \$300$ billion, so that this year's $t = 20.5\%$, then this year each of the following three values of Q will occur one-third of the time:

$t = 20.5\%$	Probability	1/3	1/3	1/3
	I	300	380	460
	Q	2,200	2,418	2,637

But if last year's I was $380 billion, then policymakers will assume that this year's I will also be $380 billion, so that this year's t is set at 25%. We have already calculated that with $t = 25\%$

$t = 25\%$	Probability	1/3	1/3	1/3
	I	300	380	460
	Q	2,000	2,200	2,400

Finally, if last year's I was \$460 billion, then policymakers will assume that this year's I will also be \$460 billion, so that this year's t is set at 29.5%. If I does turn out to be \$460 billion, then Q will be \$2,200 billion. But if I turns out to be \$300 billion, then with $t = 29.5\%$

$$Q = 0.8(Q - 0.295Q + 250) + 300 + 300$$
$$Q = 1,835$$

If I turns out to be \$380 billion, then with $t = 29.5\%$

$$Q = 0.8(Q - 0.295Q + 250) + 380 + 300$$
$$Q = 2,018$$

Thus, with $t = 29.5\%$

$t = 29.5\%$	Probability	1/3	1/3	1/3
	I	300	380	460
	Q	1,835	2,018	2,200

Let us now summarize the results of the three probability tables with $t = 20.5\%$, $t = 25\%$, and $t = 29.5\%$. Last year, each of the three values of I had a one-third chance of occurring. Therefore, this year, each of the three values of t will be set one-third of the time. Thus, each outcome for Q in the three probability tables will occur one-ninth of the time $(1/3 \times 1/3 = 1/9)$. The outcome 2,200 occurs once in each table, so it occurs three-ninths of the time. Ordering the outcomes from the lowest to the highest value of Q, we have

Countercyclical Policy

Probability	1/9	1/9	1/9	3/9	1/9	1/9	1/9
Q	1,835	2,000	2,018	2,200	2,400	2,418	2,637

Let's contrast this result with the constant policy when t is set at 25%:

Constant Policy ($t = 25\%$)

Probability	1/3	1/3	1/3
Q	2,000	2,200	2,400

The countercyclical policy produces a wider range of values of total output Q. Note that under the countercyclical policy (compared to the constant policy), the lowest value of Q is lower (1,835 versus 2,000) and the highest value of Q is higher (2,637 versus 2,400). Also note that the lowest three values of Q under the countercyclical policy, taken together, occur with a probability of 1/3 and can be compared to the 2,000 value of Q under the constant policy. Their *mean* (average) value is 1,951 (1,835 + 2,000 + 2,018/3), which is clearly less than 2,000. Similarly, the mean value of the highest three values of Q under the countercyclical policy is 2,485 (2,400 + 2,418 + 2,637/3), which is clearly greater than the 2,400 value of Q under the constant policy.

Let's be sure we understand the source of the extreme outcomes under the countercyclical policy — the low value 1,835 and the high value 2,637. $Q = \$1,835$ billion results when last year's I was high (\$460 billion), so that t was set high at 29.5% to achieve fiscal restraint. However, this year's I turns out to be low (\$300 billion). In this case, fiscal restraint occurs when I is low, causing a severe decline in Q. Under the constant policy, the low I would be accompanied by the neutral constant policy, so that Q would not be as low (\$2,000 billion). Symmetrically, $Q = \$2,637$ billion results when a fiscal expansion accompanies a high I.

We have reached an important conclusion:

▶ Under certain conditions, a countercyclical policy will result in more variation in total output Q away from its targeted value, compared to a constant policy.

▶ In particular, if a countercyclical policy has a significant probability of applying fiscal restraint when fiscal expansion would be needed and applying fiscal expansion when fiscal restraint would be needed, then it will result in more variation of total output Q away from its targeted value, compared to a constant policy.

CONSTANT VERSUS COUNTERCYCLICAL POLICY

We have intentionally constructed a case that is favorable to constant policy and unfavorable to countercyclical policy. We should note several aspects of this example.

First, we have assumed that this year's investment I is completely independent of last year's I. However, countercyclical policy adjusts t according to the forecast that I will remain constant. Hence, the countercyclical policy in this example utilizes an extremely poor forecasting technique.

If forecasting were perfectly accurate, then countercyclical policy would always achieve the targeted output and would therefore be superior to constant policy. Thus

▶ When forecasting accuracy is very poor, constant policy is superior to countercyclical policy. As forecasting accuracy improves, countercyclical policy becomes superior at some point. If forecasting becomes perfectly accurate, then countercyclical policy is clearly superior to constant policy.

Second, we have assumed that constant policy sets the tax rate at $t = 25\%$. If t were set at some other constant value, then constant policy would not perform as effectively.

▶ The performance of constant policy depends on the constant value that is chosen.

To summarize:

▶ Neither a constant policy nor a countercyclical policy always produces a superior outcome.

Consequently, when the economy is characterized by normal, moderate fluctuations, it is not obvious whether a constant or a countercyclical policy is preferable. A more complex analysis is required to determine which policy is superior.

But when the economy is in a genuine depression, as it was in the 1930s, there is no doubt that countercyclical policy is highly desirable. In a depression, I remains low in successive years. Fiscal expansion that is enacted this year, based on this year's low I, is virtually certain to be needed when it has its impact next year. Thus

▶ In a depression, countercyclical policy is highly desirable.

▶ Even if constant policy is judged to be superior to countercyclical policy for a "normal" economy with moderate fluctuations, an exception should be made if the economy declines into depression. In such an emergency, countercyclical policy would be urgently needed and highly desirable.

8.2 Lags and Automatic Stabilizers

POLICY LAGS

The example given in Section 8.1 leads directly to an appreciation of the importance of *policy lags*. Suppose that policymakers could wait until they observed this year's investment I before they set this year's tax rate t. Because this year's I is the only source of uncertainty in our simple model, certain knowledge of I would enable countercyclical policy to always achieve the targeted total output of $Q = \$2,200$ billion. Countercyclical policy would then clearly be superior to constant policy.

In our example, the problem with countercyclical policy is the policy lag. This year's t must be decided last year, before this year's I is known.

Suppose, instead, that the tax rate for this year was decided four years earlier. Then this year's I would almost surely be independent of the I four years earlier when t was decided. If t were set according to the prevailing I four years ago, then it would almost surely lead to worse results four years later than a constant policy based on the t appropriate for the "normal" value of I. But if the policy lag is only one year—if the tax rate for this year is decided last year—then there is a better chance that the countercyclical policy will yield superior results.

Let's consider the role of policy lags more generally. We know that countercyclical policy would be worthwhile if policy could operate instantaneously the moment a discrepancy between total output Q and its targeted value occurred. In this hypothetical, ideal situation there would be no need for forecasting. The policy could be adjusted until its magnitude was exactly at the required level to achieve the targeted value of Q; this adjustment would happen instantaneously.

Unfortunately, policy lags pervade every aspect of the stabilization process. It is useful to consider the following distinct lags:

1. *Recognition lag:* Suppose that the economy is initially at $I = \$380$ billion, $t = 25\%$, and the targeted value of $Q = \$2{,}200$ billion. Then I drops to \$300 billion and Q decreases to \$2,000 billion. Data must be collected to show that I and Q have, in fact, declined. This *recognition lag* may last for several months before policymakers are certain that significant decreases in the levels of investment and total output have occurred.

2. *Legislative lag:* As soon as total income Q declines, the tax revenue T collected by withholding on paychecks automatically declines. There is no *legislative lag* for this automatic drop in taxes paid; in effect, the legislation has been enacted in advance. But suppose that Congress wanted to go further and cut tax rates to further cut taxes paid. At the present time in the United States, such tax-rate changes have not been legislated in advance. A tax bill would have to work its way through Congress; the process might take several months. The same would be true of an increase in government-expenditure rates.

   The Federal Reserve's Open Market Committee (FOMC) meets roughly once a month to "legislate" monetary policy—in particular, to decide the volume of new bond purchases, which determines the increase in the money supply (see Chapter 13). The legislative lag for monetary policy is therefore much shorter than the legislative lag for tax-rate or government-expenditure changes.

3. *Implementation lag:* After a change in the tax rate or government expenditures is enacted, there is an *implementation lag* (in some cases, for several months) before the change goes into effect. Once

again, the delay for monetary policy is much shorter. Open-market purchases of bonds occur within a few days of the decision by the FOMC (see Chapter 13).

4. *Impact lag:* When the tax rate changes, how quickly do households respond to a change in *disposable* (after-tax) income? (We will investigate this issue in Chapter 12, where we analyze consumption behavior.) When the Fed buys bonds, as we explain in Chapter 13, the sellers deposit Fed checks at their banks. The inflow of reserves enables banks to expand loans, resulting in an increase in the money supply and a decline in the interest rate. The lower interest rate stimulates investment and spending on consumer durables; the multiplier effect further raises consumer spending and income. The time that this process takes is the *impact lag.* The first three lags are clearly quite short for monetary policy, but the length of the impact lag is less certain. (We will consider this lag in the impact of monetary policy in Chapter 9.)

AUTOMATIC STABILIZERS

Our analysis of lags leads directly to an appreciation of *automatic stabilizers.* In Chapter 1, we introduced the concept of an automatic stabilizer:

A tax system in which tax revenue varies automatically in the same direction as income is an AUTOMATIC STABILIZER. It results in a smaller multiplier *m* than would occur under a constant tax revenue policy, which yields the same tax revenue regardless of income.

Our tax function (1.32) $T = tQ$, embodies this automatic stabilizer.

In this chapter, we have been focusing on changing the tax rate t and have taken the importance of the tax function $T = tQ$ for granted. Even if the tax rate t is held constant, this tax system automatically reduces the fluctuation of total output Q. To appreciate its role, let's replace the tax function (1.32) with a *constant tax revenue:*

(8.1) $T = T_0$ at any Q

where T_0 = some tax revenue that is independent of income

Initially, we will assume that $T_0 = \$550$ billion. In Chapter 1, we saw that with $I = \$380$ billion initially, $Q = \$2,200$ billion. The initial equilibrium would be the same under the constant tax revenue (8.1) as it would be under the tax function (1.32) with $t = 25\%$.

In Chapter 1, we also showed that with the tax function (1.32), the multiplier $m = 2.5$ (for $c = 0.8$ and $t = 25\%$); with the constant tax revenue, the multiplier $m = 5$.

A "constant" policy means that the policy instrument is kept constant. Under an income tax that results in $T = tQ$, the tax rate t is the policy instrument. Constant policy would mean keeping t constant (for example, at $t = 25\%$). However, under a constant tax revenue, the policy instrument is the tax revenue T_0. Constant policy would mean keeping T_0 constant (for example, at $T_0 = \$550$ billion).

Consider what would happen under a constant policy in each case when investment I may decline to \$300 billion or rise to \$460 billion. If t is constant at 25%, then when I changes by \$80 billion, total income Q changes by \$200 billion. If T is constant at $T_0 = \$550$ billion, then when I changes by \$80 billion, Q changes by \$400 billion. Thus, the fluctuation in total income Q under constant policy would be twice as great with a constant tax revenue (8.1) as it would be with the tax function (1.32).

We have emphasized the problems that arise when a policy instrument must be changed in response to economic events and have reviewed the various policy lags. Now consider what would happen under a constant tax revenue. If $I = \$380$ billion, then $T = \$550$ billion is the desired level of tax revenue. But if I assumes the value of \$300 billion or \$460 billion, T should be changed. Lags will prevent a change from being prompt or necessarily in the right direction.

With a tax-rate system (1.32), tax revenue T varies automatically and promptly in the desired direction. In the United States, as total income Q changes, tax revenue withheld by firms for the Internal Revenue Service promptly changes. This promptness avoids the possibility, shown earlier, that with long delays, policy may move total output Q away from its targeted value when it finally takes effect.

▶ An appreciation of lags and the problems of discretionary, countercyclical policy should lead to an appreciation of the value of automatic stabilizers.

Our analysis shows that it is quite consistent to question the desirability of discretionary countercyclical fiscal policy, given the significant cumulative lag, and — at the same time — strongly favor automatic stabilizers implemented through the tax-rate and government-expenditure systems. Thus, while macroeconomists disagree about whether countercyclical fiscal policy should normally be attempted, they agree about the importance of a system of automatic fiscal stabilizers. (We will return to this subject in Chapter 9.)

8.3 The Role of Forecasting and Policy-Instrument Variation

No policy instrument is instantaneous in effect, and some instruments can have a significant cumulative lag. In our example in Section 8.1, we assumed that under countercyclical policy, policymakers would use the current value of investment I to set the tax rate t for the following year. In effect, we supposed that policymakers follow the simple forecast rule: Assume that next year's I will equal this year's I.

However, if policymakers could forecast next year's I with great accuracy, they could use this forecast to set t. Clearly, if their forecasts were always perfectly accurate, then countercyclical policy would be superior to constant policy; it would always place total output Q at its targeted value.

Unfortunately, no forecaster is always perfectly accurate. The question becomes: How accurate must forecasting be to make a countercyclical policy based on forecasting techniques superior to a constant policy?

Consider an extreme example. Suppose that a forecasting technique is no more accurate than a random guess, and next year's actual I bears no relation to this year's forecast of I. Is it harmful to set t according to this forecast? We have already answered this question in Section 8.1 in the case of one forecasting rule: Forecast that next year's I will equal this year's I. With I independent of last year's I and, hence, independent of the forecast, the countercyclical policy based on the forecast was inferior to the constant policy (with $t = 25\%$). On average, Q deviated more from its targeted value under the countercyclical policy.

But suppose that the forecast for next year's I is always the same ($380 billion) and always calls for $t = 25\%$. In this case, even though the forecast is no more accurate than a random guess, the policy based on the forecast produces the same result as the constant policy, because it is, in fact, the constant policy.

Thus, there are two relevant elements of forecasting: (1) the degree of accuracy of the forecast, and (2) the variation in the policy instrument in response to the forecast. The greater are the inaccuracy of the forecast and the variation in the policy instrument based on the forecast, the greater is the variation in Q under the countercyclical policy.

To summarize our analysis, at one extreme, when the forecast is perfectly accurate, it is better to vary t in order to aim precisely at the targeted value of Q; in this case, less variation in t will produce inferior results. At the other extreme, when the forecast is no more accurate than a random guess, it is better to hold t constant at the value appropriate for the average I. It therefore seems plausible that if the forecast accuracy ranges between these two extremes, it is best to vary t around its normal value, but by less than the variation that would be best if the forecast were perfectly accurate.

In other words, given some inaccuracy in the forecast, t should not be varied enough to attempt to bring Q all the way back to its targeted value. A smaller variation in t would produce better results. For example, suppose that the forecast for next year's I is $300 billion. If this forecast is perfectly accurate, then t should be varied from its normal rate of 25% to 20.5%, so that next year's Q achieves its targeted value of

$2,200 billion. But if there is some inaccuracy in the forecast, then better results would occur, on average, if t is set somewhere between 25% and 20.5%.

The importance of policy lags should be evident. Suppose that forecasts become less accurate as they project further into the future. This would not be the case if I varied randomly from month to month, with no relation between the values in any two adjacent months. But if I tends to vary smoothly, so that it is highly unlikely that a very low value this month will be followed by a very high value next month, then forecasting one month ahead should be easier than forecasting one or two years ahead. Such *smooth variation* seems to be a characteristic of variables such as I.

If the cumulative lag between policy implementation and impact is six months, then only a six-month forecast is required; if the cumulative lag is two years, then a two-year forecast is required. If the six-month forecast is more accurate than the two-year forecast, then greater variation in the policy instrument is warranted as the cumulative lag becomes shorter.

If the cumulative lag is longer and more variable, then a constant policy is more likely to be superior. A sufficiently long and variable lag would make the forecast no better than a random guess. We have seen that, in this case, a constant policy is preferable to a countercyclical policy, provided that the appropriate constant value is set.

Thus, the length of policy lags and forecast accuracy are important factors to be considered when evaluating the appropriate conduct of policy.

8.4 Uncertainty About the Impact of the Policy Instrument

Thus far, the only uncertainty in our model is the value of investment I. If I were known, then the tax rate t required to achieve the targeted value of total output Q would be known with certainty. But in reality, even if I were known, the value of t needed to achieve $Q = \$2,200$ billion would not be known with certainty. Let's see why.

Thus far, we have assumed that we know, with certainty, that the consumption function (1.31) is

(1.31)
$$C = C_a + c(Q - T + R)$$
$$C = 0 \ + 0.8(Q - T + R)$$

But suppose we are uncertain about the true values of the marginal propensity to consume c and autonomous consumption C_a. Why should such uncertainty occur? Recall our discussion concerning the values of the responsiveness parameter h and the constant inflation unemployment rate U_c in equation (6.1), $\Delta w = h \ (U_c - U)/U$. We explained that economists "run a regression" to obtain the numerical values of h and U_c that best fit the data. Economists use the same statistical (econometric) technique to obtain values for C_a and c. Suppose that $C_a = 0$ and $c = 0.8$ are obtained based on a particular sample of years for the economy. Why can't we be certain of these values?

Any simple consumption function must exclude factors that may influence consumption C in a given year. These excluded factors are at work during the sample period, but economists, in effect, ignore them when they try to find the values of C_a and c that best fit the data. Unless, by coincidence, these factors happen to cancel each other out, they will affect the best estimates of C_a and c. (If these factors had taken on different magnitudes during the sample years, economists would have estimated different values for C_a and c.) Thus, the values obtained will probably differ from the true values of C_a and c due to these excluded factors.

Here, we will assume that in the true consumption function, $C_a = 0$ and $c = 0.8$ but that, based on the statistical analysis of a sample, policymakers believe that $C_a = \$380$ billion and $c = 0.6$, so that

$$C = C_a \quad + \quad c(Q - T + R)$$

True consumption function: $C = 0 \quad + 0.8(Q - T + R)$
Policymakers' C function: $C = 380 + 0.6(Q - T + R)$

Note that according to the policymakers' C function, if $I = \$380$ billion, $R = \$250$ billion, $G = \$300$ billion, and $t = 25\%$, then $Q = \$2,200$ billion:

$$Q = 380 + 0.6(Q - 0.25Q + 250) + 380 + 300$$
$$Q = 2,200$$

Now suppose that next year's I is forecast to decline to \$300 billion and assume that the forecast will prove to be correct. The tax rate t must be cut below 25% to keep total income Q at \$2,200 billion next year. Of course, the required value of t depends on the consumption function. We calculated earlier that if $C_a = 0$ and $c = 0.8$, then t must be cut to 20.5%. By the same method, we can calculate the value of t that is required to achieve $Q = \$2,200$ billion under the policymakers' C function. First, we must find the required tax revenue. Since we want Q to be \$2,200 billion:

$$Q = 380 + 0.6(Q - T + 250) + 300 + 300$$
$$2,200 = 380 + 0.6(2,200 - T + 250) + 300 + 300$$
$$T = 417$$

$$t = \frac{T}{Q} = \frac{417}{2,200} = 0.189 = 18.9\%$$

With $I = \$300$ billion, in order to achieve $Q = \$2,200$ billion

True consumption function: $t = 20.5\%$
Policymakers' C function: $t = 18.9\%$

Why is the required value of t smaller with the policymakers' C function? Since c is smaller (0.6 instead of 0.8), the tax cut must be greater to achieve the required increase in consumer demand.

When policymakers set $t = 18.9\%$, we can use the true consumption function to calculate the value of Q:

$$Q = 0.8(Q - 0.189Q + 250) + 300 + 300$$
$$Q = 2,278$$

Now suppose that I is correctly forecast to be \$460 billion next year. Then policymakers will need to raise t to achieve $Q = \$2,200$ billion next year. But, once again, the value of t they believe is required depends on the consumption function they believe is correct. Only if they assume the true consumption function will the t they set actually achieve $Q = \$2,200$ billion. By the same method used in the case of $I = \$300$ billion, we find that with $I = \$460$ billion, in order to achieve $Q = \$2,200$ billion

True consumption function: $t = 29.5\%$
Policymakers' C function: $t = 31.1\%$

When policymakers set $t = 31.1\%$, we can use the true consumption function to calculate the value of Q to be \$2,139 billion.

Now that we recognize the possibility of misjudging the impact of a change in a policy instrument, it is no longer clear that a countercyclical policy that always tries to achieve the targeted value of Q is superior to a constant tax-rate policy. Which is better in our example?

Once again, we will assume that the three values of I (\$300 billion, \$380 billion, and \$460 billion) each occur one-third of the time and that they are correctly forecast. A constant tax-rate policy results in

	Constant Policy ($t = 25\%$)			
$t = 25\%$	Probability	1/3	1/3	1/3
	I	300	380	460
	Q	2,000	2,200	2,400

Under a countercyclical policy that varies t in an attempt to achieve $Q = \$2,200$ billion, the result will depend on the degree of error concerning the impact of a change in the policy instrument. Once again, we will assume that I is correctly forecast, so that

Probability	1/3	1/3	1/3
I	300	380	460
Q	2,278	2,200	2,139

In this example, the countercyclical policy results in a better outcome than the constant policy; the variation in Q is not as great. However

▶ Even if the forecast of I is perfectly correct, uncertainty about the impact of a change in the policy instrument causes countercyclical policy to miss the targeted value of Q. Whether or not countercyclical is superior to constant policy depends on the degree of error concerning the impact of a change in the policy instrument.

In this example, to isolate the effect of policy-instrument uncertainty, we have assumed that there is no forecast error. In fact, policymakers must face both uncertainties — *forecast uncertainty* and *policy-instrument uncertainty*. Together, both uncertainties work against the effectiveness of countercyclical policy.

▶ To summarize, countercyclical policy would clearly be superior to constant policy in the absence of uncertainty. But uncertainty is central to actual policymaking. Once forecast uncertainty and policy-instrument uncertainty are recognized, it is no longer clear which policy is superior. Only more careful analysis of the degree of the uncertainty can indicate which policy is preferable.

8.5 Institutional and Political Constraints

Once again, consider our three-equation model (1.30), (1.31), (1.32), where the tax rate t is the policy instrument. Suppose that conditions are favorable to countercyclical policy. Lags are short, forecasting is accurate, and the impact of a change in t is accurately estimated. Nevertheless, a further aspect — *political* and *institutional constraints* — must be considered before countercyclical policy is judged superior to constant policy.

ASYMMETRICAL DISCRETIONARY FISCAL POLICY

Suppose that when I declines from $380 billion to $300 billion, thereby reducing Q from $2,200 billion to $2,000 billion, Congress and the President can be easily motivated to cut t to stimulate demand. But when I rises from \$380 billion to \$460 billion, it is politically very difficult to raise t to reduce demand.

In the world of pure economics, raising t is as easy as cutting t. But in the real economy, there may be a *political asymmetry*. Fiscal policy in the 1960s illustrates this problem. In the early 1960s, Congress enacted President Kennedy's proposed tax cut in order to raise demand. But in the late 1960s — with the economy overheated by the rise in government spending due to the Vietnam War — Congress and President Johnson delayed the required tax increase.

Economists sympathetic to active countercyclical fiscal policy correctly point out that the Council of Economic Advisors, led by Chairman Gardner Ackley, strongly urged a tax increase. The argument is made that countercyclical fiscal policy is economically sound; the obstacles are "only" political.

▶ Economists should assess the political and institutional constraints that are likely to affect the implementation of any economic policy. If it will usually prove politically easier to cut t than to raise t, then discretionary, countercyclical fiscal policy will, at best, be effective about 50% of the time.

But there is a further implication. Suppose, as in our example, that when $I =$ \$380 billion and $t = 25\%$, the budget is *balanced*. If I declines to \$300 billion, then t will be cut. When I rises back to \$380 billion, suppose that there is political resistance to raising t back to 25%. Thus, when I returns to its normal value of \$380 billion, the budget will be in *deficit*.

A tighter monetary policy will now be needed to keep Q from rising above the targeted value of \$2,200 billion. If the tight monetary policy is not forthcoming, then Q will rise above constant inflation output Q_c (\$2,200 billion) and the inflation rate p will rise. If the Fed does implement the tight monetary policy needed to keep Q at Q_c, then the interest rate will rise, reducing investment. We saw in Chapter 2 that this easy fiscal–tight monetary mix favors consumption relative to investment when the economy is at Q_c.

Thus, if discretionary, countercyclical fiscal policy is often used to expand demand but is seldom used to contract demand, then such ASYMMETRICAL FISCAL POLICY may, over time, gradually increase the budget deficit.

▶ In Chapter 2, we saw that an increase in the budget deficit, when the economy is kept at Q_c by a tightening of monetary policy, reduces capital accumulation; an easy fiscal–tight monetary mix favors consumption relative to investment at Q_c. If deficits at Q_c are judged harmful, then this possible consequence of discretionary fiscal policy should be weighed.

A lesson can be learned from contrasting fiscal policy with monetary policy. In late 1979, the Federal Reserve embarked on a tightening of monetary policy. The Fed expressed a willingness to accept very high interest rates as a temporary byproduct of its policy to achieve disinflation.

Interest rates rose to record levels in the early 1980s, producing a strong outcry, especially from sectors dependent on credit. The tight monetary policy threw the economy into the deepest recession since the 1930s. Still the Fed did not relent until the unemployment rate surpassed 10% and disinflation was successfully launched.

Would a President or Congress, subject to reelection pressures, have been able to implement this disinflation policy? As Chapter 9 will show, the twelve members of the Federal Open Market Committee who implement monetary policy are certainly more insulated from such pressures. It can be argued that this difference favors reliance on monetary rather than discretionary fiscal policy to achieve stabilization.

At the trough of the recession, with the unemployment rate near 11% and fears of a world depression widespread, the Fed shifted from brake to accelerator. The money-supply growth rate increased, and interest rates came down. The economy turned around and began a strong recovery. Whether the change in Fed policy was the key to the turnaround is debatable, but one thing is clear. The Fed acted aggressively to stimulate the economy.

▶ In recent years, the Federal Reserve has demonstrated an ability to conduct policy *symmetrically*—to implement both contractionary and expansionary monetary policy. This symmetry suggests that even if monetary policy is left to the discretion of the Fed and is not governed by an externally imposed rule, symmetrical countercyclical monetary policy appears feasible due to the Fed's insulation from political pressure.

▶ By contrast, discretionary fiscal policy appears to operate *asymmetrically*. It can therefore be argued that Congress and the President should be discouraged from implementing discretionary fiscal policy—except in the extreme emergency of a depression, when fiscal as well as monetary stimulus would be urgently needed.

It is important to recognize that *automatic* fiscal policy operates symmetrically. We can illustrate this point by comparing a constant tax revenue

$$(8.1) \qquad T = T_0$$
$$T = 550$$

with a constant tax rate

(1.32) $T = tQ$
          $T = 0.25Q$

Suppose that the economy is initially at $Q = Q_c$ ($2,200 billion), with $I = 380 billion; then I rises to 460 billion. According to the constant tax-revenue equation (8.1), Congress and the President would need to act (the decision would be at their "discretion") to raise tax revenue T. Politically, this might prove difficult. According to the constant tax-rate equation (1.32), without any discretionary action by Congress and the President, tax revenue T would rise automatically with total income Q. As a result, Q would not rise as far above constant inflation output Q_c, and the rise in the inflation rate would not be as great.

▶ Although recognition of political and institutional constraints may lead to skepticism about the value of *discretionary* fiscal policy, it should also lead to an appreciation of the value of *automatic* fiscal stabilizers.

▶ Automatic, symmetrical fiscal policy (countercyclical or constant) would be desirable if it could be politically achieved.

CHOICES FOR MONETARY POLICY

How should monetary policy be conducted? We must distinguish between two choices, which are often confused:

1. Should monetary policy be discretionary or governed by an externally imposed rule?
2. Should monetary policy be constant or countercyclical?

The first choice asks: should the twelve members of the Federal Open Market Committee (FOMC) be permitted to use discretion (their judgment) in deciding how to vary the main instrument of monetary policy—open-market operations? Or should Congress or a constitutional amendment prescribe a rule that the FOMC would be required to follow?

Let's consider two possible rules:

▶ Rule 1: The FOMC would be required to keep the money-supply growth rate m constant at a rate of $q_c - v$, the rate that should, on average, achieve an inflation rate of near 0%.

▶ Rule 2: The FOMC would be required to vary the money-supply growth rate m continuously to keep the nominal demand growth rate y constant at a rate of q_c, the rate that should, on average, achieve an inflation rate of near 0%.

Under either rule, the FOMC would not have the discretion to determine what target to pursue with its open-market operations.

As these two rules show, a rule can prescribe either a constant policy (rule 1), or a countercyclical policy (rule 2) where m would be varied continuously to offset changes in fiscal policy and private-sector demand to keep y constant.

This brings us to the second choice: should monetary policy be constant or countercyclical? Whether Fed discretion or an externally imposed rule governs monetary policy, this choice must be faced.

▶ In the end, a particular conduct of monetary and fiscal policy should be advocated in light of the political and institutional constraints that govern such policy.

THE COORDINATION PROBLEM

Suppose that both fiscal and monetary policy are discretionary; rules govern neither policy. Congress and the President use their judgment, each year, to set fiscal policy; the members of the Federal Open Market Committee (FOMC) use their judgment, each month, to adjust monetary policy.

When both policies are discretionary, each group of policymakers is uncertain about what the other group will do. When Congress and the President set fiscal policy, they cannot be sure what the Fed will do about monetary policy. Similarly, when the FOMC members set monetary policy, they cannot be sure what Congress and the President will do about fiscal policy.

This has been called the *coordination problem*. It is easily expressed using an *IS – LM* diagram. If fiscal policymakers know the position of the *LM* curve, then they can try to position the *IS* curve so that the two curves intersect at constant inflation output Q_c. If they are uncertain about monetary policy, they cannot know the position of the *LM* curve. Similarly, if monetary policymakers know the position of the *IS* curve, then they can try to position the *LM* curve so that the two curves intersect at Q_c. If they are uncertain about fiscal policy, they cannot know the position of the *IS* curve.

If both monetary and fiscal policy are discretionary, the best that can be done is to improve communication. This is where a knowledge of institutions is important. Who can speak for discretionary fiscal policy? Discretionary fiscal policy is the outcome of decisions made by Congress and the President. None of the participants can accurately control or predict the outcome.

Clearly, one way to mitigate the coordination problem would be to make at least one of the two policies automatic (subject to a rule). For example, if fiscal policy followed a rule (constant or countercyclical), then monetary policymakers could better estimate the position of the IS curve when planning monetary policy.

If only one of the two policies is to remain discretionary, which one should it be? Suppose that monetary policy followed a rule and fiscal policy remained discretionary. From our earlier discussion, it is doubtful that Congress and the President would be able to make effective use of the knowledge of the monetary rule. By contrast, if fiscal policy followed a rule and monetary policy remained discretionary, then monetary policymakers could make positive use of this knowledge.

▶ The *coordination problem* provides another argument for an automatic fiscal policy (countercyclical or constant).

8.6 Why the Degree of Stability of the Private Economy Matters

Two properties of the economy must be distinguished: (1) how frequently does Q move away from Q_c, and (2) how quickly does Q automatically return to Q_c after a deviation? We will call the first property the *disturbability* of the economy and the second property the *stability* of the economy.

It has been suggested that if the private economy is inherently very "disturbable," then it is clearly desirable for the government to implement an active, countercyclical policy. But this policy conclusion is not necessarily correct. Suppose that the private economy is subject to frequent, large disturbances when government adheres to a constant policy; in any particular year, Q may deviate markedly from Q_c. Thus, the private economy exhibits significant disturbability. But suppose that policy lags are significant, forecasting is highly inaccurate, and the impact of changes in policy instruments is highly uncertain. Given these conditions, we have seen that a countercyclical policy might result in even more severe fluctuations than a constant policy.

▶ Even though economic fluctuations may be severe under a constant policy, they can be even worse under a countercyclical policy. Thus, a highly disturbable private economy does not necessarily imply that countercyclical policy is desirable.

Although the disturbability of the economy does not indicate whether countercyclical policy is desirable, the stability of the economy does. To see this, let's return to our simple, three-equation model with numerical values inserted:

$$(1.30) \qquad Q = C + 380 + 300$$
$$(1.31) \qquad C = 0.8(Q - T + 250)$$
$$(1.32) \qquad T = 0.25Q$$

From Chapter 1, we know that $Q = \$2,200$ billion. If I declines from $\$380$ billion to $\$300$ billion, Q will decline from $\$2,200$ billion to $\$2,000$ billion. If the tax rate were instantly cut and the impact of the tax cut were immediately effective in raising demand, then Q could easily be prevented from decreasing to $\$2,000$ billion. But we know that countercyclical policy cannot be instantaneously effective. The cumulative lag of any countercyclical policy, such as a cut in the tax rate, is significant. Thus, we must ask what will the position of the economy be when countercyclical policy actually becomes effective (perhaps in six months or a year).

Suppose that private investment demand I is inherently very stable. In other words, suppose that any deviation of I from its normal value is temporary. Automatically, in the absence of countercyclical policy, I would rapidly move back to its normal value (in our example, to $\$380$ billion, so that Q would move back to $\$2,200$ billion). Then by the time today's countercyclical policy becomes effective in six months or a year, the economy would be back to its normal position if the tax rate t remains unchanged.

Clearly, a constant policy would be superior to a countercyclical policy. Any time we observe a deviation of Q from its targeted value, there is no point in trying to change t from 25% to restore the targeted value; by the time the change in t actually affects the economy, I will have returned to its normal value of $\$380$ billion and $t = 25\%$ will keep Q at $\$2,200$ billion. Any other t would move Q away from its target. Thus, if I quickly and automatically returns to its normal value after a deviation, then a constant policy might be superior.

Now, let's consider the reverse case. Suppose that I seldom deviates from its normal value; when it does deviate, it does so moderately. The disturbability of the economy due to I is therefore low. However, when I does deviate moderately, the deviation persists over time. If I is significantly below normal today, then six months from now it is more likely to be below normal than to be above normal. The stability of the economy is therefore low.

If $I = \$300$ billion and $Q = \$2,000$ billion today, both values will probably still be below normal ($I = \$380$ billion, $Q = \$2,200$ billion) in six months or a year, when today's countercyclical policy becomes effective. Thus, it is likely that countercyclical policy would be superior to constant policy.

▶ To summarize, the key determinant in the choice of a stabilization policy is not the inherent *disturbability* of the economy (the frequency with which Q deviates from Q_c) but the inherent *stability* of the economy (the tendency of Q to return quickly to Q_c after a deviation). If the stability of the economy is low, it is more likely that countercyclical policy, enacted today, will help—rather than hurt—when its impact is felt in the future.

According to the models we have developed in Parts 1 and 2, what determines the degree of stability of the economy? Let's begin with the *IS–LM* model we derived in Part 1. For convenience, we will rewrite the equations of our *IS–LM* system:

(1.30) $Q = C + I + G$

(1.31) $C = C_a + c(Q - T + R)$

(1.32) $T = tQ$

(2.1) $I = I_a - jr$

(2.6) $\dfrac{M^D}{P} = \dfrac{M_a}{P} + kQ - hr$

(2.7) $\dfrac{M^D}{P} = \dfrac{M}{P}$

Assume that the government policy variables (G, R, t, and M) are held constant and that the economy is initially at $Q = Q_c$. The *IS* and *LM* curves intersect at $Q = Q_c$. For convenience, we will assume that all coefficients (c, j, k, and h) also remain constant and that P is considered constant. We will focus on the autonomous elements C_a, I_a, and M_a.

If C_a or I_a declines, then the *IS* curve will shift to the left and Q will fall below Q_c. Alternatively, if M_a increases, then the *LM* curve will shift to the left and Q will fall below Q_c. Now let's consider two contrasting modes of behavior for C_a, I_a, and M_a:

1. If Q falls below Q_c, then C_a and I_a will rise and M_a will fall by amounts that tend to restore Q_c.
2. If Q falls below Q_c, then C_a and I_a will fall and M_a will rise, thereby further reducing Q_c.

If case (1) holds, then the economy will be relatively stable. A decline in Q below Q_c will provoke changes in C_a, I_a, and M_a that tend to restore Q to Q_c. With the *IS* and *LM* curves intersecting at a Q below Q_c, these changes will shift both curves to the right, so that they tend to return to the intersection point at Q_c.

If case (2) holds, then the economy will be relatively unstable. A decline in Q below Q_c will provoke changes in C_a, I_a, and M_a that tend to move Q still further below Q_c. With the *IS* and *LM* curves intersecting at a Q below Q_c, these changes will shift both curves to the left, so that they tend to move to an intersection point at a still lower Q.

Is case (1) or case (2) more likely to occur? Suppose that a decline in Q below Q_c generates pessimism, anxiety, and the conviction that Q will decline further. In this case, firms are likely to cut I_a, and consumers are likely to cut C_a. Wealth-holders may fear that bonds will default and may therefore try to increase their liquidity, thereby raising M_a. All of these reactions would result in case (2) and, therefore, in low stability for the economy.

By contrast, suppose that the public believes that any decline in Q below Q_c is likely to be followed by a sharp rise in Q. The public looks beyond the current recession and already anticipates a robust recovery. In this case, firms may actually raise I_a, and consumers may raise C_a. Wealth-holders may even shift their wealth into bonds, thereby reducing M_a. All of these reactions would result in case (1) and, therefore, in high stability for the economy.

In our analyses of consumption and investment in Chapter 12 and of money demand in Chapter 13, we will attempt to shed some light on this question. In particular, we will find that the "accelerator" hypothesis of investment suggests that I_a will generally behave according to case (2), rather than case (1), thereby reducing the stability of the economy.

Now let's consider how the $DG-SG$ model we derived in Part 2 affects the stability of the economy. An extreme case will demonstrate our point. Suppose that expectations are inertial and that the SG curve is perfectly flat, so that a rise in unemployment is assumed to cause no reduction in the wage inflation rate w or in the price inflation rate p. In period 0, the DG_0 and SG_0 curves intersect at $Q = Q_c$ and $p = 0\%$, as shown in Figure 8.1.

In period 1, suppose that the adjusted nominal demand growth rate $\hat{y}_1$ becomes negative, so that DG_1 lies below DG_0. Since SG_1 coincides with SG_0, Q_1 is less than Q_c ($p_1 = 0\%$); the economy goes into recession.

Now suppose that beginning in period 2, the adjusted nominal demand growth rate $\hat{y}$ returns to its normal value of 0%, so that the $\hat{y}_2$ line coincides with the horizontal axis. What happens in period 2? Using our earlier plotting rule, go to the last period's intersection point (Q_1, 0%) and move vertically to the $\hat{y}$ line (but you are already there); hence, DG_2 coincides with DG_1. Return to intersection point (Q_1, 0%) and move horizontally to Q_c; when you draw the horizontal SG_2 line through this point, it coincides with SG_1. Thus, in period 2, DG_2 and SG_2 intersect at the same point (Q, 0%). The identical result would occur in period 3. Hence, the economy would be stuck in a permanent recession.

By contrast, suppose that the SG curve is relatively steep, so that a rise in unemployment is assumed to cause a significant reduction in w

FIGURE 8.1 INSTABILITY DUE TO A FLAT *SG* CURVE

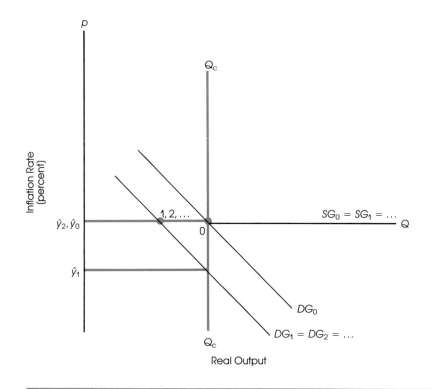

Initially, the economy is at $\hat{y} = 0\%$, $p = 0\%$, and $Q = Q_c$. In period 1, $\hat{y}$ declines to $\hat{y}_1$. The DG_0 curve shifts downward to DG_1 but, with inertial expectations, SG_1 coincides with SG_0, which is flat. The economy moves to point 1. In period 2 and thereafter, $\hat{y}$ is once again 0%. In period 2, DG_2 coincides with DG_1 and SG_2 coincides with SG_1. The economy stays at the same point; point 2 coincides with point 1. The same is true in subsequent periods. The economy remains permanently in recession.

and p. Also suppose that the initial $DG_0 - SG_0$ intersection point is again at $(Q_c, 0\%)$ and that, in period 1, the same reduction in the adjusted nominal demand growth rate $\hat{y}_1$ occurs; thus, DG_1 in Figure 8.2 and DG_1 in Figure 8.1 are in the same position.

Due to the positive slope of SG_1, which coincides with SG_0, the recession is milder in Figure 8.2. Q_1 does decline below Q_c, but to a lesser degree than it does in Figure 8.1. p_1 is negative.

Suppose that, beginning in period 2, the adjusted nominal demand growth rate $\hat{y}$ returns to its normal value of 0%, so that the $\hat{y}_2$ line coincides with the horizontal axis. What happens in period 2? Using our plotting rule, go to the last period's intersection point (Q_1, p_1) and

FIGURE 8.2 STABILITY DUE TO A STEEP SG CURVE

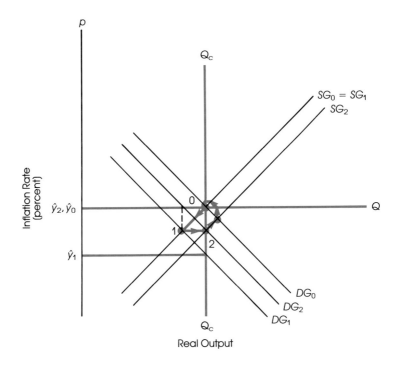

Initially, the economy is at $\hat{y} = 0\%$, $p =)\%$, and $Q = Q_c$. In period 1, $\hat{y}$ declines to $\hat{y}_1$. The DG_0 curve shifts downward to DG_1 but, with inertial expectations, SG_1 coincides with SG_0, which is steep. The economy moves to point 1. In period 2 and thereafter, $\hat{y}$ is once again 0%. In period 2, DG_2 lies above DG_1 and SG_2 lies to the right of SG_1. The economy moves to point 2, which happend to be at Q_c. The economy has automatically recovered.

move vertically to the $\hat{y}$ line; when you draw DG_2 through this point, it lies above DG_1. Return to intersection point (Q_1, p_1) and move horizontally to the Q_c line; when you draw SG_2 through this point, it lies to the right of SG_1. For convenience, we have drawn the slope of the SG curve so that Q_2 happens to be equal to Q_c. Thus, in period 2, the economy would return to its normal value of Q_c.

In the case of the horizontal SG curve in Figure 8.1, the absence of $w-p$ adjustment reduces stability. Even if the adjusted nominal demand growth rate returns to its normal value of 0%, the economy remains permanently in recession. In this case, the implementation of countercyclical policy to raise $\hat{y}$ above its normal value of 0% would be worthwhile. When the policy has its impact in the future, the economy will still be stuck in a recession and in need of a stimulus.

By contrast, with the relatively steep SG curve in Figure 8.2, the significant $w - p$ adjustment provides stability. If $\hat{y}$ returns to its normal value of 0%, then the economy will recover automatically from the recession. The implementation of countercyclical policy to raise $\hat{y}$ above its normal value of 0% would be harmful. When the policy has its impact in the future, it would cause Q to move above Q_c.

▶ Low responsiveness of wage and price inflation to a rise in the unemployment rate results in low economic stability and tends to make countercyclical policy more desirable.

8.7 Stabilizing Structural Policies

Stabilization policy is often equated with fiscal and monetary policy ("demand management" policy). Chapters 8 and 9 are primarily devoted to the proper conduct of fiscal and monetary policy, but the conclusion reached in Section 8.6 implies the following important point:

▶ Any "structural" policy that increases the responsiveness of wage and price inflation to fluctuations in nominal demand growth will improve the stability of the economy and reduce the deviations of output and unemployment from their targeted values.

In Section 6.6, we considered several structural policies that should raise wage and price responsiveness. Under the *flexible compensation* ("gain-sharing") strategy, part of a worker's compensation varies automatically with the gain (or loss) of the firm, measured in terms of profit or revenue. Let's see why the economy would be more stable under flexible compensation.

If the nominal demand growth rate y falls below its normal value, shifting the DG curve downward, then the nominal profit or revenue growth of the average firm will also fall below its normal value. Under flexible compensation, wage growth automatically declines. The SG curve is steeper with flexible compensation than it is with *fixed compensation,* because a decline in output Q causes a larger decline in the wage and price inflation rates (w and p). Hence, the downward shift of the DG curve will result in less recession under flexible compensation.

As we noted in Chapter 6, flexible compensation can be encouraged by a tax incentive. If share compensation is taxed at a lower rate than fixed compensation, then flexible compensation will be encouraged.

It is worth repeating that economists have only begun to analyze the long-run properties of a share economy. These properties are not well understood. Nevertheless, it appears that flexible compensation would improve the stability of the economy.

Two other structural policies that might increase wage responsiveness are simultaneous wage setting and the banning of multi-year, long-term labor contracts. Simultaneous wage setting might enable a firm to reduce its w without causing a decline in its relative w. Banning long-term labor contracts would compel more frequent wage setting and should cause w to respond more quickly to changes in the unemployment rate.

Objections can be raised to each policy. Long-term labor contracts reduce the frequency of negotiations and strikes. How to make wage setting "simultaneous" is not clear. The cons as well as the pros must be weighed.

These and other structural policies deserve more attention and consideration than they often receive. The importance of stabilizing monetary and fiscal policy is clear. However, the importance of stabilizing structural policies is not always recognized. It should be included in any serious analysis of stabilization policy.

8.8 The Keynesian and Classical Legacies

In this section, some historical perspective to the controversy over stabilization policy will be provided. Prior to the 1930s, most economists did not advocate countercyclical monetary or fiscal policy. The opposition to activist, countercyclical policy is a central feature of the "classical" view.

Then came the Great Depression. In late 1929, after a prosperous, "roaring" decade, the stock market collapsed and the economic downturn began. It deepened through 1930 and into 1931; bank failures multiplied. Recession deepened in other industrial countries as well. By 1932, in the United States, the unemployment rate was nearly 25% and real output was roughly 30% below potential (Q_c). Hardship was widespread.

Despite two modest recoveries during the 1930s, the unemployment rate never fell below 14%; in 1940, it was roughly 14% and real output was still significantly below potential. Only the mobilization for war finally brought the unemployment rate down to pre-Depression levels.

KEYNES'S GENERAL THEORY

The Great Depression of the 1930s jolted not only the economy but economic theory. In 1936, John Maynard Keynes from Cambridge University in England, a highly respected economist and economic advisor, published his *General Theory of Employment, Interest, and Money*. His book launched the "Keynesian Revolution" in economic theory.

Keynes's *General Theory* is a complex, challenging, and powerful work. The brief comments here cannot do it justice. We will focus on its implications for stabilization policy.

Keynes argued that the private economy is inherently unstable. The chief villain is investment demand I, which depends on expectations of future profitability, which, in turn, depends on future economic events we are unable to forecast accurately. Hence, I can fluctuate with waves of optimism and pessimism concerning the economic future. Once a wave of pessimism reduces I, the resulting decline in Q intensifies the pessimism and holds I down. The failure of I to revive quickly and automatically is a central reason for the instability of the economy.

Writing in the midst of the Great Depression, Keynes contended that a severe downward fluctuation in output might not reverse itself automatically over several years. A depression could persist, and sound economic theory should be able to account for such persistance.

To explain fluctuations in output, Keynes introduced a simple model of equilibrium output—essentially, the same model presented in Chapter 1. Keynes contended that fluctuations in I are multiplied through a "consumption function" to yield greater fluctuations in output. If I declines and fails to revive, then output will be held down as well. Keynes's *General Theory* introduced the consumption function and the "multiplier."

Keynes rejected the argument of classical economists that wages and prices would decline promptly and significantly in a recession and that this decline would generate a rapid recovery. He argued that workers resist wage cuts and, therefore, that such cuts can only occur gradually, even in a severe recession. Without a significant decline in wages and unit costs, price declines would be limited. In terms of our $DG-SG$ model, Keynes believed that expectations are inertial (not rational) and that the SG curve is relatively flat.

Thus, Keynes concluded that once the economy enters a severe recession, the recession is likely to persist; automatic and rapid recovery is unlikely. It follows that the government should act to stimulate the economy with expansionary monetary and fiscal policy.

It is important to remember the state of the world economy when Keynes published his *General Theory*. By 1936, Keynes had witnessed a depression that had persisted for more than half a decade in advanced industrial countries. In his view, it was obvious that depression could persist. The questions were why and what could be done about it.

Keynes did not draw an $IS-LM$ diagram, but his analysis led to the construction of that diagram by John Hicks in 1937, after reading Keynes's *General Theory*. In terms of that diagram, Keynes advocated shifting both the IS and LM curves to the right in response to a severe recession.

It is true that Keynes considered the possibility that monetary expansion alone might not be sufficient in a severe depression. Later, some would infer that Keynes believed in fiscal policy, not monetary policy. But a careful reading of his *General Theory* suggests that Keynes advocated a combined fiscal and monetary expansion to combat severe recession.

Keynes's central message then was not to choose fiscal over monetary policy. It was to choose *active, expansionary policy* over passivity in response to a severe recession.

In the three decades following the publication of Keynes's *General Theory*, the majority of macroeconomists worked to refine and develop the basic Keynesian framework (for example, Paul Samuelson, James Tobin, Franco Modigliani, and Lawrence Klein). Some economists even suggested using active, countercyclical monetary and fiscal policy to "fine tune" the economy to offset even relatively minor fluctuations and keep output near the full-employment level.

This period was the calm before the storm. Before turning to the upheaval that soon ushered in the classical counterrevolution, let's pause to compare the Keynesian view of the early 1960s with Keynes's own view expressed in his *General Theory*.

In his book, Keynes prescribed active, countercyclical policy to combat a depression, not just a routine economic downturn. Not one of the possible objections to active, countercyclical policy examined in this chapter is valid in a depression. There is little danger in a depression that the economy will become overheated when such a policy becomes effective perhaps a year later. There is little danger that a stimulus will mistakenly propel the economy above the constant inflation level of output Q_c, thereby increasing inflation.

Keynes himself did not promise that countercyclical (activist) policy could be used to prevent even minor economic fluctuations. He emphasized that unpredictable changes in business psychology can move I and, hence, Q. Due to business psychology and expectations, he was skeptical of early attempts to forecast economic fluctuations on the basis of a statistical (econometric) model of the economy. By contrast, Keynes focused on what to do in response to a depression.

THE CLASSICAL COUNTER-REVOLUTION

We now turn to the storm. The 1960s and 1970s witnessed a gradual upsurge in inflation in most economically advanced countries. In the United States, as inflation began to develop in the mid-1960s, Keynesians recommended fiscal and monetary contraction to combat it. However, there was political resistance to such contraction, which would have entailed a tax increase, or spending cuts, or tight money with high interest rates. To the public, Keynesian economics appeared to permit inflation.

It is also true that some Keynesians accepted the original Phillips curve view that a lower unemployment rate would result in a higher but a stable inflation rate. Many of these Keynesians were politically "liberal," and some of them advocated implementing expansionary monetary and fiscal policy to achieve a very low unemployment rate and accepting the higher, stable inflation rate that would probably follow.

In Part 2, we presented the current mainstream analysis of inflation and unemployment. According to the view held by the majority of macroeconomists today, the economy possesses a constant inflation unemployment rate U_c in the range of 6% to 7%. Any implementation of monetary and fiscal policy to hold the unemployment rate below this U_c would accelerate inflation. In retrospect, the advocacy by some Keynesians in the 1960s of demand expansion to achieve a low unemployment rate was a mistake. The rise in inflation provided the opportunity for a classical counterrevolution. Most macroeconomists would have placed themselves in the Keynesian tradition in the early 1960s, but an important minority dissented. Although they would come to be known as "monetarists," it is perhaps more accurate to call them "classical economists" who remained faithful to the basic tenets of the classical tradition (for example, Milton Friedman).

These classical economists believe that Keynes exaggerated the instability of the private economy and that Keynesian "fine tuning" would do more harm than good. In their view, monetary policy should be implemented to achieve long-run price stability — not to offset fluctuations in employment and output. Hence, the Fed should seek to keep the money-supply growth rate low and steady and should refrain from countercyclical variations in money-supply growth.

Similarly, fiscal policy should be limited to automatic stabilizers. In other words, a tax system in which taxes vary automatically with income, yielding a tax function like equation (1.32) of $T = tQ$, is useful. But no attempt should be made to vary tax rates or government expenditures countercyclically; instead, they should be set so that the budget is balanced if output and unemployment are normal.

How do these classical economists account for the Great Depression, which inspired Keynes's *General Theory* and persuaded many economists to accept the Keynesian outlook? In their view, the Depression would have been only a routine recession that corrected itself if the Fed had only acted to keep the money supply stable. During the Depression, the money supply collapsed by one-third in a wave of bank failures. Today, both classical and Keynesian economists are highly critical of the Fed's inaction as the Depression deepened.

But note an important distinction. Classical economists do not claim that the Fed should have undertaken active, countercyclical monetary policy. This, after all, is what the Keynesians assert. Classical economists argue that it would have been sufficient for the Fed to keep the money supply constant.

Both classicals and Keynesians therefore agree that the Fed should have acted aggressively as the lender of last resort to try to prevent bank failures and keep the money supply from contracting. They differ in that the classicals believe that this would have been a sufficient action, while Keynesians suspect that an active expansion of the money supply — reinforced by expansionary fiscal policy — was required to prevent the Depression.

In the 1960s, the classicals mounted a counterattack on the Keynesian mainstream. They advocated a low, steady money-supply growth rate, under which the economy would gravitate to its "natural rate" of unemployment and output, inflation would be close to 0%, and fluctuations would be relatively mild. According to the classicals, the Keynesians had tried to achieve an unattainably low unemployment rate, and the result was, predictably, accelerating inflation.

With inflation high due to Keynesian policies, the classicals advocated a gradual reduction in the money-supply growth rate and the acceptance of a temporary recession as the necessary cost of disinflation. Thereafter, active, countercyclical policy should be avoided.

By the early 1980s, the majority of macroeconomists probably agreed with the classical prescription. The monetary deceleration by the Fed, which achieved disinflation, received support from many macroeconomists. Furthermore, a majority of macroeconomists appeared to be skeptical of the use of countercyclical monetary or fiscal policy to combat routine fluctuations in employment and output.

A NEW SYNTHESIS

It may be that a new synthesis of the classical and Keynesian legacies is now emerging. The extreme classical economist would advocate no use of countercyclical policy; the extreme Keynesian (although not Keynes himself) would support activist "fine tuning." Faced with the Great Depression and the classical tradition against activism, most economists helped to swing the pendulum toward active, countercyclical policy. Faced with accelerating inflation in the 1960s and the 1970s — partly resulting from the activist pursuit of a low unemployment rate — many economists have swung the pendulum back toward the classical constant policy.

We can therefore draw the following conclusions:

▶ There is merit in the classical view that the economy often exhibits automatic stability and that — given policy lags, uncertainties, and political and institutional constraints — active, countercyclical policy may do more harm than good.

▶ There is also merit in the Keynesian view that it is possible for the economy to experience a severe fluctuation and for a severe recession to persist. In response to severe fluctuations in employment and output, the Keynesian remedy of active, countercyclical policy would be urgently needed and highly desirable.

Of course, compromise and synthesis do not necessarily produce the best result. Perhaps one legacy, if followed in its pure form, will prove more effective. Keep these competing legacies in mind as we consider the conduct of fiscal and monetary policy.

SUMMARY

1. The task of keeping the economy near its targeted inflation and unemployment rates is called *stabilization*. Stabilization policy is difficult to implement due to *uncertainty* and *political* and *institutional constraints*.

2. Two basic stabilization strategies are *constant policy* and *countercyclical (activist) policy*. Under constant policy, policymakers keep the policy instrument at a *constant value;* they do not attempt to adjust the value each year. By contrast, under countercyclical policy, policymakers adjust the policy instrument each year in an attempt to achieve the targeted constant inflation unemployment rate U_c and inflation rate p^*.

3. Neither a constant policy nor a countercyclical policy always produces a superior outcome. Under certain conditions, a countercyclical policy will result in more variation in total output Q away from its targeted value Q_c, compared to a constant policy; under other conditions, the reverse is true.

4. *Discretionary policy,* which requires action by policymakers, is affected by four *policy lags:* the *recognition lag*, the *legislative lag*, the *implementation lag*, and the *impact lag*. These lags are obstacles to successful discretionary, countercyclical policy and make *automatic fiscal stabilizers* particularly valuable.

5. Two kinds of uncertainty make the implementation of stabilization policy more difficult: *forecast uncertainty*, and *policy-instrument uncertainty*.

6. It is important for economists to assess the political and institutional constraints that are likely to affect the implementation of any economic policy. For example, if Congress and the President are more willing to provide fiscal *stimulus* than fiscal *restraint*, then such an *asymmetrical fiscal policy* may, over time, gradually increase the budget deficit.

7. In recent years, the Federal Reserve has demonstrated an ability to

conduct discretionary monetary policy *symmetrically*—to implement both contractionary and expansionary monetary policy, thereby providing restraint as well as stimulus.

8. According to one perspective, Congress and the President should be encouraged to adopt automatic, symmetrical fiscal policies (countercyclical or constant) but should be discouraged from implementing discretionary, countercyclical fiscal policy, except in the extreme emergency of a depression. If discretionary countercyclical policy is to be attempted, it should be implemented by monetary policy.

9. The key determinant in the choice of a stabilization policy is not the inherent *disturbability* of the economy (the frequency with which total output Q deviates from its targeted value of Q_c) but the inherent *stability* of the economy (the tendency of Q to return quickly to Q_c after a deviation). If the stability of the economy is low, it is more likely that countercyclical policy, enacted today, will help—rather than hurt—when its impact is felt in the future.

10. Low responsiveness of wage and price inflation to a rise in the unemployment rate results in low economic stability and makes countercyclical policy more desirable.

11. A compromise perspective would be to accept *classical* constant policy during normal, routine fluctuations in employment and output but to accept *Keynesian* countercyclical policy during severe fluctuations.

TERMS AND CONCEPTS

asymmetrical fiscal policy	implementation lag
automatic fiscal policy	institutional and political
automatic stabilizer	constraints
classical economists	Keynesian legacy
(monetarists)	legislative lag
classical legacy	policy instrument
constant policy	policy-instrument uncertainty
constant tax revenue ($T = T_0$)	policy lags
countercyclical (activist) policy	political asymmetry
discretionary fiscal policy	recognition lag
disturbability of the economy	smooth variation
fiscal restraint (contraction)	stability of the economy
fiscal stimulus (expansion)	stabilization
forecast uncertainty	stabilization policy
forecasting	symmetrical fiscal policy
impact lag	the coordination problem

QUESTIONS

8.1 In our three-equation model (1.30), (1.31), and (1.32), suppose that $C = 0.75(Q - T + R)$, $T = tQ$, $G = \$300$ billion, and $R = \$200$ billion. The targeted value of $Q_c = \$2,500$ billion, and the policy instrument is the tax rate t.

a. Find the value of t that will make $Q = \$2,500$ billion for $I = \$550$ billion. For $I = \$450$ billion. For $I = \$650$ billion.

b. Assume that each of the three values of I in (a) has a one-third chance of occurring. Complete the following table for the constant policy under the tax rate t that achieves the targeted value Q_c for $I = \$550$ billion:

Probability	1/3	1/3	1/3
I	450	550	650
Q	___	___	___

c. Suppose that policymakers implement a countercyclical policy based on the assumption that investment I will remain constant. In fact, however, this year's I is independent of last year's I. Complete the following table:

Probability	1/9	1/9	1/9	1/3	1/9	1/9	1/9
Q	___	___	___	___	___	___	___

d. Which is preferable: the countercyclical policy outcome shown in (c), or the constant policy outcome shown in (b)? Why?

e. Now suppose that this year's I does depend on last year's I. Specifically:

If last year's I was $\$450$ billion, then this year

Probability	1/2	1/2
I	450	550

If last year's I was $\$550$ billion, then this year

Probability	1/3	1/3	1/3
I	450	550	650

If last year's I was $\$650$ billion, then this year

Probability	1/2	1/2
I	550	650

Complete the following table:

Probability	2/18	3/18	8/18	2/18	3/18
Q	___	___	___	___	___

f. Which is preferable: the countercyclical policy outcome shown in (e), or the constant policy outcome shown in (b)? Why?

g. Suppose that a constant policy employs the value of t that achieves the targeted value Q_c for $I = \$450$ billion. Complete the following table:

Probability	1/3	1/3	1/3
I	450	550	650
Q	___	___	___

h. Which is preferable: the countercyclical policy outcome shown in (e), or the constant policy outcome shown in (g)? Why?

i. What conclusions can you draw from these examples?

8.2 Now consider policy-instrument uncertainty with $I = \$550$ billion. Assume that

$$C = C_a + c(Q - T + R)$$

True consumption function: $C = 0 + 0.75(Q - T + R)$

Policymakers' C function: $C = 330 + 0.60(Q - T + R)$

a. If $I = \$450$ billion is correctly forecast, what t is required to achieve $Q = \$2,500$ billion, according to the policymakers' C function?

b. Given the true consumption function, what level of Q will the t in (a) achieve?

c. If $I = \$650$ billion is correctly forecast, what t is required to achieve $Q = \$2,500$ billion, according to the policymakers' C function?

d. Given the true consumption function, what level of Q will the t in (c) achieve?

e. Under a constant policy with $t = 20\%$:

Probability	1/3	1/3	1/3
I	450	550	650
Q	___	___	___

f. Under a countercyclical policy:

Probability	1/3	1/3	1/3
I	450	550	650
Q	___	___	___

8.3 Suppose that expectations are inertial and the *SG* curve is perfectly flat; hence, a rise in the unemployment rate is assumed to cause no reduction in w and p. In period 0, the DG_0 and SG_0 curves intersect at $Q = Q_c$ and $p = 0\%$. If the adjusted nominal demand growth rate $\hat{y}$ becomes negative in period 1 but returns to its normal value of 0% in period 2, construct a $DG - SG$ diagram to show what happens to the economy.

8.4 If, instead, the *SG* curve is steep but all other assumptions in Question 8.3 hold, show what happens to the economy in the $DG - SG$ diagram.

9   Fiscal and Monetary Policy

In Chapter 8, we considered the basic obstacles that confront stabilization policy. Stabilization policy must be implemented by fiscal and/or monetary policy. In this chapter, we will examine the roles of fiscal policy and monetary policy in implementing stabilization policy and discuss how each policy should be designed and conducted.

9.1   Fiscal Policy

AUTOMATIC STABILIZERS

There is broad agreement among macroeconomists that automatic stabilizers play a useful role in stabilizing the economy. In Chapters 1 and 8, we emphasized the stabilizing effect of a tax system in which tax revenue T varies directly and automatically with total income Q.

In this section, we will expand our analysis of automatic stabilizers. First, we will explain why a *progressive* tax is more stabilizing than a *proportional* tax. Second, we will explain why certain transfer programs are automatic stabilizers.

Progressivity and Stability

We begin our comparison of a progressive and proportional tax with a definition:

Under a PROPORTIONAL TAX schedule (a "flat tax"), the tax rises at the same rate as a household's income, so that the ratio of tax to income remains constant as household income rises. Under a PROGRESSIVE TAX schedule, the tax rises more rapidly than a household's income, so that the ratio of tax to income rises as household income rises. Under a REGRESSIVE TAX schedule, the tax rises more slowly than a household's income, so that the ratio of tax to income declines as household income rises.

Consider three tax schedules—progressive, proportional, and regressive—with rates set so that they raise the same total tax revenue. From the definitions just given, it follows that

▶ The progressive tax raises a greater share of total tax revenue from high-income households and a smaller share from low-income households, compared to the proportional tax. The proportional tax raises a greater share of total tax revenue from high-income households and a smaller share from low-income households, compared to the regressive tax.

Should Congress make the income tax progressive, proportional, or regressive? The choice affects the degree of consumption inequality and the incentive to earn. But our interest here, is how the choice affects economic stability.

We will see that

▶ A progressive tax is more stabilizing than a proportional tax or a regressive tax.

Let's consider the case of extreme regressivity in which the tax stays constant as household income rises. (Note that "regressive" means that the tax rises more slowly than household income; in this extreme case, the tax does not rise at all as household income rises.) This extreme regressivity is actually a constant tax revenue policy, because tax revenue does not vary at all with income. In Chapter 1, we showed that a proportional (flat) tax with a tax rate t is more stabilizing than a constant tax revenue policy.

To carry this argument one step further, let's compare the proportional (flat) tax $T = tQ$ to a progressive tax and see how the economy would respond to the decline in I from $380 billion to $300 billion under the progressive tax.

Under the proportional tax, with $t = 25\%$, each household pays a tax equal to 25% of its income. For every household, each $100 of income is taxed $25. For the whole economy, when total income Q increases by $100 billion, T increases by $25 billion. When $Q = $2,200 billion for the economy, total tax revenue $T = $550 billion. The tax function for the economy is then $T = 0.25Q$.

Now suppose that a progressive tax replaces this proportional tax. For every household, the first $100 of income is taxed at a low tax rate; the second $100, at a somewhat higher rate; the third $100, at a still higher rate; and so on. The rates are set so that when total income for the economy $Q = $2,200 billion, total tax revenue $T = $550 billion (the same value under the proportional tax).

We must now distinguish between a household's *average tax rate* ATR and its *marginal tax rate* MTR:

The AVERAGE TAX RATE ATR is the ratio of a household's total tax to its total income (T/Q). Starting from that total income and that total tax, the MARGINAL TAX RATE MTR is the ratio of a (small) change in a household's tax to a (small) change in its income ($\Delta T/\Delta Q$).

▶ Under a proportional tax, the ATR for each household is the same as its MTR. Moreover, the ATR and the MTR are the same for all households in the economy.

For example, under a proportional tax with $t = 25\%$, if a household's total weekly income $Q = \$300$, its total tax $T = \$75$, so that its ATR = 25%. Starting from a weekly income of $300 and a weekly tax of $75, if a household's weekly income decreases by $10, its tax decreases by $2.50 (25%), so that its MTR is also 25%. However

▶ Under a progressive tax, the ATR for each household is less than the MTR for that household.

Why? Let's consider the average household with a weekly income of $300. Suppose that it is taxed 0% on its first $100, 25% on its second $100, and 50% on its last $100. For convenience, we will assume that if the household earned another $100, it would also be taxed 50% on that $100. This household therefore pays a total tax of $75 (0 + $25 + $50), and its ATR is 25% ($75/$300). But its MTR is 50%; if, for example, it lowers (or raises) its weekly income by $10, its tax will decrease (or increase) by $5, so that $\Delta T/\Delta Q = 50\%$.

Under a progressive tax, the tax rates must be set so that if $Q = \$2,200$ billion for the whole economy, then $T = \$550$ billion. Thus, the average household must have an ATR of 25%, as in our example. Low-income households will clearly have an ATR less than 25%; high-income households will have an ATR greater than 25%.

However, because each household's MTR exceeds its ATR, the average MTR of all households will clearly exceed 25%. For example, the average household has an ATR of 25% but an MTR of 50%. For convenience, let's assume that the average MTR of all households is 50%. This means that if there is a (small) change in the total income of the whole economy, then $\Delta T/\Delta Q = 50\%$.

The tax function for the economy under such a progressive tax might be

(9.1) $\qquad T = 0.5(Q - 1,100)$

If $Q = \$2,200$ billion, then

$$T = 0.5(2{,}200 - 1{,}100)$$
$$T = 550$$

If Q varies by \$100 billion, then T will vary by \$50 billion. For example, if Q declines to \$2,100 billion, then

$$T = 0.5(2{,}100 - 1{,}100)$$
$$T = 500$$

Thus, under the progressive tax, $\Delta T/\Delta Q = 0.50$ for the whole economy. By contrast, under the proportional tax, $\Delta T/\Delta Q = 0.25$ for the whole economy.

This progressive tax would cause equation (9.1) to replace $T = 0.25Q$. We can quickly see that with investment at its initial level of $I = \$380$ billion, the new tax function would, in fact, result in $Q = \$2,200$ billion. Substituting the new tax function into our three-equation system, we obtain

$$Q = C + I + G = C + 380 + 300$$
$$C = c(Q - T + R) = 0.8(Q - T + 250)$$
$$T = 0.5(Q - 1{,}100)$$

Substituting into the first equation

$$Q = 0.8[Q - 0.5(Q - 1{,}100) + 250] + 680$$
$$Q = 2{,}200$$
$$T = 0.5(2{,}200 - 1{,}100) = 550$$

Note that with $Q = \$2,200$ billion, $T = \$550$ billion, just as it did under the proportional tax. But now more tax is being paid by affluent households and less tax is being paid by low-income households.

If I declines to \$300 billion, then we repeat the same steps, except that $300 + 300 = 600$ (instead of 680) in the first equation:

$$Q = 0.8[Q - 0.5(Q - 1{,}100) + 250] + 600$$
$$Q = 2{,}067$$
$$T = 0.5(2{,}067 - 1{,}100) = 484$$

Recall the result under the proportional tax of 25%:

$$Q = 2{,}000$$
$$T = 500$$

Thus, under the progressive tax, Q declines by $133 billion (from $2,200 billion to $2,067 billion); under the proportional tax, Q declines by $200 billion (from $2,200 billion to $2,000 billion). Why?

Under the progressive tax, for each dollar that real output Q declines, the tax T declines by $0.50; under the proportional tax, T declines by only $0.25. In fact, even though Q declines by less under the progressive tax, T declines by more (from $550 billion to $484 billion, instead of from $550 billion to $500 billion).

▶ Compared to a proportional tax, a progressive tax results in a greater automatic reduction in the tax T (in response to the same decline in real output Q), a smaller decline in household *net* (disposable) income and consumer demand, and, therefore, a smaller decline in equilibrium output.

Under the progressive tax, the multiplier is $m = 1.7 \, (133/80)$; under the proportional tax $m = 2.5$. An automatic stabilizer is a policy that reduces the multiplier. Without any tax or with a constant tax revenue, the multiplier would be 5. Thus

▶ Compared to a proportional tax, a progressive tax is a more powerful automatic stabilizer because it causes a greater reduction in the multiplier m.

Transfers and Stability

Thus far, the tax system has been the only automatic stabilizer. But components of the *transfer system*—in particular, unemployment compensation and welfare—are also automatic stabilizers in most advanced economies, including that of the United States. We will now turn to the stabilizing effect of the transfer system.

To simplify our model, we have treated government transfers R as independent of total income Q. But it is important to recognize that this is not so in the actual economy. Transfers vary automatically with income. In contrast to tax revenue, which varies automatically in the same direction as income, transfers vary automatically in the opposite direction. For example, when Q declines in a recession, transfer payments for unemployment compensation and welfare automatically rise.

It is easy to see why this automatic variation is stabilizing. We have seen that when total income Q declines, the automatic decrease in tax revenue T is stabilizing because it cushions disposable household income, preventing it from declining as far and thereby limiting the decrease in consumer demand. Similarly

▶ When total income (output) declines, the automatic rise in government transfers R (such as unemployment compensation and welfare) is stabilizing because it reduces the decrease in net (disposable) household income and, hence, the decrease in consumer demand.

Let's illustrate this in our model. Previously, we set government transfers R at $250 billion, independent of total income Q. But now, just as we have a tax function, we need a *transfer function*, such as

(9.2) $R = 250 + 0.2(2,200 - Q)$

If Q = $2,200 billion, then clearly R = $250 billion. However, if Q falls below $2,200 billion, then R increases. In particular, if Q falls $100 billion below $2,200 billion, then R will increase by $20 billion. The *transfer rate* is therefore 0.2 (20%).

First, let's check that this transfer function will still result in Q = $2,200 billion if I = $380 billion. We follow the usual steps, but this time we use the transfer function for R instead of setting R at $250 billion, so that

$$Q = 0.8[Q - 0.25Q + 250 + 0.2(2,200 - Q)] + 380 + 300$$
$$Q = 2,200$$

Now what happens if I decreases from $380 billion to $300 billion? The steps are the same, except that $300 billion replaces $380 billion in the preceding equation, so that we obtain

$$Q = 2,057$$

Without the transfer system given by equation (9.2), Q declines by $200 billion (from $2,200 billion to $2,000 billion); with it, Q declines by only $143 billion (from $2,200 billion to $2,057 billion). The multiplier is reduced from m = 2.5 (200/80) to m = 1.79 (143/80). Thus

A TRANSFER SYSTEM reduces the multiplier m and is therefore an automatic stabilizer.

If the benefit per unemployed person is larger, then the transfer rate is greater (the transfer rate is 0.2 in our example). Why? When Q declines by a given amount, if the benefit per unemployed person is larger, then the automatic increase in transfers is greater to those who have become unemployed.

At a transfer rate of 0.3 instead of 0.2, we can calculate that Q will decline from $2,200 billion to $2,075 billion, instead of to $2,057 billion; the multiplier m = 1.56 (125/80), instead of 1.79 (143/80). Thus

▶ If the benefit per unemployed person is greater, then the transfer rate is larger, the multiplier m is smaller, and the stabilizing impact of the transfer system on the economy is greater.

Now that we see that a transfer system is an automatic stabilizer, this "demand-side" role can be weighed against the "supply-side" impact of transfer programs on the constant inflation unemployment rate U_c (discussed in Chapter 7). Recall that a decrease in unemployment compensation per recipient should reduce U_c, because unemployed persons are compelled to accept a job more quickly.

We now have an additional consideration — stabilization. An increase in unemployment compensation per recipient increases the stability of the economy. Thus, the positive contribution of the transfer system to stabilization must be weighed against its U_c-raising effect.

THE "NORMAL" OUTPUT SURPLUS OR DEFICIT (Q_c SURPLUS OR DEFICIT)

Suppose that the economy is initially at $Q = Q_c$ and that the government budget is balanced. Then a reduction in investment I moves the economy into a recession. As total income Q declines, tax revenue automatically falls and transfer expenditures automatically rise, so that the government budget automatically moves into deficit.

If the tax revenue and government expenditures were independent of total income, then a recession would not automatically convert a balanced budget into a deficit budget. But as we showed in Chapter 1, constant tax revenue and government expenditures would result in a less stable economy. The automatic decline in tax revenue and the automatic rise in transfer expenditures reduce the decrease in consumer demand and, therefore, in output. Thus, the automatic deficit due solely to a decline in output below the Q_c level is desirable, not undesirable.

Now suppose that the economy is once again at Q_c. But Congress cuts tax rates or raises government expenditures, so that if the economy remains at $Q = Q_c$, then the budget will run a deficit. Of course, a tax-rate cut or an expenditure increase will shift the IS curve to the right and raise the equilibrium level of output Q above Q_c. But suppose that monetary policy simultaneously tightens, shifting the LM curve to the left, so that Q stays at Q_c. The budget will then be in deficit at Q_c.

Now suppose that the Fed tightens monetary policy even further, so that the leftward shift of the LM curve more than offsets the rightward shift of the IS curve, moving the economy into a recession and further increasing the budget deficit.

It is useful to divide the budget deficit into two components: the *structural deficit* and the *cyclical deficit*.

The tax-rate and expenditure-rate changes by Congress would have resulted in a deficit even if Q had stayed at Q_c. The deficit that would have occurred at Q_c is called the STRUCTURAL DEFICIT or, alternatively, the *normal output deficit*, the Q_c *deficit*, or the *full-employment deficit*.

The automatic decline in tax revenue T and the automatic rise in transfer expenditures increase the budget deficit as Q declines below Q_c. This increase in the budget deficit that is solely due to the decline in Q below Q_c is called the CYCLICAL DEFICIT.

Comparing the Q_c deficit with the actual deficit provides useful information. In the first example, the budget would remain balanced if Q stayed at Q_c, so that the Q_c deficit would be 0; the actual budget deficit is solely due to the decline in Q below Q_c. Comparing the Q_c deficit of 0 to the actual budget deficit quickly tells us that the deficit is due solely to the recession.

By contrast, in the second example, the budget would run a deficit even if Q stayed at Q_c. When the economy goes into recession, the actual budget deficit is even larger. Some might claim that the deficit is solely due to the recession. But the existence of a Q_c deficit (although it is smaller than the actual deficit) refutes this claim.

Suppose that with the economy in recession, the Q_c deficit is $100 billion but the actual deficit is $150 billion. Then only $50 billion of the deficit is due to the recession; $100 billion would remain under current tax and government expenditure rates, even if Q were at Q_c.

Comparing the Q_c deficit with the actual deficit not only enables the cause of the deficit to be detected, but it also enables the impact of fiscal policy to be evaluated. If the budget moves from balance to an actual deficit, has fiscal policy moved in an expansionary direction? Not necessarily.

Fiscal policy moves in an expansionary direction when it shifts the *IS* curve to the right. It does so when it raises the expenditure rate or cuts the tax rate *at a given Q*. But this means that the Q_c deficit will increase (or the Q_c surplus will decrease). Thus, a change in the Q_c deficit or the Q_c surplus tells us whether fiscal policy has moved in an expansionary or a contractionary direction.

Suppose that the Q_c deficit (or surplus) remains constant (tax and government expenditure *rates* remain constant), but a decline in investment I throws the economy into a recession, so that the actual deficit increases. Then the increase in the actual deficit does not mean that fiscal policy has moved in an expansionary direction. The fact that the Q_c deficit (or surplus) is constant shows that it has not.

One problem with working with the Q_c deficit or surplus is that it must be estimated. First, the constant inflation unemployment rate U_c must be estimated, as we did in Chapter 6. Then the Q_c that would result at that U_c must be estimated. Finally, the tax revenue and government expenditures that would occur, given the current tax and government expenditure *rates*, must be estimated. All three steps involve some uncertainty, so that the estimated Q_c deficit or surplus will be sensitive to the methods used and to the assumptions made.

Fortunately, what matters most for stabilization is not the level of the Q_c surplus or deficit but how it changes from one year to the next. As long as the same methods and assumptions are used each year, the estimated *change* in the Q_c surplus or deficit should reveal which way fiscal policy has moved and why the actual deficit or surplus has changed.

Table 5.1 (page 207) presented an estimate of the Q_c deficit for the past two decades. The Q_c deficit or surplus is based on a U_c of 5.6% at the beginning of the period that rises gradually to a U_c of 7% at the end of the period. We can see that in the mid-1960s, an increase in the Q_c deficit helped to cause the increase in the nominal demand growth rate that generated the rise in inflation.

In the early 1980s, the economy went into a severe recession, even though the Q_c deficit increased in 1982. Because fiscal policy was moving in an expansionary direction, it was clearly tight monetary policy — not fiscal policy — that caused the recession. The *LM* curve must have moved further to the left than the *IS* curve moved to the right due to fiscal policy. The further increase in the Q_c deficit may, however, have helped to stimulate the recovery in 1983.

▶ To summarize, to judge the role of fiscal policy in moving the economy, it is crucial to focus on changes in the *normal* (constant inflation) output Q_c deficit or surplus rather than on changes in the *actual* budget deficit or surplus.

AUTOMATIC FISCAL POLICY

In this section, we will examine an *automatic fiscal policy* that is based on what we have learned in Chapters 1, 2, and 8.

At the end of Chapter 1, we concluded that

▶ It would be undesirable to require that the government budget *always* be balanced, because such an always-balanced budget rule would be destabilizing.

▶ A full-employment balanced budget rule would not be destabilizing; it would not require fiscal action that would worsen a recession.

▶ A full-employment *normally* balanced budget rule would not be destabilizing and would prescribe fiscal action that tries to keep the economy operating at the full-employment level of output.

According to this rule, if Q is on target this year, then government expenditures and the tax rate must be set so that the budget would be balanced next year if the economy is operating at the full-employment level of output Q. But if Q is below its targeted value this year, then government expenditures must be raised and/or the tax rate must be lowered to stimulate demand. If Q is above its targeted value this year, then government expenditures must be cut and/or the tax rate must be raised to restrain demand. The amounts by which government expenditures and the tax rate must be adjusted would be specified in a formula.

In Chapter 2, we studied the importance of the fiscal–monetary policy mix for the division of output between consumption C and investment I. To restate our discussion there:

> Suppose that a citizen favors a consumption–investment mix that requires a deficit of 0 (a balanced budget) when the economy is held at the full-employment level of output by an offsetting monetary policy. This citizen might support a full-employment normally balanced budget rule. Such a rule would, on average, tend to achieve the citizen's desired consumption–investment mix. It would also avoid destabilization and prescribe fiscal action that tries to keep the economy operating at the full-employment level of output.

Finally, in Chapter 8, we drew these conclusions concerning fiscal policy:

▶ Economists should assess the political and institutional constraints that are likely to affect the implementation of any economic policy.

▶ Thus, if discretionary, countercyclical fiscal policy is often used to expand demand but is seldom used to contract demand, then such asymmetrical fiscal policy may, over time, gradually increase the budget deficit.

▶ Automatic, symmetrical fiscal policy (countercyclical or constant) would be desirable, if it could be politically achieved.

In Chapter 8, we also saw that it is not clear whether countercyclical policy—even if implemented automatically and symmetrically—is superior to constant policy. We will therefore consider two rules for fiscal policy: a constant policy rule, and a countercyclical policy rule.

A Constant Policy Rule

Consider the following hypothetical statute proposal (or constitutional amendment):

> The President shall transmit to the Congress a budget for the coming fiscal year that is estimated to be balanced on the assumption that the economy will have a "normal" unemployment rate in that fiscal year. The "normal" unemployment rate shall be defined as the average unemployment rate in the preceding decade. The official estimate for the President's proposal shall be provided by the Office of Management and Budget (OMB).
>
> The Congressional Budget Resolution under the Congressional Budget Act of 1974 shall enact a budget for the coming fiscal year that is estimated to be balanced on the assumption that the economy will have a normal unemployment rate in that fiscal year. The official estimate for Congress' Budget Resolution shall be provided by the Congressional Budget Office (CBO).

The aim of this statute is to require that the *planned* Q_c deficit (structural deficit) be 0. As we explained in the last section, there is uncertainty about the value of U_c and, hence, about the value of Q_c. An approximation for U_c, which removes ambiguity, is the *average* unemployment rate over, say, the preceding decade.

The OMB provides technical analyses for the President; the CBO provides technical analyses for Congress. Once the CBO states that the estimated deficit is 0 on Congress' Budget Resolution, then the statute is fulfilled. The statute does not apply to the actual budget outcome, only to the official estimate.

This rule would avoid destabilization. Let's compare it to the proposal that requires the actual budget to always be kept balanced. If the economy goes into a recession, creating a cyclical deficit, then immediate action must be taken to raise the tax rate or to cut government expenditures. As we saw in Chapter 1, these actions would reduce total demand in the economy, making the recession worse. Hence, the always-balanced budget proposal is destabilizing. But the actual budget outcome is not subject to our proposed statute; it will never require any fiscal action. Hence, destabilization is avoided.

The statute does not depend on forecast accuracy. The OMB and the CBO do not forecast the unemployment rate. Rather, they estimate tax revenues and government expenditures based on the assumption that the unemployment rate will be normal (the average of the last decade).

Under the statute, the average actual deficit–GNP ratio over a decade should not deviate substantially from 0%. Moreover, the deviation is as likely to be negative as positive. The estimated structural deficit in this statute is based on the *normal unemployment rate* (the average of the unemployment rates over the last decade), not on the full-employment unemployment rate. Thus, OMB and CBO estimates focus on a realistic unemployment rate. Because the Q_c deficit–GNP ratio has been 5% in recent years, the statute should call for a gradual phase-in (for example, a 3% ratio in year 1, a 2% ratio in year 2, a 1% ratio in year 3, and a 0% ratio thereafter).

A Countercyclical Policy Rule

As we noted in Chapter 1, the constant policy rule avoids destabilization, but it prevents the adjustment of government spending and/or the tax rate to try to achieve the targeted $Q = Q_c$ for the coming fiscal year. In Chapter 8, we saw that it is not clear whether such an adjustment, even if it is automatic and symmetrical, would do more good than harm. If the adjustment is judged desirable, then the following hypothetical statute (or constitutional amendment) might be offered:

> The President shall transmit to the Congress a budget for the coming fiscal year that is estimated to achieve the "targeted" ratio of deficit to gross national product on the assumption that the economy will have a "normal" unemployment rate in that fiscal year. The "normal" unemployment rate shall be defined as the average unemployment rate in the preceding decade. The official estimate for the President's proposal shall be provided by the Office of Management and Budget (OMB).
>
> The "targeted" ratio of deficit to gross national product shall depend on the current unemployment rate:

> 1. If the current unemployment rate equals the normal unemployment rate, then the targeted ratio shall be 0%.
> 2. If the current unemployment rate is greater than the normal rate, then the targeted ratio shall be raised 0.5% for each 1% by which the current rate exceeds the normal rate.
> 3. If the current unemployment rate is less than the normal rate, then the targeted ratio shall be reduced by 0.5% for each 1% by which the normal rate exceeds the current rate.

> The Congressional Budget Resolution under the Congressional Budget Act of 1974 shall enact a budget for the coming fiscal year that is estimated to achieve the targeted ratio of deficit to gross national product on the assumption that the economy will have a normal unemployment rate in that fiscal year. The official estimate for Congress' Budget Resolution shall be provided by the Congressional Budget Office (CBO).

Under this statute, automatic fiscal policy would attempt to stabilize the economy—to move Q toward its targeted value of Q_c. For example, suppose that the economy is initially at the normal unemployment rate of 7% and that the budget is balanced. Then the economy falls into a recession, and the unemployment rate rises from 7% to 9%. This statute provides increased fiscal stimulus by raising the targeted structural deficit ratio from 0% to 1%. (Because the current unemployment rate exceeds the normal unemployment rate by 2%, the targeted ratio rises by 1%.) Symmetrically, if the economy overheats and the unemployment rate declines from 7% to 5%, then the targeted ratio declines from 0% to -1%, thereby decreasing fiscal stimulus.

The 2%-to-1% adjustment rule was chosen as follows. According to Okun's Law (page 260), a 2% rise in the unemployment rate implies a 4% decline in GNP. If the fiscal multiplier is assumed to be $m = 2$, then a 2% increase in the structural deficit ratio will be required to close the entire GNP gap.

Instead, our rule prescribes a 1% increase in the structural deficit ratio to close one-half of the GNP gap. Why only one-half of the gap? Recall our discussion of forecast uncertainty. If our forecast is uncertain, then it is better to attempt to close less than the expected GNP gap. Also, a countercyclical monetary policy could be implemented to close the remainder of the gap.

This adjustment rule is purely illustrative. Further study might improve the adjustment rule.

Several aspects of this countercyclical rule should be noted. First, no attempt is made to forecast what next year's unemployment rate will be or to estimate what fiscal stimulus is desirable based on this forecast. Instead, this year's (the "current") unemployment rate determines the fiscal stimulus.

In principle, it would be better to try to forecast next year's unemployment rate and to base the fiscal stimulus on this forecast. In practice, however, there are problems. First, would Congress and the President allow a technical agency (for example, the Congressional Budget Office) to decide the targeted structural deficit ratio (the fiscal stimulus)? In the past, despite the appeals of economists, Congress and the President have been reluctant to delegate the adjustment of tax or government expenditure rates to an independent agency. The preceding statute accepts this unfortunate political constraint.

Second, under the proposed statute, tax and government expenditure rates would be set prior to the beginning of the fiscal year and would therefore be fixed regardless of how the economy actually behaved during that year. For example, suppose that prior to the fiscal year, the current unemployment rate is normal, so that tax and government expenditure rates are set to achieve a targeted ratio of 0. But as the year begins, the economy falls into a severe recession. It would be too late, under the proposed statute, to adjust tax or expenditure rates for that fiscal year to provide immediate, additional stimulus.

A prompt, mid-year adjustment of tax or government expenditure rates might seem desirable, but it would also impose costs. For example, consider the tax system. When the budget is enacted prior to the start of the fiscal year, tax rates for the next year are set and households and business firms plan accordingly. If mid-year changes do occur, then planning becomes more difficult. Moreover, it is not clear how rapidly a change in tax withholding can be implemented. Firms must be given sufficient time to implement any change in withholding rates.

Although mid-year rate adjustments might therefore prove unfeasible and undesirable, it should be recognized that automatic stabilizers would work immediately. With a progressive tax system and a transfer system, stimulus is automatically and immediately provided as the unemployment rate rises above normal. Also, the budget for the coming fiscal year, based on the high current unemployment rate, would contain a positive structural deficit.

Constant Versus Countercyclical Policy

Is a constant or a countercyclical rule preferable? If an above-normal unemployment rate today makes it very likely that next year's unemployment rate will be above normal (in the absence of policy), then the countercyclical policy rule is probably preferable. If next year's unemployment rate (in the absence of policy) is independent of today's unemployment rate, then the constant policy rule is probably preferable.

It is useful to refer back to the unemployment rates given in Table 5.1 (page 207). The unemployment rates in any two adjacent years are *positively correlated*. For example, in 1982 and 1983, the unemployment rate was above normal; in 1967 and 1968, the unemployment rate was below normal. It is exceptional for the unemployment rate to move from below normal to above normal, or vice versa, in a single year.

▶ The positive correlation of adjacent-year unemployment rates implies that the countercyclical policy rule is probably superior to the constant policy rule.

The case for choosing the countercyclical policy statute is strengthened by the following consideration:

▶ It may be prudent to regard the choice between constant policy and countercyclical policy as permanent — to be maintained if the economy is operating normally or if it is in a depression. According to this viewpoint, a risk-averse citizen might choose countercyclical policy, whether or not it is inferior in a normal economy, because it guarantees stimulus in a depression.

The Balanced Budget Act of 1985

It is instructive to compare our two hypothetical statutes to the Balanced Budget and Emergency Deficit Control Act of 1985 (the Gramm – Rudman – Hollings Bill) that has actually been passed by Congress and signed by the President. The Balanced Budget Act prescribes a six-year phase down of the target deficit to achieve a balanced budget in fiscal year 1991. At the beginning of each fiscal year (October), the OMB and the CBO estimate the deficit that should be forthcoming, given the tax and government expenditure rates enacted by Congress. The General Accounting Office (GAO) averages the OMB and CBO estimates. If the GAO's projected deficit exceeds the prescribed target, then across-the-board expenditure cuts, estimated to achieve the targeted deficit, are mandated.

An important provision of the Balanced Budget Act is the "recession suspension." The Act requires a vote (which will presumably be positive) on a suspension of the targeted deficit for the coming year if the CBO or the OMB forecast negative real economic growth ($q < 0\%$) for the next two quarters. The Act also requires a vote (which will presumably be positive) on a mid-year suspension of that year's targeted deficit if the Department of Commerce reports that real economic growth has been less than 1% ($q < 1\%$) in the past two quarters.

The Balanced Budget Act will approximate our countercyclical statute if suspensions are voted during recessionary periods. Our statute prescribes an increase in the targeted deficit/GNP ratio in response to a projected recession (a high, "current" unemployment rate). With a recession suspension, the Balanced Budget Act will almost surely result in increased fiscal stimulus during a recession, because Congress and the President will undoubtedly take advantage of the suspension to increase spending or to cut taxes.

Our two hypothetical statutes do not address the problem of enforcement; they assume that Congress and the President will adopt a budget estimated to meet the targeted deficit. The Balanced Budget Act addresses enforcement. If Congress and the President do not enact a budget estimated to meet the targeted deficit, then across-the-board spending cuts are automatically mandated at the beginning of the fiscal year.

Under the political compromise embodied in the Act, Social Security, certain programs that assist the poor, and interest on the federal debt are exempt from these automatic spending cuts. One-half of the expenditure cuts are to be in defense programs and one-half are to be in nondefense programs.

▶ The Balanced Budget Act of 1985 is a new attempt to achieve deficit reduction without destabilizing the economy. Whether or not it will be successful remains to be seen.

9.2 Monetary Policy

THE INSTITUTIONAL AND POLITICAL FRAMEWORK

In our analysis of fiscal policy, we saw that discretionary policy implemented by Congress or the President would probably do more harm than good, except in response to very severe economic fluctuations.

Either the delay before action is taken would be substantial, or a political asymmetry would operate, biasing policy toward stimulus and against restraint. We concluded that the institutional and political framework favors automatic — but not discretionary — fiscal policy.

The Relative Insulation of the Fed

The institutional and political environment is more favorable to a discretionary, countercyclical monetary policy. The Federal Reserve's Open Market Committee (FOMC) meets monthly, and its decisions concerning open-market operations can be implemented almost immediately. This contrasts sharply with discretionary fiscal policy, which must be implemented by Congress; such action inevitably takes months to debate and several more months to implement.

The FOMC consists of the seven members of the Board of Governors of the Federal Reserve System, including the Chairman of the Fed, and the presidents of the twelve regional Federal Reserve Banks. Only five of the presidents vote on a rotating basis (except that the New York Fed president always votes), so that there are twelve voting members at any FOMC meeting. The FOMC is advised by a large staff of professional economists.

The FOMC is more insulated from popular pressure than Congress or the President. Much of the public is unaware of its existence or of its crucial role in economic policy. Moreover, members of the FOMC are not reelected every two, four, or six years. The seven members of the Board of Governors serve fourteen-year terms. The other five voting members are presidents of regional Federal Reserve Banks. The Chairman of the Fed is appointed by the President to a four-year term that does not coincide with the President's term of office.

Let's consider the Fed's behavior from late 1979 to the present. In response to roughly a 10% inflation rate that threatened to escalate even higher, the FOMC, led by Chairman Paul Volcker, committed itself to a tight monetary policy. The FOMC pledged to persist in this policy, even though it would temporarily generate very high interest rates, low credit availability, and a recession.

Volcker had been appointed chairman by President Carter, but this did not prevent the FOMC from permitting a significant rise in interest rates during the election year of 1980 (see Table 5.1, page 207). When President Reagan took office in 1981, the Fed nevertheless permitted interest rates to reach record levels, finally throwing the economy into the most severe recession it had experienced since the 1930s. As the recession deepened but before it succeeded in cutting inflation, public dismay with the economy was widespread and appeals were made to the President to reduce interest rates. The President, whom the public held responsible, was on the defensive. Yet relatively little pressure was exerted directly on the FOMC; the public was generally unaware of its role.

It is instructive to ask what would have happened if monetary policy had been directly controlled by Congress or by the President. Could the tight monetary policy of the early 1980s have been sustained long enough to achieve disinflation, given its very unpopular side effects (record high interest rates, then deep recession)?

To help answer the question, it is instructive to compare what happened to fiscal policy during the same period. Confronted with a 10% inflation rate that threatened to rise, Congress and the President significantly widened the normal output deficit, moving fiscal policy in an expansionary direction.

Thus, Congress and the President chose not to use fiscal policy to try to slow the nominal demand growth rate. A fiscal contraction is politically difficult to achieve, because cutting government spending and raising the tax rate generate significant opposition. Congress and the President, subject to reelection pressures, normally appear unwilling to undertake a fiscal contraction.

It seems hard to escape the conclusion that if monetary policy had also been placed in the hands of Congress or the President, the disinflation might never have occurred. The disinflation was apparent by the time President Reagan decided to reappoint Volcker as Chairman of the Fed. This episode is likely to strengthen the ability of the Fed to operate subject to far less political pressure than Congress or the President.

▶ Recent economic history suggests that the current institutional and political framework makes possible a discretionary, countercyclical monetary policy that largely overcomes the two shortcomings of discretionary fiscal policy: a lengthy decision lag, and a political bias against contractionary policy.

But is the current institutional framework desirable? The experience of the early 1980s appears to confirm the wisdom of the institutional insulation of monetary policy from immediate electoral pressures and from the governmental authorities that control spending and taxation.

This is not a new lesson. Economic history provides many examples of the temptation of governmental authorities to spend more than they tax and to print money to finance the deficits. Many citizens are aware of the importance of checks and balances among the legislative, executive, and judicial branches of government. But most citizens are unaware of the importance of checks and balances concerning the authority to spend and tax and the authority to control the money supply.

To a citizen who believes that important public policy should be legislated by officials who are subject to frequent reelection pressures, it should be sobering to review the disinflation of the early 1980s and to contrast the insulated Fed and the uninsulated Congress and Presidency. Such a citizen is inclined to ask: Shouldn't elected officials — or at least officials subject to prompt reelection pressures — directly control monetary policy?

The same question can be asked of the Supreme Court. Yet, the consensus is that it is better to insulate the high court from reelection pressures, implying that the general public should not be able to pressure those who may be charged with protecting the rights of citizens who express unpopular views. The same argument can be made for the Fed. The public should not be able to pressure those who may have to implement policies that are unpopular and impose hardship in the short run in order to preserve a more stable economy in the long run.

The case for *insulation* is enhanced by recalling our discussion of hyperinflation in Chapter 5. There, we noted that virtually every historical *hyperinflation* — an inflation that accelerates out of control — has occurred when the governmental authority that sets expenditures also has the power to print money and expand the money supply. When political resistance makes it difficult or impossible for the monetary authority to raise taxes to match desired government expenditures, the authority prints new money to finance the deficit.

Insulation surely reduces the chance of hyperinflation. Congress and the President set expenditures and taxes, but they do not have the power to print money to finance a deficit that they create. The independent Fed can refuse to print new money to buy the Treasury's bonds; it can refuse to inject new money into the economy to finance the deficit. The Treasury is then forced to borrow from the public. A monetary expansion does not necessarily follow a widening of the budget deficit.

A Rule Versus Discretion

Although most analysts support insulation of the Fed, some would want to go further. Not only must monetary policy be protected from electoral pressures and from the authorities that spend and tax, but it must also be protected from the members of the FOMC. Why?

Two opposite arguments can be advanced to support this view. The first holds that FOMC members are still subject to excessive pressure; insulation is *ineffective*. This view seems to be supported by the gradual rise in the money-supply growth rate and in the inflation rate in the 1960s and 1970s, with such episodes as the monetary expansion in the 1972 election year (then Fed Chairman Arthur Burns had been appointed by President Nixon, who was seeking reelection). But the Fed's conduct in the early 1980s weakens this criticism.

The opposite argument is that insulation is *effective* and that excessive power is now concentrated in the hands of persons who can use it

which it contended was consistent with the targeted short-run interest rate.

But in October 1979, the FOMC decided to focus primarily on achieving its money-growth target in the short run, even at the expense of fluctuations in interest rates. The Fed would no longer try to peg the federal funds rate in the short run.

Some analysts and participants claim that the October 1979 decision was only a change in emphasis — not a major turning point. All observers agree that the FOMC did move toward money-growth targeting and away from interest-rate targeting.

Why did this change of emphasis occur? In late 1979, the inflation rate rose to nearly 10%, resulting in overwhelming public sentiment for strong action to control inflation. For many years, monetarist economists had been emphasizing the long-run relationship between the money-growth rate and the inflation rate and insisting that disinflation would follow a consistent, disciplined effort to reduce money growth. Virtually all macroeconomists — monetarist and nonmonetarist — agree that economies with a high inflation rate almost always have a high money-growth rate and that economies with a low inflation rate almost always have a low money-growth rate. With inflation as its number-one priority, the Fed shifted toward money-growth targeting.

From Table 5.1 (page 207), it is clear that the FOMC's decision did significantly reduce the stability of interest rates, which fluctuated much more sharply after 1979. Ironically, the FOMC's decision did not result in a more stable money-growth rate. The Fed "let go" of the interest rate, but it did not hit the targeted money-growth rate with much accuracy.

We can use our *IS–LM* diagram to analyze the choice between a money-growth target and an interest-rate target.* Note that a particular level of the money supply M in this period, given last period's money supply, implies a particular money-growth rate m. In the *IS–LM* diagram, however, it is more convenient to focus on M than on m.

Suppose that the Fed wants to achieve $Q = Q^*$. (Assume that the Fed must set either the interest rate or the money-growth rate first; only later does it learn the positions of the *IS* and *LM* curves and, hence, the real output Q that results.)

Consider these two possibilities:

1. The Fed knows the position of the *IS* curve, because goods demand is stable. The Fed does not know the position of the *LM* curve that will result from a given money supply, because money demand is unstable.

---

* See William Poole, "Optimal Choice of Monetary Policy Instruments in a Simple, Stochastic Macro Model," *Quarterly Journal of Economics* (May 1970).

2. The Fed knows the position of the *LM* curve that will result from a given money supply, because money demand is stable. The Fed does not know the position of the *IS* curve, because goods demand is unstable.

Let's examine each possibility in turn.

1. In this case, shown in Figure 9.1, the position of the *IS* curve is known, so that achieving the interest rate r* results in Q*. The money supply should be adjusted until the *LM* curve intersects the *IS* curve at r*. If, instead, the Fed sets a targeted money supply M*, then since the resulting position of the *LM* curve is not known (due to money-demand instability), the *LM* curve could turn out to be LM_H (right of) or LM_L (left of) the expected LM^e curve and Q could therefore turn out to be Q_H (higher) or Q_L (lower) than Q*. Hence, an interest-rate target is superior to a money-growth target.

FIGURE 9.1 MONETARY POLICY WHEN MONEY DEMAND IS UNSTABLE

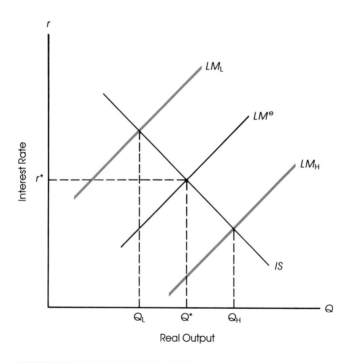

The position of the *IS* curve is known, because goods demand is stable. If the money supply is adjusted so that the *LM* curve intersects the *IS* curve at r*, then Q* will result. However, if a targeted money supply M* is set, instead, then due to money demand instability, the *LM* curve could turn out to be LM_H (resulting in Q_H) or LM_L (resulting in Q_L). Hence, an interest-rate target is superior.

2. In this case, as Figure 9.2 shows, the position of the *IS* curve is un-known due to goods demand instability. Although it is expected to be *IS^e*, the *IS* curve could turn out to be *IS$_H$* or *IS$_L$*. Under an interest-rate target, the Fed adjusts the money supply until the *LM* curve intersects the *IS* curve at *r**. With *IS$_H$*, *LM$_H$* is required, resulting in *Q$_H$*; with *IS$_L$*, *LM$_L$* is required, resulting in *Q$_L$*.

For a targeted money supply, since money demand is stable, the position of the *LM* curve is known. With *IS$_H$*, *Q$_h$* results; with *IS$_L$*, *Q$_l$* results. Since *Q$_h$* is less than *Q$_H$* and *Q$_l$* is greater than *Q$_L$*, a money-growth target would cause less variation in *Q* than an interest-rate target. Hence, a money-growth target is superior to an interest-rate target.

FIGURE 9.2 MONETARY POLICY WHEN GOODS DEMAND IS UNSTABLE

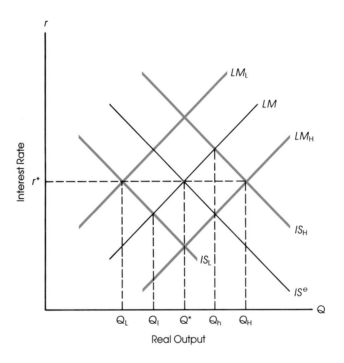

The position of the *IS* curve is unknown, due to goods demand instability. Although it is expected to be *IS^e*, the *IS* curve could turn out to be *IS$_H$* or *IS$_L$*. Under the interest-rate target, the money supply is adjusted so that the *LM* curve intersects the *IS* curve at *r**. With *IS$_H$*, *LM$_H$* is required, resulting in *Q$_H$*; with *IS$_L$*, *LM$_L$* is required, resulting in *Q$_L$*. For a targeted money supply, since money demand is stable, the position of the *LM* curve is known. With *IS$_H$*, *Q$_h$* results; with *IS$_L$*, *Q$_l$* results. Hence, the money-growth target causes less variation in *Q* than the interest-rate target.

Are we more confident of the accuracy and stability of goods demand (and the *IS* curve) or money demand (and the *LM* curve)? The answer may vary over time.

In the mid-1960s, the *IS* curve shifted right due to a fiscal expansion (military spending for the Vietnam War after an earlier tax cut). Interest rates moved up. An interest-rate target would have required the Fed to reinforce the fiscal expansion with a monetary expansion, further overheating the economy. Some analysts believe that the Fed actually did raise the money-growth rate in an effort to peg the interest rate.

Thus, it can be argued that an interest-rate target in the mid-1960s may have caused money growth in response to a fiscal expansion, initiating a sharp rise in *Q* and an acceleration of inflation. By contrast, a money-growth target might have avoided the acceleration of inflation.

In recent years, financial innovation and deregulation have made the *LM* curve more unstable. Some economists believe that the *LM* curve currently may be less reliable than the *IS* curve. If so, then focusing more on interest-rate targets may have merit. Other economists claim that the *LM* curve is still more stable than the *IS* curve, so that money-growth targets will still produce better results.

Political and Popular Constraints

Two arguments for targeting *money aggregates* instead of interest rates deserve consideration. The first concerns political pressure. Voters and members of Congress can quickly decide whether they consider a particular interest rate to be "too high." If a rise in the interest rate were required, such a target might generate pressure on the FOMC to retreat. The FOMC might prove willing to set a lower interest-rate target but unwilling to set a higher one. Thus, interest-rate targeting could create a bias in monetary policy toward stimulus and away from restraint.

This argument is very similar to the one made earlier against discretionary fiscal policy (Congress and the President could prove more willing to cut than to raise taxes). Given the long terms of its members, the Fed should be less subject to political pressures than Congress. Still, it may be true that the Fed can accomplish restraint more easily under a money-growth target than under an interest-rate target.

As an example, consider the disinflation in the early 1980s. The money-growth rates and the interest rates in the early 1980s appear in Table 5.1 (page 207). Given the initially high inflation rate of roughly 10%, the Fed needed to generate a 20% interest rate to provoke a severe recession and accomplish disinflation. But under its money-growth target, the Fed stated that its goal was to reduce money growth several percentage points over several years. The effects of this strategy on interest rates and employment were not made clear and therefore generated less opposition. If the Fed had explicitly stated that its interest-rate target was 20%, there might have been severe political opposition. Thus, money-aggregate targets may help to avoid the bias toward stimulus—and against restraint—that plagues discretionary fiscal policy.

The second argument in support of money-aggregate targeting concerns the widespread confusion among the public between real and nominal interest rates. In Chapter 5, we asserted that investment demand I—and therefore the total demand for goods and services—should depend on the expected real interest rate i^e (the nominal interest rate r minus the expected inflation rate p^e). Thus, the same volume of investment demand I should occur at an r of 3% when $p^e = 0\%$ as occurs at an r of 13% when $p^e = 10\%$ (as explained in Chapter 12).

Thus, the tightness of monetary policy cannot be gauged by the nominal interest rate r without considering the expected inflation rate p^e. Again, consider the disinflation in the early 1980s. Beginning at a 10% inflation rate, the nominal interest rate needed to be raised to 20% to achieve a real interest rate of 10%. A nominal rate of 12%—although it would have seemed high to the public—would have been no tighter than a 2% nominal rate at a 0% inflation rate.*

Thus, when much of the public focuses only on the nominal interest rate, it may be politically difficult to raise the real interest rate to the required level. Thus, the disinflation in the early 1980s would have been very difficult to achieve under nominal interest-rate targets for two reasons. First, a sharp rise in the interest rate was required to generate a severe recession. Second, because the economy began at a 10% inflation rate, the nominal rate needed to reach 20% to achieve a real rate of 10%.

Of course, as tight monetary policy is being implemented, it is evident to the public that the nominal interest rate has been raised to a high level. But the FOMC can claim to the public that it is committed to achieving a money-growth target, not an interest-rate target per se. Some observers believe that this distinction does reduce the political pressure on the FOMC and makes it more willing to apply monetary restraint.

Complexity and Discretion

Given the pros and cons of each kind of target, it should be evident that a case can be made for the use of both interest-rate and money-growth targets. If both targets cannot be achieved simultaneously, then the Fed will compromise. Instead of trying to hit one target, regardless of what

---

* Tax rules such as the deductibility of interest must also be considered when evaluating the impact of a given nominal interest rate on investment demand and, hence, on the tightness of monetary policy.

happens to the other, it would monitor both. It might assign equal or unequal weights to the two targets, depending on the economic period and its degree of confidence in each.

The Fed can watch other targets as well. As described in Chapter 13, there are several monetary aggregates (M1, M2, and so on) and several interest rates (r_1, r_2, and so on). Measures of credit and debt, according to some researchers, could also prove superior to money-growth or interest-rate targets. Thus, the Fed may monitor many targets and try to spread the discrepancy among all of them, instead of focusing on one or a few targets to the exclusion of the rest.

▶ If the Fed decides to watch several targets, weighing each according to the period and circumstances, then it would be too difficult to write a rule to cover such a complex task. Monetary policy could only be implemented at the discretion of the FOMC and its technical staff.

THE USE OF AN ECONOMETRIC MODEL FOR COUNTERCYCLICAL MONETARY POLICY

Macroeconomists who advocate countercyclical monetary policy believe that it is possible to forecast with sufficient accuracy to make the continuous adjustment of monetary policy stabilizing and therefore desirable. Many of these economists argue that we can achieve sufficiently accurate forecasting by building an *econometric model* to guide the implementation of discretionary, countercyclical monetary policy. In this section, we will explain how an econometric model is constructed and how it can be used to guide monetary policy. We will also consider a fundamental critique against the use of an econometric model for policymaking.

We began the construction of an econometric model in Chapter 2, when we built our six-equation *IS–LM* system. In Chapter 3, we added a simple supply equation to the demand equation to tentatively complete our model. In Part 2, we refined our supply equation with a deeper analysis of wage–price behavior; in Appendix 6A, we then constructed several equations to describe this behavior. In Chapters 12 and 13, we will refine our understanding of consumption, investment, and money demand; these refinements can be used to expand and complicate the *IS–LM* system of equations.

When all of these equations are combined, the result is a complete macroeconomic model. But what is needed to make it an *econometric* model? In Chapter 6, we described how econometric (statistical) technique is applied to actual data generated by the U.S. economy to estimate the numerical values of h and U_c in the wage equation $\Delta w = h(U_c - U)/U$. This same technique can be applied to all behavioral relationships in a macroeconomic model.

Consider our *IS–LM* system, described in Chapter 2. In each equation, for the purpose of illustration, we used particular numerical values for each behavioral parameter. To describe the real economy with some empirical accuracy, however, these values should be obtained by statistical analysis of the data.

An ECONOMETRIC MODEL is an economic model that obtains the numerical value of each parameter through the statistical analysis of actual data.

For example, consider the consumption function

$$(1.31) \qquad C = C_a + c(Q - T + R)$$

Our basic assumption is that there are "true" values of C_a and c that apply to the whole sample. How do we estimate these numerical values of C_a and c? Suppose that we use a sample of U.S. data from the past 20 years. We then observe variations in net income $(Q - T + R)$ and in consumption C. If we assign a single numerical value to C_a and a single numerical value to c for the whole sample, then the equation will predict a particular value for C in each year that can be compared to its actual value. The discrepancy between the prediction and the actual value in period t is the *error* in period t.

The best estimates of the "true" values of C_a and c will be the values that make the errors between their predicted and actual values as small as possible. A computer can find the values of C_a and c that minimize the errors for the sample (more precisely, that minimize the sum of the squares of the errors).

The Role Played by Policy Lags

Our policy problem now compels us to focus on an aspect that we have ignored until this point — the *lag structure*. In our equations, we have simply written that consumption varies with net income, or that investment varies with the interest rate, or that real money demand varies with real income and the interest rate.

But how quickly do these variations occur? Let's reconsider our consumption function. Statistical investigation has generally found that consumption in the current quarter is influenced by net income in several previous quarters. To simplify, we will assume that this quarter's consumption depends partly on this quarter's net income and partly on last quarter's net income.

How can we indicate that consumption in quarter t depends not only on net income in quarter t but also on net income in quarter $t - 1$? Suppose that X is an economic variable, like consumption C or net income $Q - T + R$, and let X_t indicate the value of X in quarter t and X_{t-1} denote the value of X in quarter $t - 1$. Then our new consumption function is expressed

$$(9.3) \qquad C_t = C_a + c(Q - T + R)_t + c_1(Q - T + R)_{t-1}$$

For example, if this quarter's consumption is influenced equally by this quarter's net income and last quarter's net income, then c and c_1 would have the same value.

Econometric technique can be used to estimate the lag structure that fits the data best. If only this quarter's net income influences this quarter's consumption, then the computer will discover that $c_1 = 0$ best fits the data. This term would therefore drop out of equation (9.3) and only this quarter's net income would remain in the consumption function.

In practice, however, in a quarterly econometric model, which uses quarterly data for each variable, the computer rarely finds that lagged variables are not influential. Lagged variables are important in almost all relationships, and virtually every econometric model of the economy is characterized by many lagged variables. Let's consider the implications for our policy problem.

Suppose that the Fed increases its purchases of bonds in the open market, thereby raising high-powered money (the monetary base) H in the economy. There may be a lag before this action reduces interest rates and another lag before it fully influences investment and consumption.

To be more concrete, suppose that a change in H in quarter 1 reduces the nominal interest rate r in quarter 1 and again in quarter 2. This, in turn, raises investment (and GNP) in quarters 2 and 3. In our consumption function, $Q - T + R$ will increase in quarters 2 and 3.

Then C will increase in quarter 2 due to the increase in $Q - T + R$ in quarter 2, and C will increase in quarter 3 due to the immediate effect of the increase in $Q - T + R$ in quarter 3 and the lagged effect of the increase in $Q - T + R$ in quarter 2. In quarter 4, even if $Q - T + R$ is the same as it is in quarter 3, C will increase further due to the lagged effect of the increase in $Q - T + R$ in quarter 3.

Let's see how this works in an example. Suppose that $Q - T + R = \$1,000$ billion in both quarter 0 and quarter 1; $Q - T + R$ then increases by \$100 billion to \$1,100 billion in quarter 2 and by another \$100 billion to \$1,200 billion in quarter 3; in quarter 4, $Q - T + R$ remains at \$1,200 billion. If $C_a = 0$, $c = 0.4$, and $c_1 = 0.4$, then

$$\begin{aligned} C_1 &= 0.4(Q - T + R)_1 + 0.4(Q - T + R)_0 \\ &= (0.4)(1,000) + (0.4)(1,000) \\ &= 800 \end{aligned}$$

$$C_2 = 0.4(Q - T + R)_2 + 0.4(Q - T + R)_1$$
$$= (0.4)(1,100) + (0.4)(1,000)$$
$$= 840$$
$$C_3 = 0.4(Q - T + R)_3 + 0.4(Q - T + R)_2$$
$$= (0.4)(1,200) + (0.4)(1,100)$$
$$= 920$$
$$C_4 = 0.4(Q - T + R)_4 + 0.4(Q - T + R)_3$$
$$= (0.4)(1,200) + (0.4)(1,200)$$
$$= 960$$

When lags pervade virtually every equation of an econometric model, the impact of a change in monetary policy will clearly reflect these lags. Let's consider an example.

In Chapter 3, we set the nominal money supply M at a particular value ($500 billion) and then solved our equations to find the values of real output Q ($2,200 billion) and the price level P (1.00) that would result in our model. We then set the nominal money supply at a different value ($600 billion) and again solved our equations (assuming inertial expectations) to find the values of Q ($2,271.4 billion) and P (1.018). Thus, a change in M results in a change in Q and P.

In an econometric model, there are usually more equations and many lagged variables. It remains true that if we change M_t (the value of M in quarter t), we will change Q_t (the value of Q in quarter t) and P_t (the value of P in quarter t). Now, however, the lags that appear in many of the behavioral equations of the model will influence the relationship between M_t and Q_t or P_t. In practice, the computer is assigned the task of solving for Q_t and P_t, given the numerical value of M_t.

To detect the role of lagged variables, we will compare the paths of Q_t and P_t, given two alternative paths for M_t. Under the first path for M_t (the "control solution"), we will set M_t equal to $500 billion in all quarters. Under the second path for M_t (the "disturbed solution"), we will set M_t equal to $600 billion in quarter 1 but equal to $500 billion in all subsequent quarters.

The computer is assigned the task of solving, quarter by quarter, for Q_t and P_t, given M_t. Obviously, in quarter 1, the computer will find values of Q_1 and P_1 for the control solution and higher values of Q_1 and P_1 for the disturbed solution.

Due to lags, the same will also be true in quarter 2, even though M_2 is the same in both cases. Why? Consider the consumption function with lags, given by equation (9.3). In quarter 1, $Q - T + R$ is higher under the disturbed solution than it is under the control solution. Therefore, consumption in quarter 2 is higher under the disturbed solution, because C_2 is affected by $(Q - T + R)_1$ according to equation (9.3). The values of Q_3 and P_3 will also differ under the control solution and the disturbed solution due to lagged effects. Only after many quarters will the solutions become identical and the lagged effects finally vanish.

If there were no lags, then the computer would find that the control and disturbed solutions only differ in quarter 1. Q_2 and P_2 would be the same under both control and disturbed solutions; similarly, Q and P would be the same for all subsequent quarters. Let's focus on nominal GNP Y ($Y = PQ$). If we plotted the difference between the disturbed solution and the control solution in each quarter with no lags, then we would find that a difference exists only in quarter 1, the quarter in which the nominal money supply M differs. The graph would tell us that there is no lag, because the two solutions would be identical in all subsequent quarters.

But in an actual econometric model with lags, our graph looks different, as shown in Figure 9.3. We observe a difference between the disturbed and control values of nominal GNP Y — not only in quarter 1, but in subsequent quarters — until the lagged effects completely vanish.

Given a change in monetary policy, in standard econometric models, the difference between disturbed and control solutions builds up over several quarters, reaches a peak, then declines, and eventually converges to 0 (see Figure 9.3). However, it is important to note that the impact does begin almost immediately; the solutions differ even in the first quarter.

This brings us to the concept of a *dynamic multiplier*. In Chapter 1, we defined the *multiplier* as the ratio of the change in real output Q to the change in investment demand that precipitated it. We will now broaden the concept of a multiplier in two ways. First, we need to distinguish between an *endogenous* variable and an *exogenous* variable.

The value of an ENDOGENOUS VARIABLE is determined *within* the model; the model is used to solve for its value.

The value of an EXOGENOUS VARIABLE is determined *outside* the model.

Then

A MULTIPLIER is the ratio of the change in an *endogenous* variable to the change in an *exogenous* variable that precipitated it.

If the endogenous variable is real output Q and the exogenous variable is any component of autonomous demand (such as I_a), then our new, broader definition is consistent with our old definition of a multiplier. But now, for example, we can also consider the multiplier of nominal GNP Y (an endogenous variable) with respect to the nominal

FIGURE 9.3 THE LAGGED IMPACT OF MONETARY POLICY

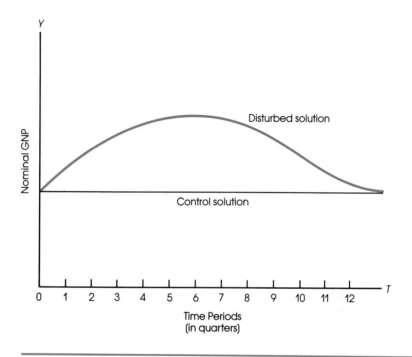

Under the "control solution," the nominal money supply M is held constant at $500 billion in all quarters. Under the "disturbed solution," the nominal money supply M is set at $600 billion in quarter 1 but at $500 billion in all subsequent quarters. In quarter 1, nominal GNP Y is higher under the disturbed solution than it is under the control solution. This gap persists (in fact, widens) in quarter 2, even though M is the same ($500 billion), due to the lagged impact of the higher M in quarter 1. The gap reaches a peak in several quarters; it is eventually eliminated when the lagged impact disappears.

money supply M (an exogenous variable)—that is, the ratio of the change in nominal GNP to the change in the nominal money supply.

A *dynamic multiplier* considers the time pattern of impact. For example, if the nominal money supply is changed only in the first quarter, then nominal GNP will change in the first quarter and in subsequent quarters due to lagged effects.

A DYNAMIC MULTIPLIER indicates the change in the endogenous variable in quarter $t + n$ in response to a change in the exogenous variable in quarter t.

Note that the change in the endogenous variable in quarter $t + n$ is always measured as the difference between its value under the disturbed solution and its value under the control solution in quarter $t + n$.

One important contribution of an econometric model is that it provides estimates of dynamic multipliers for monetary and fiscal policy instruments. What conclusion can we draw? According to estimates of dynamic multipliers from prominent econometric models, a change in monetary policy in quarter 1 will have some impact in quarter 1 but will also have an impact in subsequent quarters. In fact, the impact builds to a maximum in roughly four to eight quarters, as shown in Figure 9.3.

One monetary policy strategy is to try to hit the GNP target next quarter without worrying about the impact in future quarters. For example, suppose that GNP growth is forecast to be too low next quarter if the money-supply growth rate is kept normal at $m = q_c - v$. Then the Fed can increase the money supply this quarter by an amount that, according to the model, will hit the nominal GNP growth target next quarter. This will build to an excessive impact in later quarters if no other action is taken. But the Fed, in subsequent quarters, can reduce the money-supply growth rate below normal, thereby producing the mirror image of the first impact and tending to cancel its impact in later quarters.

But this might prove to be a tricky, even unsustainable strategy. Further investigation shows that for certain lag patterns and shocks to the economy the Fed seeks to offset, the strategy may require ever-widening gyrations in the money-supply growth rate to cancel undesired lag effects. Unfortunately, the problem is complicated, and it is unlikely that we can determine, with great confidence, whether the offsetting strategy is feasible.

▶ The Fed should consider the *lagged impact* of its actions as it weighs how aggressively to pursue next quarter's target.

The Controversy Over Econometric Models

Should monetary policy depend on an econometric model for guidance? A review of the evolution of econometric models provides background for the current controversy.

Early pioneers in the development of the econometric model were Jan Tinbergen in the late 1930s and Lawrence Klein in the late 1940s. The first models contained only a small number of equations and variables and were based on annual data. As work continued, the models grew in size and complexity and often made use of quarterly data. In the early decades, econometric models were used primarily by academic economists for research purposes and by government agencies for forecasting and policy development.

But by the 1960s, it had become apparent to some model builders that private firms would be willing to pay for the insights of an econometric model — particularly a model that could describe not only the economy as a whole but also specific industries within the economy. Thus, several new corporations were formed to sell commercial services to private firms.* Although the Federal Reserve benefits from these and other econometric models, it also relies heavily on its own MPS model (originally developed by economists at the Fed, MIT, the University of Pennsylvania, and the Social Science Research Council).

The degree of accuracy of these models is the subject of much controversy. Why is there room for so much difference of opinion among professional economists concerning model accuracy? It may seem straightforward to compare published forecasts with actual data and to judge model accuracy by the size of the discrepancies observed, but the issue is more complex.

Even a model that performs perfectly accurately in every equation, so that its equations exactly reflect the behavior of the economy, still will not result in completely accurate forecasts. To forecast nominal GNP for next quarter accurately, the model user must insert correct values for all exogenous variables, such as the monetary base H, the tax rate t, and government expenditures $G + R$. (The link between the monetary base H and the money supply M will be discussed in Chapter 13.) But the values of these variables depend on what policymakers will do.

Thus, even if the model is perfectly accurate, if the model user is a poor forecaster of the values of the exogenous variables, then the model will give a poor forecast for nominal GNP. Inaccurate forecasts do not necessarily mean that the model itself is inaccurate; exogenous variables may be hard to forecast accurately.

We can examine model accuracy by assuming that the exogenous variables have been forecast correctly and comparing the model forecast with actual data. This is accomplished by inserting the actual values of the exogenous variables into the model, instead of the forecast values. Of course, even when this is done, no model is perfectly accurate. Every behavioral equation of every model inevitably simplifies reality and excludes factors that have an impact in various quarters. Also, some equations may embody an incorrect hypothesis and include variables that are not the true causal agents.

In a fundamental critique of the use of an econometric model for policy evaluation, Robert Lucas of the University of Chicago, a propo-

---

* Today, the leading econometric-model corporations are DRI (Data Resources Incorporated), founded by Otto Eckstein of Harvard; WEFA (Wharton Econometric Forecasting Associates), founded by Lawrence Klein of the University of Pennsylvania; and CHASE (Chase Econometric Associates, Inc.), founded by Michael Evans, a former protégé of Klein who has since left CHASE to head Evans Econometrics.

nent of the rational expectations hypothesis, argues that a change in policy strategy—in the "policy regime"—may change behavioral relationships. Thus, an econometric model fitted to data generated under an old policy regime would yield incorrect answers if the policy strategy changes.

Our "game of strategy" analysis in Chapter 5 illustrates this critique. Suppose that demand management strategy has been lax. An econometric model, fitted to data generated under this lax policy regime, might contain a wage equation that implies a constant inflation unemployment rate U_c of 7% and a relatively modest response of the wage inflation rate w to a rise in the unemployment rate U. If the policy regime now becomes disciplinary and the new stance is publicized effectively, we know that the U_c for the economy may decline and w may become more responsive to a rise in U. The econometric model based on past data would not capture this change in the "policy regime."

Even most model builders concede that there is some validity to this basic critique. The issue is whether the problem raised by the critique is important only in certain equations under certain conditions, so that it serves as a useful warning, or whether it is pervasive and renders the model useless in most policy analyses.

The recent forecasting records of leading econometric models has been mixed. Most models did not forecast the recession of the early 1980s until shortly before it began, generally underestimated its depth, and were premature in forecasting recovery. It would be useful for economists to determine how much of this forecast inaccuracy was due to model inaccuracy and how much was due to inaccurate forecasting of the exogenous variables.

An episode of large forecasting errors often broadens our understanding of the economy and stimulates improvement in the econometric model. Let's consider an example of such a learning experience—the acceleration of inflation in the 1960s.

In the mid-1960s, leading econometric models generally contained wage equations that embodied the old Phillips curve, which graphed the relationship of a particular, stable level of the wage inflation rate w to a particular unemployment rate U. At that time, it was not generally recognized that the wage inflation rate w is also dependent on the expected price inflation rate p^e, which is usually equal to last period's actual price inflation rate p.

But the acceleration of inflation in the late 1960s in response to a steady unemployment rate in the 3–4% range, showed econometric modelers that their wage equation was inaccurate. At a roughly constant unemployment rate, the wage inflation rate became higher each year. What was missing from the wage equation was last year's price inflation rate. When this variable was added, the wage equation fit the data much more accurately. The new wage equation, embodying the new relationship, results in a U_c for the economy and the $DG-SG$ analysis we presented in Part 2.

It is true that some economists, purely on theoretical grounds, had insisted that the economy should contain a natural rate of unemployment U^*; as a result, the old Phillips curve was incorrect. Sometimes theoretical reasoning leads to correct predictions, and sometimes it does not. But econometric modelers are compelled, as they try to track actual data, to make continuous adjustments, such as the wage equation adjustment just described. They often do not anticipate important changes in advance but generally adjust quickly to them; they cannot afford to cling to any theory that does not monitor actual data successfully.

As model builders continuously try to refine the accuracy of each component — consumption, investment, the money market, and so on — progress is made in understanding macroeconomics. The pragmatic task of the modelers is a useful check on theorists. Some hypotheses that are attractive in theory perform poorly in practice; others that are unappealing to some theorists seem to work well in practice.

To summarize, some macroeconomists oppose countercyclical monetary policy; others believe that an econometric model will yield poor guidance if such policy is attempted. However, others feel that countercyclical monetary policy will, on average, be stabilizing and that such policy should be guided by an econometric model. Clearly, this is one aspect of macroeconomics on which there is substantial disagreement.

SUMMARY

1. A *progressive tax* is a more powerful *automatic stabilizer* than a *proportional tax*, because it causes a greater reduction in the multiplier.

2. The *transfer system* reduces the multiplier m and is therefore an automatic stabilizer.

3. It is useful to divide the actual deficit into two components: (1) the *structural deficit*, which would occur at the constant inflation output Q_c, and (2) the *cyclical deficit*, the part of the deficit resulting solely from a decline in Q below Q_c.

4. To analyze how fiscal policy has changed, we focus on the change in the Q_c deficit or Q_c surplus, not on the change in the *actual* budget deficit or surplus.

5. To avoid the political asymmetry and policy lags that characterize discretionary fiscal policy, an automatic fiscal policy can be prescribed by statute or Constitutional amendment. Automatic fiscal policy can implement a constant policy rule or a countercyclical (activist) policy rule. One purpose of both rules is to avoid destabili-

zation. In contrast to the constant policy, the countercyclical policy attempts to counter a recession with fiscal stimulus and a boom with fiscal restraint.

6. Recent economic history suggests that the current institutional and political framework makes possible a discretionary, countercyclical monetary policy that largely overcomes the two shortcomings of discretionary fiscal policy: a lengthy decision lag, and a political bias against contractionary policy.

7. The implementation of monetary policy according to an established rule versus discretion entails this trade-off. There is a risk in giving twelve members of the FOMC (Federal Reserve's Open Market Committee) the power to set monetary policy according to their own discretion (judgment). On the other hand, there is a risk in constraining monetary policy by a rule that may be highly undesirable in situations that cannot be anticipated in advance.

8. An *interest-rate target* is preferable if policymakers are more confident of the position of the *IS* curve. A money-growth target is preferable if policymakers are more confident of the position of the *LM* curve.

9. An *econometric model* can be used to guide the implementation of discretionary, countercyclical monetary policy. One important feature of such a model is that it attempts to account for the *lag structure* of economic relationships.

TERMS AND CONCEPTS

actual budget surplus/deficit
automatic fiscal policy
average tax rate (ATR)
constant policy rule
"control solution"
countercyclical (activist) policy rule
cyclical deficit
"disturbed solution"
dynamic multiplier
econometric model
endogenous variable
exogenous variable
federal funds rate
Federal Reserve's Open Market Committee (FOMC)

high-powered money (H)
interest-rate target
lag structure
marginal tax rate (MTR)
monetary base
money aggregates
money-growth target
normal output Q_c surplus/deficit
progressive tax schedule
proportional (flat) tax schedule
regressive tax schedule
structural deficit
transfer function
transfer system

9.1 Consider the following two tax schedules (functions):

(1) $T = 0.2Q$
(2) $T = 0.4(Q - 1{,}250)$

Based on the simple three-equation model given in Chapter 1, with the values

$$C = 0.75(Q - T + R)$$
$$R = 200$$
$$G = 300$$

a. Explain why schedule 2 results from a *progressive tax*.
b. When Q declines by $100 billion, by how much does T decline under schedule 1? Under schedule 2?
c. If $I = \$550$ billion, find equilibrium Q under tax schedule 1. Under tax schedule 2.
d. If I declines to $450 billion, find equilibrium Q under tax schedule 1. Under tax schedule 2. Which tax schedule results in the smaller multiplier m?

9.2 Consider the two transfer schedules

(1) $R = 200$ for any Q
(2) $R = 200 + 0.2(2{,}500 - Q)$

Based on the simple three-equation model given in Chapter 1, with these values

$$C = 0.75(Q - T + R)$$
$$T = 0.2Q$$
$$G = 300$$

a. When Q declines by $100 billion, by how much does R increase under schedule 2?
b. If $I = \$550$ billion, find equilibrium Q under transfer schedule 1. Under transfer schedule 2.
c. If I declines to $450 billion, find equilibrium Q under transfer schedule 1. Under transfer schedule 2. Which transfer schedule results in the smaller multiplier m?

9.3 An automatic fiscal policy can implement either a constant policy rule or a countercyclical policy rule.

a. State the constant policy rule given in this chapter.

b. State the countercyclical policy rule given in this chapter.

c. Explain why a simple always-balanced budget rule is destabilizing but why the constant and countercyclical policy rules in (a) and (b) are not destabilizing.

d. State the pros and cons of the constant and countercyclical policy rules in (a) and (b).

9.4 Consider the choice between a money-growth target and an interest-rate target:

a. Suppose that the *IS* curve is stable but that money demand is unstable. Using an *IS–LM* diagram, explain which target would be superior.

b. Suppose that money demand is stable but that the *IS* curve is unstable. Using an *IS–LM* diagram, explain which target would be superior.

9.5 Consider the use of an econometric model to guide countercyclical monetary policy:

a. What makes an economic model "econometric"?

b. Explain why lags make the implementation of effective countercyclical policy more difficult.

c. What fundamental critique of the use of econometric models for policy evaluation has been proposed?

d. How have the builders of econometric models replied to this critique?

4 Accumulation and Growth, and the Open Economy

CHAPTER

10 Capital Accumulation and Economic Growth

What determines the rate of improvement in the standard of living of the average household over the long term in a given country? Why is the average standard of living higher in country A than in country B in a given year? Can anything be done to raise the growth rate of the standard of living? If so, is a sacrifice inevitably required? What policies should be adopted to raise the growth rate of the standard of living?

This chapter addresses these questions. Our subject is *capital accumulation* and *economic growth*. Before beginning, it is important to understand how our subject differs from inflation and unemployment (Chapters 4–7) and from stabilization (Chapters 8–9).

Suppose that inflation has been brought under control and that the economy is usually kept close to the constant inflation unemployment rate U_c by proper stabilization policy. In other words, suppose that the lessons of Parts 2 and 3 have been implemented. Does this mean that macroeconomic performance is satisfactory? Not necessarily.

As we will see, the satisfactory treatment of inflation, unemployment, and stabilization does not, in itself, guarantee that the standard of living of the average household will rise over time at the "optimal" (best possible) rate. Even after these important problems are treated adequately, this fundamental macroeconomic task will remain—to achieve the best possible rate of capital accumulation, economic growth, and progress in the standard of living.

10.1 The Role of Capital Accumulation

Let's return to the first two questions asked at the beginning of this chapter: What determines the rate of improvement in the standard of living over the long term in a given country? Why is the average standard of living higher in country A than in country B in a given year? Not one but many factors influence the rate of improvement in the standard of living in one country over time and the disparity in the average standard of living between countries at a given moment in time. We will find that careful empirical research has cast doubt on the claim that there is a single source of economic growth.

Nevertheless, there are two reasons to devote particular attention to one source of economic growth — capital accumulation. First, both economic theory and empirical evidence generally lead to the conclusion that capital accumulation plays an important role in raising the standard of living, provided we define "capital" broadly rather than narrowly. The broad definition of *capital* includes not only physical capital but also human and "knowledge" capital. In general, we will use this broad definition of capital throughout this chapter.

Second, it is possible to design policies to raise the rate of capital accumulation if a society desires to do so. Some other sources of economic growth, although important, may be difficult to influence with economic policy. Not only can capital accumulation be raised by employing alternative policies, but choice among these policies is controversial. It therefore seems sensible to devote special attention to capital accumulation but to recognize that it is not the only important source of economic growth.

A BROAD CONCEPT OF CAPITAL

What is capital accumulation? When people use the term "capital," they often mean *financial capital* (funds that finance investments). In our analysis of growth, however, the term indicates *real capital,* which, when combined with labor, produces real output. Capital is a basic factor of production. Real capital is a man-made asset, produced by past economic activity, that raises the productivity of labor.

Real capital includes machinery and structures (factories, roads, bridges, airports, and so on), but it also encompasses several other kinds of capital of great importance. Real capital includes the stock of technical knowledge accumulated from past experience in production and inventive activity. This stock of "blueprints" prescribes both technical and organizational methods for producing specific goods and services. Each year, the blueprints are improved, as better methods are developed for producing old products and new products are invented. *Knowledge capital* (the stock of blueprints) is a vital, although sometimes neglected, component of the real capital stock.

Real capital also includes the skill of the labor force that is acquired by education and training. The stock of blueprints is not very effective unless the work force has accumulated the *human capital* (skills) needed to follow the blueprints. Similarly, the stock of machinery is not very effective unless the work force can supply the human capital required to operate the machinery. Human capital is, of course, embodied in human beings.

Human capital also includes the health of the labor force, as well as its skill. Skill does little good if a worker's poor health prevents its full utilization. Some of the factors that contribute to the accumulation of *health capital* are good nutrition, public-health measures, environmental policy, and the application of modern medicine. Like skill, health is capital embodied in particular human beings and, hence, is a component of human capital.

Capital is a broad concept that includes much more than physical capital such as machinery and factories. At times, nevertheless, we may use machinery to *illustrate* capital. Do not be misled. Knowledge capital and human capital are also genuine components of capital; they raise the productivity of workers and deserve the same recognition as physical capital. Workers will be far less productive in an economy that accumulates primarily physical capital and neglects knowledge and human capital than in an economy that accumulates a balance of physical, knowledge, and human capital.

▶ A broad definition of "capital"—one that includes knowledge and human as well as physical capital—also conveys a basic point. Capital accumulation, which raises future productive capacity, requires a sacrifice in the present. In order to build machinery (physical capital), improve our skills (human capital), or invent new technology (knowledge capital), time and resources must be diverted from producing goods and services for current consumption. Thus, accumulating physical, human, or knowledge capital generally entails a sacrifice of present consumption.

The use of machinery to illustrate capital may appear to imply that capital accumulation occurs only in the private, profit-seeking sector. Again, do not be misled. One important component of physical capital —facilities such as roads, bridges, and airports—is accumulated in the government sector. Although part of knowledge capital is certainly accumulated in private, profit-seeking firms, part is also accumulated in nonprofit universities and research institutions. Although part of human capital is accumulated in private, profit-seeking firms via on-the-job training and learning by doing, part is also accumulated in public and nonprofit schools and universities. Similarly, much of health capital is accumulated in the household or the public sector.

Thus, workers will be far less productive in an economy that confines its capital accumulation primarily to the private, profit-seeking sector and neglects the nonprofit, government, and household sectors than in an economy that accumulates capital in all sectors in a balanced manner.

To summarize, although machinery may be used to illustrate capital throughout this chapter, always remember that the broad, inclusive definition of *real capital* is actually meant.

ACCUMULATION, THE STANDARD OF LIVING, AND PRODUCTIVITY

How does an economy accumulate real capital? The accumulation of real capital requires *real investment*. When people use the term "investment," they often mean *financial investment* (funds that finance business ventures). In our analysis of economic growth, however, the term will mean the increase in the stock of *real capital*. Note an important distinction. Capital is a *stock* at a moment in time; investment is a *flow* during a period of time. Thus, we might say that the capital stock of country X on January 1, 1988, is $1,000 billion; if the investment in country X is $200 billion during the following year (from January 1 to December 31) and if none of the capital wears out, then the capital stock of country X on January 1, 1989, will be $1,200 billion.

This example raises another basic point. Let's assume that, more realistically, some of the capital held on January 1, 1988, does wear out or *depreciate* during the year. For example, suppose that $100 billion of capital depreciates and is useless by the following January 1, 1989. Then, although *gross investment* is $200 billion (new machinery and equipment is $200 billion), *net investment* (the net increase in the capital stock) is only $100 billion, and the capital stock of country X on January 1, 1989, will be only $1,100 billion. Net investment ($100 billion) equals gross investment ($200 billion) minus depreciation ($100 billion). The new capital stock on January 1, 1989, equals the capital stock on January 1, 1988, plus *net* investment. Thus

▶ To accumulate capital (to raise the capital stock), a society must achieve *positive net investment* (gross investment must exceed depreciation).

We will now consider a simple *aggregate production function* for the economy, which states that output is a function of capital and labor:

(10.1) $Q = F(K, L)$, where Q increases if either K or L increases.

where Q = output

K = capital

L = labor

Recall that equation (3.11) expressed the same production function.

Consider a simple rural economy in which output is food. Initially, suppose that there is no physical capital (no tools or machinery). If labor increases, then more food will be grown (output will increase). If labor remains constant but capital increases (tools or machinery are acquired), then more food will be grown (output will increase).

Equation (10.1) is a simple production function that ignores other determinants of output to focus attention on capital and labor. In the rural economy, land and natural resources are also important; so is technological change. In Chapter 16, we will consider the roles of natural resources and technological change in the aggregate production function; here, equation (10.1) will serve our purpose.

Equation (10.1) shows how total output varies with capital and labor, but our real concern is *output per person*. In our rural economy, suppose that 100 persons, given the capital stock, produce 10,000 units of food, so that output (food) per person is 100 units. If labor increases by 10% to 110 persons and output also rises by 10% to 11,000, then output (food) per person will still be 100 units (11,000/110); the standard of living will not change. If, instead, output only rises by 5% to 10,500 but labor increases by 10% to 110 persons, then output (food) per person will actually decline to 95.5 units; the standard of living will decline.

To improve the standard of living of the average person, real output must grow at a faster rate than the number of persons. If the population grows by 1% and real output grows by only 1%, then output per person will remain constant. If real output grows by 3%, however, then output per person will grow by 2%, and the standard of living will rise. If we make the initial, simplifying assumption that the labor force is a constant fraction of the population, so that the labor force and population grow at the same rate, then we can say that real output must grow faster than the labor force to raise the standard of living. Output per worker — labor productivity — must rise.*

But what causes *labor productivity* or *output per worker Q/L* to rise? As we will see, there are many sources of *productivity growth*. In this chapter, however, we focus primarily on one source: the accumulation of *real capital per worker K/L*, where real capital includes physical, knowledge, and human capital.

Let's rephrase the two questions at the beginning of the chapter by replacing the standard of living per household with labor productivity. Why is the productivity of the average American worker today so much higher than the productivity of the average American worker 80 years ago or so much higher than the average worker in a developing country today? One important reason is that today's American worker has more education and skill (human capital) and utilizes more and better machinery and technology (physical capital) and a more advanced set of blueprints (knowledge capital).

---

* Note that *labor productivity* is usually defined as *output per hour*, as in Chapters 3 and 4. In Chapter 10, however, we will define labor productivity as *output per worker*.

Compare the primitive farmer, who lacks both a tractor and the skill to operate it, with the modern farmer, who possesses both the tractor (physical capital) and the knowledge to operate it (human capital). Moreover, the modern farmer utilizes knowledge capital that (based on past experience, research, and invention) indicates which farming techniques will be most productive. Is it any wonder that output per worker is much higher for the modern farmer? Countless urban and industrial as well as rural examples make the common-sense point: raising capital per worker generally raises output per worker. Thus, output per worker is a function of capital per worker, so that q increases if k increases:

(10.2) $\qquad q = f(k)$

where $q \equiv Q/L$ = output per worker (labor productivity)

$\qquad k \equiv K/L$ = capital per worker (capital–labor ratio)

▶ A word on notation is in order here. In Parts 2 and 3, a lower-case letter generally indicates a *percentage growth rate;* for example, q is the percentage growth rate of Q. In the economic literature on capital accumulation and economic growth, however, a lower-case letter indicates "per worker"; hence, q indicates Q/L (output per worker). We will adopt this convention throughout Chapter 10 and the related supplement Chapters 15 and 16.

If q rises, then more output (equivalently, more real income) is being produced per worker. Thus, it follows that real income received per household will rise. Part of that higher real income will be labor income, and part will be capital income.

If we use a narrower definition of capital and exclude human capital, then capital income becomes *property income* from the ownership of stocks (dividends), bonds and savings accounts (interest), and land and dwellings (rent), and labor income becomes *compensation* (wages, salaries, fringe benefits). But if we use the broader definition of capital and include human capital, then part of compensation is really a return to human capital and only part is a wage for "raw" or unskilled labor.

10.2 The Trade-Off Between Present and Future Consumption

If we raise capital accumulation in the present, we can produce more output and enjoy more consumption in the future. Unfortunately, raising capital accumulation in the present inevitably requires a sacrifice of present consumption. Why?

Assume that we want to run the economy at the constant inflation level of real output Q_c, but we seek to raise capital accumulation. Recall

FIGURE 10.1 THE TRADE-OFF BETWEEN CONSUMPTION AND INVESTMENT

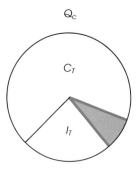

If real output Q is kept at constant inflation output Q_c, then more total investment I_T can only be obtained by reducing total consumption C_T.

from Part 2 that Q_c is the level of real output that results in an unemployment rate — the U_c of the economy — at which the inflation rate p remains constant. If Q is raised above Q_c, then the inflation rate will rise steadily without limit.

Our problem, then, is to shift the composition of Q_c toward more investment. But this requires a sacrifice, which is evident if we recall our basic national income accounting relationship from Chapter 1 for a closed economy with government

(1.24) $Q \equiv C_T + I_T$

which states that total output is divided between total consumption (private plus government) and total investment (private plus government).*

If Q is to be kept at Q_c, then equation (1.24) becomes

(10.3) $Q_c = C_T + I_T$

Our fundamental problem is evident in equation (10.3). Consumption plus investment must be kept equal to Q_c. It is apparent that raising investment requires reducing consumption.

This basic point is illustrated in Figure 10.1. The size of the "pie" chart, which represents total output, must be kept equal to Q_c. Given

---

* Throughout Chapter 10, we will assume a "closed" economy with no foreign trade or capital flows. In Chapter 11, we will see how our analysis here must be modified in an "open" economy.

this constraint, more total investment I_T requires less total consumption C_T. The key issue is the division of the "pie" between C_T and I_T. The only way to get a bigger "slice" for I_T is to accept a smaller "slice" for C_T.

▶ The reduction in present consumption constitutes the *cost* of capital accumulation. Given that real output Q must be kept equal to constant inflation output Q_c, raising investment requires reducing present consumption below what it otherwise would be.

The phrase "otherwise would be" is important. A numerical example will illustrate. Consider Table 10.1. This year, given relatively low investment, 80% of GNP ($800 billion) is allocated to consumption; given relatively high investment, only 78% of GNP ($780 billion) is allocated to consumption. Raising I_T from 20% to 22% of GNP (from $200 billion to $220 billion) requires that C_T be reduced below *what it otherwise would be this year*. However, note that in this example, C_T for this year ($780 billion) is still greater than C_T for last year ($777 billion). With GNP 3% greater this year ($1,000 billion) than last year ($971 billion), even after a decline in the consumption percentage from 80% to 78%, consumption will be greater this year than last year.

Thus, it is *not* necessarily true that raising capital accumulation requires consumption this year to be less than it was last year. This is not what we mean when we say that more capital accumulation requires a *reduction* in consumption. What is true is that consumption must be made less than it otherwise would be this year. As long as the rise in the *investment rate* (the percentage of GNP allocated to investment) is moderate (in our example, the investment rate rises from 20% to 22%), consumption will not actually decline from last year to this year; it will simply grow more slowly than it otherwise would have (from $777 billion to $780 billion, instead of at the 3% growth rate to $800 billion).

Keeping this basic distinction in mind, we will often say that more capital accumulation requires "slower consumption growth" or "less

TABLE 10.1

THE SACRIFICE IN CONSUMPTION

	GNP	I_T		C_T	
This Year (Low Investment)	1,000	200	(20%)	800	(80%)
This Year (High Investment)	1,000	220	(22%)	780	(78%)
Last Year	971	194	(20%)	777	(80%)

consumption." The phrase "less than it otherwise would be this year" should always be understood.

To summarize:

▶ Raising capital accumulation today leads to higher consumption tomorrow. However, raising capital accumulation today requires reducing consumption today below what it otherwise would be. Hence, society faces a trade-off between present and future consumption.

▶ Once it is recognized that capital accumulation has a cost as well as a benefit, it is clear that investment should be raised (and present consumption sacrificed) only as long as the marginal benefit exceeds the marginal cost. We will return to the problem of "optimal" capital accumulation in Section 10.5.

It is useful to express the sacrifice of present consumption in terms of the concept of *saving*, which is income that is not consumed. If total income is kept at Q_c, then raising total saving requires reducing total consumption. From our national income accounting relationships in Chapter 1, we know that total investment equals total saving:

$$(1.29) \qquad I_T \equiv S_T$$

▶ To raise total investment I_T, total saving S_T must be raised. If real output Q is kept at constant inflation output Q_c, then an increase in total investment will require an increase in total saving at Q_c.

10.3 Shifting the Composition of Demand at the Constant Inflation Output Q_c

Suppose that society wants to accumulate capital at a faster rate. How can the composition of output be shifted to provide more investment and less consumption?

▶ The composition of *demand* must be shifted. *Total consumption demand C_T must be decreased and *total investment demand I_T must be increased, so that total demand remains equal to Q_c.*

Thus

$$(10.4) \qquad Q_c = C_T + I_T$$

In accounting identity (10.3), C_T is actual total consumption and I_T is actual total investment. In equation (10.4), C_T is total consumption demand *(planned consumption)* and I_T is total investment demand *(planned investment)*.

▶ As we explained in Chapter 1, our analysis throughout this text assumes that the economy moves rapidly to an output level at which actual consumption equals consumption demand and actual investment equals investment demand. Based on this assumption, we use the same symbol C_T to denote actual and planned consumption and the same symbol I_T to denote actual and planned investment.

The sum of the two components of demand must be kept equal to Q_c. But C_T must be reduced and I_T must be increased, so that the composition of demand shifts toward investment. Recall from our national income accounting relationships in Chapter 1 that

(1.22) $\qquad C_T \equiv C + G_C$

where C = private consumption

$\qquad G_C$ = government consumption

and

(1.23) $\qquad I_T \equiv I + G_I$

where I = private investment

$\qquad G_I$ = government investment

Thus, either private consumption demand C or government consumption demand G_C must be reduced, and either private investment demand I or government investment demand G_I must be increased.

Many popular discussions focus solely on reducing consumption demand (raising saving) or solely on raising investment demand. As examples, some encourage households to save more (equivalently, to consume less); others encourage business firms to invest more in real capital equipment. Yet these discussions often ignore the necessity of simultaneously reducing C_T and raising I_T so that the economy remains at Q_c. Our problem is to shift the composition of demand toward more I_T and less C_T, while keeping Q at Q_c. Both the increase in investment demand I and the reduction in consumption demand C must be given attention.

▶ If the economy is initially at Q_c and consumption demand is reduced but investment demand is not increased, then total demand will fall below Q_c and the economy will go into recession. If investment demand is increased but consumption demand is not reduced, then total demand will rise above Q_c, and the inflation rate p will rise steadily. Thus, it is crucial both to reduce consumption demand and to raise investment demand such that total demand remains equal to Q_c.

In our *IS–LM* analysis in Chapter 2, we addressed this problem. Recall that we considered a shift to a tight fiscal–offsetting monetary policy mix. We examined two versions of tight fiscal policy: a high tax rate *t* tight fiscal policy, and a low transfer *R* tight fiscal policy. Let's review our Chapter 2 analysis of the fiscal–monetary policy mix.

Under a shift to a high *t* tight fiscal policy, the tax rate *t* is raised (holding government spending constant); the resulting reduction in consumer demand (at any interest rate *r*) will shift the *IS* curve to the left. Under a shift to a low *R* tight fiscal policy, government transfers are cut (holding taxes and other government spending constant); the resulting reduction in consumer demand (at any interest rate *r*) will again shift the *IS* curve to the left. Under the high *t* tight fiscal policy, taxpayer consumption declines; under the low *R* tight fiscal policy, transfer-recipient consumption declines. But in both cases, total consumption demand C_T declines at any interest rate *r*.

It should be emphasized that a citizen may prefer a tight fiscal policy that combines an increase in the tax rate and a decrease in government transfers. Under a high *t*, low *R* tight fiscal policy, both taxpayer and transfer-recipient consumption will fall, shifting the *IS* curve to the left.

When any tight fiscal policy is implemented, the Federal Reserve must simultaneously adjust monetary policy (increase the level of the money supply) so that the *LM* curve shifts to the right by the exact amount needed to keep the *IS–LM* intersection at Q_c. As shown in Figure 10.2, the shift to the tight fiscal–offsetting monetary policy mix holds Q at Q_c, but reduces the interest rate from r_0 to r_1. A lower *r* results in increased investment demand, which offsets the decline in consumer demand, so that total demand remains equal to Q_c.

▶ A shift to a tight fiscal–offsetting monetary policy mix that holds real output at the constant inflation output Q_c will reduce consumption and raise investment.

It is important to emphasize the following point concerning the offsetting monetary policy.

▶ The offsetting monetary policy does *not* entail a permanent increase in the money-supply growth rate; such an increase would raise the inflation rate *p*, as we saw in Chapter 4. Instead, the offsetting monetary policy entails a one-time increase in the level of the money supply, thereby shifting the *LM* curve to the right so that Q remains at Q_c. Thereafter, the money-supply growth rate is kept low to prevent inflation.

The offsetting monetary policy is sometimes called an "easy monetary policy," and the fiscal–monetary policy mix is called a "tight

FIGURE 10.2 A SHIFT TO A TIGHT FISCAL POLICY AT Q_c RAISES INVESTMENT

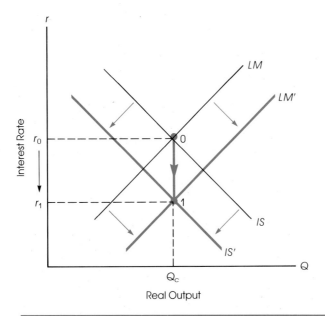

If the tax rate t is raised or government transfers R are cut, then this shift to a tight fiscal policy will shift the IS curve to the left to IS'. An offsetting monetary policy will raise the real money supply, shifting the LM curve to the right to LM', so that the $IS-LM$ intersection point remains at Q_c. But the interest rate will decline from r_0 to r_1 and investment I will rise to match the decrease in consumption C due to the tax increase or the transfer cut.

fiscal–easy monetary mix." We have generally avoided the word "easy" because it may give the false impression that the money-supply growth rate would be permanently raised, with inflationary consequences. Under our offsetting monetary policy, the money-supply growth rate is not permanently raised, and Q is never pushed above Q_c.

From Figure 10.2, we can indirectly infer that total investment I_T has increased because the interest rate r has declined. Figure 10.3 gives us a direct view of the impact of the shift in the fiscal–monetary policy mix on total saving, total investment, and the interest rate. Here, the total saving S_T curve shows total Q_c saving (the total saving that would occur when $Q = Q_c$). Why is the S_T curve a vertical line? Recall the accounting identity

(1.28) $$S_T \equiv Q - C_T$$

In our model, consumption function (1.31) does not contain the interest rate r. Private consumption demand depends on private net

FIGURE 10.3 TOTAL SAVING, TOTAL INVESTMENT, AND THE INTEREST RATE AT Q_c

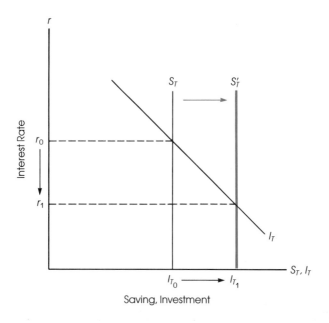

The S_T curve (a vertical line) shows total saving at Q_c. The I_T curve shows total investment demand. The S_T curve reflects the same initial fiscal policy embodied in the IS curve in Figure 10.2. When fiscal policy tightens in Figure 10.2, shifting the IS curve to the left to IS', the S_T curve shifts to the right to S_T'. With an offsetting monetary policy keeping $Q = Q_c$, the interest rate declines from r_0 to r_1 in both figures, and total investment increases from I_{T_0} to I_{T_1}.

income $Q - T + R$ and is assumed to be independent of r. Hence, C_T is independent of r. From equation (1.28), with $Q = Q_c$, S_T is therefore independent of r, so the S_T curve in Figure 10.3 is a vertical line.

The diagram is easily modified if C_T and, hence, S_T depend on the interest rate r. If an increase in r causes consumption to decrease and saving to increase at Q_c, then the S_T curve will have a positive slope. If an increase in r causes consumption to increase and saving to decrease at Q_c, then the S_T curve will have a negative slope.

The I_T curve, which has a negative slope in Figure 10.3, shows that total investment demand I_T increases when the interest rate r decreases.

The S_T curve in Figure 10.3 reflects the same initial fiscal policy embodied in the IS curve in Figure 10.2. S_T is the sum of private saving S plus government saving S_G that would occur at Q_c under the given fiscal policy. The I_T and S_T curves intersect at r_0 in Figure 10.3 — the same r_0 shown in Figure 10.2.

When fiscal policy tightens in Figure 10.2, shifting the IS to the left to IS', total consumption C_T at Q_c declines (due to a tax increase or a government transfer cut). From equation (1.28), this implies that S_T increases at Q_c. In Figure 10.3, the vertical S_T curve shifts to the right to S_T'. The intersection of S_T' and I_T now occurs at r_1 (the same r_1 shown in Figure 10.2). r_1 is lower than r_0. Total investment increases from I_{T_0} to I_{T_1}.

▶ If offsetting monetary policy keeps the economy at Q_c, then an increase in total saving S_T (achieved, for example, by a tightening of fiscal policy to reduce total consumption C_T) results in an equal increase in total investment I_T and a lower interest rate r.

Our analysis implies that a tax increase can result in an increase in investment. How can this be true?

▶ A tax increase, of course, does not directly stimulate investment; it reduces consumption. But this enables the Fed to ease monetary policy, reduce the interest rate, and stimulate investment without causing real output Q to rise above the constant inflation output Q_c. Without the tax increase, the Fed's attempt to stimulate investment would be inflationary.

CAPITAL ACCUMULATION AND THE GOVERNMENT DEFICIT

Our analysis reveals clear implications concerning the relationship between budget deficit reduction and capital accumulation:

▶ Reducing the budget deficit either by raising the tax rate or by cutting government transfers (a tightening of fiscal policy), while maintaining output at Q_c through an offsetting monetary policy, will reduce consumption and raise investment.

▶ Thus, any citizen who favors more investment relative to consumption should favor reducing the deficit that occurs at Q_c. One citizen will favor deficit reduction through an increase in taxes; another citizen will favor deficit reduction through a decrease in transfers; still another citizen will favor deficit reduction through a combination of both methods.

A shift to a tight fiscal policy will primarily reduce consumption but may also reduce *private* saving. For example, a tax increase of $100 billion may cause households to cut consumption by $90 billion and private saving by $10 billion. But the shift to the tight fiscal policy will raise government saving, as we explained in Section 2.5 (page 99). For example, a tax increase of $100 billion (holding government spending constant) will raise government saving by $100 billion. As long as the decrease in private saving is less than the increase in government saving, total saving will increase. In this example, if private saving decreases by $10 billion and government saving increases by $100 billion, then total saving will increase by $90 billion. Thus

▶ A switch to a tight fiscal – offsetting monetary policy mix that holds real output Q constant at Q_c will reduce private saving but almost certainly will raise total saving and total investment. What determines the impact on total investment is not the change in private saving alone but the change in *total* saving (the sum of government saving plus private saving).

If significant budget deficits have occurred frequently, a citizen who favors more investment relative to consumption may find a balanced budget rule, implemented by statute or constitutional amendment, appealing. It is important to restate the conclusions we reached in our discussions of balanced budget rules in Chapters 1, 2, and 9:

▶ An *always-balanced budget rule* is undesirable because it is destabilizing; it would require fiscal action that would worsen a recession.

▶ A Q_c *balanced budget rule* is not destabilizing; it would not require fiscal action that would worsen a recession.

▶ A Q_c *normally balanced budget rule* is designed to avoid destabilization and to prescribe fiscal action that attempts to keep the economy at Q_c.

Note that we have replaced "full-employment output" with "constant inflation output Q_c," based on our analysis in Part 2.

Under the Q_c *balanced budget rule*, planned government expenditures and tax rates must be set so that the budget would be balanced next year if the economy is at $Q = Q_c$. Under the Q_c *normally balanced budget rule*, if Q is at Q_c this year, then planned government expenditures and tax rates must be set so that the budget would be balanced next year if the economy is at $Q = Q_c$. But if Q is below Q_c this year, then planned government expenditures must be raised and/or tax rates must be lowered to stimulate demand. And if Q is above Q_c this year, then planned government expenditures must be cut and/or tax rates must be raised to restrain demand. The amounts by which the expenditure and tax rates must be adjusted can be specified in a formula.

THE FISCAL-MONETARY MIX AND SUPPLY-SIDE ECONOMICS

Now let's consider how the *supply-side economics hypothesis* affects our conclusions concerning a shift to the high t, tight fiscal – offsetting monetary policy mix.

The SUPPLY-SIDE ECONOMICS HYPOTHESIS contends that if the tax rate t is increased in the *relevant range* (a moderate rate increase starting from the current rate), then constant inflation output Q_c will decline *significantly* due to a reduction in the effective labor supply.

According to the supply-side economics hypothesis, a higher tax rate reduces both the incentive to work and the incentive to work hard to obtain a promotion. Therefore, it should significantly reduce the number of people who want to work (the labor force), the hours they want to work, and the intensity (productivity) with which they work. If so, then a higher tax rate will significantly reduce Q_c, the output of the economy that is produced when the unemployment rate is at the U_c of the economy (roughly 7%)—the rate required to keep the inflation rate p constant.

In Chapter 15, we will examine supply-side economics in more detail. Here, we simply note that a shift to a high t, tight fiscal policy (an increase in the tax rate, holding government spending constant) may reduce the Q_c of the economy. If so, will investment still increase?

The answer depends on how the decline in Q_c compares to the decline in C_T. If the Fed keeps total demand equal to Q_c, then

(10.4) $$Q_c = C_T + I_T$$

If Q_c decreases by less than C_T, then I_T will still increase. If Q_c decreases by as much as C_T, then I_T will stay constant. Only if Q_c decreases by more than C_T will I_T decrease.

For example, suppose that a higher tax rate reduces C_T by $90 billion. Previously, we assumed that Q_c remains constant; if so, then when the Fed adjusts monetary policy to keep total demand at Q_c, I_T will increase by $90 billion.

Now suppose that the higher tax rate reduces the labor supply, so that Q_c decreases, and that the Fed adjusts the *LM* curve, so that it intersects the *IS* curve at the new, lower Q_c. Assume that C_T still decreases by $90 billion. If Q_c decreases by $40 billion, then I_T increases by $50 billion. If Q_c decreases by $90 billion, then I_T remains constant. If Q_c decreases by $140 billion, then I_T decreases by $50 billion.

▶ A shift to a high t, tight fiscal–offsetting monetary policy mix that keeps the economy at Q_c will raise investment as long as any supply-side reduction in constant inflation output Q_c is less than the decline in consumption due to the higher tax rate. Q_c must decrease by more than consumption for investment to decline.

▶ Even if the supply-side economics hypothesis is correct that a shift to a high t, tight fiscal policy (entailing a tax-rate increase)

will significantly reduce Q_c, the shift will still raise investment unless the magnitude of the decline in Q_c is very large.

In Section 15.2, we will consider some estimates of the impact of tax-rate changes on the labor supply and on Q_c. There, we will draw the following conclusion:

▶ For tax-rate increases in the *relevant range,* most economists believe that Q_c will not decrease by a sufficient amount to reverse the standard conclusion: a shift to a high t, tight fiscal – offsetting monetary policy mix will raise investment.

SHIFTING PRODUCTION FROM C GOODS TO I GOODS

Let's examine the shift in the composition of output from another per- spective. The economy can be viewed as consisting of two production sectors: the *consumption C goods sector,* and the *investment I goods sector.* Once again, we are referring to the broad concept of capital, so that investment includes the production of new knowledge and new skills, as well as new machines. Initially, suppose that the C sector has experienced demand for $1,600 billion worth of goods and has pro- duced and supplied this quantity. The I sector has experienced demand for $400 billion worth of goods and has produced and supplied this quantity.

Now suppose that the demand for C goods is reduced to $1,500 billion, so that C-sector producers reduce production to $1,500 billion. At the same time, an increase in the money supply and a decline in the interest rate cause all producers of C and I goods to raise their demand for I-sector goods to $500 billion, so that I-sector producers increase production to $500 billion. Total production Q remains at $2,000 bil- lion.

Of course, this shift in the composition of demand—the decline in C_T and the rise in I_T—requires that labor, capital, and materials be reallocated from C-sector to I-sector producers. If the decrease in con- sumption were really as large as it is in our example, then this realloca- tion would pose a problem in the short run.

Table 10.2 shows the allocation desired this year when the one-year reduction in C_T is large. This year the large decrease in consumption causes C to be not only less than it otherwise would be this year ($1,500 billion versus $1,600 billion) but also less than it was last year ($1,500 billion versus $1,520 billion). Thus, an actual contraction in C-good production results, creating layoffs of workers in the C sector and an underutilization of real physical capital already allocated to the C sector.

For every layoff in the C sector, a new job slot will be opening up in the I sector. In practice, it will take time for laid-off C-sector workers to

TABLE 10.2

THE TRANSITIONAL COST OF A SHARP CUT IN CONSUMPTION

	Q	C		I	
Last Year: $C_T = 0.8Q$	1,900	1,520	(80%)	380	(20%)
This Year: $C_T = 0.8Q$	2,000	1,600	(80%)	400	(20%)
This Year: $C_T = 0.75Q$	2,000	1,500	(75%)	500	(25%)

locate these new jobs in the I sector and receive the training required to qualify for them. Too large a shift in the composition of demand therefore entails a significant transitional cost. It temporarily raises the unemployment rate and temporarily reduces the *capacity utilization rate* (as some capital remains idle in the C sector).

Now suppose that the decrease in consumption is smaller, so that consumption is reduced from 80% to 78% of GNP. Table 10.3 shows the allocation desired this year when the one-year reduction in C_T is small. This smaller decrease in consumption demand from a consumption rate of 80% to only 78% (instead of 75%, as in the preceding example) still causes C_T to be less than it otherwise would be this year ($1,560 billion versus $1,600 billion), but now C_T is *not* less than it was last year; it still exceeds last year's level ($1,560 billion versus $1,520 billion), although by less than it otherwise would have.

The fact that C production does not actually decline in this example but only grows more slowly than it otherwise would have, eliminates the transitional cost. The C sector does not need to layoff any workers; it just hires new workers at a slower rate. New entrants into the labor force will find most of the new jobs opening up in the I sector. Similarly, no reduction in capacity utilization will occur in the C sector.

The role of *gradualism* in eliminating—or at least in reducing—transition cost can be stated more generally. It is not just a change in the

TABLE 10.3

AVOIDING TRANSITIONAL COST THROUGH GRADUALISM

	Q	C		I	
Last Year: $C_T = 0.8Q$	1,900	1,520	(80%)	380	(20%)
This Year: $C_T = 0.8Q$	2,000	1,600	(80%)	400	(20%)
This Year: $C_T = 0.78Q$	2,000	1,560	(78%)	440	(22%)

I sector versus the C sector that can produce a transitional problem. Any economy makes many products. In a flexible economy, the relative sizes of the product sectors are constantly changing. If they change gradually, then the transitional cost is small; if they change too rapidly, then layoffs and idle capacity accompany the process.

In designing policies to reduce C_T and to raise I_T, it is important to keep in mind the potential transitional problem of *sectoral reallocation*. The shift should be sufficiently gradual to keep the transitional cost low.

10.4 Policies to Reduce Consumption and to Raise Investment

In this section, we will highlight two consumption-reducing policies (tight fiscal policy and the personal consumption tax) and one investment-raising policy (offsetting monetary policy). (Other policies to reduce consumption and raise investment will be examined in Chapter 16.) Either consumption-reducing policy (tight fiscal policy or the personal consumption tax) will shift the IS curve to the left. The investment-raising policy (offsetting monetary policy) will shift the LM curve to the right. The Fed should always adjust monetary policy so that the $IS-LM$ intersection remains at Q_c.

In Chapters 2 and 9, we have seen how an offsetting monetary policy can be conducted; the mechanics of monetary policy are reserved for Chapter 13. In this section, we will therefore focus on the two consumption-reducing policies.

TIGHT FISCAL POLICY AND THE GOVERNMENT DEFICIT

A tightening of fiscal policy, whether through raising taxes, or cutting transfers, or cutting government consumption, reduces consumption demand, thereby releasing resources for investment. Yet the early 1980s witnessed a significant easing of fiscal policy in the United States.

To detect an easing of fiscal policy, we must compare two years with similar unemployment rates. In 1984, the unemployment rate was 7.4%; in 1980, it was 7.0%. A comparison of 1984 and 1980 therefore enables us to assess the change in fiscal policy. Note that in 1979, the unemployment rate was 5.8%; thus, a comparison of 1984 with 1979 would be inappropriate.

In Chapter 6, we estimated that the constant inflation unemployment rate U_c of the economy appears to be roughly 7%. Thus, in both 1984 and 1980, the economy was near its U_c, generating output near its constant inflation output Q_C. Thus, the deficit in each year is roughly the structural deficit (Q_c deficit).

The government budget consists of federal, state, and local expenditures and revenues. We will focus on the federal budget for two reasons. First, in recent years, the federal budget has experienced the most dramatic change. Second, the federal budget is properly regarded as an instrument of fiscal policy that can be adjusted to achieve national economic goals, such as stabilization and faster capital accumulation. By contrast, each state and local government sets its budget without regard for national economic objectives.

In 1980, federal tax receipts were 20% of GNP and government expenditures were 22%, so that the federal budget deficit was 2% of GNP. In 1984, tax receipts were 18% of GNP and government expenditures were 23% of GNP, so that the budget deficit was 5% of GNP. Thus, the structural deficit more than doubled. By historical standards, this was a very substantial increase in the structural deficit.

▶ In 1980, tax revenue financed about 90% of all federal spending. In 1984, tax revenue financed only about 80% of all federal spending.

Let's analyze the impact of this significant easing of fiscal policy and increase in the federal Q_c deficit. We begin with an important accounting identity from Chapter 1. In a closed economy, the following accounting identity always holds:

(1.20) $$I \equiv S + Su$$

where I = private investment

   S = private saving

   Su = government (budget) surplus $(Su \equiv T - R - G)$

   T = tax revenue

   R = government transfers

   G = government purchases

The validity of the derivation of identity (1.20) does not depend on any hypothesis about behavior, such as the impact of the budget deficit on the interest rate or the impact of the interest rate on investment. It must be true due to accounting relationships.

Suppose that the economy is initially at $Q = Q_c$, as shown in the $IS-LM$ diagram in Figure 10.4. Then the tax rate is cut or government transfers are increased (we will consider an increase in government purchases G shortly). In the $IS-LM$ diagram, this shifts the IS curve to the right due to the increase in consumption demand at any interest rate r. Assume that the Fed simultaneously tightens monetary policy, shifting the LM curve to the left, so that Q remains at Q_c; assume that Q_c itself stays constant. The rightward shift of the IS curve and the leftward shift of the LM curve raise the interest rate r. This shift to an easy fiscal–tight monetary mix raises consumption demand and reduces

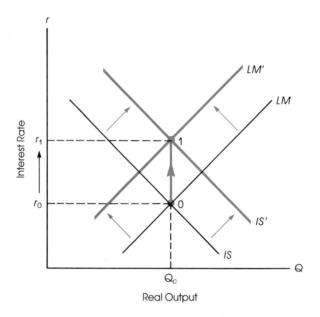

If the tax rate is cut or government spending is raised, then this shift to an easy fiscal policy will shift the IS curve to the right to IS'. An offsetting monetary policy will reduce the real money supply, shifting the LM curve to the left to LM', so that the IS–LM intersection point remains at Q_c. But the interest rate r will rise and private investment I will decline to match either the rise in C (due to the tax cut or transfer increase) or the rise in G. Total investment I_T will decline unless the rightward shift of the IS curve is due solely to an increase in government investment G_I. In that case, I_T will remain constant, because the rise in G_I will match the decline in I.

investment demand (in response to the higher interest rate), while holding total demand constant at Q_c.

▶ A rise in the structural Q_c deficit, with an offsetting monetary policy holding real output Q at constant inflation output Q_c, will reduce private investment I at Q_c.

Let's examine what has happened in the accounting identity (1.20). Private investment I has decreased. Because total income remains at $Q = Q_c$, the tax cut or government transfer increase has probably caused a modest increase in private saving S. For example, if the tax cut or transfer increase is $100 billion, then disposable income will be increased by $100 billion, which may increase private saving by $10 billion (and raise consumption by \$90 billion). But with tax revenue cut by \$100 billion, the government surplus Su will be cut by \$100 billion. Thus, private investment I will decline by \$90 billion, exactly matching the increase of \$90 billion in consumption.

Now suppose that, instead of a tax cut or a government transfer increase, the government raises its purchases G. The impact on private investment I will be the same. An increase in G shifts the IS curve to the right, as shown in Figure 10.4, compelling the Fed to shift the LM curve to the left to keep Q at Q_c. The rise in the interest rate will reduce private investment I.

It is important to distinguish between the two components of G: government consumption G_C, and government investment G_I. If G_C increases, then when private investment I declines, total investment I_T $(I + G_I)$ clearly declines. But if G_I increases, then the decline in private investment I is matched by the increase in G_I, so that total investment I_T stays constant. Thus

▶ An increase in the structural Q_c deficit due to an increase in government investment G_I (complemented by an offsetting monetary policy that keeps Q at Q_c) will reduce private investment I but will keep total investment I_T constant at Q_c.

▶ An increase in the structural Q_c deficit (except through an increase in G_I), with an offsetting monetary policy keeping Q at Q_c, will raise total consumption C_T and reduce total investment I_T.

Does an increase in the structural Q_c deficit raise the interest rate? Our analysis emphasizes that the answer depends on whether monetary policy keeps the economy at Q_c. If monetary policy keeps Q at Q_c, then Figure 10.4 makes it clear that the answer is yes.

A tax cut or a spending increase that raises the structural Q_c deficit is a fiscal policy expansion (an easing of fiscal policy) that shifts the IS curve to the right. If this easing of fiscal policy is offset by a tightening of monetary policy that shifts the LM curve to the left and keeps Q at Q_c, then the result is to raise the interest rate. Thus

▶ An increase in the structural Q_c deficit (with Q held at Q_c by an offsetting monetary policy) will raise the interest rate r at Q_c.

The U.S. Experience in the 1980s

At first glance, the U.S. experience in the early 1980s may appear to contradict this conclusion. First, as the economy reached the trough of the 1982 recession, the actual budget deficit rose but the interest rate fell. Second, during the first half of the decade, fiscal policy eased but the nominal interest rate declined. Actually, these two observations are fully consistent with our conclusion.

First, consider the 1982 recession. Initially, tight money policy shifted the LM curve to the left, raising the interest rate along a fixed IS curve and reducing Q, thereby launching the recession. But the recession soon generated business pessimism and reduced autonomous investment I_a, shifting the IS curve to the left, reducing the interest rate r, and further reducing Q. Automatically, tax revenue T declined and the actual budget deficit (not the structural Q_c deficit) increased. As the recession deepened, the actual deficit increased and the interest rate declined.

Our conclusion, however, does not refer to an economy that is approaching the trough of a recession. It refers to an economy that is kept at Q_c by an offsetting monetary policy. The same IS–LM analysis explains why the actual budget deficit and the interest rate vary inversely in a recession but vary in the same direction when an offsetting monetary policy keeps $Q = Q_c$.

Second, consider the disinflation of the early 1980s. We saw in Chapter 5 that according to Fisher's hypothesis, the nominal interest rate should decline by roughly the same percentage as the inflation rate. Let's review why.

The impact of this disinflation is shown in Figure 10.5. Initially, suppose that the inflation rate $p = 10\%$ and that the nominal interest rate $r_0 = 13\%$, so that the real interest rate $i = 3\%$. Thus, IS_0 intersects LM_0 at point 0 ($r_0 = 13\%$, $Q = Q_c$). At the end of the disinflation (after a transitional recession), suppose that the inflation rate is reduced by 6% to $p = 4\%$. Then IS_1 intersects LM_1 at point 1 ($r_1 = 7\%$, $Q = Q_c$). The real interest rate is still $i = 3\%$, because the nominal interest rate r and the inflation rate p have both declined by 6%.

Suppose that at the end of this disinflation process, the Q_c deficit is raised. This fiscal policy expansion in itself will shift the IS curve to the right to IS_2, requiring a leftward (upward) shift of the LM curve to LM_2 to hold Q at Q_c. If the nominal interest rate rises to $r_2 = 10\%$, then the real interest rate will rise to $i = 6\%$ ($10\% - 4\%$).

If the economy moves first from 0 to 1, due to disinflation, and then from 1 to 2, due to the increase in the Q_c deficit (and the offsetting monetary policy), then there would be no confusion. The shift to the easy fiscal–tight monetary mix will move the economy from point 1 to point 2, raising the interest rate r and reducing private investment I.

But what if the shift to the easy fiscal–tight monetary mix occurs while the disinflation is proceeding. Then the economy will move directly from point 0 to point 2. An observer might note that the Q_c deficit increases but the interest rate declines.

It is essential to separate the move from point 0 to point 2 into two distinct steps: (1) the move from 0 to 1, due to disinflation, and (2) the move from 1 to 2 due to an increase in the Q_c deficit and an offsetting monetary policy. The move from 0 to 1 reduces the nominal interest

FIGURE 10.5 A SHIFT TO AN EASY FISCAL–TIGHT MONETARY MIX DURING DISINFLATION

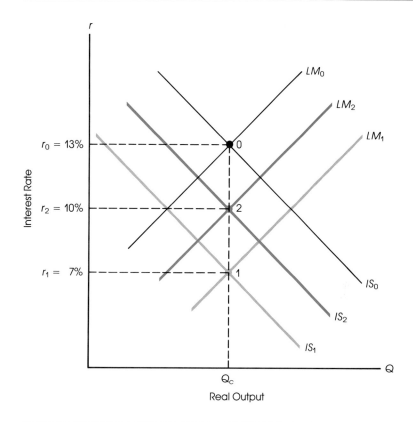

Initially, the inflation rate $p = 10\%$, the nominal interest rate $r = 13\%$, and the real interest rate $i = 3\%$. IS_0 and LM_0 intersect at point 0. Due to the disinflation and the shift in the fiscal–monetary mix, the economy moves to point 2. The 6% disinflation (from 10% to 4%) will, in itself, move the economy from point 0 to point 1; r_1 will be 7%, the real interest rate will still be $i = 3\%$, and private investment I will be unchanged. The shift to the easy fiscal–tight monetary mix will move the economy from point 1 to point 2. This move will raise the nominal interest rate by 3% (from 7% to 10%), raise the real interest rate by 3% (from 3% to 6%), and reduce private investment I.

rate r by 6% (from 13% to 7%) but does not affect either the real interest rate, which remains at $i = 3\%$, or private investment I. The move from 1 to 2 due to the shift in the fiscal–monetary mix raises both the nominal and real interest rates by 3% and reduces private investment.

During a period when the inflation rate is not constant, we should focus on the real interest rate i to discern the impact of a change in the Q_c deficit, because the change in the inflation rate, in itself, changes the nominal interest rate but not the real interest rate, according to Fisher's hypothesis. For example, during the first half of the 1980s, disinflation reduced the nominal interest rate, but the increase in the Q_c deficit kept the real interest rate relatively high at Q_c. (The real interest rate would have been even higher if capital had not flowed in from abroad, as we will see in Chapter 11.)

It is useful to view the impact of the government deficit in light of identity (1.20). We should recall, however, that this identity is true only for a closed economy with no foreign trade; it can offer only a first approximation. First, we divide each term in identity (1.20) by Q to obtain

(1.21) $$\frac{I}{Q} \equiv \frac{S}{Q} + \frac{Su}{Q}$$

Note that identity (1.21) holds whether I and S are both gross or both net of depreciation. Recall that *net investment* equals gross investment minus depreciation and that *net saving* equals gross saving minus depreciation. As long as the same value for depreciation is subtracted from both sides, the identity continues to hold. It will be useful to focus on net investment and net saving, because net investment is the increase in the capital stock.

The ratio of *net private saving* (gross private saving minus depreciation) to GNP—the *net saving rate S/Q*—has remained roughly 7% in the United States. For example, in 1984, gross private saving was 18% of GNP and depreciation was 11% of GNP, so that net saving was 7% of GNP. In the mid-1980s, the government (federal, state, and local) deficit was roughly 3% of GNP. In a closed economy, this would result in a net investment rate I/Q of roughly 4% of GNP:

$$\frac{I}{Q} \equiv \frac{S}{Q} + \frac{Su}{Q}$$
$$4\% = 7\% + (-3\%)$$

Now suppose that Su/Q is 0% instead of -3%; in other words, suppose that the deficit is converted to a balanced budget. Assume that this occurs due to the policy shift illustrated in Figure 10.2 (raising taxes or cutting transfers and shifting to a tight fiscal–easy monetary mix to hold Q at Q_c). The easy monetary policy will reduce the interest rate r and stimulate private investment I. S/Q should stay at 7%. (When disposable income declines by 3% of GNP, saving, which is 6% of disposable income, will decline by 0.18% of GNP.) In a closed economy, the net investment rate I/Q would then increase to 7%:

$$\frac{I}{Q} \equiv \frac{S}{Q} + \frac{Su}{Q}$$

$$7\% = 7\% + 0\%$$

In other words, converting the 3% deficit to a balanced budget would almost double the net investment rate (from 4% to 7%) if the United States were a closed economy.

This conclusion must be qualified because identity (1.21) ignores foreign trade. We will redo the calculation at the end of Chapter 11, recognizing that the United States is an open economy.

▶ Our calculation using identity (1.21) suggests that eliminating the U.S. government deficit would significantly increase the U.S. net private investment rate.

A Dissenting View

Throughout this text, we have emphasized the importance of the fiscal–monetary mix for the allocation of total output between consumption and investment. Although most economists accept this analysis, we should note a dissenting view.

According to this hypothesis, the average person will reason:

> A tax cut now, resulting in a deficit, will require a tax increase in the future to pay interest on the debt issued today. In response to today's tax cut, I'd better hold consumption constant and save the full tax cut in order to earn interest to pay the future tax increase.

If the average person reasons this way, then the tax cut would have no effect on consumption demand and no effect on the position of the IS curve. Hence, the Fed would not need to shift the LM curve to keep Q at Q_c. The interest rate would stay constant, as would the allocation of output between investment and consumption at Q_c.

In accounting identity (1.20), this argument contends that when the government surplus Su decreases by $100 billion due to a $100 billion tax cut or government transfer increase, then private saving S will increase by $100 billion; the entire increase in disposable income will be saved, and private investment I will remain unchanged. The possibility that a person might reason this way was considered and rejected by nineteenth-century economist David Ricardo. Recently, Robert Barro, a proponent of rational expectations, has argued that individuals do indeed reason this way and that budget deficits therefore do not affect consumption and investment.

Most economists reject this hypothesis because they believe that the average person is unlikely to save an entire tax cut to pay future interest on the debt. Empirical evidence that we will review in Chapter 12 strongly implies that only a fraction of a sustained increase in disposable income is saved. Hence, most economists conclude that the dissenting hypothesis is theoretically implausible and empirically unsupported.

To summarize our analysis of tight fiscal policy and the government deficit:

▶ A reduction in the Q_c deficit (with an offsetting monetary policy holding Q at Q_c) will raise private investment I.

▶ A reduction in the Q_c deficit, except by a cut in government investment G_I (with an offsetting monetary policy holding Q at Q_c), will reduce total consumption C_T and raise total investment I_T. If the Q_c deficit is reduced by cutting G_I, then C_T and I_T will stay constant; a rise in private investment I will match the decline in government investment G_I, so that investment would be reallocated from the public to the private sector.

In Chapter 15, we will further analyze government deficits and debt.

THE PERSONAL CONSUMPTION (EXPENDITURE) TAX

Consumption can be reduced by converting the income tax to a *personal consumption (expenditure) tax,* under which each household would be taxed according to its consumption (expenditure) instead of according to its income. Saving (and personal investment) would then be tax deductible; every dollar saved (or invested), instead of spent, would reduce the tax owed by the household.

The U.S. income tax has incorporated several savings incentives that move in the direction of a consumption tax. When an employer contributes $500 to an employee's pension fund, the $500 is really income for the employee. But because this income is saved in a pension fund, it is not subject to tax. Similarly, when a person places $2,000 in an Individual Retirement Account (IRA), the $2,000 is tax deductible; the income that is subject to tax can be reduced by $2,000.

These savings incentives, however, fall short of a conversion of the income tax to a consumption (expenditure) tax. First, they may primarily encourage asset shifting, rather than an increase in total saving and a reduction in total consumption. For example, a person may simply shift $2,000 from a money-market fund or bank account into an IRA. In this case, the $2,000 was saved in the past; there is no new saving—no reduction in current consumption—but the person still enjoys a tax cut by shifting assets from the money-market fund or bank account to the IRA.

Second, the savings incentives that have been enacted in the United States only affect saving for retirement. Saving for any other purpose is not favored. Yet our analysis makes clear that saving for any purpose — reducing consumption for any reason — releases resources for investment.

Third, and most fundamentally, the savings incentives enacted under the income tax do not result in equal tax for persons with equal consumption. Consider two persons with equal consumption but different sources of financing. Neither takes advantage of any savings incentive. The "lazy heir" earns no labor income but finances his consumption by "spending down" his large inheritance. The "diligent worker" finances her consumption entirely from her own labor earnings. Under the income tax with savings incentives, if the "lazy heir" earns less income than the "diligent worker," he will pay less tax, even though both individuals have the same consumption and cause the same reduction in potential investment.

▶ Economists who specialize in taxation are divided about the desirability of converting the income tax to a consumption tax. But most of them agree that *if* our tax system is to encourage saving, then it would be better to convert the income tax to a consumption (expenditure) tax than to expand the list of particular saving incentives under the income tax.

Taxing each household according to its consumption (expenditure) rather than its income has attracted significant support among economists for many years. But until recently, it was widely assumed that the implementation of a personal consumption tax would create too many practical problems.

In the last several years, however, a number of tax experts have concluded that a personal consumption tax would not be any more difficult to implement than an income tax. Two major studies undertaken by tax specialists — the U.S. Treasury's *Blueprints for Basic Tax Reform* (1977), and the U.K. Institute for Fiscal Studies' *The Structure and Reform of Direct Taxation* (1978) — both conclude that replacing the income tax with a personal consumption tax is both feasible and desirable.

Under the personal consumption tax, each household would add all *cash receipts* (including wages, salaries, interest, dividends, and receipts from the sale of such assets as stocks and bonds) and subtract the purchase of *investment assets* (such as stocks and bonds), the net increase in its savings-account balance, and its actual tax payments. The difference — *consumption expenditure* — would be subject to tax rates given in the tax tables (after the subtraction of any appropriate exemptions and deductions). Each household would file a return once a year, just as under the income tax. In fact, the consumption-tax return would contain many of the same items as the current income-tax return.

A common reaction to the consumption-tax proposal is the mistaken belief that it favors the affluent, because they consume a smaller fraction of their income. It must be emphasized that Congress can distribute the tax burden across income classes in any way that it desires, simply by adjusting the tax rates in the tax tables.

For example, suppose that Congress decides that the affluent should continue to pay the same share of total tax revenue. The affluent do consume a smaller fraction of their income, and if the income-tax tables are retained after conversion to the consumption tax, then the share of total tax revenue paid by the affluent will decline. However, Congress can easily remedy this by raising the consumption tax rates that apply to the affluent until they are paying the same share of total tax revenue as before.

▶ The choice between a personal consumption tax and an income tax should not be made on the mistaken belief that the consumption tax inherently favors the affluent. Under a personal consumption tax, Congress can apportion the tax burden among different income classes in any way that it desires, simply by adjusting the tax rates in the tax tables.

Conversion to a consumption tax should reduce total consumption in two distinct ways: (1) the horizontal redistribution effect, (2) the incentive effect.

First, within each income class, a consumption tax would reduce the tax of households with a relatively low propensity to consume and raise the tax of households with a relatively high propensity to consume. Thus, within each income class, disposable income would be shifted from "high" consumers to "low" consumers. This *horizontal redistribution effect* should reduce total consumption.

The horizontal redistribution effect is not significant for low-income households because the propensity to consume is close to 1 and exhibits little variation. But it is very significant for affluent households, which exhibit great variation in the propensity to consume. According to one study, the horizontal redistribution effect could raise aggregate household saving by 11%.*

Second, because saving and personal investment are tax deductible, the average household may be induced to raise its propensity to save (reduce its propensity to consume), as the reward for saving is higher. The tax deductibility of saving would raise the future consump-

---

* Stephen Maurer and Laurence Seidman, "The Consumption Tax, Horizontal Redistribution, and Aggregate Saving," *Mathematical Modeling* 5 (1984): 205–22.

tion that can be enjoyed or the future bequest that can be given for a given sacrifice of present consumption. This *incentive effect* should reduce total consumption.

Some economists dispute this incentive effect. They correctly explain that a rise in the return to saving — the interest rate — may either lower or raise consumption. According to standard microeconomic analysis, the *substitution effect* tends to reduce consumption, but the *income effect* tends to raise consumption, because individuals can now afford to consume more at all ages; in this sense, they become richer when the interest rate rises.

While this analysis of a rise in the interest rate is correct, the argument misses a crucial point:

▶ Conversion from an income tax to a consumption tax differs fundamentally from a rise in the interest rate. As a first approximation, there is no *income effect* under tax conversion; because one tax replaces another, the individual generally does not become richer. The *substitution effect* determines the outcome, so the result should be less consumption.

For example, suppose that the consumption-tax rate is set so that a worker who saves for retirement can afford the same consumption path over life as under the income tax. In Chapter 16, we will see that this worker will reduce consumption.

A consumption tax has been compared to a *labor income tax,* because both offer a higher reward to saving. Under a labor income tax, saving is encouraged because the capital income earned from past saving is not taxed.

Reducing the effective tax rate on capital income is a step toward converting the income tax (a tax on both labor and capital income) into a labor income tax. As examples, the exclusion of 60% of long-term *capital gains* (capital income that results from a rise in the market value of corporate stock) from taxation reduces the effective tax rate on this form of capital income; the exclusion from taxation of interest income on state and local bonds reduces the effective tax rate on this form of capital income to 0%.

But although both the consumption tax and the labor income tax increase the incentive to save, one fundamental difference between the two should be emphasized:

▶ A consumption tax is fairer than a labor income tax. A "lazy heir" who inherits a fortune, never works, and enjoys high consumption pays no tax under a labor income tax but pays a high tax under a consumption tax.

▶ The consumption tax assures that anyone enjoying high consumption pays a high tax; the labor income tax does not. The fairness of the income tax versus the consumption tax continues to be vigorously debated, but few economists would argue that a labor income tax is fair.

The conversion from an income tax to a personal consumption tax should occur gradually. It would be prudent to repeat the history of the income tax by initially limiting the conversion to a consumption tax to the very affluent. Once the practical problems of implementation are overcome and experience is gained, the conversion can be gradually extended to the rest of the population. The personal consumption tax will be discussed in greater detail in Chapter 16.

10.5 Capital Accumulation and the Reduction of Poverty

We have analyzed how to raise capital accumulation. In doing so, we have found that raising capital accumulation requires a sacrifice in present consumption. We now ask: What is the "optimal" rate of capital accumulation?

We will consider three perspectives that help to answer this question. In this section, we will examine the impact of capital accumulation on the reduction of poverty. In Section 10.6, we will see how international competition over the relative standard of living may influence the "optimal" saving rate. In Section 10.7, we will develop the concept of "efficient capital accumulation."

CAPITAL ACCUMULATION AND THE REAL WAGE

To understand the role of capital accumulation in reducing poverty, we must analyze its impact on the real wage of low-skilled workers. As capital accumulation occurs over time, *real* (inflation-adjusted) *compensation per worker* rises with output per worker. This happens for two reasons. First, the average worker accumulates additional human capital over time; the personal "ownership" of this human capital (training, education, and skill) yields human capital income. Second, even the low-skilled worker with relatively little human capital receives an increasingly higher real wage; in other words, the real wage per unit of "raw" labor rises. Together, these two factors raise real compensation per worker.

Although it is conceptually useful to divide compensation per worker into a wage for "raw" (unskilled) labor and a return to human capital, we will ignore this distinction for the moment and focus on compensation per worker. How does real compensation per worker (equivalently, the *real wage per worker w*) behave as the *capital–labor ratio k* and *output per worker q* rise?

Empirical evidence provides a decisive answer. As k and q grow over time in a country, w also grows. Similarly, at a moment in time, countries with a relatively high k and q generally have a relatively high w. These general statements do not mean that an $X\%$ increase in k or q will always result in the same $X\%$ increase in w, or that the link between k, q, and w is always tight in the short run (several years), or that there are no exceptions. More careful empirical work is required to examine these refinements. But the general statement that the real wage per worker w rises with the capital–labor ratio k and output per worker q receives strong empirical support.

Why does the real wage per worker w rise with k and q? Most economists are persuaded by the "neoclassical" explanation, which is often called the *marginal productivity theory* of the real wage. Conveniently, we have already encountered it in Section 3.2; the labor demand–labor supply diagram in Figure 3.3 (page 124) embodies this theory of the real wage. We will now see how capital accumulation affects the labor demand–labor supply diagram and thereby affects the real wage.

In Figure 10.6, for convenience, we assume that labor supply is fixed (completely "inelastic") with respect to the real wage. The labor

FIGURE 10.6 THE RISE IN THE REAL WAGE

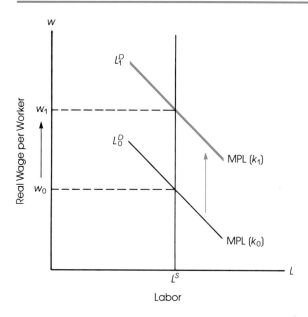

The real wage per worker w is given by the intersection of the labor supply L^S curve and the labor demand L^D curve. The L^D curve is the marginal product of labor MPL curve. The MPL varies directly with the capital–labor ratio k. As capital accumulation occurs, k rises from k_0 to k_1, raising the L^D curve from MPL(k_0) to MPL(k_1). Hence, the real wage per worker rises from w_0 to w_1.

demand curve is the marginal product of labor MPL curve, which depends on the capital–labor ratio k; if k is higher, then the MPL is higher. The intersection of the labor supply L^S curve with the labor demand L^D curve, which is the MPL curve, gives the equilibrium real wage per worker w. In period 0, if the capital–labor ratio is k_0, so that the MPL curve is MPL(k_0), then the real wage per worker is w_0.

A rise in the capital–labor ratio from k_0 to k_1 shifts the MPL curve up to MPL(k_1). At the period 0 real wage w_0, there is now an excess demand for labor; with workers more productive but the real wage still at w_0, firms will want to hire (demand) an amount of labor that exceeds the available supply L^S. In response to this excess demand, competitive firms will bid up the real wage per worker until equilibrium is reached at w_1.

Thus, a higher k raises the MPL or L^D curve, thereby "pulling up" the equilibrium real wage. Most economists would agree that Figure 10.6 captures an important cause of the rise in the real wage and, therefore, in the standard of living of the average worker. Capital accumulation that raises the capital–labor ratio raises the marginal product of labor; competition for labor among profit-seeking firms then bids up the real wage until it equals the higher marginal product of labor.

Thus, the real wage is a function of the capital–labor ratio:

(10.5) $w = f(k)$, where w increases if k increases.

where w = the real wage per worker

k = the capital–labor ratio

As knowledge capital accumulates through new inventions, new technology is instituted with new physical capital. The productivity of worker A's human capital directly raises her compensation. But even worker B, who has minimum education and training, will experience a rise in his compensation. Despite his relatively low human capital, his marginal product rises because he interacts with more physical capital (embodied in machines) and with more knowledge and human capital (embodied in other workers such as A). Profit-seeking firms will therefore be willing to pay a higher real wage to obtain worker B, and competition will cause the real wage to rise to his marginal product.

We have shown that by raising the capital–labor ratio k, capital accumulation not only raises output per worker q but also benefits the average worker. By raising *marginal* as well as *average* productivity, a rising k also results in a rising w.

Due to capital accumulation, a low-skilled worker today earns a much higher real wage than a low-skilled worker 50 years ago. Due to greater capital accumulation, today's low-skilled American worker earns a much higher real wage than today's low-skilled worker in an economically less developed country.

▶ Capital accumulation is a genuine, effective, anti-poverty process and has been a very important poverty-reducing mechanism throughout economic history.

▶ The faster we accumulate capital today, the higher the standard of living of tomorrow's low-skilled workers will be.

"PROGRESSIVE" CAPITAL ACCUMULATION

To raise the rate of capital accumulation, society must make a greater sacrifice of present consumption. Whose consumption should fall below what it otherwise would be? If the motive for raising capital accumulation is to raise the standard of living of low-skilled workers, then it should be recognized that

▶ Raising capital accumulation can be — but need not be — in the best interest of *today's* low-skilled worker. The determining factor is the amount of consumption that today's low-skilled worker must sacrifice in the short run in order to achieve a higher real wage and higher consumption in the future.

If capital accumulation is progressive, it will benefit today's low-skilled worker. The term "progressive" is borrowed from the field of taxation. A *progressive tax* imposes most of its burden on affluent households and little or none of its burden on low-income households. ("Affluent" denotes households with above-average incomes, not the elite rich or the wealthy.) We will consider capital accumulation *progressive* if it imposes most of its burden of consumption reduction on affluent households and little or none of its burden on low-income households.

▶ Faster, progressive capital accumulation results in faster poverty reduction, without imposing a sacrifice on today's low-skilled workers.

What policies can implement progressive capital accumulation? It is worth reemphasizing that an increase in investment demand must be stimulated by an easing of monetary policy, which shifts the *LM* curve to the right and reduces the interest rate r. The tougher challenge is how to reduce consumption demand *by the affluent*, thereby shifting the *IS* curve to the left, so that Q remains at Q_c despite the increase in investment generated by monetary policy.

Consider our two consumption-reducing policies: tight fiscal policy, and the personal consumption tax. To make consumption reduction progressive, each policy must focus on reducing affluent consumption and exempting low-income consumption. A tight fiscal policy is progressive if taxes are raised on the affluent but are not raised on low-skilled workers. A personal consumption tax is progressive if the affluent are subject to much higher tax rates than low-skilled workers.

Faster progressive capital accumulation means that resources (labor, capital, and materials) that would have been used to make consumption goods for the affluent are used instead to make investment goods, which raise the productivity and real wage of low-skilled workers:

> ▶ Faster progressive capital accumulation converts potential affluent consumption into poverty-reducing investment.

Every citizen will favor a different degree of sacrifice of affluent consumption to raise the real wage of low-skilled workers. Our analysis of capital accumulation, however, leads to the following conclusion:

> ▶ A citizen who wants the wages of low-skilled workers to increase at a faster rate, without imposing a sacrifice on these workers, can advocate faster progressive capital accumulation, implemented by a tight fiscal policy that raises taxes on the affluent and by the conversion of the income tax to a progressive, personal consumption tax.

10.6 International Competition and the "Optimal" Saving Rate

International competition over the relative standard of living provides an argument for raising our saving rate. Americans may care about how the U.S. standard of living and U.S. economic strength will compare with those of other countries in the future.

The hypothesis that people care about relative position was given its classic formulation in economics by James Duesenberry in 1949.* Duesenberry's *relative income hypothesis* will be discussed in more detail in Chapter 12. Recently, Robert Frank has presented new analysis and evidence to support the relativity hypothesis.[†]

In Section 10.8, we will see that the United States has a relatively low saving rate, investment rate, and productivity growth rate, compared with several other economically advanced countries. This implies that the standard of living will grow more slowly in the United States than in these other countries. Although the U.S. *absolute* standard of living will rise, the U.S. *relative* standard of living will deteriorate.

---

* James Duesenberry, *Income, Saving, and the Theory of Consumer Behavior* (Cambridge, MA: Harvard University Press, 1949).
[†] Robert Frank, *Choosing the Right Pond: Human Behavior and the Quest for Status* (New York: Oxford University Press, 1985).

Just as we may want to "keep up with the Joneses," we may want to keep up with the Japanese. We may wish that Japan would reduce its high saving and growth rate. But if Japan maintains its growth pace, threatening to surpass our standard of living, we may decide that we have no choice but to raise our own.

In response, it can be argued that we should ignore relative comparisons. If Japan, Germany, and France make the sacrifice to achieve a higher productivity growth rate, then that's their decision. We should make our own decision without reference to their behavior. But concern about relativity may be deeply ingrained. Despite our best efforts, we and our children may be unable to shrug off a deterioration in our relative standard of living. We may suffer "disutility" from a loss of relative status, just as we suffer "disutility" from a loss of absolute income.

▶ It can be argued that to avoid the *disutility* that may accompany a deterioration in the U.S. relative standard of living, we should raise our rate of capital accumulation to match the rate of the leading economically advanced countries.

This argument should not be confused with the often-made claim that we must grow faster or we will suffer a calamity in international markets; our exports will decline, our imports will rise, and our trade deficit will increase drastically, eventually causing a macroeconomic crisis. This claim is not correct.

As we will explain in Chapter 11, a relatively low saving rate does generate a trade deficit. But if the gap between the U.S. saving rate and the saving rates of other economically advanced countries stays constant, then a *stable trade deficit–GNP ratio* should result. This ratio presents no obstacle to the achievement of a low inflation rate, a normal unemployment rate, and a reasonably stable economy through the implementation of the policies prescribed in Parts 2 and 3.

▶ The real issue is not that a future macroeconomic crisis will develop from an ever-rising trade deficit. It is international competition over the relative standard of living.

Finally, the standard of living is not the sole aspect of international competition. Relatively low U.S. saving and productivity growth rates might have important implications for defense and foreign policy. A slower productivity growth rate than the growth rates of potential adversaries might result in a deterioration of the relative strength of U.S. military and foreign policy. A slower growth rate than the growth rates of the allies might result in a decline of U.S. leadership and influence within the alliance.

▶ Defense and foreign policy provide a possible argument for raising capital accumulation.

10.7 Efficient Capital Accumulation

Another perspective on "optimal" capital accumulation is provided by the concept of *efficient capital accumulation*. We will begin our explanation of efficient capital accumulation with a very simple, imaginary, rural economy, consisting of only one person. Initially, our farmer devotes all of his working time to growing food. Annual food output is 100 units, and his consumption is 100 units. Assume that this output requires full-time, year-round work.

One day, our farmer recognizes that if he had tools, he would be able to plant and harvest more food per year. But to have tools next year requires making them this year. Our farmer must become a farmer–toolmaker this year, spending part of his time making tools instead of growing food.

Our farmer realizes that a variety of tools can help him produce food and that some tools are more productive than others. For convenience, we will assume that the farmer must spend the same amount of time to make any tool; each tool he makes this year will result in a loss of 10 units of food this year. However, there is no depreciation; each tool will last for the rest of his life.

Our farmer ranks each tool according to its productivity. Suppose that the most productive tool would raise food output by 5 units per year for the rest of the farmer's life; the next tool, 4 units per year; the next, 3 units per year; the next, 2 units per year; and the last tool, 1 unit per year.

Each tool requires a loss of 10 units of consumption this year. Tool 1 yields a gain of 5 units of consumption per year, so we say that the *marginal rate of return mrr* on this "investment" is 50% (5/10). Section 12.5 will precisely define the *rate of return on investment* and show that if an investment of 10 yields a gain of 5 per year indefinitely, then the marginal rate of return *mrr* is indeed 50%. Similarly, the *mrr* on tool 2 is 40% (4/10); and so on.

This relationship between the rate of return on investment and the marginal rate of return *mrr* is plotted in Figure 10.7. Total investment, as measured by the total loss in present consumption, is graphed on the horizontal axis. If total investment is 10 units (the loss in consumption required to make tool 1), then the *mrr* on tool 1 is 50%. If total investment is 20 units (the total loss in consumption required to make tools 1 and 2), then the *mrr* on the *last tool* (tool 2) is 40%; and so on. If total investment is 50 units, then the *mrr* on the last tool (tool 5) is 10%.

How much consumption should our farmer sacrifice this year to raise his consumption in all future years? This depends on his subjective preference. It is crucial to understand that there is no "economically

FIGURE 10.7 OPTIMAL INVESTMENT

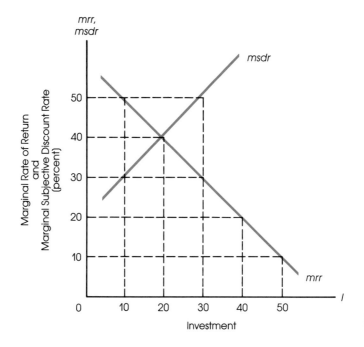

If a farmer invests 10 units (sacrifices 10 units of consumption this year) to obtain tool 1, then the *mrr* is 50% but the *msdr* is only 30%; hence, the investment in tool 1 raises the farmer's lifetime subjective utility. If the farmer invests another 10 units in tool 2 (raising total investment *I* to 20 units), then the *mrr* slightly exceeds 40% and the *msdr* is slightly less than 40%, so that the investment is just worthwhile. Tool 3 is not worthwhile; the *mrr* would be 30%, and the *msdr* would be 50%. Hence, the farmer's *optimal* investment is 20 units, the point at which the *mrr* equals the *msdr*.

correct" preference between present and future consumption, just as there is no "economically correct" preference between apples and oranges. Our problem is to determine our farmer's best decision, given his preference concerning present versus future consumption. Here's how we find the answer.

Assume that starting with present and future consumption at 100 units per year, we ask the farmer: If you give up 10 units of present consumption, how much more consumption per year must you obtain in all future years to "compensate you" — to make you just as well off (to keep your subjective "utility" constant)? Suppose that his honest answer is 3 units per year. Then we say that the farmer's *marginal subjective discount rate msdr* is 30% (3/10).

But we have good news for our farmer. From Figure 10.7, an investment of 10 units (a sacrifice of 10 units of present consumption), which enables him to make tool 1, will have an *mrr* of 50% — more than enough to cover his required *msdr* of 30%. Clearly, the farmer should invest 10 units (accept a 10-unit loss in present consumption) and make tool 1.

After deciding to make tool 1, our farmer has a present consumption of 90 units this year and a future consumption of 105 units per year. Starting with this (90, 105) combination, let's ask our farmer again: If you give up *another* 10 units of present consumption, how much more consumption per year must you obtain in all future years to "compensate you?"

This time the farmer may answer that he requires 4 units more per year, so that his *msdr* now rises to 40%. Why does his *msdr* rise? Because he is now starting with a (90, 105) combination instead of a (100, 100) combination. With present consumption having declined to 90 units and future consumption having risen to 105 units per year, the farmer is likely to place a higher value on present consumption.

The news we have for our farmer is now less exciting. From Figure 10.7, it is evident that investing *another* 10 units (sacrificing another 10 units of present consumption) to make tool 2 has an *mrr* of only 40%. Since his *msdr* is also 40%, this is just enough to maintain his current position. In fact, if both the *mrr* and the *msdr* were exactly 40%, the farmer would not care if he made tool 2; he would be "indifferent." For convenience, we will assume that either the *mrr* is slightly above 40% or the *msdr* is slightly below 40%, so that the farmer will want to make tool 2. His present–future consumption combination will then move from (90, 105) to (80, 109).

It is clear that the farmer should not make tool 3. After making tools 1 and 2 — investing 20 units (sacrificing 20 units of present consumption), so that his combination is now (80, 109) — his *msdr* will be even higher. For example, as shown in Figure 10.7, the farmer's *msdr* on another 10-unit sacrifice could be 50%, but the *mrr* on another 10-unit investment (tool 3) would be only 30% — not enough to compensate him for the sacrifice. We can therefore draw the following conclusion:

▶ It is *optimal* for the farmer to keep investing in tools as long as the *mrr* exceeds the *msdr* and to stop when the *mrr* equals the *msdr*. After that point, further investment will result in an *mrr* that is less than the *msdr* and will reduce the farmer's well-being as he perceives it.

Note that the *mrr* is *objective;* it is dependent on the physical productivity of tools. By contrast, the *msdr* is *subjective;* it is dependent on the subjective preference of the farmer. To determine the farmer's optimal investment, we must consider both the productivity of the farmer's tools (the *mrr*) and the farmer's preference for present versus future consumption (the *msdr*).

INTERTEMPORAL EFFICIENCY

Once again, refer to the *mrr*–*msdr* diagram in Figure 10.7. Initially, when the farmer's present–future consumption combination is tentatively (100, 100), the *mrr* on a 10-unit investment (tool 1) is 50%; but his *msdr* is only 30%. Thus, the farmer can improve his position by reallocating 10 units from consumption to investment. Once he has invested 20 units, so that the *mrr* on the last investment equals the *msdr*, however, it is no longer possible to reallocate further and improve the farmer's position.

Economists would call the initial resource allocation (100 units for consumption, 0 units for investment) "inefficient."

An allocation is INEFFICIENT if it is possible to make everyone better off by a reallocation.

By contrast, economists would call the final resource allocation (80 units for consumption, 20 units for investment) "efficient."

An allocation is EFFICIENT if it is *not* possible to make everyone better off by a reallocation.

In our one-person economy, the allocation is efficient if the *mrr* equals the *msdr*. Since we are considering the choice between consumption at different times, we will call this *intertemporal efficiency*.

By similar reasoning, it can be shown that in an economy with many persons and many firms, efficiency requires that the *mrr* of all firms must be the same, the *msdr* of all persons must be the same, and the common *mrr* must equal the common *msdr*.

INTERTEMPORAL EFFICIENCY requires that the marginal rate of return on real investment *mrr* equal the marginal subjective discount rate *msdr*.

We will now explain why, under certain ideal conditions, a competitive economy will automatically achieve intertemporal efficiency. Suppose that capital markets are "perfect," so that every person and every firm can borrow or lend without limit at the going market interest rate for the economy r. Assume that there is no tax on capital (interest) income, so that the interest rate r paid by a borrower is fully received by the lender.

Each person will maximize his or her subjective utility (welfare) by borrowing or lending, thereby reallocating consumption between the present and the future, until $msdr = r$. For example, initially, if $msdr = 8\%$ when r is 12%, a person will raise saving by $100, because the 12%

return *r* exceeds the 8% *msdr* required to make it just worthwhile. If the individual saves another $100, then 9% may be required, and so on, until finally the *msdr* rises to 12% (equal to *r*). At this point, the individual will stop, satisfied with the allocation between present and future consumption.

▶ To maximize subjective utility, each person will allocate between consumption and saving so that the marginal subjective discount rate *msdr* equals the market interest rate *r*.

Now let's consider firms. Each firm faces different investment opportunities. As long as the *mrr* that a firm receives on real investment exceeds *r*, the firm will find it profitable to borrow and invest until its *mrr* finally declines to equality with *r*. For example, suppose that an investment has an *mrr* of 15% when *r* is 12%. Clearly, it will be profitable for the firm to borrow at 12% to finance an investment that will yield 15%. The next investment may have an *mrr* of only 14%. Eventually, the *mrr* on an investment will decline to equality with *r* at 12%. Further investment will yield an *mrr* below 12% and will therefore not be profitable. Thus

▶ To maximize profit, each firm will invest until its marginal rate of return on investment *mrr* equals the market interest rate *r*.

It should now be apparent that the outcome for society is intertemporally efficient. People act in a way that sets their *msdr* equal to *r*. Firms act in a way that sets their *mrr* equal to the same *r*. Thus, without any participant planning it

▶ In a competitive economy, under certain ideal conditions (including the absence of a tax on capital income), the marginal rate of return on real investment *mrr* will equal the marginal subjective discount rate *msdr*, so that the allocation is *intertemporally efficient.*

This desirable outcome under ideal market conditions is an example of Adam Smith's famous "invisible hand" principle. Each person or firm intends only to promote self-interest: the person seeks to maximize his or her utility; the firm, to maximize its profit. Neither cares about contributing to an efficient allocation of resources between the *C* and *I* sectors, but through a competitive market, they are led by an "invisible hand" to achieve this desirable result.

We will now show that a *capital income tax* will cause an inefficient allocation between the *C* and *I* sectors. In particular, too few resources will be allocated to the *I* sector; the investment rate of the economy will be inefficiently low.

We must now distinguish between the *gross interest rate* r_g that a firm (borrower) pays and the *net interest rate* r_n that a person (saver–lender) receives. For example, if $r_g = 15\%$ and the capital income tax rate is 33%, then $r_n = 10\%$.

▶ To maximize utility, each person sets his or her *msdr* equal to the net interest rate r_n; to maximize profit, each firm sets its *mrr* equal to the gross interest rate r_g. If r_g exceeds r_n, then the *mrr* will exceed the *msdr* and allocation will be inefficient.

Thus, the allocation between the C and I sectors that occurs under the capital income tax is wasteful, because it is possible to raise every individual's utility by moving resources from the C sector to the I sector.

Consider the impact of starting from the allocation under the capital income tax and then shifting $100 worth of resources from the C sector to the I sector. Assume that the tax results in a gross interest rate $r_g = 15\%$ and a net interest rate $r_n = 10\%$. (Our conclusion does not depend on the value of r_g, but only on the existence of a "wedge" between r_g and r_n.) The reduction in C goods requires a corresponding reduction of $100 in present consumption by some person (or persons). However, because every person has an *msdr* equal to r_n (10%), each individual will be just as well off as long as the sacrifice results in an increase in future consumption of $10 per year.

But since $r_g = 15\%$, the *mrr* is also 15%. It follows that a machine produced in the I sector with the $100 of resources will raise future output — and, hence, consumption — by $15 per year. If $10 per year is given to the person(s) who made the original sacrifice, then they are just as well off as before. The $5-per-year surplus can then be divided among all persons, so that everyone's utility increases.

▶ Starting at the allocation under the capital income tax, when the *mrr* exceeds the *msdr,* it is possible to raise everyone's utility by raising the investment rate of the economy, because the *msdr* that each person subjectively requires is less than the *mrr* that real investment can yield.

▶ It follows that eliminating the capital income tax by switching from an income tax to a consumption tax (or a labor income tax) would eliminate intertemporal inefficiency.

▶ Because capital income is taxed under the U.S. personal and corporate income tax, the rate of capital accumulation is inefficiently low. Conversion of the income tax to a consumption tax (or a labor income tax) would promote efficient capital accumulation.

It should be noted, however, that switching to a consumption tax (or a labor income tax) might worsen another inefficiency by distorting the choice between leisure and consumption. Some researchers have compared the reduction in intertemporal inefficiency with the possible increase in leisure–consumption inefficiency and have estimated that a net reduction in inefficiency would occur. Although this result is not unanimous, it seems reasonable to conclude that

▶ Converting the income tax to a consumption tax (or a labor income tax) would probably result in a net reduction in inefficiency.

10.8 U.S. Output and Productivity Growth

THE UNITED STATES VERSUS OTHER COUNTRIES

Figure 10.8 compares the investment rates and productivity growth rates (in manufacturing) of the United States and several other economically advanced countries during the 1970s. Investment is defined narrowly as new physical capital; productivity, as output per hour.

▶ Figure 10.8 shows that investment rates and productivity growth rates (in manufacturing) are highly correlated.

Japan's net investment (gross investment minus depreciation; the increase in the capital stock) averaged nearly 20% of GNP, and its growth rate of output per hour in manufacturing averaged over 7%. For the United States, net investment averaged less than 7% of GNP, and the growth rate of output per hour in manufacturing averaged about 2.5%.

In the 1980s, U.S. gross private investment has averaged 15% of GNP, roughly the same as in the 1970s. By contrast, in the 1970s, the gross private investment rate was 28% in Japan and 19% in both West Germany and France.*

Figure 10.9 compares the *personal saving rates*—the ratio of personal (household) saving to personal (household) disposable income —of several economically advanced countries in the mid-1970s. At one end of the spectrum, Japan's personal saving rate is above 20%. At the other end, the U.S. personal saving rate is near 6%. In the 1980s, the U.S. personal saving rate remains at roughly 5%–6%.

Private saving is composed of business saving as well as personal (household) saving. In 1984, U.S. personal saving was 4% of GNP and gross business saving was 14% of GNP, so that total gross private saving was 18% of GNP. In the 1980s, the U.S. *gross private saving rate* (the

---

* Barry Bosworth, *Tax Incentives and Economic Growth* (Washington, D.C.: The Brookings Institute, 1984) 92.

FIGURE 10.8 INTERNATIONAL COMPARISON OF INVESTMENT AND
PRODUCTIVITY GROWTH (1971–1980)

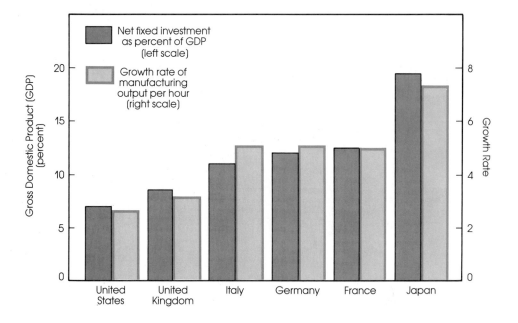

SOURCES: Organization for Economic Cooperation and Development and *Economic Report of the President 1983*, p. 82.

A higher investment rate generally implies a higher productivity growth rate. The United States has a relatively low investment rate and a relatively low productivity growth rate.

ratio of gross private saving to GNP) is averaging 17%, roughly the same as in the 1970s. By contrast, in the 1970s, the gross private saving rate was 30% in Japan and 21% in both West Germany and France.*

To summarize:

▶ Compared with several other economically advanced countries, the United States has a low saving rate, a low investment rate, and a low productivity growth rate.

SOURCES OF ECONOMIC GROWTH

In Section 10.1, we explained the importance of a broad concept of capital that encompasses human and knowledge capital as well as phys-

---

* Bosworth, *Tax Incentives*, 92.

FIGURE 10.9 INTERNATIONAL COMPARISON OF PERSONAL SAVING RATES (MID-1970s)

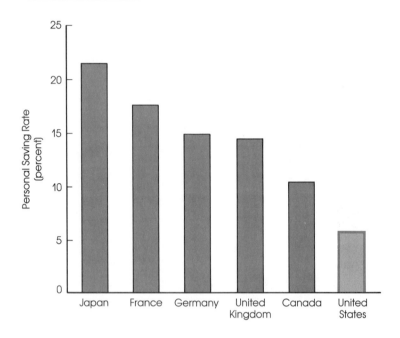

Note: Due to discrepancies in data collection, international saving rates are not exactly comparable.

SOURCES: U.S. Department of Commerce (*Survey of Current Business*) and International Trade Administration; *Federal Reserve Bank of New York Quarterly Review* (Spring 1981), p. 26.

The United States has a relatively low personal saving rate.

ical capital. Such a concept of capital includes technological change and the improvement of the quality—as well as the quantity—of capital.

Capital accumulation does not simply consist of an increase in machinery of unchanged quality. It consists of an increase in machinery of improved quality, in the skills of workers, and in the blueprints that indicate how to produce new products and old products more efficiently. In the actual economy, technological change, invention, and improvement of skills are all part of the process of capital accumulation.

Although the broad concept of capital is useful, researchers have also sought to quantify the contribution of each of its components to economic growth. In Section 16.4 on the sources of economic growth, we will consider this work carefully. In this section, we will provide a summary of the research.

Two early, influential studies by Moses Abramowitz in 1956 and Robert Solow in 1957 reach similar conclusions. During the first half of the twentieth century in the United States, the rise in physical capital per worker appears to explain only a small fraction of the rise in output per worker. These early results have, at times, been interpreted as showing that capital accumulation is not an important determinant of economic growth. But this inference is incorrect. In these studies, the dollar value of the stock of physical capital is the measure of capital. Each worker or hour of labor is assumed to have the same level of efficiency.

But according to our broader concept of capital accumulation, resources are diverted away from producing consumer goods and into not only the production of physical capital goods but also invention and organizational planning (the production of knowledge capital) and education and skill (the production of human capital).

▶ Because the accumulation of knowledge and human capital normally requires a sacrifice in consumption and because technical knowledge and skill raise the productivity of an hour of labor, they should be regarded as capital.

But these components of capital were excluded in the early studies of the contributions of capital to economic growth. It is interesting that physical capital appears to account for a fraction of economic growth. But this does not mean that capital accumulation, when capital is defined broadly, is unimportant for growth. Subsequent research has focused on the other components of capital.

Some of the most careful studies of the sources of economic growth have been performed by Edward Denison of The Brookings Institution.* Let's review some of his conclusions.

First, consider total output (in the nonresidential business sector, which excludes housing and government), which grew at an annual rate of 3.8% from 1948 to 1973. Of this growth rate, 15% was due to the increase in physical capital; 15%, to the change in employment and hours; 14%, to education; 10%, to improved resource allocation (mainly, the shift out of farming); 37%, to advances in technological, managerial, and organizational knowledge; 11%, to economies of scale; and, finally, −2%, to certain legal and human-environment changes.

---

* See Edward Denison, *Trends in American Economic Growth, 1929–1982* (Washington, D.C.: The Brookings Institution, 1985); a summary of Denison's research, "The Contribution of Capital to Economic Growth," appeared in *American Economic Review, Papers and Proceedings* (May 1980).

Thus, even after isolating human capital (education) with a 14% contribution, the "residual"—advances in knowledge—remains the largest single source of economic growth.

Next, consider output per worker, the main focus of the early Solow study. The increase in physical capital per worker accounts for 15% of the rise in output per worker (the same as the percentage for total output).

If the whole economy (instead of the nonresidential business sector) is considered, then the capital contribution rises to 18%–19%. Thus, the contribution of physical capital—either to the growth rate of total output or output per worker—is estimated to be between 15% and 19% over this postwar period in the United States.

Next, Denison turns to an international comparison of growth rates. Although physical capital accumulation sometimes contributes to economic-growth differences, it is far from the sole cause. For example, in two countries with faster growth rates than the United States—Italy and France—capital contributed no more to economic growth and, hence, explains none of the difference.

Japan has the highest growth rate of the economically advanced countries Denison studied. Japan did secure a higher contribution from physical capital accumulation than other countries. However, it also benefited from changes in working hours, age–sex composition of employment, resource allocation, new production knowledge, and economies of scale. Physical capital is one—but only one—source of the higher Japanese growth rate.

Denison emphasizes this last point in an interesting way by asking what *investment rate* (ratio of investment to national income) would the United States need to adopt to match the Japanese growth rate of output? In other words, if the United States were to rely solely on raising physical capital accumulation, what would it take to reach Japan's productivity growth rate?

Initially, Denison calculates that the U.S. net investment rate, which averaged less than 8% in the postwar years up to 1973, would have to rise to 60% of national income. He then adds that due to diminishing returns to capital, an even higher investment rate would be required.

▶ Denison estimates that each 1% increase in the U.S. net investment rate will raise the growth rate of output by roughly 0.1%.

From 1948 to 1973, the growth rate of output averaged 3.8% per year. According to Denison's estimate, an increase in the net investment rate from 8% to 9% will raise the growth rate to 3.9%.

It is worth quoting Denison's interpretation of his findings:

> How important to economic growth in advanced countries is the accumulation of physical capital? My short answer is that

increased capital is one of several important sources of output growth. This appraisal, which is amply supported by research results, should surprise no one — but doubtless it will. . . .

Why many people share a vision of growth that assigns exclusive attention to capital I do not know. . . .

To deny that capital is everything is not to imply that it is nothing. I do not share the other extreme view, sometimes encountered, that capital can be ignored because its significance is hard to establish if one fits a production function by correlation analysis. I stress again: capital is an important growth source. It has sometimes contributed importantly to differences in growth rates between periods and places. More capital formation would raise the growth rate.*

Whenever Denison mentions "capital," he is referring to physical capital. Denison's own work shows that education (human capital) makes an important contribution. Knowledge capital — advances in technological, organizational, and managerial knowledge — is the single most important source of economic growth. New products and techniques are not normally created or implemented without an investment of resources. In general, resources must be diverted to these activities in order to produce new inventions, techniques, and "blueprints."

One of the most careful and thorough studies of the contribution of capital to economic growth, broadly defined, has been conducted by John W. Kendrick, who writes:

> This study rests squarely on the concept of capital as output- and income-producing capacity and of investments as outlays that maintain or enhance productive capacity. On the basis of this definition, it is argued that total investment and the associated stocks of capital should include not only the tangible, nonhuman capital outlays of all sectors but also rearing costs (tangible human investment) and intangible investments that are embodied in, and improve the quality or productive efficiency of, tangible factors. The intangibles are viewed as including outlays for research and development, education and training, health and safety, and mobility.†

When this broad concept of capital is applied, Kendrick finds that

> In contrast to the declining secular trend shown by the conventional series, all of our measures of total capital formation indicate a significant rise in the proportion of income and prod-

---

* Edward Denison, "The Contribution of Capital to Economic Growth," *American Economic Review, Papers and Proceedings* (May 1980), 220.
† John W. Kendrick, *The Formation and Stocks of Total Capital* (New York: National Bureau of Economic Research, 1976) 126–27.

uct saved and invested between 1929 and 1969. By 1969, virtually half of the adjusted GNP was devoted to forward-looking outlays we term "total gross investment," up from around 43% in 1929.*

The categories of investment, which are usually excluded from a narrow definition of capital, account for the increase.

▶ The research of Denison, Kendrick, and others suggests that physical capital is not the sole or primary determinant of economic growth, although it is one important contributor. But if capital is broadly defined to include knowledge and human capital as well as physical capital, then capital does appear to be a major determinant of economic growth—particularly of output per worker.

THE SLOWDOWN IN U.S. PRODUCTIVITY GROWTH

Over the past two decades, the labor productivity growth rate has declined from over 3% to roughly 1% per year. Productivity growth resurged during the strong 1983–1984 recovery, but it is too early to know whether this resurgence is temporary or whether it marks the beginning of a more permanent upturn in productivity growth.

According to one study,[†] once the estimated effect of the cyclical upturn is removed, the underlying trend in labor productivity growth remains about 1% per year—roughly the same rate as in the 1970s and roughly one-half of the 2% average productivity growth rate this century. Many possible sources of this slowdown have been suggested. Let's review them.

First, the past decade saw two severe recessions—the first in 1975, the second in 1982. Labor productivity declines in recessions because firms do not layoff workers immediately when sales begin to decline. It is costly to recruit and train new workers when recovery comes. Therefore, firms initially retain workers during a slowdown; they cut back their hours, and require less output per hour. Hence, output per worker declines.

It is not clear how much of the slowdown in productivity growth can be attributed to this normal, cyclical effect; however, most analysts believe that the recessions explain only part of the productivity slowdown.

---

* Kendrick, "The Formation," 127.
† Peter K. Clark, "Productivity and Profits in the 1980s: Are They Really Improving?" *Brookings Papers on Economic Activity,* 1 (Washington, D.C.: The Brookings Institution, 1984).

In another study,* Martin N. Baily tries to estimate what the labor productivity growth rate would have been without the 1975 and 1982 recessions by estimating the normal relationship between a rise in the unemployment rate and a decline in the labor productivity growth rate over the 1949–1968 period. Based on his estimate of this relationship, Baily determines how much the high unemployment rates of the two recessions reduced productivity growth. He concludes that much of the productivity slowdown cannot be explained by the recessions.

Most analysts believe that the productivity slowdown is not primarily due to the recessions of the past decade. Between 1976 and 1979, real output in the private business sector increased 4.5% per year and total employment increased 13%.[†] Yet productivity growth was very poor over these four years.

Next, attention has focused on investment and capital accumulation as sources of the economic slowdown. International comparison suggests a high correlation of investment rates and labor productivity growth rates. It therefore seems natural to look for a decline in the U.S. investment rate or in the growth rate of the capital–labor ratio during the past decade. Did either occur?

The investment rate, at most, declined moderately during the 1970s. Its precise behavior depends on whether the whole economy or the private business sector is studied, and on whether gross or net investment and gross or net output are used. Figure 10.10 illustrates the trend in the investment rate.

The investment rate shown is the ratio of net, private, nonresidential, fixed investment as a percentage of GNP, based on five-year, centered moving averages. Measured in this way, the investment rate declined from about 4% in the 1960s to 3% in the 1970s, thereby returning to its level in the 1950s. It should be noted, however, that according to other measures, the investment rate remained constant or rose modestly in the 1970s. We can conclude that a clear, significant decline in the investment rate is not evident in the 1970s, although a modest decline did occur by some measures.

By contrast, the growth rate of the capital–labor ratio did decline significantly in the 1970s, as is evident in Figure 10.10. The growth rate of the capital–labor ratio in Figure 10.10 is the percentage change in real, net, private, nonresidential fixed capital stock per worker in the business sector, based on five-year, centered moving averages. From nearly 4% in the late 1960s, this growth rate declines to less than 1% in the late 1970s.

---

* Martin N. Baily, "Productivity and the Services of Capital and Labor," *Brookings Papers on Economic Activity,* 1 (Washington, D.C.: The Brookings Institution, 1981).
† Baily, "Productivity and the Services," 5.

FIGURE 10.10 U.S. INVESTMENT AND CAPITAL PER WORKER

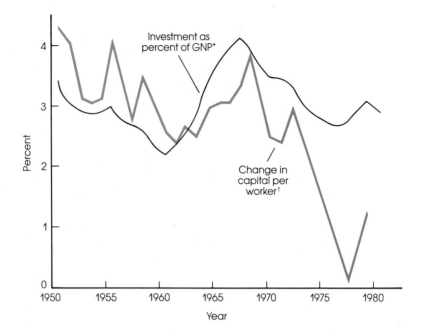

*Net private nonresidential fixed investment as percent of GNP; five-year centered moving averages.
†Percent change in real net private nonresidential fixed capital stock per worker in the business sector; five-year centered moving averages.

SOURCES: U.S. Department of Commerce, U.S. Department of Labor, and Council of Economic Advisers; *Economic Report of the President 1983*, p. 80.

The U.S. investment rate declined slightly while the growth rate of capital per worker declined sharply in the 1970s.

This sharp decline occurred for two reasons, despite the rough constancy of the investment rate. First, output grew somewhat more slowly, partly due to the recession, so that a given investment percentage rate yielded a smaller increase in the capital stock. Second, the labor force grew more rapidly. Even with the 1975 recession, actual employment increased by 2.0% per year from 1973 to 1978, compared to 1.5% per year from 1948 to 1973.

Another suspect in the productivity slowdown is energy. OPEC's quadrupling of the world oil price in 1974 significantly slowed the growth rate of energy use over the remainder of the decade. For convenience, thus far, we have worked with the simple production function

(10.1), where Q depends on K and L. But given the magnitude of the energy supply shock in the 1970s, it is important to add energy E as a third input, along with K and L. If the growth rate of E is reduced, then Q may grow more slowly relative to K or L.

Baily has suggested an intriguing interaction between energy and the effective capital–labor ratio that might help to explain the productivity slowdown. His hypothesis is that the sharp rise in the price of energy caused a significant fraction of the capital stock to become economically obsolete. Firms that were stuck with high energy-use capital when the high price of energy called for low energy-use capital may have found it optimal to reduce the utilization of their high energy-use capital.

The conventional measure of the capital–labor ratio, shown in Figure 10.10, ignores the possibility that some of the capital may have become underutilized due to the energy price rise. The growth rate of the effective capital–labor ratio may have declined even more sharply than the conventional measure. Baily notes that the stock market could have been depressed in the late 1970s, partly because investors recognized that a portion of the capital stock had become obsolete.

Let's list some other possible suspects that may have contributed to the productivity slowdown: the change in the composition of the labor force; environmental and safety regulation; a possible decline in research and development spending and in the opportunity for significant innovation; and a shift in the composition of output.

An alternative hypothesis,* emphasizing social and motivational factors, argues that the productivity slowdown is due primarily to a reduction in the managerial ability to compel or induce intense effort by workers and to a reduction in competitive pressure on firms, which has caused business innovation to decline.

International comparison gives some perspective to the recent U.S. productivity slowdown. Virtually all other economically advanced countries also experienced a significant productivity slowdown in the 1970s. It might be noted that all of these countries, like the United States, were subject to the world oil-price shock of 1974 and the world recessions of 1975 and 1982. The low relative position of the United States remained unaltered.

To summarize:

▶ The productivity slowdown is probably due to a number of causes. The recessions of 1975 and 1982, the slowdown in the growth rate of the effective capital–labor ratio, and the reduc-

---

* Samuel Bowles, David Gordon, and Thomas Weisskoff, "Hearts and Minds: A Social Model of U.S. Productivity Growth," *Brookings Papers on Economic Activity*, 2 (Washington, D.C.: The Brookings Institution, 1983).

tion in the growth rate of energy use probably deserve special attention, although several other suspects warrant questioning as well.

▶ Faster capital accumulation — where "capital" is broadly defined to include physical, human, and knowledge capital — will raise the productivity growth rate. Whatever the source of the productivity slowdown, it can be combatted by policies that achieve faster capital accumulation.

SUMMARY

1. *Capital accumulation*, which raises future productive capacity, requires a sacrifice of present consumption. Whether we build machinery *(physical capital)*, improve our skills *(human capital)*, or invent new technology *(knowledge capital)*, time and resources must be diverted from producing goods and services for current consumption.

2. With real output Q kept equal to constant inflation output Q_c, raising investment requires reducing present consumption below what it otherwise would be.

3. To shift the composition of output toward more investment, the composition of demand must be shifted. *Total consumption demand C_T* must be decreased and *total investment demand I_T* must be increased, so that total demand remains equal to Q_c.

4. A shift to a tight fiscal–offsetting monetary policy mix that holds real output Q at Q_c will reduce consumption and raise investment.

5. Reducing the government budget deficit by raising taxes or by cutting government transfers (a tightening of fiscal policy), while maintaining output at Q_c through an offsetting monetary policy, will reduce consumption and raise investment.

6. Two consumption-reducing policies are *tight fiscal policy* and the *personal consumption (expenditure) tax*.

7. Eliminating the Q_c deficit could significantly increase the U.S. net (private) investment rate.

8. An important lesson of economic history is that capital accumulation raises the *standard of living* of the average worker.

9. Faster capital accumulation in the present will reduce poverty among low-skilled workers in the future.

10. *Progressive* capital accumulation raises the standard of living of future low-skilled workers without imposing a sacrifice on today's low-skilled workers.

11. An increase in the U.S. *saving rate* is necessary to prevent a future

deterioration of the U.S. standard of living relative to the standard of living of several other countries with higher saving rates.

12. It is optimal for the farmer in our example to invest in tools until the *marginal rate of return mrr* equals the *marginal subjective discount rate msdr.*

13. Eliminating the *capital income tax* by switching from an income tax to a consumption tax would eliminate *intertemporal inefficiency.*

14. Cross-country data indicate that the *productivity growth rate* is correlated with the *investment rate.*

15. In comparison with other economically advanced countries, the United States has a low saving rate, a low investment rate, and a low productivity growth rate.

16. The U.S. productivity slowdown in the 1970s and early 1980s is probably due to a number of causes. The recessions of 1975 and 1982, the slowdown in the growth rate of the effective capital–labor ratio, and the reduction in the growth rate of energy use probably deserve special attention.

17. Whatever the source of the productivity slowdown, it can be combatted by policies that achieve faster capital accumulation.

TERMS AND CONCEPTS

aggregate production function
capacity utilization rate
capital
capital gains
capital income tax
capital–labor ratio (k)
compensation
consumption C goods sector
depreciation
economic growth
efficient capital accumulation
financial capital
flow
gross interest rate (r_g)
gross investment
gross private saving

health capital
horizontal redistribution effect
human capital
incentive effect
income effect
intertemporal efficiency
investment I goods sector
knowledge capital
labor income tax
marginal rate of return *(mrr)*
marginal subjective discount
    rate *(msdr)*
net interest rate (r_n)
net investment
net investment rate (I/Q)
net private saving

net saving rate (S/Q)

offsetting monetary policy

output per worker (Q/L)

personal consumption (expenditure) tax

physical capital

production function

productivity growth

progressive capital accumulation

property income

rate of return on investment

real capital

real capital per worker (K/L)

real investment

real wage per worker (w)

stock

substitution effect

supply-side economics hypothesis

QUESTIONS

10.1 Suppose that the economy is initially at r_0 and Q_c on the $IS-LM$ diagram. Then taxes are raised or government transfers are cut, and monetary policy is adjusted to keep the economy at Q_c. The final $IS-LM$ intersection point is r_1 and Q_c. Assume that Q_c is unaltered.

   a. Construct the $IS-LM$ diagram to show the initial equilibrium.

   b. How does the IS curve shift?

   c. How does the LM curve shift?

   d. How does r_1 compare with r_0?

   e. What is the relationship between the Q_c deficit and the interest rate r?

   f. What happens to consumption and investment? Why?

   g. If the tax increase reduces Q_c, then what happens to consumption and investment? Explain.

10.2 If a citizen wants the wages of low-skilled workers to increase at a faster rate, without imposing a burden on today's low-skilled workers, then what capital accumulation policies should the citizen advocate? Why?

10.3 Consider a simple rural economy with one farmer. Initially, the farmer devotes all of his working time to growing food. Annual food output is 200 units, and his consumption is 200 units. Then the farmer becomes aware of the option of making tools. To make a tool requires a sacrifice of 20 units of food this year. Once made, a tool never depreciates.

   Suppose that the most productive tool will raise food output by 10 units per year for the rest of the farmer's life; the next tool, by 8 units per year; the next, by 6 units per year; the next, by 4 units per year; and the last, by 2 units per year.

   At present and future consumption levels of 200 units per year, the farmer is willing to sacrifice 20 units this year to obtain 6 additional units per year in all future years. But the next 20 units that are sacrificed will require 8 additional units per year; the next 20 units, 10 additional units per year; and so on.

a. What is the *mrr* on the first tool?

b. Draw the *mrr* schedule.

c. Draw the *msdr* schedule.

d. How many tools should the farmer make? Explain.

10.4 How important is *capital* as a source of economic growth?

10.5 Why did U.S. productivity growth slow down in the 1970s?

11

Macroeconomics in an Open Economy

Thus far, we have ignored foreign trade and capital flows and have treated the U.S. economy as if it were *closed*. But virtually any actual economy is an *open economy*, subject to international trade and capital flows. In this chapter, we will modify our analysis to recognize the openness of the U.S. economy.

Although the U.S. economy has traditionally been relatively closed compared to the economies of most European countries and Japan, it has become more open in recent years. For example, in 1964 exports were 6% of GNP; in 1984, exports were 10% of GNP. Similarly, in 1964 imports were 5% of GNP; in 1984, imports were 12% of GNP. Open-economy macroeconomics is therefore relevant to the U.S. economy and to the design of U.S. macroeconomic policy.

11.1 National Income Accounting in an Open Economy

In our first example in Section 1.1, the farmer adds $100 of value and sells the $100 of wheat to the miller, the miller adds $150 of value and sells $250 of flour to the baker, and the baker adds $100 of value and sells $350 of bread to the consumer. Total (final) output is $350.

Now suppose that the farmer lives in another country, so that the $100 worth of wheat is imported. The value-added in our country is then the miller's $150 plus the baker's $100 (a total of $250). It is clearly improper to claim that $350 is the output of our economy, yet $350 is the final product sold to the consumer. Final product expenditure therefore equals the sum of domestically produced output and imports.

Now suppose that of the $350 worth of bread, $150 worth is exported (sold abroad) and $200 worth is sold to domestic consumers.

When foreign trade is included, the sum of domestically produced output and imports is divided between domestic uses (consumption, investment, and government purchases) and exports. Thus

(11.1) $\quad Q + Z \equiv C + I + G + X$

where Z = imports
$\qquad X$ = exports

Subtracting Z from both sides of equation (11.1) and letting $NX \equiv X - Z$, we obtain

(11.2) $\qquad Q \equiv C + I + G + NX$

where NX = net exports (the trade surplus)

In our simple example, with $C = \$200$, $I = G = 0$, $X = \$150$, and $Z = \$100$, we have

$$250 = 200 + (150 - 100)$$

Dividing government expenditure G into its two components, consumption G_C and investment G_I, equation (11.2) becomes

$$Q \equiv C + I + G_C + G_I + NX$$

Recognizing that total consumption C_T is the sum of C and G_C and that total investment I_T is the sum of I and G_I, we obtain

(11.3) $\qquad Q \equiv C_T + I_T + NX$

This identity is the same as identity (1.24) for a closed economy with government, except for the inclusion of the term net exports NX.

SAVING AND INVESTMENT

How does the existence of foreign trade affect our conclusions in Chapter 1 concerning saving and investment? It is still true that total saving equals total income minus total consumption, or

(1.28) $\qquad S_T \equiv Q - C_T$

Moving C_T to the left of equation (1.28) gives us

$$Q = C_T + S_T$$

Substituting this expression for Q into identity (11.3) and canceling

C_T on both sides, we obtain

(11.4) $S_T \equiv I_T + NX$

TOTAL SAVING S_T equals *total investment I_T* plus *net exports NX*. In an open economy, total saving exceeds total investment by the amount of net exports.

Now suppose that an offsetting monetary policy keeps the economy at the constant inflation output level Q_c, so that

(11.5) $Q_c = C_T + I_T + NX$

What happens if total saving S_T increases at Q_c—or, equivalently, if total consumption C_T decreases at Q_c (for example, due to a tightening of fiscal policy through a tax increase or to a cut in government transfers or government consumption)?

First, let's focus on total saving S_T in equation (11.4). In a closed economy, an increase in S_T is matched by an equal increase in I_T. But according to equation (11.4), an increase in S_T in an open economy may be shared between I_T and NX. If net exports NX increases, then the increase in domestic investment I_T will be less than the increase in total saving S_T.

Now, let's focus on total consumption C_T in equation (11.5). In a closed economy, the decrease in C_T is matched by an equal increase in I_T, as is evident in Figure 10.1 (page 436). But according to equation (11.5), total domestic investment I_T would not increase as much as C_T decreases if NX increases. Thus, it is possible that the rise in domestic investment I_T will be less than the decrease in total consumption. This possibility is evident if we look at Figure 11.1. If C_T decreases, it is possible that the two other "slices" of the constant inflation output Q_c pie, I_T and NX, will share the increase.

Our analysis in Section 11.6 will demonstrate that this possibility will generally occur. An increase in S_T will be shared by I_T and NX.

Because S_T is the sum of private saving S and government saving S_G, equation (11.4) can be rewritten

$$S + S_G \equiv I + G_I + NX$$

Moving G_I to the left side gives us

$$S + S_G - G_I \equiv I + NX$$

Using identity (1.26), we replace $S_G - G_I$ with Su (the government surplus) to obtain

---

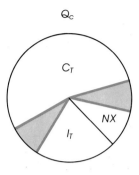

If real output (income) Q is kept at the constant inflation level Q_c, then more total consumption C_T can be obtained only by reducing the sum of total investment I_T and net exports NX. If C_T increases due to an easing of fiscal policy and an offsetting monetary policy holds Q at Q_c, then I_T and NX will "share" the decline. Hence, the rise in C_T will partly crowd out I_T and partly crowd out NX.

(11.6) $$S + Su \equiv I + NX$$

▶ *Private saving S plus the government surplus Su equals private investment I plus net exports NX.*

We will derive a final accounting relationship for later use: *world saving* equals *world investment*. Letting * indicate the rest of the world, we rewrite equation (11.4) for the U.S. economy and for the rest-of-the-world economy:

$$S_T \equiv I_T + NX$$
$$S_T^* \equiv I_T^* + NX^*$$

If U.S. net exports NX are \$100 billion (a *trade surplus* of \$100 billion), then rest-of-the-world net exports NX^* must be $-\$100$ billion (a *trade deficit* of \$100 billion). The sum $NX + NX^*$ must be \$0. If we add the two previous equations, we therefore obtain

$$S_T + S_T^* \equiv I_T + I_T^*$$

The left side of this equation is *total world saving* S_W; the right side is *total world investment* I_W. Thus

(11.7) $$S_W \equiv I_W$$

▶ Total world saving S_W equals total world investment I_W.

We can now summarize:

▶ In a closed economy, total saving equals total investment. This is true whether the closed economy is one country or the whole world. In an open economy with foreign trade, however, total saving exceeds total investment by the amount of net exports.

11.2 Net Exports, Real Output, and the Relative Price

U.S. imports vary directly with U.S. real output (income). When the United States raises its output, producers generally require more materials from abroad. Also, when U.S. income increases, American consumers spend more on imports. U.S. exports depend on the real output (income) of other countries and are largely independent of U.S. output. Because an increase in real output (income) Q raises imports but has little effect on exports

▶ Net exports NX decrease when real output (income) Q increases, as shown in Figure 11.2.

FIGURE 11.2 NET EXPORTS DECREASE AS REAL OUTPUT INCREASES

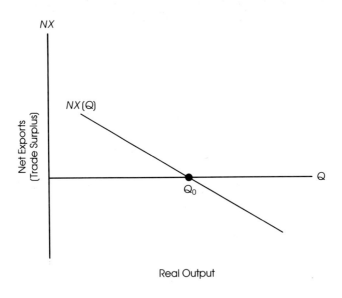

If real output (income) Q increases, then imports Z will increase, so that net exports NX (exports X minus imports Z) will decrease. The NX (Q) curve shows how NX varies with Q. At $Q = Q_0$, $NX = 0$.

U.S. net exports *NX* also vary with the relative price of foreign goods. To compare the prices of foreign and U.S. goods meaningfully, both prices must be expressed in the same currency (for convenience here, the dollar). To convert the price of foreign goods to dollars, we must know the exchange rate *e*.

The EXCHANGE RATE *e* is the dollar price of a unit of foreign currency.

There are many exchange rates—the dollar price of a Japanese yen, a French franc, a German mark, a British pound, and so on. To facilitate the analysis in this chapter, we will combine the rest of the world into a single country, Alpha-Land, with a single currency, the alpha α. The exchange rate *e* is the dollar price of an alpha.

Suppose that the price of 1α is \$2, so that $e = \$2$. If the price of an Alpha good (a good produced in Alpha-Land) is 4α, then its dollar price is $4 \times \$2 = \$8$. More generally:

▶ If P^* is the price of foreign goods in foreign currency, then eP^* is the dollar price of foreign goods.

We define the RELATIVE PRICE *c* as eP^*/P, the ratio of the *dollar price of foreign goods* eP^* to the *dollar price of U.S. goods P*.

We will sometimes write eP^*/P, rather than *c*, because it reminds us that the foreign price is in the numerator and the U.S. price is in the denominator. At other times, *c* will be used to conserve space.

The symbol *c* also denotes U.S. COMPETITIVENESS. An increase in *c* is an increase in U.S. competitiveness, because the foreign price rises relative to the U.S. price.

Suppose the price of Alpha goods P^* rises by 5%, while the exchange rate *e* and the U.S. price level *P* remain constant. The rise in P^* raises the relative price eP^*/P. What happens to expenditures on U.S. exports measured in dollars *X* and expenditures on U.S. imports measured in dollars *Z*?

Alpha-Landers will demand a greater quantity of U.S. exports because U.S. goods are now less expensive relative to Alpha goods. With the dollar price *P* held constant, the *dollar expenditure* (quantity multiplied by dollar price) on U.S. exports *X* will increase.

Americans will demand a smaller quantity of U.S. imports because U.S. goods are now less expensive relative to Alpha goods. With the dollar price of Alpha goods eP^* 5% higher, the dollar expenditure on U.S. imports *Z* will remain constant if quantity is cut by 5%, rise if quantity is cut by less than 5%, and decline if quantity is cut by more than 5%.

Since *X* rises, if *Z* declines, then *NX* rises. Even if *Z* rises, *NX* will rise as long as the rise in X exceeds the rise in Z. Empirical studies show that Z may rise more than X in the short run. However, because the reduction in the quantity of imports increases as time passes, Z will generally rise less than X or decline in the long run. Based on these studies, we will assume that

▶ A rise in the relative price eP^*/P will raise net exports NX in the long run, as shown in Figure 11.3.

If we let parentheses indicate "is a function of" ("varies with"), then

$$(11.8) \qquad NX = NX\left(Q, \frac{eP^*}{P}\right)$$

where a decline in Q or a rise in eP^*/P increases NX in the long run.

NET EXPORTS AND THE *IS* CURVE

Let's reexamine equation (11.2):

$$(11.2) \qquad Q = C + I + G + NX$$

FIGURE 11.3 A RISE IN THE RELATIVE PRICE INCREASES NET EXPORTS

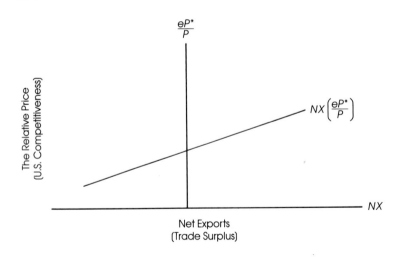

If the relative price eP^*/P (the ratio of the dollar price of foreign goods eP^* to the dollar price of U.S. goods P) increases, then net exports NX will increase in the long run. The NX (eP^*/P) curve shows how NX varies with eP^*/P.

interpreting the right side as components of demand. Just as an increase in *I* or *G* at a given (*r*, *Q*) shifts the *IS* curve to the right, so an increase in *NX* at a given (*r*, *Q*) shifts the *IS* curve to the right. By equation (11.8), a rise in the relative price eP^*/P increases *NX* in the long run at a given (*r*, *Q*). Thus

▶ A rise in the relative price eP^*/P shifts the *IS* curve to the right in the long run.

11.3 The Balance of Payments

The *balance of payments BP* is the record of a country's transactions with the rest of the world. Balance-of-payments accounting follows this rule:

▶ Any transaction that entails a payment *to* U.S. residents (by foreigners) is a *surplus item* in the U.S. balance-of-payments accounts. Any transaction that entails a payment *by* U.S. residents (to foreigners) is a *deficit item*.

For example, the sale of U.S. exports and financial assets (stocks and bonds) to foreigners are surplus items; the purchase of foreign imports and financial assets by Americans are deficit items.

The balance of payments consists of two main accounts: the *current* account and the *capital* account.

The *current account* records trade in goods and services (exports *X* and imports *Z*) and in international transfer payments. Exports *X* include not only goods (merchandise) but also services. For example, when U.S. residents sell capital services abroad, these services (measured in terms of the dividends and interest paid by foreigners) are a component of U.S. exports *X*. Symmetrically, when U.S. residents buy capital services from foreigners, these services (measured in terms of the dividends and interest paid to foreigners) are a component of U.S. imports *Z*. Net transfers to U.S. residents is a surplus item.

The CURRENT ACCOUNT SURPLUS equals *net exports NX* plus *net transfers* to U.S. residents.

In recent years, much attention has been paid to the *merchandise trade balance,* which focuses on goods and excludes services. The *merchandise trade surplus* equals exports of goods (not services) minus imports of goods (not services). Note that the merchandise trade surplus does *not* equal net exports *NX*, which includes services, and does *not* equal the current account surplus, which includes services and transfers.

The *capital account* records purchases and sales of assets, such as stocks, bonds, bank deposits, and land. A *capital account surplus* results when receipts from the sale of U.S. assets exceed payments for foreign assets.

We say that a *capital inflow* occurs when foreigners buy U.S. financial assets, such as stocks and bonds; a capital inflow is a *surplus* item. The "export" of bonds, like the export of goods, gives rise to a payment to U.S. residents (by foreigners) and is therefore a surplus item.

We say that a *capital outflow* occurs when U.S. residents buy foreign assets, such as stocks and bonds; a capital outflow is a *deficit* item. The "import" of bonds, like the import of goods, gives rise to a payment by U.S. residents (to foreigners) and is therefore a deficit item.

The NET CAPITAL INFLOW equals the *capital inflow* minus the *capital outflow*. The net capital inflow is the CAPITAL ACCOUNT SURPLUS.

Combining the two accounts

The BALANCE-OF-PAYMENTS SURPLUS equals the *current account surplus* plus the *capital account surplus.*

The current account surplus equals net exports *NX* plus net transfers to Americans. To focus on net exports *NX*, we combine net transfers with the capital account surplus to obtain the *adjusted net capital inflow CF,* which is "adjusted" to include the current account item, net transfers. Thus

(11.9) $$BP \equiv NX + CF$$

where BP = the balance-of-payments surplus

NX = net exports

CF = the adjusted net capital inflow (the capital account surplus plus net transfers to Americans)

When *CF* is used, the adjustment for net transfers is included. We will refer to *CF* simply as the *net capital inflow* (omitting the word "adjusted").

11.4 The Foreign Exchange Market

Let's consider two alternative "regimes" — a *flexible (floating)* exchange rate and a *fixed* exchange rate. As before, for convenience, we will assume that the rest of the world is a single country, Alpha-Land, with a single currency, the alpha α.

▶ Under both *flexible* and *fixed* exchange rate regimes, the exchange rate e — the dollar price of a unit of the foreign currency (here, the alpha α) — is governed by the supply of and the demand for alphas. If supply equals demand, then e will remain

---

FIGURE 11.5 THE NET CAPITAL INFLOW INCREASES AS THE INTEREST RATE RISES

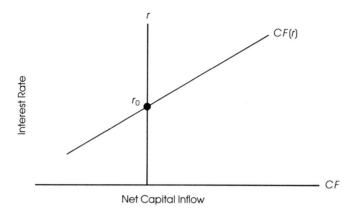

If the U.S. interest rate r increases, then wealth-holders will shift their portfolio demand toward U.S. bonds, so that the net capital inflow CF will increase. The $CF(r)$ curve shows how CF varies with r. At $r = r_0$, $CF = 0$.

capital inflow CF. Hence, the net capital inflow CF is a function of the interest-rate differential

(11.10) $CF = CF(r - r^*)$

where an increase in $r - r^*$ raises CF, as shown in Figure 11.5.

Given the Alpha-Land interest rate r^*, there is some U.S. interest rate r (call it r_0) at which the U.S. net capital inflow $CF = 0$. r_0 is indicated in Figures 11.4 and 11.5.

At the point (r_0, Q_0) in Figure 11.4, $NX = 0$ and $CF = 0$; thus, by equation (11.9), $BP = 0$ also. Hence, the BP curve passes through point (r_0, Q_0). If Q increases above Q_0, from Figure 11.2, NX becomes negative; a trade deficit occurs. To maintain balance-of-payments equilibrium $BP = 0$, a positive net capital inflow CF of equal magnitude must offset the trade deficit. In Figure 11.5, r must rise above r_0 to induce the required, positive CF. Thus

▶ The BP curve has a positive slope because a rise in the domestic interest rate r is required to raise the net capital inflow CF and to keep $BP = 0$ when a rise in real output Q reduces net exports NX.

Starting from any point on the BP curve, if Q increases, with r held constant, then NX decreases and BP in equation (11.9) becomes negative. Symmetrically, if Q decreases, with r held constant, then NX increases and BP becomes positive. Thus, as shown in Figure 11.4

▶ At any point to the right of the BP curve, there is a BP deficit ($BP < 0$). At any point to the left of the BP curve, there is a BP surplus ($BP > 0$).

What determines whether the BP curve is steep or flat? If the responsiveness of wealth-holders to a change in the interest-rate differential is greater (that is, if *capital mobility* is greater), then the CF curve in Figure 11.5 is flatter and the rise in r required to raise CF to offset the negative NX is smaller. Hence, the BP curve is flatter.

▶ If *capital mobility* is greater, then the CF curve is flatter and the BP curve is flatter.

What shifts the BP curve? A shift in the NX curve in Figure 11.2 or a shift in the CF curve in Figure 11.5 will shift the BP curve.

If the NX curve in Figure 11.2 shifts to the right, then a level of real output Q larger than Q_0 is required to achieve $NX = 0$. In Figure 11.4, a Q larger than Q_0 is required to achieve $BP = 0$ at $r = r_0$. Hence

▶ A rightward shift of the NX curve causes a rightward shift of the BP curve.

From Figure 11.3, an increase in the relative price c raises NX at a given Q and shifts the NX curve in Figure 11.2 to the right. Hence

▶ An increase in the relative price c shifts the BP curve to the right.

If the CF curve in Figure 11.5 shifts downward, then a domestic interest rate r smaller than r_0 is required to achieve $CF = 0$. In Figure 11.4, an r smaller than r_0 is required to achieve $BP = 0$ at $Q = Q_0$. Hence

▶ A shift of the CF curve downward (rightward) shifts the BP curve downward (rightward).

11.6 Saving, Investment, and the Trade Surplus

Let's restate accounting identity (11.4):

(11.4) $S_T \equiv I_T + NX$

In this section, we will show that an increase in total saving S_T at the constant inflation output level Q_c is shared by total investment I_T and net exports NX in the long run; hence, an increase in saving increases both domestic investment and the trade surplus.

In Chapter 10, we saw that in a closed economy, future consumption can be increased and future poverty can be reduced by raising current investment. Raising investment, however, requires raising saving (equivalently, reducing consumption). We also found that saving can be raised (consumption can be reduced) by tightening fiscal policy (raising taxes, cutting government transfers, or reducing government consumption). A simultaneous easing of monetary policy reduces the interest rate and assures that the reduction in consumption is matched by an equal increase in investment, so that Q remains equal to Q_c.

Here, we will examine the effects on an open economy of an increase in total saving S_T (equivalently, a decrease in total consumption C_T) at Q_c.

Suppose that the IS, LM, and BP curves initially intersect at point (r_0, Q_c), as shown in Figure 11.6. To ease exposition, we will assume that this is the same point (r_0, Q_0) shown in Figure 11.4, so that $NX = 0$ and $CF = 0$.

In Figure 10.2 (page 441), an increase in total saving S_T at Q_c is achieved by a tightening of fiscal policy (a leftward shift of the IS curve). The Fed conducts an offsetting monetary policy that repositions the LM

FIGURE 11.6 AN INITIAL EQUILIBRIUM WITH $Q = Q_c$ AND $BP = 0$

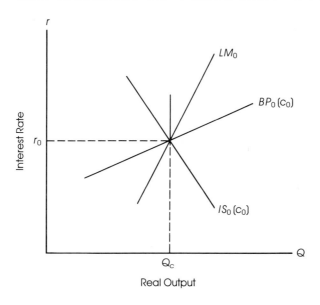

Both the IS and the BP curves depend on the relative price c. With $c = c_0$, IS_0 and BP_0 intersect at point (r_0, Q_c). We assume that the Fed then positions LM_0 to intersect IS_0 at point (r_0, Q_c). For convenience, we also assume that r_0 is identical to r_0 in Figure 11.5, so that $CF = 0$, and that Q_c is identical to Q_0 in Figure 11.2, so that $NX = 0$.

curve so that it intersects the new IS curve at Q_c. The tighter fiscal policy represents an increase in the tax rate, a decrease in government transfers, and/or a decrease in government consumption. Total consumption C_T declines (equivalently, total saving S_T rises).

In a closed economy, the increase in total saving S_T must be matched by an equal increase in total investment I_T, according to accounting relationship (1.29). This result is illustrated in Figure 10.3 (page 442), where an increase in total saving at Q_c from S_T to S_T' results in an equal increase in total investment from I_{T_0} to I_{T_1} and a reduction in the interest rate from r_0 to r_1.

What happens in an open economy when total saving at Q_c increases? First, we will ascertain the long-run equilibrium that must eventually result. Then, we will compare the transition paths to this long-run equilibrium under flexible and fixed exchange rate regimes.

▶ By "long-run equilibrium," we mean that $Q = Q_c$ and $BP = 0$. Hence, in the IS–LM diagram, the long-run equilibrium is characterized by the intersection of the IS, LM, and BP curves at a single point (r, Q_c).

Figure 11.7 illustrates the long-run equilibrium (omitting the LM curve to simplify the diagram). The Fed conducts an offsetting monetary policy that always positions the LM curve so that it intersects the IS curve at $Q = Q_c$. Thus, the LM curve always passes through the intersection of the IS curve and the vertical Q_c line and need not be drawn explicitly.

Recall that the positions of both the IS and BP curves depend on the relative price c, which equals eP^*/P:

▶ An increase in the relative price c shifts both the IS and BP curves to the right.

Initially, the relative price is c_0. If the relative price were to remain constant at c_0, then the IS curve would shift to the left from $IS_0(c_0)$ to IS' (c_0), as shown in Figure 11.7, in response to a tightening of fiscal policy. The interest rate would decline from r_0 to r', and the economy would move from point (r_0, Q_c) to point (r', Q_c). This is the closed economy result shown in Figure 10.2 (page 441).

But point (r', Q_c) lies below the BP_0 curve, so that, with $c = c_0$, a BP deficit would occur at (r', Q_c). Long-run equilibrium requires that $BP = 0$. Therefore, the relative price c must adjust until the BP and IS curves intersect at $Q = Q_c$.

If the relative price c increases above c_0, both the IS and BP curves will shift to the right. Focus on the vertical Q_c line in Figure 11.7. Beginning at BP_0, the BP curve shifts to the right as c increases, and the BP–Q_c intersection moves downward below point 0 along the Q_c line.

FIGURE 11.7 THE LONG-RUN IMPACT OF AN INCREASE IN SAVING AT Q_c

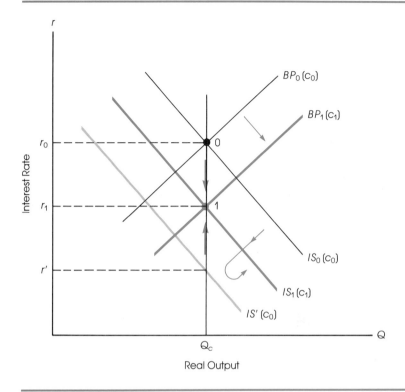

The initial equilibrium is at point 0 (which coincides with the equilibrium point in Figure 11.6); the initial relative price is c_0. The increase in saving (due to a tightening of fiscal policy) would shift the IS curve to the left to $IS'(c_0)$ if c_0 remained constant. But point (r', Q_c) lies below the $BP_0(c_0)$ curve, so that a BP deficit would be created. Long-run equilibrium requires that $BP = 0$, which is achieved if c rises to c_1. As c rises, both the IS curve (beginning at IS') and the BP curve shift to the right; at $c = c_1$, they intersect at point 1 (r_1, Q_c). Hence, the interest rate r declines to only r_1 in an open economy, compared to r' in a closed economy.

Beginning at IS', the IS curve shifts to the right as c increases, and the $IS - Q_c$ intersection moves upward along the Q_c line above point (r', Q_c). Eventually, the BP and IS curves intersect at a point on the Q_c line (r_1, Q_c). Let c_1 be the relative price at which $BP_1 (c_1)$ and $IS_1 (c_1)$ intersect at (r_1, Q_c). The long-run equilibrium is then $c = c_1, r = r_1$, and $Q = Q_c$ in an open economy.

We can compare the open and closed economy results by focusing on equation (11.5):

(11.5) $$Q_c = C_T + I_T + NX$$

In the closed economy case, $NX = 0$ always. In the open economy case, $NX = 0$ at the initial equilibrium shown in Figure 11.6. In both cases, the tightening of fiscal policy results in the same decline in C_T. In the closed economy case, the reduction in r to r' induces a rise in I_T that equals the cut in C_T. But in the open economy case, r decreases only to r_1 (which is greater than r'), so that the rise in I_T is less than the decline in C_T. The increase in the relative price c raises NX so that the rise in I_T and NX, taken together, equals the decline in C_T.

Because the initial value of NX is 0, the final value is positive. The increase in total saving S_T at Q_c generates a trade surplus. If NX is initially positive (a trade surplus), then the surplus will become larger. If NX is initially negative (a trade deficit), then the deficit will become smaller or be converted to a surplus.

▶ An increase in total saving S_T at the constant inflation level of output Q_c raises domestic investment I_T and the trade surplus NX.

▶ A country's *saving rate* is an important determinant of its (international) competitiveness and trade position. An increase in the saving rate increases competitiveness and either reduces the trade deficit or increases the trade surplus.

Although the increase in U.S. investment is less than the increase in U.S. saving, accounting identity (11.7) offers insight:

(11.7) $S_W \equiv I_W$

The increase in total world investment must match the increase in total world saving.

If we assume that Alpha-Land saving remains constant, then the increase in world saving equals the increase in U.S. saving. Hence, the rise in Alpha-Land investment plus the rise in U.S. investment must equal the rise in U.S. saving.

Consider equation (11.5) for the Alpha-Land economy:

(11.5) $Q_c = C_T + I_T + NX$

When U.S. NX moves from 0 to surplus, Alpha-Land NX moves from 0 to deficit. With C_T held constant (because we are assuming that Alpha-Land saving S_T is constant), I_T increases in Alpha-Land. Thus

▶ In an open or a closed economy, an increase in U.S. saving causes an equal increase in total world investment, which reduces future poverty by raising the real wage. But in an open economy, part of the poverty reduction occurs among low-skilled workers in Alpha-Land because part of the investment occurs in Alpha-Land.

We now focus on equations (11.4) and (11.9):

$$(11.4) \qquad S_T \equiv I_T + NX$$

$$(11.9) \qquad BP \equiv CF + NX$$

With $BP = 0$, subtracting equation (11.9) from equation (11.4) yields a relationship that holds in long-run equilibrium:

$$(11.11) \qquad S_T = I_T + (-CF)$$

Since CF is the net capital inflow, $-CF$ is the *net capital outflow* — the net "import" of Alpha-Land bonds by U.S. wealth-holders. When U.S. total saving S_T increases, U.S. total investment I_T and net capital outflow $-CF$ share the increase, just as I_T and Alpha-Land investment share the increase according to equation (11.7). Hence, the increase in the U.S. net capital outflow $-CF$ equals the increase in Alpha-Land investment. U.S. savers acquire Alpha-Land bonds that match the increase in Alpha-Land investment. Thus

▶ An increase in U.S. saving results in the same increase in future U.S. consumption in an open economy as in a closed economy. Although part of the increase in investment occurs in Alpha-Land, the future capital income on both U.S. and Alpha-Land investment will be received by U.S. savers.

THE TRANSITION UNDER ALTERNATIVE REGIMES

We have seen that an increase in U.S. total saving at the constant inflation level of output Q_c requires an increase in the relative price eP^*/P to restore $BP = 0$ in the long run. Let's consider how this increase in eP^*/P is accomplished under a flexible exchange rate and under a fixed exchange rate.

When the IS curve shifts to the left to IS' in Figure 11.7, the new IS–LM intersection moves below the BP_0 (c_0) curve. As indicated in Figure 11.4, this implies that the economy experiences a BP deficit.

In the absence of central-bank intervention, the BP deficit implies an excess demand for foreign currency. Under a flexible exchange rate, e appreciates (the dollar depreciates). The rise in e raises the relative price eP^*/P until the long-run equilibrium value c_1 is reached.

▶ Under a flexible exchange rate regime, an appreciation of the foreign currency (a depreciation of the dollar) raises the relative price eP^*/P to its required long-run equilibrium value.

Under a fixed exchange rate, central banks supply foreign currency (and demand dollars) so that the supply of and the demand for foreign currency are equal at the initial value of e, despite the U.S. BP deficit. Hence, e remains fixed, which implies that the required increase in the relative price eP^*/P must be accomplished by raising the price ratio P^*/P.

The increase in P^*/P can be achieved by temporarily increasing the growth rate of P^* or decreasing the growth rate of P. According to our earlier $DG - SG$ analysis, either Alpha-Land must temporarily hold Q above Q_c (U below U_c) or the United States must temporarily hold Q below Q_c (U above U_c).

▶ Under a fixed exchange rate regime, a temporary divergence in the unemployment rate U from the constant inflation unemployment rate U_c must occur in either the United States or Alpha-Land to increase P^*/P and thereby raise eP^*/P to its required long-run equilibrium value.

11.7 Inflation in an Open Economy

Returning to the balance-of-payments equilibrium shown in Figure 11.6, where the IS and BP curves intersect at $Q = Q_c$ when $c = c_0$, we will assume that both the U.S. and Alpha-Land inflation rates are initially 0. What happens if the Alpha-Land central bank permanently raises the growth rate of nominal demand by X%, so that the Alpha-Land inflation rate eventually rises to X%?

The long-run equilibrium relative price is still c_0, because at $c = c_0$, the U.S. BP and IS curves continue to intersect at $Q = Q_c$. However, if eP^*/P is to remain constant with P^* growing at the rate of X%, then either e must decline at the rate of X% or P must rise at the rate of X%.

Suppose that initially e and P are held constant as P^* begins to rise. As shown in Figure 11.8, the relative price c rises to c', shifting the BP and IS curves to the right. The $IS - LM$ intersection occurs at point 1, which lies above the new BP curve, indicating a BP surplus and an excess supply of foreign currency.

Under a flexible exchange rate, e declines, reducing c until the BP and IS curves once again intersect at $Q = Q_c$. This requires that c return to c_0. To maintain $c = c_0$, e must decline at the same rate that P^* rises (X%). The dollar therefore appreciates at the rate of X%.

▶ Under a flexible exchange rate, if the Alpha-Land inflation rate exceeds the U.S. inflation rate by X%, then the dollar will appreciate at the rate of X%. Symmetrically, if the U.S. inflation rate exceeds the Alpha-Land inflation rate by X%, then the dollar will depreciate at the rate of X%.

To restore the balance-of-payments equilibrium ($BP = 0$) under a fixed exchange rate, the Fed can raise the nominal demand growth rate

FIGURE 11.8 THE IMPACT OF A RISE IN ALPHA-LAND'S INFLATION RATE

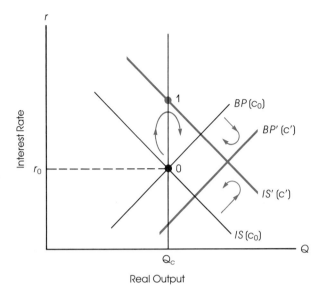

Real Output

The initial equilibrium is at point 0 (which coincides with the equilibrium point in Figure 11.6); the initial relative price is c_0. The increase in the Alpha-Land inflation rate would raise c to c' if the nominal exchange rate e and the domestic price level P remained constant (because $c = eP*/P$) and would move the economy from point 0 to point 1 by shifting the IS curve to $IS'(c')$. But because BP would also shift to the right to $BP'(c')$, a BP surplus would occur at point 1. To restore $BP = 0$, c must be kept at c_0. Under a flexible exchange rate, e must decline at the rate that $P*$ rises to keep the relative price $eP*/P$ constant; under a fixed exchange rate, P must rise at the same rate as $P*$.

y by X%, so that the U.S. price level P grows at the same rate as the price of Alpha goods $P*$, thereby maintaining the relative price c at c_0. The United States must raise its inflation rate to match the inflation rate in Alpha-Land.

If the Fed refused to raise the nominal demand growth rate and the U.S. inflation rate, then the relative price $eP*/P$ will rise, the IS and BP curves will shift to the right, and the U.S. BP surplus will increase steadily. As the excess supply of foreign currency increases, the Fed will be forced to increase its demand for foreign currency (its supply of dollars); the Fed has a sufficient inventory of dollars to keep the exchange rate e from declining. Because a BP surplus tends to increase the U.S. money supply, the Fed must offset the impact of this surplus through sterilization in the form of a continuous open-market contraction.

However, the Fed may refuse to support the exchange rate e. The Alpha-Land central bank does not have an unlimited inventory of dollars with which to demand alphas and support e. Eventually, the Alpha-Land central bank will face one of two options: (1) let e decline at the rate of $X\%$, thereby converting the fixed exchange rate into a flexible exchange rate, or (2) reduce its inflation rate to 0.

11.8 The Real Exchange Rate

A comparison of the saving analysis in Section 11.6 and the inflation analysis in Section 11.7 will provide insight concerning the concept of the *real exchange rate*.

Assuming a flexible exchange rate regime, an increase in U.S. saving results in a rise in the exchange rate e and a rise in the relative price eP^*/P. An increase in the U.S. inflation rate relative to the Alpha-Land inflation rate results in a rise in e but no change in eP^*/P.

In both cases, the dollar depreciates (e rises). In the saving case, the dollar depreciation increases U.S. competitiveness. In the inflation case, the dollar depreciation does not change U.S. competitiveness; it merely offsets the decline in P^*/P.

The term "real exchange rate" has recently been used to emphasize that a change in the "nominal" exchange rate e may or may not imply a change in the relative price eP^*/P. When we use the phrase "the alpha's real exchange rate," we mean the relative price eP^*/P, in contrast to the alpha's nominal exchange rate e.

In the saving case, the alpha appreciation (the rise in e) results in a rise in the alpha's real exchange rate eP^*/P. Equivalently, the dollar depreciation results in a decline in the dollar's real exchange rate. In the inflation case, the alpha appreciation does not change the alpha's real exchange rate. Equivalently, the dollar depreciation does not change the dollar's real exchange rate.

▶ A change in the *real exchange rate* (the relative price eP^*/P) — not a change in the nominal exchange rate e per se — affects competitiveness and therefore the trade surplus (net exports).

11.9 Flexible Versus Fixed Exchange Rates

According to our saving and inflation analyses, long-run equilibrium is independent of the exchange rate regime. Long-run equilibrium, where $Q = Q_c$ and $BP = 0$, requires a particular relative price c, which equals eP^*/P. The transition path to long-run equilibrium, however, depends on the regime. Under a flexible exchange rate, e adjusts to achieve the required c. Under a fixed exchange rate, either P^* or P adjusts to achieve the required c.

Is a flexible or a fixed exchange rate preferable? First, let's consider some disadvantages of a fixed exchange rate.

▶ Under a fixed exchange rate, the transition to long-run equilibrium may require a transitional recession to raise $eP*/P$ to its long-run equilibrium value. Under a flexible exchange rate, the transition to long-run equilibrium can maintain Q at Q_c because e adjusts to achieve the required value of $eP*/P$.

In our inflation analysis, we saw that if Alpha-Land raises its inflation rate by $X\%$, then the United States can keep its inflation rate at 0 under a flexible exchange rate. Thus, e will depreciate at the rate of $X\%$, thereby keeping the relative price $eP*/P$ constant. Under a fixed exchange rate, however, $BP = 0$ requires that the United States raise its inflation rate by $X\%$.

Even if the United States maintains a BP surplus by refusing to raise its inflation rate by $X\%$, it will experience *supply inflation,* as the rising price of imports increases U.S. costs. With a flexible exchange rate, an appreciation of the dollar should keep the dollar price of imports constant, thereby avoiding supply inflation. Thus

▶ Under a fixed exchange rate, a country is vulnerable to "importing" inflation that originates abroad. Under a flexible exchange rate, a country should be insulated from foreign inflation.

Finally, as we will see when we briefly review the history of the exchange rate regime

▶ A fixed exchange rate is vulnerable to a "speculative attack" that generates an economic crisis. Central banks may be forced to "surrender" to speculators and to change the value of the exchange rate. Hence, it may not be feasible to maintain fixed exchange rate values. It can be argued that a sharp change in the exchange rate caused by a speculative attack is less desirable than gradual adjustment under a flexible exchange rate.

We will now consider some disadvantages of a flexible exchange rate. Under a flexible exchange rate, the relative price $eP*/P$ may fluctuate more sharply than it would under a fixed exchange rate. Hence, the output of the export sector and of the import-competing sector may fluctuate more sharply. Such fluctuations may be economically wasteful. For example, suppose that private speculation is periodically destabilizing, moving the relative price $eP*/P$ away from its long-run equilibrium value. Then

▶ Under a flexible exchange rate, destabilizing speculation may induce undesirable fluctuations in the output of the export sector and of the import-competing sector.

Sharper fluctuations in the relative price $eP*/P$ may make planning more difficult for exporters, importers, and producers of import-competing goods. Thus

▶ Under a flexible exchange rate, a *risk premium* may raise the cost of exporting and importing, resulting in a decline in the volume of international trade.

Managed floating may reduce these disadvantages.

Under MANAGED FLOATING, central banks try to limit fluctuations in the relative price eP^*/P due to destabilizing speculation, so that changes in eP^*/P are gradual and reflect changes in the long-run equilibrium.

Economists disagree over how effectively central banks can perform this task.

THE EVOLUTION OF THE EXCHANGE RATE REGIME

In choosing the exchange-rate system, it is important to keep in mind the actual history of alternative exchange-rate regimes. Let's briefly review exchange-rate history.

In the 1930s, exchange rates fluctuated, and many observers reacted negatively to the experience. In 1944, a fixed exchange rate regime was established—the *Bretton Woods system,* named for the New Hampshire town in which the international agreement was reached. The Bretton Woods system lasted until 1973.

Under Bretton Woods, each country's central bank agreed to peg the dollar exchange rate of its own currency; hence, the exchange rate between any two countries was automatically fixed. Countries were permitted to alter the dollar exchange rate if a "fundamental disequilibrium" persisted. Such changes were expected to be the exception, however, not the rule.

The post-World War II period saw an expansion of world trade and a reduction in trade restrictions. Many observers believed that the fixed exchange rate system was effective. But in the 1960s, the U.S. inflation rate increased relative to Germany's inflation rate, reducing U.S. competitiveness and generating a U.S. trade deficit and a German trade surplus. An excess demand for German marks (and an excess supply of U.S. dollars) resulted. Under a flexible exchange rate, the mark would have appreciated. Under a fixed rate system, the German government was required to intervene, supplying marks (and demanding dollars).

This necessary intervention became so great that speculators eventually expected the German government to declare a "fundamental disequilibrium" and "revalue" the mark upward. A speculator who expects the mark to be revalued upward should demand marks; once the mark is revalued, the speculator can then convert marks back to dollars and make a profit. If the rate remains fixed, then the speculator will lose nothing.

So, in the face of an excess demand for marks, speculators raised the demand for marks still further. This turned the problem into a crisis, raising the degree of German central-bank intervention required to keep the exchange rate fixed. The pressure from speculators forced several revaluations of the mark.

The British central bank faced a tougher problem. An excess supply of the British pound developed several times. To keep the exchange rate fixed, the British central bank intervened, demanding pounds and supplying U.S. dollars or other currencies. But such intervention required an adequate inventory of these "reserves" and therefore could not occur indefinitely.

Hence, speculators "attacked" the pound by supplying pounds and demanding other currencies; they planned to convert these currencies back to pounds after the pound was devalued. This attack greatly magnified the excess supply of pounds. The speculators forced the British government to "surrender," making a profit on the devaluation.

These crises reveal a basic problem of a fixed exchange rate system; speculators have little risk of losing. These speculators knew that the mark would either be revalued upward or held fixed and that the British pound would either be devalued or held fixed. They had little to lose by betting on these changes, but their actions created economic crises.

In contrast, a flexible exchange rate may move in either direction, so that speculators, in general, risk losing as well as winning. This tends to limit the magnitude of speculation.

In 1971, an attempt was made to save the fixed exchange rate system by significantly altering exchange rates. Before long, however, speculative attacks began, and the system broke down in 1973. Since then, dollar exchange rates have fluctuated for most of the major currencies, including the yen, mark, franc, and pound.

Once again, it is misleading to characterize the end of the Bretton Woods system as simply a conversion from fixed to flexible exchange rates. First, the fluctuations of dollar exchange rates have often been tempered by significant interventions at various times by various governments. "Managed floating" is a more accurate description of normal operations since 1973. Second, most European countries have maintained relatively fixed exchange rates within Europe, while floating their currencies relative to the dollar. Thus, a mixed exchange rate system is still evolving.

11.10 The U.S. Trade Deficit in the 1980s

Figure 11.9 documents the emergence of a significant U.S. trade deficit ($NX < 0$) in the early 1980s. During the 1970s, the current account balance was usually near 0. In the second half of the decade, a merchandise (goods) deficit of roughly 1% of GNP ($20 billion) was offset by

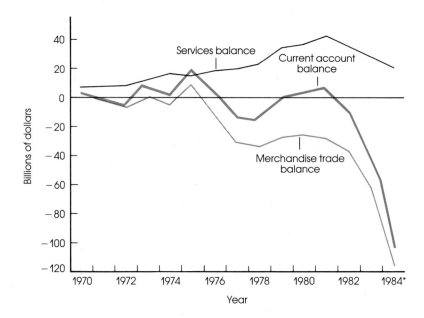

*First three quarters at annual rate; seasonally adjusted.

SOURCE: U.S. Department of Commerce; *Economic Report of the President 1985*, p. 100.

In the early 1970s, the current account balance was usually near 0. In the second half of the 1970s, a merchandise-good deficit of roughly 1% of GNP ($20 billion) was offset by a services surplus of roughly 1% of GNP. In the early 1980s, however, the merchandise deficit tripled as a fraction of GNP, rising to 3% ($100 billion), so that the current account deficit rose above 2% of GNP.

a services surplus of similar magnitude. In the early 1980s, however, the merchandise (goods) deficit tripled as a fraction of GNP, rising to 3% ($100 billion), and the services surplus declined somewhat. Hence, the current account deficit rose above 2% of GNP.

Although several factors probably contributed to this rise in the U.S. trade deficit, we will emphasize two: (1) the relative cyclical effect, (2) the shift to an easy fiscal–tight monetary mix. Let's briefly review each factor.

First, the United States and its trading partners suffered a severe recession in 1982. The U.S. recovery in 1983 and 1984 was much stronger than that of most of its trading partners. The U.S. unemployment rate fell to near the constant inflation unemployment rate U_c (7%), while the unemployment rate in Canada and several European countries remained well above U_c. U.S. imports vary directly with U.S. output; exports depend on the output of other countries that import U.S. goods and services. Thus, the stronger recovery in the United States, relative to other countries, raised U.S. imports relative to U.S. exports and worsened the trade deficit.

Second, the United States shifted to an easy fiscal–tight monetary mix in the early 1980s. In our saving analysis, we saw that a shift to a tight fiscal–easy monetary mix increases U.S. competitiveness and raises the trade surplus. A symmetrical analysis shows that a shift to an easy fiscal–tight monetary mix reduces U.S. competitiveness and raises the trade deficit.

In fact, from 1980 to 1984, U.S. competitiveness declined by about 60%.* This decrease in the relative price $eP*/P$ occurred through a decline in the exchange rate e—an appreciation of the dollar. (The $P*/P$ ratio changed very little.) The 65% rise in the dollar's *nominal* exchange rate was matched by a comparable rise in the dollar's *real* exchange rate.

Given these two causes of the large U.S. trade deficit, what is the prospect for the future? If U.S. trading partners eventually enjoy a strong recovery that reduces the unemployment rate to U_c, then the cyclical effect will reverse itself and U.S. exports will rise relative to U.S. imports. This should reduce part of the deficit.

A tightening of fiscal policy—a reduction in the government budget deficit—is the key to raising investment and reducing the trade deficit. To assess the impact of balancing the budget, let's restate equation (11.6):

(11.6) $$S + Su \equiv I + NX$$

After subtracting depreciation from both sides, S is *net saving* and I is *net investment*. Dividing both sides of equation (11.6) by Q, we obtain

(11.12) $$\frac{S}{Q} + \frac{Su}{Q} = \frac{I}{Q} + \frac{NX}{Q}$$

In the mid-1980s, these four numbers were roughly

$$7\% + (-3\%) = 6\% + (-2\%)$$

Suppose that the budget is balanced, so that $Su/Q = 0$. An increase in taxes or a cut in government transfers should cause a very modest

---

* *Economic Report of the President 1985*, pp. 103–104.

reduction in private saving S; S/Q should stay at 7%. (When disposable income declines by 3% of GNP, saving, which is 6% of disposable income, will decline by 0.18% of GNP.) Then the left side of this equation will increase by 3% (from 4% to 7%).

Now suppose that I increases by 2% and that NX increases by 1%. Then balancing the budget yields

$$\frac{S}{Q} + \frac{Su}{Q} = \frac{I}{Q} + \frac{NX}{Q}$$
$$7\% + 0\% = 8\% + (-1\%)$$

Under this assumption, net investment increases by 33% (from 6% to 8%) and the U.S. trade deficit decreases by 50% (from 2% to 1%).

If, instead, I increases by 1% and NX increases by 2%, then balancing the budget yields

$$7\% + 0\% = 7\% + 0\%$$

Under this assumption, net investment increases by 17% (from 6% to 7%) and the U.S. trade deficit decreases by 100% (from 2% to 0%).

▶ Eliminating the government budget deficit will significantly raise U.S. net investment and/or significantly reduce the U.S. trade deficit.

Whether or not the President and Congress will balance the U.S. budget remains to be seen.

SUMMARY

1. When an economy is "open" to foreign trade and capital flows, accounting identities are changed as follows:

Closed Economy	Open Economy
$Q = C + I + G$	$Q = C + I + G + NX$
$I = S + Su$	$I + NX = S + Su$
$I_T = S_T$	$I_T + NX = S_T$

2. In an *open economy*, *total saving* S_T exceeds *total investment* I_T by the amount of *net exports NX* (the *trade surplus*). *Total world saving* S_W equals *total world investment* I_W.

3. Net exports NX decrease when real output (income) Q increases, because imports Z increase.

4. The *exchange rate e* is the dollar price of a unit of foreign currency. The *relative price c* is eP^*/P, the ratio of the *dollar price of foreign*

goods eP^* to the *dollar price of U.S. goods P*. The symbol c also represents *U.S. competitiveness*.

5. A rise in the relative price eP^*/P will raise net exports NX in the long run and shift the *IS* curve to the right.

6. Any transaction that entails a payment *to* U.S. residents (by foreigners) is a *surplus item* in the U.S. *balance-of-payments (BP) accounts*. Any transaction that entails a payment *by* U.S. residents (to foreigners) is a *deficit item* in the U.S. *BP* accounts.

7. The *balance-of-payments surplus* equals the *current account surplus* plus the *capital account surplus*. Thus, $BP \equiv NX + CF$, where CF is the *net capital inflow*.

8. Under a *flexible exchange rate* regime, central banks do not intervene to adjust either the supply of or the demand for foreign currency. Under a *fixed exchange rate* regime, central banks do intervene to adjust either the supply of or the demand for foreign currency to equalize them at a fixed *target exchange rate*.

9. A *BP surplus* implies an excess supply of foreign currency; a *BP deficit* implies an excess demand for foreign currency.

10. A flexible exchange rate will tend to achieve *balance-of-payments equilibrium* $(BP = 0)$ in the long run.

11. Under a fixed exchange rate, a U.S. *BP* deficit tends to decrease the U.S. money supply held by the public and a U.S. *BP* surplus tends to increase the U.S. money supply held by the public. The money supply can be held constant by *sterilization*.

12. The *BP curve* connects all points (r, Q) for which $BP = 0$. It is drawn for a given relative price c. The *BP* curve has a positive slope because a rise in the interest rate r is required to raise the net capital inflow CF and to keep $BP = 0$ when a rise in real output Q reduces net exports NX. An increase in c shifts the *BP* curve to the right.

13. In *long-run equilibrium* $(Q = Q_c$ and $BP = 0)$, an increase in total saving S_T at the constant inflation level of output Q_c raises domestic investment I_T and the trade surplus NX. A country's *saving rate* is an important determinant of its (international) competitiveness and its trade position. An increase in the saving rate increases competitiveness and either reduces the trade deficit or increases the trade surplus.

14. Under a flexible exchange rate, if the Alpha-Land inflation rate exceeds the U.S. inflation rate by $X\%$, then the dollar will appreciate at the rate of $X\%$.

15. A change in the *real exchange rate* (the relative price eP^*/P) — not a change in the *nominal* exchange rate e per se — affects competitiveness and the trade surplus (net exports).

16. A fixed exchange rate may require a transitional recession to achieve $BP = 0$ and is subject to a "speculative attack" that generates an economic crisis. Under a flexible exchange rate, destabilizing speculation may induce undesirable fluctuations in the output of the export sector and of the import-competing sector.

17. Eliminating the government budget deficit will significantly raise U.S. net investment and/or significantly reduce the U.S. trade deficit.

TERMS AND CONCEPTS

balance of payments (BP)
balance-of-payments deficit ($BP < 0$)
balance-of-payments equilibrium ($BP = 0$)
balance-of-payments surplus ($BP > 0$)
BP curve
Bretton Woods system
capital account
capital account surplus
capital mobility
current account
current account surplus
deficit item
depreciation/appreciation
devalue
dollar price of foreign goods (eP^*)
dollar price of U.S. goods (P)
exchange rate regime
exports (X)
fixed exchange rate
flexible (floating) exchange rate
foreign-currency reserves
government surplus (Su)

imports (Z)
interest-rate differential
managed floating
merchandise
net capital inflow (CF)
net capital outflow
net exports (NX)
(nominal) exchange rate (e)
open-market contraction
open-market expansion
private saving (S)
real exchange rate (eP^*/P)
relative price (c or eP^*/P)
reserves
revalue
risk premium
speculative attacks
sterilization
surplus item
supply inflation
total investment (I_T)
total saving (S_T)
trade deficit
trade surplus
U.S. competitiveness
world investment (I_W)
world saving (S_W)

QUESTIONS

11.1 Derive these three accounting identities:
   a. $S_T \equiv I_T + NX$
   b. $S + Su \equiv I + NX$
   c. $S_W \equiv I_W$

11.2 Use a diagram that relates NX and Q and one that relates CF and r to explain why the BP curve has a positive slope.

11.3 Use a diagram that relates c and NX to explain why an increase in the relative price c:
   a. shifts the IS curve to the right.
   b. shifts the BP curve to the right.

11.4 Use an $IS-BP$ diagram to show that in long-run equilibrium ($Q = Q_c$, $BP = 0$), a decrease in S_T that is induced by an easing of fiscal policy will reduce U.S. competitiveness, investment, and the trade surplus (or raise the trade deficit).

11.5 Use an $IS-BP$ diagram to show that in long-run equilibrium under a flexible exchange rate, if the Alpha-Land inflation rate exceeds the U.S. inflation rate by $X\%$, then the dollar will appreciate at the rate of $X\%$.

11.6 Is the U.S. trade deficit in the 1980s consistent with the theory presented in this chapter? Explain your answer.

Supplements

12 Consumption and Investment

Prerequisite: Chapter 2

In Chapter 2, we adopted a simple hypothesis for consumption behavior, and a simple hypothesis for investment behavior. We assumed that consumption varies directly with net (disposable) income, and that investment varies inversely with the interest rate. In this chapter, we will look more carefully at consumption and investment.

Private sector demand can be divided into two components: consumption C and investment I. Consumption demand is contributed almost exclusively by households. Investment demand is contributed largely by firms. The official accounts divide C into two components: C_n, consumption of nondurable goods and services; and C_d, consumption of durable goods (goods which are not fully consumed in the year of purchase). Examples of C_n are food, clothing, fuel, electricity, transportation, and shelter (the rental value of housing). Examples of C_d are automobiles, furniture, and household equipment. The purchase of a house, the most durable of consumer durables, is classified under investment rather than under C_d. While C_d is similar to C_n in that the decision to buy is made by and for the household, and not the business firm, C_d is also similar to I in that what is purchased is durable, so that borrowing to finance the purchase is often warranted. This means that interest rates and credit availability are especially important for both C_d and I.

Thus far, we have used the three categories used by the official national income accounts. But we should note that, from a theoretical perspective, consumption in a given year really consists of nondurable consumption plus the flow of services from the stock of consumer durables (including housing). For example, in any given year, all autos in use — regardless of when they were purchased — yield transportation service to households which should be regarded as part of this year's consumption. When we examine the theory of consumption, we should keep in mind the difference between the pure theoretical concept, and the categories C_n and C_d actually reported in the national income accounts.

12.1 The Theory of Consumption

Before we begin, we must recall the distinction between C_n, C_d, and the theoretical concept of consumption: C_n plus the service from the stock of consumer durables. It is the theoretical concept of consumption that we will generally have in mind in this section. Most of the analysis will also apply to C_n, but will usually not apply directly to C_d, this year's expenditure on consumer durables. Because our main focus here is stabilization policy, we will concentrate on the short-run variation in consumption. But we should briefly note, as background, how the long-run behavior of consumption has influenced the theory of consumption.

THE CROSS-SECTION, TIMES-SERIES PARADOX

Any theory of consumption must confront the following apparent conflict. In a cross section of households, the saving ratio rises (the consumption ratio falls) as current household income rises. This might seem to imply that as national income rises over time, the national saving ratio should likewise rise (the national consumption ratio should fall). But this has not happened. The time series of these ratios do not show a clear trend, and appear to be roughly constant over the long run (while fluctuating in the short run).

In 1949, James Duesenberry proposed the *relative income hypothesis* to reconcile the cross-section and time-series facts.* According to this hypothesis, a household's saving ratio depends on its relative income, not its absolute income. Table 12.1 illustrates. Suppose there are just two persons in a simple economy, L and H. In period 1, L has $10,000 of income while H has $20,000 of income; the mean income is $15,000. Note that L's income is 33% below the mean, while H's income is 33% above the mean. L consumes 100% of income, while H consumes 80% of income. For the economy, consumption is 87% of income. In period 2, each person's income is twice as great. But L's is still 33% below the new mean of $30,000 and H's is still 33% above the new mean. Relative incomes have not changed.

According to the relative income hypothesis, since L's income remains 33% below the mean, it will keep the same consumption ratio

---

* James Duesenberry, *Income, Saving, and the Theory of Consumer Behavior* (Cambridge, Mass.: Harvard University Press, 1949).

TABLE 12.1

THE RELATIVE INCOME HYPOTHESIS

	Period 1		Period 2	
	income	**consumption**	**income**	**consumption**
household L	$10,000	$10,000 (100%)	$20,000	$20,000 (100%)
household H	$20,000	$16,000 (80%)	$40,000	$32,000 (80%)
total	$30,000	$26,000 (87%)	$60,000	$52,000 (87%)

(100%). Since H's income remains 33% above the mean, it, too, will keep the same consumption ratio (80%). If this is so, then for the economy, consumption will remain 87% of income. Thus, the relative income hypothesis can account for the cross-section and time-series facts. In either period, as we move from person L to person H, the saving ratio rises from 0% to 20%. But over time, the saving ratio of the economy stays constant at 13%. Duesenberry argued that people are primarily concerned with their relative position in society—"keeping up with the Joneses." Hence, regardless of the absolute level of income, persons with below-average income feel more pressure to consume than people with above-average income. Recently, new evidence in support of this relativity hypothesis has been provided.*

In the 1950s, an alternate explanation was offered by Franco Modigliani† and Milton Friedman‡ working separately. Modigliani called his *the life-cycle hypothesis,* while Friedman called his *the permanent income hypothesis.* Although differing in certain respects, they are nevertheless similar. An example given in Table 12.2 illustrates. Consider a simple economy where a person follows a life cycle of two stages. He works in stage 1 and retires in stage 2. Assume that the two stages are of equal length. In any period, there are only two persons in the economy: the worker W (in stage 1) and the retiree R (in stage 2). In the table, W in period 1 is R in period 2. Assume that each person wants to equalize consumption in stages 1 and 2. To simplify, suppose there is no interest from saving. Then the worker must consume only 50% of his income in stage 1, so that he can consume the other 50% in stage 2. In Table 12.2,

---

* Robert Frank, *Choosing the Right Pond: Human Behavior and the Quest for Status* (New York: Oxford University Press, 1985).
† Albert Ando and Franco Modigliani, "The Life Cycle Hypothesis of Saving: Aggregate Implications and Tests," *American Economic Review* 53 (1963): 55–84.
‡ Milton Friedman, *A Theory of the Consumption Function* (Princeton, N.J.: Princeton University Press, 1957).

TABLE 12.2

THE LIFE-CYCLE HYPOTHESIS

	Period 1		Period 2	
	income	**consumption**	**income**	**consumption**
household W	$20,000	$10,000 (50%)	$40,000	$20,000 (50%)
household R	$ 0	$ 5,000	$ 0	$10,000
total	$20,000	$15,000 (75%)	$40,000	$30,000 (75%)

W in period 1 consumes $10,000; then R in period 2 also consumes $10,000. If we assume that in each period the productivity of the economy grows such that the income of a worker doubles, then in any period the retiree R will always consume half as much as the worker W.

In Table 12.2, total consumption is 75% of total income (the saving ratio is 25%) in both periods. Yet consider a cross section in either period. The retiree's current income is 0, while the worker has a high current income. The retiree consumes more than current income, while the worker consumes 50% of current income. Thus, moving from R to W, as current income rises, the saving ratio rises.

The life-cycle–permanent income hypothesis, then, like the relative income hypothesis, can potentially account for the cross-section and time-series facts. It is possible that the actual data are determined by both the behavior described by the relative income hypothesis and the behavior described by the life-cycle–permanent income hypothesis. The two hypotheses may be complements, rather than substitutes, in reconciling the cross-section and time-series facts concerning long-run consumption behavior.

PERMANENT INCOME, WEALTH, AND CONSUMPTION

With this background, let us turn to the short-run behavior most relevant for stabilization policy. Beginning in Chapter 1, we have used a simple consumption function:

(1.31) $$C = C_a + c(Q - T + R)$$

In equation (1.31), we have not specified what influences C_a. The key determinant of consumption in equation (1.31) is current disposable income $Q - T + R$. Equation (1.31) has been a useful simplification. But now that we are seriously studying consumption behavior, it requires more careful scrutiny.

In *The General Theory of Employment, Interest, and Money* (1936), John Maynard Keynes emphasized the importance of current disposable income for consumption. But by the 1950s, economists began to question this emphasis. Two theories with much in common were developed: the permanent income hypothesis of Friedman, and the life-cycle hypothesis of Modigliani. Both attributed a smaller role to current disposable income. Why?

According to the permanent income hypothesis, the representative household bases its current consumption on its expected, permanent (or normal) income, not its current income. Thus, if there is a temporary deviation in income from its normal level, this transitory change will have little effect on consumption. If current income falls below normal income, the household will use past savings, or borrow, to maintain consumption.

In the life-cycle hypothesis, the representative household seeks a smooth consumption path over its lifetime. Yet earnings are not smooth; they are low in youth, peak in middle age, and decline sharply in retirement. Consumption in a given year should not be set according to current income, but according to lifetime earnings. The life-cycle hypothesis has another important implication: wealth should be a variable in the consumption function. Why? Consider a simple example. Suppose a person wishes a constant level of consumption for the remainder of his life, regardless of fluctuations in earnings. He is age 55, will retire at 65, and expects to die at 75. His labor earnings will be $20,000 per year for the next 10 years, and then none during retirement. To simplify the calculation, assume the interest rate is 0% and that there is no Social Security program (we will consider the impact of Social Security on the consumption–saving decision in Chapter 16). If at age 55 he has accumulated no wealth, then he will set his consumption at $10,000 per year ([$20,000 × 10]/20) for the remaining 20 years of his life (we assume he does not intend to leave a bequest to his heirs at death). But if he has $100,000 of wealth at age 55, then he should set his consumption at $15,000 per year ([$20,000 × 10 + $100,000]/20) for the remaining 20 years of his life.

Clearly, then, the greater a person's wealth, the greater should be that person's consumption. Thus, the life-cycle hypothesis leads to a consumption function with two variables: wealth and expected normal labor earnings:

(12.1) $\qquad C = a_1 W + a_2 E$

$\qquad$ where W = wealth

$\qquad\qquad E$ = expected normal labor earnings

The coefficient a_1 indicates the increase in consumption C that will follow an increase in wealth W; a_1 is the marginal propensity to consume wealth, $\Delta C/\Delta W$. The coefficient a_2 indicates the increase in C that will follow an increase in expected normal labor earnings E; a_2 is the marginal propensity to consume labor earnings, $\Delta C/\Delta E$.

Once wealth is recognized as an influence on consumption, then the stock market becomes important for consumption. Fluctuations in the stock and bond markets alter the wealth held by households. These changes in wealth, according to the life-cycle hypothesis, influence consumption. A new route for monetary policy to influence consumption emerges. When the Fed expands the money supply by purchasing bonds in the open market, it raises the price of bonds, reduces interest rates, and generally raises the price of stocks. The rise in the value of stocks and bonds raises household wealth, and therefore raises consumption.

Both theories contend that current disposable income is not very important to consumption. If current income drops, consumption remains roughly constant, since it is based on permanent income, or lifetime earnings. So how does the household finance its steady consumption? If it possesses *liquid assets*—assets easily converted to cash to finance consumption—then some of these assets can be sold. If not, the household can borrow and is able to repay if it has based its consumption properly on its permanent income or lifetime earnings.

But suppose the household faces a *liquidity constraint*, that is, it has liquid assets of little value and cannot obtain credit, or can do so only at a prohibitively high interest rate. Then it may not be able to keep consumption pegged to permanent income or lifetime earnings. If this is the case, it is forced, by lack of liquidity, to vary its consumption with current disposable income. If a liquidity constraint is characteristic of many households, then current disposable income influences consumption after all.

12.2 Do Temporary Tax Changes Influence Consumption?

One important implication of the permanent income and life-cycle hypotheses is that a household income-tax change that is declared to be temporary has a relatively small impact on consumption—C_n plus services from the stock of consumer durables. Some analysts believe that the 1968 temporary tax surcharge provides support for these theories and against the hypothesis that current disposable income is the main determinant of consumption.

In the mid-1960s, the rise in military spending propelled an expansionary fiscal policy, and the unemployment rate moved below 4%—well below the U_c of roughly 6%. Inflation began to rise. To reduce demand, the Johnson Administration succeeded in getting Congress to enact a one-year, temporary tax surcharge on the personal income tax. After the surcharge went into effect, consumption as a percentage of before-tax income stayed roughly constant, despite the surcharge, while the household saving rate declined. When the surcharge expired, the saving rate returned to normal. Such behavior is exactly what the permanent income and life-cycle hypotheses predict — namely, that consumption is largely unaffected by a temporary tax change because households gear consumption to permanent income.

But the issue is not that clear-cut. Suppose that, without the surcharge, other forces would have raised the ratio of consumption to before-tax income and reduced the saving rate. It is possible that the surcharge made the ratio of consumption to before-tax income less than it otherwise would have been — that is, kept it constant when it would have risen. We need to control for the influence of other forces that might influence consumption in order to isolate the impact of the surcharge. Economists do this by the econometric technique *regression analysis* — fitting a consumption function to the data. (A brief explanation of regression technique was given in our discussion of the relationship between inflation and unemployment in Chapter 6.) Several economists have applied such econometric techniques to the tax surcharge of 1968 and the tax rebate of 1975 (a temporary tax cut). The outcomes have not been uniform, and the resulting debate has been lively.* From these studies, we can draw the following conclusion:

▶ A temporary income-tax change has perhaps one-half to one-third of the impact of a permanent income-tax change of the same magnitude. Thus, a temporary tax change would need to be made two to three times as large as a permanent tax change in order to achieve the same impact.

---

* Arthur Okun, Chairman of the Council of Economic Advisors when the surcharge was proposed, used the consumption equations from four prominent econometric models to examine the impact of the 1968 surcharge (Okun, "The Personal Tax Surcharge and Consumer Demand, 1968–70," *Brookings Papers on Economic Activity* 1971: 1). Okun concluded that, according to these equations, the surcharge made consumption less than it otherwise would have been; its impact was as effective as if the surcharge had been permanent, instead of temporary. Springer disputed Okun's conclusion (Springer, "Did the 1968 Surcharge Really Work?" *American Economic Review* [September 1975]). He performed similar tests based on his own consumption equation. He concluded that the surcharge had virtually no effect. In a rejoinder (*American Economic Review* [March 1977]), Okun replied that the score in favor of the surcharge's impact was now four equations to one, instead of four to none. He noted that the equations he used had not been developed specially to test the impact of the surcharge, in contrast to Springer's.

Several other researchers report intermediate results, where consumption is affected roughly half as much by a temporary tax change as by a permanent tax change. (See Modigliani and Steindel, "Is a Tax Rebate an Effective Tool for Stabilization Policy?" *Brookings Papers on Economic Activity* 1977: 1; Dolde, "Temporary Taxes as Macroeconomic Stabilizers" *American Economic Review* [May 1979]; and Blinder, "Temporary Income Taxes and Consumer Spending" *Journal of Political Economy* [February 1981].)

In light of the permanent income and life-cycle hypotheses, why should the impact be this large? First, many households may face a liquidity constraint. Second, while these hypotheses predict that consumption—C_n plus the services of the stock of durables—will change little, expenditures on consumer durables may be affected. Such expenditures are really a form of investment and may be altered even when consumption is being kept fairly constant.

The entire debate has been over *income*-tax changes. In Chapter 10, we explained that to encourage saving and capital accumulation, some economists advocate converting the income tax to a personal consumption tax. Under such a conversion, each household is annually taxed according to its consumption expenditure, not its income. Under a personal consumption tax, temporary tax changes have a substantial impact according to the life-cycle hypothesis. For example, if the consumption tax rate is lower this year than it is next year, it makes sense for a household to shift some of next year's consumption to this year; symmetrically, if the consumption tax rate is higher this year than it is next year, then a household should postpone some consumption until next year.

▶ Temporary consumption tax changes should promptly and significantly affect consumer expenditure.

12.3 Consumption and Monetary Policy

Monetary policy affects the interest rate and credit availability; these, in turn, influence expenditure on durables. Durables, by definition, last several years. Since a durable provides a flow of services over several years, it makes sense to spread the cost over a comparable period through borrowing.

While monetary policy primarily influences investment and expenditure on consumer durables, it also influences consumption, and its component C_n, through the stock market wealth effect of the life-cycle hypothesis. Moreover, it has an important impact whenever a liquidity constraint is preventing the desired adjustment to permanent income or lifetime earnings. For example, suppose the economy plunges into a recession which reduces current disposable income. With permanent income and lifetime earnings hardly affected, households may want to hold consumption fairly constant. But this may require borrowing. A monetary policy expansion that reduces interest rates and raises credit availability raises consumption, and its component C_n.

According to this analysis, monetary policy influences consumption and C_n most when liquidity constraints are binding. But this is the situation most relevant to the potency of countercyclical monetary policy in a recession. It is in recession that liquidity constraints are likely to be severe. It is therefore incorrect to assume that monetary policy can only combat a recession by stimulating investment or durable consumption. The stock market wealth effect may raise consumption. But even more importantly, given liquidity constraints in a recession, expansionary monetary policy also stimulates nondurable consumption.

12.4 The Theory of Investment: The Accelerator

The ACCELERATOR HYPOTHESIS OF NET INVESTMENT states that *net* investment depends on the expected *change* in output.

Consider a representative firm. We will suppose that for any level of output there is a most profitable level of real capital that should be used to produce that output. Since output is produced by capital, labor, and other factors, the desired capital stock depends on the relative costs of the different factors. At any moment in time, these relative costs can be estimated, and an *optimal (profit-maximizing) capital stock* corresponding to each level of output can be found.

Let v^* be the most profitable capital–output ratio for the representative firm. Then the desired capital stock K^* is equal to the product of v^* and the expected output Q^e:

(12.2) $K^* = v^* Q^e$

For example, if v^* is 2, and expected output Q^e is 1,000, then the desired capital stock K^* is 2,000. The most profitable capital–output ratio v^* depends on relative factor costs. In particular, it is influenced by the interest rate and the tax treatment of investment. For the moment, we will consider these as given.

Net investment I_n is defined as the increase in the capital stock in a given year. It is equal to gross investment I_g minus depreciation (the capital stock that wears out during the year) D:

(12.3) $I_n \equiv I_g - D$

For example, if gross investment (the production of new capital) is 150, but 100 of the old capital stock wears out during the year, then net investment I_n is 50. Net investment therefore equals the increase in the capital stock:

(12.4) $I_n \equiv \Delta K \equiv K - K_{-1}$

K is the capital stock at the end of the year, and K_{-1} is the capital stock at the end of last year (the beginning of this year). In the simplest version of the accelerator hypothesis, it is assumed that the net investment required to achieve the desired capital stock in a single year is always undertaken. Thus, the actual capital stock is always kept equal to the desired capital stock. With this simplifying assumption, the basic idea behind the accelerator is easily illustrated. If the optimal capital–output ratio v^* is assumed to stay constant, then the desired capital K^* will change only if expected output Q^e changes. For example, if v^* is 2, then as long as Q^e stays at 1,000, K^* stays at 2,000, and desired net investment I_n is 0 (desired gross investment I_g just equals depreciation D).

But suppose Q^e increases by 100 to 1,100. If v^* remains 2, then the desired K^* increases to 2,200. Hence, net investment is 200. If Q^e stays constant, then net investment is 0. It is positive only if Q^e increases. Hence, investment depends on the expected change in output. We can show this more formally. If the actual capital K is always kept equal to the desired capital K^*, then we can rewrite equation (12.4) as

(12.5) $I_n = K^* - K^*_{-1}$

If we substitute equation (12.2) into equation (12.5) and assume that v^* stays constant, we have

$$I_n = v^*Q^e - v^*Q^e_{-1}$$
$$I_n = v^*(Q^e - Q^e_{-1})$$

If ΔQ^e is the change in Q^e $(Q^e - Q^e_{-1})$, then

(12.6) $I_n = v^*(\Delta Q^e)$

Equation (12.6) indicates that net investment I_n is proportional to the expected change in output ΔQ^e. For example, suppose output is not expected to change; then $I_n = 0$. This makes sense — the firm already has the capital stock that is optimal for that particular output. If output is expected to stay the same, then the firm wants no change in its capital stock; hence, net investment is 0.

Of course, net investment of 0 requires positive gross investment to match depreciation. If depreciation D is 100, then gross investment must be 100 to keep the capital stock constant. We can write an equation for gross investment I_g, making the simplifying assumption that depreciation D is a constant fraction δ of the previous year's capital stock K_{-1} (for example, if 20% of the capital stock wears out in a year, δ will be 20%) as follows:

(12.7) $D = \delta K_{-1}$

Equation (12.3) can be rewritten:

(12.8) $I_g \equiv I_n + D$

Substituting equation (12.7) and equation (12.6) into equation (12.8) yields

(12.9) $I_g = v^*(\Delta Q^e) + \delta K_{-1}$

For example, suppose that $v^* = 2$, $\Delta Q^e = 100$ (Q^e increases from 1,000 to 1,100), the depreciation rate δ is 20%, and K_{-1} is 2,000. Then, from equation (12.6), net investment $I_n = 2(100) = 200$ and, from equation (12.7), depreciation $D = 0.2(2,000) = 400$. Using equation (12.9), we find that $I_g = 600$. Thus, gross investment depends on two things. First, the capital that depreciated in the preceding year must be replaced to restore the capital stock. Second, if the desired capital stock has increased, then net investment must be undertaken.

Why is this hypothesis called the accelerator? Suppose that the representative firm expects the output it can sell to decline. Then ΔQ^e is negative and the firm wants negative net investment in order to keep its capital–output ratio optimal. Hence, it reduces its gross investment I_g below depreciation D. This reduction of I_g, a component of aggregate demand, in itself causes a further decline in equilibrium Q as we showed in Chapter 1. Thus, an initial downturn is accelerated by this kind of investment behavior. The instability of the economy is increased because any initial downturn gets magnified.

THE FLEXIBLE ACCELERATOR

The simple accelerator can be made more flexible and realistic in several ways. The simple accelerator assumes that the optimal capital–output ratio v^* remains constant. But as we will see shortly, v^* varies; it is dependent on the cost of capital. Monetary and fiscal policy affect v^*. But v^* may also change automatically. For example, suppose a decline in output is expected. Net investment is therefore negative and gross investment falls below depreciation in order to reduce the capital stock. Output (income) falls and in the IS–LM diagram, the IS curve shifts to the left while both Q and r fall. A lower interest rate means a lower cost of capital. Hence, the optimal capital–output ratio v^* rises. This automatic change in v^* is stabilizing; it raises the desired capital stock K^*, and thereby limits the fall in investment and output. The Fed can further increase the optimal v^* by instituting an expansionary monetary policy in the recession. The shift right of the LM curve further reduces the interest rate, and therefore the cost of capital, making a higher v^* profitable. This stimulates investment demand, and helps to end the recession.

Now consider another example. Suppose that a large increase in output is expected. At the initial optimal capital–output ratio v^* a large net investment I_n, and hence a large gross investment I_g, would be forthcoming. Given consumption C and government purchases G, we assume that this large investment I results in an equilibrium output Q well above Q_c, such that if no policy action were taken to reduce aggregate demand, inflation would rise (as shown in Chapter 4). Faced with the threat of excess demand that has been propelled by the accelerator, the Fed decides to tighten monetary policy in order to reduce Q to Q_c. The tightening of monetary policy shifts the LM curve to the left, raising the interest rate, and thus the cost of capital as well. The subsequent reduction in v^* spurs a reduction in I. A tight monetary policy, then, if applied with sufficient strength, can counter the pressure from the accelerator and keep the economy from overheating, despite the fact that business firms expect a large increase in expected output Q^e.

These examples contain a very important lesson. The simple accelerator, with a constant optimal capital–output ratio v^*, appears to make the economy volatile. To be sure, Q^e is probably volatile, depending as it does on expectations of the future. Swings in Q^e (up or down) may be large and, were v^* constant, would cause large swings in I_g and hence in aggregate demand. Thus, the economy appears subject to large fluctuations from investment behavior. The automatic variation of v^*, however, provides some stability:

▶ The optimal capital–output ratio v^* generally varies automatically in a stabilizing direction. The automatic variation in v^* tends to reduce the fluctuation in I. Moreover, countercyclical monetary policy can further move v^* in a stabilizing direction. Hence, investment is not as destabilizing as the simple accelerator implies.

The simple accelerator assumes that the desired capital stock is always achieved by the required amount of net investment. But the flexible accelerator allows for the possibility that net investment may only close a fraction of the gap between the initial capital stock, and the desired capital stock. Why? Firms may face adjustment costs that make gradual adjustment optimal. Also, firms may not believe the change in expected output Q^e is permanent.

12.5 The Rate of Return on Investment

In the preceding section, we assumed that the representative firm knows the most profitable capital–output ratio v^*. Once Q^e is estimated, the firm then knows the most desirable capital stock K^*, and hence, the investment required to achieve it. But how does the firm determine v^*? Equivalently, how does it decide how much investment will maximize its profit?

The firm needs to estimate the *rate of return (yield)* on each potential investment project. Let's illustrate the rate of return in a simple example. Suppose a machine costs $100. It is purchased in year 0, and can be used in year 1. At the end of year 1, it is completely used up. If its use in year 1 enables the firm to earn $110 more net revenue (revenue minus operating cost) than it could have earned without the machine, then the yield, or return, is 10%.

Consider another example. Suppose the $100 machine lasts forever, instead of completely depreciating in one year. Then if it enables the firm to earn $10 more net revenue in every year of its use, the yield, or return, is also 10%. While this 10% seems intuitively plausible in both examples, let's define the yield, or return, more precisely so that we can see that the return is in fact 10% in both of these cases.

We first need to define the concept of *present value*. Suppose you are given the choice of being paid $100 this year, or $100 next year. Which would you choose? You should prefer $100 this year, because you could invest the $100 and earn interest. For example, if the interest rate is 10%, the $100 you receive this year grows to $110 next year (interest of $10 plus the principal of $100). Thus, $100 this year is better than $100 next year. It is, in effect, equivalent to $110 next year if the interest rate is 10%. We say that the present value of $110 next year is $100 when the interest rate is 10%. Finding the present value of a future revenue is the opposite of compounding, and is called *discounting*. Let the present be year 0. Then to find the present value PV of a revenue in year 1, S_1, we divide (discount) S_1 by 1 plus the interest rate r (the discount rate):

(12.10) $$PV = \frac{S_1}{1 + r}$$

If S_1 is $110 and r is 10%, then

$$PV = \frac{110}{1.1} = 100$$

Suppose we receive a revenue in year 2. If the interest rate is 10%, then $121 in year 2 is equivalent to $100 in year 0; $100 in year 0 grows to $110 in year 1, and $121 in year 2. Hence, the present value of $121 in year 2 is $100. Formally

$$PV = \frac{S_2}{(1 + r)^2}$$

In our example, $r = 10\%$ and $(1 + r)^2 = 1.21$.

To generalize, consider revenue in year t, S_t. Its present value is given by

$$PV = \frac{S_t}{(1 + r)^t}$$

We define the RATE OF RETURN (yield) R on an investment as the discount rate that makes the present value of the additional net revenue generated by the investment equal to the cost of the investment.

In our first example, the additional net revenue all occurs in year 1 — $110. The cost of the investment in year 0 is $100. Thus, we have

$$100 = \frac{110}{1 + R}$$

Clearly, R is 10%. Hence, the rate of return on this investment is 10%.

Should this investment be undertaken? The answer depends on how the rate of return R compares with the market interest rate r at which the firm can borrow. Suppose the market interest rate r is 10%. If the firm borrows $100, it must repay $110 in year 1. Since the rate of return R is 10%, this is exactly the additional net revenue the investment generates in year 1. Hence, the result is a draw. If, however, the market interest rate r is less than 10%, then less than $110 needs to be repaid, and the investment should be made. For example, if r is 8%, then the firm repays $108 in year 1. Since it earns an additional $110 of net revenue, it gains $2 of profit by making the investment. Symmetrically, if r is greater than 10%, then more than $110 must be repaid, and the investment should not be made. The firm, then, should undertake all investments for which the rate of return R exceeds the market interest rate r. Thus, we reach an important conclusion.

▶ An investment is profitable if and only if its rate of return (yield) R exceeds the market interest rate r.

THE RETURN ON A DURABLE INVESTMENT

Now consider the second example where $10 of additional net revenue is generated in all future years, beginning with year 1. The rate of return R is the discount rate that makes the present value of future additional net revenue equal to the cost of the investment:

$$100 = \frac{10}{1 + R} + \frac{10}{(1 + R)^2} + \frac{10}{(1 + R)^3} + \cdots$$

This series of terms never ends. But the sum can still approach 100. For example, if we add $40 + 20 + 10 + \cdots$, we gradually approach 80, even though the series never ends. To find the rate of return R, we divide every term on both sides by $1 + R$, and write the new equation under the original equation. When the first term $10/1 + R$ is divided by $1 + R$, the result is $10/(1 + R)^2$. For each subsequent term, the power of $1 + R$ in the denominator is raised by 1. Thus, we have

$$100 = \frac{10}{1 + R} + \frac{10}{(1 + R)^2} + \frac{10}{(1 + R)^3} + \cdots$$

$$\frac{100}{1 + R} = \frac{10}{(1 + R)^2} + \frac{10}{(1 + R)^3} + \cdots$$

When we subtract the second equation from the first, all terms on the right drop out except the first term of the first equation:

$$100 - \frac{100}{1 + R} = \frac{10}{1 + R}$$

Multiplying each term on both sides by $1 + R$ gives us

$$100(1 + R) - 100 = 10$$
$$100(1 + R) \qquad = 110$$
$$1 + R = \frac{110}{100} = 1.1$$
$$R = 0.1 = 10\%$$

Thus, the rate of return R is 10%.

We have given two simple examples of an investment with a return of 10%. In the first, the machine lasts one year; in the second, the machine lasts forever and generates the same additional net revenue in all years. Most machines last several years. But R can always be found. Its value makes the cost $\mathscr{C}$ of the machine equal to the present value of additional net revenue over the life of the machine. Thus, if n is the life of the machine, then the rate of return R is the value that satisfies the following equation:

(12.11)
$$\mathscr{C} = \frac{S_1}{1 + R} + \frac{S_2}{(1 + R)^2} + \cdots + \frac{S_n}{(1 + R)^n}$$

where $\mathscr{C}$ = the cost of the machine

Whatever the life of the machine, the result stated earlier still holds: the firm should undertake all investments for which the rate of return (yield) R exceeds the market interest rate r.

Suppose that potential investment projects of all firms are ranked, beginning with the project with the highest rate of return R. As investment increases, the rate of return R falls. In Figure 12.1, we plot the rate of return R curve for the economy. At each investment I, the height of the curve is equal to the rate of return R on the last project undertaken. Using the R curve, we can tell how much investment occurs at a given market interest rate r by drawing a horizontal line with height r. We know that it is profitable for a firm to undertake any project where the rate of return R exceeds the market interest rate r. Hence, investment projects are undertaken until the r line intersects the R curve.

This rate of return R curve is our investment I curve from Chapter 2. In that chapter, we postulated that when the market interest rate r decreases, investment I increases; we drew a curve that told us the investment I at each market interest rate r. We now see that the investment I curve is the rate of return R curve because the R curve tells us the investment that occurs at each r.

Given formula (12.11), it would be easy for a firm to decide what its total investment should be if it knew with certainty the values of future net revenues S_1, S_2, and so forth. But as Keynes emphasized in the *General Theory*, we can only guess at the future. Hence, the expected

FIGURE 12.1 THE RATE OF RETURN ON INVESTMENT

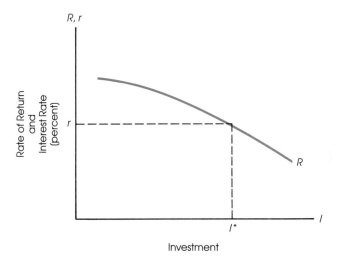

At each level of I, the height of the R curve indicates the rate of return on the last (marginal) investment project undertaken. It is profitable to raise total investment I until the rate of return declines into equality with the market interest rate r. Hence, I^* is the level of investment that is undertaken at interest rate r. This means that the R curve coincides with the I curve of Chapter 2.

rate of return R will vary with optimism and pessimism about the future. In a famous passage in the *General Theory,* Keynes writes:

> The outstanding fact is the extreme precariousness of the basis of knowledge on which our estimates of prospective yield have to be made. Our knowledge of the factors which will govern the yield of an investment some years hence is usually very slight and often negligible. If we speak frankly, we have to admit that our basis of knowledge for estimating the yield ten years hence of a railway, a copper mine, a textile factory, the goodwill of patent medicine, an Atlantic liner, a building in the City of London amounts to little and sometimes to nothing; or even five years hence.*

12.6 Investment, Inflation, and the Real Interest Rate

Now that we have explained the rate of return on investment, we can clarify an assertion made in Chapter 5 in our discussion of the consequences of inflation: that investment demand I depends on the expected real interest rate i^e, where:

The EXPECTED REAL INTEREST RATE i^e is defined as the nominal interest rate r minus the expected inflation rate p^e.

If investment I depends on i^e, then I is the same for both of the following two combinations of r and p^e: $r = 3\%$, $p^e = 0\%$; and $r = 13\%$, $p^e = 10\%$. In each case, i^e is 3%, and hence I is the same. Furthermore, if I depends on i^e, then an increase in p^e of 10% shifts the investment curve up by 10% when the nominal interest rate r is on the vertical axis as shown in Figure 5.1 (page 207). Why? If investment I depends on the expected real interest rate i^e $(r - p^e)$, then the nominal interest rate r must rise by 10% to keep investment constant when the expected inflation rate p^e rises by 10%.

In general:

▶ If p^e rises by $X\%$, then when the nominal interest rate r is on the vertical axis, the investment I curve shifts up by $X\%$.

To explain this, let's return to our first example from Section 12.5 where the machine costs $100 in year 0 and raises net revenue by $110 in year 1. With no inflation, the rate of return R is 10%. If the nominal interest rate r is 10%, then the investment is a draw. But suppose that the inflation rate is 10%. This means prices are 10% higher in year 1 than in year 0. The machine still costs $100 in year 0, but because all prices are 10% higher in year 1 than in year 0, it now raises net revenue in year 1 by

---

* John Maynard Keynes, *General Theory of Employment, Interest, and Money* (New York: Harcourt Brace Jovanovich, Inc., 1936) 149–50.

110×1.10, or approximately \$121. Therefore, the nominal rate of return R is approximately 20% (the original rate of return, 10%, plus the inflation rate, 10%).

▶ The nominal rate of return on investment R rises by X% when the expected inflation rate rises by X%.

With the expected inflation rate at 10%, the same investment project is a draw if the nominal rate of interest r is 20%. Thus:

▶ If the nominal interest rate r rises by X% when the expected inflation rate p^e rises by X%, then investment stays the same. Hence, investment depends on the expected real interest rate i^e.

In Figure 5.1, the expected inflation rate rises from 0% to p^e and the investment curve I shifts up by p^e because a higher nominal interest rate (higher by p^e) corresponds to the same expected real interest rate i^e, and hence the same investment I. A specific investment I results from a particular expected real interest rate i^e, and so does a specific equilibrium output Q. Thus, equilibrium output Q depends on the expected real interest rate i^e. This means that if the expected inflation rate rises from 0% to p^e, then the IS curve shifts up by p^e (because it is plotted with the nominal interest rate r on the vertical axis).

If the $IS-LM$ intersection is initially at Q_c, then as Figure 12.2 shows, the rise in the expected inflation rate from 0% to p^e raises equilibrium output Q above Q_c when the LM curve stays fixed, by shifting up the IS curve by p^e. But if the Fed shifts the LM curve left to keep Q at Q_c, then the nominal interest rate r rises by the same percent as the expected inflation rate p^e. The real interest rate i stays constant. This result is called *Fisher's hypothesis,* after the American economist Irving Fisher who developed it early in this century:

FISHER'S HYPOTHESIS states that a change in the expected inflation rate p^e causes roughly an equal percentage change in the nominal interest rate r, and hence no change in the real interest rate i.

Since the expected inflation rate often approximates the actual inflation rate, it follows that an economy with a high inflation rate will have a high nominal interest rate. Thus, the inflation rate is a central determinant of the nominal interest rate of the economy. Note, however, that according to Fisher's hypothesis, the inflation rate has roughly no effect on the real interest rate, and hence no effect on investment. This conclusion ignores the impact of the tax system. Tax rules may cause a shift in IS when the inflation rate changes, and may result in different nominal and real interest rates. Thus, Fisher's hypothesis should be viewed as a first approximation only—one that may require modification in an economy with taxes.

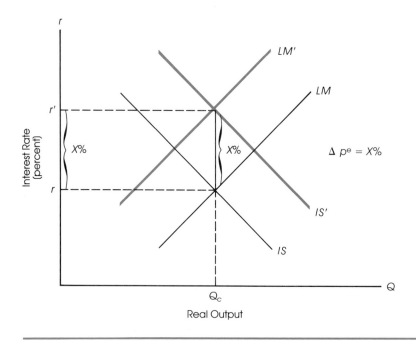

Real Output

Initially, the economy is at point (r, Q_c). When the expected inflation rate p^e rises by $X\%$, the I curve shifts up by $X\%$, causing the IS curve to shift up by $X\%$. To hold Q at Q_c, monetary policy must tighten, shifting up the LM curve by $X\%$. Hence, the nominal interest rate rises $X\%$ from r to r'. This is Fisher's hypothesis, which states that a rise in the expected inflation rate of $X\%$ raises the nominal interest rate by $X\%$.

12.7 The Impact of Monetary and Fiscal Policy on Investment

We turn now to the responsiveness of investment to monetary and fiscal policy. Policy can influence investment by changing the optimal capital–output ratio v^*.

▶ The desired capital–output ratio v^* increases when the cost of capital falls.

From equation (12.2) it is obvious that when the optimal capital–output ratio v^* increases, the optimal capital stock K^* increases for a given expected output Q^e. This increase in K^* results in an increase in net investment I_n. Previously, we assumed that the optimal capital–output ratio v^* was constant. However, suppose v^* falls from year 0 to year 1. Equation (12.6) is no longer valid. Suppose that in year 0 the optimal capital–output ratio v_0^* is 2, the expected output Q_0^e is 1,000, and thus capital K_0 is 2,000. If v^* remains constant in year 1 such that v_1^* is 2, then by setting the expected output in year 1 Q_1^e at 1,100 so that ΔQ^e is 100, we see that the net investment for year 1 $I_{n_1} = 2(100) = 200$. But if in year 1 an expansionary monetary policy reduces the interest rate and the cost of capital such that v^* increases to 2.1, then with $Q_1^e = 1,100$, $K_1^* = 2.1(1,100) = 2,310$. Thus, $I_{n_1} = 2,310 - 2,000 = 310$.

This example shows that equation (12.6) must be modified when v^* changes from year 0 to year 1. Let's redo the derivation. We continue to assume that net investment I_n is sufficient to keep the capital stock at the desired level:

(12.5) $$I_n = K^* - K_{-1}^*$$

But now equation (12.2) must include the change in v^* from year 0 to year 1. In what follows, for any variable the current year is indicated by the variable, while the variable with a subscript -1 is its value in year 0.

(12.2) $$K^* = v^* Q^e$$
$$K_{-1}^* = v_{-1}^* Q_{-1}^e$$

If we subtract the second equation from the first, we obtain

$$K^* - K_{-1}^* = v^* Q^e - v_{-1}^* Q_{-1}^e$$
(12.12) $$I_n = v^* Q^e - v_{-1}^* Q_{-1}^e$$

Equation (12.12), unlike equation (12.6), allows for the possibility that v^* may change from period 0 to period 1.

(12.13) $$v^* = v_{-1}^* + \Delta v^*$$
where $\Delta v^* =$ the change in the optimal capital–output ratio

Substituting equation (12.13) into equation (12.12) gives us

$$I_n = (v_{-1}^* + \Delta v^*) Q^e - v_{-1}^* Q_{-1}^e$$

Multiplying out the first term, we obtain

$$I_n = v_{-1}^* Q^e + \Delta v^* Q^e - v_{-1}^* Q_{-1}^e$$

Note that v_{-1}^* is a common factor of the first and last terms. When these are combined, and recalling that $\Delta Q^e = Q^e - Q_{-1}^e$, we have

(12.14) $$I_n = v_{-1}^* \Delta Q^e + \Delta v^* Q^e$$

If v^* is constant such that $\Delta v^* = 0$ and $v^*_{-1} = v^*$, then equation (12.14) is the same as equation (12.6). But if v^* changes, Δv^* is not 0 and v^*_{-1} is not equal to v^*, then equation (12.14) is the relevant equation for net investment I_n. In our example, where $v^*_{-1} = 2$ and $v^* = 2.1$, we have

$$I_n = 2(100) + 0.1(1{,}100) = 200 + 110 = 310$$

Note that the first term in equation (12.14) shows what net investment would have been if the optimal capital–output v^* had not changed. The second term shows the impact of the change of v^*.

Thus, equation (12.14) shows clearly that if monetary or fiscal policy changes the optimal capital–output ratio v^*, it also changes net investment I_n for a given ΔQ^e. But how can policy change v^*? We will now consider the *neoclassical theory of investment*, which gives special emphasis to the role of the *user cost of capital* in determining the optimal capital–output ratio v^*.

THE NEOCLASSICAL THEORY OF INVESTMENT AND THE USER COST OF CAPITAL

Figure 12.3 shows the basic problem. The representative firm can choose among various combinations of labor L and capital K that achieve a given output Q. The output Q curve is called an isoquant. The firm seeks to choose the (K, L) combination that minimizes its cost. If policy seeks to raise net investment I_n, it must shift the cost-minimizing combination (K, L) from point 1 to point 2, and thereby raise the desired K to Q ratio which is the optimal capital–output ratio v^*. To induce a shift from point 1 to point 2, the cost of capital must be reduced relative to the cost of labor such that it is profitable for the firm to substitute capital for labor — to raise its K/L ratio for a given output Q; hence raise its desired K/Q ratio (the optimal capital–output ratio).

From standard microeconomics, cost-minimization occurs where a cost line is tangent to the isoquant (the Q curve in Figure 12.3). It can be shown (see the adjacent box) that the absolute value of the slope of the cost line equals the *ratio of factor prices* — the ratio of the cost of capital to the cost of labor; and that the absolute value of the slope of a tangent to the isoquant at any point equals the ratio of marginal products. Cost-minimization occurs where the two slopes are equal — where the ratio of marginal products equals the ratio of factor prices:

(12.15) $$\frac{\text{MPK}}{\text{MPL}} = \frac{c}{w}$$

where c = the user (or rental) cost of capital

w = the cost of labor

In this box, we review the standard microeconomics of cost-minimization. There is a family of parallel cost lines. Each line contains all (K, L) combinations with the same total cost $\mathscr{C}$, given current user cost of capital c and cost of labor w. The equation of a cost line with cost $\mathscr{C}$ is

$$\mathscr{C} = wL + cK$$

With L plotted on the vertical axis as shown in Figure 12.3, the slope of a cost line is the coefficient of K when the equation is solved for L:

$$L = \left(\frac{-c}{w}\right)K + \frac{\mathscr{C}}{w}$$

Hence, the absolute value of the slope of the cost line equals the factor price ratio c/w. Note that with factor prices given, the lower the cost line (L-intercept $\mathscr{C}/w$) is, the lower is the cost $\mathscr{C}$.

Now consider the isoquant. The slope of the isoquant equals $\Delta L/\Delta K$, where ΔL and ΔK hold output Q constant. The change in Q resulting from the change in L must exactly offset the change in Q resulting from the change in K. But:

$$\Delta Q \text{ resulting from } \Delta K = (\text{MPK})\Delta K, \text{ since MPK} \equiv \frac{\Delta Q}{\Delta K}$$

and

$$\Delta Q \text{ resulting from } \Delta L = (\text{MPL})\Delta L, \text{ since MPL} \equiv \frac{\Delta Q}{\Delta L}$$

To hold Q constant, the two ΔQs must sum to 0:

$$(\text{MPK})\Delta K + (\text{MPL})\Delta L = 0$$
$$\frac{\text{MPK}}{\text{MPL}} = \frac{-\Delta L}{\Delta K} \text{ (where } Q \text{ is held constant)}$$

Hence, the absolute value of the slope of the isoquant equals the ratio of marginal products. The point on the isoquant with minimum cost is the point on the lowest cost line. At this point, the cost line is tangent to the isoquant. Since the two slopes are equal, the ratio of factor prices equals the ratio of marginal products.

FIGURE 12.3 COST MINIMIZATION AND THE OPTIMAL K/Q RATIO (v^*)

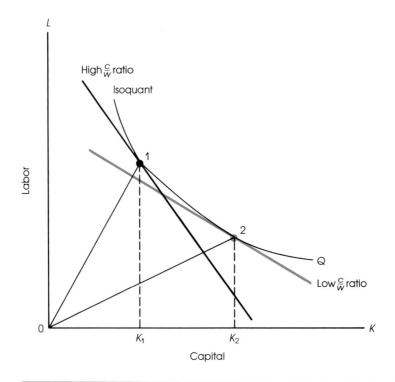

The representative firm seeks to produce a given output Q at minimum cost. The isoquant contains all combinations of (K, L) that achieve the given output Q. The least-cost (K, L) depends on the ratio of factor prices. The slope of the cost line equals the c/w ratio multiplied by -1. When c/w falls, the cost line becomes flatter. The optimum (K, L) occurs at the tangency of the isoquant and the cost line. When c/w falls, the optimum (K, L) shifts from 1 to 2. A larger capital K for the same output Q implies a larger optimal capital–output ratio v^*.

If policy reduces the user cost of capital c, then c/w falls, the cost line becomes flatter and the firm shifts from point 1 to point 2.

What is the user cost of capital? Standard microeconomics says that profit is maximized if each factor is hired until its marginal product equals its cost per unit.

▶ The user cost of capital c is the cost to which the firm should compare the MPK in order to maximize profit, just as the cost of labor w is the cost to which the firm should compare the MPL in order to maximize profit.

What constitutes user cost? Suppose the firm wants to raise its real capital stock permanently by one dollar. This raises its output by the marginal product of capital MPK (which is defined as the increase in output due to an increase in capital of one dollar, holding other factors constant). For example, if output is increased by $0.25 per year, so that the marginal product of capital MPK is 25%, what is the cost to which this 25% should be compared in order to decide whether adding another dollar's worth of capital permanently is profitable? If we assume that the dollar of capital that is acquired is perfectly durable—it does not depreciate—and that the firm borrows an amount of $1 with an annual interest payment of $0.10, or 10%, to finance $1 of capital, then the user cost of capital is the interest payment of 10% per year.

The user cost is the same even if the firm does not borrow, but rather, finances its purchase out of retained earnings because the firm could have earned 10% interest by lending out its dollar of retained earnings, but now must forego this interest.

If the capital depreciates, then each year part of the $1 of capital wears out and must be replaced. For example, a $0.15 depreciation per year requires the firm to replace $0.15 per year to keep the capital stock permanently larger by $1. In this case, the user cost of capital c is the 15% depreciation cost plus the 10% interest cost, or 25%. In this example, the firm is indifferent to the addition of another $1 of capital because the marginal product exactly equals the user cost—both are 25%.

The USER COST OF CAPITAL (expressed as a percentage) is the sum of the interest rate plus the depreciation rate (ignoring taxes and subsidies).

Thus far, we have worked with the gross marginal product. In our example it is 25%. An equivalent approach is to work with the net marginal product. The net marginal product is the gross marginal product minus depreciation. In our example, it is 10% (25% − 15%). Thus, profitability is determined by comparing either the gross marginal product to the user cost (interest rate plus depreciation rate) or the net marginal product to the interest rate.

The impact of monetary policy should be clear. If the Fed eases monetary policy and reduces the interest rate, the user cost of capital is reduced, and the optimal capital–output ratio v^* is raised. For any expected change in output ΔQ^e in equation (12.14), the increase in v^* implies a larger net investment I_n. This in turn implies a larger gross investment I_g in equation (12.9).

TAX POLICY AND INVESTMENT

Now let us turn to fiscal policy, and in particular, tax policy. Thus far, the marginal product is compared to the interest rate plus the depreciation rate. If, however, tax policy is designed such that the purchase of an additional $1 of new capital reduces the tax liability of the firm, then clearly the user cost of capital c is reduced. In our example, both the marginal product of capital MPK and the user cost c are 25% (10% interest rate plus a 15% depreciation rate) and the firm is indifferent to the additional dollar of capital. But if tax policy reduces the tax of the firm when it adds another $1 of capital, then the user cost c is reduced to below 25% and the firm finds it profitable to add additional capital.

How might tax policy reduce the user cost of capital? One method is the *investment tax credit* ITC. Under a 10% ITC, for each $100 of new investment, the firm's taxes are reduced by $10. Since the 1960s, the United States has used the ITC method, varying its average rate between 7% and 10%.

Another method for reducing the user cost of capital is *accelerated depreciation*. To understand it, a distinction must be kept in mind between genuine economic depreciation and artificial tax-law depreciation. Under the corporate income tax, a corporation deducts cost from revenue and arrives at its income (profit). The tax rate is applied to this income. Depreciation is a component of cost. If a measure of genuine income is to be obtained, then *genuine economic depreciation*—the actual reduction in the real value of the asset—should be subtracted. Under accelerated depreciation, however, the tax law allows the firm to artificially inflate its measure of depreciation for a new asset. The greater is the depreciation permitted for tax computation, the lower is the reported income. A lower income, in turn, results in a lower tax.

Under accelerated depreciation, the tax law permits the firm to depreciate an asset more rapidly than its actual economic depreciation. Total reported depreciation over the life of the asset does not change. Because of the artificial acceleration, the firm reports less profit and pays less tax when the asset is relatively new. Toward the end of the asset's life, the firm reports more profit and pays more tax. This shift benefits the firm because money now is worth more than the same money later as a result of the interest earned. When a tax is postponed, the present value of the tax is reduced. Thus, under accelerated depreciation, each $1 of investment results in a greater present value of depreciation cost over the life of the asset, a smaller present value of tax, and a larger present value of after-tax profit.

Given the corporate income tax, the ITC and accelerated depreciation reduce the user cost of capital below what it would be under a corporate income tax without these provisions. But what is the impact of the corporate income tax itself on the most profitable capital stock? With no corporate income tax, it is profitable to add capital if the gross marginal product exceeds the *no-tax user cost*—the sum of the interest rate plus the economic depreciation rate. Suppose that the income tax permits interest and economic depreciation to be deducted as a cost such that only the excess of marginal product over the no-tax user cost is taxed. As long as the tax rate is less than 100%, the firm still gains by adding capital whenever the marginal product exceeds the no-tax user cost. Hence, the firm's investment decision should not change. The corporate income tax is neutral and does not affect user cost.

If, however, an interest deduction is not permitted when the firm finances its new capital by retained earnings, or by issuing new stock (equity financing), then the tax raises user cost and discourages investment. A reduction in the tax rate reduces user cost and raises investment. If, on the other hand, interest is deductible and the depreciation that can be deducted for tax computation exceeds true economic depreciation, then the tax reduces user cost and encourages debt-financed investment. Its reduction raises user cost and discourages investment.

Thus, given the actual, complex provisions of the corporate income tax, we see that its impact on investment is ambiguous. A cut in the corporate income tax rate does not have a clear impact on the profitability of investment or on the user cost of capital. This discussion of the impact of the corporate income tax leads us to modify our definition of the user cost:

The USER COST OF CAPITAL (expressed as a percentage) is the sum of the interest rate plus the economic depreciation rate plus or minus a tax adjustment.

▶The introduction of a corporate income tax may raise or lower the user cost, depending on its provisions. Hence, cutting the tax rate may or may not lower user cost. But given a corporate income-tax rate, the introduction of an investment tax credit ITC or of accelerated depreciation reduces the user cost below what it otherwise would be under the income tax, and therefore stimulates investment.

There is another route, however, by which a cut in the corporate income tax might encourage investment. Some analysts believe that *liquidity*, or *cash flow*, stimulates investment. They maintain that firms are more likely to undertake investment if they have cash on hand and are in a relatively liquid position. According to this view, a cut in the corporate tax rate which increases retained earnings stimulates investment.

Can a tax policy that influences investment be used to stabilize the economy? It is instructive to compare a temporary change in the investment tax credit with a temporary tax change to influence consumption. In our discussion of the latter, we saw that according to the life-cycle and permanent income hypotheses, a temporary income-tax change should not have much impact. In practice, however, a temporary income-tax change does have some impact — perhaps one-half to one-third of what a permanent change of the same magnitude accomplishes — due to the role of liquidity. We also saw that if the personal tax is a tax on consumption expenditure instead of on income, then the life-cycle hypothesis predicts a significant impact for a temporary tax change. Why? Because it makes sense to shift consumption to a period of relatively low tax.

A tax change on investment expenditure is similar to a tax change on consumption expenditure. A temporary increase in the ITC should be effective in shifting investment to the period with a relatively high tax saving. For example, suppose a firm is planning to purchase new capital equipment with a life of five years. If a downturn in the economy occurs, the firm is inclined to delay its purchase. But if the government announces a temporary sharp increase in the ITC along with a pledge that it will be terminated as soon as recovery has begun, then it may be profitable for the firm to make the purchase during the downturn, instead of waiting for recovery.

A possible problem, however, has been raised. If the ITC is expected to be so generous in recession that many firms hold back investment during prosperity while waiting for the recession, then the variable ITC generates the recession, even though it also assures a quick recovery. Thus, the evaluation of a variable ITC must take account of this possible destabilizing response.

In the 1950s and 1960s, Sweden attempted to stabilize investment by releasing funds to subsidize investment during recession. Like a variable ITC, the Swedish investment funds system reduced the cost of investment goods during recession. In a careful study, John Taylor concludes:

> The main empirical findings of this study indicate that the Swedish investment funds system reduced the cyclical fluctuations in investment during the late 1950s and 1960s. The system had a major impact on the effective price that firms paid for investment goods, and in general this impact was countercyclical with the price being relatively low during recessions and high during booms. Such countercyclical price effects would be expected to shift firms' investment plans in a countercyclical direction. . . . Although the analysis indicates that such a scheme could in principle destabilize investment for certain forecasting procedures used by firms, no evidence of such destabilizing effects was found in the empirical analysis.[*]

---

[*] John Taylor, "The Swedish Investment Funds System as a Stabilization Policy Rule," *Brookings Papers on Economic Activity* 1 (1982): 96.

Finally, it is important to mention the *q theory of investment*, which emphasizes the influence of the stock market on investment, and is therefore another channel by which monetary and fiscal policy can influence investment. The q theory holds that if the value of corporate stock exceeds the replacement cost—that is, the current and not the historical cost—of the real capital owned by the firm, then stockholders gain when the firm raises its real investment. Why? Because $100 spent on investment instead of paid out as dividends raises the value of corporate stock more than $100, and thereby more than compensates stockholders for the foregone dividends. The variable q is the ratio of the value of corporate stock to the replacement cost of corporate capital. Fluctuations in q should influence investment.

If the q theory has validity, then monetary and fiscal policy can influence investment through the stock market. A monetary expansion generally raises the value of corporate stock. With money more abundant, wealth-holders initially try to shift out of money and into corporate stock. Only the resulting rise in the price of corporate stock induces wealth-holders to hold more money in their portfolios. Thus, a monetary expansion should raise q, and hence should stimulate real investment.

A cut in the effective tax rate on capital gains should stimulate investment as well. Under a pure income tax, a rise in the value of stock—a *capital gain*—is fully taxed like other income. But if part of the capital gain is tax-exempt, reducing the effective tax rate, then corporate stock becomes more attractive to wealth-holders. The price of stock rises, raising q, and hence stimulates real investment by firms.

Thus, both the neoclassical theory of investment and the q theory of investment suggest that monetary and fiscal policy can significantly influence investment.

12.8 Residential Investment and Inventory Investment

While the major component of investment is *fixed business investment* —the increase in capital equipment and structures by firms—we should briefly note two other components of investment: residential investment (housing), and inventory investment.

Housing is a consumer durable. As we noted earlier, all consumer durables are capital goods that yield a flow of services over time. Hence, expenditure on all consumer durables can be regarded as investment. But in the official national income accounts, only housing is classified as an investment. Our earlier comments on consumer durable expenditure apply to housing. In particular, the interest rate is a key determinant of such expenditure. Liquidity constraints and credit restrictions are especially important. Monetary policy therefore has a strong influence on housing expenditure.

An increase in inventories is another component of investment. Recall from Chapter 1 that inventories consist of materials, goods in process, and finished goods held by firms but not yet sold. Since an increase in inventories is available for future use, it is classified as investment. But often, actual inventories do not equal desired inventories. One determinant of desired inventories is the interest rate. There is a similarity between choosing optimal money and choosing optimal inventories. In both cases, the holder weighs the advantage of holding the asset against the foregone interest.

Inventories fluctuate significantly during a business cycle. When a recession begins, it usually catches firms by surprise. Undesired inventories accumulate as firms are unable to sell as much as they intended. Production does not fall as fast as demand, and thus there exists a temporary excess of output over demand. Before long, however, firms cut production in an attempt to reduce inventories to the desired level. This intentional inventory decumulation often causes a sharp drop in production. The fluctuation of inventories over the business cycle is called the *inventory cycle*. It is important for short-term forecasting.

SUMMARY

1. Three theories of consumption are the *permanent income hypothesis*, the *life-cycle hypothesis*, and the *relative income hypothesis*. All three attempt to reconcile the following two facts: in a cross section of households, the saving rate rises as income rises, and the saving rate of the economy does not appear to rise as household income rises over time.

2. Because consumption depends on permanent income as well as on current income, temporary income-tax changes do not affect consumption as much as permanent changes. Based on empirical studies, it seems reasonable to conclude that a temporary income-tax change has perhaps one-half to one-third of the impact of a permanent income-tax change of the same magnitude.

3. Monetary policy influences consumer durable expenditure through the interest rate and through credit availability. It influences consumption through the value of stock market wealth.

4. The *accelerator hypothesis* of net investment states that net investment depends on the expected change in output. Such investment behavior implies that if output begins to decline, the decline is accelerated because investment declines. Hence, investment behavior is destabilizing.

5. The simple accelerator ignores the fact that the *optimal capital–*

output ratio v* generally varies automatically in a stabilizing direction. The automatic variation in v^* tends to reduce the fluctuation in investment.

6. The *rate of return R* on an investment is the discount rate that makes the *present value PV* of the additional revenue generated by the investment equal to the cost of the investment.

7. A firm should undertake all investments for which the rate of return R exceeds the market interest rate r.

8. Investment demand depends on the expected real interest rate i^e. According to *Fisher's hypothesis,* a change in the expected inflation rate p^e does not alter the expected real interest rate i^e. Hence, it does not alter investment demand.

9. The *neoclassical theory of investment* emphasizes that the desired capital–output ratio increases if the cost of capital falls.

10. The *user cost of capital c* (expressed as a percentage) is the sum of the interest rate plus the economic depreciation rate plus or minus a tax adjustment. The corporate income tax may raise or lower user cost, depending on its provisions. Given the corporate rate, an *investment tax credit ITC* or *accelerated depreciation* reduces the user cost, and thereby stimulates investment.

11. The *q theory of investment* holds that if the value of corporate stock exceeds the replacement cost of the real capital owned by the firm, then stockholders gain if the firm raises its real investment.

12. Residential and inventory investment are each sensitive to the interest rate, credit availability, and hence, monetary policy.

TERMS AND CONCEPTS

accelerated depreciation
accelerator hypothesis
capital gain
consumption of durable goods
    (C_d)
consumption of nondurable
    goods and services (C_n)
discounting
disposable income
Fisher's hypothesis
fixed business investment
flexible accelerator
genuine economic depreciation
investment tax credit (ITC)
life-cycle hypothesis
liquid assets

liquidity (cash flow)
liquidity constraint
neoclassical theory of
    investment
optimal capital–output ratio
    (v^*)
optimal (profit-maximizing)
    capital stock
permanent income hypothesis
present value (PV)
q theory of investment
rate of return on investment (R)
ratio of factor prices
regression analysis
relative income hypothesis
user cost of capital (c)

12.1 Using Table 12.1 as a guide, make up an example to show how the relative income hypothesis reconciles the cross-section and time-series facts about consumption.

12.2 Using Table 12.2 as a guide, make up an example to show how the life-cycle hypothesis reconciles the cross-section and time-series facts about consumption.

12.3 If the optimal capital–output ratio v^* is constant, then derive the accelerator hypothesis.

12.4 If a fall in the user cost of capital c raises v^*, show how the equation for net investment is altered.

12.5 Suppose an investment I with a cost of \$200 generates an additional \$10 of net revenue in all future years. What is the rate of return R on this investment?

12.6 Using the $IS-LM$ diagram, explain Fisher's hypothesis.

CHAPTER

13 Money, Banking, and the Federal Reserve System

Prerequisite: Chapter 2

In Chapter 2, we briefly defended the hypothesis that real money demand varies directly with real income, and inversely with the interest rate. We stated that the supply of money is controlled by the Federal Reserve. In this chapter, we will analyze more carefully the demand for and supply of money.

13.1 What Is Money?

Money is a means of payment (medium of exchange). In an era where definitions of money have proliferated, and where controversy has arisen over which definition is most useful, the basic concept of a means of payment is a comforting anchor.

The *M1 definition of money* is currency plus checkable (demand) deposits. *Checkable deposits* are deposits at commercial banks and thrift institutions against which checks can be written. Both currency and checkable deposits are directly used as a means of payment. In the United States in 1984, M1 was about $550 billion compared to a nominal GNP of roughly $3,700 billion. The nominal GNP to M1 ratio was just under 7. Recall from Chapter 4 that the ratio of nominal GNP to money supply is the *velocity of money V*. Of the $550 billion of M1, just over one-fourth was currency and just under three-fourths was checkable deposits. Checkable deposits are held in commercial banks and *thrift institutions* (*thrifts* include savings and loan associations, mutual savings banks, and credit unions). Roughly two-thirds of checkable deposits are held by businesses and one-third are held by households.

All this seems straightforward. Why, then, the multiple definitions of money? While currency and checking deposits are clearly means of payment, other assets are close substitutes for money and highly *liquid* —that is, they are easily convertible into a means of payment. The *M2 definition of money* includes M1 plus savings and small time deposits at banks and thrift institutions, money-market funds, and several other liquid assets. These assets are easily converted into a means of payment. For example, a money-market fund invests in short-term, interest-bearing securities (such as Treasury bills), pays interest on deposits, and permits the owner to write checks exceeding a minimum sum. A money-market fund is a close substitute for checkable deposits at banks or thrifts. The *M3 definition of money* includes M2 plus several other somewhat less liquid assets.

Obviously, there is nothing right or wrong about a definition per se. The key question is which definition is most useful for the economic analysis of output and inflation? While the majority of macroeconomists probably favor M1, many argue that M2 and M3 should be watched as well. The basic problem is that there is a continuum of assets with respect to liquidity. Some are directly usable as a means of payment; others are easily convertible into a means of payment. Still others—like consumer or producer durable goods—are difficult to convert into a means of payment. It is therefore not obvious where to draw the line and declare all assets to the liquid side of the line to be "money." This ambiguity creates problems for the conduct of monetary policy.

The past few years have witnessed some important financial innovations which have complicated the classification problem. For example, money-market funds began in the early 1970s. Prior to 1982, banks were not permitted to issue money-market accounts. But as soon as the prohibition was removed, money-market deposit accounts at banks mushroomed from zero to over $300 billion in 1983. Hence, changes in financial market regulation and private sector innovation must always be kept in mind when analyzing the growth of a particular concept of money, such as M1. In the past, money was sometimes defined as a noninterest-bearing asset. Clearly, currency meets this definition and, until recently, checking accounts were legally prohibited from earning interest. But that restriction has been repealed for checkable deposits other than demand deposits. While more than half of M1 pays no interest, an important fraction of M1 now pays interest.

While we have defined money as a means of payment, it has several other traditional functions as well. Money is a store of value, a unit of account, and a standard of deferred payment (in which long-term transactions can be defined). What can be used as money? The history of money is one of the more fascinating tales of human evolution. At one time or another, and in one place or another, a variety of commodities, from cattle to cigarettes, has played the role of money. The basic fact remains that money is what money does. Whatever is generally accepted as a means of payment is money. Certain features of a commodity, such as perishability, may rule it out, but if people accept something as a means of payment, it is money.

13.2 The Demand for Money

In Chapter 2, we introduced the demand for money in our explanation of the *LM* curve. We will now deepen the analysis of money demand. Before we begin, let's re-emphasize a basic assumption made in Chapter 2. We assumed that wealth-holders care about real money M/P, and are interested in the purchasing power of a given quantity of nominal money. Thus, we mean the real demand for money when we use the phrase "demand for money."

The starting point is to recognize that each household, firm, and governmental unit has a *portfolio problem*. At any given moment, it has a particular total wealth. In what form should it hold this wealth? It has many assets to choose from; one is the means of payment — money.

One component of money — currency and demand deposits — pays no interest. Even the component of money — other checkable deposits — that pays interest is likely to pay a lower rate than can be earned on alternate assets. Why? If the interest rate on bonds were no greater than the interest rate on money, few wealth-holders would demand bonds because money can finance transactions while bonds generally cannot. Hence, the price of bonds would decline — that is, the interest rate on bonds would rise above the rate paid on money. The final asset market equilibrium would therefore entail a higher interest rate on bonds than on money. Suppose the stock of money is reduced while the stock of bonds remains fixed. Then to induce people to want to shift their portfolios away from money toward bonds, the interest rate differential must widen.

In our introduction to Chapter 2, we assumed initially that money paid no interest and spoke of the interest rate on bonds. But we can generalize by recognizing that it is the interest rate differential between bonds and money that matters for portfolio allocation. Although it will be convenient to continue to focus on the interest rate on bonds, it is really the interest rate differential that is the key variable for money demand.

MONEY DEMAND MOTIVES AND THE IMPACT OF THE INTEREST RATE

Three motives for demanding money have traditionally been given: the transactions motive, the precautionary motive, and the speculative motive. The *transactions motive* is the desire to hold money to make payments. Consider two extremes: most wealth can be held in the form of money at all times so that it is available whenever a transaction occurs. Alternatively, holding money can be avoided, except just before a transaction. This requires conversion of other assets to money just before each transaction.

Clearly, two things must be balanced: the greater the interest rate differential of bonds over money, the smaller the amount of money that should be held; but the greater the cost of converting from other assets to money before each transaction, the larger the amount of money that should be held. In this formulation of the problem, money acts as an inventory. How much of this inventory is it optimal to keep on hand? William Baumol and James Tobin analyzed this problem carefully, and showed precisely how money demand rises as the conversion cost rises and as the interest rate differential falls.* One important example of the impact of the cost of conversion is the innovation in the 1970s that allowed transfers by telephone instruction between savings and checking accounts. A trip to the bank was no longer necessary. This reduction in conversion cost reduced the demand for M1.

Next, we consider the *precautionary motive*. Here, uncertainty plays the key role. Households and firms are not sure how much they will want to transact. If desired transactions rise unexpectedly, they may be caught illiquid. To finance the transactions, they may be compelled to sell illiquid assets at a price well below value. Hence, to avoid this cost, extra money is held. This, too, must be balanced against the lost interest.

Finally, we turn to the *speculative motive*. Suppose the wealth-holder has a choice between two assets: money and a risky bond. The bond is risky because its return is variable, although on average it will be positive and greater than the certain return on money. James Tobin argued that a risk averse investor prefers to hold some money, even though its return on average is lower, because it is safer.† As in the inventory analysis of transactions demand, under the speculative motive, the greater is the interest rate differential of bonds over money, the lower is the demand for money. According to all three motives, then, a greater interest rate differential reduces the demand for money.

THE ROLES OF WEALTH AND INCOME

Thus far we have focused on the role of the interest rate differential in determining money demand. Now let us turn to the role of wealth, and of income. We have explained that money demand should be approached as a portfolio problem of allocating wealth among alternative

---

* See William Baumol, "The Transactions Demand for Cash: An Inventory Theoretic Approach," *Quarterly Journal of Economics* (November 1952); and James Tobin, "The Interest Elasticity of Transactions Demand for Cash," *Review of Economics and Statistics* (August 1956).
† See James Tobin, "Liquidity Preference as Behavior Toward Risk," *Review of Economic Studies* (February 1958).

assets. When wealth increases, the wealth-holder can afford more of all assets and will raise M^D/P, unless it is an "inferior asset"—as wealth goes up, the wealth-holder reduces demand for the asset. Wealth is a key determinant of any asset demand, including the demand for money.

The volume of transactions in the economy is not the same as national income, but exceeds it. Recall from national income accounting that GNP avoids double counting. Nevertheless, the volume of transactions is correlated with income. Income is a proxy for transactions. Hence, we expect the demand for money to vary directly with income. The real money demand, then, is a function of real income Q, the interest rate r, and real wealth W/P (recall that real wealth is nominal wealth divided by the price level).

We should also recognize two other influences on real money demand. First, the psychological attitude and expectations of wealth-holders can affect asset demand—and in particular, money demand. Second, as we noted earlier, innovations such as telephone transfers and money-market checking accounts can alter real money demand. Since these factors are independent of Q, r, and W/P, we will indicate their influence by an autonomous component of real money demand, M_a/P.

(13.1) $$\frac{M^D}{P} = f\left(Q, r, \frac{W}{P}, \frac{M_a}{P}\right)$$

In Chapter 2, we ignored real wealth in order to simplify and concentrate on real income and the interest rate:

(2.6) $$\frac{M^D}{P} = \frac{M_a}{P} + kQ - hr$$

where $k > 0$ and $h > 0$.

We arbitrarily assigned numerical values to k (0.5), h (7,500), and M_a/P (0). To determine the actual responsiveness of real money demand M^D/P to real income Q, the interest rate r, and real wealth W/P, economists perform statistical (econometric) analysis of data generated by the actual economy. We explained econometric technique in Chapter 6, where we analyzed the response of inflation to a rise in the unemployment rate.

Empirical results generally support the hypothesis that real money demand responds to the interest rate, real income, and real wealth.* Let

---

* For example, see a review of the literature by John Judd and John Scadding, "The Search for a Stable Money Demand Function," *Journal of Economic Literature* (September 1982); and Stephen Goldfield, "The Demand for Money Revisited," *Brookings Papers on Economic Activity* 1973: 3.

us note an implication of this hypothesis for the velocity of money. The velocity of money V is defined as the ratio of nominal GNP PQ to the money stock M:

$$(13.2) \qquad V \equiv \frac{PQ}{M} \equiv \frac{Q}{M/P}$$

When the money market is in equilibrium, real money demand M^D/P equals the real money supply M/P. Hence, if the money market is in equilibrium, from equation (13.2) we have

$$(13.3) \qquad V = \frac{Q}{M^D/P}$$

Our hypothesis states that, with real income Q held constant, an increase in the interest rate r reduces real money demand M^D/P. It follows that if the interest rate rises, then the denominator in equation (13.3) falls and the right side rises. Hence

▶ The velocity of money varies directly with the interest rate.

According to Fisher's hypothesis, a rise in the inflation rate eventually raises the nominal interest rate. Since we have just seen that an increase in the nominal interest rate increases the velocity of money, we can draw the following conclusion:

▶ In the long run, the velocity of money varies directly with the inflation rate.

13.3 The Money-Supply Process

In Chapter 2, we stated that there is a money supply and that it is, in principle, determined by the Federal Reserve. In this section, we will examine more carefully how the money supply is determined. As we said in Section 13.1, the money supply M that is owned by the public consists of currency C plus checkable deposits D:

$$(13.4) \qquad M = C + D$$

How is M determined? In a modern economy, the public, the banks, and the central bank interact to determine the money supply. We will begin, however, with a hypothetical economy without a bank, and explain why a bank is created, and how it affects the money supply. We will then extend our discussion to the creation of many banks. In Section 13.4, we will explain why a central bank is created, and how it influences the money supply.

Imagine a simple economy without banks. There are no checkable deposits; money consists solely of currency. Suppose the currency consists of identical gold coins, which are the only generally accepted means of payment. Why might a bank be created? First, there is the matter of theft. A bank promises safekeeping. Second, there is the matter of convenience. A bank offers check-writing privileges.

How do checks work? If there is a single bank, persons A and B both have an account at that bank. A writes a check to B for 100 coins which B deposits at the bank. The bank subtracts 100 from A's account and adds 100 to B's account. Coins do not move from the bank's vault, and the horse-drawn coin carriages sadly make their way to the museum.

So it comes to pass that a single bank is created. The bank charges a fee for the safekeeping of coins and check-writing privileges; initially, this is its sole means of earning income. Suppose that, before the bank opens, the public holds 1,300 gold coins; hence the money supply is 1,300. When the bank opens, the public decides to deposit 1,000 in coins and retain 300 as currency. The bank's balance sheet initially reads

Assets		Liabilities	
Gold Coins	1,000	Deposits	1,000

The banker soon recognizes that there is no need to keep an amount of gold coins equal to deposit liabilities. Experience shows that the bank can get by if gold coins are only 20% of deposits. Although the bank is committed to provide coins to any depositor at any time, depositors, in fact, only withdraw modest amounts from time to time. True, they often write checks. But since there is only one bank, when A writes a check to B there is no withdrawal of coins.

The banker concludes that the bank should make loans, giving borrowers deposits, even though the bank does not have coins to match the new deposits. The bank will earn interest on the loans and greatly enhance its income. The loans can take the form of specific arrangements with specific borrowers, or the purchase of bonds issued by firms or by the government.

The question arises as to how much it is safe to lend. The bank must retain gold coins equal to 20% of total deposits—that is, maintain a reserve ratio of 20%. The *reserve ratio* is the ratio of bank reserves (gold coins) to bank deposits. First, we will present the banker's solution; then we will show how it is obtained.

In the economy, there are 1,300 gold coins. By depositing 1,000, and keeping 300 as currency, the public shows that it likes to hold 30% as much currency as checkable deposits — that is, its *currency ratio* is 30%. With the reserve ratio at 20%, and the currency ratio at 30%, the bank should create 2,080 in loans and new deposits. With more deposits, the public will want to hold more currency (to satisfy its currency ratio of 30%), so the public will end up withdrawing 480 of the 1,000 coins, leaving the bank with 520 in coins. The bank's balance sheet will end up as follows:

Assets		Liabilities	
Reserves (coins)	520	Deposits	2,600
Loans	2,080		

Note that the reserve ratio is 20% (520 of reserves for 2,600 of deposits). Also, the public holds currency of 780 (the original 1,300 minus the 520 now in the bank), which is 30% of the 2,600 of deposits, so that the public's currency ratio is satisfied.

Let's see how the banker arrived at this solution. If D represents deposits and R represents bank reserves, then, since experience indicates that bank safety requires that reserves equal 20% of deposits, we have

(13.5) $\qquad R = 0.2D$

The public wants currency to be 30% of deposits, so that

(13.6) $\qquad C = 0.3D$

where C = currency

Total gold coins in the economy (1,300) must equal the sum of currency C held by the public plus reserves R held by the bank:

(13.7) $\qquad C + R = 1,300$

Substituting equation (13.5) and equation (13.6) into equation (13.7) yields

$$C + R = 1,300$$
$$0.3D + 0.2D = 1,300$$
$$0.5D = 1,300$$
$$D = 2,600$$

From equation (13.5)

$$R = 0.2(2,600) = 520$$

and from equation (13.6)

$$C = 0.3(2,600) = 780$$

Loans L must equal the difference between total deposits and reserves:

(13.8) $\qquad L = D - R = 2,600 - 520 = 2,080$

In addition, we know from equation (13.4) that the money supply is

(13.4) $\qquad M = C + D = 780 + 2,600 = 3,380$

The decision of the bank to make loans raises the money supply from the original 1,300 to 3,380.

But suppose the safe reserve ratio changes, or the currency ratio of the public changes, or the total number of gold coins changes. How will the banker know the right amount of loans to make?

The steps are the same. If e is the reserve ratio, c is the currency ratio, and H is the total gold coins in the economy, then for equation (13.5) and equation (13.6) we now have:

(13.5) $\qquad R = eD$
(13.6) $\qquad C = cD$

We will call the total gold coins in the economy the *high-powered money* and designate it H. Another name for H is "the monetary base." *The monetary base H* is the sum of currency C held by the nonbank public and reserves R held by the bank. Equation (13.7) then becomes:

(13.7) $\qquad C + R = H$

Substituting equation (13.5) and equation (13.6) into equation (13.7) gives us

$$eD + cD = H$$
$$(e + c)D = H$$
(13.9)
$$D = \frac{H}{e + c}$$

In our example, we see that

$$D = \frac{1{,}300}{0.2 + 0.3} = 2{,}600$$

Substituting equation (13.9) into equation (13.5) yields

(13.10)
$$R = e\,\frac{H}{e + c}$$

Substituting equation (13.9) into equation (13.6) yields

(13.11)
$$C = c\,\frac{H}{e + c}$$

Finally, substituting equation (13.9) and equation (13.11) into equation (13.4) gives the money supply M:

(13.4)
$$M = C + D$$
$$M = c\,\frac{H}{e + c} + \frac{H}{e + c}$$
(13.12)
$$M = \frac{1 + c}{e + c}\,H$$

Equation (13.12) gives the formula for the money supply in terms of high-powered money (the monetary base) H, the reserve ratio e, and the currency ratio c.

THE MONEY MULTIPLIER

The ratio of the money supply M to high-powered money H deserves a name. We call it the *money multiplier* μ:

(13.13)
$$\mu = \frac{M}{H}$$

where $\mu =$ the money multiplier

If we divide both sides of equation (13.12) by H, we have

$$(13.14) \qquad \frac{M}{H} = \mu = \frac{1+c}{e+c}$$

The last term in equation (13.14) must be greater than 1, because the reserve ratio e is a fraction less than 1. Hence, the money multiplier μ must exceed 1. In our example, we see that

$$\mu = \frac{1+0.3}{0.2+0.3} = 2.6$$

This means that an increase in gold coins results in an increase in the money supply that is 2.6 times as great. Since H is 1,300, and with μ equal to 2.6, M is 3,380. If 100 more gold coins enter the economy for use as money, then the money supply rises by 260.

From equation (13.12), it is clear that if the reserve ratio e decreases, the money supply M will increase (because e is in the denominator). For example, if bank safety requires a reserve ratio of only 10%, then with H equal to 1,300, the money supply is

$$M = \left(\frac{1+0.3}{0.1+0.3} \right) (1,300) = (3.25)(1,300) = 4,225$$

Finally, suppose the currency ratio c preferred by the public decreases. It may not be immediately obvious what happens to the money multiplier because both the numerator and denominator decrease. But it turns out that because e is less than 1, a fall in c increases μ. For example, if the currency ratio fell to 20%, then we see that

$$\mu = \frac{1+0.2}{0.2+0.2} = 3.0$$
$$M = (3.0)(1,300) = 3,900$$

Although pleased with the solution, the banker remains troubled by one question. Suppose the depositors find out that there are gold coins —reserves—equal to only 20% of the deposits. What if they get nervous and come in asking for gold coins? The bank, nevertheless, begins to make loans. We will return to the consequences shortly.

We must now ask: What happens if there are many banks instead of just a single bank? It turns out that the results for the whole economy, and the whole banking system, are the same. If H is high-powered money (gold coins), e is the reserve ratio all banks use for safety, and c is the public's currency ratio, then with many banks the formulas derived above are still valid. Why? Because if we view all banks together in the aggregate, all of the relationships above hold. If each bank requires the reserve ratio e for safety, then for the whole economy the ratio of total bank reserves to total deposits must be e. Similarly, the currency ratio applies to the whole economy. Thus, the relationships we derived above hold in an economy with many banks.

13.4 The Fed and the Money Supply

Now we must recognize the banker's fears. In normal times, when optimism prevails, depositors are unconcerned about this detail of banking — that each bank holds reserves (gold coins) equal to only 20% of its deposits. When a depositor occasionally needs to withdraw coins, the bank meets its obligation. But unfortunately, times are not always normal. Business does, now and then, turn down and pessimism spreads. Some businesses default on their loans and the banks holding these loans begin to face problems. Rumors begin to spread: is it true that bank X may be unable to provide gold coins to meet its depositors' needs? Suddenly, the secret of modern banking is out and on every depositor's mind. Each resolves to withdraw his coins tomorrow. But when he goes to the bank the next day, the line of depositors is long. A "run on the bank" has begun.

If only one bank is in trouble, it can borrow gold coins from other banks, pay every depositor that requests coins, and by doing so, calm its other depositors. Soon the run is over. But when pessimism is wide-spread, many banks experience a run simultaneously. Then where can the bank get gold coins? Once a few banks fail, and the public sees that depositors have lost everything, the panic spreads. Bank panics have been a periodic feature of economic history. It is easy to understand why. In normal times, banks that maintain high reserve ratios and limit loans sacrifice profit. Few can resist the temptation of risking a low reserve ratio in order to raise earnings on loans. But when times go bad, only a very high reserve ratio can save a bank once panic spreads. Thus, the financial system is unstable.

How can it be made more stable? We can consider two techniques. First, if there were a central bank acting as a lender of last resort, so that any embattled bank could quickly borrow the gold coins needed to calm depositors, then perhaps a run could be defeated. Second, if depositors were insured so that, even if their bank fails, they would be reimbursed by an insurer, then a run might never gain momentum in the first place.

Which technique is likely to be more effective? In the aftermath of the panic of 1907, Congress began work on the first technique, culminating in the creation of the Federal Reserve System (the Fed) in 1913. Its central purpose was to act as a lender of last resort in order to combat panics. It is inconvenient for the prestige of the Fed that the next 20 years witnessed the worst bank panics in U.S. history, culminating in the "bank holiday" of March 1933 when all banks were temporarily closed and only safe ones were permitted to reopen. Only then was the second technique tried. In 1934, the Federal Deposit Insurance Corporation (FDIC) was created, guaranteeing to reimburse depositors in the event that their bank failed. It is surely more than coincidental that the United States has not experienced a serious bank panic since the creation of the FDIC.

HOW THE FED CONTROLS THE MONEY SUPPLY

Although the Fed needs the FDIC to stabilize the banking system, it assumes sole responsibility for controlling the money supply. How does it perform this task? In a gold coin economy in which there are banks, but no central bank, the money supply depends on gold discoveries. A new influx of gold raises high-powered money H, and therefore raises the money supply M. We saw in Chapter 4 that money-supply growth m is an important determinant of the nominal demand growth rate y. We learned that to keep the inflation rate at 0, the nominal demand growth rate y should equal the normal growth rate of real output q_c, which equals the sum of normal labor-force growth f and normal productivity growth a. For example, if $f = 1\%$ and $a = 2\%$, then the nominal demand growth rate y must be 3% to keep prices stable.

In a gold coin economy where there is no central bank, no authority is controlling money growth, and hence no authority is controlling nominal demand growth. Suppose gold discoveries become more rapid such that the money supply increases significantly faster than the normal growth rate of real output q_c. Inflation then occurs. Or suppose the gold discoveries stop. Then the economy is thrown into a transitional recession; eventually, the recession ends and the wage and price level is forced down to a lower level. Inflation and recession are thus at the mercy of gold discoveries. Needless to say, such a situation is highly unsatisfactory. A major purpose of the central bank is to get control of the money supply. How does the central bank do this?

Let's see how the Federal Reserve can, in principle, control the U.S. money supply owned by the public. In our gold coin economy, a bank's reserves consist of the currency—gold coins. But clearly, it is not essential for the gold coins to be in the bank's own vault. The bank might instead hold deposits at the central bank, convertible to gold coins whenever the bank requests. In the United States, the currency consists of coins and paper, so a bank's reserves consist of such currency, plus deposits at the Fed convertible into currency.

Thus, in the gold coin economy, high-powered money H consists of currency held by the public, plus bank reserves, (the gold coins in the bank's vault). Under the Federal Reserve System, high-powered money H again consists of currency held by the public, plus bank reserves; but now bank reserves consist of currency in the bank's vault plus deposits at the Fed.

In the gold coin economy, high-powered money enters the economy through gold discoveries. The key to the Fed's control of the money supply is its control over high-powered money. How does the Fed control H?

First, gold or silver discoveries are not permitted to influence the currency. Only the Fed (and, to a limited extent, the Treasury) can issue *currency*—minted coins or printed notes. Neither commercial banks nor private firms are permitted to do so. Although this prevents discoveries of gold or silver from influencing H, how does the Fed exercise its influence? The most important method is *open-market operations*.

Open-Market Operations

The Fed buys or sells government securities, or bonds, in the open market. How does this work and how does it influence H? Each month the Federal Open Market Committee (FOMC) meets in Washington. The FOMC meeting goes largely unnoticed by a general public unaware of its existence or its importance. Yet the fate of the economy is greatly influenced by the decisions made at FOMC meetings.

The FOMC consists of the seven governors of the Federal Reserve, including the Chairman of the Fed, and the presidents of the twelve regional Federal Reserve Banks. Only five of these presidents vote (these five are selected on a rotating basis, except for the New York Fed president who always votes) so that there are twelve voting members at any FOMC meeting. The FOMC is advised by a large staff of professional economists. The FOMC arrives at a decision and sends a directive to the open-market manager of the system, located at the New York Fed. In response to the directive, the manager executes an order to buy or sell a certain dollar amount of government securities, paying with a check written on the Fed.

Suppose that this decision is a bond purchase of $1 million. The sellers deposit Fed checks for most of the $1 million in their banks and keep the rest as currency. Assume $950,000 is deposited and $50,000 is held as currency. Then the banks are credited with $950,000 in deposits at the Fed. Thus, high-powered money H—the currency held by the public plus bank reserves—has increased by $1 million as a result of the Fed's $1 million bond purchase. If the banks want to convert part of the $950,000 to vault cash—say, $100,000—then the Fed stands ready to convert $100,000 of deposits to currency—printed notes or minted coins. But where does the Fed get this currency? It simply has it printed, or minted. The Fed is legally empowered to issue new currency.

Clearly, then, the Fed can raise high-powered money H simply by raising its open-market purchases. Symmetrically, the Fed can reduce

H by selling bonds. If the bond sale is $1 million, then the buyers write checks on their banks that total $1 million. The Fed receives these checks and cancels bank deposits at the Fed totaling $1 million. Bank reserves, and hence high-powered money H, are cut by $1 million.

▶ Open-market operations is the most important tool by which the Fed controls the money supply.

The Discount Rate and Availability of Reserves

The second method used by the Fed to influence the money supply is to set the discount rate and the availability of reserves to member banks. The *discount rate* is the interest rate the Fed charges member banks when they borrow reserves. Member banks may be permitted to borrow reserves at the discount rate, at the discretion of the Fed. When a bank borrows reserves of $100,000, high-powered money H increases by $100,000.

If the Fed sets a low discount rate and lets banks borrow as much as they want, then banks tend to increase their borrowing from the Fed. Hence, high-powered money H rises more than if the Fed sets a high discount rate and limits the amount banks are permitted to borrow.

The discount rate (and reserve availability) is not as precise a tool for controlling high-powered money H as open-market operations. The Fed can only estimate how much banks will want to borrow under the conditions it sets. In contrast, under open-market operations, the Fed can directly control the change in H. This is one important reason why the Fed generally relies on open-market operations.

Reserve Requirements

In our formula for the money supply, there are three key variables: high-powered money H, the reserve ratio e, and the currency ratio c. The first two tools of the Fed, open-market operations and the discount rate, focus on H. The public determines c. While the banks in our gold coin economy were free to determine the reserve ratio e, the Fed prescribes a minimum e^* for banks. One reason for this is to prevent banks from being tempted to risk a low reserve ratio e that may prove unsafe when times turn bad. We can now see that the Fed's *reserve requirement* gives it a third tool with which to alter the money supply.

Suppose that the Fed reduces the minimum reserve ratio e^*. Banks are free to increase loans and reduce their e. This raises the money supply. If banks always kept their reserve ratio e at the exact minimum requirement of the Fed, e^*, it would help the Fed in its task of controlling the money supply.

However, banks are free to keep their e above the legal minimum e^*; that is, they are free to hold excess reserves. Banks face a trade-off. If they hold exactly the minimum e^*, then an unexpected currency withdrawal by depositors forces the bank to immediately sell nonreserve assets, such as bonds, to obtain reserves to maintain e^*. Excess reserves prevent this forced bond sale. On the other hand, the bank earns no interest on excess reserves.

The higher the interest rate, the smaller the excess reserves the bank prefers. Hence, the reserve ratio e that the banks choose must be at least as great as the legal minimum. But e also varies inversely with the interest rate. Recall that e influences the money supply M in equation (13.12):

(13.12)
$$M = \frac{1+c}{e+c} H$$

Since e is influenced by the interest rate r, it follows that, for a given H and c, the money supply M is affected by the interest rate. Hence, not only does money demand M^D depend on the interest rate, so does the money supply. When the interest rate rises, banks reduce their reserve ratio e toward the legal minimum; this raises the money supply. Thus, when the interest rate rises, money demand falls and money supply increases.

For a given H and c, suppose that the money market is initially in equilibrium, with money demand equal to money supply. Then suppose real output Q increases. This raises real money demand such that real money demand exceeds real money supply. This begins to bid up the interest rate r. In our discussion of the LM curve, we assumed that the real money supply stays constant as the interest rate r rises. Thus, r rises until real money demand is reduced to the constant money supply.

But now, as the interest rate r rises, for a constant H and c, banks choose to lower the reserve ratio e, thereby raising loans and the money supply, as predicted by equation (13.12). The real money supply moves up as real money demand declines. Real money demand and real money supply become equal after a smaller rise in the interest rate. This implies that the LM curve still has a positive slope, but is flatter than would be the case if the money supply were independent of the interest rate r. Why?

We have just seen that for a given increase in Q, the interest rate r must rise less before money demand equals money supply. This is because money demand does not have to decline all the way back to a constant money supply. So when we plot the LM curve, a given increase in Q requires a smaller increase in r to restore money-market equilibrium. Our basic lessons from the $IS-LM$ analysis continue to hold. But we must now recognize that, for a given H and c, the money supply is endogenous — when real output Q increases, the rise in the interest rate r in itself raises the money supply by reducing the reserve ratio e banks choose.

This does not mean, however, that the Fed cannot control the money supply. It only means that the Fed's job is somewhat more difficult. If the Fed is choosing high-powered money H and the minimum reserve ratio e^* in an attempt to achieve a particular money supply M, it must take into account the fact that banks will adjust their reserve ratio e according to the interest rate. For example, suppose the Fed wants to raise M to a particular level by changing H. Equation (13.12) gives the required H if the correct values of e and c are used. The Fed must be sure to use the reserve ratio e that banks choose at the interest rate r that results, and not assume that e will stay constant as r changes.

Finally, it is important to recognize that fear of a bank "run" causes a bank to raise its reserve ratio e above the legal requirement e^*. With Federal Deposit Insurance and an economy that has avoided a depression for over 40 years, the threat of such a run is generally remote. If insurance were weakened or if a depression should develop, however, many banks might then raise e as a defense against a run. This would, in itself, tend to reduce the money supply and intensify the depression. The Fed could offset such a rise in e, however, by raising H through open-market operations, and thereby prevent the money supply from contracting.

13.5 The Fed and the Treasury

The Treasury receives tax payments T from the public, writes checks to finance government expenditures (transfers R and government purchases of goods and services G), issues securities (bonds) whenever it is necessary to finance a deficit (whenever $R + G$ exceeds T), and conducts *debt management operations* — that is, decides the mix of long-term and short-term bonds it will issue. The Fed is the central bank, and as we have just explained, conducts open-market operations in which it buys or sells Treasury bonds, paying with (or withdrawing) high-powered money, thereby influencing the money supply.

It is very important to recognize that the U.S. Treasury and the Fed are two separate institutions. Fiscal policy and monetary policy are made by different decision makers. The Treasury's activities — taxing, spending, borrowing, and debt management — are determined by Congress and/or the President. Authorization and appropriations bills, enacted by Congress and signed by the President, determine tax payments T, government purchases G, and government transfers R, and hence the size of the deficit.

The Fed's open-market operations are determined by the twelve voting members of the Federal Open Market Committee (FOMC) of the

Federal Reserve System. Each governor of the Federal Reserve is appointed by the President and confirmed by the Senate to serve a 14-year term and can serve only one term; terms are arranged so that they expire every two years. The regional bank presidents are selected by their banks' directors; neither Congress nor the President play a role in their selection.

Thus, a new President, on taking office, initially has no influence on the membership of the FOMC. If he serves two terms, only by the end of his second term will he have appointed four of the seven governors, which is still only four out of twelve FOMC members. The President does, however, choose the Chairman (and Vice Chairman) of the Federal Reserve Board (who is also Chairman of the FOMC) from among the seven governors. The Chairman serves a four-year term and can be reappointed. The term begins roughly mid-way through the President's term.

The Fed is institutionally separated from Congress, from the President, and from the Treasury (a department in the executive branch under the control of the President). This institutional separation must always be kept in mind.

Let's consider the impact of the institutional separation on the consequence of government budget deficits. If the Treasury runs a deficit, it must issue bonds. It is sometimes thought that whenever the government runs a deficit, it prints new money to finance it, and the increase in money growth leads to inflation. By this reasoning, deficits must be inflationary.

In many countries, and in many historical periods, such a description has been accurate. But the institutional separation that exists in the United States means that this is not necessarily so. The Treasury must issue bonds (borrow) to finance a deficit. But this, in itself, does not lead to an increase in the money supply. The fate of the money supply is determined by the reaction of the FOMC.

Suppose that when the Treasury issues $10 billion of new bonds to finance a $10 billion deficit, the FOMC raises its bond purchase by $10 billion. In effect, the new bonds are bought by the Fed, which pays with high-powered money. The money supply will increase by more than $10 billion as a result of the money multiplier. In this case, although bond certificates are sent from the Treasury to the Fed, it is useful to treat this as internal bookkeeping of the government. In effect, the government—Treasury plus the Fed—has financed its deficit by injecting money into the economy. This case illustrates the claim that the government finances its deficits by printing money. Such financing raises the nominal demand growth rate y and, if continued, is inflationary.

But the FOMC may act differently. Faced with the issue of $10 billion of new bonds by the Treasury, the FOMC may refuse to increase its purchase of bonds; it may refuse to inject more money into the economy. The Treasury therefore finds that it must lower bond prices (equivalently, raise the interest rate on its bonds) to induce the public to buy them. The bonds are sold, and the Treasury finances its deficit. The money supply, however, does not increase.

Even if there were no institutional separation, a deficit need not mean an increase in the money supply. The government might choose to borrow from the public rather than print money. But without institutional separation, it is more likely that money creation accompanies deficits. Interest rates rise immediately as the government tries to sell its bonds to the public, and this is invariably unpopular.

But with institutional separation, the FOMC may refuse to create money in response to deficits created by Congress and the President. It is possible, therefore, for money growth to slow even while deficits widen. This, in fact, occurred in the early 1980s.

Is it desirable to have this institutional separation? What is the best institutional structure for monetary and fiscal policy? These important questions are discussed in Chapter 9.

13.6 Deregulation of the Banking System

In 1980, Congress passed a banking reform act that called for the gradual phasing out of bank interest-rate ceilings (except on demand deposits) by 1985. The end of interest-rate ceilings means that, for the first time since the Great Depression of the 1930s, banks are free to pay any interest rate they choose on checking and savings accounts (other than demand deposits). It is important to look back, briefly, at the impact of interest-rate ceilings and to look forward to the impact of their repeal.

In the past, whenever market-determined interest rates rose significantly above the regulated ceiling, savers shifted funds out of banks and into unregulated bonds to take advantage of the higher yields. Thus, during a period of tight money policy and high interest rates, the financial intermediaries (banks and savings and loan institutions) suffered sharp fund withdrawals. Savers, in effect, were lending directly to corporations and government, buying their unregulated bonds, instead of lending indirectly through banks. The process was called *disintermediation*. Borrowers especially dependent on these financial institutions experienced reduced access to credit and experienced high interest rates as well. Housing, in particular, was hit hard. The severe impact on housing and financial institutions made it difficult for the Fed to sustain a tight money policy for a long period.

In Chapter 5, we explained that in the mid-1960s fiscal and monetary expansion generated a rise in the inflation rate. The fiscal expansion, which shifted the *IS* curve to the right, could have been countered by a monetary contraction, which would have shifted the *LM* curve to the left, and thereby held output Q at Q_c. But the result would have been a sharp rise in interest rates. This in turn would have caused disintermediation and severe trouble for housing and financial institutions. It can be argued that one reason the Fed did not stick to a tight money policy in the second half of the 1960s—a policy that might have curbed the rise in inflation—was the disintermediation problem. Thus, the termination of interest-rate ceilings has an important implication:

▶ If a tight monetary policy is needed to achieve disinflation or to prevent inflation, then the policy can now be pursued without causing a disintermediation problem.

SUMMARY

1. *Money* is a means of payment. It is also a store of value, a unit of account, and a standard of deferred payment (in which long-term transactions can be defined).

2. By the *M1 definition of money,* money consists of *currency* and *checkable deposits.* Broader definitions such as the *M2 definition of money* and the *M3 definition of money* include other liquid assets. There is no strong consensus as to which definition is most useful for explaining variations in output and inflation.

3. The demand for money results from the attempt of each wealth-holder to solve a *portfolio problem.* The wealth-holder must choose between money and other assets.

4. Three motives for holding money are usually given: the *transactions motive,* the *precautionary motive,* and the *speculative motive.* From these motives, it follows that money demand rises when income and wealth rise, and when the interest rate on bonds falls. Psychology and expectations also affect the demand for money. Empirical studies generally confirm these relationships.

5. The velocity of money V varies directly with the nominal interest rate r. Because r rises with the inflation rate p, according to Fisher's hypothesis, the velocity of money varies directly with the inflation rate.

6. The money supply M increases when *high-powered money* (the *monetary base*) H increases, when the *reserve ratio e* decreases, and when the *currency ratio c* decreases.

7. The Federal Deposit Insurance Corporation (FDIC) established in 1934 may be more important in preventing bank failures than the Federal Reserve System established in 1913, but the Fed is a useful complement to the FDIC for avoiding financial panics.

8. *Open-market operations*—the buying and selling of government bonds by the Fed—is the most important instrument of monetary

policy. The Federal Open Market Committee (FOMC) meets monthly to adjust monetary policy.

9. The Treasury and the Fed are two separate institutions. If the Treasury runs a deficit, it must issue bonds. It is up to the Fed to decide whether to buy the bonds and thereby finance the deficit with an increase in the money supply. The Fed can refuse to increase the money supply when the Treasury runs a deficit.

10. Recent interest-rate deregulation has enabled the Fed to conduct a tight monetary policy without causing a disintermediation problem.

TERMS AND CONCEPTS

currency
currency ratio (c)
debt management operations
discount rate
disintermediation
Federal Deposit Insurance
    Corporation (FDIC)
Federal Open Market
    Committee (FOMC)
high-powered money (H)
liquidity
loans
M1 definition of money
M2 definition of money

M3 definition of money
monetary base
money
money multiplier (μ)
open-market operations
portfolio problem
precautionary motive
reserve ratio (e)
reserve requirements
bank "run"
speculative motive
thrift institutions
transactions motive
velocity of money (V)

QUESTIONS

Imagine a simple economy that is initially without banks or a central bank. The public holds 2,600 of currency. Then a bank is created. The public decides to deposit 2,000 in coins and retain 600 in currency (a currency ratio of 30%).

13.1 Initially, what is the bank's balance sheet?

13.2 Suppose that safety calls for a reserve ratio of 20%. After loans are made, what is/are (a) the bank's balance sheet; (b) deposits; (c) bank reserves; (d) currency held by the public; (e) loans; (f) the money supply?

13.3 Derive the formula for the money supply M in terms of high-powered money (the monetary base) H, the currency ratio c, and the reserve ratio e. What is the money multiplier?

13.4 Use the formula you derived in Question 13.3 to explain why the money supply increases when the interest rate rises.

CHAPTER

14

Unemployment and Vacancies

Prerequisite: Chapters 4–7

In this chapter, we will develop a model of the labor market and use it to analyze the impact of policies. At the outset, we should emphasize that the modeling of the labor market is one of the more challenging and difficult tasks of macroeconomics. While progress has been made, there is no strong consensus among economists as to which labor-market model best captures the properties of the actual economy. This means that we must draw our policy conclusions tentatively.

We will set out one model of the labor market. It is intended for illustration. Most macroeconomists accept at least certain features of the model, although few are completely satisfied with it. Some reject it, strongly preferring an alternate model. Our purpose is to show how a model can be used to analyze the labor market and the impact of policies on the constant inflation rate of unemployment CIRU. Conclusions, however, should be regarded as tentative.

14.1 Employment, Unemployment, and Vacancies

Suppose 100 persons want to work (supply labor) and firms want to employ (demand) 98 persons. With *labor supply* L^S equal to 100 and *labor demand* L^D equal to 98, what is the unemployment rate?

It is natural to answer that 98 people are employed while 2 people are unemployed, so the unemployment rate is 2% (2/100). But this answer is incorrect. The unemployment rate is higher. To illustrate, the answer might be as follows:

Labor supply L^S = 100	Labor demand L^D = 98
Employment E = 93	Employment E = 93
Unemployment U = 7	Vacancies V = 5

In this case, the unemployment rate is 7% (7/100) and the vacancy rate is approximately 5% (5/98). But why don't 5 of the 7 people who are unemployed fill the 5 vacancies and thereby reduce the unemployment rate to 2% and the vacancy rate to 0%? There are several reasons. First, some of the unemployed may prefer to wait for a better job to open up. Second, some of the employers with vacancies may prefer to wait until more productive employees are available. Third, unemployed workers may have difficulty locating available vacancies while employers may have difficulty locating available workers. We have reached an important conclusion:

▶ Unemployment and vacancies exist simultaneously in the labor market. Employment is less than both labor demand and labor supply.

Equation (14.1) defines *unemployment;* equation (14.2) defines *vacancies:*

(14.1) $$U \equiv L^S - E$$

where U = unemployment
L^S = labor supply
E = employment

(14.2) $$V \equiv L^D - E$$

where V = vacancies
L^D = labor demand

If we subtract equation (14.2) from equation (14.1), we obtain

$$U - V \equiv L^S - E - (L^D - E)$$
$$U - V \equiv L^S - E - L^D + E$$
(14.3) $$U - V \equiv L^S - L^D$$

Using the values from our example and substituting them into equation (14.3) gives us

$$7 - 5 = 100 - 98$$

In equation (14.3), we call $L^S - L^D$ the *excess labor supply.* Equation (14.3) states that

▶ Excess supply in the labor market is equal to unemployment minus vacancies.

In our example, excess supply is 2. It is possible for excess supply to be negative. For example, if labor supply L^S is 98 and labor demand L^D is 100, then excess supply is -2. Equivalently, we can say that *excess demand* is 2.

If unemployment minus vacancies, $U - V$, increases, then we know that labor supply has increased relative to labor demand (equivalently, labor demand has decreased relative to labor supply). Thus, we can tell what is happening to excess supply by focusing on the term $U - V$.

ENTRANTS AND EXITS

Will the economy remain at the position just described? This position may generate wage and price changes that cause either labor demand L^D or labor supply L^S to change. But even before we consider wage and price changes, we must ask: if L^S stays at 100 and L^D stays at 98, will E remain at 93, U at 7, and V at 5?

If the economy is in this position, then we can assume that the 7 unemployed persons are searching for jobs, and the firms with the 5 vacancies are searching for workers. In a month's time, we expect a particular number of successful matches to occur. Given our 7 unemployed workers and our 5 vacancies, suppose that in one month 3 successful matches are likely to occur. In this one month period, 3 unemployed persons enter into employment. We say that *entrants n* is 3 per month.

But during the same month, we expect that some of the 93 employed persons exit from employment. Some voluntarily quit. Others are laid off. For example, suppose that with 93 employed persons, in one month 3 of these exit from employment. We say that *exits x* is 3 per month.

If entrants n equals exits x, then employment stays constant. Thus, in this example, since entrants and exits are both 3, employment stays constant. If entrants n exceeds exits x, then employment rises. If entrants n is less than exits x, then employment declines.

(14.4)   If $n = x$, then E stays constant.

If $n > x$, then E increases.

If $n < x$, then E decreases.

At any moment in time, if labor demand L^D and labor supply L^S remain constant, there is a particular value of employment E which tends to remain constant — that is, where n equals x. We call this value of E the *equilibrium level of employment E^**. If E stays constant at E^*, then U stays constant at the equilibrium level of unemployment U^*, and

V stays constant at the equilibrium level of vacancies V^*. In our example, where L^D is fixed at 98 and L^S is fixed at 100, if E stays constant at 93, then U stays constant at 7, and V stays constant at 5. Thus, $n = x$ is the condition for equilibrium employment, equilibrium unemployment, and equilibrium vacancies.

Note that we have not said anything about wage and price behavior. Even if E^* is 93 at this moment, this does not necessarily mean that wage and price inflation stay constant at this E^*. When we say "equilibrium," we mean only that E tends to remain constant as long as L^D and L^S stay constant, and not that wage and price inflation necessarily stay constant.

What determines the number of entrants n per month? In our example, there are 7 unemployed workers and 5 job vacancies. But suppose that there are 14 unemployed workers and still only 5 vacancies. We expect more contacts per month between unemployed workers and job vacancies because more workers are searching for jobs; with more contacts, the number of entrants is greater. Similarly, if there are 7 unemployed workers and 10 job vacancies, more contacts per month occur because firms have more vacancies. Hence, the number of entrants, again, is greater.

▶ The number of entrants into employment per month increases when unemployment increases and when vacancies increases, because when there are more unemployed workers and more job vacancies, there are more *contacts*. More contacts result in more entrants.

But the number of entrants n per month is also influenced by how workers and firms search. If workers are willing to accept any job and search with great intensity, then the number of entrants is higher than if workers are choosy about a job or do not search very actively. Similarly, if firms are willing to accept any worker and search with great intensity, then the number of entrants is higher than if firms are choosy about a worker or do not search very actively.

Finally, the number of entrants per month is affected by how well the skills of the unemployed match the skills required by the employer to fill their vacancies. Even if the unemployed and employers with vacancies locate each other, the probability of employment depends on a satisfactory matching.

It is useful to write an equation for entrants n that expresses these ideas. We need an equation where n increases when any of the following increase: unemployment U, vacancies V, intensity of search by workers i_w, intensity of search by firms i_f, and the degree of matching of worker skills and vacancy skill requirements m:

(14.5) $n = m(i_w U)(i_f V)$

where n = entrants

i_w = intensity of worker search

i_f = intensity of firm search

U = number of unemployed

V = number of vacancies

m = degree of matching of skills of the unemployed and skills required by the vacancies

For example, if $U = 7$, $V = 5$, $i_w = 3/7$, $i_f = 1/5$, and $m = 1$, then

$$n = 1\left[\left(\frac{3}{7}\right)(7)\right]\left[\left(\frac{1}{5}\right)(5)\right] = 3 \text{ per month}$$

In equation (14.5), n increases if either m, i_w, U, i_f, or V increases. If either U or V doubles, then n doubles. Of course, this may not be empirically correct. But equation (14.5) is a simple functional form that enables us to illustrate the basic ideas.

Since $U \equiv L^S - E$ and $V \equiv L^D - E$, we can rewrite equation (14.5) to specify the n *curve:*

(14.6) $n = m[i_w(L^S - E)][i_f(L^D - E)]$

Equation (14.6) shows how the number of entrants n varies with employment E when given fixed values for m, i_w, i_f, L^S, and L^D. For example, suppose that labor supply L^S is fixed at 100 and labor demand L^D is fixed at 98. The parameter values are $m = 1$, $i_w = 3/7$, and $i_f = 1/5$. By substituting these values into equation (14.6), we arrive at an n curve equation with $L^D = 98$ and with $L^S = 100$:

$$n = 1\left[\left(\frac{3}{7}\right)(100 - E)\right]\left[\left(\frac{1}{5}\right)(98 - E)\right]$$

(14.7) $n = \left(\frac{3}{35}\right)(100 - E)(98 - E)$

The n curve shows how entrants per month n varies with employment E. We can plot several points on this curve. To do so, we take a particular value of E, insert it into equation (14.7), and calculate n:

E	n
91	5.40
93	3.00
95	1.29
98	0.00

Clearly, as E increases, n falls. Why? Because as employment E rises, with labor supply L^S fixed at 100, unemployment U (labor supply L^S minus employment E) declines; with labor demand L^D fixed at 98, vacancies V (labor demand L^D minus employment E) declines. As U and V fall, the number of successful matches falls, and hence the number of entrants into employment falls.

The n curve is plotted in Figure 14.1. Note that when E reaches 98, so that $V = 0$, there can be no successful contacts because there are no vacancies. The number of entrants $n = 0$. Hence, the n curve hits the E axis at $E = 98$. Suppose L^D increases from 98 to 102. Then the n curve

FIGURE 14.1 EQUILIBRIUM EMPLOYMENT

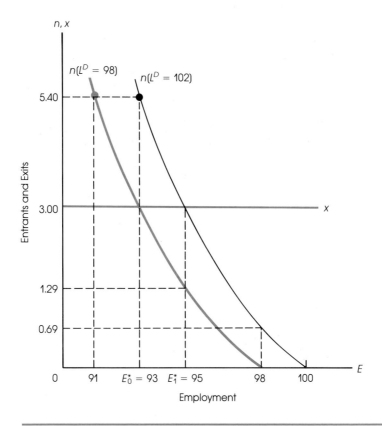

The intersection of the entrants n curve and the exits x line determines equilibrium employment E^*. Each n curve corresponds to a given labor demand L^D. For a particular L^D, as employment E increases, n declines. We assume that x is independent of E. When L^D increases, the n curve shifts to the right. In this example, when L^D increases from 98 to 102, equilibrium employment increases from $E_0^* = 93$ to $E_1^* = 95$.

equation becomes

$$(14.8) \qquad n = \left(\frac{3}{35}\right)(100 - E)(102 - E)$$

We can plot several points on this new n curve. It is convenient to compare the new values of n given by equation (14.8), where L^D is fixed at 102, with the old values of n given by equation (14.7), where L^D is fixed at 98:

E	$n(L^D = 98)$	$n(L^D = 102)$
91	5.40	8.49
93	3.00	5.40
95	1.29	3.00
98	0.00	0.69

At each employment E, the number of entrants n is now greater. With labor demand L^D greater (102 as opposed to 98), vacancies V is greater. With V greater, there are more contacts and thus n is greater. The new n curve from equation (14.8) is also shown in Figure 14.1. It lies above the old n curve.

▶ An increase in labor demand L^D shifts the n curve up.

What determines the number of exits x per month? Some analysts have made the simple assumption that the number of exits per month is a constant fraction of employment E. For example, if the constant fraction is $1/31$, and if E is 93, then the number of exits x is 3 per month.

If this simple hypothesis is correct, then an even simpler hypothesis is approximately correct: exits per month x is constant. Why? If the constant fraction is $1/31$, and if E increases to 96, then x increases to 3.10; if E decreases to 90, then exits x decreases to 2.90. In practice, if labor supply L^S is 100, employment E generally fluctuates in the 90–96 range; hence, x fluctuates in the 2.90–3.10 range.

It will greatly simplify the exposition of our model to assume that exits per month x is constant. We shall therefore make this assumption.

▶ The number of exits per month x from employment is constant.

In our example, we will assume that the number of exits x per month is constant at 3 per month. Figure 14.1 shows how x stays constant as E increases. The x line is horizontal; x is the same at all values of E.

Observe the intersection of the n curve with $L^D = 98$ and the x line with $x = 3$. The intersection gives the equilibrium employment E^*. If employment is at E^*, it stays constant because entrants n equals exits x.

But suppose that E initially differs from its equilibrium value E^*. Does E move to E^*? Is the equilibrium stable? The answer is yes. The stability of the equilibrium can be seen in Figure 14.1. If E is initially less than E^*, then from Figure 14.1 it is clear that n exceeds x; by relationship (14.4), E then increases toward E^*. Symmetrically, if E is initially greater than E^*, then from Figure 14.1 it is clear that n is less than x; by relationship (14.4), E then decreases toward E^*.

What is the numerical value of E^*? We must set x (where $x = 3$) equal to n, as given by the n curve equation (14.7) where L^D is fixed at 98:

$$\left(\frac{3}{35}\right)(100 - E)(98 - E) = 3$$

If we multiplied out the left side of this equation, one of the terms would contain E^2 (E squared); thus, our equation is a *quadratic equation*. In Appendix B, we solve for E in this example and find that $E = 93$. We can easily confirm that this satisfies the equation by inserting 93 in place of E:

$$\left(\frac{3}{35}\right)(100 - 93)(98 - 93) = 3$$

$$3 = 3$$

Thus, with L^S fixed at 100 and L^D fixed at 98, our equilibrium values are

Labor supply L^S	= 100	Labor demand L^D	= 98
Employment E	= 93	Employment E	= 93
Unemployment U =	7	Vacancies V	= 5

Note that these are the same values given at the beginning of this section. We now see that with L^S fixed at 100 and L^D fixed at 98, the values for E, U, and V are equilibrium values (given the numerical values of the parameters m, i_w, and i_f).

WHAT CAUSES EMPLOYMENT TO CHANGE?

Now suppose that L^D increases from 98 to 102. What happens? The n curve shifts up (as shown in Figure 14.1) and E moves to its new equilibrium E_1^* from E_0^*. How does employment move from E_0^* to E_1^*? When

L^D rises by 4, the immediate effect is to raise V ($L^D - E$) by 4 (from 5 to 9). With U still at 7, contacts increase. Entrants n rises above 3 per month; in fact, with V increasing by 80% (from 5 to 9) and U initially remaining unchanged, from equation (14.5) entrants n also rises by 80% (from 3 to 5.4). With n greater than x, E begins to rise.

But as E rises, n begins to decline. First, V declines below 9. Then U, which equals $L^S - E$, declines. As both V and U decline, contacts decline, and n declines below 5.4. Thus, when E rises, it reaches a value at which n again equals $x = 3$. This is the new equilibrium value of employment E_1^* that results when L^D is fixed at 102 and L^S is fixed at 100. What is the numerical value of E_1^*? We must set x (3) equal to n, as given by the n curve equation (14.8) where L^D is fixed at 102:

$$\left(\frac{3}{35}\right)(100 - E)(102 - E) = 3$$

In Appendix B, we solve for E in this example and determine that $E = 95$. We can confirm this by inserting 95 in place of E:

$$\left(\frac{3}{35}\right)(100 - 95)(102 - 95) = 3$$
$$3 = 3$$

Our new equilibrium values are then

Labor supply L^S	= 100	Labor demand L^D = 102	
Employment E	= 95	Employment E	= 95
Unemployment U =	5	Vacancies V	= 7

Let's compare these values to the values with $L^D = 98$:

Labor supply L^S	= 100	Labor demand L^D = 98	
Employment E	= 93	Employment E	= 93
Unemployment U =	7	Vacancies V	= 5

What can we conclude? An increase in labor demand L^D of 4 raises employment E by 2 (from 93 to 95). Hence, vacancies V increases by 2. With labor supply L^S fixed, the rise in employment E implies an equal decline in U. Note that the decline in U is less than the increase in L^D.

From this, we can draw the following conclusions:

▶ With labor supply L^S fixed, an increase in labor demand L^D raises equilibrium employment E^* and equilibrium vacancies V^*, and reduces equilibrium unemployment U^*.

Thus far, we have kept the parameters m, i_w, and i_f constant. Now let's consider how an increase in each parameter affects the equilibrium where L^S and L^D are fixed.

Recall the n curve equation (14.6):

(14.6) $$n = m[i_w(L^S - E)][i_f(L^D - E)]$$

We saw that with m, i_w, i_f, and L^S fixed, an increase in L^D raises n at each E. In other words, an increase in L^D shifts the n curve up. Similarly, an increase in m, i_w, or i_f also raises n at each E:

▶ An increase in any of the parameters m, i_w, or i_f shifts the n curve upward (to the right).

This makes sense. Recall that m is the degree of matching of the skills of the unemployed and the skills required by the vacancies. If m increases, then more contacts between unemployed persons and job vacancies result in employment. Hence, an increase in m raises entrants per month at any E.

Recall that i_w is the intensity of worker search and i_f is the intensity of firm search. If i_w or i_f increases, then more contacts occur between unemployed persons and firms with vacancies. Hence, an increase in i_w or i_f raises entrants per month at any E.

In Figure 14.1, if the n curve shifts upward, then equilibrium employment E^* increases from E_0^* to E_1^*. Although this upward shift is a result of an increase in L^D, an increase in E^* also occurs when the upward shift is due to an increase in m, i_w, or i_f.

In our earlier example, an increase in L^D from 98 to 102 raises equilibrium employment E^* from 93 to 95 and reduces equilibrium unemployment U^* from 7 to 5. Now suppose that L^D is once again fixed at 98. Let's find the increases in m, i_w, or i_f that achieves an E^* of 95 and a U^* of 5.

With L^S fixed at 100 and L^D fixed at 98, we can rewrite the n curve equation as

(14.9) $$n = m i_w i_f (100 - E)(98 - E)$$

In this equation, we have moved all three parameters together.

At the initial equilibrium of $E^* = 93$, we see that

$$3 = m i_w i_f (100 - 93)(98 - 93)$$
$$3 = m i_w i_f (35)$$
$$\frac{3}{35} = m i_w i_f$$

Recall that the initial parameter values are $m = 1$, $i_w = 3/7$, $i_f = 1/5$. Hence, mi_wi_f is initially the required 3/35.

If $E = 95$ is the new equilibrium, then

$$3 = mi_wi_f(100 - 95)(98 - 95)$$
$$3 = mi_wi_f(15)$$
$$\frac{1}{5} = mi_wi_f$$

Hence, to increase E^* from 93 to 95, mi_wi_f must increase from 3/35 to 1/5. When 3/35 is multiplied by 7/3, we obtain 1/5. Thus, if the initial value of any parameter is multiplied by 7/3 (slightly more than doubled), then E^* rises from 93 to 95 and U^* falls from 7 to 5. What matters is that the combined product mi_wi_f be multiplied by 7/3. If this is so, then the new equilibrium values are

Labor supply L^S	= 100	Labor demand L^D = 98	
Employment E	= 95	Employment E	= 95
Unemployment U =	5	Vacancies V	= 3

Note that this increase in the parameters reduces equilibrium vacancies V^* from 5 to 3. This is in contrast to the impact of raising L^D from 98 to 102 where V^* rises from 5 to 7.

We can now draw the following conclusion:

▶ For a given labor supply L^S and labor demand L^D, equilibrium employment E^*, equilibrium unemployment U^*, and equilibrium vacancies V^* depend on the *degree of skill match m*, the *intensity of worker search i_w*, and the *intensity of firm search i_f*. An increase in these parameters raises equilibrium employment and reduces equilibrium unemployment and equilibrium vacancies.

THE CONSTANT UNEMPLOYMENT (*CU*) CURVE

Thus far, our model has been described by one diagram, Figure 14.1, which plots the n curve and the x line. We will now introduce a second diagram, Figure 14.2, which plots a new curve — the *constant unemployment (CU) curve*.

The CONSTANT UNEMPLOYMENT *CU* CURVE contains all points (U, V) for which entrants n equals exits x, so that employment, unemployment, and vacancies all remain constant.

If we replace n with x in equation (14.5), we obtain the equation of the *CU* curve:

FIGURE 14.2 EQUILIBRIUM UNEMPLOYMENT, VACANCIES, AND INFLATION

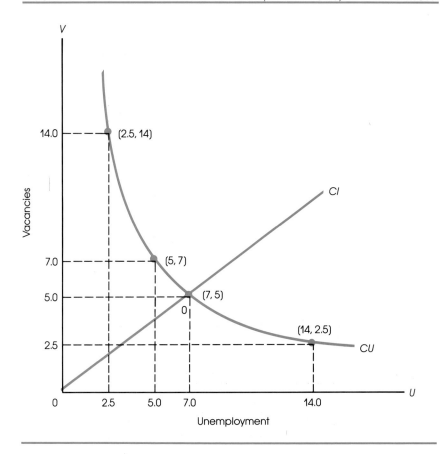

At each point on the *CU* curve, unemployment *U* and vacancies *V* remain constant. At each point on the *CI* line, the inflation rate remains constant. At the *CU*–*CI* intersection point, unemployment, vacancies, and inflation are all constant. At this point, the unemployment rate *U* divided by the labor supply L^S equals the constant inflation rate of unemployment (CIRU) of the economy.

(14.10) $m(i_w U)(i_f V) = x$

For example, with $m = 1$, $i_w = 3/7$, $i_f = 1/5$, and $x = 3$, we see that

$$1\left(\frac{3}{7}U\right)\left(\frac{1}{5}V\right) = 3$$

(14.11) $$UV = 35$$

$$U = \frac{35}{V}$$

If the values of m, i_w, i_f, and x are given, then for any V, there is a unique U that satisfies equation (14.10). At this combination of U and V, entrants n equals exits x so that employment, unemployment, and vacancies all remain constant. Moreover, as V increases, U decreases. In our example, for any V, U must equal $35/V$. We plot this curve in Figure 14.2:

V	U
2.5	14.0
5.0	7.0
7.0	5.0
14.0	2.5

It is important to understand precisely the phrase "constant unemployment." Obviously, as we move along the curve, both U and V vary. But if the economy is at any point (U, V) on the curve, unemployment stays constant because entrants n equals exits x. At any point (U, V) off the curve, unemployment does not stay constant because entrants does not equal exits.

For example, at any point (U, V) northeast of the curve, unemployment declines. Why? At any point on the curve, entrants equals exits. Starting from a point on the curve, we can move horizontally right and vertically up, to a point northeast of the curve. With an increase in U (moving horizontally) an increase in V (moving vertically), there are more contacts between unemployed persons and job vacancies, so that entrants exceeds exits; employment increases, and unemployment declines.

Thus, at any point northeast of the CU curve, unemployment is decreasing. Symmetrically, at any point southwest of the CU curve, unemployment is increasing. If E, U, and V are to stay constant, the economy must be at some point on the CU curve. But what determines which point? With L^S fixed, the value of L^D determines the point on the CU curve to which the economy moves.

In our first example, with $L^D = 98$, the economy moves to $E = 93$, $U = 7$, and $V = 5$, which is point $(7, 5)$ in Figure 14.2. With $L^D = 102$, the economy moves to $E = 95$, $U = 5$, and $V = 7$, which is point $(5, 7)$ in Figure 14.2. Thus

▶ As labor demand L^D increases (with labor supply L^S and the parameters m, i_w, and i_f remaining fixed), the equilibrium of the economy moves northwest along the constant unemployment CU curve.

What shifts the CU curve? The answer is clear from equation (14.10). If m, i_w, or i_f increases, then for a given U, a smaller V is required to make the left side of equation (14.10) equal to the constant x. This makes sense. For a given U, even with a smaller V, entrants can be the same if the degree of skill matching m is greater, if the intensity of search by the unemployed i_w is greater, or if the intensity of search by firms i_f is greater.

▶ An increase in the parameters m, i_w, or i_f shifts the CU curve downward (to the left).

14.2 Unemployment, Vacancies, and Inflation

Thus far, we have ignored the impact of unemployment and vacancies on wage and price inflation. Now we will ask what happens to the inflation rate in our economy where L^D is fixed at 98, the unemployment rate is 7%, and the vacancy rate is 5%.

Let's assume, as we did throughout Part 2, that workers and employers focus on the expected real wage gain $w - p^e$ when they bargain over the money wage increase w. Suppose that expectations are inertial, so that $p^e = p_{-1}$. If w is set so that the expected real wage gain $w - p^e$ equals labor productivity growth a (so that $p^e = w - a$), then since $p = w - a$, $p = p^e = p_{-1}$ and inflation stays constant. For a given expected inflation rate p^e, what influences the money wage increase w?

Unemployed workers tend to put downward pressure on w. On the other hand, vacancies tend to put upward pressure on w. The more intense is the search by unemployed workers and the more willing are the unemployed to accept any job, the greater is the downward pressure. The more intense is the search by firms with vacancies and the more willing are employers to accept any worker, the greater is the upward pressure.

There is a final, important aspect that must be considered: the *effectiveness of unemployment* and the *effectiveness of vacancies* in exerting pressure on wage increases. When a specific number of unemployed persons are searching with a particular intensity, how effective are they in exerting downward pressure on wage increases? If the economy has strong labor unions, then the effectiveness of the unemployed is lower than if such unions are absent. Strong unions limit the ability of employers to threaten current employees with replacement by unemployed workers.

Let's consider the effectiveness of vacancies in exerting upward pressure on wage increases. Suppose that an effective wage–price policy, implemented by a tax incentive or regulation (as described in Chapter 6), applies downward pressure to wage increases. Then a specific level of vacancies is less effective in raising wage increases due to the downward pressure of the wage–price policy.

We can hypothesize that wage and price inflation stay constant at any point (U, V), where

(14.12) $e_U i_w U = e_V i_f V$

where e_U = the effectiveness of the unemployed in applying downward
          pressure on the wage increase w

     e_V = the effectiveness of vacancies in applying upward
          pressure on the wage increase w

For example, if $e_U = 1/3$, $i_w = 3/7$, $e_V = 1$, and $i_f = 1/5$, then

$$\left[\left(\tfrac{1}{3}\right)\left(\tfrac{3}{7}\right)\right] U = \left[(1)\left(\tfrac{1}{5}\right)\right] V$$

(14.13) $5U = 7V$

Note that $U = 7$, $V = 5$ is one $U - V$ combination that satisfies the equation.

The left side of this equation is the downward pressure on wage increases resulting from unemployment. The right side is the upward pressure on wage increases resulting from vacancies. When the two sides are equal, wage inflation stays constant and price inflation stays constant. In this example, unemployment $U = 5$ exerts as much pressure as vacancies $V = 7$.

The term $e_U i_w U$ increases if unemployment, the intensity of worker search, or the effectiveness of the unemployed to exert pressure increases. The term $e_V i_f V$ increases if vacancies, the intensity of employer search, or the effectiveness of vacancies to exert pressure increases.

In equation (14.12), let's isolate V by dividing through by $e_V i_f$:

$$V = \frac{e_U i_w}{e_V i_f} U$$

The slope of the CI line is therefore $e_U i_w / e_V i_f$. For example, if $e_U = 1/3$, $i_w = 3/7$, $e_V = 1$, and $i_f = 1/5$, then we have

$$V = \frac{(1/3)(3/7)}{(1)(1/5)} U$$

$$V = \frac{5}{7} U$$

The slope of this CI line is 5/7.

If the economy is at any point (U, V) that satisfies equation (14.12), then the inflation rate stays constant. Hence, we call the line joining all such points the *constant inflation CI line*.

Figure 14.2 plots equation (14.12) as a ray (line) from the origin with a positive slope. Since the slope is $e_U i_w / e_V i_f$, the slope need not be 1; in our example, the slope is 5/7. Hence, the ray does not necessarily appear at a 45° angle. One unemployed worker may not exert the same pressure as one vacancy. Thus, it is not necessarily true that inflation stays constant if unemployment equals vacancies—that is, if the $V-U$ ratio equals 1.

Let us designate $(V/U)_c$ as the *constant inflation $V-U$ ratio*. In our example, $(V/U)_c = 5/7$. We then adopt the following hypothesis:

▶ If $\dfrac{V}{U} = \left(\dfrac{V}{U}\right)_c$, then the inflation rate stays constant.

If $\dfrac{V}{U} > \left(\dfrac{V}{U}\right)_c$, then the inflation rate rises.

If $\dfrac{V}{U} < \left(\dfrac{V}{U}\right)_c$, then the inflation rate declines.

In Figure 14.2, if the economy is at a point (U, V) that lies northwest of the *CI* line, then V/U exceeds $(V/U)_c$, so that the inflation rate rises. If the economy is at a point (U, V) that lies southeast of the *CI* line, then V/U is less than $(V/U)_c$, so that the inflation rate declines.

Because the slope of the *CI* line equals $e_U i_w / e_V i_f$, the following is true:

▶ The *CI* line becomes steeper if e_U or i_w increases or if e_V or i_f decreases.

If e_U or i_w increases, then a given U results in more downward pressure on w. For inflation to stay constant, there needs to be a rise in V relative to U. This keeps the two pressures equal. If e_V or i_f decreases, then a given V results in a decrease in upward pressure on w. For inflation to stay constant, there needs to be a rise in V relative to U to keep the two pressures equal.

14.3 Equilibrium Unemployment and Inflation

The intersection of the *CU* curve and the *CI* line gives the only point (U, V) that keeps both unemployment and inflation constant. We designate this intersection as point (U_c, V_c). In our example, we can find the numerical values for this equilibrium unemployment U_c and equilibrium vacancies V_c. With $m = 1$, $i_w = 3/7$, $i_f = 1/5$, and $x = 3$, we saw that the equation of the CU curve is equation (14.11):

(14.11) $UV = 35$

With $e_U = 1/3$, $i_w = 3/7$, $e_V = 1$, and $i_f = 1/5$, we saw that the equation of the CI line is equation (14.13):

(14.13) $5U = 7V$

To solve for U, we multiply equation (14.11) by 7 and equation (14.13) by U:

$$7UV = 245$$
$$5U^2 = 7UV$$

Since $7UV$ appears in both equations, it follows that

$$5U^2 = 245$$
$$U^2 = 49$$
$$U = 7$$
$$V = 5$$

Thus, while any point on the CU curve keeps U constant, and any point on the CI curve keeps inflation constant, only point (7, 5) keeps both unemployment and inflation constant in our example.

If L^S is fixed, and the parameters are given, we know that there is a particular L^D associated with each point on the CU curve. Thus, there is a particular L^D that moves the economy to the intersection point (7, 5) where both unemployment and inflation stay constant. In our example, with the initial parameter values, that value of L^D is 98 because we calculated that with L^D fixed at 98, the equilibrium values $E = 93$, $U = 7$, and $V = 5$ result.

Now let's review the general behavior of our model. Our two basic relationships are the constant unemployment CU curve, given by equation (14.10), and the constant inflation CI line, given by equation (14.12):

(14.10) $m(i_w U)(i_f V) = x$

(14.12) $e_U i_w U = e_V i_f V$

These two equations can be solved for the two unknowns, U and V. The solution is the intersection point (U_c, V_c). If the CU curve shifts or the CI line rotates, then the intersection point (U_c, V_c) changes. We know that an increase in m, i_w, or i_f shifts the CU curve downward; we also know that the CI line becomes steeper if e_U or i_w increases or if e_V or i_f decreases. Thus, a change in any of these parameters changes the point (U_C, V_C) of the economy.

If the intersection U_C (7) is divided by the labor supply L^S (100), then we obtain *the constant inflation rate of unemployment (CIRU)*, denoted by U_c (7%). If the intersection V_C (5) is divided by the labor demand L^D (98), then we obtain *the constant inflation rate of vacancies (CIRV)*, denoted by V_c (approximately 5%). Thus, our model determines the U_c of the economy. A change in any of the parameters of the model changes U_c. We will now turn to an analysis of policies that might reduce the intersection U_C—that is, reduce the constant inflation rate of unemployment CIRU.

14.4 Policies to Reduce the Constant Inflation Rate of Unemployment (CIRU)

In this section we will use our labor-market model to show how various policies or institutional changes reduce the constant inflation rate of unemployment (CIRU) of the economy. We want to emphasize that a citizen need not regard a policy as socially desirable simply because it reduces the CIRU. As we shall see, a citizen's view of a particular CIRU-reducing policy depends partly on his or her philosophical values.

Our strategy is straightforward. For each policy, we consider which of the parameters of our model—m, i_w, i_f, e_U, or e_V—are affected. We then shift either the CU curve or the CI line, or both, appropriately, and observe the change in the intersection U_C.

Consider an institutional change: the *weakening of unions*. If unions are weaker, then the effectiveness of unemployed workers to exert downward pressure increases. Employers have more freedom to threaten current employees with replacement by the unemployed unless they accept smaller wage increases. What is the impact of this change in our model?

We know from equation (14.12) that an increase in e_U makes the CI line steeper (as shown in Figure 14.3). The new intersection has a lower U_C and a higher V_C.

▶ A weakening of unions reduces the constant inflation rate of unemployment (CIRU) and raises the constant inflation rate of vacancies (CIRV).

Next, consider the impact of a *reduction in unemployment compensation benefits*. A worker who is laid off is entitled to unemployment compensation benefits. Such benefits help ease the hardship of unemployment. At the same time, because they make the unemployed less desperate, they reduce the intensity of search by the unemployed. The

FIGURE 14.3 WEAKENING UNIONS

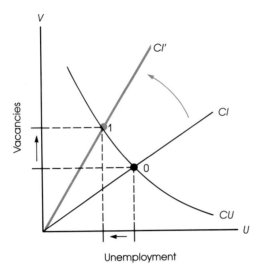

A weakening of unions shifts the *CI* line to *CI'*, so that the constant inflation rate of unemployment (CIRU) declines and the constant inflation rate of vacancies (CIRV) rises.

unemployed who receive benefits can afford to search more selectively and less urgently.

Reducing unemployment compensation benefits raises i_w. The parameter i_w affects both the *CU* curve and the *CI* line; hence, an increase in i_w shifts both. We know that an increase in i_w shifts the *CU* curve downward and makes the *CI* line steeper. The impact is shown in Figure 14.4. The new intersection clearly has a lower U_c, but it is not certain whether V_c is higher or lower.

▶ A reduction in unemployment compensation benefits reduces the constant inflation rate of unemployment (CIRU); the impact on the constant inflation rate of vacancies (CIRV) is uncertain.

Next, consider three policies that raise the degree of match *m* between the skills of the unemployed and the skills required by vacancies: *manpower training*, a *wage subsidy* for low-skilled workers, and a *reduction in the legal minimum wage* relative to the average wage in the economy. The objective of manpower training is to provide skills that are demanded by job vacancies. If it succeeds, then a worker who would have been rejected by a firm might be accepted for employment. Manpower training tries to adjust the worker to the skill requirements of available vacancies. It therefore raises *m*.

FIGURE 14.4 REDUCING UNEMPLOYMENT COMPENSATION

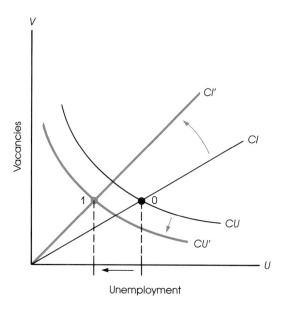

A reduction in benefits per unemployed worker shifts the *CI* line to *CI'*, and the *CU* curve to *CU'*, so that the constant inflation rate of unemployment (CIRU) declines. The constant inflation rate of vacancies (CIRV) may rise or fall.

Many of the unemployed are low-skilled and are therefore less productive. It is not profitable for firms to hire such persons unless the wage cost to the firm is less than the person's productivity. Wage subsidies for low-skilled workers and a reduction in the legal minimum wage relative to the average wage enable employers to create vacancies that require the skills of many of the unemployed.

Under a wage subsidy, the government reimburses the firm for a fraction of its wage payment; this reduces the wage cost to the firm. A reduction in the legal minimum wage permits firms to lower the wage; this also reduces the wage cost to the firm. Hence, both policies induce firms to create more vacancies for low-skilled workers. Because more of the unemployed are now suitable for the vacancies, m increases.

We know that an increase in m shifts the *CU* curve downward, as shown in Figure 14.5. Both the new U_c and the new V_c are lower.

▶ An increase in manpower training, a wage subsidy for low-skilled workers, and a reduction in the legal minimum wage all reduce both the constant inflation rate of unemployment (CIRU) and the constant inflation rate of vacancies (CIRV).

FIGURE 14.5 IMPROVED MATCHING OF VACANCY SKILLS AND UNEMPLOYED SKILLS

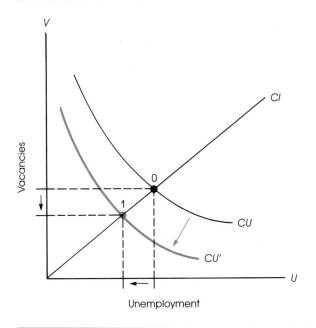

An increase in manpower training, a wage subsidy for low-skilled workers, and a reduction of the legal minimum wage all improve the matching of vacancy skills and unemployed skills. Each policy shifts the *CU* curve downward to *CU′*, so that the constant inflation rate of unemployment (CIRU) declines and the constant inflation rate of vacancies (CIRV) declines.

Next, consider a permanent *tax-incentive inflation policy* (TIP) (described in Chapter 6). Recall that such a policy gives a tax incentive to each covered firm to hold down its price and wage increase. If TIP provides an effective incentive, then each covered firm will find it optimal to give a smaller wage increase than it otherwise would. This means that TIP reduces the effectiveness of vacancies to exert upward pressure on wage increases. Any given level of vacancies now results in a smaller wage increase because firms must now weigh the tax incentive.

We know that a reduction in e_V makes the *CI* line steeper, as shown in Figure 14.6. The new intersection at point 1 has a lower U_C and a higher V_C.

▶ If a permanent tax-incentive inflation policy (TIP) provides an effective incentive, it reduces the constant inflation rate of unemployment (CIRU) and raises the constant inflation rate of vacancies (CIRV).

FIGURE 14.6 TAX-INCENTIVE INFLATION POLICY

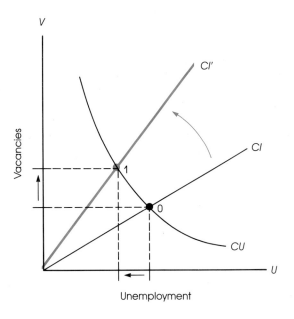

A tax-incentive inflation policy (TIP) shifts the *CI* line to *CI'*, so that the constant inflation rate of unemployment (CIRU) declines and the constant inflation rate of vacancies (CIRV) rises.

Now consider the *market anti-inflation plan* (MAP) (described in Chapter 6). Recall that such a policy attempts to achieve a targeted average price increase of p^*. A firm that sets its p above p^* is required to buy MAP permits. A firm that sets its p below p^* is entitled to sell MAP permits. If MAP is administered effectively, then price raising ($p > p^*$) by some firms is always matched by price cutting ($p < p^*$) by other firms, so that the average p of all MAP-covered firms stays roughly equal to p^*.

But this means that the inflation rate is p^* — and therefore constant — regardless of the vacancy–unemployment combination. As shown in Figure 14.7, there is no longer a constant inflation line. The inflation rate is constant (at p^*) at any point (U, V) in the diagram. In equilibrium, the economy still needs to be at some point on the *CU* curve.

▶ If a permanent market anti-inflation plan (MAP) is effective, it makes any unemployment rate a constant inflation rate of unemployment (CIRU) and any vacancy rate a constant inflation rate of vacancies (CIRV).

FIGURE 14.7 MARKET ANTI-INFLATION PLAN

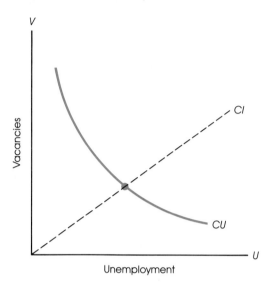

A market anti-inflation plan (MAP) eliminates the *CI* line, so that any point on the *CU* curve is a potential equilibrium.

Each of the policies or institutional changes we have considered reduce the CIRU of the economy in our model. Two comments are warranted. First, we have only considered one labor-market model. Perhaps an alternate labor-market model would prove more realistic and would yield a different conclusion concerning a particular policy change. Second, as we emphasized at the outset, a policy is not necessarily socially desirable simply because it reduces the CIRU. Each of these CIRU-reducing policies has disadvantages as well as advantages that must be weighed. Let's briefly note these possible disadvantages.

Weakening unions reduces their positive role in protecting workers against arbitrary and unfair treatment by some employers. Reducing unemployment compensation benefits increases the hardship of the unemployed who genuinely cannot find work. Manpower training and wage subsidies for low-skilled workers are government expenditures that must be financed by an increase in taxes. Reducing the legal minimum wage reduces the earnings of many low-skilled workers who would have been employed at the higher minimum wage. A permanent TIP or MAP imposes administrative costs on covered firms and the Internal Revenue Service and causes inefficiencies and distortions.

Thus, both the pros and cons of CIRU-reducing policies must be weighed. A citizen may choose to support some CIRU-reducing policies and to oppose others. To reiterate, our conclusions are tentative. Other labor-market models might lead to different conclusions concerning various policies.

SUMMARY

1. This chapter illustrates how the labor market can be modeled. Macroeconomists disagree about how to model the labor market. Policy conclusions from the model, therefore, should be regarded as tentative.

2. *Unemployment U* and *vacancies V* exist simultaneously in the labor market. *Employment E* is less than both *labor demand L^D* and *labor supply L^S*.

3. Unemployment equals labor supply minus employment; vacancies equals labor demand minus employment. Excess supply in the labor market equals labor supply minus labor demand. This equals unemployment minus vacancies.

4. Employment stays constant when the number of *entrants per month n* equals the number of *exits per month x*. Entrants per month *n* increases when unemployment increases and when vacancies increases.

5. The *constant unemployment (CU) curve* contains all points (U, V) for which unemployment, employment, and vacancies stay constant because the number of entrants equals the number of exits. Given the hypothesis that exits per month is constant, the *CU* curve has a negative slope.

6. The *constant inflation (CI) line* contains all points (U, V) for which the inflation rate stays constant because downward pressure on the money wage increase *w* equals upward pressure on *w*. The *CI* line has a positive slope.

7. Unemployment and inflation are both constant at the point (U, V) at which the *CU* curve and the *CI* line intersect. Expressed as a percentage of labor supply, this unemployment *U* gives the *constant inflation rate of unemployment (CIRU) U_c* of the economy. Expressed as a percentage of labor demand, this vacancies *V* gives the *constant inflation rate of vacancies (CIRV)* of the economy.

8. In this model, the impacts of particular policies are as follows:
   a. A *weakening of unions* makes the constant inflation (*CI*) line steeper, thereby reducing the CIRU and raising the CIRV.
   b. A *reduction in unemployment compensation benefits* per unem-

ployed person makes the *CI* line steeper and shifts the *CU* curve downward; it therefore reduces the CIRU. Its impact on CIRV is uncertain.

c. *Manpower training* or a *wage subsidy* for hiring low-skilled workers shifts the *CU* curve downward, thereby reducing the CIRU and the CIRV.

TERMS AND CONCEPTS

constant inflation (*CI*) line
constant inflation rate of
   unemployment (CIRU)
constant inflation rate of
   vacancies (CIRV)
constant unemployment (*CU*)
   curve
contacts
CU–CI diagram
degree of skill match (*m*)
effectiveness of unemployment
   (e_U)
effectiveness of vacancies (e_V)
employment (*E*)
entrants per month (*n*)
equilibrium level of
   employment (*E**)
excess labor supply
exits per month (*x*)

intensity of firm search (i_f)
intensity of worker search (i_w)
labor demand (L^D)
labor supply (L^S)
manpower training
market anti-inflation plan (MAP)
n curve
quadratic equation
reduction in the legal minimum
   wage
reduction in unemployment
   compensation benefits
tax-incentive inflation policy
   (TIP)
unemployment (*U*)
vacancies (*V*)
wage subsidy
weakening of unions

QUESTIONS

14.1 Suppose that labor supply L^S is 100, exits per month *x* is 3, and entrants per month *n* is given by the following *n* curve: $n = m[i_w(L^S - E)][i_f(L^D - E)]$.

a. If $m = 1$, $i_w = 1/2$, $i_f = 1/4$, and $L^D = 98$, then write the *n* curve equation.

b. Complete the following table for this *n* curve:

E	*n*
90	_____
92	_____
94	_____
96	_____
98	_____

c. Plot this n curve on a graph.

d. What is equilibrium employment E^*?

e. If labor demand L^D increases to 102, write the equation for the new n curve.

f. Complete the following table for this new n curve:

E	n
90	_____
92	_____
94	_____
96	_____
98	_____

g. Plot the new n curve on a graph.

h. What is the new equilibrium employment?

14.2 The constant unemployment CU curve is given by the following equation: $m(i_w U)(i_f V) = x$. The constant inflation CI line is given by the following equation: $e_U i_w U = e_V i_f V$.

a. What is the meaning of the CU equation? Of the CI equation?

b. Given the values for m, i_w, i_f, and x in Question 14.1, write the CU equation.

c. Plot this CU curve.

d. With $e_U = 1/3$, $e_V = 1$, and the same values for i_w and i_f, write the CI equation.

e. Plot this CI line.

f. Find the point (U, V) at which the CU curve and the CI line intersect.

14.3 Using the CU–CI diagram, explain how each of the following alters the constant inflation rate of unemployment (CIRU) and the constant inflation rate of vacancies (CIRV) of the economy in this model:

a. a weakening of unions

b. a reduction in unemployment compensation

c. a wage subsidy for hiring low-skilled workers

d. a permanent tax-incentive inflation policy (TIP)

APPENDIX
14 A

THE LABOR-MARKET MODEL AND THE DG–SG AND L^D–L^S DIAGRAMS

In Appendix 14A, we will consider how the labor-market model presented in this chapter relates to the demand growth–supply growth (DG–SG) diagram we examined in Chapter 4 and to the labor demand–labor supply (L^D–L^S) diagram we examined in Chapter 3.

14.A.1 The Labor-Market Model and the *DG–SG* Diagram

How does our labor-market model relate to our analysis using the *DG–SG* diagram? For convenience, assume our economy is a no-growth economy, that at the initial equilibrium both wage and price inflation are 0% (productivity growth is 0%), and that the nominal demand growth rate is 0%. In the *DG–SG* diagram, Figure 14.A.1(a), the two curves intersect at $Q = Q_c$, $p = 0\%$. In the *CU–CI* diagram, Figure 14.A.1(b), assume that the *CU* curve and the *CI* line intersect at $U_c = 7$ and $V_c = 5$ and that the economy is at the following equilibrium values:

Labor supply L^S	= 100	Labor demand L^D = 98	
Employment E	= 93	Employment E	= 93
Unemployment U =	7	Vacancies V	= 5

FIGURE 14.A.1 THE RESPONSE TO A PERMANENT INCREASE IN THE NOMINAL DEMAND GROWTH RATE

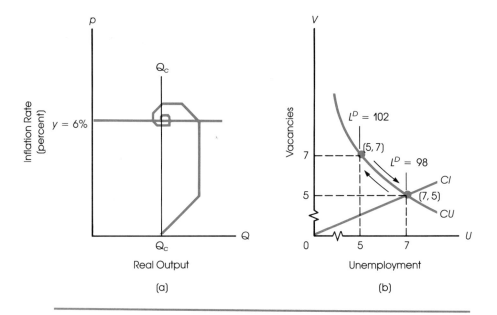

(a) Real Output

(b) Unemployment

Initially, the economy is at a real output of $Q = Q_c$ and an inflation rate of $p = 0\%$ in the *DG–SG* diagram in (a) and at point 0 ($U = 7$, $V = 5$) in the *CU–CI* diagram in (b). In period 1, the nominal demand growth rate rises to $y = 6\%$. In *DG–SG* diagram (a), Q rises above Q_c and p rises above 0%. In *CU–CI* diagram (b), the economy moves northwest along the *CU* curve to point ($U = 5$, $V = 7$). In the *DG–SG* diagram, the economy converges to $Q = Q_c$ and $p = 6\%$ in the long run. In the *CU–CI* diagram, the economy returns to point 0 ($U = 7$, $V = 5$).

Now if the nominal demand growth rate increases in period 1 as a result of an increase in money growth from $y = 0\%$ to $y = 6\%$, assuming inertial expectations, then DG_1 lies above DG_0. But SG_1 coincides with SG_0. Hence, both real output Q and price inflation p increase. Let's consider what happens in the labor-market model.

To produce a higher Q, firms demand more labor. Hence, labor demand L^D increases. For example, suppose L^D increases from 98 to 102 in period 1. We calculated earlier that the economy moves to the following equilibrium values:

Labor supply L^S	= 100	Labor demand L^D =	102
Employment E	= 95	Employment E	= 95
Unemployment $U =$	5	Vacancies V	= 7

In period 1 in Figure 14.A.1(b), the economy moves northwest along the CU curve to point $(5, 7)$. Recall that an increase in L^D raises E and V and reduces U, moving the economy northwest along the CU curve. In Figure 14.A.1(b), the CI line stays fixed; none of the parameters that determine its position (e_U, i_w, e_V, i_f) have changed. Thus, in period 1, the economy moves to point $(5, 7)$ northwest of the CI line. Recall that when the economy is at a (U, V) point northwest of the CI line, so that V/U exceeds $(V/U)_c$ (the slope of the CI line), the inflation rate rises. This is the same conclusion that the $DG - SG$ diagram provides.

If the nominal demand growth rate remains constant at $y = 6\%$, we know from our $DG - SG$ analysis that as shown in Figure 14.A.1(a) the economy spirals in to $Q = Q_c$ $(U = U_c)$ and that the inflation rate p becomes equal to the nominal demand growth rate y. What happens in the $CU - CI$ diagram?

As Q returns to Q_c, the labor demand of firms returns to the initial 98. Hence, the economy moves back down the CU curve in Figure 14.A.1(b) to its original equilibrium point $(7, 5)$ at the intersection of the CU curve and the CI line. Although E, V, and U return to their initial values, the inflation rate p is now constant at 6%, instead of 0%. But the intersection point in the $CU - CI$ diagram implies only that the inflation rate stays constant; it is consistent with any level of p.

In the $CU - CI$ diagram, then, a permanent increase in nominal demand growth causes the economy to move temporarily northwest up the fixed CU curve and then to reverse direction and move back down the CU curve to the initial intersection. The CU curve and the CI line remain fixed during the process, because an increase in nominal demand growth does not affect any of the parameters that determine the positions of the CU curve and CI line.

14.A.2 The Labor-Market Model and the Labor Demand – Labor Supply Diagram

How does our labor-market model relate to the labor demand – labor supply diagram shown in Figure 3.3 (page 124)? The L^D and L^S curves are drawn in Figure 14.A.2. To simplify our labor-market model, we have assumed that labor supply L^S is fixed. Thus, instead of a labor supply curve with a positive slope (Figure 3.3), we draw a vertical L^S curve (Figure 14.A.2).

Let's briefly review the rationale for the L^D and L^S curves. The L^D curve is the marginal product of labor MPL curve. Profit maximization causes firms to seek labor until the MPL equals the real wage W/P. The L^S curve reflects worker preferences between work and leisure. We make the assumption that they choose to hold labor supply constant at any real wage (in the relevant range). In Chapter 3, we assumed that the labor market is "frictionless." We made the standard assumption that

FIGURE 14.A.2 THE EMPLOYMENT CURVE

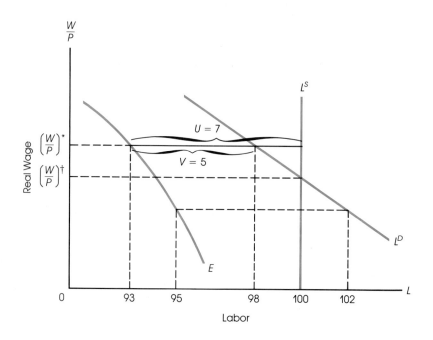

Due to frictions, actual employment E is always less than labor supply L^S and less than labor demand L^D. The E curve lies to the left of the L^S curve and the L^D curve. In our example, equilibrium occurs at $(W/P)^*$, which exceeds $(W/P)^\dagger$ at which L^S and L^D intersect. Unemployment $U = L^S - E$, and vacancies $V = L^D - E$. At $L^D = 98$ and $L^S = 100$, $E = 93$, $U = 7$, and $V = 5$.

equilibrium occurs where labor supply equals labor demand. Thus, we assumed that the intersection of the L^S and L^D curves indicates the equilibrium level of labor actually employed and the equilibrium real wage.

Why is such a labor market frictionless? At the intersection, employment E equals both labor supply L^S and labor demand L^D. But recall equation (14.1) and equation (14.2):

$$\text{(14.1)} \quad U \equiv L^S - E$$
$$\text{(14.2)} \quad V \equiv L^D - E$$

If $E = L^S$, then $U = 0$; if $E = L^D$, then $V = 0$. When we say that the labor market is "frictionless," we mean that in equilibrium there is neither unemployment nor vacancies.

By "frictionless," we also mean that at any real wage above the L^D–L^S intersection in Figure 14.A.2, E equals L^D and both are less than L^S. Hence, U is positive and V is 0. Symmetrically, at any real wage below the intersection, E equals L^S and both are less than L^D. Hence, V is positive and U is 0. Thus, in a frictionless market, even when the economy is out of equilibrium, either unemployment or vacancies exists, but not both.

THE EMPLOYMENT E CURVE

The actual economy, however, is always characterized by the simultaneous existence of unemployment and vacancies. We noted at the beginning of this chapter that there are several reasons why unemployment and vacancies coexist even when the labor market is in equilibrium. First, some of the unemployed may prefer to wait for a better job to open up. Second, some of the employers with vacancies may prefer to wait until more productive employees are available. Third, unemployed workers may have difficulty locating available vacancies, and firms may have difficulty locating workers to fill their vacancies.

Our labor-market model has tried to account for the simultaneous existence of unemployment and vacancies, even when the labor market is in equilibrium. How can these "frictions" be incorporated into the labor demand–labor supply diagram? The answer is shown in Figure 14.A.2. To the left of both the L^D curve and the vertical L^S curve is drawn an employment E curve. At any real wage W/P, the L^D curve indicates labor demand L^D, the vertical L^S curve indicates labor supply L^S, and the E curve indicates actual employment E, which must be less than both L^S and L^D.

At any real wage W/P and given L^D and L^S, E can be determined from our labor-market model. Recall that given the parameters m, i_w, and i_f, with $L^S = 100$ and $L^D = 98$, we can set the n curve equation (14.7) equal to x (3), and solve for the equilibrium employment E^*:

(14.7)
$$n = \left(\frac{3}{35}\right)(100 - E)(98 - E)$$

Substituting equation (14.7) into equation (14.4), we obtain

(14.4)
$$n = x$$

$$\left(\frac{3}{35}\right)(100 - E)(98 - E) = 3$$

$$E = 93$$

Corresponding to this example, the vertical L^S curve in Figure 14.A.2 is positioned at 100. At the real wage $(W/P)^*$, where $L^D = 98$, $E = 93$. The horizontal distance between E and L^S equals U (7); the horizontal distance between E and L^D equals V (5).

In general, when we are given the values of the parameters and the values of L^D and L^S, we can find E^* by setting the general n curve equation (14.6) equal to x and solving for E:

(14.6)
$$n = m[i_w(L^S - E)][i_f(L^D - E)]$$

Substituting equation (14.6) into equation (14.4) gives us

$$m[i_w(L^S - E)][i_f(L^D - E)] = x$$

We can now solve for E. The equilibrium employment E^* is shown in Figure 14.1 (page 577) at the intersection of the n curve and the x line. Since an increase in m, i_w, or i_f shifts the n curve upward, its intersection with the x line occurs at a larger E. Hence, with L^S and L^D fixed, an increase in m, i_w, or i_f raises E and reduces U and V. Therefore, in our labor demand–labor supply diagram, the following is true:

▶ With the L^D and L^S curves held constant, an increase in m, i_w, or i_f shifts the E curve to the right, closer to the L^D and L^S curves.

Recall that an increase in these same parameters—and only these parameters—shifts the CU curve downward (to the left) in the CU–CI diagram.

▶ With the L^D and L^S curves held constant, the E curve shifts to the right if and only if the CU curve shifts downward (to the left).

The CU–CI diagram is shown in Figure 14.2 (page 583). Given the initial parameter values and $L^S = 100$, the CU–CI intersection point 0 is at $(U = 7, V = 5)$; $L^D = 98$ is associated with this equilibrium point. The corresponding $E = 93$. In Figure 14.A.2, this equilibrium requires a real wage $(W/P)^*$ that happens to be above the intersection $(W/P)\dagger$ such that $L^D = 98$ and $E = 93$. In contrast to the assumption made in Chapter 3, this implies that equilibrium may occur when L^D does not equal L^S and, therefore, when V does not equal U.

In our labor-market model, equilibrium may occur when L^S and L^D are unequal (equivalently, when U and V are unequal). We said that equilibrium occurs when the downward pressure on wage increases from unemployment balances the upward pressure from vacancies. But it is not obvious that one unit of unemployment exerts the same pressure as one unit of vacancies. Our model therefore allows for the possibility that $(V/U)_c$ may differ from 1.

To emphasize this possibility, $(V/U)_c = 5/7$ in our example. This does not mean that the equilibrium $(W/P)^*$ must always be greater than the intersection $(W/P)\dagger$. Different parameter values provide a different (U_C, V_C) intersection point in the $CU\text{-}CI$ diagram and a different associated L^D. The equilibrium $(W/P)^*$ might turn out to be equal to or less than the intersection $(W/P)\dagger$.

This refinement of the $L^D\text{-}L^S$ diagram affects the position, but not the slope, of the long-run aggregate supply curve S_{LR} (Figure 3.2, page 122). Let's review the rationale for the vertical S_{LR} curve.

In Chapter 3, we said that labor must be L^* in long-run equilibrium. When L^* and long-run equilibrium capital K^* are inserted into the production function given by equation (3.11), the long-run equilibrium level of output Q^* results. Moreover, L^* depends on the positions of the L^D and L^S curves, which are independent of the price level P. Hence, in long-run equilibrium, Q^* is supplied at any P. The long-run aggregate supply curve S_{LR} is vertical at Q^*.

Our refinement implies that in long-run equilibrium, labor actually employed is not the $L\dagger$ at the intersection of the L^D and L^S curves. Instead, it is the E^* at the point on the E curve that corresponds to the $CU\text{-}CI$ intersection. Only that point implies the U, V, and L^D at the $CU\text{-}CI$ intersection.

When this E^* is substituted into the production function along with K^*, Q^* results. While this Q^* is less than the one implied by $L\dagger$, it is still true that Q^* is the same, regardless of the price level P. Why? Nothing in our labor-market model depends on the price level P per se. The parameters that determine the $CU\text{-}CI$ intersection are independent of P. Hence, so is E^*. It is still true, then, that the long-run aggregate supply curve S_{LR} is vertical.

Our basic conclusion from Chapter 3 remains valid. If demand for output shifts permanently, there is no change in real output Q in the long run; the sole impact is on the price level P.

In Section 14.A.1, we examined how our labor-market model relates to the $DG-SG$ diagram. We looked at an example where the nominal demand growth rate is raised from $y=0\%$ to $y=6\%$. Figure 14.A.1(a) shows what happens in the $DG-SG$ diagram, and Figure 14.A.1(b) shows what happens in the $CU-CI$ diagram. Now we ask what happens during this episode in the labor demand–labor supply (L^D-L^S) diagram. The answer is shown in Figure 14.A.3.

Why does the labor demand curve shift from L^D to $L^{D\prime}$? When output growth rises above normal, *capital utilization* (also called *capacity utilization*) rises above its normal, equilibrium value. At any point in time, the economy has a fixed capital stock. But the intensity of use of that stock can vary. When demand for output grows faster than the normal (expected) rate, it may be profitable for firms to raise capital utilization above normal.

FIGURE 14.A.3 A CYCLICAL INCREASE IN EMPLOYMENT

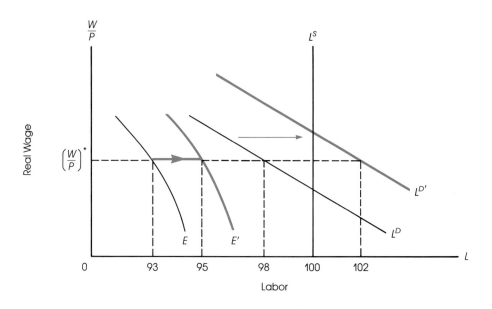

In response to an increase in nominal demand growth, the L^D curve temporarily shifts upward to $L^{D\prime}$ because a temporary increase in capital utilization raises the marginal product of labor MPL at each level of L. The shift to $L^{D\prime}$ causes the E curve to shift to $E\prime$. Employment E rises from 93 to 95 as L^D rises from 98 to 102. In this example, the real wage W/P stays constant at $(W/P)^*$. In the long run, $L^{D\prime}$ shifts back to L^D, $E\prime$ shifts back to E, and the economy returns to its initial equilibrium.

But recall from Chapter 3 that an increase in capital actually utilized raises the marginal product of labor MPL at each level of labor. Thus, if capital utilization temporarily increases during this phase of the cycle, then the L^D curve, which is the MPL curve, temporarily shifts upward. For convenience, in Figure 14.A.3, the L^D curve shifts so that $L^D = 102$ (instead of 98) at the initial real wage $(W/P)^*$.

The E curve depends on the positions of the L^D curve and the L^S curve. When the L^D curve shifts to the right to $L^{D\prime}$, the E curve shifts to the right to $E^\prime$. At the initial $(W/P)^*$, with L^D now fixed at 102, we know that E rises to 95. Thus, with these shifts of the L^D and E curves, there is no change in the real wage; it remains at $(W/P)^*$, while actual employment moves from 93 on the initial E curve to 95 on the new $E^\prime$ curve.

In the long run, capital utilization returns to normal, the L^D curve returns to its initial position, and the economy returns to the initial equilibrium point shown in Figure 14.A.3.

POLICIES TO REDUCE THE CIRU

In Section 14.4, we analyzed policies to reduce the constant inflation rate of unemployment (CIRU). Now let's consider how each policy to reduce the CIRU affects the labor demand–labor supply diagram.

We will see that in the L^D–L^S diagram, each policy (except MAP) increases equilibrium employment from E_0^* to E_1^*. When E_1^* replaces E_0^* in the production function, the result is Q_1^* instead of Q_0^* (where Q_1^* exceeds Q_0^*). In the aggregate demand–long-run aggregate supply diagram shown in Figure 3.2 (page 122), the vertical S_{LR} curve shifts to the right. In long-run equilibrium, regardless of the level of nominal demand, the economy converges to a real output of Q_1^*, instead of Q_0^*.

With our assumption that the labor supply L^S curve is vertical, an increase in equilibrium employment from E_0^* to E_1^* implies a decrease in equilibrium unemployment from U_0^* to U_1^*, since U is the horizontal distance between E and the fixed L^S. None of the CIRU-reducing policies shift the L^D curve (the MPL curve) or the L^S curve (which depends on worker preferences between work and leisure). We will see that the impact of the policy results either from shifting the E curve or from moving along the E curve.

In our analysis of the impact of each policy, we will employ an earlier conclusion, restated here:

▶ With the L^D curve and the L^S curve held constant, the E curve shifts to the right if and only if the CU curve shifts downward (to the left).

We will continue to assume that the initial equilibrium is at a $(W/P)^*$ above the intersection $(W/P)^\dagger$, so that L^D is less than L^S and the initial V/U ratio is therefore less than 1 (5/7 in our example). Equivalently, at our initial equilibrium, we will assume that V (5) is less than U (7). Because some conclusions drawn in the following sections depend on this assumption, it is worth repeating the warning that this assumption may not be empirically correct.

Weakening Unions

The impact of weakening unions on the $CU-CI$ diagram is shown in Figure 14.3 (page 590); its impact on the labor demand–labor supply diagram is shown in Figure 14.A.4. We saw earlier that the CU curve does not shift. Hence, as just emphasized, the E curve does not shift.

Weakening unions makes the CI line steeper. With a constant CU curve, the economy moves to a new $CU-CI$ intersection point at a lower unemployment rate U. In Figure 14.A.4, U is the distance between L^S and E. To narrow this distance, the economy must move down the E

FIGURE 14.A.4 WEAKENING UNIONS

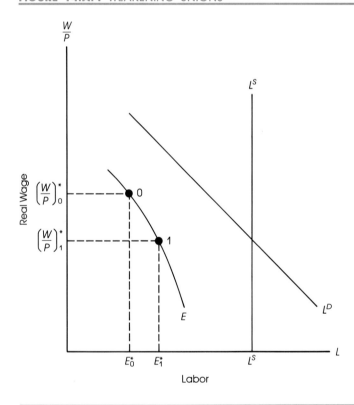

A weakening of unions moves equilibrium employment E^* from point 0 to point 1 along a fixed E curve.

curve from E_0^* to E_1^*. Hence, the real wage must decline from $(W/P)_0^*$ to $(W/P)_1^*$.

Reducing Unemployment Compensation Benefits

The impact of reducing unemployment compensation benefits on the CU–CI diagram is shown in Figure 14.4 (page 591); its impact on the L^D–L^S diagram is shown in Figure 14.A.5. We saw earlier that the CU curve shifts downward. Hence, the E curve shifts to the right, from E to E'.

Reducing unemployment compensation benefits also makes the CI line steeper. In Figure 14.4, the economy moves to a point with a higher V/U ratio. In Figure 14.A.5, the initial V/U ratio is 5/7. To achieve a higher V/U ratio, the economy must move to a point on the E' curve that has a lower real wage of $(W/P)_1^*$. Why?

FIGURE 14.A.5 REDUCING UNEMPLOYMENT COMPENSATION

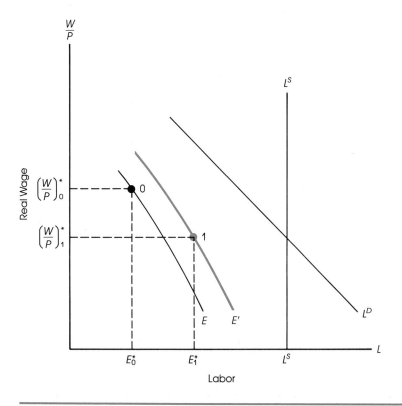

A reduction in the benefit per unemployed worker shifts the E curve right to E' and moves equilibrium employment E^* from point 0 to point 1.

If the real wage stayed at $(W/P)_0^*$, then the economy would move horizontally to the right, and V and U would decline by the same amount. For example, if each fell by 2, then the new V/U ratio would be $3/5$. However, $3/5$ is less than $5/7$, indicating that the V/U ratio would have declined. Since, according to Figure 14.4, the V/U ratio must increase (not decrease), the economy must move down the E' curve. Moving down the E' curve raises V and reduces U, thereby raising the V/U ratio to its required level.

Improved Matching Through Manpower Training, Wage Subsidies for Low-skilled Workers, and a Reduction in the Legal Minimum Wage

The impact of improved matching through manpower training, wage subsidies for low-skilled workers, and a reduction in the legal minimum wage on the CU–CI diagram is shown in Figure 14.5 (page 592); the impact on the L^D–L^S diagram is shown in Figure 14.A.6. We saw earlier that the CU curve shifts downward. Hence, the E curve shifts to the right from E to E'.

Improved matching does not affect the CI line. Hence, in Figure 14.5, the economy moves to a point with the same V/U ratio. In Figure 14.A.6, the initial V/U ratio is $5/7$. To maintain this ratio, the economy must move to a point on the E' curve that has a lower real wage $(W/P)_1^*$. Why?

If the real wage stayed at $(W/P)_0^*$, then the economy would move horizontally to the right, and V and U would fall by the same amount. For example, if each fell by 2, then the new V/U ratio would be $3/5$. However, $3/5$ is less than $5/7$, indicating that the V/U ratio would have declined. Since, according to Figure 14.5, the V/U ratio must remain constant (not decrease), the economy must move down the E' curve. Moving down the E' curve raises V and reduces U, thereby restoring the V/U ratio to its initial value.

TIP

The impact of the tax-incentive inflation policy (TIP) on the CU–CI diagram is shown in Figure 14.6 (page 593); its impact on the L^D–L^S diagram is shown in Figure 14.A.7. We saw earlier that the CU curve does not shift. Hence, the E curve does not shift.

TIP makes the CI line steeper. With a constant CU curve, the economy moves to a new CU–CI intersection point at a lower unemployment rate U. In Figure 14.A.7, U is the distance between L^S and E. To narrow this distance, the economy must move down the E curve from E_0^* to E_1^*. Hence, the real wage must decline from $(W/P)_0^*$ to $(W/P)_1^*$.

FIGURE 14.A.6 IMPROVED MATCHING OF VACANCY SKILLS AND UNEMPLOYED SKILLS

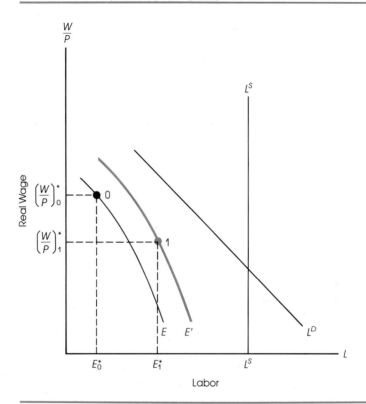

An increase in manpower training, a wage subsidy for low-skilled workers, and a reduction of the legal minimum wage all improve the matching of vacancy skills and unemployed skills. Each policy shifts the E curve to the right to E' and moves equilibrium employment E^* from point 0 to point 1.

▶ All four of these CIRU-reducing policies shift the vertical, long-run aggregate supply S_{LR} curve to the right. Each policy raises equilibrium employment from E_0^* to E_1^*. When E_1^* replaces E_0^* in the production function, output rises from Q_0^* to Q_1^*. Equilibrium employment E^* is independent of the price level P, which does not affect any of the determinants of our model. Hence, in the long run, Q_1^* is supplied at any P.

MAP

The impact of the market anti-inflation plan (MAP) on the $CU-CI$ diagram is shown in Figure 14.7 (page 594); its impact on the L^D-L^S

FIGURE 14.A.7 TIP

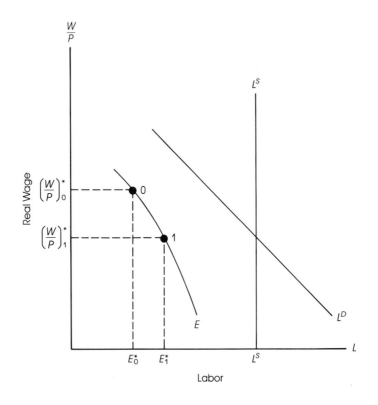

A tax-incentive inflation policy (TIP) moves equilibrium employment E^* from point 0 to point 1 along a fixed E curve.

diagram is shown in Figure 14.A.8(a). We saw earlier that the CU curve does not shift. Hence, the E curve does not shift.

MAP eliminates the CI line. MAP keeps the inflation rate constant (at p^*) at any point (U, V). In contrast to the preceding four policies, with MAP there is no longer a unique point (U_C, V_C) at which the CU curve and the CI line intersect. An equilibrium with a constant inflation rate can occur at any point on the CU curve. Thus, the economy is at equilibrium at any point on the E curve, rather than at a unique point on the E curve.

With $p^* = 0\%$, the long-run aggregate supply S_{LR} curve is not vertical. As shown in Figure 14.A.8(b), it is horizontal at the initial price level $\overline{P}$ that MAP holds constant. The horizontal long-run aggregate supply curve has a maximum real output, denoted by $\overline{Q}$, that is produced if actual employment E is equal to the labor supply L^S shown in Figure

FIGURE 14.A.8 MAP

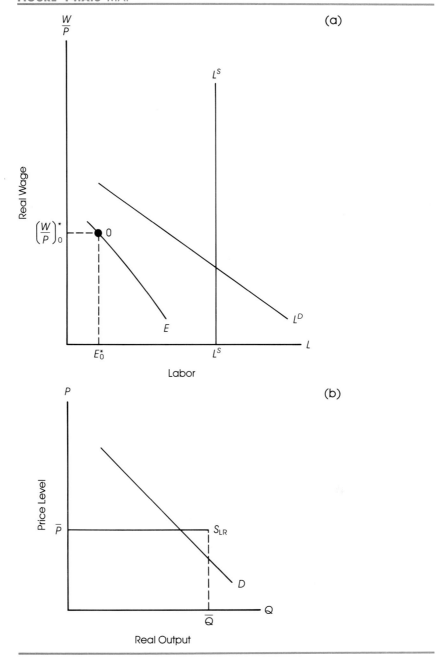

A market anti-inflation plan (MAP) makes any point on the E curve in (a) a potential equilibrium. The equilibrium is determined by the D–S intersection in (b).

14.A.8(a). Actual employment can never quite reach this maximum (unemployment can never quite reach 0), so that $\overline{Q}$ is an upper bound on equilibrium real output.

What then determines the long-run output Q of the economy? The answer is the position of the aggregate demand curve. As always, the intersection of the aggregate demand curve and the long-run aggregate supply curve determines the long-run point (Q, P) of the economy. But instead of the situation shown in Figure 3.2 (page 122), where the S_{LR} curve is vertical, Figure 14.A.8(b) illustrates the case under MAP, where the S_{LR} curve is horizontal until it terminates at $\overline{Q}$. Without MAP, the S_{LR} curve is vertical, so that in the long run, the aggregate demand curve has no effect on Q, but only determines P. With MAP, and the resulting horizontal S_{LR} curve, the reverse is true. The position of the aggregate demand curve has no effect on P—which is fixed by MAP—but does determine Q.

To which point in Figure 14.A.8(a) does the economy go in long-run equilibrium? To the point E_1^* that, in the production function, yields the Q_1^* (the intersection of the aggregate demand curve and the horizontal S_{LR} curve). Point E_1^* also indicates the equilibrium real wage $(W/P)_1^*$.

With MAP holding the inflation constant at 0, why not raise the level of nominal demand, and thereby shift the aggregate demand curve upward in Figure 14.A.8(b), until the unemployment rate is driven down close to 0? The answer requires a full analysis of the MAP economy. A few brief comments will suffice here.

First, an economy with a very high V and a very low U might be characterized by low effort from its work force. Although many persons work hard to win a promotion or out of commitment to the work ethic, others work only out of fear of discharge. But if V is high and U is low, employers are reluctant to discharge workers and workers know that they can easily obtain another job. Thus, some workers may relax their efforts, and productivity may be reduced.

Second, suppose that the aggregate demand curve is shifted so far to the right that the intersection of the demand curve and the horizontal supply curve occurs at a Q greater than $\overline{Q}$. In this case, product markets are characterized by a general condition of *shortage*, or *excess demand*. Buyers are not able to obtain as much as they want of various products at the going price; some frustrations and inefficiency therefore result. In the L^D–L^S diagram, the real wage W/P is forced down as actual employment E moves down the E curve toward the limit of the vertical L^S. If the L^S curve remains vertical as the real wage falls drastically, then the W/P is forced down toward 0.

These observations suggest that the level of nominal demand should be set under MAP to achieve a moderately low, not an extremely low, unemployment rate. At this level of demand, work effort remains satisfactory, product market shortages do not generally occur, and the real wage is not forced down significantly.

It should be noted that little analysis of "the MAP economy" has been done by economists. Further research is needed to make progress on the properties of a MAP economy.

SOLVING FOR EQUILIBRIUM EMPLOYMENT

In Appendix 14B, we will solve the quadratic equation to obtain equilibrium employment E^*. In the text (pages 579–580), we presented the solutions for two quadratic equations:

$$\left(\frac{3}{35}\right)(100 - E)(98 - E) = 3$$

$$E = 93$$

$$\left(\frac{3}{35}\right)(100 - E)(102 - E) = 3$$

$$E = 95$$

Once the solution is obtained, it is easy to confirm that it satisfies the equation:

$$\left(\frac{3}{35}\right)(100 - 93)(98 - 93) = 3$$

$$3 = 3$$

$$\left(\frac{3}{35}\right)(100 - 95)(102 - 95) = 3$$

$$3 = 3$$

Now we will show how to solve an equation of this form to obtain E. If the left side of either equation is multiplied out, it contains an E-squared term. Each equation is therefore a quadratic equation. Instead of solving these two equations, we will solve for the general case. We begin with the equilibrium condition equation (14.4):

(14.4) $\qquad n = x$

The general n curve equation, which describes how n varies with E, is equation (14.6):

(14.6) $n = m[i_w(L^S - E)][i_f(L^D - E)]$

Substituting equation (14.6) into equation (14.4) yields our general quadratic equation:

(14.B.1) $m[i_w(L^S - E)][i_f(L^D - E)] = x$

If m, i_w, L^S, i_f, L^D, and x are given, then this equation can be solved for E. We want to rearrange equation (14.B.1) into the standard form for a quadratic equation, where $E = X$:

(14.B.2) $AX^2 + BX + C = 0$

Once the equation is in this form, we can apply the standard quadratic formula for X:

(14.B.3) $X = \dfrac{-B \pm \sqrt{B^2 - 4AC}}{2A}$

Note that every quadratic equation has two *roots* (solutions). One root is obtained by using the *positive* square root; the other, by using the *negative* square root. We will see shortly that only the negative square root case is economically relevant.

To convert equation (14.B.1) into the form of equation (14.B.2), with $E = X$, we multiply out equation (14.B.1):

$$mi_w i_f(L^S L^D - L^S E - L^D E + E^2) = x$$
$$mi_w i_f(E^2) + [-mi_w i_f(L^S + L^D)]E + (mi_w i_f L^S L^D - x) = 0$$

We can now apply the quadratic formula (14.B.3) using the following designations:

$A = mi_w i_f$
$B = [-mi_w i_f(L^S + L^D)]$
$C = (mi_w i_f L^S L^D - x)$

Let's solve the first equation given at the beginning of the appendix. We have $m = 1$, $i_w = 3/7$, and $i_f = 1/5$, so that $mi_w i_f = 3/35$, $L^S = 100$, $L^D = 98$, and $x = 3$. Hence

$$A = \frac{3}{35}$$

$$B = \left(\frac{-3}{35}\right)(100 + 98) = \left(\frac{-3}{35}\right)(198) = \frac{-594}{35}$$

$$B^2 = \left(\frac{9}{1{,}225}\right)(39{,}204) = \frac{352{,}836}{1{,}225}$$

$$C = \left[\left(\frac{3}{35}\right)(100)(98)\right] - 3 = \left[\left(\frac{3}{35}\right)(9{,}800)\right] - 3$$

$$= \left(\frac{29{,}400}{35}\right) - \left(\frac{105}{35}\right) = 837$$

$$4AC = \left(\frac{12}{35}\right)(837) = \frac{10{,}044}{35} = \left(\frac{10{,}044}{35}\right)\left(\frac{35}{35}\right) = \frac{351{,}540}{1{,}225}$$

$$B^2 - 4AC = \frac{1{,}296}{1{,}225}$$

Substituting these values into equation (14.B.3) gives us

$$E = -\frac{(-594/35) \pm \sqrt{1{,}296/1{,}225}}{2(3/35)}$$

$$E = \frac{594/35 \pm 36/35}{6/35}$$

$$E = \quad 93 \text{ (using the } -)$$

$$E = 105 \text{ (using the } +)$$

Clearly, $E = 105$ is not possible economically, because E exceeds L^D (98) and L^S (100). Hence, $E = 93$ is the economically relevant solution.

Every quadratic equation has two roots (solutions). We can prove that, given the parameters chosen to yield Figure 14.1 (page 577), where an $n - x$ intersection occurs at a positive E, equation (14.B.1) has one and only one economically relevant root (one and only one root that is positive and less than both L^D and L^S). To yield the intersection at a positive E in Figure 14.1, parameters must be chosen such that:

(14.B.4) $mi_w i_f L^S L^D > x$

Why? In n curve equation (14.6), if $E = 0$, then $n = mi_w i_f L^S L^D$. Thus, $mi_w i_f L^S L^D$ is the height of the n curve at $E = 0$. As long as this height is greater than x, the downward-sloping n curve intersects the x line at a positive E. As long as the parameters are chosen to satisfy equation (14.B.4), there is one economically relevant root. It is the only such root because there is another root greater than L^D and L^S that satisfies equation (14.B.1).

CHAPTER

15

Topics in Accumulation and Growth I

Prerequisite: Chapter 10

This chapter extends the analysis begun in Chapter 10 of government deficits and debt and supply-side economics. We will begin with a discussion of government deficits and debt, and follow with a discussion of supply-side economics. Each topic is self-contained.

15.1 Government Deficits and Debt

Government deficits and debt have long been a concern of citizens. But in the 1980s, concern has risen in response to a rise in the federal government deficit and debt relative to GNP. What are the consequences of government deficits and debt, and what are the implications for policy?

SAVING, INVESTMENT, AND THE GOVERNMENT BUDGET

In Chapter 10, we focused on the impact of an increase in the Q_c deficit (with an offsetting monetary policy that keeps real output Q at the constant inflation level of output Q_c) on private investment I. We focused on the accounting identity (1.20):

(1.20) $I \equiv S + Su$

where I = private investment

S = private saving

Su = government surplus

We saw in Chapter 10 that an increase in the Q_c deficit shifts the *IS* curve to the right and that an offsetting monetary policy shifts the *LM* curve to the left to hold Q at Q_c, as shown in Figure 15.1. The result is a rise in the interest rate r and a decline in private investment I.

FIGURE 15.1 AN INCREASE IN THE Q_c DEFICIT RAISES THE INTEREST RATE

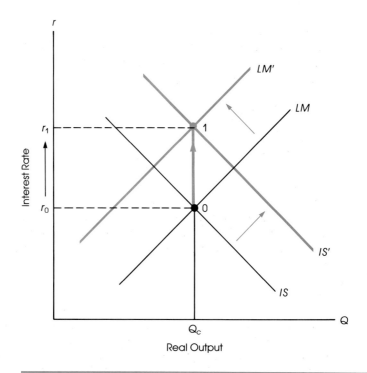

Initially, the economy is at point ($Q = Q_c$, $r = r_0$). A subsequent tax cut or transfer increase raises disposable income at Q_c. We will assume that this raises private consumption C and shifts the IS curve to the right to IS'. An offsetting monetary policy shifts the LM curve to LM', holding Q at Q_c. The interest rate rises from r_0 to r_1.

In the accounting identity (1.20), an increase in the Q_c deficit means a reduction in the government surplus Su. Suppose that the Q_c deficit increases by $100 billion due to either a tax cut of $100 billion or a transfer increase of $100 billion. Su then falls by $100 billion. The $100 billion increase in disposable income might raise consumption by $90 billion and private saving S by $10 billion. Thus, in equation (1.20), I decreases by $90 billion, exactly matching the increase in consumption of $90 billion.

In Chapter 10, we noted that a few economists reject this analysis. They argue that consumption is unaffected by the increase in disposable income and that the IS curve does not shift (contrary to Figure 15.1). In this example, when disposable income increases by $100 billion, private saving S also increases by $100 billion. Hence, in equation

(1.20), the $100 billion increase in S cancels the $100 billion reduction in Su, and I remains unchanged.

As we indicated in Chapter 10, most economists find this claim implausible. If we reviewed the empirical studies of consumption behavior, we would clearly see that virtually all studies find that consumption varies directly with disposable income, that the relationship is statistically significant, and that the long-run marginal propensity to consume disposable income is closer to 1 than to 0. We will therefore continue to assume, as we have throughout this text, that consumption varies directly with disposable income, so that a shift to an easy fiscal–tight monetary mix (as shown in Figure 15.1) raises consumption and reduces investment at Q_c.

Government Investment and the Deficit

Now let's consider another important accounting identity (for a closed economy) from Chapter 1, equation (1.29):

(1.29) $I_T \equiv S_T$

where I_T = total investment

S_T = total saving

Let's review the example of the $100 billion tax cut or transfer increase while keeping equation (1.29) in mind. A $100 billion tax cut or transfer increase reduces government saving S_G by $100 billion. If private saving S increases by $10 billion, then total saving and total investment decline by $90 billion. In this case, the decline in total investment I_T is the same as the decline in private investment I because we are holding government investment G_I constant.

Instead of a tax cut or transfer increase, let's consider an increase in government (public) investment G_I. For example, the government may increase its spending on the construction of highways, schools, or hospitals. Like factories, these facilities will yield productive services in the future. They are clearly part of the nation's capital stock. In contrast to tax cuts and transfers, which promote private consumption, G_I spending promotes public investment.

The increase in G_I, with taxes and other spending held constant, shifts the IS curve to the right. Once again, we assume that a tightening of monetary policy simultaneously shifts the LM curve to the left, so that Q remains at Q_c.

With Q and tax revenue T the same, disposable income is the same; we assume consumption is therefore the same. Thus, total investment must be the same in order to keep Q at Q_c. But this means that the rise in the interest rate must have caused a decline in private investment to match the increase in government investment.

Let's consider this example in light of our two accounting identities, equation (1.20) and equation (1.29). Suppose that the increase in G_I is $100 billion. In equation (1.20), private saving S is unchanged because disposable income is the same. The government surplus Su declines by $100 billion. Hence, private investment I declines by $100 billion, exactly matching the increase in G_I. In equation (1.29), private saving S is unchanged. Government saving S_G is also unchanged because G_I does not affect government saving. Hence, total saving and total investment remain unchanged.

Thus, when an increase in government investment G_I reduces the budget surplus Su, private investment declines but total investment remains unchanged. There is a reallocation of investment from the private to the public sector, with the total remaining the same.

▶ A reduction in the budget surplus or an increase in the budget deficit reduces private investment I; it does not necessarily reduce total investment I_T. If the budget surplus is reduced by an increase in public investment, so that government saving remains the same, then total investment remains constant.

It is important to ask whether a reduction in the government surplus Su (equivalently, an increase in the government deficit Df) is due to an increase in G_I. If so, then while it reduces private investment I, it does not reduce total investment I_T.

A reduction in total investment makes the capital stock and output smaller in the future than it otherwise would be. In this sense, the reduction in total investment imposes a burden on the future citizenry. A reduction in government saving S_G, which is almost certain to reduce total saving and total investment, therefore imposes a burden on the future population.

A reduction in the government surplus Su, unless it is due to an increase in government investment G_I, also reduces government saving S_G and also imposes a burden on the future citizenry. Suppose that initially $Su = 0$. It is then reduced, and the resulting deficit is financed by issuing government debt. The debt is purchased by the public, which then holds the bonds. The phrase "burden of the debt" can be interpreted to mean the lower future capital stock and output that follows from the reduction in total saving and investment.

It might be better, however, to avoid using the phrase "burden of the debt" for the following reason. Suppose that initially $Su = 0$ but is subsequently reduced by an increase in government investment G_I. The deficit must again be financed by issuing government debt. And once again, the public purchases and holds government bonds. But there is no reduction in the future capital stock; the private sector capital stock becomes smaller, while the public sector capital stock becomes larger. Thus, the existence of government debt per se does not mean that the future capital stock has been reduced more than it otherwise would be. A burden has not necessarily been imposed on the future citizenry.

THE OPTIMAL DEFICIT AND DEBT

Suppose that a simple economy is born today. It consists of households, firms, and government. Households consume and save but perform no real investment. Firms and government perform real investment but we will make the simplifying assumption that they do not save or consume. Total saving, then, equals household saving, and total investment is the sum of firm and government investment. To finance investment, firms and government each must borrow by issuing debt (here, to simplify, we will ignore the option of issuing money in place of debt). Each runs a deficit. Households lend, buy the firm and government debt, and run a surplus.

This emergence of deficits and debt may be socially optimal. When households choose to save, they are revealing that they are willing to sacrifice some present consumption for future consumption. Households, in our simple economy, cannot physically transform resources into future output; they do not perform real investment. But firms and government do. Through deficits and debt, firms and government act as agents of households, transforming resources into future output.

Would it be socially optimal for only firms to invest, issue debt, and run deficits, while the government performs no investment, issues no debt, and always balances its budget? Suppose that if all investment occurred in firms, then the *marginal rate of return mrr* on the last $1,000 of real investment is 5%. But also suppose that government can undertake a $1,000 investment project that yields a return of 15%. Then a reallocation of $1,000 of investment from firms to government would raise the return by 10%.

It would therefore be inefficient (not socially optimal) for all investment to be conducted by firms. In fact, investment should be reallocated until the marginal rate of return is the same on private and public investment. In general it is not socially optimal for government to avoid all debt and never run a deficit, just as it is not optimal for firms to avoid all debt and never run a deficit. Thus:

▶ A balanced budget rule is not socially optimal in this simple economy. It would prevent the government from performing investment that would raise the well-being of the representative person.

The deficits and debt in this simple economy are socially desirable because the accumulation of debt is matched by the accumulation of real capital that yields a return at least as great as the interest rate on the debt. When debt is issued to purchase productive real assets, the *net worth* (assets minus liabilities) of the government is not reduced.

Suppose that an accountant of a private firm reports only one side of a balance sheet (liabilities) showing debt outstanding, but does not report the other side of the balance sheet (assets). Obviously, the accountant is presenting an incomplete and misleading picture of the financial health of the firm. A firm that might be quite healthy may appear to be quite sick. The same is true for the government.

In our simple economy, we have assumed that government and firms do not save. Recall that government saving is defined as government net income $T - R$ minus government consumption G_C:

(1.25) $$S_G \equiv T - R - G_C$$

Recall further that the government surplus Su is given by

$$Su \equiv T - R - G_C - G_I$$

But from equation (1.25), we know that $T - R - G_C$ can be replaced by S_G, so that

(1.26) $$Su \equiv S_G - G_I$$

If $S_G = 0$, then equation (1.26) becomes

(15.1) $$Su = -G_I$$

Thus, if government saving $S_G = 0$, then the government deficit equals government investment G_I.

It can be argued that the government should remain neutral concerning the choice between present and future consumption, leaving this choice to households. Firms and government, as agents of households, should implement household preferences via real investment. But government should set its saving $S_G = 0$, so that total saving S_T equals private saving S and thereby reflects the preferences of households.

▶ If *government neutrality* is desired, then the proper rule for government is not a balanced budget rule — a *zero surplus rule* ($Su = 0$) — but a *zero saving rule* ($S_G = 0$), which prescribes a government deficit equal to government investment.

But how should the proper level of government investment be determined? If efficiency is the only criterion, then government should undertake all investment projects that are socially profitable at the current interest rate. *Social profitability* means that measured benefits — even if they are not fully collected as revenues — exceed the cost of the project. This assures that the social marginal rate of return on government and private investment are equal to one another. This is the condition for an efficient allocation of investment. In the absence of a tax on capital income, it also assures intertemporal efficiency; the *marginal social discount rate msdr* equals the social marginal rate of return *mrr* on real investment. To implement this policy, a separate capital budget is utilized. Government investment projects are financed by borrowing, so that deficit financing of government investment is the rule.

Some Objections

Although this simple economy provides insight, it is time to consider objections to adopting the rule that government saving $S_G = 0$:

1. The line between government investment G_I and government consumption G_C is not always easy to draw. There is no question that construction of physical assets, such as roads and bridges, are components of G_I. But should acquisition of military weapons be treated as G_I? Further, we emphasized in Chapter 10 that capital should be defined broadly to include human and knowledge capital as well as physical capital. Shouldn't government expenditure on research and development, education, training, and perhaps even health be counted as G_I? Clearly, drawing the line between G_I and G_C is not easy.

   We have pointed out that a competent accountant should list assets as well as liabilities in presenting a balance sheet for any firm, including the government. But which assets just mentioned should be included? Also, the government cannot sell many of its assets to finance either principal or interest payments on its debt. Thus, potential and actual bondholders may grow nervous if the debt to GNP ratio rises, even if the rise is matched by a rise in the assets to GNP ratio.

2. Politicians would have an incentive to define favorite spending projects as G_I, rather than G_C because such projects could be financed by borrowing instead of by taxation. Political strength, not economic merit, may govern this process.

3. Each G_I project should, in principle, be subject to the criterion of social profitability, or *cost–benefit analysis*, and should not be undertaken if it fails this test. In practice, however, this standard might not prove an effective check on the expansion of the capital budget. A public investment project often does not collect revenue as great as the social benefit of the project. For example, a highly beneficial

road may collect little or no revenue from users. Thus, the benefit must be estimated. This uncertainty may create an opening for politicians to justify an excessive volume of such projects.

4. It seems likely that G_I would increase its share of total government spending at the expense of G_C and R. It is possible, then, that permitting G_I to be financed by borrowing, while still requiring that G_C and R be financed by taxation, would reduce the net contribution of government to efficiency and equity.

5. It can be argued that the only practical deterrent to an overexpansion of government spending — whether it be G_I, G_C, or R — is the requirement that politicians be compelled to vote for a matching increase in taxes. According to this view, even if a hypothetical, benevolent social planner should be permitted to finance G_I by borrowing, Congress and the President should not be permitted to do so. Top priority must be assigned to compelling Congress and the President to weigh cost against benefit before raising any kind of spending.

These five objections to the zero saving rule are practical. We will now consider a more fundamental objection. It is possible to reject the goal of government neutrality. Government should perhaps not simply accept private sector saving but should seek to augment it. For example, in Chapter 10 we saw that capital accumulation is a central mechanism for reducing poverty and preventing a deterioration in our standard of living relative to other countries.

▶ A citizen may judge that private sector saving, which is the result of each individual's pursuit of self-interest, is too low to reduce poverty rapidly or to maintain our relative standard of living.

If a citizen's goal for government saving is positive (not 0), then the government deficit should be less than government investment. If a citizen's goal for government saving is sufficiently positive (greater than government investment), then even the government surplus should be positive because the government surplus Su equals government saving S_G minus government investment G_I.

▶ Thus, despite the insight from the simple economy governed by a benevolent social planner, it is possible to argue that a balanced budget rule is nevertheless a desirable constraint to impose on Congress and the President.

▶ Our analysis has shown, however, that deciding the optimal level of deficits and debt is more complex than most people realize.

When a government runs a deficit, it can finance the difference in two ways: by borrowing from the public or by printing money. Historically, printing money has often been the choice. Consequently, deficits have often led to monetary expansion. With monetary expansion reinforcing the fiscal expansion, the result has often been inflation.

In the United States, however, there is an important institutional separation of function between the Treasury and the Federal Reserve. When the government runs a deficit of $100 billion, the Treasury must borrow $100 billion; it is not empowered to cover the deficit by printing money. Hence, it must sell $100 billion worth of bonds.

Although the $100 billion worth of bonds may be sold to the public, this does not mean that the debt held by the public necessarily rises by $100 billion. How much the debt rises depends on the behavior of the Federal Reserve. If the Fed simultaneously buys $100 billion worth of bonds from the public (via open-market operations), then the debt held by the public remains unchanged. Instead, *high-powered money H* increases by $100 billion. In Chapter 13 we explain that bond sellers would deposit most of the Fed checks for $100 billion in their bank accounts. *Bank reserves* then would increase by almost $100 billion. These reserves enable banks to expand loans, further raising the money supply. If the Fed buys only $30 billion worth of bonds, then the debt held by the public increases by $70 billion.

Thus, even though the Treasury may directly sell all its bonds to the public, a share of the bonds may be bought indirectly by the Fed. That share results in an equal increase in high-powered money. The sum of the increase in the debt held by the public ΔB and the increase in high-powered money ΔH must equal the deficit Df:

(15.2) $$Df = \Delta B + \Delta H$$

where Df = deficit

B = debt held by the public (excluding the Fed)

H = high-powered money

If for example, Df = $100 billion, ΔB = $70 billion, and ΔH = $30 billion, then 70% of the deficit is *debt-financed* and 30% is *money-financed*. The Fed *monetizes* 30% of the deficit.

If we viewed the Treasury and the Fed together as "the government," then we could say that the deficit is financed either by issuing debt or high-powered money to the public. The institutional separation of function, however, is very important. It is the Fed's responsibility to decide how the deficit will be divided between debt growth and high-powered money growth. In recent years, the Fed has refused to monetize more than a small fraction of the large deficit. Thus, a very large share of the deficit has gone to increase the debt held by the public. This behavior by the Fed suggests that it is willing—and able—to try to offset fiscal policy to keep the economy near the constant inflation level of output Q_c. Thus, a fiscal expansion is more likely to result in an offsetting monetary contraction than in a reinforcing monetary expansion.

If the Fed implements an offsetting monetary policy, then the historical association between deficits and inflation will be broken. This policy will keep Q near Q_c, and, as we explained in our IS–LM analysis, a rise in the deficit at Q_c will reduce investment but will not increase inflation. The Fed can therefore determine whether the increase in the Q_c deficit raises inflation.

We should note, however, that to implement an offsetting policy, the Fed must be willing to permit the interest rate to rise, as shown in Figure 15.1. If the Fed proves unwilling to permit a sufficient rise in the interest rate, then the shift right of the IS curve due to an increase in the Q_c deficit is not fully offset by a shift left of the LM curve. Thus, Q rises above Q_c, and a rise in inflation results.

▶ A large increase in the Q_c deficit may, therefore, make it more difficult politically for the Fed to implement a fully offsetting monetary policy that avoids a rise in inflation.

THE U.S. DEFICIT AND DEBT

As is evident in Figure 15.2, after averaging 1–2% of GNP since 1950, the federal deficit climbed to 5% of GNP in the first half of the 1980s. Part of this climb was due to a severe recession in 1982. But projections for the second half of the 1980s suggest that, at current expenditure and tax rates, the deficit may remain at 5% of GNP even if there is no recession and the economy is at its normal unemployment rate. It is the projected jump in the Q_c deficit (not merely in the actual deficit) from 2% to 5% of GNP that seriously concerns many economists and citizens.

At the outset, we should emphasize that any deficit projection is subject to significant uncertainty. This uncertainty has sometimes been emphasized by those who claim that concern about the deficit is premature. This inference is not warranted. The projected deficit can prove to be too low as well as too high.

Figure 15.3 shows the ratio of federal debt held by the public and the Federal Reserve to GNP since 1950. World War II financing required a very sharp rise in this ratio. But since the end of the war and until the late 1970s, the ratio declined (from over 80% in 1950 to less than 30% in the late 1970s). Beginning in the late 1970s, however, the ratio has risen

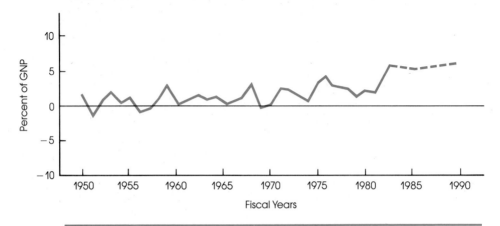

FIGURE 15.2 FEDERAL DEFICITS

The federal deficit as a percentage of GNP rose significantly in the 1980s. In the 1950s and 1960s, the deficit averaged 1% of GNP; in the 1970s, 2% of GNP; in the 1980s, 5% of GNP.

Sources: Office of Management and Budget; U.S. Department of Commerce, Bureau of Economic Analysis; Congressional Budget Office, *The Economic Outlook* (February 1984), p. 60.

TABLE 15.1

BUDGET OUTLAYS AND RECEIPTS AS PERCENT OF GNP
(FISCAL YEARS 1960, 1970, AND 1980–1985)*

Item	1960	1970	1980	1981	1982	1983	1984	1985
Total outlays	18.5	20.2	22.4	22.8	23.8	24.7	23.1	24.0
National defense	9.7	8.4	5.2	5.5	6.1	6.5	6.2	6.4
Net interest	1.4	1.5	2.0	2.4	2.8	2.8	3.0	3.3
Other	7.5	10.3	15.1	15.0	15.0	15.4	13.9	14.3
Non-OASDHI	5.1	6.5	9.3	8.8	8.4	8.4	—	—
OASDHI	2.3	3.8	5.8	6.2	6.6	6.9	—	—
Social Security	2.3	3.1	4.6	4.8	5.1	5.3	—	—
Medicare	0	0.6	1.2	1.4	1.5	1.6	—	—
Total receipts	18.6	19.9	20.1	20.8	20.2	18.6	18.0	18.6
OASDHI	2.1	3.9	5.3	5.6	5.8	5.7	—	—
Other	16.4	16.0	14.8	15.2	14.4	12.9	—	—
Deficit	−0.1	0.3	2.3	2.0	3.6	6.1	5.0	5.4

Sources: *Economic Report of the President 1984*, Table 1–1 for 1960–1983 data; and Congressional Budget Office, *The Economic and Budget Outlook* (February 1986) for 1984–1985 data.
* Percent of GNP in each fiscal year.

FIGURE 15.3 PUBLICLY HELD FEDERAL DEBT

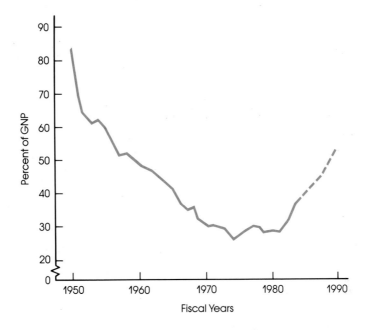

Publicly held federal debt as a percentage of GNP declined steadily from the end of World War II to the mid-1970s, held constant at 30% in the late 1970s, and then rose significantly in the 1980s, exceeding 40% by 1985 (with 50% projected for 1990).

SOURCES: Office of Management and Budget; U.S. Department of Commerce, Bureau of Economic Analysis; Congressional Budget Office, *The Economic Outlook* (February 1984), p. 60.

to roughly 40% in 1985 and is projected to reach almost 50% by the end of the decade.

Table 15.1 shows how the components of the federal budget changed from 1980 to 1983. Outlays (expenditures) rose from 22.4% to 24.7% of GNP, while receipts fell from 20.1% of GNP to 18.6% of GNP. Hence, the deficit rose from 2.3% to 6.1% of GNP. In 1983, roughly 25% of all outlays were financed by borrowing.

Why did outlays rise by 2.3% and receipts decline by 1.5% from 1980 to 1983? As we see in Table 15.1, national defense rose by more than 1%, net interest by nearly 1%, and Social Security and Medicare (OASDHI) by 1%. This more than 3% increase was partly offset by a 1% decline in non-OASDHI domestic spending. The main cause of the 1.5% decline in receipts was the tax cut of 1981.

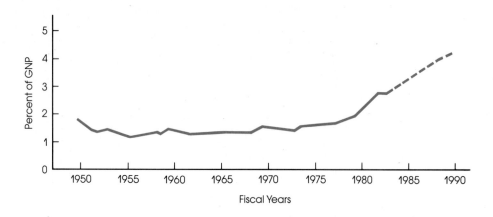

FIGURE 15.4 FEDERAL NET INTEREST PAYMENTS

Federal net interest payments as a percentage of GNP stayed constant at 1.5% from the 1950s to the late 1970s, rose above 2% at the end of the 1970s, and rose above 3% by the mid-1980s (with over 4% projected for 1990).
SOURCES: Office of Management and Budget; U.S. Department of Commerce, Bureau of Economic Analysis; Congressional Budget Office, *The Economic Outlook* (February 1984), p. 64.

The Congressional Budget Office (CBO) projects that with normal economic growth for the rest of the decade, under current expenditure and tax rates, outlays will stay near 24% of GNP and that receipts will stay near 19% of GNP, so that the deficit will remain close to 5% of GNP. As shown in Figure 15.4, the CBO projects net interest payments on the debt to rise from the current 2% to 4% of GNP by 1990.

Note that if the interest–GNP ratio doubles from 2% to 4%, while the outlay–GNP ratio remains at 24%, then interest on the debt rises from 8% to 16% of federal spending. Thus, the projected deficits imply a rising debt–GNP ratio and a rising interest–GNP ratio. Clearly, these ratios must not be permitted to rise indefinitely.

A Critique of the Conventional View

Some economists have asserted that conventional measures and interpretations of the U.S. deficit and debt are misleading. A recent study by Robert Eisner and Paul Pieper* presents this view. Let's consider several points they make.

First, the conventional measure of debt in the debt–GNP ratio is the

---

* Robert Eisner and Paul Pieper, "A New View of Federal Debt and Budget Deficits," *American Economic Review* 74 (1984): 11–29.

par value of gross debt—the book value of the gross financial liabilities of the federal government. Eisner and Pieper estimate that the *market value of gross debt* was only 93% of the par value in 1980. More importantly, the federal government possesses financial assets (such as its gold stock) as well as financial liabilities. *Net debt* equals financial liabilities *(gross debt)* minus financial assets. Eisner and Pieper estimate that the market value of net debt was roughly 50% of the market value of gross debt in 1980.

Second, the federal government possesses tangible assets, such as structures, equipment, and land. Eisner and Pieper estimate that if tangible assets and financial assets are added, total assets would actually exceed total liabilities of the federal government. In other words, the federal government, despite its debt, has a positive *net worth* (assets minus liabilities):

> Looking at what would for a private business be the bottom line, the net worth figures tell a different story, although a story that would hardly be unfamiliar to any successful large corporation. For all the while that gross Treasury debt, or even the difference between total liabilities and total financial assets which we have been calling net debt, was growing, so was net worth. . . . Our federal government, like many individuals and business that borrowed heavily in an inflationary period, came out pretty well with its investments in tangible assets—and in gold.*

We discussed this point in the preceding section, where the deficit and debt resulted only from the financing of socially optimal government investment (accumulation of real capital assets).

Third, Eisner and Pieper claim that in an economy with inflation, the conventionally measured deficit overstates the properly measured deficit. In fact, in many years, deficits become surpluses if they are properly measured. Suppose that expenditures exceed revenues by $100 billion in a given year, so that the government issues $100 billion of new debt. However, during that year, also assume that the real (inflation-adjusted) value of previously issued debt declines by $120 billion due to inflation. (For the moment, we will assume that assets are 0 and net debt equals gross debt.) Outstanding real debt is then $20 billion less at the end of the year. Eisner and Pieper would argue that there is a real surplus of $20 billion, even though, by the conventional measure, a deficit of $100 billion is reported:

> A proper measure of the government's current surplus is the reduction in real value of the government's net debt . . . or the amount of additional expenditures that can be made while keeping net debt intact.†

---

* Eisner and Pieper, "A New View of Federal Debt," 14–15.
† Eisner and Pieper, "A New View of Federal Debt," 16.

In this example, *real net debt* declines by $20 billion. An additional expenditure of $20 billion could be made (the conventional deficit could be raised to $120 billion), while keeping net debt constant.

Inflation reduces the real value of debt, but it also may reduce the value of government assets. Both sides of the balance sheet must be considered to obtain the annual change in real net debt. Eisner and Pieper calculate that inflation reduces the real value of net debt for the U.S. government. Measuring the real surplus (deficit) in this way, they estimate that in many post-war years, the conventional deficit masked a real surplus. In 1980, for example, the officially reported deficit was $61 billion, but Eisner and Pieper estimate a real surplus of $7 billion for that year.

Let's reconsider our earlier analysis and conclusions in light of this claim about mismeasurement. In Chapter 10, we concluded that an increase in the Q_c deficit (or a reduction in the Q_c surplus) reduces private investment at Q_c. With Q held at Q_c, the inflation rate stays constant as the economy shifts to an easier fiscal–tighter monetary mix. The reduction in the real value of net debt due to inflation is unaltered because the inflation rate stays constant. When the tax rate is cut or government spending is raised, the conventional deficit at Q_c might rise (for example, from $100 billion to $150 billion), while the properly measured real surplus might fall (from $50 billion to $0). However, the conclusion still holds:

▶ An increase in the conventionally measured Q_c deficit raises the real interest rate and reduces private investment at Q_c.

Next let's consider our closed economy estimate, using accounting identity (1.21):

(1.21)
$$\frac{I}{Q} \equiv \frac{S}{Q} + \frac{Su}{Q}$$

The conventional measure is then

$4\% = 7\% + (-3\%)$ (currently projected)
$7\% = 7\% +\ \ 0\%$ (if deficit is ended)

Here, the government (federal, state, and local) deficit is measured conventionally. Suppose that if the deficit is properly measured, then the current projection is a 1% deficit (Eisner and Pieper estimated a gap of 2% for 1980). But if properly measured Su/Q is 2% larger (-1% instead of -3%), then properly measured S/Q is 2% smaller (5% instead of 7%). Why?

If inflation reduces the real value of net debt held by the public, then the private sector suffers a capital loss. Capital losses and gains are excluded from the conventional (national income accounting) measure of income and, hence, from saving. But if the capital gain of the government is to be counted, the capital loss of the private sector must also be counted, which would reduce private income and saving. The two adjustments exactly cancel one another, and the proper measure preserves accounting identity (1.21):

(1.21)
$$\frac{I}{Q} \equiv \frac{S}{Q} + \frac{Su}{Q}$$

$4\% = 5\% + (-1\%)$ (currently projected)

$7\% = 5\% + (+2\%)$ (if conventional deficit is ended)

Thus, there is no change in our previous estimate for a closed economy. Eliminating the conventionally measured projected deficit at Q_c almost doubles the net (private) investment rate at Q_c—from 4% to 7%.

THE CONSTITUTIONAL APPROACH TO THE DEFICIT PROBLEM

Can Congress and the President keep deficits under control? Analysts disagree. Some observers believe that the answer is yes. They argue that deficits have been successfully controlled until very recently. While the United States has run a deficit (conventionally measured) in most years, the deficit has been sufficiently small that the debt–GNP ratio declined over the post-World War II period until the late 1970s. The recent rise in the deficit and in the debt–GNP ratio are regarded as temporary aberrations resulting from particular mistakes that Congress and the President will prove able to correct. Other observers are more pessimistic. They concede that the debt–GNP ratio only began rising recently, but they fear that the rise is not a temporary aberration and that it represents a permanent trend. In Chapter 10, we described the Balanced Budget and Emergency Deficit Control Act of 1985. Optimists cite this statute as evidence that Congress and the President are controlling the deficit. Pessimists argue that the statute will prove ineffective.

Let us sketch one argument that supports the pessimistic view. Both liberal and conservative politicians believe that it is politically profitable to make deficit reduction a second priority. Liberals believe that protecting domestic spending must be given top priority; conservatives believe that cutting tax rates and increasing military spending must be given top priority. If liberals possessed a clear Congressional majority as well as the Presidency, they would attempt to control the deficit without sacrificing domestic spending. Similarly, if conservatives possessed a clear Congressional majority as well as the Presidency, they would attempt to control the deficit without sacrificing tax cuts and military spending.

The problem results from the current political stalemate between the liberals and the conservatives — a stalemate that may persist. Each side protects its first priority at the expense of its second — deficit reduction. But since the public overwhelmingly supports deficit reduction, isn't it politically profitable for liberals or conservatives to make deficit reduction their first priority? Not necessarily.

Consider two liberals competing in a Democratic primary election. Both promise to reduce the deficit. The first insists that it can and should be done by raising taxes on the affluent and cutting military spending — not by cutting domestic spending. The second is willing to cut domestic spending to reduce the deficit if that should be necessary. Given such a scenario, liberal voters may elect the first candidate.

Now consider two conservatives competing in a Republican primary election. Both promise to reduce the deficit. The first insists that it can and should be done by cutting domestic spending — not by raising taxes or cutting military spending. The second is willing to raise taxes and cut military spending to reduce the deficit. Given this scenario, conservative voters may elect the first candidate.

Every politician, liberal or conservative, can genuinely oppose the large deficit and propose a package that reduces it. A sincere case can always be made that the other side is preventing the solution. In the meantime, the stalemate leaves the problem unsolved. These and other pessimistic arguments lead us toward a constitutional approach to the problem. This strategy calls for an amendment to the U.S. Constitution that is designed to compel Congress and the President to bring down the deficit.

The effort to enact a constitutional amendment has intensified in recent years. As we shall see, some advocates of the constitutional approach propose a limit on spending or tax revenue as a complement to — or a substitute for — a requirement that the budget be balanced. By 1983, over 30 state legislatures had passed a resolution calling for a constitutional convention to enact such an amendment. An amendment obtained the necessary two-thirds vote in the Senate, but fell short of a two-thirds vote in the House. If an amendment receives a two-thirds vote in both houses of Congress, then it must be ratified by 38 states.

It is convenient to begin our analysis by presenting the amendment (S.J. Res. 58, proposed on August 4, 1982) that obtained a two-thirds vote in the U.S. Senate:

> *Section 1.* Prior to each fiscal year, the Congress shall adopt a statement of receipts and outlays for that year in which total outlays are no greater than total receipts. The Congress may amend such statement provided revised outlays are no greater than revised receipts. Whenever three-fifths of the whole num-

ber of both Houses shall deem it necessary, Congress in such statement may provide for a specific excess of outlays over receipts by a vote directed solely on that subject. The Congress and the President shall, pursuant to legislation or through exercise of their powers under the first and second articles, ensure that actual outlays do not exceed the outlays set forth in such statement.

Section 2.   Total receipts for any fiscal year set forth in the statement adopted pursuant to this article shall not increase by a rate greater than the rate of increase in national income in the year or years ending not less than six months nor more than twelve months before such fiscal year, unless a majority of the whole number of both houses shall have passed a bill directed solely to approving specific additional receipts and such a bill has become law.

Section 3.   The Congress may waive the provisions of this article for any fiscal year in which a declaration of war is in effect.

Section 4.   Total receipts shall include all receipts of the United States except those derived from borrowing and total outlays shall include all outlays of the United States except those for repayment of debt principal.

Section 5.   The Congress shall enforce and implement this article by appropriate legislation.

Section 6.   On and after the date this article takes effect, the amount of Federal public debt limit as of such date shall become permanent and there shall be no increase in such amount unless three-fifths of the whole number of both Houses of Congress shall have passed a bill approving such increase and such a bill has become law.

Section 7.   This article shall take effect for the second fiscal year beginning after its ratification.

Several features of this amendment warrant attention:

The Planned Budget Versus the Actual Budget

The amendment requires that the planned budget be balanced. Tax and expenditure rates must be set so that revenues and expenditures are forecast to balance in the coming fiscal year.

Suppose that the forecast assumes that the economy will remain at a normal unemployment rate, but that a recession occurs instead. The actual budget automatically moves into deficit. Under Section 1 of the amendment, Congress is not required to act to correct a deficit due to an automatic drop in tax revenue in response to recession. Thus, Section 1 of the amendment does *not* require Congress to raise taxes or to cut spending immediately in an attempt to keep the actual budget balanced in the midst of a recession.

This feature of Section 1 is very important. Why? Recall our analysis in Part 1. In our Chapter 1 model, an increase in the tax rate t or a decrease in government transfers R reduces disposable income and consumption (consumer) demand C. Hence, an increase in taxes or a cut in government spending (R or G) reduces total demand and equilibrium output, thereby worsening the recession. In our Chapter 2 *IS–LM* analysis, an increase in taxes or a cut in government spending is a fiscal contraction that shifts the *IS* curve to the left, reducing equilibrium output and worsening the recession.

▶ Most economists strongly oppose an amendment that requires Congress to raise taxes or to cut spending immediately in the midst of a recession, because either action would make the recession worse.

We should note, however, that Section 1 requires Congress to prevent an automatic rise in outlays in response to a recession. Actual outlays must not exceed statement outlays. But we have seen that transfers increase automatically during a recession. Presumably, Congress would permit such transfers as unemployment compensation to increase but would cut other expenditures immediately to prevent total outlays from increasing. Transfers would continue to help the unemployed. But government expenditure would no longer act as an automatic stabilizer.

The amendment also prevents Congress from cutting tax rates or raising expenditure rates in the midst of a recession to combat the recession, because this might result in a Q_c deficit as well as an actual deficit. Thus, the amendment rules out active, countercyclical fiscal policy, although it preserves the role of the tax system as an automatic stabilizer.

The amendment does not specify the assumption concerning the unemployment rate that should be made in the forecast. A specific set of tax and expenditure rates might result in a balanced budget if a 5% unemployment rate is assumed but might result in a large deficit if a 9% unemployment rate is assumed. The following provision could be included:

> The estimate of receipts and outlays should assume that the unemployment rate will equal the average unemployment rate for the preceding decade.

Such a provision accomplishes two things. First, it reduces the vagueness concerning the basis for the estimates of planned revenues and expenditures and prevents possible abuse from the assumption of an unrealistically low unemployment rate each year. Second, it addresses the following problem. Suppose that at the time the statement is adopted the economy is in a deep recession — one that is forecast to persist through the coming fiscal year. A realistic forecast might assume a high unemployment rate. It would therefore require higher tax rates or lower expenditure rates than if a normal unemployment rate were assumed to achieve a planned balance. But this would tighten fiscal policy in the midst of a deep recession. Many economists view such a tightening as undesirable.

The Permanent Public Debt Ceiling

Section 6 was not part of the original amendment but was adopted during debate. Its intent is to ensure that the actual budget is always balanced by preventing new borrowing. It therefore goes beyond Section 1, which requires only that the planned budget be balanced.

Contrary to Section 1, Section 6 does not permit an actual deficit in recession, because any actual deficit requires an increase in the public debt. The inclusion of Section 6 therefore disturbs many economists. It requires immediate elimination of a deficit in the midst of a recession; hence, it compels action that reduces aggregate demand and makes the recession worse.

We should note that there is a statutory debt ceiling under current law. It can be raised, however, by a simple majority of those voting; such an increase in the debt ceiling has been a routine annual event. Under Section 6, 60% of the membership of both houses — instead of 50% of those voting — must vote for an increase in the debt ceiling. It is therefore much more likely that the debt ceiling would prove to be fixed, even in recession.

The Limit on the Government Spending – GNP Ratio

Section 2 limits the growth rate of planned receipts to the recent growth rate of national income. Since planned receipts must equal planned outlays and actual outlays must equal planned outlays, the amendment limits the government spending – GNP (national income) ratio. The ratio can be raised by a majority of the members of both houses.

The merit of limiting the government spending – GNP ratio can be judged separately from the merit of requiring a planned balanced budget. It would be possible to omit Section 2 from a balanced budget amendment.

Proponents of the spending limit are concerned that without Section 2, the budget would be balanced by raising taxes rather than by cutting spending, so that the government spending – GNP ratio would continue to rise. They point out that with a progressive tax system, tax revenue automatically rises faster than GNP, so that legislators need not go on record as having voted for a tax increase.

Section 2 addresses this bias of a progressive tax system. It permits an increase in the spending–GNP ratio, but it requires the majority of Congress to go on record as having voted for the tax (and spending) increase.

The Pros and Cons of the Constitutional Approach

Critics of the constitutional approach to the deficit problem have made the following points:

1. If the amendment proves to be enforceable, it will prevent active, countercyclical fiscal policy. If a severe recession or depression should occur, the government will probably be unable to fight it with active fiscal policy because a three-fifths vote of the whole Congress will be very difficult to obtain.

2. On the other hand, the amendment may well prove to be unenforceable. What happens if Congress violates it? Who is punished? What sanctions are imposed? The amendment does not address these issues.

3. The amendment will cause Congress to find ways around it that can cause further harm. Expenditures will be moved off of the budget and may be replaced by the regulation of private firms and households.

4. It is unwise to place a rule in the Constitution that may be temporarily desirable but that can cause unanticipated problems in the future.

5. Although the debt–GNP ratio should not be permitted to rise rapidly, this does not mean that a balanced budget is desirable. A balanced budget actually causes the debt–GNP ratio to decline. A moderate deficit–GNP ratio is consistent with a constant debt–GNP ratio. Our simple economy illustrates the point that the optimal deficit–GNP ratio may well be positive, not 0.

6. The spending limit might prevent a rise in the spending–GNP ratio, even if the public prefers an increase. Liberals fear a squeeze on social insurance and welfare spending. Conservatives fear a squeeze on military spending. Both may fear a squeeze on public investment.

7. Proper measurement of the deficit as the annual increase in the real (inflation-adjusted) net debt shows that the deficit is not out of control. In fact, until very recently, real surpluses generally occurred. Thus, no serious problem needs to be addressed by statute or by a constitutional amendment.

Advocates of the amendment might offer the following responses to each criticism:

1. Congress is very poor at conducting active, countercyclical fiscal policy anyway, so little is lost by preventing it. If countercyclical policy is to be conducted, it should be implemented through monetary policy. In a genuine depression, a three-fifths vote of the whole Congress may well be attainable. The role of the tax system as an automatic stabilizer will be preserved.

2. Although it may be difficult to enforce full compliance, deficits should be significantly smaller than they otherwise would be. Sanctions devised by Congress or the Supreme Court may have some effect. Moreover, neither legislators nor the President will be eager to violate the Constitution openly. The amendment will exert much more pressure on their behavior.

3. Congress will probably try to move some expenditures off of the budget or to substitute regulation for spending, but these options are limited. Harm from such behavior should be compared to the harm of widening deficits.

4. This rule belongs in the Constitution because it is permanently desirable. Without it, politicians will always have an incentive to give the deficit second priority.

5. It may be true that the optimal deficit – GNP ratio is not necessarily 0, but it is important to make politicians weigh cost against benefit when they enact spending programs. If they are permitted to finance an increase in expenditures with borrowing instead of with a tax increase, more waste will result. Even with a balanced budget, there will undoubtedly be slippage, but at least deficits will be smaller. Without a clear rule, deficits will get out of control. The only rule that can command public understanding and support is a balanced budget (a 0 deficit).

6. The spending limit can be raised if a majority of Congress votes for the increase. The point of the amendment is that it requires them to go on record. It is true that all government expenditures will feel more pressure, but this is desirable. Government should only spend if the benefit is judged to exceed the cost. Legislators should be compelled to confront the cost.

7. Even if proper measurement of the deficit and debt shows a different picture, this does not change the fact that requiring the planned budget (conventionally measured) to move from deficit to balance will raise capital accumulation (provided monetary policy adjusts to keep the economy at Q_c).

In conclusion, it is safe to say that the controversy over government budget deficits, debt, and the constitutional strategy will be with us for some time.

15.2 Supply-side Economics

Since Keynes's *General Theory* was published in 1936, macroeconomics has focused much attention to demand. It is not true, however, that macroeconomists have ignored supply. Many of the leading Keynesian economists of the past few decades have contributed to the development of *neoclassical growth theory*, which emphasizes the role of the supply of capital in the evolution of the economy over time.

Since the late 1970s, however, the term *supply-side economics* has come to stand for something more specific:

Advocates of SUPPLY-SIDE ECONOMICS assert the hypothesis that a *substantial* decrease in marginal tax rates would *significantly* increase the supplies of labor, capital, and full-employment output (constant inflation output Q_c).

By "substantial" and "significantly," most advocates mean that cutting marginal tax rates by perhaps one-third does not reduce tax revenue at Q_c, due to the resulting rise in Q_c and the reduction in tax evasion and avoidance.

▶ Advocates of supply-side economics unite on a particular policy: a substantial cut in marginal tax rates.

It is this specific hypothesis and policy, and certain related assertions — not the general importance of supply in economics — that has generated controversy. The 1981 personal income tax cut, which cut tax rates by 23% over three years, represents an attempt to implement supply-side economic policy. Whether a particular cut in marginal tax rates is desirable is, as we shall see, a complex question. Public finance economics has long examined the issue of optimal tax rates and has applied the criteria of efficiency and equity. We will consider this analysis shortly.

THE MARGINAL TAX RATE MTR AND THE AVERAGE TAX RATE ATR

The MARGINAL TAX RATE MTR is the tax rate that applies to an additional dollar of earnings:

$$(15.3) \quad \text{MTR} \equiv \frac{\Delta T}{\Delta E}$$

where T = tax

E = earnings

By contrast, the AVERAGE TAX RATE ATR is the ratio of the household's total tax to its total earnings:

$$(15.4) \qquad \text{ATR} \equiv \frac{T}{E}$$

To illustrate the difference between the MTR and the ATR, let's consider the following two alternative tax schedules relating a household's tax T to its earnings E:

$$(15.5) \qquad T = 0.2E$$

$$
\begin{aligned}
(15.6) \qquad & T = 0 & E < 10{,}000 \\
& T = 0.3(E - 10{,}000) & E > 10{,}000
\end{aligned}
$$

Under the *proportional tax schedule* given by equation (15.5), each household pays a tax T equal to 20% of its earnings. Under the *progressive tax schedule* given by equation (15.6), for any household with earnings less than $E = \$10{,}000$, $T = 0$; for any household with earnings greater than $E = \$10{,}000$, $T = 30\%$ of the E in excess of $\$10{,}000$. Figure 15.5(a) plots the two tax schedules, which cross at $\bar{E}$, where T is the same. Equating the two expressions for T gives us

$$
\begin{aligned}
0.2\bar{E} &= 0.3(\bar{E} - 10{,}000) \\
\bar{E} &= 30{,}000
\end{aligned}
$$

Suppose that we switch from the progressive to the proportional schedule and assume that each household holds its earnings E constant in response to the switch. (We will reconsider this assumption shortly.) Then any household with earnings less than $E = \$30{,}000$ pays more tax under the proportional schedule; any household with earnings more than $E = \$30{,}000$ pays less tax under the proportional schedule.

Figure 15.5(b) shows the MTR and the ATR under each schedule. For the proportional schedule, the MTR and the ATR are 20% at any E because

$$T = 0.2E$$

$$\text{MTR} \equiv \frac{\Delta T}{\Delta E} = 0.2$$

$$\text{ATR} \equiv \frac{T}{E} = 0.2$$

For the progressive schedule, where $E < \$10{,}000$, both the MTR and the ATR are clearly 0%. Where $E > \$10{,}000$, the following is true:

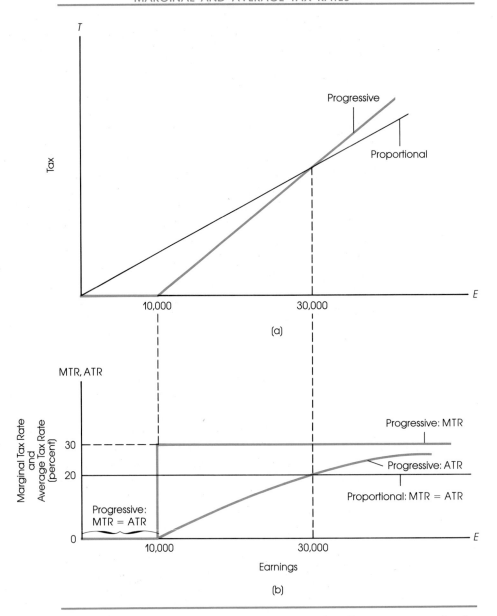

(a)

(b)

Under the proportional tax, MTR = ATR = 20% for all earnings E. Under the progressive tax, MTR = ATR = 0% for all earnings E less than \$10,000 and MTR = 30% for all earnings E greater than \$10,000. The ATR rises as E rises in the limit approaching 30%. At E = \$30,000, both taxes have the same ATR (20%); the proportional tax has a higher ATR for $E <$ \$30,000 and a smaller ATR for $E >$ \$30,000.

$$T = 0.3(E - 10,000) = 0.3E - 3,000$$

$$\text{MTR} \equiv \frac{\Delta T}{\Delta E} = 0.3$$

$$\text{ATR} \equiv \frac{T}{E} = 0.3 - \frac{3,000}{E}$$

The MTR = 30% for any E above \$10,000; if E increases by \$100, then T increases by \$30. The ATR, on the other hand, varies with E. At $E = \$10,000$, the ATR = 0%. As E gets larger, the ATR rises; for example, when $E = \$30,000$, the ATR = 20% (its value under the proportional tax). As E becomes so large that the second term approaches 0, then the ATR approaches 30% (the value of the MTR). Because the ATR is constant as E rises from \$0 to \$10,000 and then increases as E rises beyond \$10,000, this schedule is progressive. A tax schedule is defined as progressive if the ATR rises as E rises.

Now suppose that we switch from the progressive to the proportional schedule. Once again, we will assume that each household holds its earnings constant in response to the switch. Then for the ATR, the dividing point $E = \$30,000$; for the MTR, the dividing point $E = \$10,000$. If E is less than \$30,000, then the ATR increases; if E is greater than \$30,000, then the ATR decreases. If E is less than \$10,000, then the MTR increases; if E is greater than \$10,000, then the MTR decreases.

▶ The average tax rate ATR determines a household's tax burden. The marginal tax rate MTR influences a household's incentive to earn additional income.

In our example, a switch from the progressive to the proportional schedule reduces the MTR for most households in the population (households with $E > \$10,000$). Hence, it increases the incentive to earn additional income for most households. It also raises the tax burden on households with income below \$30,000 and reduces the tax burden on households with income above \$30,000. The tax switch therefore has both an *incentive effect* and a *distributional effect*.

The U.S. Income Tax

Now let's consider the U.S. income tax. Taxpayers determine the tax they owe by using a rate table. According to this rate table, the first several thousand dollars is taxed at the lowest rate, the next several thousand dollars at a higher rate, and the next several at a still higher rate until the last dollar is taxed at the household's *apparent marginal tax rate*. This apparent MTR is often called the household's *tax bracket*. For example, a high-income household with an apparent MTR of 50% is said to be "in the 50% tax bracket." The rate table gives the apparent

MTR (tax bracket) and the average tax rate ATR for a household with any earnings E. Both the apparent MTR and the ATR rise as E rises; the rate table schedule is clearly progressive.

The rate-table MTR, however, is misleading. It is not true that all additional income is taxed at this MTR. If a household is in a 50% tax bracket and if a member of the household earns another $100 in cash salary, its tax rises by $50; its MTR on this kind of income is 50%.

But under the current tax law, if the household earns another $100 in fringe benefits (such as an employer contribution to health insurance or a pension fund), it pays no additional tax; its MTR on this kind of income is 0%. If the household earns another $100 in *capital gains income* (income that results from selling corporate stock for $100 more than it cost), then 60% of the gain is excluded and only $40 is taxed at the 50% rate. Hence, the household's tax rises by only $20; its MTR on this kind of income is 20%.

▶ The marginal tax rate MTR given in the rate table applies only to certain kinds of additional income (for example, cash wages and salaries). Other kinds of additional income are taxed at a lower MTR or not at all.

The rate-table ATR is also misleading. Under current law, a household is permitted various exclusions, deductions, exemptions, and credits. The household's taxable income is often significantly less than its true comprehensive income. Only part of the household's comprehensive income is subject to tax. There has been significant erosion of the tax base.

▶ The average tax rate ATR given in the rate table is significantly greater than the ratio of tax to the comprehensive income of the household.

How high are marginal tax rates in the United States? We will present some facts concerning the apparent MTR given in the rate table — the highest MTR that applies to any kind of additional income. Keep in mind that the MTR on other kinds of income is, in fact, lower.

Prior to the 1981 tax cut, the rate-table MTR ranged from 14% on low-income taxpayers to 70% on the most affluent taxpayers. Under the 1981 tax cut, the range is now from 11% to 50%. Knowing that the range of MTR was 14–70% in 1981 does not tell us the rate-table MTR faced by the average household. More precisely, consider the household with the *median* income. By the definition of median, 50% of all households earn a higher income and 50% of all households earn a lower income than the household with the median income. What apparent MTR does this median household face, and how has this MTR changed over time?

Table 15.2 shows how the apparent MTR facing the household with

TABLE 15.2

MARGINAL PERSONAL INCOME TAX RATES FOR FOUR-PERSON
FAMILIES* FOR SELECTED YEARS, 1965–1984 (PERCENT)

Family Income

Year	One-half Median Income	Median Income	Twice Median Income
1965	14	17	22
1970	15	20	26
1975	17	22	32
1980	18	24	43
Under Economic Recovery Tax Act of 1981			
1981	17.8	27.7	42.5
1982	16	25	39
1983	15	23	40
1984	16	25	38
Under Old Law			
1981	18	28	43
1982	18	28	43
1983	18	28	49
1984	21	32	49

SOURCE: *Economic Report of the President 1982*, Table 5–4.
* Excludes Social Security taxes and state and local income taxes.

the median income rose from the mid-1960s to 1981. The household with the median income faced a 17.0% MTR in 1965, but confronted a 27.7% MTR in 1981. Similarly, from 1965 to 1981, the household that earned one-half of the median income saw its MTR rise from 14.0% to 17.8%, while the household that earned twice the median income saw its apparent MTR rise from 22.0% to 42.5%.

The apparent MTR facing the typical household did not rise due to rate increases enacted by Congress. It rose because the typical household earned a higher nominal income and therefore moved into a higher tax bracket. Over time, fewer households fell into low tax brackets and more households fell into high tax brackets. The higher nominal income was due to higher real income and inflation.

The tax cut of 1981 reduced tax rates by 23% for each tax bracket. At the same time, the median household generally gains income each year. The apparent MTR of the median household in 1985 was roughly 25%.

We have presented data only for the federal income tax. Other taxes also must be considered to accurately assess the total MTR facing a household. For example, the additional consumption that a household can enjoy by earning additional income is reduced by other taxes, such as payroll and sales taxes. The *payroll tax rate* (employee plus employer) is roughly 14% until the *earnings ceiling* (above the median income) is reached. Thus, the total MTR for the median household is substantially greater than the income-tax MTR.

SUPPLY-SIDE HYPOTHESES

We can now evaluate two supply-side hypotheses. Before we begin, we must emphasize two fundamental points that are often ignored in discussions about supply-side economics.

First, suppose that the economy is initially at $Q = Q_c$ ($U = U_c = 7\%$), so that the inflation rate is constant. When tax rates are cut (holding government spending constant), there is a *demand-side effect*. The *IS* curve shifts to the right as a result of this fiscal expansion. If the Fed kept the *LM* curve fixed, then Q would increase due to the demand-side effect.

We will see that there may also be a *supply-side effect*. The tax rate cut may increase constant inflation output Q_c—the output that would be produced if the unemployment rate were kept at the constant inflation unemployment rate U_c (7%).

If the demand-side increase in Q exceeds the supply-side increase in Q_c, then U falls below U_c (7%) and the inflation rate rises. If the demand-side increase in Q is less than the supply-side increase in Q_c, then U rises above U_c (7%) and the inflation rate declines.

To avoid the complication of a changing inflation rate, it makes sense to assume that the Federal Reserve adjusts monetary policy to keep Q equal to the new Q_c, so that the unemployment rate U remains at the original U_c (7%) and the inflation rate p stays constant. In the *IS – LM* diagram, the Fed adjusts the *LM* curve so that the *IS* and *LM* curves intersect at a Q equal to the new Q_c.

▶ Our analysis, then, is "neoclassical" or "classical" in that we are investigating what happens if the economy always remains at the full-employment level, or equivalently (in this context), at the constant inflation unemployment rate U_c.

Our second fundamental point about supply-side economics is this:

▶ We want to compare the path of the economy with a low tax rate to the path of the economy with a high tax rate. We do not want to compare the economy after the tax cut to the economy before the tax cut. The correct comparison here is *with* versus *without* the tax-rate cut (not "after" versus "before" the tax-rate cut.

Consider the supply-side assertion that a tax-rate cut does not reduce tax revenue. The correct formulation follows. Imagine that the economy has two paths, each generated by a different tax rate. Real output $Q = Q_c$ (given the tax rate) along each path. Does the low tax-rate path have a lower tax revenue than the high tax-rate path?

We do *not* want to ask if the tax revenue will be greater this year than it was last year if we cut the tax rate this year. In a growing economy, a constant tax rate normally yields growing tax revenue. A before-and-after comparison is therefore misleading.

These two fundamental points reveal a fallacy that often occurs. Actual tax revenue is compared for two years: the year before the tax cut and the year after the tax cut. This has been done for the 1964 tax-rate cut as well as for the 1981 tax-rate cut. But such comparisons ignore our two fundamental points.

The correct comparison is between what tax revenue would be at the initial tax rate if the economy were at its U_c (currently 7%) and what tax revenue would be (in that same year) at the lower tax rate if the economy were at the same U_c. For example, we want to know what the 1982 tax revenue would have been at the initial tax rate with $U = 7\%$ and what the 1982 tax revenue would have been at the lower tax rate with $U = 7\%$. A correct analysis must therefore estimate the two hypothetical tax revenues for 1982. If U had been 7% in 1982 (in fact, U was 9.5%), then actual tax revenue for 1982 would be relevant. But we must still estimate what the tax revenue would have been in 1982 with $U = 7\%$ if tax rates had not been cut.

▶ At least one hypothetical tax revenue must always be estimated to make the proper comparison — the tax revenue that would have occurred if the initial tax rate had been retained and U had remained at U_c. A simple comparison of actual data in two years is not sufficient to answer the relevant question.

Keeping these two fundamental points in mind, we will now turn to the two supply-side hypotheses.

The Impact of a Tax-Rate Cut on Tax Revenue

▶ Hypothesis 1: A substantial (perhaps one-third) cut in tax rates would not reduce tax revenue at Q_c.

Tax revenue equals the average tax rate ATR multiplied by the *tax base*. For example, if the tax base is income Q, then we employ our familiar tax function:

(15.7) $T = tQ$

An across-the-board tax-rate cut reduces both marginal and average tax rates. Consider a tax-rate cut that reduces the average tax rate by 33% (roughly the original 1980 supply-side proposal). For tax revenue T to stay constant, the tax base Q must increase by 50%. For example, suppose that the tax rate is initially $t = 30\%$ and that $Q = \$1,000$ billion, so that $T = \$300$ billion. Then if t is cut to 20%, Q must increase to $1,500 billion to keep T at $300 billion.

A cut in the tax rate on labor income might raise the Q_c of the economy. This point is illustrated by a hypothetical example in Table 15.3.

Suppose that the constant inflation unemployment rate $U_c = 7\%$, the initial labor force is 100 persons, the average employee works 40 hours per week, and real output per hour worked (labor productivity) is $10. The weekly Q_c is the output that 93 workers produce per week; initially, weekly $Q_c = \$37,200$ ($93 \times 40 \times \$10$).

If the tax rate on labor income is cut by 33%, then the labor force increases by 2% to 102 because 2 persons now find it worthwhile to seek work. With a 7% unemployment rate still required to keep inflation

TABLE 15.3

A TAX CUT MAY RAISE Q_c

	High Tax Rate	Low Tax Rate
Labor Force	100	102 (+2%)
Unemployment Rate (U_c)	7%	7%
Unemployment	7	7
Employment	93	95 (+2%)
Hours per Worker	40	41 (+2.5%)
Output per Hour	$10	$10.20 (+2%)
Output (Q_c)	$37,200	$39,729 (+7%)

constant, 95 persons (roughly a 2% increase) are now employed if the economy remains at $U_c = 7\%$.

In addition, suppose that the work week increases by 2.5% to 41 hours and that labor productivity increases by 2% to $10.20 due to the increased incentive to work. Then weekly Q_c increases by roughly 7% to $39,729 (95 × 41 × $10.20). These numbers are used only for illustration. The basic point is that a cut in the tax on labor income may increase Q_c by increasing the labor force, hours per worker, and output per hour.

Supply-siders suggest two ways in which the tax base can be increased due to a tax-rate cut. First, Q_c (and therefore Q) will increase for the whole economy. Second, even if Q and Q_c remain constant for the whole economy, a greater share of Q will become taxable. Let's consider each case in turn.

First, how plausible is a 50% increase in Q_c (and Q) for the whole economy? If production is characterized by *constant returns to scale*, then to increase output (and income) by 50% requires a 50% increase in the effective labor supply and in the effective capital supply.

We have seen that the effective labor supply can increase in three ways: by increasing the labor force, by increasing hours per worker, and by increasing output per hour due to more intensive effort. If each of these three elements contributed equally to the effective labor supply, then each should increase by roughly 15%. For example, a person working 40 hours per week should increase to 46 hours per week.

Let's consider the likelihood of a 50% increase in the effective labor supply from another perspective. In Table 15.2, the median household faced an apparent marginal tax rate MTR of 27.7% in 1981. Not all labor income is subject to this MTR; moreover, the 1981 tax cut has reduced the apparent MTR. On the other hand, the total MTR facing the median household includes not only the MTR from the U.S. income tax but several other taxes, such as the payroll tax, as well.

If the total MTR on the median household is 40%, then a 33% cut will reduce the total MTR to 27%. This means that if the household earns another $100, it will gain $73 instead of $60; its gain will rise by 22% ($13 out of $60). How is this 22% increase in the net (after-tax) wage likely to affect the effective labor supply?

It is helpful to use the concept of the *elasticity of the labor supply* with respect to the net wage (the percentage change in the labor supply in response to a 1% increase in the net wage). Clearly, an elasticity of more than 2 is required if a 22% increase in the net wage is to induce a 50% increase in the labor supply.

Labor economists have performed econometric analyses of the response of the labor supply to changes in the net wage. Given many different samples of data and statistical techniques, estimates of the elasticity of the labor supply vary, but the elasticity for households is generally close to 0. A negative elasticity or an elasticity of 0 is often found for men; a positive elasticity between 0 and 1 is often found for married women. Virtually all studies imply a household elasticity that is much smaller than 2. These studies suggest that the effective labor supply will not increase by the required 50%.

Actually, the effective labor supply should be increased by more than 50%, because the capital supply cannot be raised by 50% in the short run. Even if a significant rise in the saving rate does occur, annual saving is the increment to the capital stock. A given percentage change in this year's saving represents a much smaller percentage change in the effective capital supply.

The second way in which the tax base can be increased in response to a tax-rate cut involves illegal tax evasion (operating in the *underground economy*) and legal tax avoidance. A significant amount of income goes illegally unreported and is therefore not subject to tax. The higher the tax rate, the greater the individual's incentive to risk concealing income from the Internal Revenue Service and the greater the incentive to hire accountants and lawyers to find legal methods of avoiding taxation. Supply-siders believe that a significant cut in tax rates (for example, a cut of 33%) would result in a significant increase in the share of total national income that is subject to tax.

Suppose that tax evasion and avoidance shelters 20% of total income from taxation, so that sheltered income is initially 25% of taxable income. In our example, where taxable income Q is initially $1,000 billion, assume that total income not subject to tax is $250 billion. Then even if all income became subject to tax, total taxable national income Q would rise to only $Q = $1,250$ billion (a 25% increase). It seems doubtful that more than a small fraction of the required 50% increase can be expected from a reduction in tax evasion and avoidance.

▶ It is very doubtful that a 33% tax-rate cut can maintain tax revenue if the economy is kept at $Q = Q_c$, so that the inflation rate p remains constant. It is much more likely that a significant drop in tax revenue will result.

The relationship between the tax rate and tax revenue is shown in a curve (Figure 15.6) that has recently been called the *Laffer curve,* after supply-side economist Arthur Laffer. We have argued that the most useful tax rate–tax revenue curve is based on the assumption that Q is always kept at Q_c by monetary policy, so that the inflation rate stays constant as the tax rate is altered. This enables us to focus on the pure supply-side effect of a tax-rate change. Thus, we plot the tax revenue that is collected at constant inflation output $T(Q_c)$ against the tax rate t.

There is nothing new in the observation that just as a tax rate of 0% raises 0 revenue, a tax rate of 100% on labor income also raises 0 revenue, because no one has any financial incentive to work. This

FIGURE 15.6 THE Q_c TAX REVENUE CURVE (THE LAFFER CURVE)

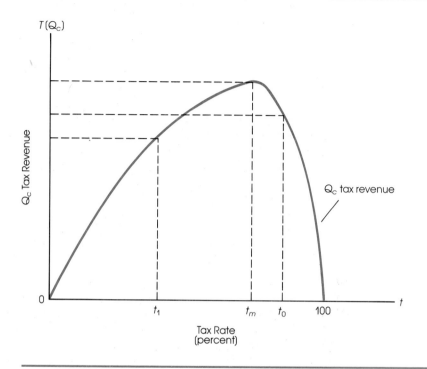

$T(Q_c)$

Q_c Tax Revenue

Q_c tax revenue

0   t_1 t_m t_0 100 t

Tax Rate
(percent)

The Q_c tax revenue (Laffer) curve shows the tax revenue that would be raised at each tax rate if the economy were kept at the Q_c associated with that tax rate (by monetary policy). If the U.S. tax rate is less than or equal to the maximum revenue rate t_m, then a rate cut would reduce Q_c tax revenue. But even if the U.S. tax rate somewhat exceeds t_m (say, equals t_0), a significant rate cut (say, from t_0 to t_1) would still reduce Q_c tax revenue.

means that some tax rate t_m yields a maximum tax revenue. It also means that two tax rates — one less than t_m and one greater than t_m — can yield any other tax revenue.

The key question here is where is the U.S. economy positioned on the Laffer curve? Laffer and other supply-siders assert that the United States is currently at a tax rate significantly greater than t_m. Hence, a "significant" (say, 33%) reduction in the tax rate raises tax revenue. Note from Figure 15.6 that a significant reduction in the tax rate reduces tax revenue if the initial tax rate is only somewhat greater than t_m. (A reduction in the tax rate from t_0 to t_1 reduces tax revenue even though t_0 somewhat exceeds t_m.)

The kind of arithmetic calculation we have just made has persuaded most economists that a significant tax-rate cut will almost certainly reduce tax revenue if Q is kept at Q_c, so that the inflation rate stays constant. This does not necessarily mean that the U.S. economy is currently at a tax rate of less than t_m. But it does mean that the U.S. economy cannot be so far above t_m that a substantial tax-rate cut will raise tax revenue.

The Impact of a Tax-Rate Cut on Investment

▶ Hypothesis 2: Cutting tax rates would raise saving and investment at Q_c.

With Q held at Q_c

(10.4) $$Q_c \equiv C_T + I_T$$

We know that total consumption C_T is equal to private consumption C plus government consumption G_C and that total investment I_T is equal to private investment I plus government investment G_I. In the tax-rate cut experiment proposed by supply-siders, G_C stays constant. Thus

▶ In response to a tax-rate cut, total investment at Q_c increases if and only if Q_c increases more than private consumption C increases.

For example, in equation (10.4), with G_C held constant, if Q_c increases by \$100 billion and C increases by \$80 billion, then I_T increases by \$20 billion. But if Q_c stays constant and C increases by \$90 billion, then I_T decreases by \$90 billion.

Supply-siders believe that a tax-rate cut causes a significant increase in the effective labor supply (and therefore in Q_c) and also causes a reduction in the propensity to consume. The labor supply increases in response to the increase in the *net (after-tax) wage*, and the propensity to save increases in response to the increase in the *net return to saving*. Together, these two effects result in an increase in total investment at Q_c.

Let's consider two polar examples and an intermediate example, all shown in Table 15.4. The first supports the supply-side conclusion that investment at Q_c increases. The second supports the standard conclusion that investment at Q_c decreases. The third illustrates the intermediate case in which investment at Q_c decreases by less than it does in the standard case.

First let's consider the supply-side example. When the tax rate is cut, if Q_c increases by \$100 billion but tax revenue remains constant, then private net income increases by \$100 billion. If private saving S increases by \$20 billion, then private consumption C increases by \$80 billion (note that the propensity to consume $c = 80\%$), so that total investment I_T increases by \$20 billion. This example assumes that the

TABLE 15.4

THE IMPACT OF A TAX-RATE CUT ON INVESTMENT

	Q_c	T	Private Net Income	C_T	I_T	S	S_G
Supply Side	+100	0	+100	+80	+20	+20	0
Standard	0	−100	+100	+90	−90	+10	−100
Intermediate	+50	−50	+100	+85	−35	+15	−50

first supply-side hypothesis is correct (a tax-rate cut does not reduce tax revenue because Q_c increases enough and tax evasion and avoidance decrease enough to offset the tax-rate cut).

If tax revenue stays constant, then the increase in Q_c implies an equal increase in private net (after-tax) income. As long as this increase in private net income raises saving, private consumption will increase by less than Q_c.

▶ If tax revenue T at Q_c remains constant when tax rates t are cut, then as long as the increase in private net income raises private saving S, total investment I_T at Q_c will increase.

Now let's consider the standard example. When the tax rate is cut, suppose that Q_c stays constant and that tax revenue declines by $100 billion, so that private net income increases by $100 billion. If private consumption C increases by $90 billion (note that the propensity to consume $c = 90\%$, 10% greater than in the supply-side case), then total investment I_T will decline by $90 billion. This example is based on the standard assumption that Q_c stays constant. This is the constant Q_c case that we emphasized in our discussion of the fiscal–monetary policy mix in Chapters 2 and 10. We saw that, with government spending held constant, a tax-rate cut—a shift to an easy fiscal policy—reduces tax revenue, raises consumption, and "crowds out" investment at a constant Q_c.

▶ If Q_c remains constant when tax rates t are cut and if tax revenue T declines at Q_c, then as long as the increase in private net income raises private consumption C, total investment I_T at Q_c will decrease.

Finally, let's consider the intermediate case. Here, Q_c increases by $50 billion and T declines by $50 billion. (Note that the propensity to consume $c = 85\%$.) Thus, I_T decreases by $35 billion.

▶The intermediate case shows that moderate supply-side effects are not sufficient to reverse the standard conclusion that a tax-rate cut will reduce total investment I_T at Q_c. These supply-side effects do, however, make the reduction in total investment smaller.

It should be noted that even with Q_c held constant, a decline in tax revenue, and a rise in private net income, it is theoretically possible for consumption to decrease, given a sufficient decrease in the propensity to consume. But how likely is this to occur?

Let's consider a household that earns $25,000 in income. The first row of Table 15.5 shows this household's position before the tax-rate cut. The data in this row are fairly realistic: the propensity to save is roughly $s = 6\%$, and a $25,000-income household pays roughly $3,000 under the U.S. income tax. The second row shows what this household's position needs to be to keep consumption from rising in response to a 33% tax-rate cut (assuming that its before-tax income remains at $25,000). If consumption is to stay at $20,600, then the household's propensity to save must increase by 67% to $s = 10\%$. How likely is such a rise to occur?

The personal saving rate (propensity to save) has ranged between 5% and 8% in the United States for several decades, even when tax rates were lower and the net real (inflation-adjusted) return to saving was higher. Moreover, some econometric studies estimate that the elasticity of saving with respect to the net return is close to 0.* However, one study[†] did find an elasticity of 0.4. We will give the benefit of the doubt to supply-siders and assume that the elasticity is 1.0.

In this example, the average tax rate ATR falls from 12% ($3,000/$25,000) to 8% ($2,000/$25,000). The marginal tax rate MTR on certain categories of capital income, however, is higher than the ATR. Suppose that the MTR declines from 36% to 24%. If the household earns a gross return of $100 on additional saving, it will now gain $76 instead of $64 — a 19% increase ($12 out of $64) in the net return to saving. An elasticity of 1.0 implies that the saving rate will increase by 19% (1.0 × 19%) of itself; thus, the saving rate increases from 6% to roughly 7%, instead of to the required 10%.

As we noted in Chapters 2 and 10 and as we have seen again here, the supply-side hypothesis is correct (and reverses the standard conclusion) if the magnitudes of the impact on Q_c, on tax evasion and avoidance, and on the propensity to consume are sufficiently large. The key

* Phillip Howrey and Saul Hymans, "The Measurement and Determination of Loanable-Funds Saving," *Brookings Papers on Economic Activity* 3 (1978): 655–706.
† Michael Boskin, "Taxation, Saving, and the Rate of Interest," *Journal of Political Economy*, 86.2 (1978): S3–S28.

TABLE 15.5

A TAX CUT THAT DOES NOT CHANGE CONSUMPTION

Income	Tax	Net Income	Consumption	Saving	Propensity to Consume	Propensity to Save
25,000	3,000	22,000	20,600	1,400	94%	6%
25,000	2,000	23,000	20,600	2,400	90%	10%

issue is whether it is likely that the magnitudes will be large enough to reverse the standard conclusion. Based on the examples and econometric evidence presented in this section, we can conclude

▶ It is very likely that a 33% tax-rate cut would reduce total investment at Q_c.

It is useful to analyze this hypothesis by focusing on the concept of saving, instead of on the concept of consumption. To do this, we need to recall several closed-economy accounting identities. The first is

$$(1.29) \qquad I_T \equiv S_T$$

Total investment I_T must equal total saving S_T. In turn, total saving is the sum of private saving S plus government saving S_G. Thus

▶ Total investment I_T increases if and only if the increase in private saving S exceeds the decrease in government saving S_G.

Recall that government saving S_G is defined as

$$(1.25) \qquad S_G \equiv (T - R) - G_C$$

Government saving S_G equals government net income (tax revenue T minus government transfers R) minus government consumption G_C.

Since government transfers R and government consumption G_C stay constant during the tax-rate cut experiment proposed by supply-siders, the change in government saving S_G equals the change in tax revenue T. For example, if T declines by $100 billion, then S_G declines by $100 billion. It then follows that

▶ Total investment I_T increases if and only if the increase in private saving S exceeds the decrease in tax revenue T.

In the supply-side case, S increases by \$20 billion and investment increases by \$20 billion. In the standard case, S increases by \$10 billion and investment decreases by \$90 billion. Finally, in the intermediate case, S.increases by \$15 billion and investment decreases by \$35 billion.

SHOULD MARGINAL TAX RATES BE SUBSTANTIALLY REDUCED?

Supply-siders propose a substantial reduction in marginal tax rates. Whatever the merit of the supply-side hypotheses, we can now ask whether the supply-side policy is desirable.

Optimal taxation is an important subject in traditional public-finance economics. According to standard analysis, any positive marginal tax rate MTR causes an inefficiency. An MTR on labor income distorts the choice between leisure and work; an MTR on capital income distorts the choice between present and future consumption. In Chapter 10, we explained how a capital income tax causes inefficiency.

According to standard analysis, reducing the MTR reduces these inefficiencies. But this does not necessarily mean that reducing the MTR is desirable. There may be losses—as well as gains—to be weighed.

It is essential to recognize that there are four different ways to reduce marginal tax rates: (1) by reducing rates without base broadening, (2) by reducing rates with base broadening, (3) by reducing the progressivity of the tax schedule, and (4) by raising revenue through another form of taxation. Let's consider each in turn.

Reducing Rates Without Base Broadening

Base broadening means reducing exclusions, deductions, credits, and exemptions, so that more income is subject to taxation (included in the tax base). If marginal tax rates are reduced without base broadening, we have seen that it is very likely that tax revenue at Q_c will be reduced. This means that government spending will need to be reduced as well. Hence, this loss must be weighed.

Reducing Rates With Base Broadening

Reducing marginal tax rates with base broadening has long been advocated by tax reformers—both liberal and conservative. Only a fraction of the comprehensive income of households is subject to taxation because the tax base has been eroded by various exclusions, deductions, exemptions, and credits. A smaller tax base requires higher tax rates to raise a target revenue. The strategy is to broaden the tax base by reducing these exclusions, deductions, exemptions, and credits. This would permit a cut in tax rates—particularly in MTRs—and still raise the same revenue.

There are two possible losses to consider. The first involves our distinction between the apparent MTR in the rate table and the actual MTR on different kinds of income. Currently, 60% of capital gains income is excluded and 100% of fringe-benefit labor income is excluded. Hence, the MTR on capital gains income is only 40% of the apparent MTR, and the MTR on fringe-benefit labor income is 0%. If both kinds of income are fully included under base broadening, then the apparent MTR (the MTR that applies to cash wage and salary income) would be cut, but the MTR on capital gains and fringe-benefit labor income would rise. The higher MTR on these kinds of income imposes a loss.

The second possible loss involves some of the credits and deductions. Do we want to eliminate the incentive for charitable giving or assistance for abnormally high medical expenses? Some deductions and credits benefit only a special interest; others serve a worthy purpose and improve the fairness of the tax.

Reducing the Progressivity of the Tax Schedule

In Section 15.1, we saw that a switch from the progressive tax schedule given by equation (15.6) to the proportional tax schedule given by equation (15.5) reduces the MTR for most households in the population (all households with earnings E greater than $10,000) from 30% to 20%. But we also saw that such a switch has an important distributional consequence. It raises the tax burden — the ATR — on all households with earnings E less than $30,000 and lowers the tax burden on all households with earnings E greater than $30,000. Thus, a citizen must weigh the impact on distribution as well as the efficiency of reducing the MTR by this method.

Recently, much attention has been given to the proposal to make the U.S. income tax a *flat tax*.

The FLAT-TAX PROPOSAL combines the preceding two methods for reducing marginal tax rates. Conversion to a flat tax has two components: base broadening and a reduction in progressivity. An evaluation of the flat-tax proposal involves weighing the pros and cons of the preceding two methods of reducing MTRs.

Raising Revenue Through Another Form of Taxation

Income-tax rates can be cut, and the revenue lost can be made up (for example, by raising taxes on business firms). But then the reduction in MTRs is only apparent. A person who earns another $100 may keep $80 instead of $70 but should recognize that $80 will purchase the same consumption as $70 did before, because the price of consumer goods now includes $10 in tax.

Relativity and Taxation

A final argument deserves our attention. If individuals feel pressure to "keep up with the Joneses," then a positive MTR may be desirable to restrain excessive relativistic competition. As Robert Frank writes in *Choosing the Right Pond:*

> . . . if people are as concerned about relative standing as the evidence we have seen suggests, it becomes clear that the supply-siders are barking up the wrong tree. The real problem is not at all that the current tax system induces people to work too little, take too few risks, and so on. On the contrary, it is a lack of taxation that would cause individually rational citizens to work too many hours, take too many risks, and spend too little time with family and friends.*

To summarize:

▶ Reducing marginal tax rates MTR entails possible losses as well as gains. Deciding what marginal tax rates are optimal involves weighing the consequences for both efficiency and equity.

SUMMARY

1. A reduction in the budget surplus or an increase in the budget deficit reduces private investment but does not necessarily reduce total investment. If the budget surplus is reduced by an increase in public investment, so that *government saving* remains the same, then total investment remains constant.

2. A balanced budget rule is not socially optimal in our simple economy. It would prevent government investments that would raise the well-being of the representative person.

3. If government "neutrality" is desired, then the proper rule for government is not a balanced budget rule (a *zero surplus rule*) but a *zero saving rule*. This rule prescribes a government deficit equal to government investment.

4. Nevertheless, due to practical objections to the zero saving rule, it is possible to argue that a balanced budget rule is a desirable constraint to impose on Congress and the President.

5. More fundamentally, a citizen may reject the goal of government neutrality that a zero saving rule implies and judge that private-sector saving is too low to reduce poverty rapidly or to maintain our

---

* Robert Frank, *Choosing the Right Pond: Human Behavior and the Quest for Status* (New York: Oxford University Press, 1985) 248.

relative standard of living. A citizen whose goal for government saving is positive may prefer a balanced budget rule.

6. A deficit need not be inflationary. Whether or not it is inflationary depends on the response of the Federal Reserve.

7. Projected federal deficits imply a rising *debt – GNP ratio* and a rising *interest – GNP ratio*. These ratios must not be permitted to rise indefinitely.

8. Some economists argue that the debt and the deficit are mismeasured.

9. A constitutional amendment to require a balanced budget has been offered. The pros and cons of such an approach should be weighed.

10. Advocates of *supply-side economics* assert the hypothesis that a substantial decrease in *marginal tax rates* MTRs would significantly increase the supplies of labor, capital, and constant inflation output Q_c. Advocates unite on the policy of a substantial cut in marginal tax rates.

11. It is very doubtful that a 33% tax-rate cut could maintain tax revenue if the economy is kept at Q_c, contrary to the claim of supplysiders.

12. It is very likely that a 33% tax-rate cut would reduce total investment at Q_c, contrary to the claim of supply-siders.

13. There are four different ways to reduce marginal tax rates: (1) by reducing rates without *base broadening,* (2) by reducing rates with base broadening, (3) by reducing the progressivity of the tax schedule, and (4) by raising revenue through another form of taxation. The possible loss of each method must be weighed against the benefit of a lower marginal tax rate.

14. If individuals feel pressure to "keep up with the Joneses," then a positive marginal tax rate may be desirable to restrain excessive relativistic competition.

TERMS AND CONCEPTS

apparent marginal tax rate	demand-side effect
average tax rate (ATR)	distributional effect
bank reserves	earning ceiling
base broadening	elasticity of the labor supply
capital gains income	flat tax
comprehensive income	government neutrality
constant returns to scale	government saving (S_G)
cost – benefit analysis	government surplus (Su)
debt-financed	gross debt
debt – GNP ratio	high-powered money (H)

incentive effect
interest – GNP ratio
Laffer curve
marginal rate of return (*mrr*)
marginal social discount rate
   (*msdr*)
marginal tax rate (MTR)
market value of gross debt
monetization
money-financed
neoclassical growth theory
net (after-tax) wage
net debt
net return to saving
net worth
optimal deficit and debt

optimal taxation
par value of gross debt
payroll tax rate
progressive tax schedule
proportional tax schedule
real net debt
relativity
social profitability
supply-side economics
supply-side effect
tax base
tax bracket
underground economy
zero saving rule
zero surplus rule

QUESTIONS

15.1 What is the impact on private investment and on total investment of a reduction in the budget deficit at Q_c that is achieved by cutting government investment G_I? Explain.

15.2 Describe a simple economy in which the emergence of government deficits and debt may be socially optimal.

15.3 List several practical objections to a zero saving rule.

15.4 List the pros and cons of a constitutional amendment requiring a balanced budget.

15.5 To assess the plausibility of the supply-side claim that a 33% tax-rate cut would not reduce tax revenue at Q_c, construct an example of the response of the labor supply (see Table 15.3, page 646).

15.6 To assess the plausibility of the supply-side claim that a tax-rate cut would raise investment at Q_c, construct an example (see Table 15.4, page 651).

15.7 List four ways to cut marginal tax rates and cite a possible loss associated with each.

16 Topics in Accumulation and Growth II

Prerequisite: Chapter 10

Like Chapter 15, this chapter discusses several topics in accumulation and growth. The topics are as follows: Social Security and capital accumulation; policies to reduce consumption and raise investment; the sources of economic growth; the neoclassical growth model; and accumulation, pollution, and depletion. The treatment of each topic is completely self-contained.

16.1 Social Security and Capital Accumulation

The Social Security program enacted during the Great Depression has helped assure a decent standard of living for retirees. Social Security taxes today are approximately 14% of covered payroll (wages), and benefits finance an important share of retirement consumption. In 1985, the ratio of Social Security retiree benefits to GNP—the *Social Security ratio*—was approximately 5%.

Given its large size, and the importance of its role in financing retirement, it seems likely that Social Security has a significant impact on saving and capital accumulation. In this section we will explain why the enactment of a gradual, moderate reduction in the ratio of Social Security expenditure to GNP should raise capital accumulation.

Two points deserve special emphasis.

▶ Throughout our analysis, we will assume that the Fed adjusts monetary policy to keep output Q at Q_c. Specifically, if the enactment of a gradual, moderate reduction in the Social Security ratio reduces consumption demand, then we will assume that the Fed simultaneously reduces the interest rate and thereby stimulates investment demand, so that total demand remains at Q_c. In the *IS–LM* diagram, if the scheduled reduction in the Social Security ratio shifts the *IS* curve to the left, then we will assume that the Fed shifts the *LM* curve to the right, so that the intersection remains at Q_c.

▶ Even if a scheduled future reduction in the Social Security ratio raises capital accumulation at Q_c, this does not necessarily mean that a citizen should favor it. We will consider the pros and cons of a scheduled phasedown in the Social Security ratio in the course of our discussion.

THE IMPACT ON CAPITAL ACCUMULATION

To analyze the impact of Social Security, it is crucial to understand that its financing is fundamentally different from the financing of a properly managed private pension fund. When such a pension fund is introduced, workers begin making contributions, but no benefits are initially paid. Only after a contributing worker retires is a benefit paid. Thus, initially there are only contributions as workers build their own funds. The pension fund grows and reflects each individual account. When workers retire, they receive in benefits only what they have contributed, plus the interest earned by their funds; they "decumulate" only what they have previously accumulated.

In contrast, our Social Security system is financed on a "pay-as-you-go" basis. Under this system, workers begin making contributions through taxation while an equal amount of benefits is immediately paid out to retirees. Each year, taxes from workers are completely paid out as benefits; no fund is accumulated. Social Security maintains an annually balanced budget, so that tax revenue roughly equals benefit payments in a given year.

Under the private pension method, each person is self-sufficient. Each worker builds an individual pension fund and then draws it down during retirement. If today's workers decide not to contribute to the fund, this will not affect today's retirees, who are dependent only on their own fund. Self-sufficient financing, of course, applies not only to properly managed private pensions but also to other forms of private saving.

In contrast, the Social Security method depends on an implicit *compact between generations*. Each generation of workers agrees, in effect, to finance the retirement of current retirees. In return, these workers expect that when they retire, the next generation of workers will do the same for them. If today's workers do not contribute—if Social Security taxes are suddenly ended—then today's retirees receive no benefits. They do not have their own funds; they are completely dependent on the contributions of today's workers.

Social Security and Consumption

In our analysis, we will consider three alternative assumptions concerning individuals. We will assume that they are *self-sufficient planners*, that they are *short-sighted spenders*, and that they are *intrafamily transferers*.

Let's begin with the *self-sufficient planners*. Here, we will assume that workers try to plan for their own retirement and that they believe they cannot count on significant support from their children. In other words, we will assume that each generation tries to be self-sufficient and tries to plan ahead.

When a permanent Social Security (SS) is suddenly introduced without several years of advanced warning that might alter behavior, workers looking ahead will regard SS taxes as a substitute for private saving. Workers expect that these taxes will be followed by benefits when they retire. Thus, the average worker may cut private saving by the amount of the new SS tax and keep consumption constant. The introduction of SS then has no impact on the consumption of workers. But it immediately raises the consumption of retirees, who unexpectedly receive benefits. Thus, aggregate consumption rises. This result is shown in row 1 of Table 16.1.

Now consider the reverse: a sudden reduction in the Social Security ratio—a reduction in both SS benefits and SS taxes (which are equal in a given year) relative to GNP. The consumption of retirees drops immediately. However, the consumption of workers stays constant, despite the reduction of SS taxes, because workers now realize that they should replace their tax contributions with private saving because there will be a smaller SS benefit when they retire. Thus, aggregate consumption declines. This is shown in row 4 of Table 16.1.

Many citizens would regard a sudden reduction in SS benefits as particularly unfair to retirees. Consider instead the enactment of a scheduled future reduction of the Social Security ratio that gives "advanced warning." If, for example, it is enacted today that, beginning in ten years, the ratio of SS benefits to GNP will be gradually reduced by one-third over the next 20 years, then what happens?

In contrast to a sudden reduction, no immediate reduction in the consumption of retirees occurs because the phasedown does not start for ten years. But there is an immediate reduction in the consumption of workers. For ten years they must continue paying the same SS tax rate. But they know that when they retire, they will have to depend less on SS and more on their own saving. They must raise their saving immediately and thereby cut consumption today. Thus, aggregate consumption declines immediately. This is shown in row 7 of our table. Thus:

TABLE 16.1

THE IMPACT OF A CHANGE IN SOCIAL SECURITY ON CONSUMPTION

	Workers' consumption	Retirees' consumption	Total consumption
Sudden Introduction			
1. Self-sufficient planners	constant	increase	increase
2. Short-sighted spenders	decrease	increase	constant
3. Intrafamily transferers	constant	constant	constant
Sudden Reduction			
4. Self-sufficient planners	constant	decrease	decrease
5. Short-sighted spenders	increase	decrease	constant
6. Intrafamily transferers	constant	constant	constant
Scheduled Future Reduction			
7. Self-sufficient planners	decrease	constant	decrease
8. Short-sighted spenders	constant	constant	constant
9. Intrafamily transferers	constant	constant	constant

▶ If workers are *self-sufficient planners,* a change in Social Security affects aggregate consumption.

These conclusions, of course, depend on the assumption that workers plan for retirement and do not privately provide primary support for their own retired parents or expect their children to support them in retirement. Each generation is assumed to be composed of self-sufficient planners. Now let's see what happens if these assumptions are violated.

Suppose that workers are completely short-sighted and do not plan ahead; they are *short-sighted spenders.* They see only the SS tax but ignore the future SS benefit. They simply consume most of their disposable (after-tax) income and do not distinguish between an SS tax and any other tax. Then when SS is introduced, they reduce their consumption by almost as much as the tax, canceling the increase in consumption by retirees, so that aggregate consumption stays constant. This result is shown in row 2 of Table 16.1.

Similarly, the sudden reduction of SS causes short-sighted workers to raise their consumption with the tax cut, canceling the cut in the consumption of retirees. This is shown in row 5 of the table. Finally, enactment of the scheduled future reduction causes no immediate change in worker or retiree consumption, as shown in row 8 of Table 16.1. Thus:

▶ If workers are *short-sighted spenders,* a change in Social
  Security does not affect aggregate consumption.

Next, suppose that workers do significantly help to support retired parents and expect the same from their children; they are *intrafamily transferers.* Prior to SS, there is already a voluntary Social Security program within each family. The introduction of SS means that the government now implements such transfers from workers to retirees. It stands to reason that workers will respond by reducing their own private transfers; consequently, there will be no change in the consumption of either workers or retirees and therefore no change in aggregate consumption. This is shown in row 3 of our table.

Similarly, a sudden reduction of SS causes no change in aggregate consumption, because workers immediately make private transfers to compensate for the reduction in transfers via the government. This is shown in row 6. Finally, the enactment of a scheduled future reduction also has no effect on either workers' or retirees' consumption, as indicated in row 9 of Table 16.1.

▶ If workers are *intrafamily transferers,* a change in Social
  Security does not affect aggregate consumption.

We have seen that the impact of Social Security depends crucially on which of the three alternative assumptions is correct. What, in fact, would happen if a scheduled future reduction in the SS ratio were enacted in the actual economy? Society consists of diverse households. Some plan ahead, intending to be self-sufficient. Others are short-sighted. Others significantly support their retired parents and expect their children to support them when they retire. The impact on aggregate consumption is a *weighted average* of these responses. Empirical analysis is necessary to try to determine the weights and to determine the resulting impact on aggregate consumption. It is difficult, however, to obtain reliable statistical estimates of the impact of SS on consumption. Two basic methods are possible: the time-series method and the cross-section method. Let's consider each briefly.

The *time-series method* examines variation over time in a single country (for example, in the United States). As SS taxes and benefits change over time, how does aggregate consumption change? At the same time, we must "control" for the effects of other variables that influence consumption, such as disposable income and private wealth. The problem, however, is that SS benefits grow steadily over time along with disposable income and private wealth. These variables are *correlated*. It is therefore difficult to pin down the degree to which each separate variable has influenced consumption.

The *cross-section method* examines variation across individuals or across countries in a given year. As SS taxes and benefits vary from person to person, how does consumption change? Once again, we must control for the influence of other variables. Because SS coverage is almost universal and because of the structure of taxes and benefits, there is once again a correlation problem. Taxes and benefits tend to increase with disposable income and wealth. It is hard to pin down the influence that each has. From country to country, does variation in the Social Security ratio influence consumption? Countries differ in tax policies and in cultural attributes that are hard to measure.

Controlling for these factors is difficult. This does not mean that data cannot help, but it does mean that statistical studies are likely to leave substantial uncertainty. Some studies have detected a large influence of SS on consumption. One study concludes that SS has significantly raised consumption and reduced the saving rate by nearly 40%.[*] However, other studies, controlling for other variables, have found much smaller effects.[†]

▶ When theory and empirical evidence are viewed together, it seems likely that enacting a scheduled future reduction in the Social Security ratio would reduce aggregate consumption and raise capital accumulation. Whether the magnitude of the impact would be small or large is more difficult to say.

THE IMPLICIT RATE OF RETURN ON SOCIAL SECURITY SAVING

We have already seen that enacting a scheduled future reduction in the Social Security ratio should raise capital accumulation. Later, we will consider the pros and cons of such a policy. In this section, we will perform an analysis that will be relevant to our pros and cons discussion.

In a simplified world with perfect certainty and identical house-

---

[*] Martin Feldstein, "Social Security and Private Saving: Reply,"*Journal of Political Economy* 90.3 (1982): 630–42.
[†] For example, see Alicia Munnell, *The Future of Social Security* (Washington, D.C.: Brookings Institute, 1977).

holds (except for age differences), the following question can be asked: Would the representative worker receive a larger or smaller *implicit return on Social Security saving* than on private saving? To answer this question, we must consider what determines each return in such a simplified economy.

The *return to private saving* is simply the marginal rate of return on real investment *mrr*. Even if there is a capital income tax, the social return to private saving equals the gross return on real investment. Although each private saver directly captures only part of the *social return*—the *net return*—the saver receives the full return if government uses the capital income tax revenue to finance services that the saver values. From this perspective, the individual's benefit from private saving should be judged equal to the gross return on real investment, regardless of whether there is a capital income tax.

We will now demonstrate that

In the steady state, the IMPLICIT REAL (INFLATION-ADJUSTED) RATE OF RETURN ON SOCIAL SECURITY SAVING (tax contributions) equals the growth rate of real income in the economy, which approximately equals the sum of the *labor-force growth rate f* and the *labor productivity growth rate a*. For example, if $f = 1\%$ and $a = 2\%$, then the implicit real return on SS saving $\bar{r}$ is approximately 3%.

We can show this most easily in a simple model in which each person lives for two equal time periods corresponding to two life stages. Each person works in stage 1 and retires in stage 2. Suppose that the Social Security payroll tax rate is 10% and that the real wage per worker is $1,000 in stage 1. Since Social Security is financed by a 10% wage (payroll) tax, the tax (saving) per worker is $100. The return on this saving depends on the Social Security benefit that this worker receives on retirement in stage 2. For example, if the benefit is $150 in stage 2, then the return is 50% ($150/$100 − 1). More generally, the implicit return on Social Security saving $\bar{r}$ is defined by

(16.1)
$$\bar{r} \equiv \frac{B_2}{T_1} - 1$$

where $\bar{r}$ = implicit rate of return on SS saving

B_2 = SS benefit per retiree in stage 2

T_1 = SS tax per worker in stage 1

Consider a person who works in time period 1 and retires in time period 2. For this person, stage 1 occurs in time period 1 and stage 2 occurs in time period 2. What is this person's benefit in stage 2 (period 2)? To find B_2, we must know the Social Security tax revenue that is collected in period 2 and the number of retirees that share the revenue equally. Tax revenue in period 2 depends on the real wage and the number of workers, as well as on the Social Security tax rate, which we will assume remains constant at 10%.

We make the assumption — based on our Chapter 10 analysis of the real wage and the marginal product of labor — that real wage growth equals productivity growth. Thus, if productivity growth is 25%, then the real wage should grow by 25% (from \$1,000 to \$1,250).* If the labor force is 10 in period 1 and has a growth rate of 20%, then in period 2 there will be 12 workers and 10 retirees. In period 2, then, we know that

$$T_{\text{SS}_2} = tw_2L_2 = 0.1(1,250)(12) = 1,500$$

where T_{SS} = total SS tax revenue

t = SS tax rate

w = real wage

L = labor force

Since the number of retirees in period 2 equals the number of workers in period 1 (10), we can find the benefit B_2 as follows:

$$B_2 = \frac{T_{\text{SS}_2}}{R_2} = \frac{1,500}{10} = 150$$

where R_2 = number of retirees in period 2

Hence, the return is 50% ($150/100 - 1$). Note that $\bar{r}$ is approximately equal to the sum of the labor-force growth rate ($f = 20\%$) and the labor productivity growth rate ($a = 25\%$).

Now let's derive the following general relationship:

(16.2) $1 + \bar{r} = (1 + f)(1 + a)$

The previous example satisfies equation (16.2):

$1 + 0.50 = (1 + 0.20)(1 + 0.25)$

Note that if we multiply out equation (16.2) and subtract 1 from both sides, we obtain

(16.3) $\bar{r} = f + a + fa$

---

* Remember that each period is roughly 30 years, so that the growth rates in our example should be much larger than annual growth rates.

In the previous example, equation (16.3) is

$$\bar{r} = 0.20 + 0.25 + (0.20)(0.25) = 0.45 + 0.05 = 0.50$$

If f and a are fractions, then fa is small relative to $f + a$, and we can conclude that $\bar{r}$ is approximately equal to $f + a$.
We now derive equation (16.2):

(16.1) $\qquad \bar{r} \equiv \dfrac{B_2}{T_1} - 1$

Adding 1 to both sides gives us

$$1 + \bar{r} \equiv \dfrac{B_2}{T_1}$$

Since $B_2 = T_{SS_2}/R_2$ (the benefit per retiree equals total SS tax revenue divided by the number of retirees), then

$$1 + \bar{r} = \dfrac{T_{SS_2}/R_2}{T_1}$$

Since $T_{SS_2} = tw_2L_2$ (total revenue equals the tax rate multiplied by the wage multiplied by the number of workers), $R_2 = L_1$ (the number of retirees in period 2 equals the number of workers in period 1), and $T_1 = tw_1$ (the tax per worker equals the tax rate multiplied by the wage), we can substitute to obtain

$$1 + \bar{r} = \dfrac{tw_2L_2/L_1}{tw_1}$$

Canceling the t in both the numerator and the denominator gives us

(16.4) $\qquad 1 + \bar{r} = \dfrac{w_2L_2}{w_1L_1}$

Equation (16.4) can be simplified further by noting that

(16.5) $\qquad 1 + a = \dfrac{w_2}{w_1}$

(16.6) $\qquad 1 + f = \dfrac{L_2}{L_1}$

Equation (16.5) is based on the assumption that the real wage grows at the same rate as productivity. Substituting equation (16.5) and equation (16.6) into equation (16.4) results in equation (16.2), and thereby completes the derivation of equation (16.2).

Subtracting 1 from both sides of equation (16.4) yields

(16.7) $$\bar{r} = \frac{w_2 L_2}{w_1 L_1} - 1$$

Hence, the implicit return on SS saving equals the growth rate of labor income wL. If labor income wL is a constant fraction s_L of total real income Q, then equation (16.7) becomes

(16.8) $$\bar{r} = \frac{s_L Q_2}{s_L Q_1} - 1 = \frac{Q_2}{Q_1} - 1$$

$$\bar{r} = q_c$$

where q_c = growth rate of real income $\left(q_c = \dfrac{Q_2}{Q_1} - 1 \right)$

Thus, the real return on SS saving equals the growth rate of real income.

Note that the above analysis assumes that a person is taxed in stage 1 before receiving benefits in stage 2. In the early years of Social Security, however, retirees received benefits even though they had paid little or no SS tax prior to retirement. From equation (16.1), someone who has paid no tax obviously earns an "infinite" return. For several decades after Social Security began in 1935, retirees paid tax for less than their entire work lives. These retirees were therefore able to receive a return greater than $f + a$, or q_c. We have now reached the point at which the system is "mature"; retirees have paid tax for their entire work lives. If the tax rate, the growth rate of the labor force, and the growth rate of productivity are reasonably constant, then the return approximately equals $f + a$, or q_c.

Although we derived equations (16.2) and (16.3) in a two-stage model, the result is also valid when the stages are not of equal length and f, a, and $\bar{r}$ are expressed as annual rates. Thus, if $f = 1\%$ and $a = 2\%$, then $\bar{r}$ is approximately 3%. It is very likely that the pre-tax real (inflation-adjusted) rate of return on investment significantly exceeds 3%. As we will report in our discussion of the sources of economic growth (Section 16.4), some researchers estimate that the real return on investment is normally in the 11% range.* Even if this estimate is several

---

* Martin Feldstein and Lawrence Summers, "Is the Rate of Profit Falling?" *Brookings Papers on Economic Activity* 1 (1977): 211–28.

points high, it is a fair assumption that the return substantially exceeds the $\bar{r}$ on SS saving.

If the return on real investment does exceed the return on SS saving, then in a simple economy with perfect certainty and identical households (except for age), it might seem desirable to end Social Security and to rely completely on private saving to finance retirement. This brings us to our discussion of the pros and cons of enacting a scheduled future reduction in the Social Security ratio.

SHOULD A SCHEDULED FUTURE REDUCTION IN THE SOCIAL SECURITY RATIO BE ENACTED?

To answer this question, we must broaden our analysis beyond our simplified economy. But even in our simple economy, there is an argument against reducing the Social Security ratio: the *transition problem*.

Suppose that each person prefers to enter the labor force, work, and retire in an economy with a lower Social Security ratio than our current one. Given the current ratio, it does not follow that it is desirable to attempt to reduce it. Once the higher ratio has been in effect, it may be difficult — if not impossible — to avoid harm to particular age cohorts if an attempt is made to reduce the ratio.

For example, suppose that this year Congress enacts a scheduled 33% reduction in the ratio, to begin in ten years and to proceed over the next 20 years. A 55-year-old person today would then pay the same SS tax rate for ten years until retirement, after which SS benefits (and taxes) would begin to decrease. Although this person may benefit from a rise in the real wage during the last ten years of work due to the increase in capital accumulation that should immediately follow enactment, this gain may be outweighed by the cut in SS benefits.

Now let's leave our simple economy. In the actual economy, would enacting a scheduled future reduction below the current 5% ratio be desirable? If so, what SS ratio would be optimal? Let's compare reliance on private saving with reliance on Social Security.

Under private saving, each person must depend on the performance of private capital markets. In the simple economy, each saver always receives a return equal to the *mrr* on real investment. In the actual economy, however, the saver is dependent on the performance of the stock and bond markets; returns on stocks and bonds do not necessarily match the return on real investment. Moreover, under private saving, retirement is dependent on what each person has earned and saved; individuals must be self-sufficient. If a depression occurs in the decade preceding retirement or if a career is subject to adversity or bad luck, then an individual may be unable to adequately prepare for retirement.

Under Social Security, each retiree must depend on the taxes that the next generation of workers will pay. If the tax rate remains constant, we saw that the return on SS saving equals the growth rate of real income in the economy. But the return is less if the tax rate is cut after a person retires. Thus, each retiree is dependent on the relative political strength of workers versus retirees during retirement.

▶ A *risk-averse citizen* who does not want "to place all his retirement eggs in one basket" might decide that it is best to have a mix of private saving and Social Security. If either system performs poorly, then the other can cushion the loss.

It is instructive to recall the period when Social Security was first enacted. During the Great Depression of the 1930s, many workers approaching retirement lost their jobs and were compelled to draw on savings originally intended for retirement. Moreover, the stock and bond markets collapsed. Complete dependence on private saving proved hazardous; one purpose of Social Security is to reduce this dependency.

Another aspect of Social Security is that it is compulsory; private saving is voluntary. Because no one can be certain about the future, each person must determine how much voluntary saving is optimal given this uncertainty. Inevitably, some will later decide that they have saved too little. They may have overestimated their future economic success or underestimated the retirement standard of living that they desire. Social Security protects against such outcomes. Thus, even if everyone appears to have the same potential lifetime earning power and ability to save, a citizen entering the work force might still favor a significant role for Social Security in financing retirement. Social Security provides insurance against the harmful outcomes that can occur due to sole reliance on private saving.

In a society in which everyone does not have the same lifetime earning power and ability to save, Social Security provides some redistribution. Under private saving, low-skilled workers may have difficulty accumulating enough to subsist during retirement. After 40 years of full-time work and in the absence of SS, many low-skilled workers would be forced to turn to welfare or private charity in old age.

Social Security recognizes differences in the ability to save and performs some redistribution from high-income to low-income workers. If worker H earns twice as much as worker L, he will receive a higher SS benefit than L, but the benefit will be less than twice as great. Thus

▶ Social Security assures an adequate minimum benefit for the low-skilled worker. Many citizens regard this as desirable.

Once it is recognized that it may be optimal to have a mix of private saving and Social Security, the question becomes: what mix is best? In this section, we have explained the impact of Social Security on capital accumulation, so that this aspect can be adequately weighed when a citizen considers enactment of a particular scheduled future reduction in the SS ratio. For example, consider a citizen who initially favors the current 5% ratio. In response to the analysis of capital accumulation, the citizen may support a scheduled future reduction in the SS ratio (for example, a reduction from 5% to 3%).

▶ In response to a proposed scheduled future reduction in the Social Security ratio, a citizen should weigh the insurance and redistributive functions of Social Security, as well as the *transition problem*—the harm that may occur to particular age cohorts during a phasedown. But each citizen should also weigh the impact of such a reduction on capital accumulation.

16.2 Policies to Reduce Consumption

In Chapter 10, we highlighted two consumption-reducing policies—tight fiscal policy and a personal consumption tax—and we devoted some attention to the personal consumption tax. Here, we will extend our analysis of the personal consumption tax, describe a consumption tax levied on business firms (the value-added tax), and note several other consumption-reducing policies.

A PERSONAL CONSUMPTION (EXPENDITURE) TAX

We will consider three aspects of the personal consumption tax: the *horizontal redistribution effect*, the *incentive effect*, and *fairness (equity)*.

The Horizontal Redistribution Effect

Let's analyze conversion to an *equally progressive consumption tax* (C-tax), under which rates are adjusted so that each income class pays the same total tax under the C-tax as it would otherwise pay under the *income tax* (Y-tax). Hence, no vertical redistribution would occur.

Consider the high-income class H, which contains many households with comparable incomes but different propensities to save (or consume). If the Y-tax is converted to an equally progressive C-tax, then the total tax revenue from class H must stay the same. But within H, households with an *average propensity to consume* APC that is above average for class H would pay more tax, and households with an APC that is below average for class H would pay less tax. Thus, within class H, *horizontal redistribution* occurs. The distribution is horizontal because it is between households of similar income. Within H, the tax burden is shifted from low consumers to high consumers; equivalently, disposable income shifts from high consumers to low consumers. As a result, total consumption is likely to decrease.

Table 16.2 provides a simple example to illustrate this *horizontal redistribution effect*. Within class H, there are just two households, S and C, each with an income of $50,000. To simplify, we will consider an extreme case: household S saves all its disposable income, and household C saves none. Under a Y-tax, suppose that the average tax rate is 20%, so that each household pays $10,000 and total tax revenue from class H is $20,000. Household S saves its $40,000 of disposable income; household C saves none. Thus, aggregate saving from class H is $40,000 and aggregate consumption is also $40,000.

If the Y-tax is converted to an equally progressive C-tax, then $20,000 in total tax revenue must still be raised from class H. But all of the $20,000 must be paid by C, because S consumes nothing. If the C-tax rate is set at 67%, then C consumes $30,000 and pays $20,000 in tax. (Note that a 67% C-tax rate imposes the same burden on C as a 40% Y-tax rate imposes, because household C would pay $20,000 of tax out of its income of $50,000.) Household S saves its $50,000 of disposable income, so that aggregate saving is now $50,000 and aggregate consumption is now $30,000. In effect, the tax conversion shifts $10,000 of disposable income from household C to household S, all of which is saved.

TABLE 16.2

		Y-tax (20%)			
Income		Tax	Disposable Income	Consumption	Saving
Household C	50,000	10,000	40,000	40,000	0
Household S	50,000	10,000	40,000	0	40,000
Total	100,000	20,000	80,000	40,000	40,000
		C-tax (67%)			
Household C	50,000	20,000	30,000	30,000	0
Household S	50,000	0	50,000	0	50,000
Total	100,000	20,000	80,000	30,000	50,000

THE HORIZONTAL REDISTRIBUTION EFFECT

TABLE 16.3

VARIATION IN SAVINGS WITHIN AN INCOME CLASS
($25,000–49,000 in 1963)

Savings	Over $25,000	10,000–24,999	5,000–9,999	2,500–4,999	0–2,499	(−1)–(−999)	Over (−1,000)
% of households	23%	23%	21%	3%	8%	0%	22%

SOURCE: Dorothy Projector, *Survey of Changes in Family Finances*, Table S 1, p. 106 (Board of Governors of the Federal Reserve System, 1968).

This example implicitly assumes that each household's *marginal propensity to save* MPS—the ratio of an *increment* of saving to an increment of disposable income—equals its *average propensity to save* APS—the ratio of its total saving to its total disposable income. The tax conversion shifts disposable income from low APS households to high APS households within each income class. But whether aggregate saving increases depends on whether the MPS of households that gain disposable income exceeds the MPS of households that lose disposable income. Aggregate saving therefore increases as long as the following is true for most households within an income class: if household A has a higher APS than household B, then it also has a higher MPS than household B.

How much do saving propensities differ within an income class? According to a widely cited study of household saving behavior conducted by the Federal Reserve Board in the mid-1960s, there is substantial variation in the APS of households within a high-income class.* For example, Table 16.3 presents variations in savings for a very high income class (disposable income from $25,000 to $49,000 in 1963).

At one extreme, 23% of these households saved more than two-thirds of their income (over $25,000 of savings out of an average disposable income of about $36,000). At the other extreme, 22% *dissaved*—that is, they consumed more than their income. We should note that part of this variation is due to differences in age and therefore to differences in stages of the life cycle. Part, however, is due to differing lifetime propensities to save, derived from differing attitudes toward thrift, accumulation, and bequests.

Variation in the APS across households does not necessarily imply a

---

* Dorothy Projector, *Survey of Changes in Family Finances*, Table S1, p 106 (Board of Governors of the Federal Reserve System, 1968).

similar variation in the MPS. It is therefore not completely certain that tax conversion would raise aggregate saving by horizontal redistribution. The impact on aggregate saving depends on the individual behavior generating the variation in the APS shown in Table 16.3.

Nevertheless, this variation suggests that horizontal redistribution would probably significantly raise aggregate saving (equivalently, reduce aggregate consumption). Using the Federal Reserve study's data and making the assumption that each household's MPS equals its APS and is unaffected by tax conversion, it has been estimated that horizontal redistribution would raise total *gross* saving in the household sector by approximately 11%.* This would increase the *net* saving rate of the economy by significantly more than 11%, because the increase in saving would be a larger fraction of net saving. Although these assumptions can surely be questioned, this estimate illustrates the possibility that horizontal redistribution might significantly increase aggregate net saving in the economy.

The Incentive Effect

To focus on the *incentive effect* of conversion to a C-tax, let's imagine that all households are identical so that we can analyze a single, representative household. How would this household respond to a C-tax that raises the same revenue from this household that the Y-tax would raise, leaving the household with the same disposable income?

The point to keep in mind is that conversion to the C-tax raises the *reward to saving* for the household, because the saving is now *tax deductible;* saving immediately reduces the tax owed by the household. An example will illustrate how switching to a C-tax would raise the future consumption made possible by a given sacrifice of current consumption; in other words, a switch from a Y-tax to a C-tax would raise the net return to saving.

First, let's consider the no-tax case. Suppose that the interest rate is 6%. A person who saves $1,000 (foregoing $1,000 of consumption today) will earn $60 of interest and will be able to enjoy $1,060 of consumption next year. The ratio of next year's to this year's consumption is 1.06. Equivalently, we say that the *net return to saving* is 6%.

Next, suppose that there is a $33\frac{1}{3}$% income tax, so that a person who earns $1,500 is taxed on $500. Saving the $1,000 (foregoing $1,000 of consumption today) will again earn $60 of interest, but this individual will owe $20 of tax on this interest (capital) income and will only be able to enjoy $1,040 of consumption next year. The ratio of next year's to this

---

* Stephen Maurer and Laurence Seidman, "The Consumption Tax, Horizontal Redistribution, and Aggregate Saving," *Mathematical Modeling* 5 (1984): 205–22.

year's consumption is only 1.04 under the $33\frac{1}{3}\%$ income tax; the net return to saving is 4%.

Now suppose that there is a consumption tax of 50% (any rate will do). Out of $1,500 of income, the person can consume $1,000, on which $500 of tax is owed, or can save $1,500 and earn $90 of interest. Out of $1,590 in the next year, the individual can consume $1,060, on which a tax of $530 is owed. The ratio of next year's to this year's consumption is once again 1.06, and the net return to saving is 6%, exactly as in the no-tax case. We can thus conclude that

▶ Conversion from an income tax (Y-tax) to a consumption tax (C-tax) raises the net return to saving.

This increase in the net return to saving should reduce consumption. As we explained in Chapter 10, this impact on saving is disputed by some economists. They correctly explain that a rise in the net return to saving due to a rise in the interest rate (ignoring taxation) may either lower or raise consumption. According to standard microeconomic analysis, the *substitution effect* tends to reduce consumption but the *income effect* tends to raise consumption, because a person can now afford to consume more at all ages; in this sense, people become richer when the interest rate rises.

Although this analysis is correct, the argument misses a crucial point:

▶ An increase in the net return to saving due to *tax conversion* differs fundamentally from an increase in the net return due to a *rise in the interest rate* (ignoring taxation). As a first approximation, there is no *income effect* under tax conversion; because one tax replaces another, the person is generally not richer. The *substitution effect* determines the outcome, so that the result should be lower consumption.

This important point is illustrated in Figure 16.1—a standard microeconomic *indifference-curve* diagram, applied to an individual's choice between *present consumption* C_p and *future consumption* C_f. The individual works in the present and retires in the future. Under the Y-tax, if the entire wage is consumed in the present, the individual chooses the point at which the *lifetime budget B_Y line* hits the C_p axis; $C_p = B_Y$, but $C_f = 0$. By saving, the individual can raise future consumption C_f above 0 by sacrificing some present consumption C_p. The B_Y line shows the feasible points (C_p, C_f) available under the Y-tax. Its slope is $-(1 + r_n)$, where r_n is the *net return to saving*. For example, if the net return to saving under the Y-tax is 4%, then the slope is -1.04; for every $1 of present consumption C_p that is sacrificed, future consumption C_f can be raised by $1.04. To maximize lifetime well-being (utility),

FIGURE 16.1 CONVERSION TO A C-TAX REDUCES PRESENT CONSUMPTION

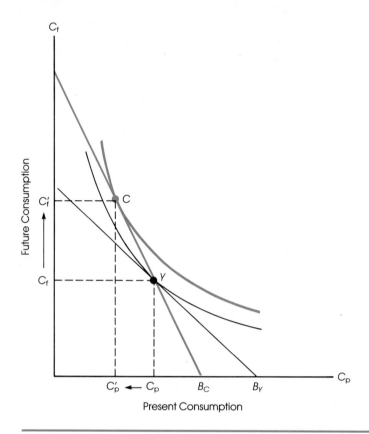

Under the income tax, the individual can choose any point on the lifetime budget line B_Y that has a slope of $-(1 + r_n)$. Choosing point Y maximizes utility. If the consumption-tax rate is set so that the individual can still afford point Y, then a new budget line B_C must pass through point Y. This budget line is steeper, with a slope of $-(1 + r_g)$. Hence, the individual now chooses point C to maximize utility, and present consumption declines from C_p to C_p'.

the individual chooses point Y—the point on line B_Y that is tangent to an *indifference curve*.

Suppose that the Y-tax is converted to a C-tax that enables the individual to continue to choose point Y. The new budget line under the C-tax, B_C, passes through point Y. But it is steeper than the slope of the B_Y line. Its slope is $-(1 + r_g)$, where r_g is the *gross return to saving*. For example, if the gross return to saving is 6%, then the slope is -1.06; for every \$1 of present consumption C_p that is sacrificed, future consumption C_f can be raised by \$1.06. To maximize lifetime well-being, the individual will now choose point C — the point on line B_C that is tangent to an indifference curve.

The crucial point is that point C must lie above and to the left of point Y. Hence, tax conversion must reduce the worker's present consumption from C_p to C_p'. The result is unambiguous because there is essentially no income effect under tax conversion. The substitution effect alone determines the outcome. Thus:

▶ The *incentive effect* should reduce consumption.

Fairness

It is sometimes claimed that a C-tax is equivalent to a *labor income tax* (W-tax) and is therefore unfair. In one respect, the C-tax and the W-tax are very similar. They embody two different methods of raising the net return to saving. Under the C-tax, the household escapes from taxation in the year that the saving occurs. Under the W-tax, saving does not immediately reduce a household's tax, but when the saving earns interest, dividends, or capital gains, tax is reduced. Thus, both taxes raise the net return to saving above its level under the Y-tax.

With respect to fairness, however, the C-tax and the W-tax differ significantly. This is most striking when we recall the case of the "lazy heir" who inherits a fortune, never works, and enjoys a very high level of consumption. The lazy heir owes no tax under a W-tax but owes a high tax (probably a higher tax than under a Y-tax) under the C-tax. Most would regard a W-tax as unfair because it permits such a person to pay little or no tax even while enjoying a high standard of living. Therefore

▶ It is *not* true that a C-tax is the same as a W-tax. True, both the C-tax and the W-tax raise the net return to saving, but the two taxes differ significantly on the crucial criterion of *equity*.

Obviously, a citizen may judge a C-tax to be fair but a W-tax to be unfair, based on the difference in the treatment of persons who earn little labor income but who finance their high consumption with inherited wealth or with wealth that results from an abnormally high return on past investment (not from a large personal sacrifice of consumption).

It is not surprising that although vigorous debate has occurred over the relative merits of the Y-tax and the C-tax, almost no one has suggested that a W-tax would be preferable. In practice, proposals to reduce the taxation of capital income are often made. But supporters of moderate reductions do not usually state that they believe the conversion of a Y-tax to a W-tax is desirable. For this reason, we have devoted much more attention to the conversion of the Y-tax to a C-tax than to the conversion of the Y-tax to a W-tax.

When conversion of a Y-tax to a C-tax is proposed, a common

assumption is that this would favor the affluent. In Chapter 10, we emphasized the error of this assumption. A personal consumption tax can be just as progressive as a personal income tax. Congress can adjust the rates in the tax table to achieve whatever distribution of the tax burden across income classes it desires.

Which is fairer: a Y-tax or a C-tax? The Y-tax advocate asks: if two households earn the same amount of income, why should they pay different amounts of tax just because they have different attitudes toward saving? Don't they have the same ability to pay? The C-tax advocate replies that a person should be taxed in proportion to use of output (consumption) — on the basis of what is taken out of the economic "pie" for the individual's own enjoyment (consumption) rather than on the basis of what is contributed to the "pie" (output, which equals income).

Neither the Y-tax nor the C-tax advocate usually emphasizes the impact of the behavior of households S and C on the well-being of others when judging which tax is the more equitable. But such an argument can be made. When S saves instead of consuming, S unintentionally helps raise the real wage of the low-skilled worker. Our Chapter 10 analysis showed that capital accumulation raises the real wage. A citizen who regards the improvement of the standard of living of the low-skilled worker as an important social goal may believe that it is fair to tax household S less than household C because S makes a greater social contribution than C.

The Y-tax advocate would respond that S's saving is motivated by self-interest, not by a desire to raise the standard of living of the low-skilled worker. Although S undoubtedly saves to promote self-interest, the question can be asked: is it S's motivation or the consequences of its action that is relevant? Some argue that only motivation matters. But it is possible for a citizen to believe that it is fair to reward S relative to C, because S's behavior contributes more to a desirable social goal than C's behavior does.

One final aspect of equity should be noted: the transition problem. It is unfair to suddenly subject older persons — in particular, retirees — to a consumption tax at full rates. During their work years, these retirees paid income tax and saved out of after-tax income. A sudden switch to a consumption tax would, in effect, tax these persons twice. Fairness therefore calls for lower rates for retirees during a transition period.

THE VALUE-ADDED TAX (VAT)

If the decision is made to switch from taxing income to taxing consumption in the United States, then the corporate income tax would lose its justification. If the corporate income tax were abolished, total tax revenue could then be held constant by raising household taxes or by introducing a consumption tax levied on business firms — the *value-added tax* VAT. The value-added tax is widely used abroad. Given the popular resistance to a household tax increase, a VAT is probably an essential element in the conversion of an income-tax system to a consumption-tax system.

To compute its value-added tax, a firm subtracts its expenditure on inputs purchased from other firms from its gross revenue. The VAT tax rate is applied to this tax base to yield the firm's tax. The important point here is that expenditure on capital equipment (investment) is subtracted and is therefore not taxed. The VAT tax base for the whole economy equals value-added (output) minus investment; hence, a value-added tax is levied on consumption. The economic effect of a VAT is therefore similar to a retail sales tax on consumer goods; it discourages consumption.

One argument for replacing the corporate income tax with a value-added tax, rather than raising the household tax, is that a VAT effectively taxes the underground economy but a household tax does not. People who legally avoid or illegally evade personal taxes must still bear the burden of a VAT when they consume, because the VAT tax is incorporated into the price of consumer goods.

A disadvantage of VAT is that its burden on households cannot be directly adjusted. The VAT is passed on uniformly. Because the affluent have a lower consumption – income ratio than low-income individuals, they will have a lower VAT tax burden – income ratio. Hence, a VAT is *regressive*.

▶ The regressivity of a value-added tax can be offset by making the personal consumption tax more progressive, so that the total tax system achieves the desired degree of progressivity.

Low-income individuals who pay no personal tax could be protected from VAT by a *refundable tax credit*. These individuals would be entitled to file for a cash payment from the government to reimburse the estimated VAT tax burden. Also, the level of welfare and unemployment compensation benefits could be raised to offset higher consumer prices due to VAT.

Both supporters and opponents of a value-added tax agree that it should enable the government to raise more total tax revenue, because it is less visible to voters than a household tax. Those who believe that the deficit problem should be solved in part by a tax increase approve of this revenue-raising ability of the value-added tax; those who want the deficit problem solved primarily through expenditure cuts dislike it.

Two other consumption-reducing policies should be noted: a *bonus system for compensation* policy, and a *required minimum down payment* and unfavorable tax treatment policy to discourage consumer borrowing. The case for these two policies is advanced by Lester Thurow in *The Zero-Sum Solution*.* According to Thurow, one-third of Japanese compensation is paid out in bonuses, given twice a year. People may adjust consumption to their nonbonus ("normal") monthly compensation. If this is done, then a bonus system raises the personal saving rate. Since the Japanese personal saving rate is 20% and the U.S. personal saving rate is 6%, it is possible that a bonus system does reduce consumption. Favorable tax treatment could be used to encourage bonuses; for example, bonus compensation might be exempt from payroll tax.

A required minimum down payment and unfavorable tax treatment policy would reduce consumer borrowing. Under the current income tax, interest payments on consumer loans are tax deductible for taxpayers who itemize (instead of taking the standard deduction). A switch to a personal consumption tax would remove this bias toward consumer borrowing. But even under the income tax, tax deductibility of interest payments can be terminated; for example, Germany does not permit deductibility for interest on consumer loans. Thurow suggests requiring a 20% minimum down payment and a phaseout of interest deductibility in the United States.

16.3 Policies to Raise Investment

In Chapter 10, we emphasized easy monetary policy as the primary means of raising investment demand. As we note other investment-raising policies in this section, it will be useful to keep the *IS–LM* diagram in mind. Assume that the *IS* and *LM* curves initially intersect at $Q = Q_c$. Consumption-reducing policies shift the *IS* curve to the left. Investment demand policy must shift the *LM* curve or the *IS* curve to the right to keep the *IS–LM* intersection at $Q = Q_c$. Easy monetary policy shifts the *LM* curve to the right. The policies we will now consider all shift the *IS* curve to the right.

The first policy is an *investment incentive* for firms implemented by tax policy. Firms can be induced to raise investment demand at any given interest rate by favorable tax treatment of investment. Two examples of investment incentives are the *investment tax credit* (ITC) and *accelerated depreciation* (see Chapter 12). Under a 10% investment tax credit, when the firm pays $100 for new capital equipment, its tax is cut

---

* Lester Thurow, *The Zero-Sum Solution* (New York: Simon and Schuster, 1985) 218–21.

by $10. The tax credit reduces the cost of new equipment, making it profitable for firms to raise investment. Under accelerated depreciation, a firm can deduct more depreciation cost in the years immediately following an investment. Over the lifetime of the capital good, the present value of depreciation increases, the present value of taxable profit decreases, the present value of tax decreases, and the present value of after-tax profit increases. Thus, acceleration of depreciation raises the after-tax profitability of investment and thereby stimulates investment demand.

A second policy, *industrial policy*, seeks to stimulate investment demand on the part of particular, targeted industries through government subsidized loans, or tax incentives, directed at those industries.

A third policy is *public investment by government* in infrastructure — roads, bridges, and so forth — or in research and development. This raises government investment G_I, one of the two components of total investment demand. We have already emphasized that investment is performed in the public as well as in the private sector.

The fourth policy is to use tax incentives, loans, or grants to encourage persons to invest in *human capital* — college and graduate education or vocational training. The demand for education and training is investment demand (where "investment" is broadly defined). This policy can be concentrated on low- and moderate-income persons.

The fifth policy, *enterprise zones*, designates poor areas and provides tax incentives to firms that locate there. Hence, investment demand by firms locating in poor areas is stimulated.

16.4 The Sources of Economic Growth

In Chapter 10, we summarized the results of research on the sources of economic growth. Here we will examine the methods used to arrive at these results.

THE THEORETICAL FRAMEWORK

Let's begin with the concept of an aggregate production function

(16.9) $$Q = F(K, L, A)$$

In equation (16.9), K is narrowly defined as physical capital (in dollars); L is the number of workers (the labor force); A is the *residual*, which incorporates the impact of advancements in knowledge and technological change not reflected in K; and Q is real output. Equation (16.9) simply states that real output depends on capital, labor, and the residual. Over time, we observe K, L, and Q increasing. How can we tell how much of the increase in Q is due to L, to K, and to A?

The problem is that A is not directly observable. In a given year, we can add up the total dollar value of real capital and add up the number of workers, but we probably can't directly measure the quantity of technical change or advancement in knowledge. If we could directly measure A, then we could "run a regression" (fit an equation to the data) to estimate the impact of K, L, and A individually on Q. Perhaps the simplest regression is

(16.10) $\hat{Q} = b_1\hat{K} + b_2\hat{L} + b_3\hat{A}$

In equation (16.10), the caret (ˆ) symbol indicates the *percentage growth rate*. For example, $\hat{Q}$ is the annual growth rate of real output. Each coefficient, b_1, b_2, and b_3, measures the impact of its variable on $\hat{Q}$. For example, we might find that

$$\hat{Q} = 0.25\hat{K} + 0.75\hat{L} + 1.00\hat{A}$$

If we could measure $\hat{A}$ as we can $\hat{K}$, $\hat{L}$, and $\hat{Q}$, we could ask the computer to find the values of the coefficients b_1, b_2, and b_3 that make the errors as small as possible over the sample period. Each coefficient is the estimate of the elasticity of that variable. For example, if $b_1 = 0.25$, then a 4% increase in $\hat{K}$, holding $\hat{L}$ and $\hat{A}$ constant, causes a 1% increase in $\hat{Q}$.

If we had such estimates, we could account for the growth in Q from the beginning to the end of the sample period. We know the average annual values of $\hat{Q}$, $\hat{K}$, and $\hat{L}$; if we also knew the average annual value of $\hat{A}$, then we could find the contribution of each in the following manner. To find the contribution of $\hat{K}$, set $\hat{L} = 0$ and $\hat{A} = 0$; then $b_1\hat{K}$ is the part of $\hat{Q}$ that is due to $\hat{K}$ alone. Similarly, $b_2\hat{L}$ is the contribution of $\hat{L}$, and $b_3\hat{A}$ is the contribution of $\hat{A}$.

The Neoclassical Assumption

Unfortunately, we probably cannot directly measure $\hat{A}$. What, then, can we do? The approach most often used is to assume that we know the coefficients of $\hat{K}$ and $\hat{L}$ (b_1 and b_2). Specifically, we will assume that b_1 is the share of national income received by capital and that b_2 is the share of national income received by labor. Hence, if property income is 25% of national income, then we can assume that $b_1 = 25\%$; if labor income is 75% of national income, then we can assume that $b_2 = 75\%$.

If we are willing to assume that the coefficients are equal to the income shares, then we would be able to compute the contributions of $\hat{K}$ and $\hat{L}$ in each year; what remains must be the contribution of the residual $\hat{A}$. But what is the justification for assuming that we know the coefficients of $\hat{K}$ and $\hat{L}$? What is the justification for assuming that we know that each coefficient is the income share of that factor?

Neoclassical theory offers a justification. In Chapter 10, we saw that according to neoclassical analysis, the real wage equals the marginal product of labor (that labor is paid its marginal product). Symmetrically, neoclassical analysis holds that the return paid to capital equals the marginal product of capital (that capital is paid its marginal product). If we are willing to make the *neoclassical assumption* that each factor is paid its marginal product, then we can show that the coefficient of $\hat{K}$ in equation (16.10) equals capital's share of national income and that the coefficient of $\hat{L}$ equals labor's share of national income. Let's demonstrate this.

The *marginal product of labor* MPL is defined as the increase in output that results from another unit of labor if all other inputs are held constant. If labor is increased—not by one unit, but by ΔL units—then the increase in output is $\text{MPL} \times \Delta L$. For example, if MPL = 2 and labor increases by 3 units, then the increase in output is 6 units.

Symmetrically, the *marginal product of capital* MPK is defined as the increase in output that results from another unit of capital if all other inputs are held constant. If capital is increased—not by one unit, but by ΔK units—then the increase in output is $\text{MPK} \times \Delta K$. For example, if MPK = 0.1 and capital increases by 3 units, then the increase in output is 0.3 units.

Thus, if K increases by ΔK and L increases by ΔL, then ΔQ (the change in Q) resulting from ΔK and ΔL, ignoring the residual, is given by

(16.11) $$\Delta Q = (\text{MPK})(\Delta K) + (\text{MPL})(\Delta L)$$

In Chapter 3, we presented the argument that MPL should equal the real wage of labor w. We saw that a profit-maximizing firm should keep hiring workers as long as the MPL exceeds w and should stop when the MPL declines into equality with w through diminishing returns. Thus, the w we observe in the economy should equal the MPL.

By the same reasoning, the return to capital r we observe in the economy should equal the MPK. For example, if $r = 10\%$, then the MPK of capital should be 10%; that is, if another $100 of capital is utilized, it should raise output by $10 per year. Thus, this profit-maximizing hiring of labor and capital results in

(16.12) $$w = \text{MPL}$$
(16.13) $$r = \text{MPK}$$

Substituting equation (16.12) and equation (16.13) into equation (16.11) gives us

(16.14) $$\Delta Q = r\Delta K + w\Delta L$$

To obtain $\hat{Q}$, which is defined as $\Delta Q/Q$, we divide both sides of equation (16.14) by Q:

(16.15)
$$\frac{\Delta Q}{Q} = \frac{r\Delta K}{Q} + \frac{w\Delta L}{Q}$$

Multiplying and dividing the first term by K and multiplying and dividing the second term by L we obtain

(16.16)
$$\frac{\Delta Q}{Q} = \left[\left(\frac{rK}{Q}\right)\left(\frac{\Delta K}{K}\right)\right] + \left[\left(\frac{wL}{Q}\right)\left(\frac{\Delta L}{L}\right)\right]$$

However, since rK is *total capital income in the economy* and Q is total income

$$s_K = \frac{rK}{Q}$$

where s_K = capital's share of national income

Similarly, since wL is *total labor income in the economy*

$$s_L = \frac{wL}{Q}$$

where s_L = labor's share of national income

Thus, equation (16.16) becomes

(16.17)
$$\hat{Q} = s_K\hat{K} + s_L\hat{L}$$
$$\text{where } \hat{Q} = \frac{\Delta Q}{Q}$$
$$\hat{K} = \frac{\Delta K}{K}$$
$$\hat{L} = \frac{\Delta L}{L}$$

In equation (16.17), the growth rate is indicated by the caret ($\hat{}$) symbol above the variable.

We have just shown that if each factor is paid its marginal product (as a result of the profit-maximizing process), then the weight b_1 in equation (16.10) is capital's share of national income s_K; and the weight b_2 in equation (16.10) is labor's share of national income s_L.

Two early, influential studies by Moses Abramowitz* and Robert Solow† assume that the weights for capital and labor, b_1 and b_2, are the *income shares*. Both reach a similar and striking conclusion. The rise in physical capital per worker k appears to explain only a small fraction of the rise in output per worker q; most of the rise in output per worker appears to be due to the residual. The box on page 686 presents some details of Solow's calculation. His results are provocative. From 1909 to 1949 in the United States, Solow finds that the increase in physical capital per worker accounts for only one-eighth of the rise in output per worker; seven-eighths is due to the residual. Abramowitz calls the residual a "measure of our ignorance." It is somewhat disconcerting that so much of this growth appears to be due to the residual.

As we pointed out in Chapter 10, these early results have, at times, been interpreted as showing that capital accumulation is not an important determinant of economic growth. Some analysts have ignored the fact that these studies focus on physical capital. But we have argued for a broader concept of capital accumulation. We have emphasized that capital consists of knowledge and human as well as physical capital. Over Solow's sample period, resources were diverted away from producing consumer goods and into the production not only of physical capital goods but also into invention and organizational planning (the production of *knowledge capital*) and into the production of education and skill (the production of *human capital*). Because knowledge and human capital raise the productivity of a man-hour of labor and because their accumulation requires a sacrifice in consumption, they should be regarded as capital.

These early studies, then, suggest that the accumulation of physical capital alone does not appear to account for a large share of the growth in real output Q. But the studies do not show that the accumulation of capital (broadly defined) is unimportant for economic growth. In fact, subsequent research has demonstrated that the accumulation of knowledge and human capital, together with physical capital, plays a central role in economic growth.

Denison's Research

Some of the most careful studies of the sources of economic growth have been performed by Edward Denison of the Brookings Institution.

---

* Moses Abramowitz, "Resource and Output Trends in the United States Since 1870," *American Economic Association Papers and Proceedings* 46 (1956): 5–23.
† Robert Solow, "Technical Change and the Aggregate Production Function," *Review of Economics and Statistics* (August 1957) 312–20.

Solow's Calculation of the Sources of Economic Growth

Solow further simplifies equation (16.10) as follows. First, since the contribution of the residual is $b_3\hat{A}$ but neither b_3 or $\hat{A}$ can be separately measured, b_3 is assumed to be 1 for convenience, so that $\hat{A}$ is the contribution of the residual. Second, since the income shares of capital and labor sum to 1, from equation (16.10) we know that

(16.18) $\hat{Q} = b_1\hat{K} + (1 - b_1)\hat{L} + \hat{A}$

If $\hat{L}$ is subtracted from both sides, we obtain

(16.19) $\hat{Q} - \hat{L} = b_1(\hat{K} - \hat{L}) + \hat{A}$

Recall that

$$q \equiv \frac{Q}{L}$$

$$k \equiv \frac{K}{L}$$

where q = output per unit labor
k = capital per unit labor

Applying the math growth-rate rule (pages 170–71), we have

(16.20) $\hat{q} = \hat{Q} - \hat{L}$
(16.21) $\hat{k} = \hat{K} - \hat{L}$

Substituting equation (16.20) and equation (16.21) into equation (16.19) gives us

(16.22) $\hat{q} = b_1\hat{k} + \hat{A}$

Equation (16.22) states that the growth rate of output per worker $\hat{q}$ equals capital's share of national income b_1 multiplied by the growth rate of capital per worker $\hat{k}$ plus the contribution of the residual $\hat{A}$. Note, once again, that Solow assumes that he knows the impact of $\hat{k}$ on $\hat{q}$ based on neoclassical theory—namely, that b_1 equals capital's share of national income.

For each year from 1909 to 1949, Solow has obtained numerical data on $\hat{q}, b_1$, and $\hat{k}$; thus, by subtracting $b_1\hat{k}$ from $\hat{q}$ for each year, he obtains the $\hat{A}$ for that year. In a typical year, the value of $\hat{A}$ is much larger than the value of $b_1\hat{k}$ and therefore accounts for a greater share of $\hat{q}$.

By adding the changes in A over all years, Solow calculates that if A is given a value of 1.00 in 1909, then its value in 1949 is 1.81. He reasons that if A had stayed constant, output per worker in 1949 would have been equal to actual output per worker in 1949 divided by 1.81. It turns out that after dividing by 1.81, output per worker would have grown by only one-eighth as much as it actually grew over that period.

We cited his studies and summarized his conclusions in Chapter 10. Here we will concentrate on his methods.

Denison makes the same neoclassical assumption made in the early studies; in equation (16.10), b_1 is assumed to be equal to the *income share of capital* (the ratio of property income to total income) and b_2 is assumed to be equal to the *income share of labor* (the ratio of labor compensation to national income). But Denison makes several improvements and refinements over the earlier studies.

One important improvement is his treatment of labor input. In effect, in his measure of the impact of human capital accumulation, Denison recognizes that all man-hours do not have the same "efficiency." As workers have become more educated and skilled, effective labor input per hour increases. Denison uses information on relative earnings to adjust labor input for human capital. For example, if a college graduate earns x times the wage of a high-school graduate in a given year, then Denison assumes that the college graduate contributes x times the effective labor of a high-school graduate.

The effect of this adjustment in labor input is that less output growth is due to the residual and more is due to the inputs of capital and labor. While Denison's technique adjusts the labor input to reflect more education and skill, the increase in labor input is due to human capital accumulation, which requires investment — a sacrifice in current consumption to devote resources to education and skill acquisition.

In Chapter 10, we referred to an interesting question asked by Denison: what investment rate (ratio of investment to national income) would the United States need to adopt to match the Japanese growth rate of output? In other words, if the United States were to rely solely on raising physical capital accumulation, what would it take to reach Japan's growth rate?

Denison calculates that the net investment rate, which averaged less than 8% in the postwar years up to 1973, would have to rise to 60% of national income. He adds that an even higher investment rate would be required due to diminishing returns to capital.

How does Denison obtain this provocative estimate? In equation (16.11), if we focus on the portion of ΔQ that is due solely to ΔK, we have

$$\Delta Q = \text{MPK}\Delta K$$

If we assume that $\text{MPK} = r$, then the above equation becomes

(16.23) $$\Delta Q = r\Delta K$$

Letting b be the *net investment (saving) rate* (the ratio of net investment to output)

(16.24) $\qquad b = \dfrac{I_n}{Q}$

where I_n = net investment

Multiplying both sides of equation (16.24) by Q gives us

(16.25) $\qquad bQ = I_n$

However, net investment, by definition, is the increase in the capital stock:

(16.26) $\qquad I_n = \Delta K$

Combining equation (16.25) and equation (16.26) yields

(16.27) $\qquad \Delta K = bQ$

Substituting equation (16.27) into equation (16.23) gives us

(16.28) $\qquad \Delta Q = rbQ$

Finally, dividing both sides by Q, we obtain *the investment – output growth equation*

(16.29) $\qquad \hat{Q} = rb$

where r = the return to capital

b = the net investment (saving) rate

Equation (16.29) is a very handy tool. It states that the contribution of investment to the growth rate of output is the return to capital multiplied by the net investment rate. In the 1948 – 1973 period, Denison estimates that the return to (marginal product of) capital averaged 8.0% (for further evidence on the return to capital in the United States, see the adjacent box) and that the net investment rate averaged 7.5%. Then the net investment in physical capital (the increase in physical capital) caused output to grow by 0.6% per year. Since the growth rate of output was, in fact, 3.8% per year, physical capital contributed roughly 15% of the growth of output, as reported earlier.

Now suppose we ask what is the increase in the growth rate of output $\Delta\hat{Q}$ if the net investment rate is raised by Δb percentage points? For example, if $\Delta b = 1\%$ (so that net investment increases from 7.5% to 8.5%), by how much does $\hat{Q}$ increase? From equation (16.29) we know that

(16.30) $\qquad \Delta\hat{Q} = r\Delta b$

16.5 The Neoclassical Growth Model

In Chapter 10, we considered policies to reduce the consumption rate (the consumption–output ratio) and to raise the investment rate (the investment–output ratio). But we did not analyze the long-run impact of such policies. If the investment rate of the economy is permanently raised, what happens to the economy in the long run?

Economic growth models have been developed in an attempt to answer this and related questions. The model most often utilized by economists is the *neoclassical growth model* developed by Robert Solow and many other economists, beginning in the 1950s. The neoclassical growth model embodies many simplifications in order to isolate the core of the growth process.

THE MODEL*

We begin with the production function. We will assume that output per unit labor q varies directly with capital per unit labor (the capital–labor ratio) k:

(16.31) $$q = f(k)$$

In equation (16.31), we are assuming that there are *constant returns to scale* in production, so that if all inputs (capital and labor) are doubled, then output doubles. (More generally, if capital K and labor L are each multiplied by x, then Q is also multiplied by x.) In equation (16.31), if K and L are doubled, then k stays constant (since $k = K/L$); equation (16.31) implies that q stays constant. Since $q = Q/L$, q stays constant if and only if Q has also doubled.

Furthermore, we assume that the production function $f(k)$ is curved, as shown in Figure 16.2. This curvature means that if, for example, k doubles, then q will less than double; if q doubled, then $f(k)$ would be a straight line. As long as capital is subject to diminishing returns, the $f(k)$ curve will exhibit this curvature.

One reason that our model is considered neoclassical is that the assumption is made that each factor of production (labor and capital) is "fully employed." Thus, we abstract from the cyclical fluctuations that were so important to the analyses in Parts 1, 2, and 3. Our purpose is to understand long-run evolution; it is therefore a sensible and defensible strategy to suppress short-term fluctuations.

Total output must be allocated between consumption and invest-

---

* A lower-case letter normally means "per unit labor." For example, K is the capital stock and k is capital per unit labor. The growth rate of a variable will be indicated by the caret (^) symbol above the variable. For example, $\hat{k}$ is the growth rate of capital per unit labor.

Martin Feldstein and Lawrence Summers have analyzed the pretax rate of return on nonfinancial corporate capital in the United States from 1948–1976* by measuring the capital income–capital stock ratio. If capital is paid a return that is equal to its marginal product, as neoclassical theory implies, then this ratio should measure the marginal product of capital.

They estimate that the pretax return to nonfinancial corporate capital averaged 11% from 1948–1976. They agree with other analysts that the return fell in the early 1970s, but Feldstein and Summers attribute most of the decline to a reduction in capacity utilization. They write: "Our analysis of these rates of return provides no support for the view that there has been a gradual decline in the rate of return over the postwar period." Thus, they estimate that if $100 is invested in new, physical capital, it should raise output by $11 per year. This estimate is higher than Denison's estimate of 8%.

---

* Martin Feldstein and Lawrence Summers, "Is the Rate of Profit Falling?" *Brookings Papers on Economic Activity* 1 (1977): 211–28.

Like equation (16.29), equation (16.30) is a very handy tool. If $\Delta b = 1\%$, then $\Delta \hat{Q}$ is simply equal to 1% of r. If $r = 8.0\%$, then $\Delta \hat{Q} = 0.08\%$. This is Denison's first estimate. But to be conservative, he supposes that each 1% increase in b raises $\hat{Q}$ by 0.12%. Then to raise $\hat{Q}$ by a full 1.00% requires an 8.5% increase in b (from 7.5% to 16.0%). To raise the growth rate by 6.00%—which would have been necessary to match Japan's growth rate—requires an increase of 6 × 8.5%, or 51%. When added to the original 7.5%, this brings the net investment rate close to 60%.

Thus, if we are willing to assume that the return to capital measures capital's marginal productivity, then equation (16.30) gives us a handy rule of thumb. Each 1% increase in the net investment rate raises the growth rate of output by 1% of the return to capital r. If the return capital is roughly 10%, then it raises the growth rate of output by 0.1

▶Given certain assumptions, each 1% increase in the net investment rate raises the growth rate of output by roughly 0.1%. Thus, doubling the net investment rate from 8% to 16% raises the annual growth rate of output by just under 1% (0.8%).

Once again, we should emphasize that "investment" here is in p ical capital. According to Denison, it is difficult to raise the growth by 1%; it requires a doubling of the net investment rate.

FIGURE 16.2 THE OUTPUT-PER-UNIT-LABOR CURVE

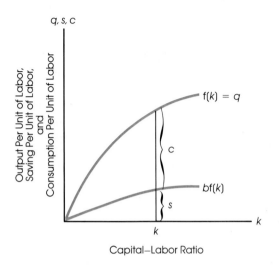

Capital–Labor Ratio

Output per unit labor q varies directly with capital per unit labor k. The curvature is due to diminishing returns to capital. Since b is the saving rate, the height of the $bf(k)$ curve at any k is saving per unit labor s and the gap between $f(k)$ and $bf(k)$ is consumption per unit labor c.

ment (saving). Equivalently, output per unit labor must be divided between consumption per unit labor c and saving per unit labor s. Let b designate the *saving rate*—the fraction of output (income) that is saved. If, for example, $b = 10\%$, then saving per unit labor s is 10% of output per unit labor q and consumption per unit labor c is 90% of q. The division of q between s and c at any k is shown in Figure 16.2.

We will assume that labor grows at the constant rate n (for example, at the rate of 1% per year). Clearly, then, if the capital stock also grows at the rate n, the capital–labor ratio k will remain constant. If the growth rate of capital $\hat{K}$ exceeds n, then k will rise; if $\hat{K}$ is less than n, then k will fall. Since k is defined as K/L, applying the math growth-rate rule gives us

(16.32) $\hat{k} = \hat{K} - \hat{L} = \hat{K} - n$

What determines the growth rate of capital $\hat{K}$? By definition of $\hat{K}$, we know that

(16.33) $\hat{K} \equiv \dfrac{\Delta K}{K}$

where ΔK = increase in the capital stock

In turn, the increase in the capital stock depends on the net investment rate b (which equals the net saving rate):

(16.34) $$\Delta K \equiv I_n = S_n = bQ$$

where I_n = net investment

S_n = net saving

For example, if the saving rate $b = 10\%$ and real output $Q = 100$, then the increase in the capital stock (net investment) will be 10. Note that from national income accounting, net investment equals net saving (gross saving minus depreciation). The saving rate b can be called either the *net saving rate* or the *net investment rate*. For convenience, we will drop the term "net," but it is always understood.

Substituting equation (16.34) into equation (16.33) gives us

(16.35) $$\hat{K} = b \frac{Q}{K}$$

Q/K is the output–capital ratio, or *capital productivity*, just as Q/L is *labor productivity*. Suppose that the saving rate b stays constant. Then

▶ The *growth rate of capital* $\hat{K}$ varies directly with *capital productivity* Q/K.

How does capital productivity vary with capital per unit labor k? If we divide the numerator and the denominator of capital productivity Q/K by L, we see that

(16.36) $$\frac{Q}{K} = \frac{Q/L}{K/L} = \frac{q}{k} = \frac{f(k)}{k}$$

At any k in Figure 16.2, if we move vertically to the corresponding $f(k) = q$, then the slope of the line from that point to the origin is $f(k)/k$. (Recall that *slope* is defined as the vertical gap/horizontal gap; $f(k)$ is the vertical gap, and k is the horizontal gap.) This means that capital productivity equals the slope of the line from the origin to the $f(k)$ curve. Thus, it is clear that

▶ Given the curvature of $f(k)$, capital productivity falls as capital per unit labor k increases.

Substituting equation (16.36) into equation (16.35) gives us

(16.37) $$\hat{K} = \frac{bf(k)}{k}$$

Substituting equation (16.37) into equation (16.32) yields

(16.38) $$\hat{k} = \frac{bf(k)}{k} - n$$

Equation (16.38) is the equation that governs our growth model. The first term on the right is the growth rate of capital $\hat{K}$ and the second term is the growth rate of labor $\hat{L}$.

Figure 16.3 illustrates the key elements of equation (16.38). A horizontal line at height n indicates that the growth rate of labor $\hat{L}$ is n at any value of k (by assumption). The growth rate of capital $\hat{K}$ curve has a negative slope. Why? We have seen that capital productivity Q/K, which equals $f(k)/k$, decreases as k increases. Thus, $bf(k)/k$, which equals $\hat{K}$, also decreases as k increases.

▶ We will assume that the saving rate b is independent of capital per unit labor k and output per unit labor q.

Suppose that the saving rate is initially b_0. Now consider the capital per unit labor k, where the n line intersects the $b_0f(k)/k$ curve. Since

FIGURE 16.3 THE EQUILIBRIUM CAPITAL–LABOR RATIO

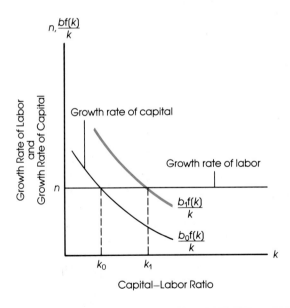

The growth rate of capital is $bf(k)/k$; the growth rate of labor is n. The equilibrium capital–labor ratio k is at the intersection of the $bf(k)/k$ curve and the n line. If the saving rate rises from b_0 to b_1, then k gradually rises from k_0 to k_1.

$b = b_0$, we will call k at this intersection k_0. At k_0, since the growth rate of capital $\hat{K}$ equals the growth rate of labor $\hat{L}$, according to equation (16.38), $\hat{k} = 0\%$; k stays constant at k_0.

▶ If the economy is initially at capital per unit labor k_0, it will stay at k_0; k_0 is the *equilibrium capital–labor ratio*, given the constant growth rate of labor n and the constant saving rate b_0.

Now suppose that the economy is initially at some k less than k_0. From Figure 16.3, clearly $b_0 f(k)/k$ exceeds n; the growth rate of capital exceeds the growth rate of labor. From equation (16.38), we know that $\hat{k}$ is positive; k rises toward k_0. This occurs because as k declines below k_0, capital productivity rises and, in equation (16.38), this raises the growth rate of capital above n.

Symmetrically, suppose that the economy is initially at some k that is greater than k_0. From Figure 16.3, clearly $b_0 f(k)/k$ is less than n; the growth rate of capital is less than the growth rate of labor. From equation (16.38), we know that $\hat{k}$ is negative; k declines toward k_0. This occurs because as k rises above k_0, capital productivity declines and, in equation (16.38), this reduces the growth rate of capital below n.

▶ Whether capital per unit labor k is initially above or below the capital per unit labor k_0, it moves toward k_0. This means that k_0 is a *stable equilibrium*.

The Impact of Raising the Saving Rate

If we assume that the economy is initially at k_0 but that the saving rate then increases permanently from b_0 to b_1, what happens? In Figure 16.3, the $bf(k)/k$ curve shifts upward, so that at k_0, $b_1 f(k)/k$ exceeds n; the growth rate of capital exceeds the growth rate of labor. According to equation (16.38), $\hat{k}$ is positive; k begins to rise. Eventually, k converges to k_1, the intersection of $b_1 f(k)/k$ and n. Thus

▶ In the long run, the permanent increase in the saving rate (from b_0 to b_1) results in a permanent increase in the capital–labor ratio (from k_0 to k_1) and, by equation (16.31), in a permanent increase in output per unit labor (from q_0 to q_1).

However, note what happens to the growth rate of output $\hat{Q}$. At the initial equilibrium, k is constant (at k_0) and q is therefore constant (at q_0). Since Q/L is constant, this means that $\hat{Q} = n$. As soon as b is raised to b_1, $\hat{k}$ becomes positive. As k rises, so does q; this means that $\hat{Q}$ is greater than n during this transition. But when k converges to k_1, q becomes constant at q_1; this means that $\hat{Q}$ returns to n.

▶ A permanent increase in the saving rate does not permanently increase the growth rate of output $\hat{Q}$. During the transition, the growth rate is raised above the constant growth rate of labor n. In the long run, however, the growth rate returns to n.

▶ It should be recognized that the transition to the new equilibrium may take many years. Thus, it is correct to say that in the short and medium runs, raising the saving rate raises the growth rate of output.

Let's briefly note the impact of an increase in the saving rate on the wage per unit labor w and on the return per unit capital r. Neoclassical theory postulates that each factor is paid its marginal product; hence, the wage equals the marginal product of labor MPL and the return to capital equals the marginal product of capital MPK. We will assume that the MPL increases as k increases; more capital per unit labor raises the marginal productivity of labor. Symmetrically, the MPK decreases as k increases; more capital per unit labor reduces the marginal productivity of capital (diminishing returns).

It then follows that a permanent increase in the saving rate b, by raising k, raises w and reduces r. In final equilibrium, since k is constant, w and r are constant at their new values.

Technical Change and Productivity Growth

We need to remedy one shortcoming of our growth model. If the saving rate b remains constant, then the economy converges to a constant k and therefore to a constant q. Hence, in equilibrium, output per unit labor q stays constant. But in most economies, output per worker has grown over time — even over periods when the saving rate has been roughly constant.

Perhaps the simplest way to resolve this discrepancy is to assume that the efficiency of each worker is improving steadily over time, so that *effective labor per worker* increases steadily. We will therefore assume that effective labor per worker increases at the constant rate a (the labor productivity growth rate).

When the economy converges to a constant capital per effective labor k and output per effective labor q, this means that capital K and output Q each grow at the same rate as effective labor L — namely, at the rate n. But since effective labor per worker grows at the rate a (for example, at a rate of 2%), then K and Q per worker also grow at that rate a.

In GROWTH-MODEL EQUILIBRIUM, output per unit of effective labor q and capital per unit of effective labor k are constant, but output per worker and capital per worker each grow at the labor productivity growth rate a.

The growth rate of effective labor n now equals the sum of the growth rate of the labor force f and the growth rate of effective labor per worker a. For example, if $f = 1\%$ per year and $a = 2\%$ per year, then $n = 3\%$. As we noted earlier, when the economy converges to a constant k, w and r will stay constant. But w is the wage per unit of effective labor. Since effective labor per worker increases at the rate a, the wage per worker will also increase at the rate a.

The growth of effective labor per worker is called *labor-augmenting technical change*. Note that the labor productivity growth rate a is assumed to be independent of the saving rate b. This hypothesis is a convenient way to make the equilibrium of the model correspond more closely to the growth of output and capital per worker and to the wage per worker that we observe in the actual economy. But we must admit that it may not, ultimately, be a valid resolution of the problem. Further analysis of technical change and growth models must be left for advanced texts.

THE OPTIMAL SAVING RATE

Let's consider a hypothetical offer. Suppose that the United Nations offers to give a new country any capital stock it requests; the country can have any initial k that it wants. But in return, the country must permanently adopt the saving rate b that will keep its k constant, given its growth rate of labor n. What k—and hence what b—should the country choose?

From Figure 16.3, we know that if the equilibrium value of k (and therefore of q) is higher, then the value of b required to sustain it is higher. If a saving rate of $b = 1$ could somehow be maintained, it would sustain a higher value of q than any lower saving rate. But a saving rate of 1 would soon confront the population with starvation.

Rather than trying to maximize q, a more sensible goal is to try to maximize consumption per unit labor c. At one extreme, a saving rate of 0 causes k, q, and c to all deteriorate toward 0 as labor grows. At the other extreme, a saving rate of 1 results in a c of 0. At some value of b between 0 and 1, c should be maximized. This maximum c will be denoted by c_g. The new country's problem is to find the b_g and k_g that yield c_g.

Return to equation (16.38). Since we are concerned only with an equilibrium, constant value of k, we set $\hat{k} = 0\%$:

(16.38) $$\hat{k} = 0\% = \frac{bf(k)}{k} - n$$

Moving n to the left side of the equation and multiplying both sides by k yields

(16.39) $nk = bf(k)$

for any equilibrium k, where $\hat{k} = 0\%$.

Figure 16.4 shows the nk line; its slope is n. Its intersection with the $bf(k)$ curve gives the equilibrium value of k. This intersection is the same as the intersection of the n line and the $bf(k)/k$ curve in Figure 16.3.

As shown in Figure 16.2, at any capital per unit labor k, since saving per unit labor $s = bf(k)$, consumption per unit labor c is given by

(16.40) $c \equiv q - s = f(k) - bf(k)$

At an equilibrium k, equation (16.39) holds, so that equilibrium c is obtained by substituting equation (16.39) into equation (16.40) to

FIGURE 16.4 THE GOLDEN RULE k_g AT WHICH CONSUMPTION PER UNIT LABOR IS MAXIMUM

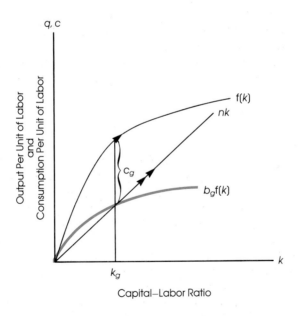

If the saving rate is held constant at b, then the economy eventually converges to the k given by the intersection of the $bf(k)$ curve and the nk line. Consumption per unit labor c is the gap between $f(k)$ and $bf(k)$—at equilibrium k, between $f(k)$ and nk. At k_g, the gap between $f(k)$ and nk is widest; here, consumption per unit labor c is maximum.

obtain

(16.41) $c = f(k) - nk$

for any equilibrium c, where $\hat{k} = 0\%$.

The new country's problem is to find the equilibrium k and the b to sustain it that will make the c given by equation (16.41) as large as possible. In Figure 16.4, we must find the k at which the gap between the $f(k)$ curve and the nk line is widest. Clearly, this occurs where the slope of (the tangent to) the $f(k)$ curve is parallel to the nk line. We will call this *capital–labor ratio* k_g.

Thus, the new country should choose k_g and agree to adopt the saving rate b_g needed to maintain it. Any other k and b would result in a lower consumption per unit labor.

This value of k has been called the *golden rule k*, which is why we have used the symbol k_g. The reason for using the phrase "golden rule" is as follows. Instead of a gift from the United Nations, suppose that each generation agrees to practice the golden rule: "Do unto others as you would have others do unto you." Specifically, each agrees to adopt the same saving rate it would have had past generations adopt. Then the best common saving rate is b_g, which yields k_g, so that all generations enjoy the highest possible common consumption per unit labor.

It can be shown that the slope of the $f(k)$ curve equals the marginal product of capital. This is plausible because as k increases, so that capital K rises relative to labor L, we expect diminishing returns to capital to reduce MPK. As k increases, the slope of the $f(k)$ curve declines. Given the neoclassical assumption that capital is paid a return equal to its marginal product, the slope of the $f(k)$ curve also equals the *return to capital* (the interest rate) in the economy r.

▶ To achieve the maximum *consumption per unit labor* c_g, the country should choose the *capital per unit labor* k_g at which the *return to capital* (the interest rate) r equals the *growth rate of labor n*.

There is another illuminating way to describe k_g. At k_g, $r = n$. Multiplying both sides by k gives us

(16.42) $rk = nk$

Substituting equation (16.39) into equation (16.42) gives us

(16.43) $rk = bf(k)$

Dividing both sides by $f(k)$ yields

$$(16.44) \qquad \frac{rk}{f(k)} = b$$

and using equation (16.36) gives us

$$(16.45) \qquad \frac{rK}{Q} = b$$

The numerator of the term on the left is capital income in the economy; the denominator is total income (output). Hence, the ratio is capital's share of national income, which, at k_g, equals the saving rate. Thus

▶ To achieve the maximum consumption per unit labor, the country must adopt a saving rate equal to capital's share of national income.

Should We Raise Our Saving Rate to b_g?

How does the actual k of most economies compare to k_g? At k_g the return to capital r equals the growth rate of effective labor n. If n is roughly 3%, then at k_g, r would be 3%. But r has been estimated to be in the 8–11% range in the U.S. economy (see the Feldstein–Summers estimate on page 689). This implies that the k of the United States lies to the left of k_g in Figure 16.4, because if k is less than k_g, then the slope of $f(k)$ (which equals r) is greater than n.

The same conclusion is suggested by comparing the net saving rate and capital's share of national income. Focusing on physical capital, the net saving rate in the United States has been in the 7% range. Yet capital's share of national income has exceeded 20%. Hence, the saving rate has been much less than capital's share, resulting in a k that is less than k_g.

Does this mean that a country should raise its saving rate to b_g, which will eventually raise k to k_g? Not necessarily. It is important to recognize the difference between the hypothetical offer presented by the United Nations to the new country and the choice facing an actual economy.

In the hypothetical situation, the new country does not need to sacrifice in order to build k up to k_g. It must only agree to adopt the saving rate necessary to maintain the k it is given by the United Nations.

But consider the situation facing an actual economy. Suppose that the economy is initially at a k_0 less than k_g (and at a b_0 less than b_g). Then if it raises its saving rate to b_g, the initial impact is to reduce c from c_0 to c_1, as shown in Figure 16.5. As k rises toward k_g, c will pass the initial c_0 at some point on its way to its final value c_g, which is the maximum equilibrium c and must therefore be greater than c_0.

FIGURE 16.5 THE SACRIFICE REQUIRED TO REACH k_g

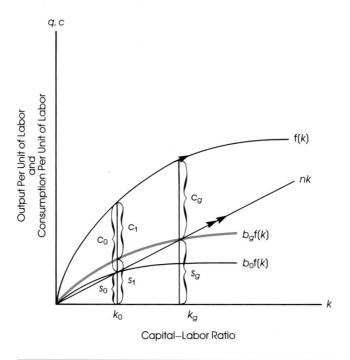

Capital–Labor Ratio

The economy is initially at k_0, which is less than k_g. The saving rate is b_0, which is less than b_g. To reach k_g in the long run, the saving rate must be raised to b_g. But in the short run, this reduces consumption per unit labor from c_0 to c_1. When c eventually reaches c_g, consumption per unit labor is greater than c_0.

▶ Any actual economy beginning at a k_0 less than k_g faces a trade-off. It must balance the long-run gain in consumption per unit labor c against the short-run reduction in c. It is therefore not obvious that it is socially optimal to raise the saving rate b to b_g.

Thus, recognition that there is a golden rule k_g at which equilibrium c is at a maximum does not resolve the problem we emphasized in Chapter 10. Society must sacrifice consumption in the present to raise consumption in the future, so that raising the saving rate is not always desirable. This point remains valid, even when the saving rate is initially below b_g and it is proposed that the rate be raised to b_g.

16.6 Accumulation, Pollution, and Depletion

In recent years, both the desirability and feasibility of economic growth have been challenged by the concern that growth generates environmental pollution and depletes natural resources. We will address this concern in this section.

To focus on the impact of capital accumulation on pollution and depletion, we will assume that the labor force and the population are constant. Raising the standard of living of a constant population will clearly cause less pollution and depletion than raising the standard of living of a growing population will. We do not mean to imply that zero population growth is socially optimal, but a discussion within such a context emphasizes that population growth and growth in output per person are two distinct sources of pollution and resource depletion.

ENVIRONMENTAL POLLUTION

Environmental pollution is a classic example of *market failure*. To economists, the reason for this failure is straightforward. In the absence of environmental policy, firms are not charged when they use up a valuable resource like clean air or water. They can pollute "for free," so it is not surprising that they use valuable resources to excess. If firms were not charged for using other inputs — labor, capital, land, materials — they would use them wastefully as well.

Why are firms not charged for using the environment but are charged for other valuable inputs? Again, the answer is straightforward. The private owners of other inputs insist that they be paid for the use of the input. But who is the private owner of air or water? Who can insist on a price? Private ownership of air and most water is either not feasible or is not desirable.

Just as most economists agree on the source of market failure, they also agree on the appropriate policy remedy:

▶ The government should assume collective ownership of the environment and charge a price to firms that seek to use this valuable resource in order to discourage pollution.

The price of a given pollutant in a particular geographical region can be established in one of two ways. The government can issue a fixed number of permits, setting the permit price according to supply and demand, or the government can set a tax per unit of pollutant. If the damage from a particular pollutant increases, fewer permits should be sold to the polluting firms or a higher tax should be set per unit of the pollutant. In the case of drastic damage from even a small level of emission, no permits should be issued; equivalently, the tax should be prohibitive. In other words, the pollutant should be banned.

Economists emphasize that there is an inevitable trade-off between the environment and output. In the absence of environmental policy, the market encourages overproduction of output at the expense of environmental quality. An appropriate set of prices on particular pollutants can restore a better balance between the two. Equally important, pollution prices can reduce the sacrifice in output that is required to achieve a given environmental quality.

Pollution prices can help to steer economic growth in a direction that reduces its harm to the environment. In macroeconomics, where aggregation is so necessary for analysis, it is sometimes easy to forget that thousands of different goods and services constitute GNP and that each is produced by a different technique with different inputs. A given growth rate of GNP can occur with sectors A–C carrying the lead or with sectors X–Z carrying the lead, and a given mix of goods and services can often be produced by alternative input mixes and techniques.

Consider, then, the impact of the introduction of a permanent set of pollution prices. The cost of goods and services that generate high pollution will rise relative to the cost of low-polluting output. The price of high-polluting goods will then rise relative to the price of low-polluting goods. Consumers will therefore shift their demand toward low-polluting output, and producers will be compelled to follow demand. Resources will be reallocated from the high-polluting sector to the low-polluting sector.

This shift from high- to low-polluting output would occur even if firms respond only to demand but do not consider altering their production techniques. Over the long run, however, the incentive to invent low-polluting techniques may prove most important. Some techniques are readily available. As soon as prices are imposed, polluters will find it profitable to switch to these low-polluting techniques to reduce their permit or tax cost, and firms will be provided with an incentive to invent new techniques.

The history of technological change is replete with examples of how a change in input prices has generated an incentive for firms to invent and adopt new techniques. In the past, the environment has been underpriced—at 0. Producers had no reason to economize on the use of this resource. The sharp rise in the price of the environment— implemented by pollution permits or taxes—would stimulate the invention of techniques to economize on this input that has now become permanently more expensive.

It is very difficult to forecast how successful the inventive process will be in making growth in output per person compatible with a high quality environment. The history of technological change is a history of surprises and breakthroughs. Fortunately, we need not forecast correctly to adopt the proper policy. A set of pollution prices should be imposed; the prices should be high enough to protect the environment adequately. This set of prices would generate the incentives for shifting the composition of output and inventing new techniques and products. Time will tell how much material growth per person would then be possible while protecting the environment.

Citizens, of course, will differ on their views as to how stiff the set of prices should be because they differ in their preferences for the environment versus output. Even an extreme environmentalist, however, should not try to limit growth per se but, instead, should advocate a set of prices stiff enough to maintain a high quality environment. Whatever growth turns out to be compatible with such an environment should surely be acceptable. Science and invention, given proper incentives, may be able to surprise even the extreme environmentalist.

NATURAL-RESOURCE DEPLETION

We will now turn to the problem of *natural-resource depletion*. In our analysis of accumulation and growth, we have focused on the inputs capital and labor and have ignored natural resources. It is now important to rewrite our aggregate production function to include R, the flow of natural resources used in a given year:

(16.46) $Q = F(K, L, R)$

Note the distinction between the *stock of natural resources* S at any moment in time and the *flow of natural resources* R in a given year. The concern, of course, is that the sum of the flows over a period of years will eventually exhaust the stock.

As stated earlier, it is convenient to regard L as constant; we will therefore focus on K, R, and Q. If output Q always requires a fixed amount of R and if the stock S is not a large multiple of the annual R, then we are indeed in trouble. So far in economic history, however, this fixed relationship between Q and R has not been present. Let's examine why.

Suppose that the stock of a particular natural resource appears to be depleting rapidly. What happens? Owners of the stock anticipate that as its flow R is reduced in the future, it will command a higher price. Owners therefore refuse to sell the stock at a low price today because they know that it will be more profitable to hold it and sell it later at a much higher price. Of course, the expected price rise must exceed the interest the owner could earn by selling the stock today and then saving. But if genuine scarcity of a valuable resource is anticipated, then this will surely be the case. This brings us to an important point. It is not profitable for owners to allow their stocks to deplete rapidly. If scarcity is on the horizon, they will find it profitable to conserve today.

Such conservation by owners may be misunderstood by the public. The public will observe a reduction in the supply of R and a consequent rise in its price. They will suspect *monopoly exploitation,* but they will be wrong on two counts. First, even if all owners are small competitors with no market power, they will find it profitable to reduce the supply of R in anticipation of higher future prices. Second, the public is not being exploited, but protected. True, owners care primarily about their self-interest, but the result is conservation of a resource that is expected to grow more valuable in the future.

Now let's follow the impact of the rise in the price of the particular resource, denoted by R_i, that follows its reduction in supply to the market. The story is the same as the one we told about the response to a pollution price. First, we must recognize that there are many goods and services; each uses R_i with a different intensity, and many do not use R_i at all. The rise in the price of R_i raises the price of goods that use R_i intensively relative to goods that do not. This relative price change causes consumers to shift demand away from goods intensive in R_i to goods that use little or no R_i. Firms then have an incentive to shift to techniques that use less R_i relative to other inputs. When such techniques are not immediately available, they have an incentive to try to invent them.

All of these responses help to minimize the depletion of the resource. The speed of depletion should be reduced as the composition of output and production techniques are shifted to conserve the resource and as new techniques and new products that are less dependent on the resource are invented.

We have intentionally saved a final escape for last. The rise in price creates an incentive to search for more of the resource. Optimists generally claim that a rise in the price of many resources should stimulate discovery of new stocks, so that the model of a fixed stock S (only a modest multiple of annual R) will prove inaccurate. Pessimists claim that the reverse will be the case for many important resources. If optimists are right, the standard of living can clearly keep rising. We will concentrate on the more pessimistic scenario.

SUBSTITUTING CAPITAL FOR RESOURCES

Suppose that the stock S cannot be significantly augmented by new discoveries. Let's return to production function (16.46). We have been assuming that labor L is constant. We will now further assume that if $R = 0$, then $Q = 0$, despite K and L. If the stock S cannot be augmented, then isn't it inevitable that as R declines, Q will eventually decline to 0?

Not necessarily. For illustration, suppose that the initial, unaugmentable stock in year 0 is 800. Obviously, if R is 100 in each year, then the stock will be depleted by the end of year 8; starting in year 9, Q will be 0. But we have just explained why profit-seeking owners begin to slow down the supply of R to the market in anticipation of higher future prices. Thus, the R supplied per year should decline as the remaining stock declines.

It is possible that R will never actually reach 0. Suppose that the path of supply is as follows. In each year, let the amount of R supplied equal one-half of the stock remaining at the beginning of the year. With $S_0 = 800$, the path is then $R_1 = 400$, $R_2 = 200$, $R_3 = 100$, $R_4 = 50$, and so on; R will never actually reach 0. Of course, profit-seeking behavior by owners might not follow this pattern exactly, but such a path is feasible. It is not true, then, that because the stock is finite, the flow of the stock per year must reach 0.

Nevertheless, it is surely true that R must decline. Is there any hope, then, of maintaining Q? Looking at equation (16.46), the source of hope is obvious:

▶ If capital K can be substituted for resources R, so that as R declines, a rise in K can sufficiently compensate, then output Q can be prevented from declining. The strategy, then, must be to accumulate real capital fast enough so that it offsets the decline in R. Capital accumulation therefore becomes the defender of the standard of living in the face of resource depletion.

Although capital accumulation may have a chance for success, there is no guarantee. Capital may not be easily substituted for natural resources. For example, if only one product is consumed in the economy and that product is completely dependent on natural resources, then the situation is hopeless.

However, the situation is clearly not that bleak. Many goods and services are consumed, with varying degrees of dependency on natural resources. There are also a variety of techniques for producing particular products, which often differ in their capital–resource ratio. It is therefore possible that substitutability may be great enough that the standard of living can be maintained if capital is accumulated fast enough.

It is important to re-emphasize the broad definition of capital first set out in Chapter 10. One central component of capital is knowledge capital. It may be that, in the context of resource depletion, accumulating knowledge capital is the most crucial factor. Economic history abounds with examples of how inventors, faced with the rising relative price of an input, discovered methods to economize on the input. One method is to develop a production technique that is less intensive in the scarce input. Another method is to develop new products that use less or none of the input but that are satisfactory substitutes to consumers.

It is possible, then, that if we mistakenly interpret K in a narrow sense as physical capital, there will be far less ground for optimism than if we recognize the broad concept of K and realize that investment in science and technology — the accumulation of knowledge capital — may prove to be the key to substitutability. Once again, there is no guarantee of success. But even if potential substitutability proves adequate, we must still accumulate capital at a sufficient rate. For example, if society consumes its whole GNP, K will not rise and the decline in R will cause a decline in Q, whatever the potential substitutability of R and K may be. Thus, the policies to raise capital accumulation that we have discussed are extremely relevant to the resource-depletion problem.

▶ Reducing the rate of resource depletion and raising capital accumulation are two ways to protect the standard of living for future generations. Both entail a sacrifice by the present generation.

Finally, let's consider how capital accumulation policy affects resource conservation. In Chapter 10, we considered two policies to reduce consumption demand (tight fiscal policy and a personal consumption tax) and one policy to raise investment demand (easy monetary policy). In the IS–LM diagram, either consumption-reducing policy shifts the IS curve to the left; the easy monetary policy shifts the LM curve to the right. Q stays at Q_c, and the interest rate r declines, thereby stimulating investment.

The reduction in the interest rate promotes resource conservation. Why? A resource owner compares the expected rise in the price of the resource to the interest rate. A high interest rate favors supplying the resource to firms now, saving the proceeds, and earning interest. A low interest rate favors holding (conserving) the resource and waiting for the resource price to rise. The IS–LM shift just described lowers the interest rate and thereby encourages resource owners to conserve more and to supply less to the market.

▶ A mix of a consumption-reducing policy (tight fiscal policy or a personal consumption tax) and an easy monetary policy will reduce the interest rate at Q_c and raise both investment and resource conservation.

SUMMARY

1. If workers are *self-sufficient planners*, then a change in Social Security affects aggregate consumption. Specifically, a scheduled future phasedown of the *Social Security ratio* (the ratio of Social Security expenditures to GNP) should reduce aggregate consumption and raise capital accumulation.

2. If workers are *short-sighted spenders* or *intrafamily transferers,* then a change in Social Security does not affect aggregate consumption or capital accumulation.

3. In the steady state, the *implicit real (inflation-adjusted) rate of return on Social Security saving* (tax contributions) equals the growth rate of real income in the economy, which approximately equals the sum of the *labor-force growth rate f* and the *labor productivity growth rate a* (roughly 3% in the United States).

4. A *risk-averse citizen* who does not want "to place all retirement eggs in one basket" may decide that it is best for the economy to offer a mix of private saving and Social Security. Policymakers should weigh the likely negative impact of Social Security on capital accumulation when they set the Social Security ratio.

5. If the income tax is converted to an *equally progressive personal consumption tax,* then each income class pays the same total tax. Within each class, however, high savers enjoy a tax cut and low savers suffer a tax increase. This *horizontal redistribution effect* should raise total saving; equivalently, it should reduce total consumption.

6. Conversion to a consumption tax raises the net return to saving. This *incentive effect* should reduce consumption because the outcome is determined by the *substitution effect.* (There is no *income effect* because one tax replaces another.)

7. A *consumption tax* is more equitable than a *labor income tax.* The "lazy heir" who inherits a fortune, enjoys high consumption, and never works pays no tax under a labor income tax but pays a high tax under a consumption tax.

8. A personal consumption tax can be made just as progressive as an income tax by appropriate adjustment of the tax rates in the tax table.

9. The income-tax (Y-tax) advocate argues that if two households earn the same income, then they have the same ability to pay and therefore should pay the same tax. The consumption-tax (C-tax) advocate responds that people should be taxed according to what they take out of the economic "pie" for their own enjoyment (consumption), not according to what they contribute to the "pie" (output, which equals income).

10. A *value-added tax* VAT is a consumption tax levied on business firms. Under a VAT, firms deduct investment expenditures, so that the tax base is output minus investment, which equals consumption. If the income-tax system is converted to a consumption-tax system, a VAT could replace the corporate income tax.

11. A *bonus system for compensation* and a required *minimum down payment* are two additional consumption-reducing policies.

12. Although easy monetary policy is the basic method of raising investment demand, other investment-raising policies are tax incentives for firms (the *investment tax credit* or *accelerated depreciation*), industrial policy, public investment, tax incentives or loans for *human capital* investment, and *enterprise zones.*

13. Most studies analyzing the sources of economic growth make the *neoclassical assumption* that each factor input is paid its marginal product.

14. Most empirical studies conclude that the accumulation of physical capital alone does not account for a large share of the growth in real output but that capital accumulation, broadly defined, plays a central role in economic growth.

15. Denison estimates that a doubling of the U.S. *net investment rate* (from 8% to 16%) would raise the annual growth rate of output by just under 1% (from 3% to 4%).

16. In a *neoclassical growth model,* a permanent increase in the saving rate results in a permanent increase in the capital–labor ratio and in output per unit labor.

17. It may not be desirable to raise the saving rate to b_g (the rate that achieves the maximum consumption per unit labor in the long run), because consumption must be sacrificed in the short run. The short-run cost must be weighed against the long-run benefit.

18. Most economists agree that government should charge a price to polluters to discourage pollution. Stiff prices can steer economic growth toward low-polluting output.

19. To attempt to maintain output and the standard of living, despite *resource depletion,* capital must be accumulated fast enough to offset the decline in resources. Capital accumulation and resource conservation are two ways to protect the standard of living of future generations.

TERMS AND CONCEPTS

ability to pay
accelerated depreciation
average propensity to consume (APC)
average propensity to save (APS)
bonus system for compensation
capital productivity (Q/K)

capital's share of national income (s_K)
compact between generations
constant returns to scale
cross-section method
effective labor
enterprise zones

environmental pollution
equally progressive
   consumption tax (C-tax)
equilibrium capital – labor ratio
fairness (equity)
flow of natural resources
future consumption (C_f)
golden rule k (k_g)
gross return to saving (r_g)
growth-model equilibrium
growth rate of capital $(\hat{K})$
horizontal redistribution
horizontal redistribution effect
human capital
incentive effect
income effect
income share of capital
income share of labor
income shares
income tax (Y-tax)
indifference curve
industrial policy
intrafamily transferers
investment incentive
investment – output growth
   equation
investment tax credit (ITC)
implicit return on Social
   Security saving $(\bar{r})$
knowledge capital
labor-augmenting technical
   change
labor-force growth rate (f)
labor income tax (W-tax)
labor productivity (Q/L)
labor productivity growth rate
   (a)
labor's share of national
   income (s_L)
"lazy heir"
lifetime budget B_Y line

marginal product of capital
   (MPK)
marginal product of labor (MPL)
marginal propensity to save
   (MPS)
market failure
monopoly exploitation
natural-resource depletion
neoclassical assumption
neoclassical growth model
net investment (saving) rate (b)
net return to saving (r_n)
percentage growth rate
present consumption (C_p)
public investment by
   government
refundable tax credit
required minimum down
   payment
residual (A)
return to private saving
reward to saving
rise in the interest rate
risk-averse citizen
self-sufficient planners
short-sighted spenders
social return
Social Security ratio
stable equilibrium
stock of natural resources
substitution effect
tax conversion
tax-deductible saving
time-series method
total capital income in the
   economy
total labor income in the
   economy
transition problem
value-added tax (VAT)

16.1 Consider the following three changes in Social Security: a sudden introduction of SS benefits, a sudden reduction of SS benefits, and a scheduled future reduction of SS benefits. Construct a table that shows the impact of these changes on workers' consumption, retirees' consumption, and aggregate consumption for the following three groups: *self-sufficient planners, short-sighted spenders,* and *intrafamily transferers.*

16.2 Derive the formula that relates the steady-state implicit return on Social Security saving $\bar{r}$ to the labor-force growth rate f and to the labor productivity growth rate a.

16.3 Construct an example of the *horizontal redistribution effect,* using households S and C.

16.4 Draw a diagram that shows how conversion from an income tax to a consumption tax reduces present consumption.

16.5 Derive equation (16.17), $\hat{Q} = s_K \hat{K} + s_L \hat{L}$.

16.6 Derive equation (16.38), $\hat{k} = bf(k)/k - n$, the fundamental equation of the *neoclassical growth model.*

16.7 Can the environment be protected from economic growth? How is capital accumulation policy related to natural-resource depletion?

Index

A 6
B 7
C 8
D 9
E 0
F 1
G 2
H 3
I 4
J 5